STREE

Cardiff, Swansea and the Valleys

First published in 1995 as
Cardiff, Swansea and Glamorgan by

Philip's, a division of
Octopus Publishing Group Ltd
2–4 Heron Quays, London E14 4JP

First colour edition 2001
Second impression with revisions 2002

ISBN 0-540-07974-X
© Philip's 2002

Ordnance Survey

This product includes mapping data licensed
from Ordnance Survey® with the permission
of the Controller of Her Majesty's Stationery
Office. © Crown copyright 2001. All rights
reserved. Licence number 100011710

Printed and bound in Spain
by Cayfosa-Quebecor

Contents

Inside front cover:
Administrative and Postcode boundaries

II **Key to map symbols**

IV **Key to map pages**

VI **Route planning**

1 **Street maps** at 2½ inches to 1 mile

218 **Street maps** at 1¼ inches to 1 mile

232 **Town maps** of Abergavenny, Carmarthen,
Chepstow and Caldicot

234 **Index** of towns and villages

235 **Index** of streets, hospitals, industrial estates, railway
stations, schools, shopping centres and universities

Digital Data

The exceptionally high-quality mapping found in this atlas is available as digital data
in TIFF format, which is easily convertible to other bit mapped (raster) image formats.

The index is also available in digital form as a standard database table. It contains
all the details found in the printed index together with the National Grid reference
for the map square in which each entry is named.

For further information and to discuss your requirements, please contact
Philip's on 020 7531 8439 or george.philip@philips-maps.co.uk

Allwedd i symbolau'r map

Trafford gyda rhif y gyffordd	Gorsaf rheilffordd
	Walsall
Prif dramwyfeydd – ffordd ddeuol/un lôn	Gorsaf rheilffordd breifat
Ffordd A – ffordd ddeuol/un lôn	Gorsaf fysiau
Ffordd B – ffordd ddeuol/un lôn	Gorsaf ambiwlans
Ffyrdd bychan – ffordd ddeuol/un lôn	Gorsaf gwylwyr y glannau
Ffyrdd bychan eraill – ffordd ddeuol/un lôn	Gorsaf Dân
Ffordd yn cael ei hadeiladu	Swyddfa'r heddlu
Mân cerddwyr	Mynedfa damwain ac argyfwng i'r ysbyty
Ffiniau codau-post	Ysbyty
Ffiniau Sir ac awdurdod unedol	Lle o addoliad
Rheilffordd	Canolfan gwybodaeth (a'r agor drwy'r flwyddyn)
Tramffordd	Parcio
Rheilffordd ar raddfa fychan	Parcio a chludo
Trac gwledig, ffordd breifat, neu ffordd mewn ardal ddinesig	Swyddfa'r post
Llidiart neu rhwystr i draffig (gall fod cyfyngiadau ddim yn ddilys ar gyfer bob amser neu i bob drafnidiaeth)	Safle gwersylla
Llwybr, llwybr march, cilffordd yn agored i bob trafnidiaeth, ffordd a ddefnyddir yn llwybr cyhoeddus	Safle carafan
	Cwrs golff
Nid yw ymddangosiad unrhyw ffordd arall neu drac neu lwybr ar yr atlas hwn yn tystio fod hawl tramwy ar hyd-ddynt	Safle picnic
Dangosydd dalennau gyffiniol (Mae lliw yr arwydd yn dangos graddfa y tudalen gyffiniol - gweler y graddfeudd isod)	Adeiladau pwysig, ysgolion, colegau, prifysgolion ac ysbytai
	Prim Sch
Dangosydd y tudalen cyffiniol yn dangos y tudalennau sy'n gyffiniol a phen a gwaelod y dudalen	River Medway Enw dŵr
	Nant
Dangosir ardal y map tu mewn i'r band glâs mewn graddfa mawr ar y tudalen a ddangosir gan y bloc glâs â'r arwydd	Afon neu gamlas – bach a mawr
	Dŵr
	Dŵr llanw
	Coed
	Tai
	House Hynafiaeth anrhufeinig
	VILLA Hynafiaeth rhufeinig

Allot Gdns	Gerddi ar osod	Meml	Coffa
Acad	Academi	Mon	Cofgolofn
Cemy	Mynwent	Mus	Amgueddfa
C Ctr	Canolfan ddinesig	Obsy	Arsyllfa
CH	Tŷ Clwb	Pal	Palas brenhinol
Coll	Coleg	PH	Tŷ tafarn
Crem	Amlosgfa	Recn Gd	Maes chwaraeon
Ent	Menter	Resr	Cronfa ddŵr
Ex H	Neuadd Arddangos	Ret Pk	Parc adwerthu
Ind Est	Ystad ddiwydiannol	Sch	Ysgol
Inst	Institiwt	Sh Ctr	Canolfan Siopa
Ct	Llys cyfraith	TH	Neuadd y dref
L Ctr	Canolfan hamdden	Trad Est	Ystad Fasnachol
LC	Croesfan wastad	Univ	Prifysgol
Liby	Llyfrgell	Wks	Gwaith
Mkt	Marchnad	YH	Hostel ieuenctid

■ Y mae'r rhifau bach o gwmpas ochrau'r mapiau yn dynodi llinelli grid cenedlaethol 1 cilomedr

■ Mae'r ffin llwyd tywyll ar ochr fewn rhai tudalennau yn dynodi nad yw'r mapio yn canlyn ymlaen i'r tudalen gyffiniol

Graddfa y mapiau yw 3.92 cm i 1km, 2½ modfedd i'r filltir 1: 25344

0		¼		½		¾		1 milltir
0		250m	500m	750m		1 km		

Graddfa y mapiau ar y tudalennau wedi ei rhifo mewn gwyrdd yw 1.96 cm i 1km, 1¼ modfedd i'r filltir 1:50688

0	¼	½	¾	1 milltir
0	250m 500m 750m	1 km		

Symbol	Description
(22a)	**Motorway** with junction number
	Primary route – dual/single carriageway
	A road – dual/single carriageway
	B road – dual/single carriageway
	Minor road – dual/single carriageway
	Other minor road – dual/single carriageway
	Road under construction
	Pedestrianised area
DY7	**Postcode boundaries**
	County and unitary authority boundaries
	Railway
	Tramway
	Miniature railway
	Rural track, private road or narrow road in urban area
	Gate or obstruction to traffic (restrictions may not apply at all times or to all vehicles)
	Path, bridleway, byway open to all traffic, road used as a public path
	The representation in this atlas of a road, track or is no evidence of the existence of a of a right of way
219 / 84	**Adjoining page indicators** (The colour of the arrow indicates the scale of the adjoining page - see scales below)
25 / 49	**Adjoining page indicator** showing the pages adjoining the top and bottom halves of the current page
1	**The map area within the blue band is shown at a larger scale on the page indicated by the blue block and arrow**

Allot Gdns	**Allotments**	Meml	**Memorial**
Acad	**Academy**	Mon	**Monument**
Cemy	**Cemetery**	Mus	**Museum**
C Ctr	**Civic Centre**	Obsy	**Observatory**
CH	**Club House**	Pal	**Royal Palace**
Coll	**College**	PH	**Public House**
Crem	**Crematorium**	Recn Gd	**Recreation Ground**
Ent	**Enterprise**	Resr	**Reservoir**
Ex H	**Exhibition Hall**	Ret Pk	**Retail Park**
Ind Est	**Industrial Estate**	Sch	**School**
Inst	**Institute**	Sh Ctr	**Shopping Centre**
Ct	**Law Court**	TH	**Town Hall/House**
L Ctr	**Leisure Centre**	Trad Est	**Trading Estate**
LC	**Level Crossing**	Univ	**University**
Liby	**Library**	Wks	**Works**
Mkt	**Market**	YH	**Youth Hostel**

Symbol	Description
Walsall	**Railway station**
	Private railway station
	Bus, coach station
	Ambulance station
	Coastguard station
	Fire station
	Police station
	Accident and Emergency entrance to hospital
H	**Hospital**
	Place of worship
i	**Information Centre** (open all year)
P	**Parking**
P&R	**Park and Ride**
PO	**Post Office**
	Camping site
	Caravan site
	Golf course
	Picnic site
Prim Sch	**Important buildings, schools, colleges, universities and hospitals**
River Medway	**Water name**
	Stream
	River or canal – minor and major
	Water
	Tidal water
	Woods
	Houses
House	**Non-Roman antiquity**
VILLA	**Roman antiquity**

■ The small numbers around the edges of the maps identify the 1 kilometre National Grid lines

■ The dark grey border on the inside edge of some pages indicates that the mapping does not continue onto the adjacent page

The scale of the maps is 3.92 cm to 1 km 2½ inches to 1 mile 1: 25344	0 ¼ ½ ¾ 1 mile 0 250m 500m 750m 1 kilometre
The scale of the maps on pages numbered in green is 1.96 cm to 1 km 1¼ inches to 1 mile 1: 50688	0 ¼ ½ ¾ 1 mile 0 250m 500m 750m 1 kilometre

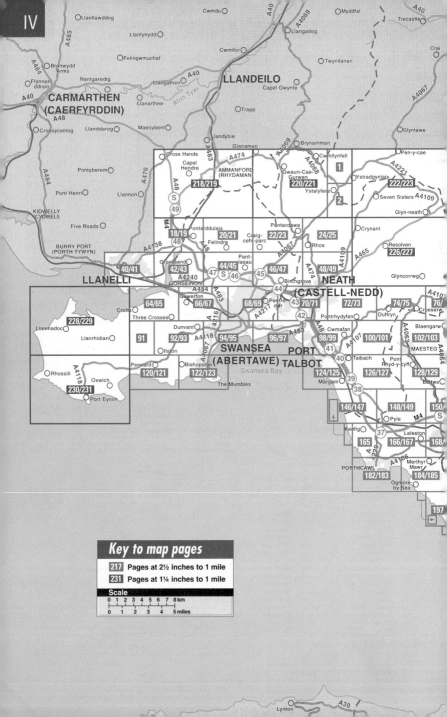

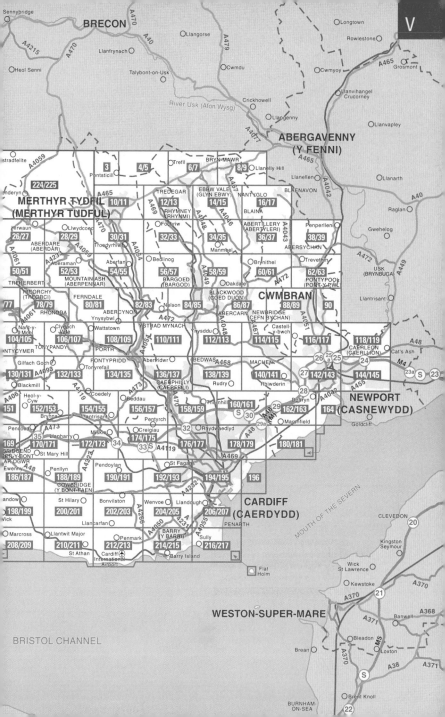

Route planning

Scale

0 1 2 3 4 5 6 7 8 km
0   1   2   3   4 5 miles

BRISTOL CHANNEL

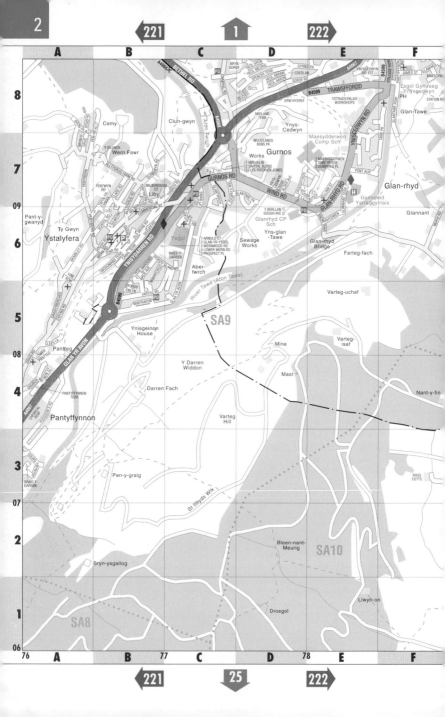

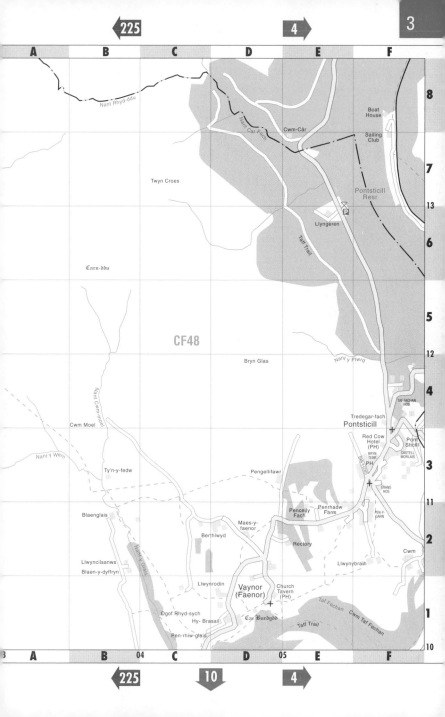

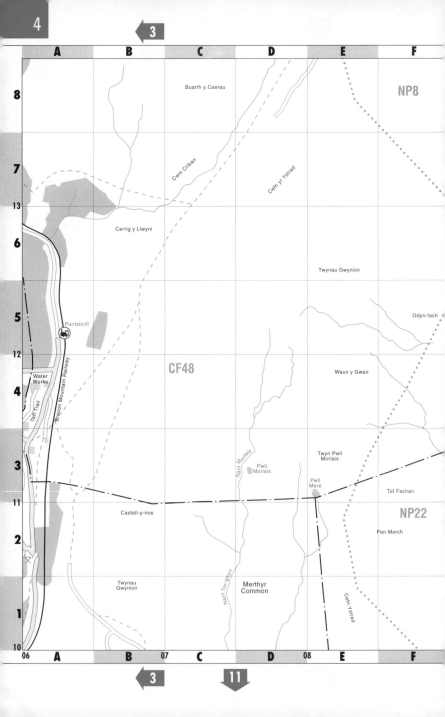

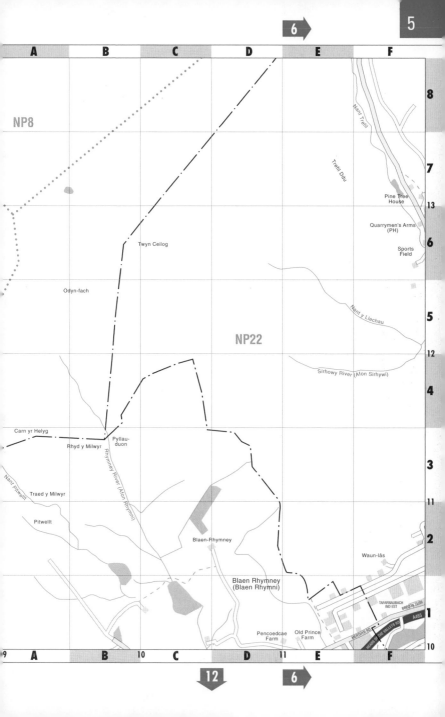

5

| A | B | C | D | E | F |

5
13

8

7

13

Trefil Las

Pen-y-lan
Farm

6

RAILWAY TERR

RHYMNEY
ROW

Trefil

Cross Brook
Cottages

SHAP
ROW

Ty Newydd
Cottage

5

Afon Sirhywi (Sirhowy River)

12

Dros-y-
lynn

Ffynnon
Sion Sieffre

4

NP22

Shon-Sheffrey's
Resr

Milgatw

Nant Milgatw

Twyn Bryn-march

NP23

RASSAU IND EST

The Castle
(PH)

NANT-Y-CROFT

RASSAU RD

A465

BRYN-SEROLAT

The Wells
Farm

Mast

Garnddu
Farm

3

Penrhyn
Farm

Blaen-y-cwm

Hirgan

Tynewydd

Tir Morgan-
Hywel

Hirgan-
Fach

Hirgan

11

Ty-gwyn

Inn

Cemy

Factory

Dukestown

CROWN
BSNS PK

Bryn Serth
(Bryn-Sarth)

2

Waundeg

STATION
TERR

WILLOW CT

WHITE
LION
COTTS

BROOKLANDS

GREENFIELD
COTTS

POLICE
ROW

ST LUKE'S RD

CROWN
AVE

HEADS OF THE VALLEYS RD

Bryn Bach
Prim Sch

Hafod-wen

MERTHYR RD

ROSE FARM
BGLWS

GREENWOOD

BRYNBACH ST

MEADOW

YELLOW
ROW

Scwrfa

ESTAD SEA

Duke's
Meadow

COACH RD

FEEDER ROW

BRYN TEG

1

TAFARNAUBACH
IND EST

A465

Visitor
Ctr

Nant-y-Bwch

WOODLANDS

GRIFFITHS

Ashvale

MARTIN

GREENWOOD AVE

BORTH

AVE

CRESCENT

Sch

COACH RD

CHARLES ST

AVALONDALE

1 EBENEZER CT
2 MECHANIC'S SQ
3 CARMEL ST
4 VARTEG PL
5 BUTLEIGH TERR
6 AVALON TERR
7 MYDRIAM PL

BEAUFORT RD

(RHOSLAN)

SGT
LADIES
ROW

A4047

PO

Sirhowy
(Sirhywi)

10

12

A

13

B

C

13

D

14

E

F

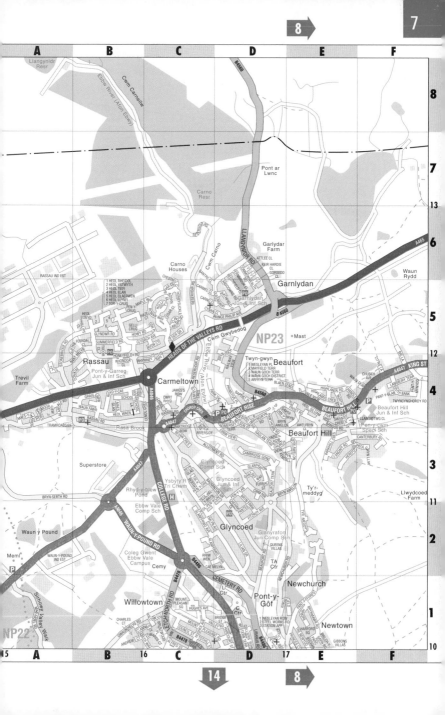

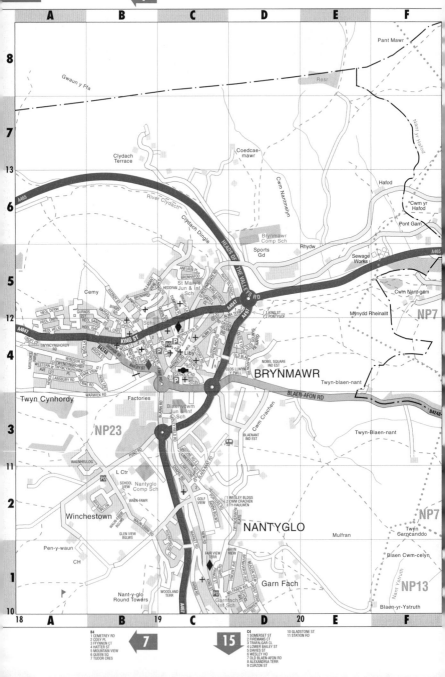

A   B   C   D   E   F

8

7

13

6

5

12

4

3

11

2

1

10

18   A   B   19   C   D   20   E   F

Pant Mawr

Gwaun y Ffa

Resr

Nant yr Hafod

Clydach Terrace

Coedcae-mawr

Hafod

Cwm Nantmelyn

Cwm yr Hafod

River Clydach

Clydach Dingle

Pont Garn

HEADS OF THE VALLEYS RD

Brynmawr Comp Sch

Sports Gd

Rhydw

Sewage Works

A465

A465

Cemy

St Mary's Jun & Inf Sch

ANEURIN PL

BRONHAFOD

HEDDFAN

BRYNMAWR

Cwm Nant-gam

Mynydd Rheinallt

NP7

HEOL DERW

GURNOS

HEOL ONEN

HEOL HAFOD

HEOL GAD

BIRCH

BANK

BIRCH BDL

BEAUFORT HILL

A4047

1 KING ST
2 PONTYGOF

HILL CRES

Sch

KING ST

HELP

BAILEY ST

TWYNCYNGHORDY RD

WINDSOR RD

TWYNCYNGHORDY

TWYNCYNGHORDY

WESTERN AVE

PINE RD

LANSBURY RD

CRUFFT

MONTON ST

Liby

NOBEL SQUARE IND EST

BRYNMAWR

Twyn-blaen-nant

WARWICK RD

CLOS LLWYN YR PWLL

Twyn Cynhordy

Factories

CATHERINE RD Sch

BLAEN-AFON RD

B4248

NP23

Blaencwm Jun & Inf Sch

Cwm Crachen

Twyn-Blaen-nant

BLAENANT IND EST

WAUNHEULOG

PENN RD

L Ctr

SCHOOL VIEW

Nantyglo Comp Sch

GOLF VIEW

1 WESLEY BLDGS
2 CWM CRACHEN
3 TY-HAULWEN

WAEN-FAWR

NP7

GLEN VIEW BGLWS

NANTYGLO

Mulfran

Twyn Garncanddo

Pen-y-waun

CH

FAIR VIEW TERR

GWYN VIEW

Blaen Cwm-celyn

NP13

Nant-y-glo Round Towers

WOODLAND TERR

Garnfach Inf Sch

Garn Fach

Blaen-yr-Ystruth

Nant Ystruth

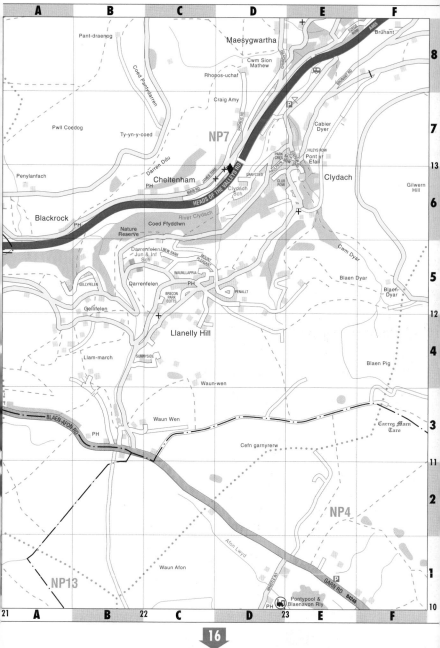

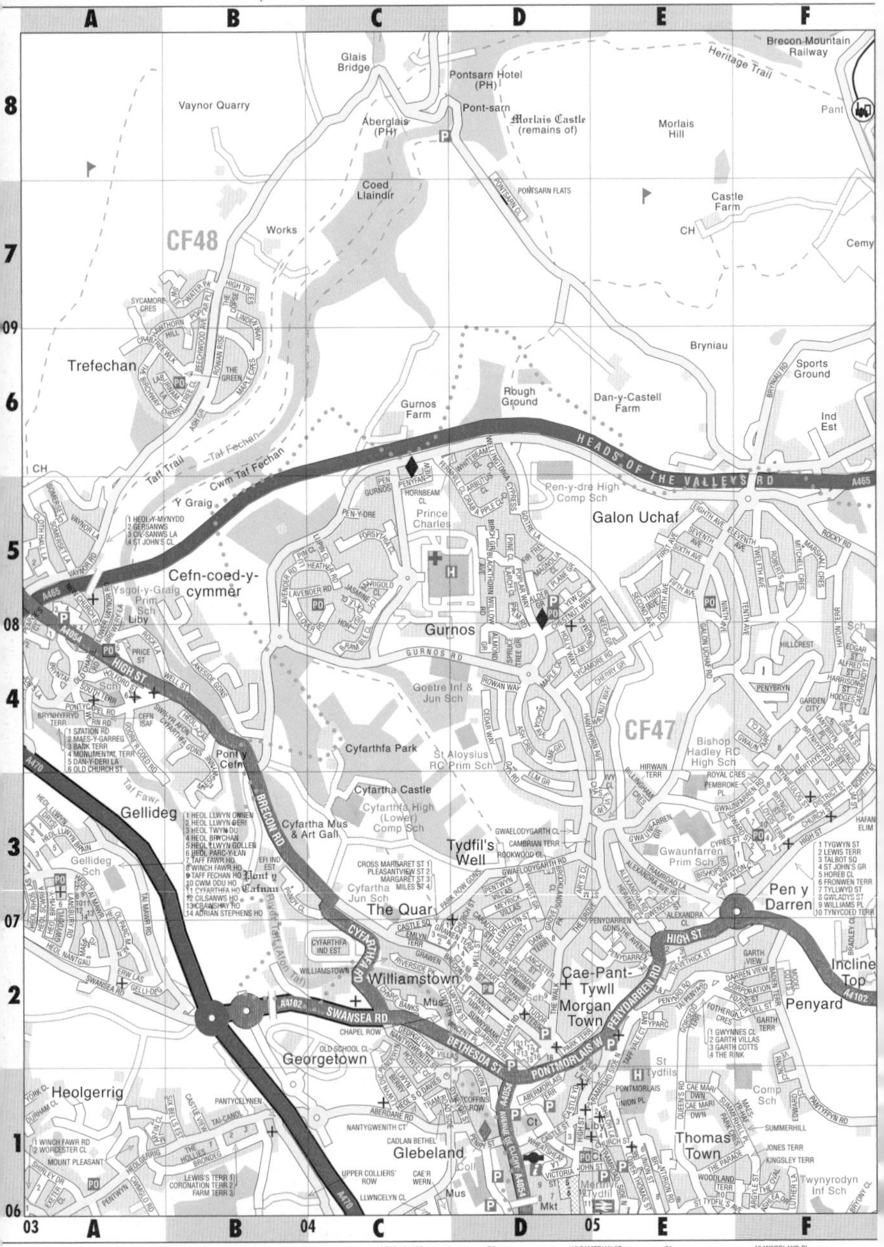

D1
1 BETHESDA ST
2 ROBERTS LA
3 POST OFFICE LA
4 GLEBELAND ST
5 MARKET SQ
6 GRAHAM ST
7 GRAHAM WAY
8 RIVER WLK
9 NEWMARKET WLK
10 THE ARCADE
11 MASONIC CL

D2
1 MOUNT ST
2 TYDFIL'S TERR
3 MOUNT TERR
4 MORGAN ST
5 CROSS MORGAN ST
6 TAIR GRAWEN
7 BRYCHAN PL
8 KING EDWARD ST
9 BRUNSWICK ST
10 CAMBRIAN ST
11 WILLIAM ST
12 SAND ST
13 LOWER EDWARD ST
14 DAVID ST
15 MORIAH ST
16 GARTH ST
17 UPPER EDWARD ST
18 BARTHINEWYDD CT

E1
1 MORLAIS BLDGS
2 NEW CASTLE ST
3 UPPER THOMAS ST
4 TRAMROAD TERR
5 LIBRARY LA
6 UNION TERR
7 SOMERSET ST
8 COURTLAND TERR
9 BRYN-TEG TERR

10 WOODLAND PL

F4
1 NIBLOE TERR
2 SUMMERFIELD DR
3 AMBERTON PL
4 BRYNMAIR TERR
5 BRYN-ONEN TERR
6 BRYNMORLAIS ST
7 AWELFRYN TERR
8 PENYBRYN VILLAS

1 TYGWYN ST
2 LEWIS TERR
3 TALBOT ST
4 ST JOHN'S GR
5 HOREB CL
6 FRONWEN TERR
7 TYLLWYD ST
8 GWLADYS ST
9 WILLIAMS PL
10 TYNYCOED TERR

1 GWYNNES CL
2 GARTH VILLAS
3 GARTH COTTS
4 THE RINK

A B C D E F

Blaen-y-garth

Garth

Pantcerddinen

Pitwellt
Pond

Nant Morlais

Blaen-
morlais

Jepson's
Pond

8

Pantcadifor

PANTSYGALLOG
TERR

Caeracca

7

Mast

Pengarnddu

09

Pant

Rhyd-y-
Bedd

HAFOD
COTTS

Warehouse

Superstores

6

1 ALPHONSO ST
2 CROSS HOULSON ST
3 HOULSON ST
4 DAVIES ST
5 GUEST COTTS

Ind Est

CROSS IFOR TERR

BRYNWERN
BARRACK ROW

UPPER ROW

LOWER ROW

HEADS OF THE VALLEYS RD

A465

Halfway
House

5

CWM GRAIG
BGLWS

THOMAS
TERR

1 GLENDOWER ST
2 CROSS FRANCIS ST
3 LIBANUS ST
4 ALMA TERR
5 WIMBORNE ST
6 BRYNTIRION ST
7 MORLAIS ST
8 OVERTON ST
9 WALTER ST
10 CROSS MORLAIS ST

REES ST
SPRING ST

Pen-y-wern

CHARLOTTE
GDNS

Dowlais Top

COEDCAE BACK

A4060

Gelli-Gaer
Common

08

MEN ROAD

MORET TERR

BLANCHE ST

STATION TERR

COEDCAE ROW

GREEN ST

GROSE BLANCHE ST

SMITHS CT

Sch

Dowlais
Inf Sch

Gwernllwyn
Jun Sch

BLACK DOWLAIS ST

4

St Illtyd's
RC Prim
Sch

Liby

Factories

JAPONICA DR

1 BODALAW
2 STABLES CT
3 DOWLAIS STABLES
4 CHURCH ST
5 COMMERCIAL ST
6 BRYN MAIR
7 MAES-Y-FFYNNON
8 CHARLOTTE ST
9 MENELAUS SQ

CF48

NEW RD

HIGH ST

Dowlais

3 WYNDHAM ST
2 MARY ST
3 MORGAN ST
4 GWERNLLWYN CL
5 Y GANOLFAN

Merthyr
Common

MERTHYR TYDFIL
(MERTHYR TUDFUL)

Tair
Carreg

07

2

CF47

Isaac Morgan
Cottages

GOAT MILL RD   A4102

MANGOED TERR

BRYN
TERR

CROSS MARGOED

PENYDRE TERR

Mountain
Hare

LC

1

06

06 A B 07 C D 08 E F

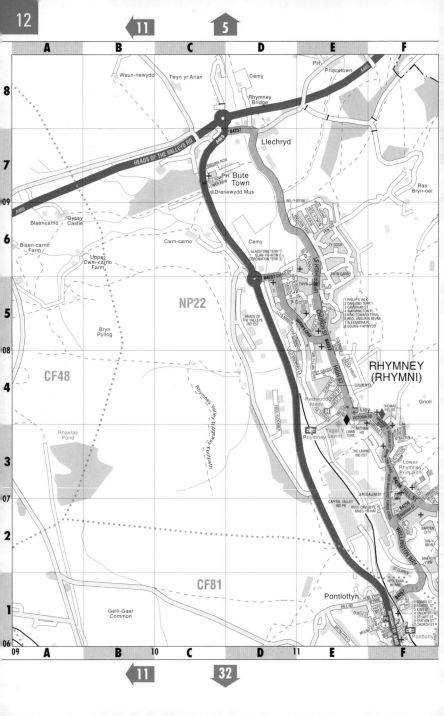

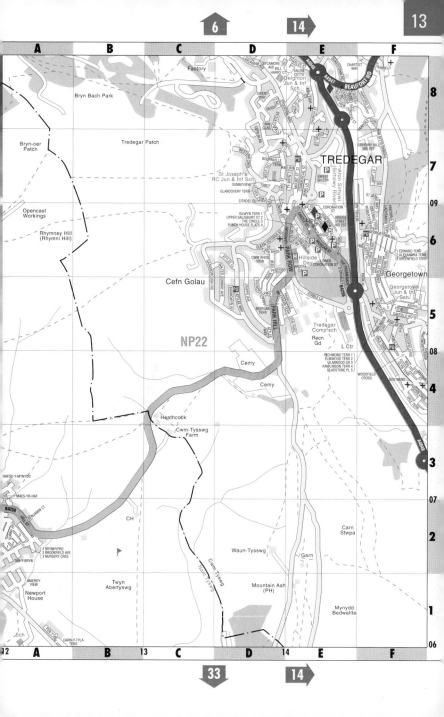

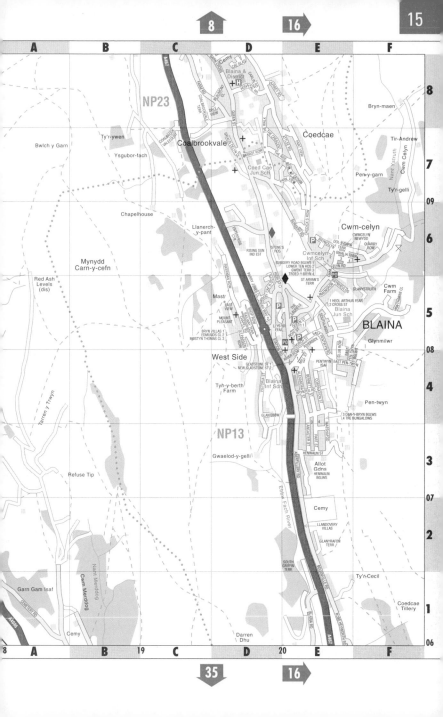

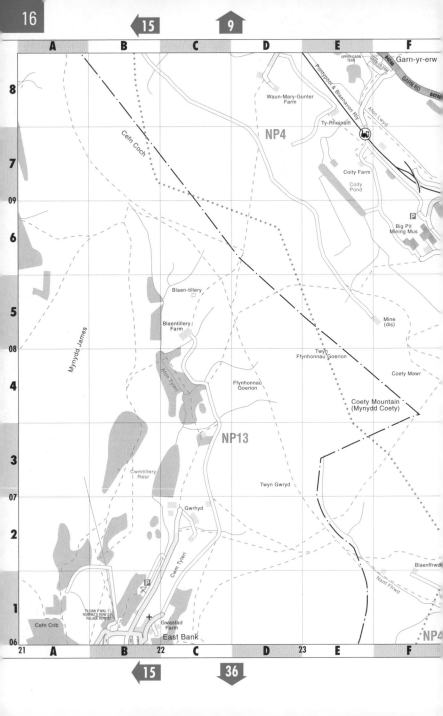

C6
1 LION CT
2 NEW QUEEN ST
3 BURFORD ST
4 DUKE ST
5 BOOT LA
6 ANNE ST

7 GEORGE ST
8 CHURCH VIEW
9 COMMERCIAL ST
10 OLD JAMES ST
11 BAKER STREET HO
12 OLD WILLIAM ST
13 MARY ST

14 LOWER HILL ST
15 SOUTHVIEW TERR
16 NEW WILLIAM ST
17 TON-MAWR ST
18 BRIDGE ST
19 BRYNAVON

C7
1 MAXWORTHY RD
2 RIFLE GN
3 CLIFTON TERR
4 ELGAM GN
5 ALMA ST
6 STACK SQ

7 VINCENT ST

D6
1 GLADSTONE TERR
2 NEW JAMES ST
3 CAPEL NEWYDD RD
4 COED TERR
5 FRANCIS MORRIS EST
6 BRIGHTS LA

D7
1 BLORENGE TERR
2 NEVILL TERR
3 GARN DYRUS MOUNT
4 LLANFOIST CRES
5 COURT RISE
6 MORRIS RISE

7 MORGAN RISE
8 GWAUNFELIN WLK
9 GILCHRIST WLK
10 CARADOC WLK
11 LOWER WOODLAND ST

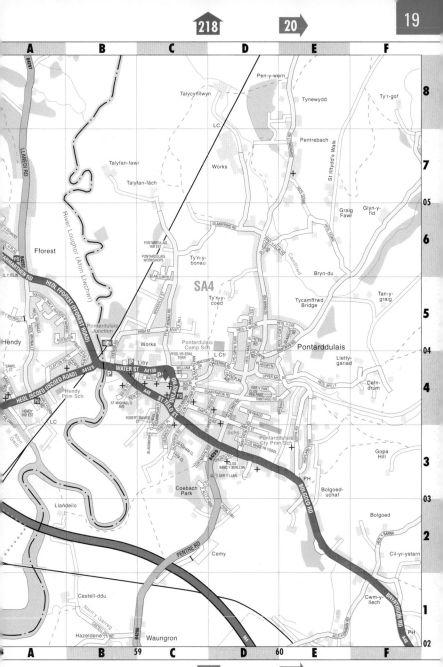

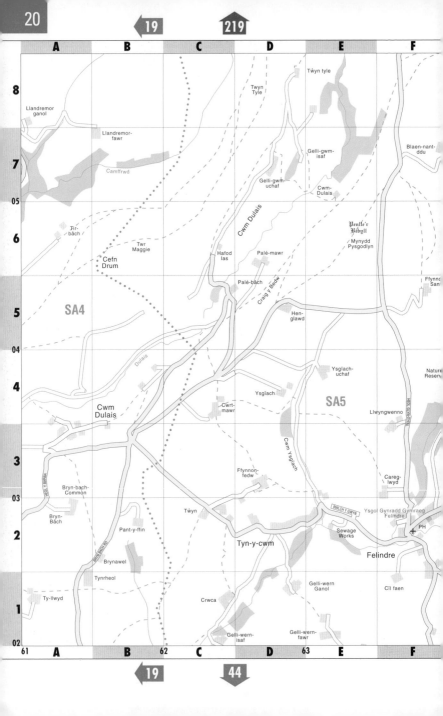

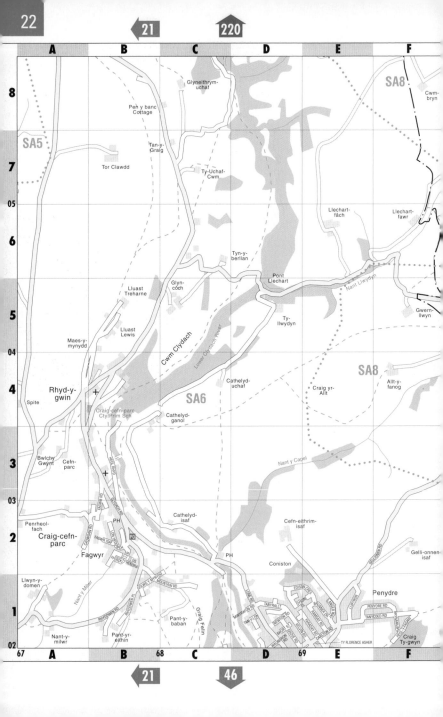

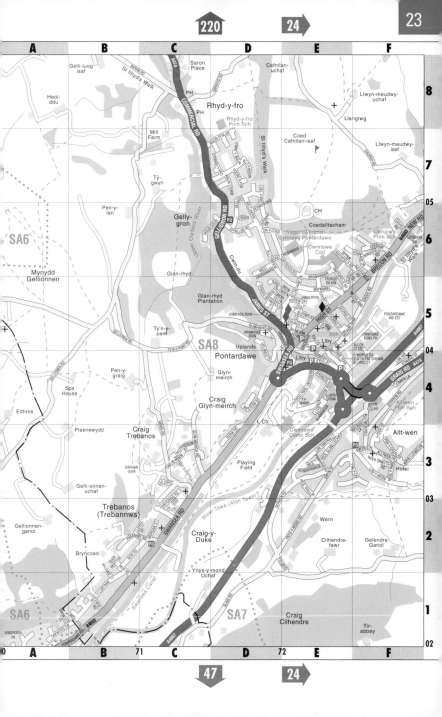

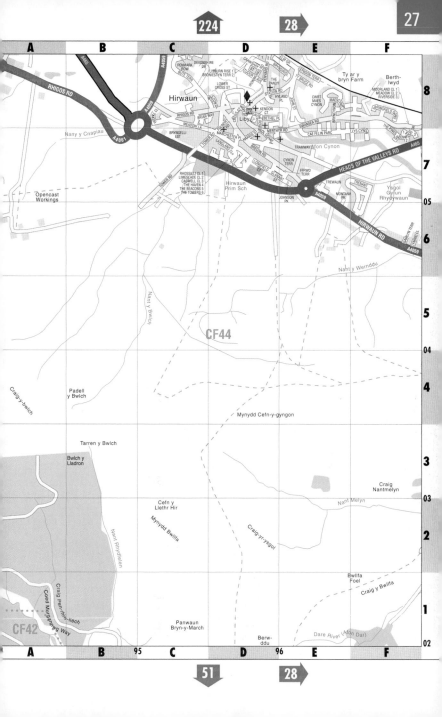

A   B   C   D   E   F

224
28

8

RHIGOS RD

A465

A4059

A4061

Hirwaun

DEVONSHIRE DR
PENMARK ROW
BUTE TERR

LISBURN RISE 1
BRYNBRES'N TERR 2

LOWER CROSS ST

MEADOW LA

RHIGOS RD

BRYNGELLI EST

MANCHESTER PL

LLWYN RD

TOWER RD

TOWER RD

THE PANDY
STATION RD
HYLAND PL

BRIAR WAY

KENDON

BETHEL PL

MERTHYR PL

CROSS ST
BRICK RD

GYNION TERR

CWRT MAES CYNON

MAES GLYN
CWM MACHEN

SWANSEA RD

CAE FELIN PARC

TRAMWAY

Afon Cynon

Ty ar y bryn Farm

Berth-lwyd

MOORLAND CL 1
MEADOW CL 2
RIVERSIDE 3

LLYS CYNON

KINGSFIELD CL

THE PINES
GREENHOLM

8

Nany y Cnapiau

Opencast Workings

RHOSSILLY CL 1
LIMESLADE CL 2
CASWELL CL 3
THE HAVEN 4
THE BEACONS 5
THE TOWERS 6

Hirwaun Prim Sch

LONGFAIR RD
ST AGNES

CYNON TERR

EFFWD TERR

HEADS OF THE VALLEYS RD

A465

7

JOHNSON PK

TREWAUN

TREVANT

Ysgol Gyfun Rhydywaun

MONTANA PK

HIRWAUN RD

A4059

CARN YN TERR
TY'N CNICL

05

6

Nant y Bwlch

Nant y Wernddu

6

CF44

5

04

4

Craig-y-bwich

Padell y Bwich

Mynydd Cefn-y-gyngon

4

Tarren y Bwich

Bwlch y Lladron

Cefn y Llethr Hir

Mynydd Bwllfa

Craig-yr-ysgol

Nant Melyn

Craig Nantmelyn

Craig y Bwllfa

Bwllfa Foel

3

03

2

Nant Rhydfelen

Coed Mnlganwg Way

Craig Pen-rhiw-llech

CF42

Panwaun Bryn-y-March

Berw-ddu

Dare River (Afon Dar)

1

02

A   B   95   C   D   96   E   F

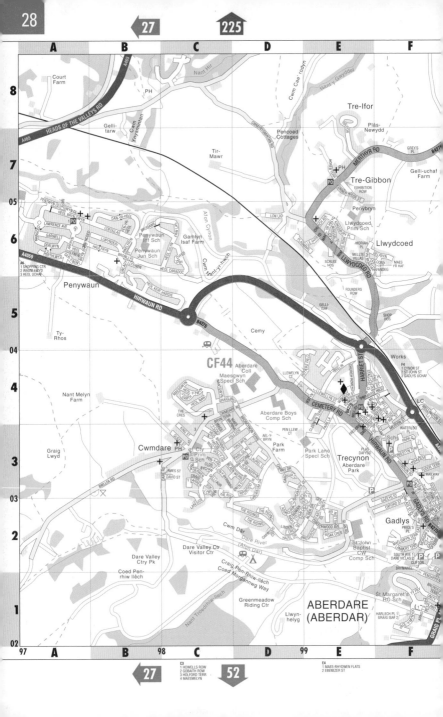

A B C D E F

Mynydd Aberdâr

yn-defaid Patch
Opencast Workings
Dyllas Farm
MERTHYR RD
B4276
Dyllas Cottage

Twyn Ddisgwylfa

Waun y Gwair

Cain Pentyle-bir

Mast

Mast

1 WINCH FAWR RD
2 TAI YSGOL FACH

CF48

8

Bryn Pica

Nant y Wenallt

Pen Llwynmelyn

Cefn Ffordd

Twyh Blaen-nant

7

05

Tir-ergyd

Bryn Mawr

Blean-nant

6

Blaencanaid

CF44

Coedcae Farm

Gwersyll

5

04

Ysgubor-wen House

Gwrhyd

Coed Morgannwg Way

Garn Las

4

sgubor-wen Farm

PH

Robertstown

Aber-nant Cty Prim Sch

Twyn y Werfa

WERFA LA

WERFA LA

Werfa House

3

Aberdare General

H

RICHMOND TERR
WINDSOR TERR

Abernant

03

Maes-y-dre

PARK VIEW TERR
BETHUEL RD

CH

ALLTWEN

WENALLT CT

us

Aberdare

A4233

GLANYNYS HO

Crichton Farm

Blaen-nant-y-groes

Nant y Groes

2

A4059

Superstore

GORDON VILLAS

CWMBACH RD

Sports Ctr

BETHEL ST

1 BROOKBANK CL
2 MEADOWBANK CL

WINDERMERE CL

NYNSCYNON TERR

KENDAL LA

INCLINE RD

WATERLOO ST

Cwmbach Jun Sch

1

oundry Town

VICTORIA SQ

CARDIFF ST
A4233

A4059

Ysgol Synrada Cymraeg Aberdar

B4275

Cwmbach

02

A B 01 C D 02 E F

A   B   C   D   E   F

8
7
05
6
5
04
4
3
03
2
02

INCLINE TOP HOUSE
Incline Top House
Tip
BOGEY RD
INCLINE SIDE
Ffos y Frân
Tai Cwm
Bargoed
Pen-coedcae
Cwm Golau
Cwmblacks
Farm
Garth Fawr
Nant Gwrawd
Bargod Taf
Merthyr Common
Bryn
Caerau
Pen-y-lan
Graweth
PENTREBACH
IND EST
CF48
Pwll-glâs
PH
Greenfield
Sch
1 CHAPEL CL
2 HAMILTON ST
3 POPLAR TERR
4 GREENFIELD TERR
5 MORLAIS ST
6 NORMAN TERR
Pentrebach
Begwns
HICKMAN
ST
Mynydd
Cilfach-yr-encil
ARTHUR
ST
Enterprise
Ctr
CF46
Bargod Taf
FURNACE
ROW
HOLLY TERR 1
HAZEL TERR 2
PLAS DERWEN 3
LABURNAM TERR 4
TY PONTRHUN 5
1 BROOKFIELD TERR
2 SOUTH VIEW
3 TYDFIL TERR
4 GREENFIELD TERR
5 PEMBROKE ST
6 KIMBERLEY PL
7 RHODFA TERR
8 LADYSMITH TERR
9 TALDWYN TERR
Pen-rhiw
ronen
ENOCH
MORRELL
Troedyrhiw
Troed-y-rhiw
Craig
Pendeugae
Cwm Bargod
Mount
Pleasant
Buarth-
weunydd
Pont
Rhûn
Afon Taf
High
Sch

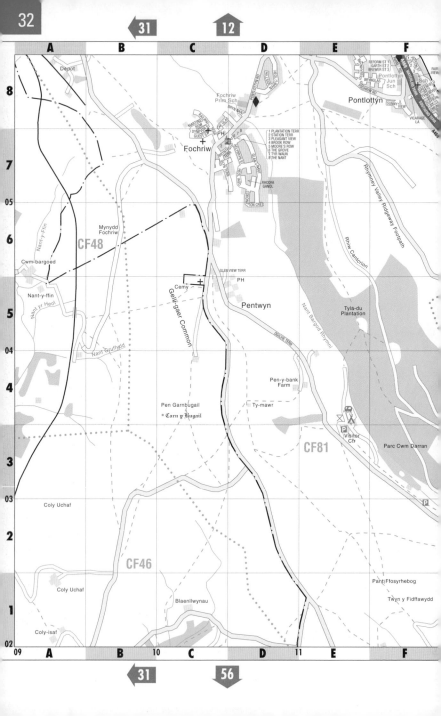

8

7

05

6

CF48

5

04

4

3

03

2

CF46

1

02

09   A   B   10   C   D   11   E   F

Depot

Fochriw Prim Sch

BRYN BACH

Fochriw

1 PLANTATION TERR
2 STATION TERR
3 PLEASANT VIEW
4 BROOK ROW
5 MOORE'S ROW
6 THE GROVE
7 TYR WAUN
8 THE NANT

Pontlottyn
Jun Sch

Pontlottyn

REFORM ST
GARTH ST
BREWER ST

A469

Nant-y-ffin

Mynydd Fochriw

Cwm-bargoed

Nant-y-ffin

Nant yr Heol

Nant Gruffydd

Gelli-gaer Common

GLEN VIEW TERR

Cemy

Pentwyn

PH

Nant Bargod Rhymni

Rhiw Cancrion

Rhymney Valley Ridgeway Footpath

Tyla-du
Plantation

Pen Garnbugail
Carn y Bugail

Ty-mawr

Pen-y-bank
Farm

CF81

Visitor
Ctr

Parc Cwm Darran

P

Coly Uchaf

Coly Uchaf

Blaenllwynau

Pant Ffosyrhebog

Twyn y Fidffawydd

Coly-isaf

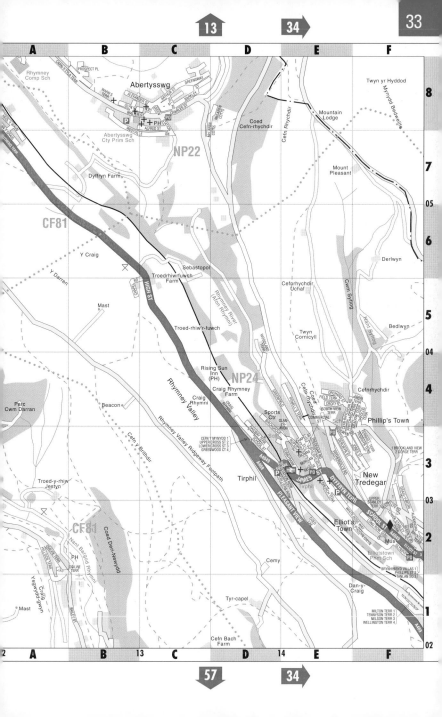

A **B** **C** **D** **E** **F**

Rhymney Comp Sch

PROSPECT PL

CEFN FFLA TERR

WARN'S TERR

Abertysswg

ALEXANDER ST

GREENDWK

ARTHUR ST

CHARLES ST

MARKLEY

GLYN TERR

WALTER ST

WESTVILLE

P

PH

ALFRED ST

Abertysswg Cty Prim Sch

MILL ROAD
COTTS

Coed Cefn-rhychdir

Twyn yr Hyddod

Mynydd Bedwellte

Mountain Lodge

Cefn Rhychdir

8

NP22

Dyffryn Farm

7

Mount Pleasant

05

CF81

Y Craig

Y Darren

Sebastopol

Troedrhiwrfuwch Farm

HIGH ST

ROAD FIELDS

Rhymney River (Afon Rhymni)

Cefnrhychdir Uchaf

Cwm Syllog

Nant Syllog

Derlwyn

Bedlwyn

6

5

Mast

Troed-rhiw'r-fuwch

WOODLAND

Twyn Cornicyll

04

Rhymney Valley

Rising Sun Inn (PH)

NP24

Craig Rhymney Farm

CRAIG ROAD

Cefnrhychdir

4

Parc Cwm Darran

Beacon

Rhymney Valley Ridgeway Footpath

Craig Rhymni

Cefn y Brithdir

Sports Ctr

GREENFIELD

POWELL'S TERR

Coed Cefn-hychdir

ORCHARD
FIELD TERR

SOUTH VIEW
TERR

CROFT

COMMERCIAL ST

FARM

Phillip's Town

03

Troed-y-rhiw Jestyn

CF81

Coed Deri-Newydd

Nant Bargod Rhymni

HAZELDENE TERR

OSBUNE TERR

PH

GLAN-YR-AFON

CEFN Y MYNYDD 1
UPPER CROSS ST 2
LOWER CROSS ST 3
GREESWOOD CT 4

SCHOOL ST

A469

BURNHAM

JAMES ST

Tirphil

CHARLES ST

MORGAN ST

P

PO ST

COMMERCIAL ST

PLEASANT VIEW

DYFFRYN TERR

Tirphil

New Tredegar

1 BROOKLAND VIEW
2 GORGE TERR

UPPER STANLEY TERR

SCHOOL ST

Elliot's Town

3

Craig Gbwyb-Gwyn

Ysgwydd

BAILEY TERR

PH

Cemy

Tyr-capel

A469

P

Mus

Elliotstown Prim Sch

PO

BRYNHYFRYD VILLAS 1
PHILLIPS ST 2
TANLAN SQ 3

2

Mast

Dan-y-Craig

MILTON TERR 1
TENNYSON TERR 2
NELSON TERR 3
WELLINGTON TERR 4

Cefn Bach Farm

A469

1

02

A **B** 13 **C** **D** 14 **E** **F**

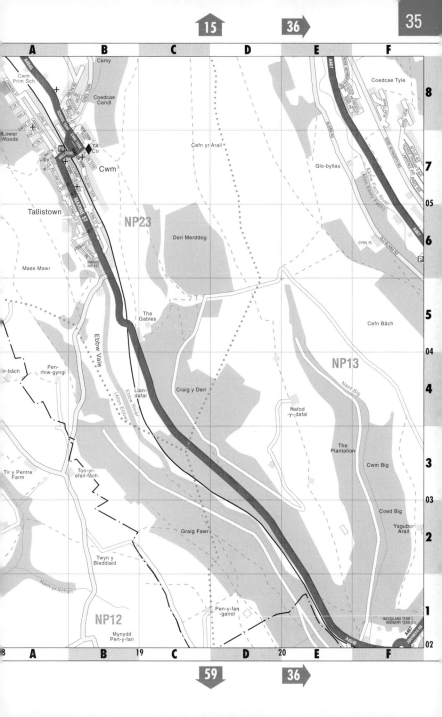

8

7

05

6

05

5

04

4

3

03

2

02

A B C D E F

Gwastad

Coed
Castellau

Cwmtillery
(Cwmtyleri)

1 SUMMER'S HOS
2 MOUNT PLEASANT ROW

Twyn Pentre

Ty Pwdr

Cwmtillery
Jun Sch

CWMTILLERY
IND EST

3 FOUNTAIN CT
8 FAIRVIEW TERR
9 GREENMEADOW TERR
9 GWERN LAS

Greenmeadow

Pen-y-Bont

Blaenau
Gwent

Abertillery
Comp Sch

Rhiw Lladron

Waun Wen

NP4

Cwm Sychan

Antwerp
Pl

Abertillery
Prim & Inf Sch

THE
BROOKLANDS

CLARENCE ST

THE
PINES

ADAM ST

ABERTILLERY
(ABERTYLERI)

10 EDWARD ST
11 ARGYLE ST
12 DIAMOND JUBILEE TERR
13 FERNFIELD TERR
14 TRYNORUG COTTS
15 RHIW PARK TERR

ROYAL LA 1
LOWER ROYAL LA 2
LOWER ROYAL LANE
TERR 3
THE OLD BAKERY 4
UPPER ROYAL LA 5
MORGAN ST 6
CORBAN CT 7
GREEN VILLAS 8
BRYNTEG HO 9

Rhiw Park

THE BUNGALOWS

PENRHIWGARREG

Liby & Mus

MOUNT PLEASANT COTTS 16
MELBOURNE RD 17
ARCADE 18
COMMERCIAL ST 19
CARMEL ST 20
DAVY EVANS CT 21
CROSS ST 22

THE
WILLOWS

Pant-y-Pwdyn

OLD BARN
WAY

Coetgae

Craig yr Arail

CWRT
ALEXANDRE

Sp Ctr

Bryngwyn
Prim Sch

Nant y Groes

Coed
y Gilfach

Cwm Nant-y-groes

Arail

LOWER LANCASTER
ST

Six
Bells

1 VIVIAN COTTS
2 ALEXANDRA TERR
3 HAFOD-FAN TERR
4 HAFOD-FAN RD

CHAPEL

NP13

Coed
Hafod-fan

Gilfach-wen

Arail
Jun & Inf Sch

ABERBEEG RD

WESTVIEW
TERR

Cwm Llwydrew

Ty-Dafydd

Nant Ddu

Aber Each River
(Afon Ebwy Fach)

VICTORIA RD

CEMETERY RD

Mast

Coetgae-coch

Mynydd-
Llanhilleth

Cemy

8

7

05

6

04

5

4

03

3

2

02

A B C D E F

NP7

Garn Clochdy

Hafod-wenog

Beili-glâs

Bryn-glâs

Henfelin

Coedcae Sal

Mynydd Garnclochdy

Pwll Cefn-y-llaw

Pant- ysgawn

Coed Peggy-Shams

Holy Well

Cwmarvon Farm

Pen-y-heol

Pen-y-ddoyga

Coed y Cam

Coed Howell

Cwm Lasgarn

Garn-wen

Tyr-ywen

Greenmeado

Mynydd Garn-wen

Drain Eos

Greenmeadow Wood

Rising Sun Bridge

VICARAGE TERR

Lasgarn Wood

Lasgarn Farm

NP4

Coedcae Ambrose

Mamhilad House Wood

Penlasgarn House

Coed Ithel

Lambrook

Company's Wood

LINTON CT
LASGARN PL
AFON CT

Freehold Wood

PLEASANT CT

Penlasgarn-isaf

CH

Little Mountain

Tir-croes Bleddyn

Troed-y-rhiw

BEECHWOOD WLK 1
FERNCROFT WAY 2
ARCADIA WAY 3

Pontnewynydd Prim Sch

Mus

Craig y Twr

Upper Govera

Pant-y-gollen

Coedcae

Trevethin

Ysgol Gyfun Gwynllyw

ORCHARD FARM EST

Church Farm

LEIGH RD

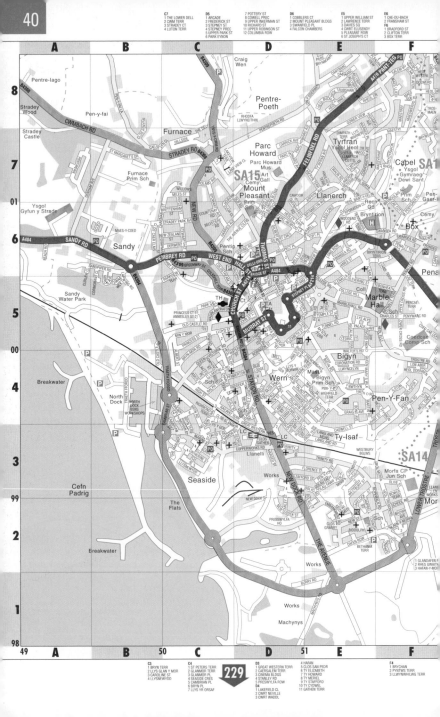

229

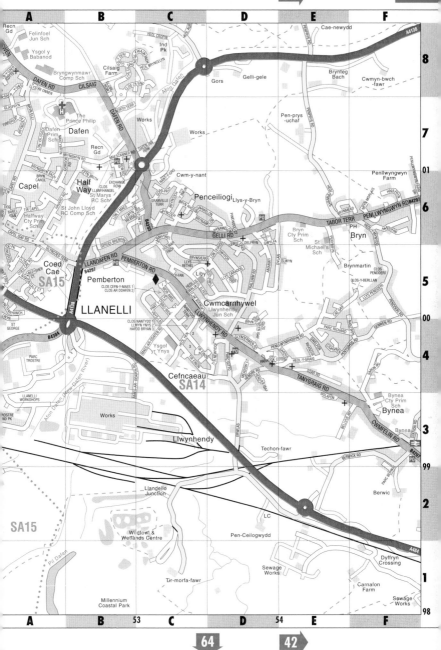

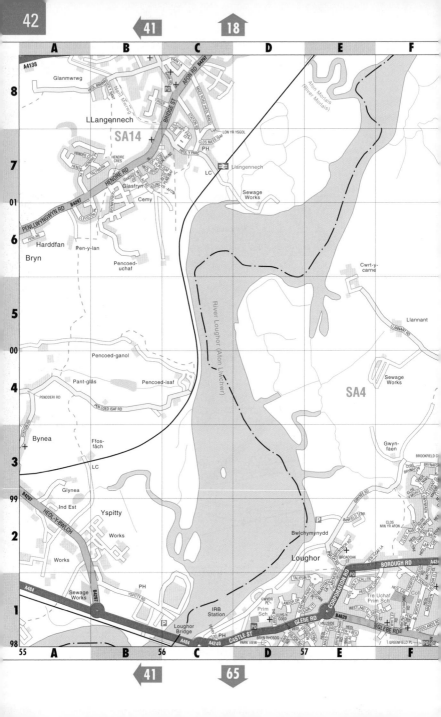

8
7
01
6
5
00
4
3
99
2
1
98

Gwenlais-fâch
Gwenlais-uchaf
Nant y Crimp
Brynawel
Fforest-newydd
Coed-cae-croes
Clordir
Pontlliw Prim Sch
Abergwenlais
Glan-lliw-uchaf
BRYNTIRION RD
BRYN RD
BRYN BACH RD
SWANSEA RD
PO
1 CARMEL RD
2 HEOL-Y-TWYN
Pontlliw

Penllergaer Forest
Pen-y-waun
Glan-Lliw
HEOL PANT-Y-LLIW
OAKLANDS RD
WOODFIELD AVE
CHRIST CHURCH RISE
VERNON LN
SA4
Craig Tyle-du
Tyle-du
Cefnfforest-fawr
SA5
The Poplars
Llwyn-y-beech Covert
Green Plantation
SWANSEA RD
Tircoed
Coed-Tremig
M4
Ty'rheol
Motel
Tredegar-fawr
Pen-deri-fawr
Swansea West Service Area
Penllergaer Forest Walks
Melin-llae
Afon Llan
Tir-ffordd
Cwm Tir-fford Wood
47
A48
A483
M4
A48
Penllergaer Prim Sch
PENLLERGAER BSNS PK
Coedwig-Hywel
GROSS HILL
A4240
GORSEINON RD
PO
PH
C. Ctr
A48
1 CLOS BRYN DAFYD
2 CLOS TIRFFORDD
Cil-fwnwr
LLEWELLYN RD
Penllergaer
Parc-mawr
1 SPRUCE WAY
2 CLOS LLANWYDDEN
ELM CRES
Parc Penllergaer
Valley Wood
Gelli-aur
A4240
A483
Y Bwthyn
Middle Lodge
Clawdd-y-duon Wood

A B C D E F

8

Bryn-caws Farm

Bryn-rhôs Cottage

Nant Rhos

Craig Tir isaf

Llwyngriffith Farm

A4109

Tan-y-rhiw

Tir-isaf Farm

7

SA10

Lletty'r-afel-fawr

01

Ty-draw

Ty-draw Brook

DERWEN FAWR

Gelli-march Farm

Deri

Micheldever

6

Craig y gigfran

OAK VIEW

Cilfrew Farm

Coed Cae-fforest

Llettybella Farm

Coed Gawdir

PH

PLEASANT HILL

Cilfrew

PO

Cae'r-graig

B4242

5

P

NEW RD

SWN-YR-AFON

Fforest Farm

Coed y Fforest

B4242

00

SCWD-YR-AFON

YMYL-YR-AFON

Aberdulais

YNYSYGERWN AVE

Ynys-y-gerwyn-fâch

Craig Gwladus

P

Cilfrew Prim Sch
Wildlife Pk

Aberdulais Falls

MAIN RD

B4434

4

Cadoxton-Juxta-Neath (Llangatwg)

Llangatwg Comp Sch

PH

A4109

Tonna

H

PEN-Y-BRYN

BRUNEL

Wenallt Wood

Noddfa Bungalow

3

MAIN RD

A4230

CANAL SIDE

B4434

DULAIS-FACH RD

PARK ST

TONNA UCHAF

DAN-Y-BRYN

Wenallt Farm

ABERDULAIS TERR

Tennant Canal

ST ANNE'S TERR

Penlan-fâch

99

2

Neath Canal

HENFAES RD

Tonna

SA11

Bryn-chwŷth

Tonnau Prim Sch

MOUNT PLEASANT

Mast

HENFAES TERR

CWRT-Y-YSGOL

Cytgoed

Gelli-dêg Farm

Castell-fforch-nant

River Neath (Afon Nedd)

NEATH RD

Cefn-y-don

Dan-y-lan Farm

Ivy Tower

1

B4434

LLANTWIT RD

FAIRYLAND RD

P

98

A B 77 C D 78 E F

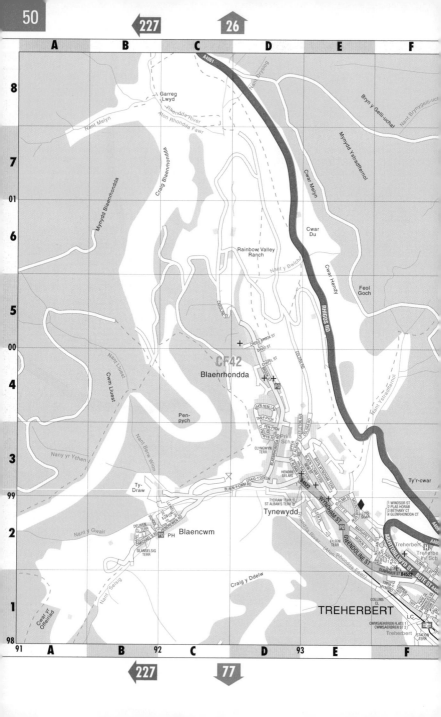

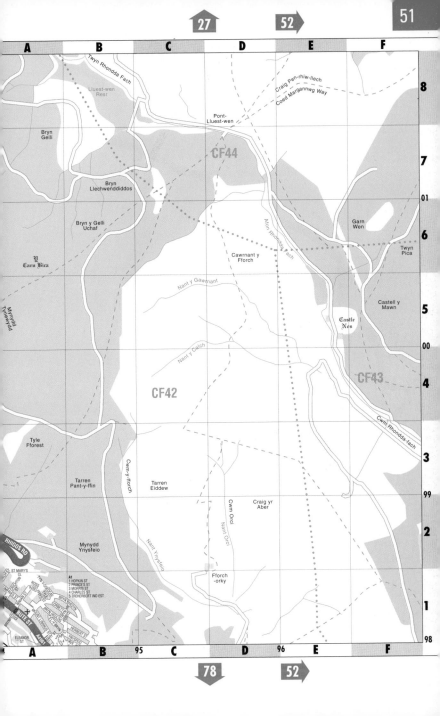

51

28

A   B   C   D   E   F

8

7

01

6

5

00

4

3

99

2

1

98

97   A   B   98   C   D   99   E   F

Troedrhiw
lech Foel

Craig Rhiw-ddu

Graig
Rhiwmynach

A4233

Dumfries
Park

Cefnrhos-
gwawr

Fire
Tower

MAERDY RD

P

Hafod-
wen

Panwen
Garreg-wen

Nant Aman Fach

CF44

Rhos-
gwawr

Pen Foel
Aman

Coed
Blaenaman-fach

Craig Fforchaman

Bryn
Du

Nant Aman Fawr

P

Glynhafod
Jun Sch.

GLYNHAFOD ST
GLANRHYD ST

KINGSBURY
PL.

BRYNHYFRYD

GLANAMAN RD

Cwm Aman

P

Twyn Croesffordd

Afon Rhondda Fach

CF43

Craig
Bedwlwyn

Craig
Tirllaethdy

Bedwlwyn

Cefn Craig Amos

Maerdy
Farm

Mynydd
y Ffaldau

Craig y Gilwern

Liby

Maerdy

STATION RD

POL

MAERDY
CT

ROWLEY
CT

MAERDY RD A4233

Cwm Rhondda-fach

Maerdy
Inf Sch

CARN
CT.

ROYAL
CLOSE

51

79

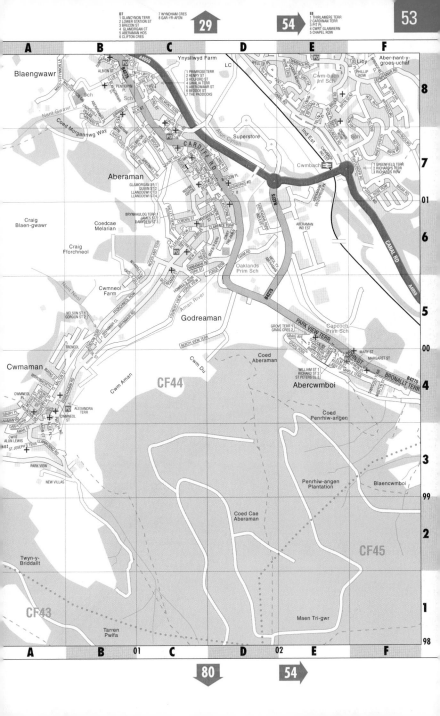

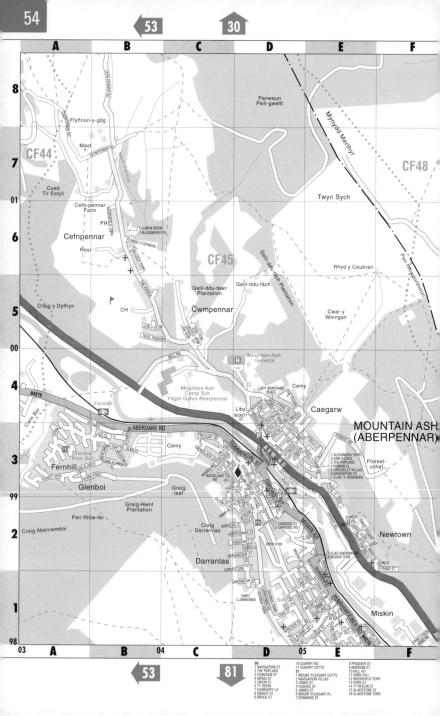

A   B   C   D   E   F

8

7

01

6

CF44

CF48

CF45

Panwaun
Pwll-gwellt

Mynydd Merthyr

Twyn Sych

Ffynnon-y-gôg

Mast

Coed
Tir Estyll

Cefn-pennar
Farm

PH

Cefnpennar

Resr

1 LLWYN BEDW
2 BLACKBERRY PL

Gelli-ddu-fawr
Plantation

Gelli-ddu-fâch

Gelli-ddu-fâch Plantation

Rhyd y Ceubren

Pen Rhiw-porthmon

5

00

4

Craig y Dyffryn

CH

Cwmpennar

Cwar y
Wningen

Mill Rd

Mountain Ash
General

H

B4275

Cwm Boi

Fernhill

Mountain Ash
Comp Sch
Ysgol Gyfun Aberpennar

Lady Abardare
Flats

Cemy

Caegarw

MOUNTAIN ASH
(ABERPENNAR)

ABERDARE RD

Liby

Beckett

Cemy

99

3

2

1

98

Glenboi Prim Sch

Fernhill

Glenboi

Graig
Isaf

Craig
Darren-las

Graig-Hwnt
Plantation

Pen Rhiw-fer

Craig Abercwmboi

Darranlas

COMMERCIAL ST

Cte

Woodland Rd

Park Hill

Oxford St

Miskin Rd

1 ALEXANDRA TERR
2 DAN-Y-COED
3 THE POPLARS
4 RUMAN CL
5 CRESSELLY VILLAS
6 NAVIGATION YD
7 GLAS -Y- DDERWEN

Fforest-
uchat

1 CARADOC RD
2 CARADOC RD

Bryn Ifor

1 CLAS GWERNIFOR
2 MISKIN TERR

Forest
Level

Newtown

John St

Strand St

Cwrt
Llanwonno

Sch

Coplestone

Swernifor

Miskin

Sch

Sch

03   A   B   04   C   D   05   E   F

D3
1 NAVIGATION ST
2 THE POPLARS
3 FOUNTAIN ST
4 GRAIG ST
5 UNION ST
6 TY SEION
7 CHANCERY LA
8 KNIGHT ST
9 BRUCE ST

10 QUARRY RD
11 QUARRY COTTS

E1
1 MOUNT PLEASANT COTTS
2 NAVIGATION VILLAS
3 JONES ST
4 HUGHES ST
5 JAMES ST
6 MOUNT PLEASANT PL
7 EDWARDS ST

8 PROSSER ST
9 MORGAN ST
10 HILL HO
11 PARK HILL
12 WOODFIELD TERR
13 PARK ST
14 TY RFELIN ST
15 GLADSTONE ST
16 GLADSTONE TERR

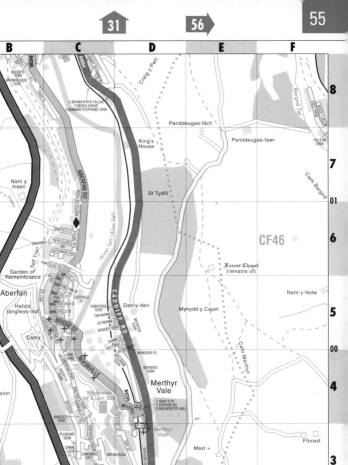

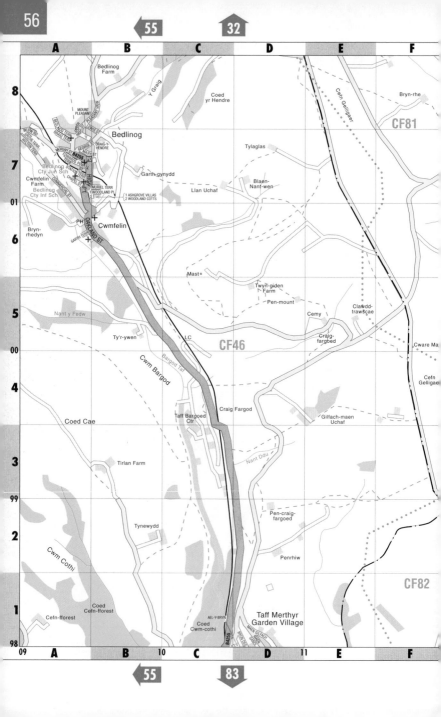

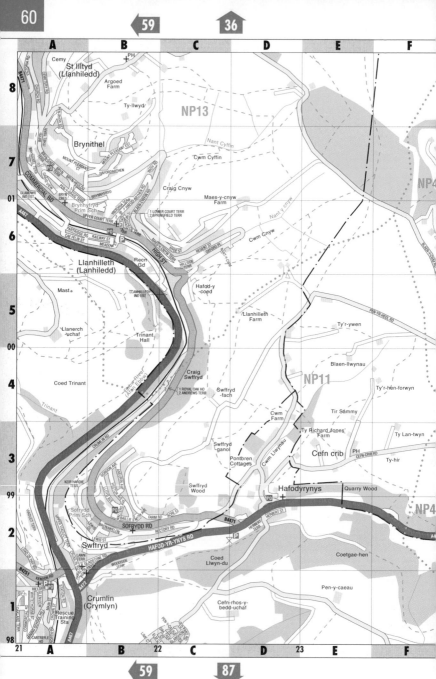

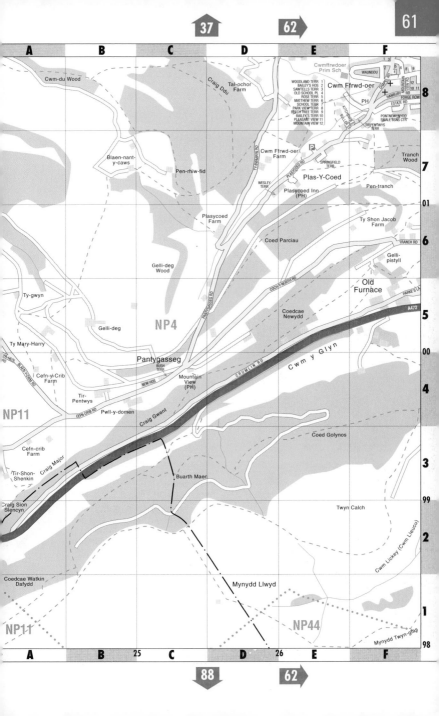

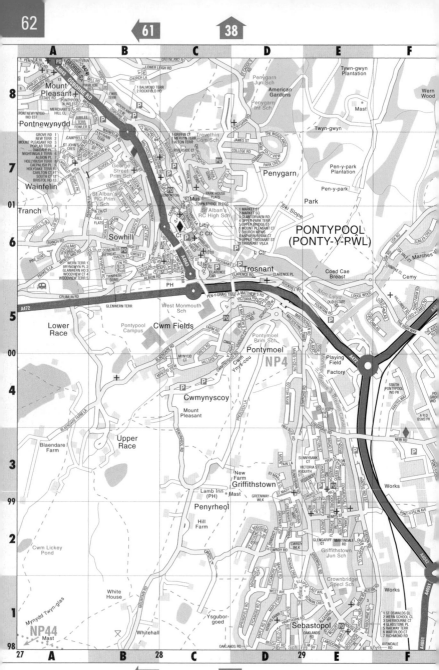

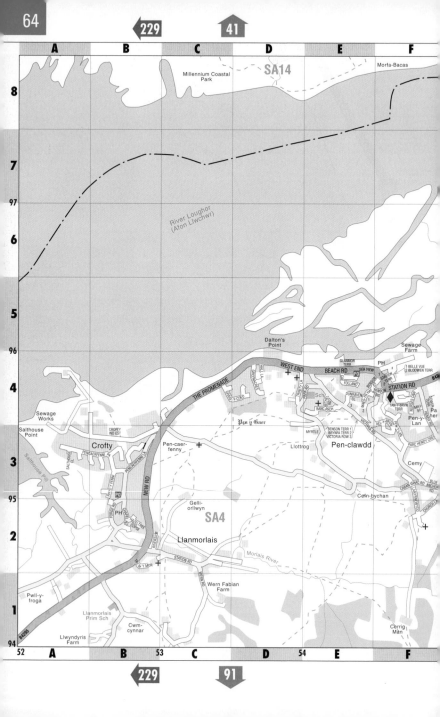

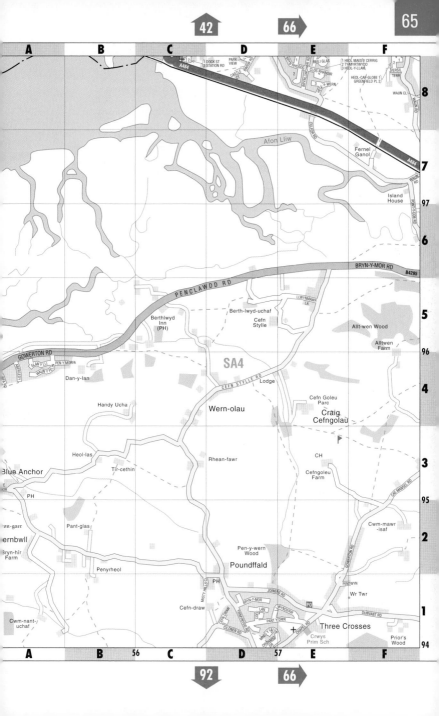

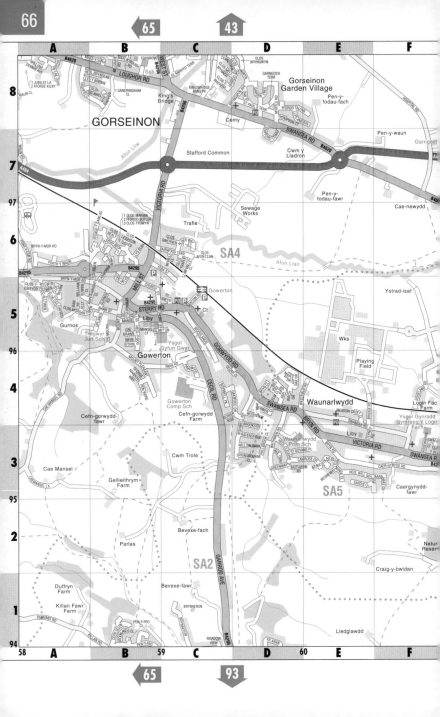

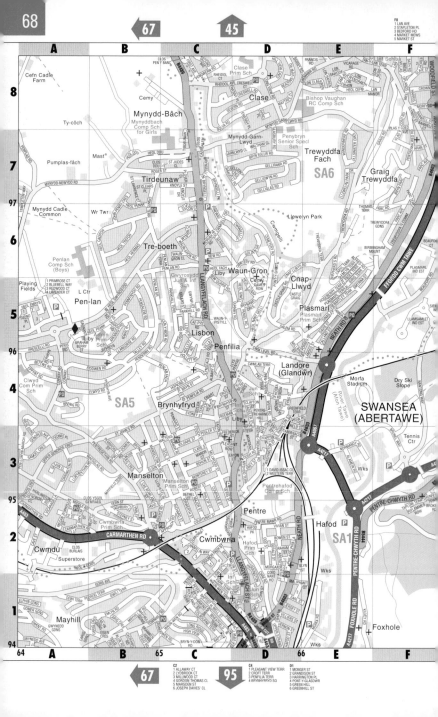

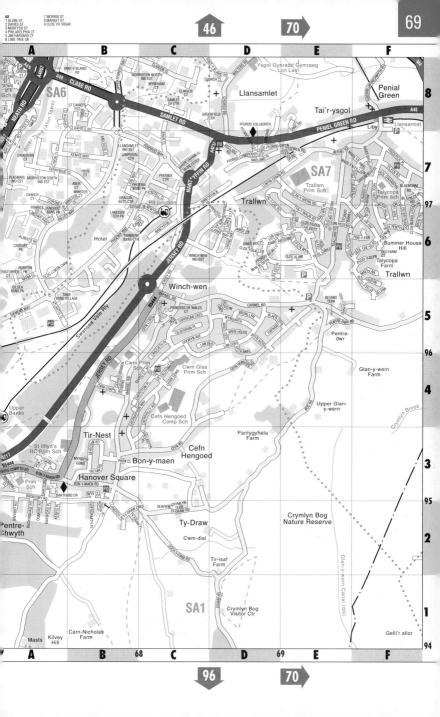

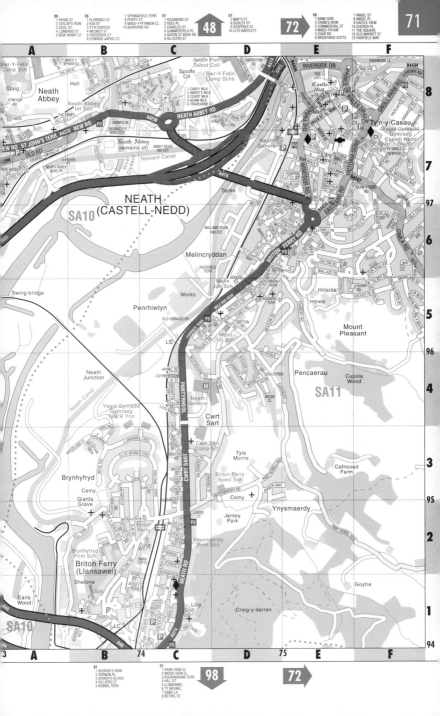

A B C D E F

8

7

97

6

5

96

4

3

95

2

1

94

B4434
LLANTWIT RD
Llantwit
Cemy
FAIRLAND
RD
Mosshouse
Wood
Mosshouse
Wood
Gnoll
Gardens
FAIRYLAND
Cefn
Morfudd
GNOLL
VIEW
Gnoll
Gds
Fishpond
Wood
Brynau
Fernbank
Preswylfa
Farm
Preswylfa
Dingle
Brynau
Wood
SA11
Nant Cae'r-bryn
Cae'r-bryn
Preswylfa Brook
Cimla
Crynallt
Jun & Inf
Schs
CASTLE DR
PO
Cefn-Saeson
Fawr
1 LARCHEL
2 HORNBEAM CL
THE
HOLLINS
Cimla
Common
AFAN VALLEY RD
CIMLA RD
1 ROWLAND HO
2 HILLARY HO
PINE GR
RAVENS AVE
Cefn Saeson
Comp Sch
Cefn-Saeson
Fâch
Baradychwallt
PH
Cimla
Level Crossing
House
Abernant
Farm
Cwm Pelenna
Ty'n-y-waun
CURWEN
TERR
Cwm Aber-nant
Cefn-
crynallt
Crythan Brook
Pen-y-star
Efail-fach
PH
Crythan
Farm
Hawdref-ganol
SA12
Tir-Evan-Llwyd
Gelli-gaer-
fâch
Mynydd
Hawdref
Cerrig
Llwydion
Gelli-gaer-
fawr
Hawdref-
fawr
Pant-Howel-
Ddu
Gaer fawr

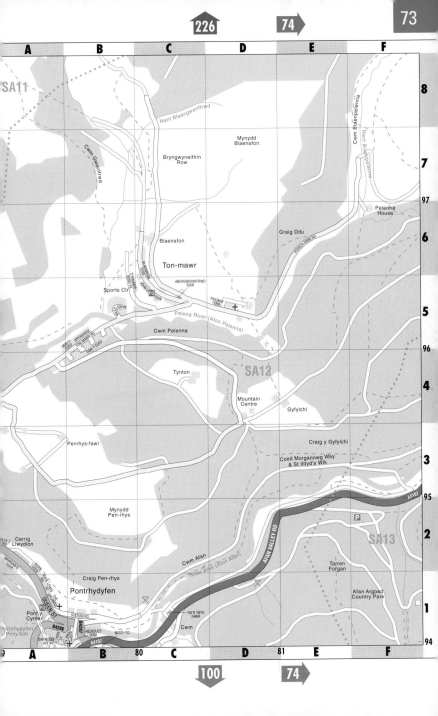

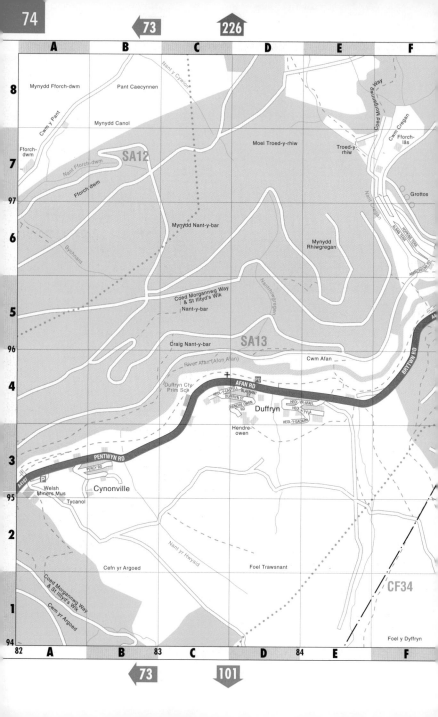

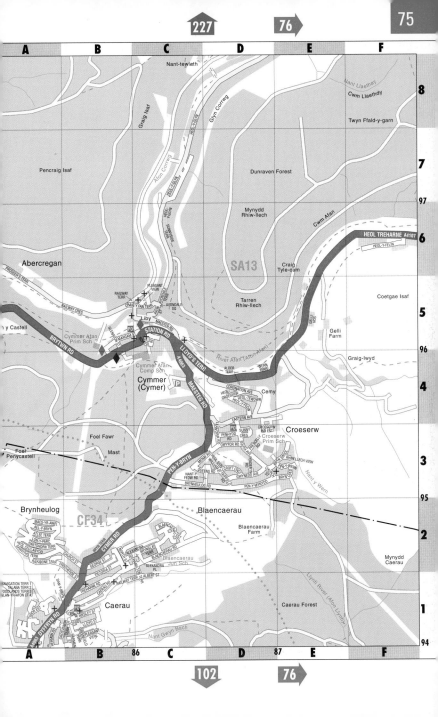

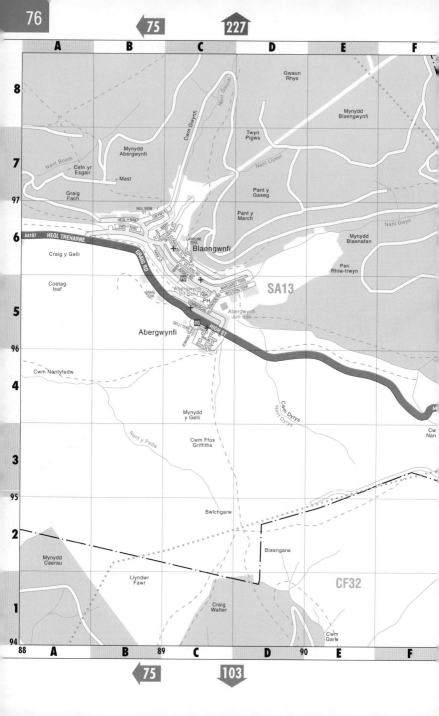

8

Gwaun Rhys

Cwm Gwynfi

Nant Gwynfi

Mynydd Blaengwynfi

7

Mynydd Abergwynfi

Nant Boeth

Cefn yr Esgair

Mast

Twyn Pigws

Nant Lluest

97

Graig Fach

Pant y Gaseg

Nant Gwyn

HILL VIEW CT

GWYNFI ST

Pant y March

Mynydd Blaenafan

6

A4107 HEOL TREHARNE

HEOL-Y-NANT

SWN-Y-NANT

MARY ST

CAROLINE TERR

Blaengwnfi

Pen Rhiw-trwyn

Craig y Gelli

GRAIG RD

Coetag Isaf

GRAIG TERR

Abergwynfi Int Sch

PH

MARGARET TERR

WESTERN TERR

SA13

5

COMMERCIAL ST

Abergwynfi Jun Sch

Abergwynfi

GELLI TERR

JENNINGS TERR

HIGH ST

CHAPEL ST

MAIN ST

SCOTT ST

96

Cwm Nantyfedw

4

Mynydd y Gelli

Cwm Dyrys

Nant Dyrys

Cw Nan

Nant y Fedw

Cwm Ffos Griffiths

3

95

Bwlchgarw

2

Mynydd Caerau

Blaengarw

CF32

Llyndwr Fawr

1

Craig Walter

Cwm Garw

94

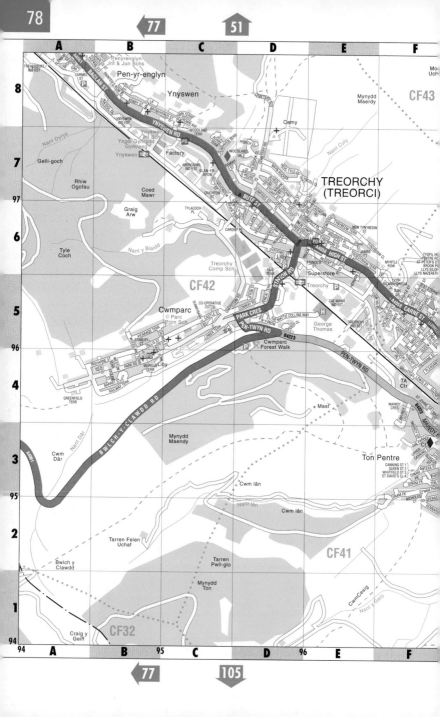

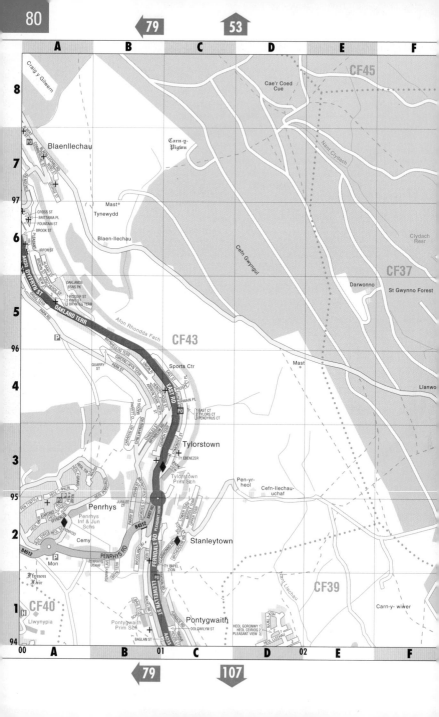

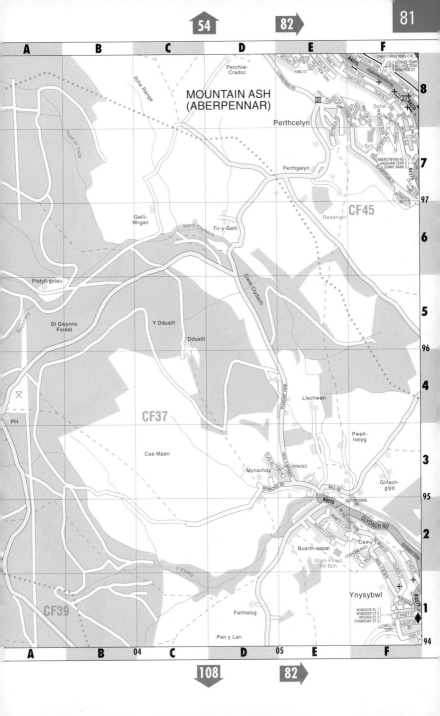

A B C D E F

8
Penrhiwceiber
Penrhiwceiber
Fforest
Isaf
Craig-yr-
efail
Ty'n-y-
cae

7
Liby
LLYS NANT
GLAS
VAUGHAN
TERR
Coed
Fforest -Isaf
Cwym
Cynon
Cefn-
glás
Pont y
Gwaith
River Taff (Afon Taf)
Penbwlcha
CF46
CARDIFF RD
Tai-yn-
Banwan
Edwardsville
Inf & Jun Sch

97
ABERCYNON RD
NEW RD

6
PENTWYN AVE
MAIN RD
HALSWELL
ST
MELBOURNE
BAGOT
HOMERTON
COMMERCIAL
PL
Ynysboeth
Inf Sch
HEBRON
VILLAS
BRYNTIRION
Ynysboeth
Jun Sch
Ynysboeth
STEINBERG ST
GLUCESTER
TERR
Darren y
Celyn
Cwyn Cynon
TAFF VALE
Quakers
Yard
Edwardsville

Tyntetown
CWRT BRYN
CYNON
Aton Cynon
B4275

5
Pen-twyn-
uchaf
Pen-twyn-
isaf
Coed Ty-
dan-
darren
ABERCYNON RD
Prince
Llewelyn

96
CF45
Nant-y-Fedw
Blaen-nant-
y-fedw
Afon Taf
Pont
Cynon
Mynydd
Goetre-coed
Goetre-
coed
INCLINE
TOP
GOETRE COED ISA

4
Ponycynon
Cemy
Abertaf
Prim Sch
STEPHEN'S
TERR

3
Gilfach-
rhydd
Gilfach-y-
rhyd
ABERCYNON
1 BETHANIA
2 GWENDOLINE TERR
WOODLAND
CRES
CALFARIA
FLATS
ALEXANDRA PL

95
Tyla-
fedw
Liby
Abercynon
North

2
CF37
Ty'n-y-
wern
Darren y Foel
Carnetown
Prim Sch
Carnetown
LITTLEWOODS
Prim Sch
DAVID DOWER CL 1
UPPER SERTRUDE ST 2
MARTINS CL 3
MARTIN'S LA 4
YNYSMEURIG RD 5
CWRT YNYSMEURIG 6
SOUTH RD
Abercynon
South
CYNON
TERR

1
Liby
LLYS BLOWN
Pen y
Foel
Pen y-
parc
Craig-Evan-
Leyshon
Common

94
06 A B 07 C D 08 E F

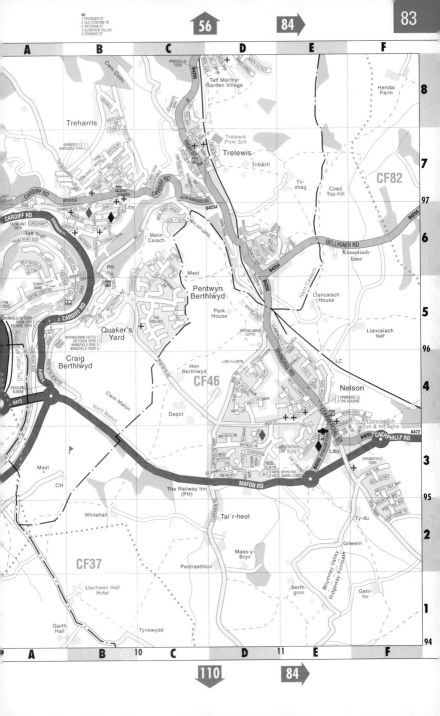

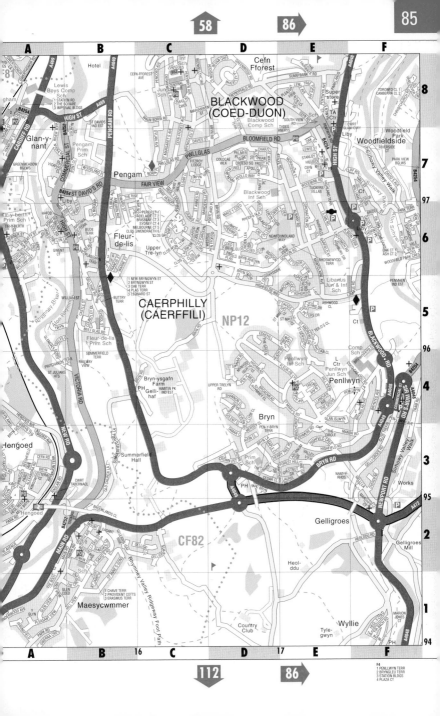

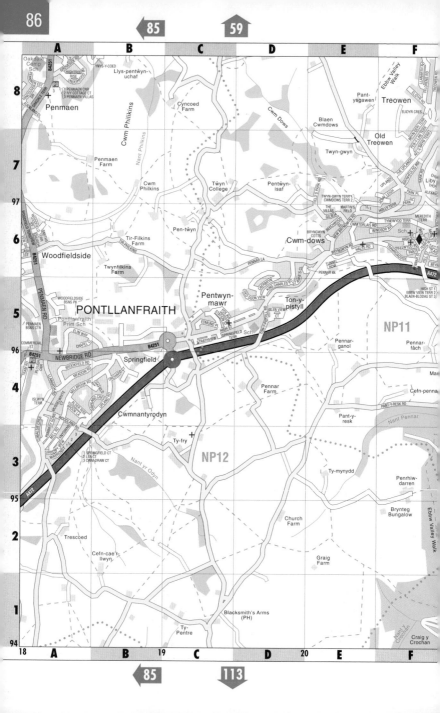

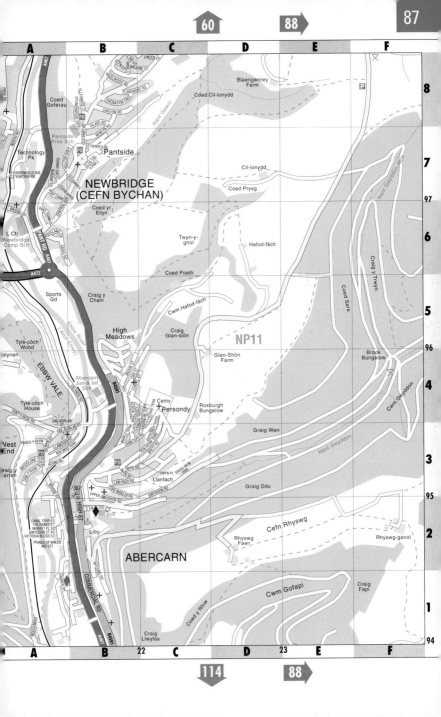

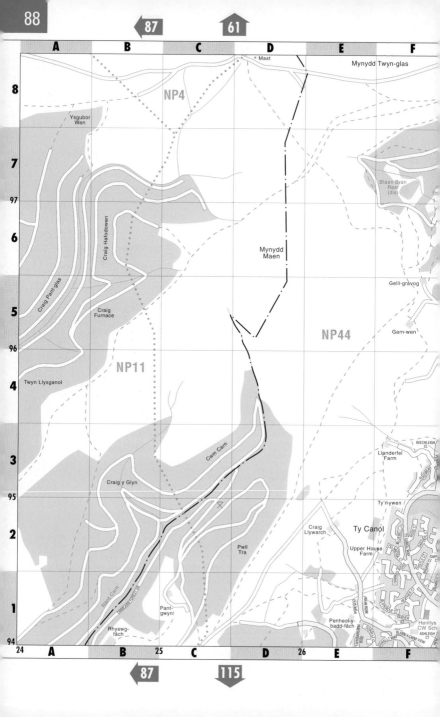

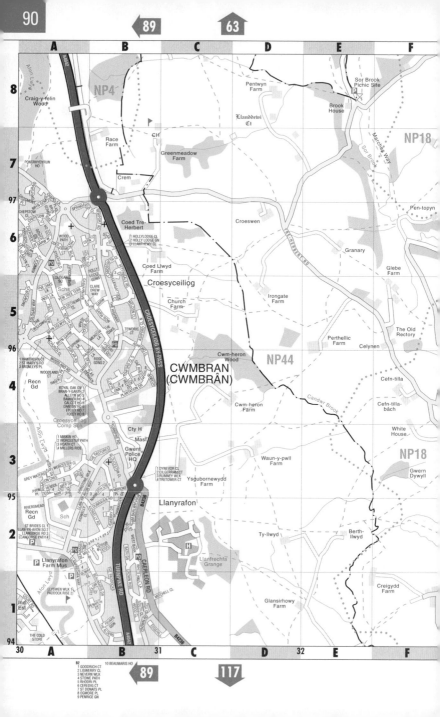

91
65

8

Cilonnen-fach

Forgemill Farm

Whitewalls Farm

CHAPEL RD BOARFIELD

Prior's Meadow

SA4

Mynydd-Bach-y-Cocs

Erw-fawr

Gelli-hîr

7

TRAWSTTO RD

Fairwood

93

Wimblewood-ganol

Caehendy Wood

Wind-Mill Wood Farm

Gelli-hîr Wood

6

Hafod Mill Wood

Fairwood Corner

B42

Wimblewood-isaf

A4118

5

Coed Bryn-côch

SA2

92

Bryncoch Farm

Fairwood Common

4

Swansea Airport

B4271

Cartersford Bridge

P

BLACKHILLS LA

Blackhills

3

91

Pen-y-banc

Worganrou Farm

2

Bryn-afel

Moorlakes

Ilston

Moorlakes Wood

SA3

1

Courthouse Farm

Carey's Wood

Canisland Wood

CANISLAND

A4118

Hams Wood

90

A B   C D   E F

91
121

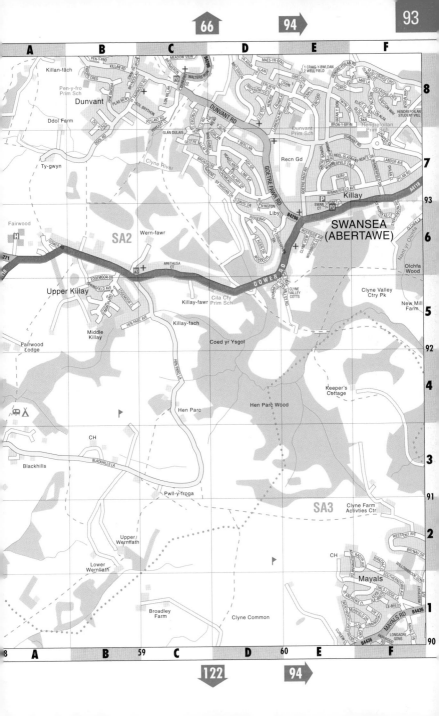

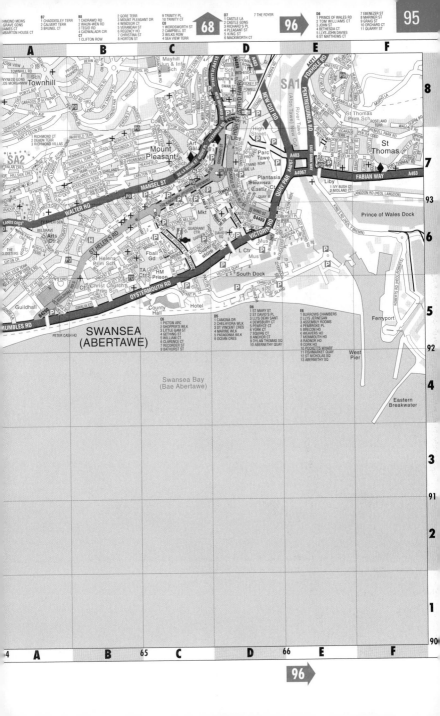

B7
1 CHADDESLEY TERR
2 CALVERT TERR
3 JAMES CT
4 ABARTON HOUSE CT

B8
1 CADRAWD RD
2 WAUN-WEN RD
3 TEGID RD
4 CADWALADR CIR

C7
1 CLIFTON ROW

2 GORE TERR
3 MOUNT PLEASANT DR
4 WINDSOR ST
5 VERANDAH ST
6 REGENCY HO
7 CHRISTINA ST
8 HORTON ST

9 TRINITY PL
10 TRINITY CT

C8
1 WORDSWORTH ST
2 CAMPBELL ST
3 WILKS ROW
4 SEA VIEW TERR

68

D7
1 CASTLE LA
2 CASTLE GDNS
3 RICHARD'S PL
4 PLEASANT ST
5 KING ST
6 MACKWORTH CT

7 THE FOYER

96

D8
1 PRINCE OF WALES RD
2 TOM WILLIAMS CT
3 JOHN ST
4 BETHESDA CT
5 LLYS JOHN DAVIES
6 ST MATTHEWS CT

7 EBENEZER ST
8 MARINER ST
9 GRAIG ST
10 ORCHARD CT
11 QUARRY ST

SA1

Townhill

SA2

Mount
Pleasant

St Thomas

SWANSEA
(ABERTAWE)

C6
1 PICTON ARC
2 SHOPPER'S WLK
3 LITTLE GAM ST
4 GETHING ST
5 WILLIAM CT
6 CLARENCE CT
7 RECORDER ST
8 BATHURST ST

D5
1 CAMONA DR
2 CHELHYDRA WLK
3 ST VINCENT CRES
4 MARINE WLK
5 PATAGONIA WLK
6 OCEAN CRES

D6
1 ST MARY ST
2 ST DAVID'S PL
3 LLYS DEWI SANT
4 DEWSBURY CT
5 PENRYCE CT
6 YORK CT
7 SQUIRE CT
8 ANCHOR CT
9 DYLAN THOMAS SQ
10 ABERNETHY QUAY

E6
1 BURROWS CHAMBERS
2 LLYS JERNEGAN
3 ASSEMBLY ROOMS
4 PEMBROKE PL
5 PRECON HO
6 WEAVERS HO
7 MONMOUTH HO
8 RADNOR HO
9 CORK HO
10 POCKETS WHARF
11 FISHMARKET QUAY
12 ST NICHOLAS SQ
13 ABERNETHY SQ

Swansea Bay
(Bae Abertawe)

Eastern
Breakwater

SWANSEA
(ABERTAWE)

Windmill
(remains of)

Pen-y-graig

Port Tennant

Cemy

Dan-y-graig

ROBERT OWEN GDNS

DAVID WILLIAMS TERR

TIR JOHN NORTH RD

SA1

Tennant Canal (dis)

Works

Works

GWYNNE TERR

DANYGRAIG RD

TEWAR ST

BELLE ST

PORT TENNANT RD

BAY ST

Danygraig
Prim Sch

VALE OF NEATH

FABIAN WAY

Works

Works

LAMBOON ROAD

SEA VIEW CRES

LC's

P 20

A483

Tanks

King's Dock

LC's

LC

Tanks

Jetties

Queen's Dock

Jetties

Jetties

Dry
Dock

Jetty

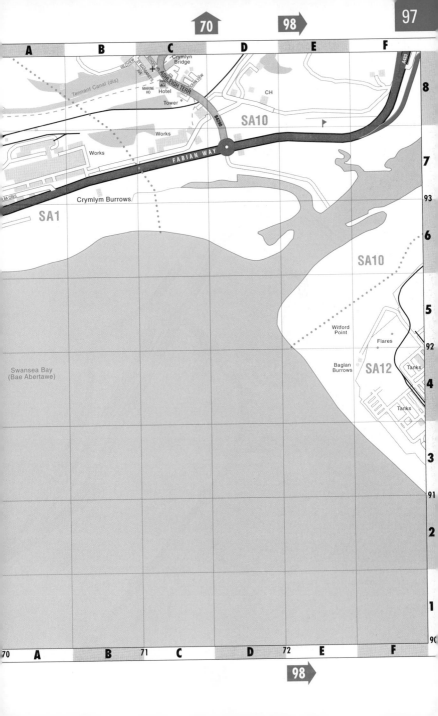

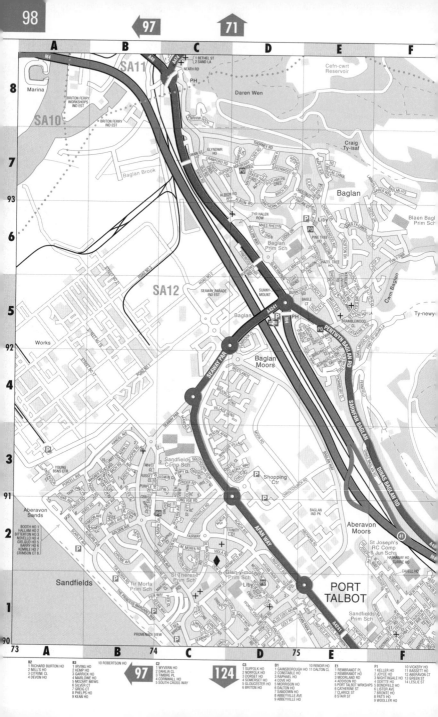

B2
1 RICHARD BURTON HO
2 MILLS HO
3 BITTERTON HO
4 DEVON HO

B3
1 IRVING HO
2 KEMP HO
3 GARRICK HO
4 MARLOWE HO
5 MOZART MEWS
6 SILVER CT
7 GREIG CT
8 PHELPS HO
9 KEAN HO
10 ROBERTSON HO

C2
1 WYVERN HO
2 DAHLIA CL
3 TIMBRE PL
4 CORNWALL HO
5 SOUTH CROSS WAY

C3
1 SUFFOLK HO
2 NORFOLK HO
3 DORSET HO
4 SOMERSET HO
5 GLOUCESTER HO
6 BRITON HO

D1
1 GAINSBOROUGH HO
2 CONSTABLE HO
3 RAPHAEL HO
4 COVE HO
5 MORRISON HO
6 DALTON HO
7 SANDOWN HO
8 ABBEYVILLE AVE
9 ABBEYVILLE HO

10 RENOIR HO
11 DALTON CL

E1
1 REMBRANDT PL
2 MOORLAND RD
3 MOORLAND RD
4 ADDISON RD
5 PORT TALBOT WKRSHPS
6 CATHERINE ST
7 CLARICE ST
8 STAIR ST

F1
1 KELLER HO
2 JOYCE HO
3 NIGHTINGALE HO
4 ODETTE HO
5 BONDFIELD HO
6 LISTER AVE
7 BRONTE HO
8 PATTI HO
9 WOOLLER HO

10 VICKERY HO
11 BASSETT HO
12 ABERAVON CT
13 GREEN ST
14 LESLIE ST

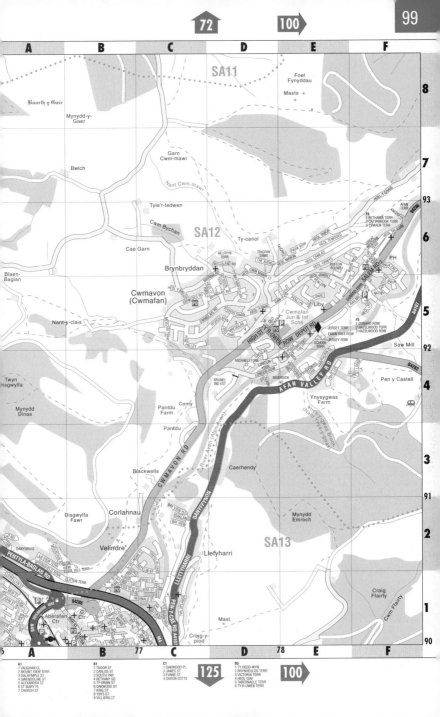

A1
1 VAUGHAN CL
2 MOUNT VIEW TERR
3 DALRYMPLE ST
4 GWENDOLINE ST
5 ALEXANDRA ST
6 ST MARY PL
7 CHURCH ST

B1
1 TUDOR ST
2 CARLOS ST
3 SOUTH PAR
4 BETHANY SQ
5 TY-DRAW ST
6 OAKWOOD ST
7 KING ST
8 YNYS ST
9 VILLIERS CT

C1
1 OAKWOOD PL
2 JAMES ST
3 EVANS ST
4 SARON COTTS

D5
1 TY HEDD-WYN
2 BRYNHEULOG TERR
3 VICTORIA TERR
4 HEOL ISAF
5 TABERNACLE TERR
6 TY R-OWEN TERR

F6
1 BETHANIA TERR
2 CATYBROOK TERR
3 TYMAEN TERR

F5
1 CUNARD ROW
2 HAZELWOOD TERR
3 HAZELWOOD ROW

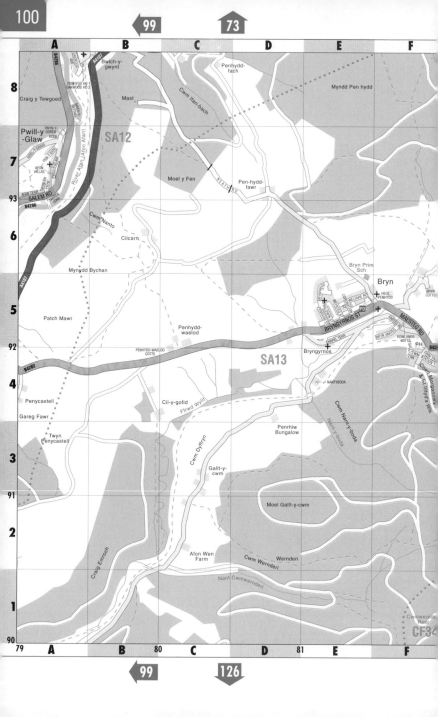

101
75

101
128

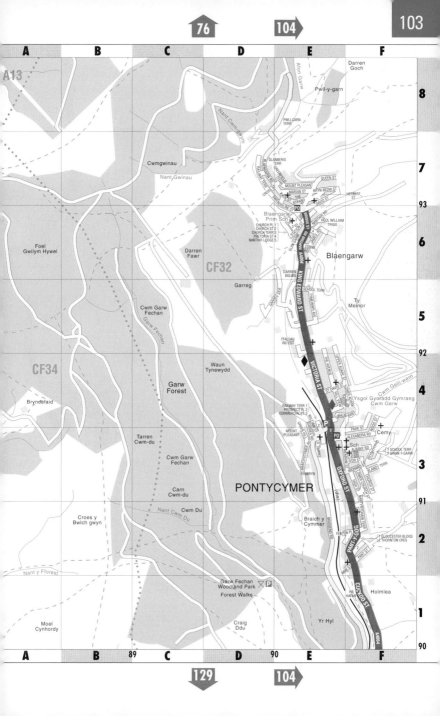

CF32

Cwm Nant-hir

Nant-Hir

Tarren y Fforch

Cwm Nant-y-Moel

Carn-yr-hyrddod

Nant y Moel

Tarren Lluest-fforch-ddu

Nant Dyfi

Cwm Gelli-wern

Cwm Gelli-wern

Rhiw Fer

Moel Garn

Mynydd Llangeinwyr

Fron-wen

Wyndham

Fforch-wen

Cwm Fforch-wen

Pant Blaenhirwr

Ogmore Vale

Cwm Cyffog

NORTH VALE VIEW

1 CRAIG-FRYN TERR
2 CHURCH TERR
3 VALVIEW TERR
4 ROWLAND TERR
5 PEMBROKE TERR
6 OGMORE TERR
7 CARDIGAN TERR
8 BLAENOGWR TERR
9 OSBORNE TERR

Talga

BWLCH-Y-CLAWDD RD

Nant-y-moel

WOODLANDS GR

DINAM CL

Nantymoel Prim Sch

BLAEN OGWR

Cemy

ABERFIELD VIEW

Craig yr Aber

ABER HOUSES

Cwm Ogwr Fawr

ABER RD

OGWR ST

Aber-House

Aber Farm

BETHANIA ROW

HIGH ST

A4061

Nant Cwm-y-fuwch

Aber Inf Sch

RHIWGLYN RD

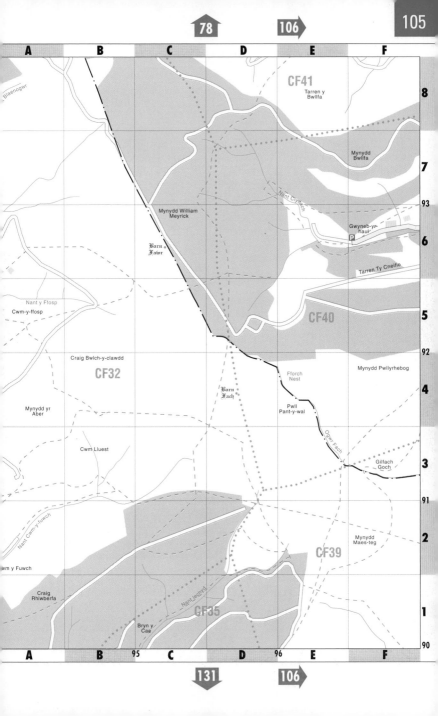

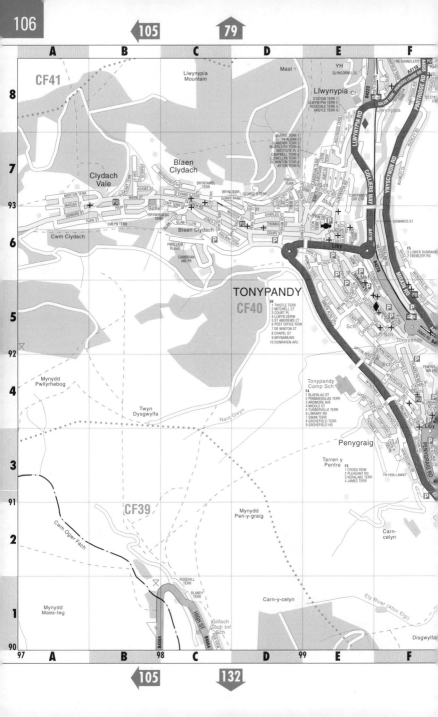

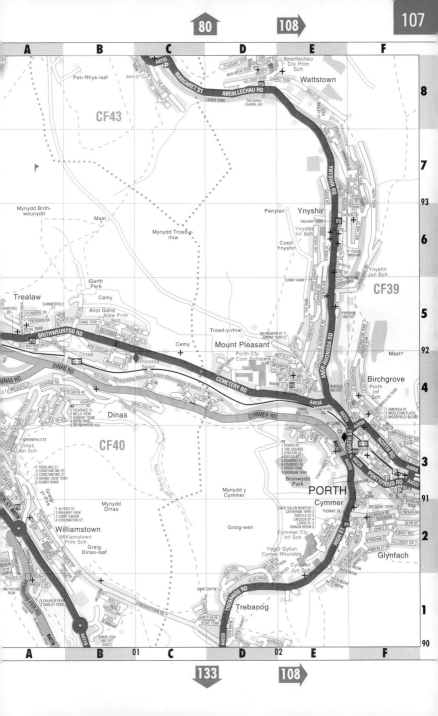

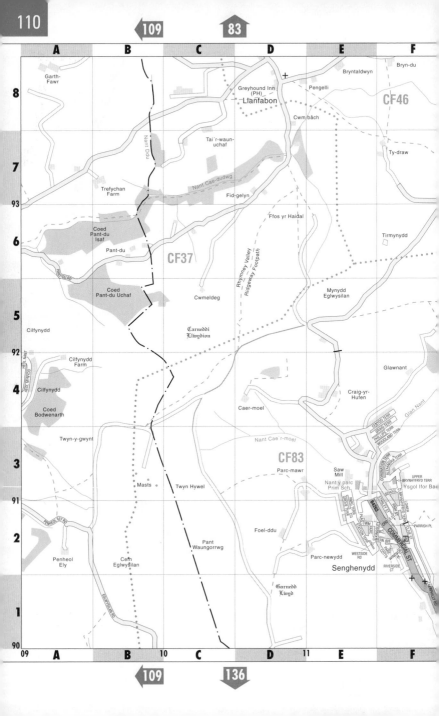

A B C D E F

Pen-yr-
heol-fawr

Castell-
llwyd

CF46

Nant Twynyrharris

Twyn-
yr-Harris

Coed y
Craig

CF82

Sports
Gd

A472 A469 Cwm-
du Wood

Ystrad Mynach
Coll

Sch

Ystrad
Mynach

COOPERS
TERR

Afon Rhymni (Rhymney)

DUFFRYN
BSNS PK

CLOS
GRADDFA

1 CLOS TIR RWYN
2 CASTELL LLWYD

Bwlch Garnygelli

Mynydd
Eglwysilan

Coed
Llanbradach

Llanbradach
Fawr

Nant Llanbradach

The
Brakes

Graddfa

Waun
Deiliaid

Maes-
diofal

CF83

COLLIERY RD

Llanbradach
Isaf

Nant Owen

GRADDFA
IND EST

Blaen-y-
fforch

Cefn-
llwyd

The
Bryn

Nant Cwm-sarn

Llanbradach

PENGERRIG ST

STATION RD

Gelli-
fanadlog

Llanbradach

13 14

8
7
93
6
5
92
4
3
91
2
1
90

F1
1 TYNYGRAIG TERR
2 PARK VIEW
3 JAMES ST
4 WOODLAND FLATS
5 OAK TERR
6 LEWIS TERR
7 PLAS CAE LLWYD
8 RICHMOND CL

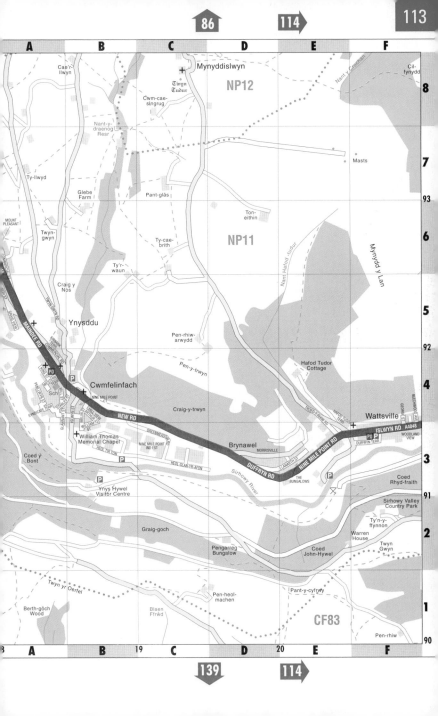

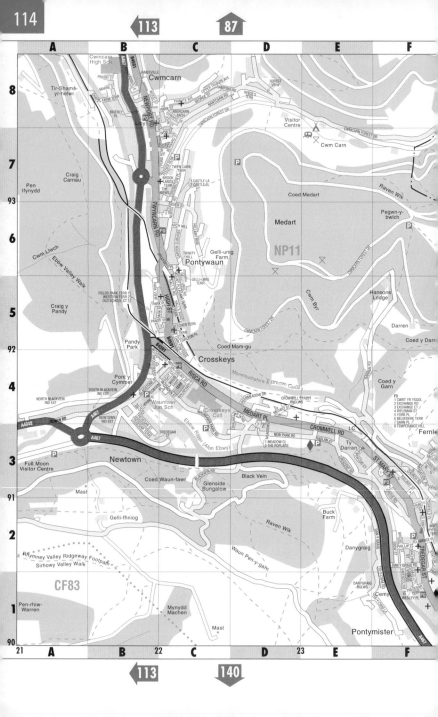

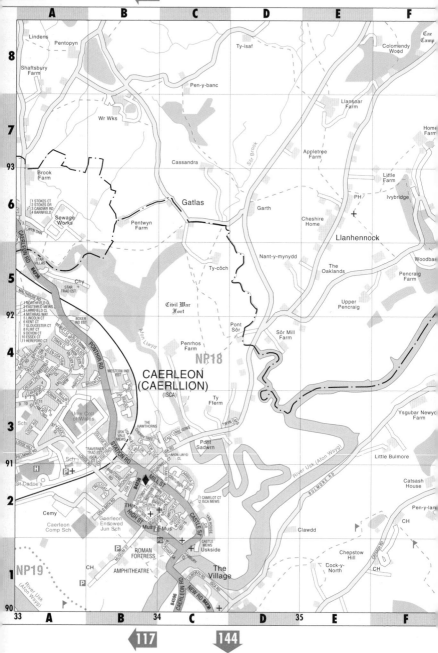

NP15

NP18

8

7

93

6

5

92

4

3

91

2

1

90

A B C D E F

Cefn-henllan Wood
Cefn-henllan
Great House
Plâs Llecha
Old Kemeys
Kennel Wood
Burnt House
Garn-fawr
Caer Licyn Motte & Bailey
Garn-fâch
Kemeys Inferior
Glen Usk
Pant-Gwyn
River Usk (Afon Wysg)
Kemeys House
Kemeys Graig
Castle Mill
Kemeys Folly
Great Caer-Licyn
Little Caer-Licyn
Abernant Farm
Woodward's Farm
Coed-y-caerau
Great Bulmore
Pen-toppen-ash
New Wood
Treclover
otel
Mount Tudor
Llanbeder
Langstone Jun & Inf Sch
Langstone Rise
Cat's Ash
Mast
Tregarn Rd
Tregarn Ho
Llanbedr Hall
Cat's Ash Farm
Priory Wood
The Gorelands
Langstone
Nursery
Tregarn Mill
PO
CHEPSTOW RD
Priory Farm
Nurseries
Nursery
Motel
PH
MAGOR RD
Ford Farm
Nursery
OLD CHEPSTOW RD
A449
B4245

CATSASH RD
CAT'S ASH RD
ROSSCROFT DR
PARK END

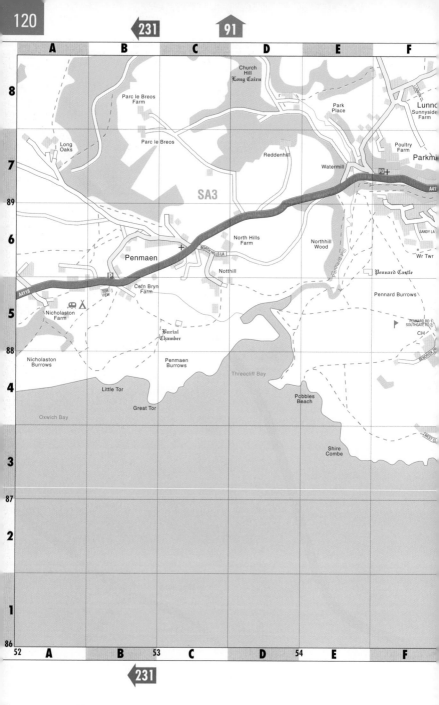

231

91

A   B   C   D   E   F

8

Church
Hill
Long Cairn

Parc le Breos
Farm

Park
Place

Lunno

Sunnyside
Farm

Long
Oaks

Parc le Breos

Reddenhill

Poultry
Farm

Parkmi

7

SA3

Watermill

A41

89

North Hills
Farm

Northhill
Wood

SANDY LA

6

Penmaen

NORTH HILLS LA

Notthill

Pennard P

Wr Twr

Pennard Castle

P

A118

TOR
VIEW

Cefn Bryn
Farm

Pennard Burrows

5

Nicholaston
Farm

PENNARD RD 1
SOUTHGATE RD 2

CH

Burial
Chamber

88

Nicholaston
Burrows

Penmaen
Burrows

BONDICOTE LR

Threecliff Bay

4

Little Tor

Great Tor

Pobbles
Beach

WEST CL

Oxwich Bay

3

Shire
Combe

87

2

1

86

231

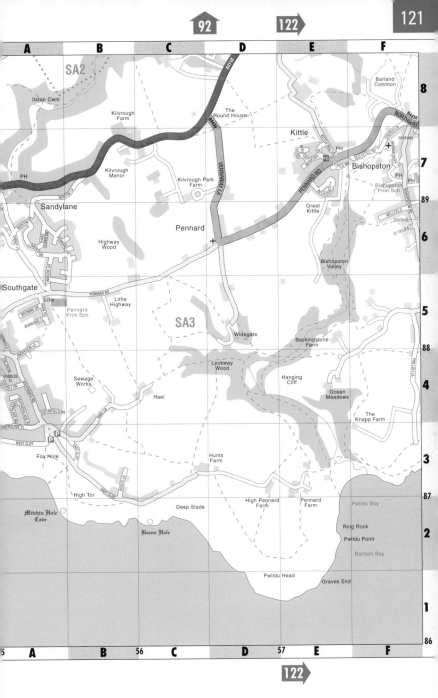

SA2

Ilston Cwm

Kilvrough Farm

The Round House

Barland Common

NORTHWAY   B4436

Kittle

PH

Kilvrough Manor

Kilvrough Park Farm

Bishopston

PORTWAY

OLD KITTLE RD

PENNARD RD

PH   PO

Bishopston Prim Sch

PH   PH

WELLFIELD

SOUTH CL

ST TEILO'S ST

Sandylane

Southgate

NORTON LA

PH

Pennard

Great Kittle

Highway Wood

Bishopston Valley

PENNARD RD

Liby

Little Highway

SA3

Pennard Prim Sch

BROWNS DR   PARK LA

BURROWS RD

Widegate

Backingstone Farm

ANDERSON LA

COBBLES CL   HOLE RD

Sewage Works

Lockway Wood

Hanging Cliff

Ocean Meadows

The Knapp Farm

EASTCLIFF DR

Hael

HAEL LA

WEST CLIFF

P   P

Fox Hole

EAST CLIFF

TOR CL

High Tor

Hunts Farm

PWLLDU LA

Mitchin Hole Cave

Deep Slade

High Pennard Farm

Pennard Farm

Pwlldu Bay

Bacon Hole

Ring Rock

Pwlldu Point

Bantam Bay

Pwlldu Head

Graves End

121 93

A B C D E F

8

7

89

6

SA3

5

88

4

3

87

2

1

86

58 A B 59 C D 60 E F

121

B4436 MAYALS RD
CONHILL 1
NORTHERON 2
BETTSLAND 3
BROADPARKS 4
LEYSHAN WLK 5
CROSS ACRE 6
WHITE GR 7
YALTON 8

THE GLADE 2
MAYALS GN 1

Sunnybank

Ryeground
Farm

B4436
PORTWAY

NORTHWAY

Nazareth
House

Clyne Common

Bishopston
Comp Sch

Murton
Green

Mansel
Green

Whitestone
City Prim Sch

Bishopston
Prim Sch

PH

Murton

Manselfield

Rushwind
Mews

Oldway

Whitestone
Cty Prim Sch

Newton
Prim Sch

Cemy

Pyle

Herberts Lodge
Farm

Lady
Housty
Ho

Newton

Colts H

Challacombe

1 DOUGLAS CT
2 PWLLDU LA

Sewage
Wks

Bishop's Wood
Nature Reserve

Hareslade

Caswell

Caswell Bay

B4593

SUMMERCLIFFE
CHALET PK

CASWELL RD

Langland

SOUTHWARD LA
B4593

Gilbertscliffe
Highcliffe
Ct
Woodridge

Ael-y-don st
Leonar

Brandy
Cove

CH

Langland Bay
Ct

Langland Bay

Newton Cliff

Whiteshell
Point

Snaple Point

Swansea Bay

St Cross

Oystermouth

SA3

The Mumbles

Mumbles Hill

Thistleboon

Limeslade

Rams Tor

Mumbles Head

Middle Head

Pier

The Knab

IRB Sta

LB Sta

Hotel

Bracelet Bay

Limeslade Bay

Mast

The Dunns

1 ALBERT PL
2 WINDSOR PL
3 WESTBOURNE PL
4 UPPER CHURCH PK
5 BROADVIEW LA
6 IRVINE CT
7 HALLBANK
8 HALLBANK TERR
9 ROCKHILL
10 TICHBOURNE ST

1 HILL ST
2 DICKSLADE
3 SOUTHEND
4 CHANDLERS REACH

1 WESTCLIFF MEWS
2 AEL-Y-BRYN
3 LIMESLADE CT

Oystermouth Castle
Oystermouth Prim Sch

Mayals Prim Sch

Mayals On The Glade

St Davids RC Prim Sch

NEWTON RD

MUMBLES RD

8
89
7
6
5
88
4
3
87
2
1
86

62
63

F8
1 FREDERICK ST
2 STATION TERR
3 THOMAS ST
4 LADY JANE ST
5 GERALD ST
6 PENDARVIS TERR

7 GREEN ST
8 SANDFIELDS RD
9 MARSH ST
10 PEMBROKE TERR
11 WELLINGTON PL
12 GLENAVON ST

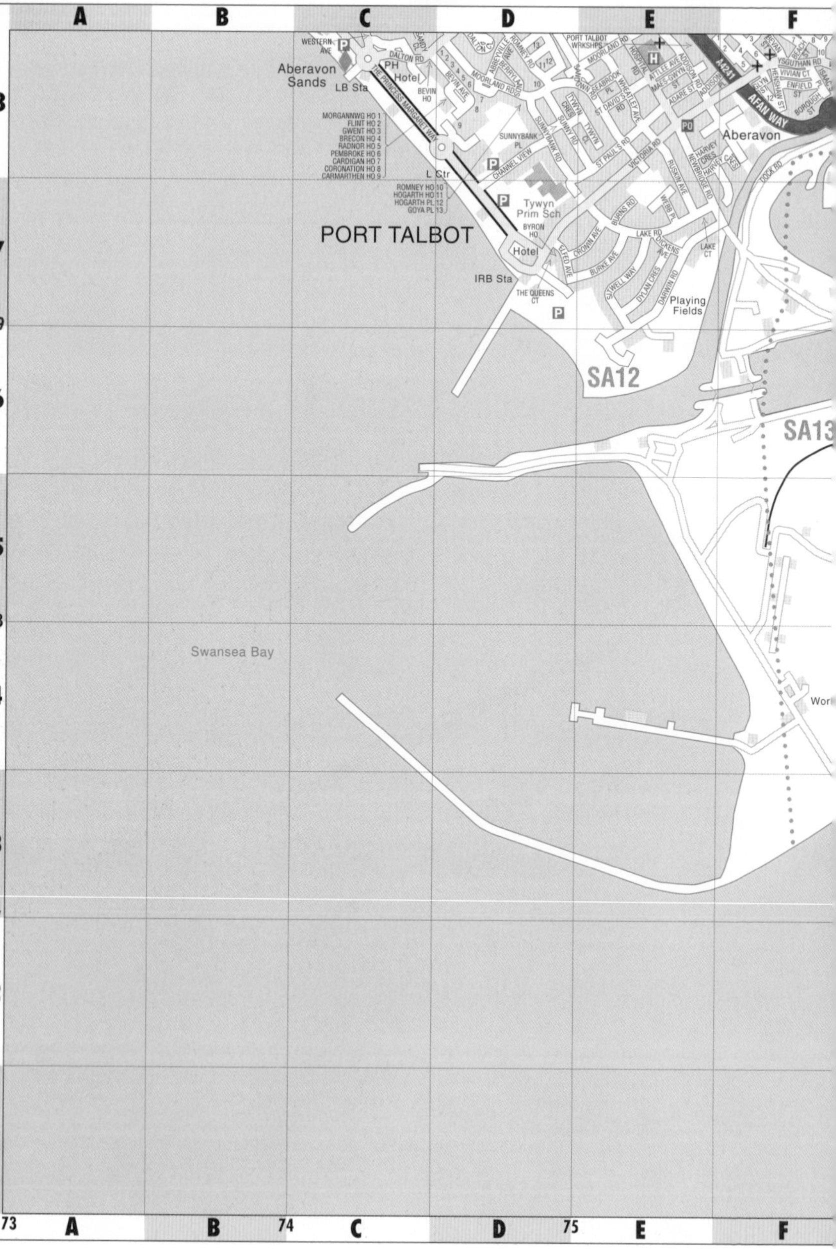

Aberavon
Sands

LB Sta

WESTERN
AVE

DALTON RD

PH

Hotel

BEVIN
HO

PORT TALBOT
WHARFS

Aberavon

MORGANNWG HO 1
FLINT HO 2
GWENT HO 3
BRECON HO 4
RADNOR HO 5
PEMBROKE HO 6
CARDIGAN HO 7
CORONATION HO 8
CARMARTHEN HO 9

SUNNYBANK

L Ctr

ROMNEY HO 10
HOGARTH HO 11
HOGARTH PL 12
GOYA PL 13

PORT TALBOT

Tywyn
Prim Sch

BYRON
HO

Hotel

IRB Sta

THE QUEENS
CT

LAKE RD

LAKE
CT

Playing
Fields

SA12

SA13

AFAN WAY

A4241

PO

Swansea Bay

Worl

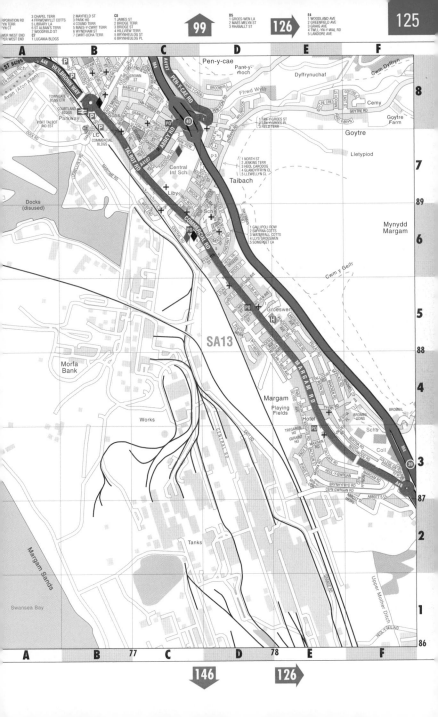

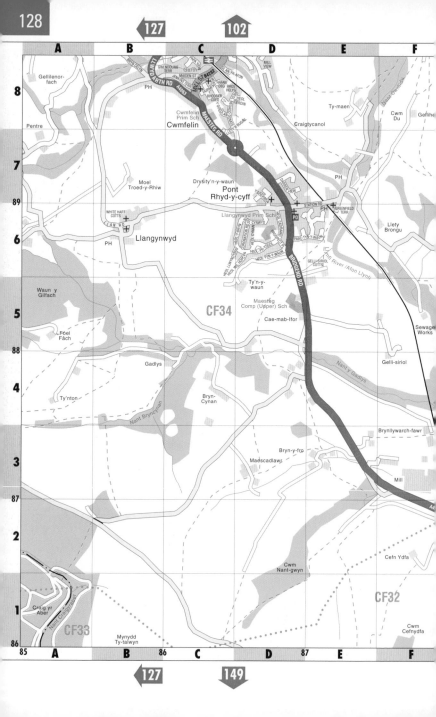

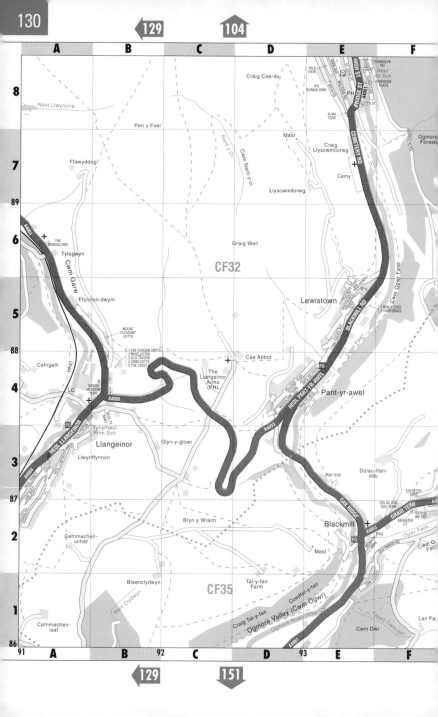

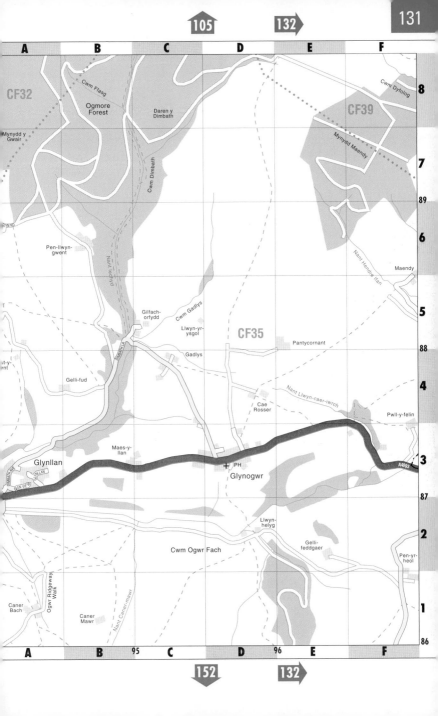

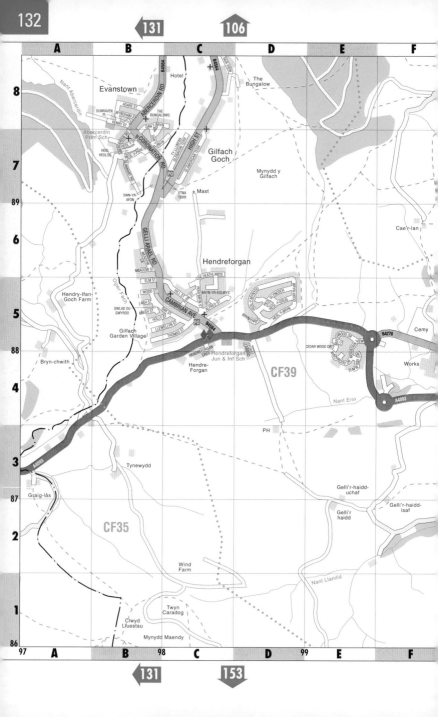

131
106
131
153

A **B** **C** **D** **E** **F**

8

Nant Abercerdin
AB4564
Hotel
B4564
FLAT TERR
Evanstown
The Bungalow
ADARE ST
WYNCHAM ST
THE BUNGALOWS
DUNRAVEN PL
DAN Y BRYN
KENRY ST
HIGH ST
TY LLWYN
Abercerdin
TREBOS ST
Gilfach
Prim Sch
Goch
HEOL-Y-RHYL
HEDL HEULOG
HEOL CENAU
CORONATION RD
Mynydd y
Gilfach

7

PLASANT RD

89
SWN-YR-
AFON
ETNA
TERR
Mast
Cae'r-lan

6

GELLI ARAEL RD
MACKY
MEADOW ST
Hendreforgan
Hendry-Ifan-
Goch Farm
ELM ST
Ogwr Fach
WOOD ST
THE HEATHLANDS
BRYN-GOCH
BRYN-Y-FFYNNON
CAMBRIAN AVE
BRYN CAMBRID
BRYN-YR-EGLWYS
HEOL TY BRYN
GWLAD DU
GWYRDD
ASH ST
BEECH ST
HILL ST
BRYN LLYS
HOLLY ST
B4278

5

Gilfach
Garden Village
LLEWELLYN ST
THOMAS ST
B4564
BRYNCETHIN
Cemy

88
Bryn-chwith
HENDREFORGAN
CRES
Hendreforgan
Jun & Inf Sch
CEDAR WOOD DR
BIRCHWOOD DR
WOOD DR
ELM DR
VIEW
B4278
Works
Hendre-
Forgan
CF39
A4093

4

Nant Erin

Tynewydd
PH
Gelli'r-haidd-
uchaf
A4093

3

87
Graig-lâs
CF35
Gelli'r
haidd
Gelli'r-haidd-
isaf

2

Wind
Farm
Nant Llanilid

1

Twyn
Caradog
Clwyd
Lluestau
Mynydd Maendy

86
97 **A** **B** **98** **C** **D** **99** **E** **F**

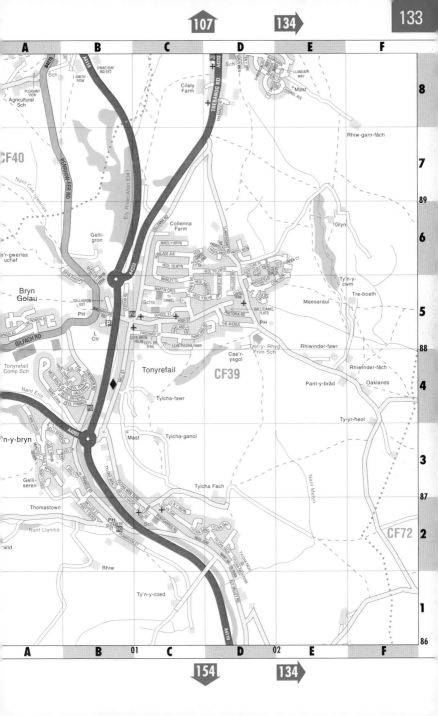

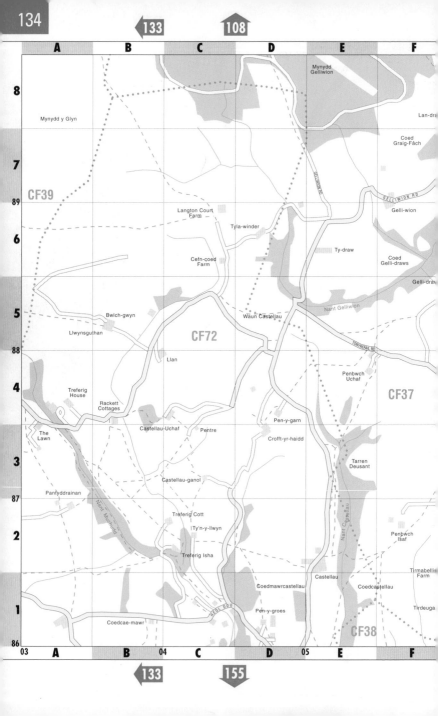

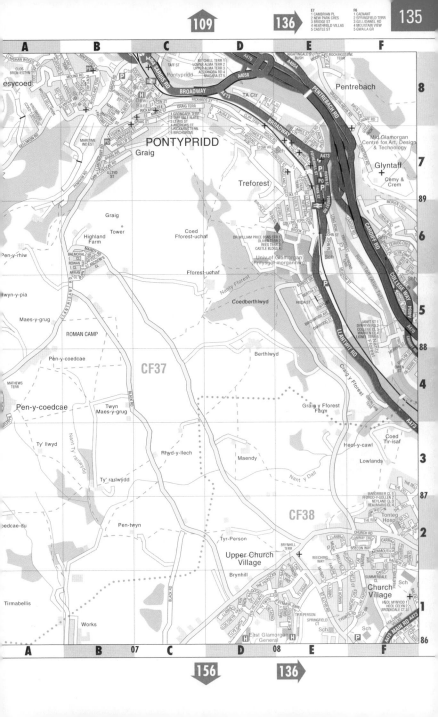

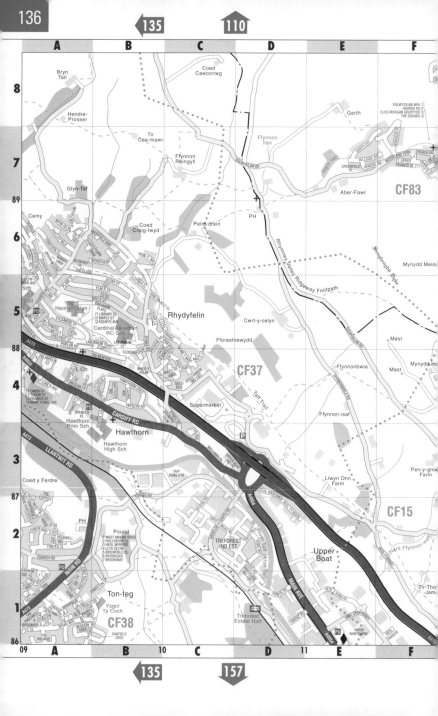

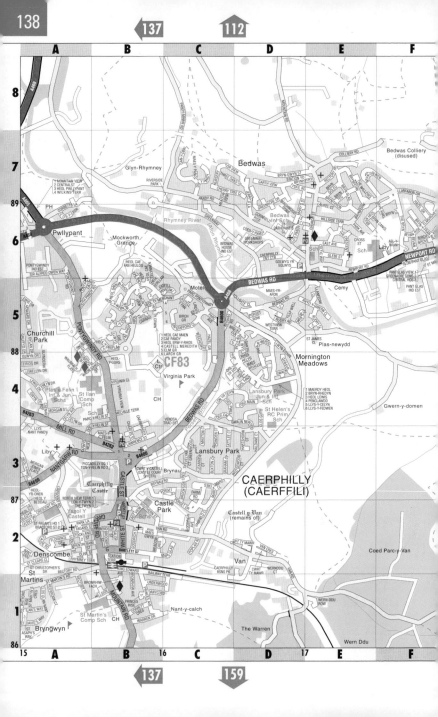

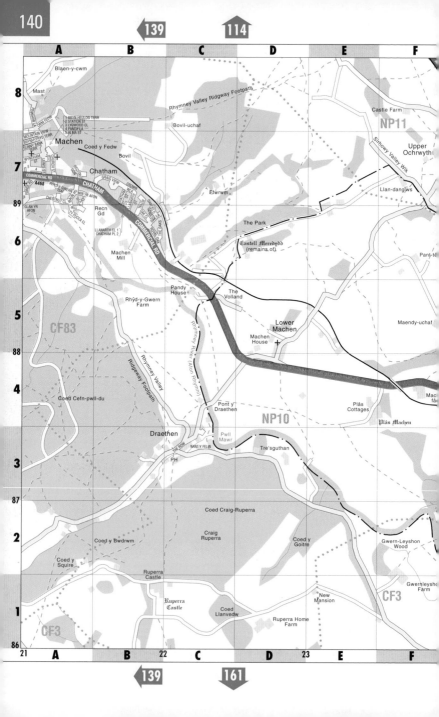

F5
1 EVESWELL LA
2 BATCHELOR RD
3 WORDSWORTH RD
4 CHAUCER CT
5 ROSENDALE CT
6 UPPER TENNYSON RD

C6
1 DENBIGH WLK
2 SALISBURY CL
3 HARLEQUIN ROBT
D6
1 GLASTONBURY CL
5 SHAFTESBURY WLK
6 UPPER TENNYSON RD

7 MALMESBURY CL
8 SHREWSBURY CL
9 CANTERBURY CL
D6
1 GLOSTER PL
2 ALFRED ST
3 GLOSTER ST

4 LORD ST
5 CAMELOT PL

E6
1 BRYNDERWEN CT
2 JACKSON CT
3 JACKSON PL
4 FAIROAK ST

5 LIVERPOOL ST
6 EXETER RD
7 VINE PL
8 FAIROAK GDNS
9 SUMMERHILL HO
10 CARDIGAN PL

2 NORTHUMBERLAND RD
3 UPLANDS CT
4 CRESCENT CT
5 WOODLAND PARK VIEW
6 KENSINGTON GDNS
7 CLEVEDON CL

117

E8
1 SCARBOROUGH RD
2 HARROGATE RD
3 BANK LA
4 WINDERMERE SQ
5 ST JULIANS
6 MARINA ST

144

E9
7 CUMBERLAND RD
8 CROYDON CT
9 STOCKTON CL
F9
1 CONISTON CL
2 ENNERDALE CT

3 BUTTERMERE WAY
4 OLD BARN
5 THIRLMERE PL
6 GAINSBOROUGH DR
7 WORCESTER CRES

143

C3
1 GROVE LA
2 HERBERT ST
3 CLYTHA CRES
4 MOUNTJOY PL
5 MOUNTJOY ST
6 MOUNTJOY ST
7 WINDMILL SQ
8 DROVERS MEWS
9 WEST MARKET ST

10 RUTLAND PL
11 DANIEL PL
12 CHARLOTTE WLK
13 CHARLOTTE CT
14 DAVIS SQ
15 LETCH SQ
16 HART GDNS
17 PARDOE-THOMAS CL
18 PINNELL PL
19 ALMA CL

20 DUNN SQ
21 FRANCIS CT
22 FRANCIS CL
23 BOWEN PL
24 SHEA GDNS
25 KNIGHT CL
26 KIRBY DANIEL CT
27 COULSON CL
28 WILLIAMS CL
29 CHAPEL CL

A4
1 BRIN WILLIAMS HO
2 BURNLEIGH RD

B4
1 WILLIAM LOVETT GDNS
2 WINDSOR TERR
3 KINGSHILL TERR
4 BEAUFORT TERR
5 SCARD ST
6 BANESWELL CTYD

164

7 ST MARYS CT
8 HAVELOCK ST
9 CATHEDRAL CT
10 ST WOOLOS CT
11 QUEEN VICTORIA
MEML ALMSHOUSES
12 SEVERN TERR
13 DEANERY GDNS

144

C4
1 FRIARS ST
2 JOHN FROST SQ
3 LLANARTH ST
4 SOVEREIGN ARC
5 KINGSWAY CTR
6 VICTORIA PL
7 VICTORIA CL
8 VICTORIA RD
9 KINGSHILL ST

E4
10 KINGSVALE
11 PALMYRA PL
12 KING LA
13 NATIONAL BLDGS
14 EBENEZER TERR
15 VICTORIA PL
16 ROBIN'S LA
17 DUMPHRIES PL
18 CROSS LA

19 EMLYN SQ
20 EMLYN ST
B5
1 QUEEN'S CHAMBERS
2 STANLEY CT
3 NEWPORT ARC
4 CAMBRIAN RET CTR
5 CAXTON PL
6 BANESWELL RD
7 PUMP ST

C5
1 MARKET ARC
2 MARKET ST
3 GRIFFIN ST
4 SKINNER LA
5 AUSTIN FRIARS

A B C D E F

8

7

85

6

82

G H

5

CF33

Kenfig Burrows

84

4

Kenfig Sands

81

4

Margam Sands

CF36

3

Swansea Bay

83

2

80

2

1

Sker Point

78 79

82

A B 77 C D 78 E F

76

Works

Margam Moors

SA13

Margam Burrows

Dunes

Afon Cynffig

Kenfig Burrows

Kenfig Sands

CF33

Upper Morfa

LC

HEOL CAED BONT

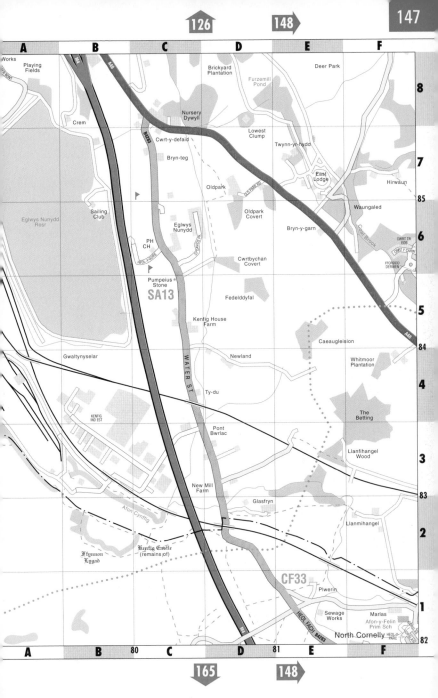

126
148

Works
Playing Fields

Crem

Brickyard Plantation

Deer Park

Furzemill Pond

8

Nursery Dywyll

Lowest Clump

Twynn-yr-hydd

7

Cwrt-y-defaid

Bryn-teg

Oldpark

East Lodge

Hirwaun

Sailing Club

85

Eglwys Nunydd Resr

Oldpark Covert

Waungaled

Eglwys Nunydd

Bryn-y-garn

Cwr Brook

6

PH CH

CWRT TIR EOS
LONT Y CARW
FFORDD DERWEN

Pumpeius Stone

Cwrtbychan Covert

SA13

Fedelddyfal

5

Kenfig House Farm

Caeaugleision

84

Gwaltynyselar

Newland

Whitmoor Plantation

WATER ST

Ty-du

4

KENFIG IND EST

The Betting

Pont Bwrlac

Llanfihangel Wood

3

New Mill Farm

83

Afon Cynffig

Glasfryn

Llanmihangel

2

Ffynnon Lygad

Kenfig Castle (remains of)

CF33

Piwerin

Sewage Works

Marlas

Afon-y-Felin Prim Sch

1

HEOL FACH B4283

North Cornelly

HEOL-Y-PARC

82

80

81

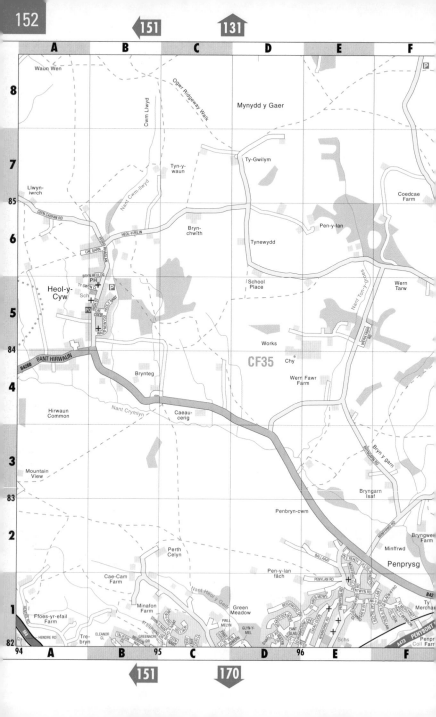

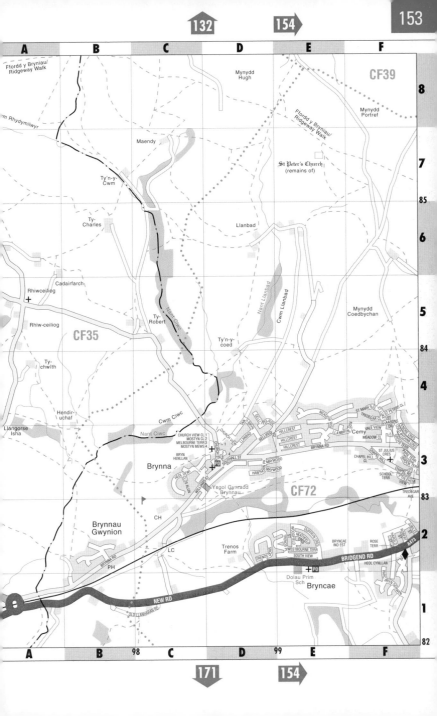

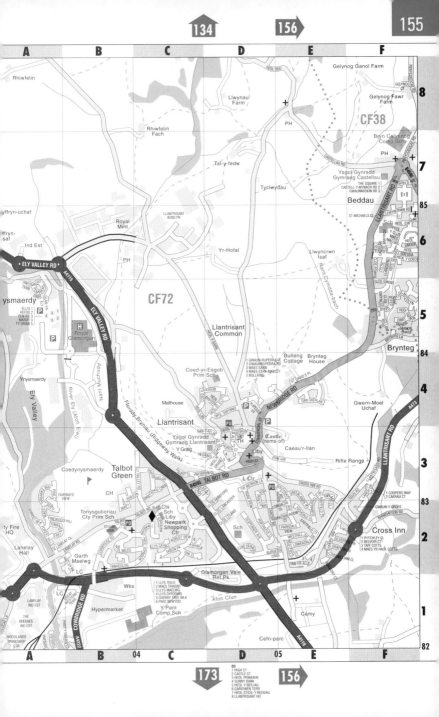

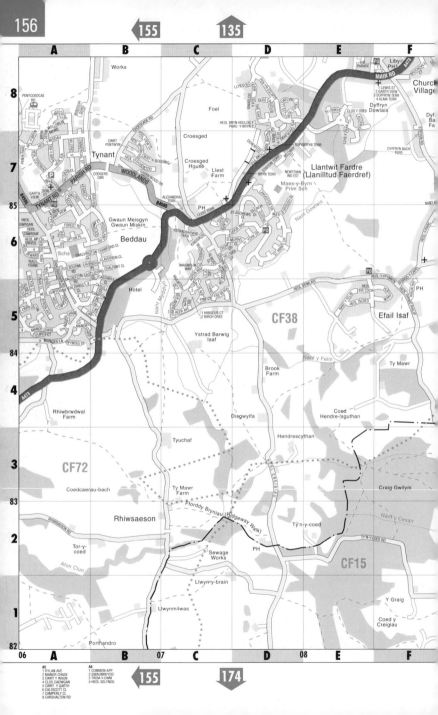

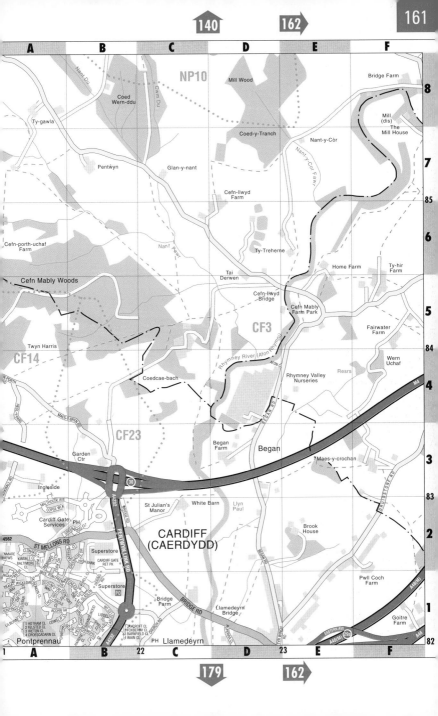

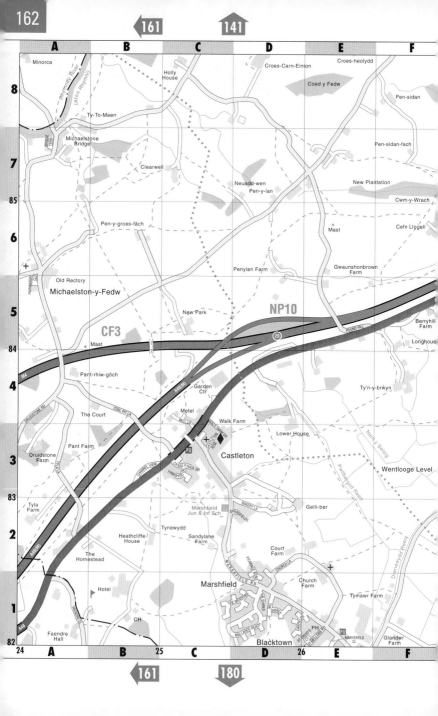

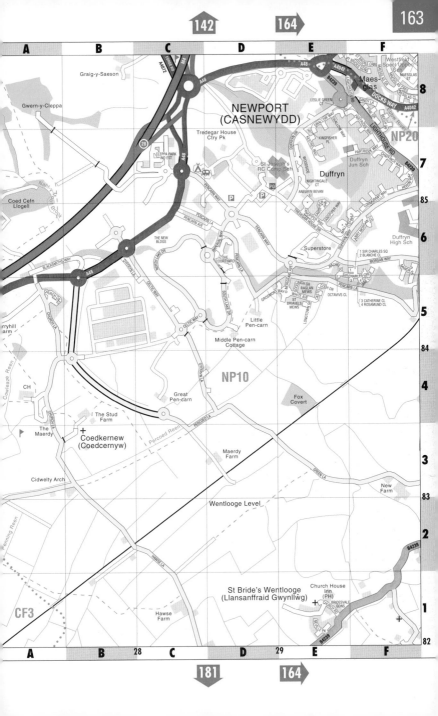

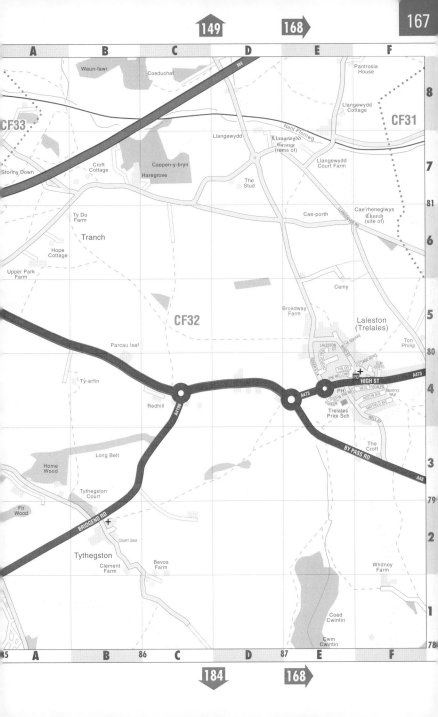

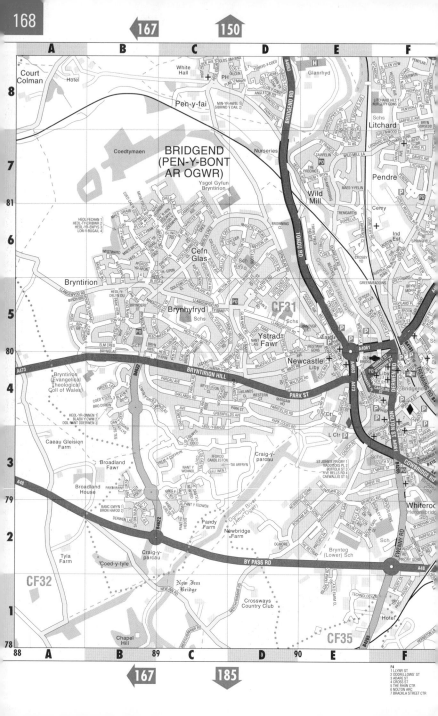

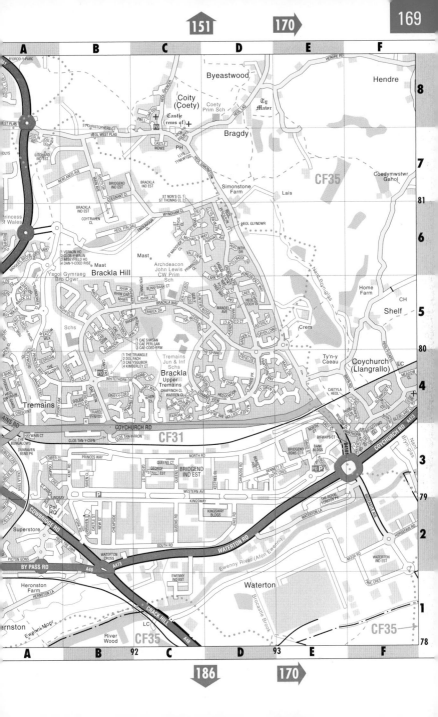

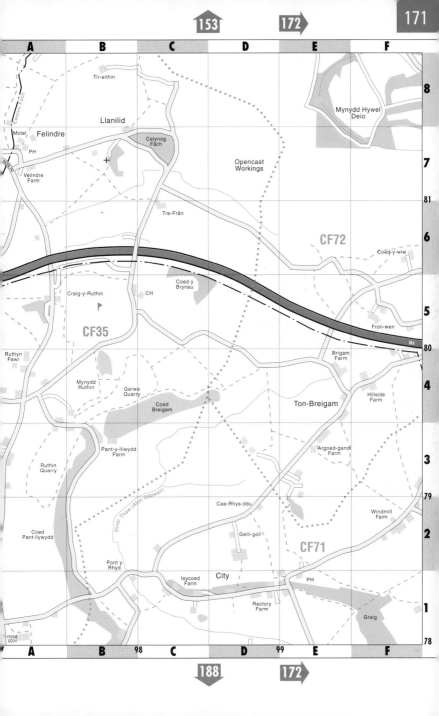

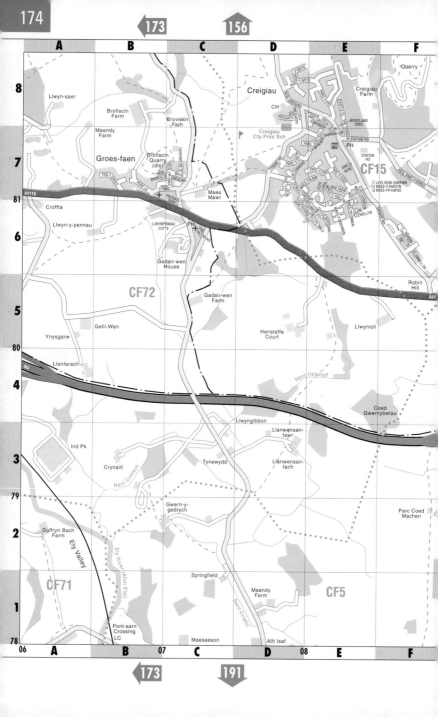

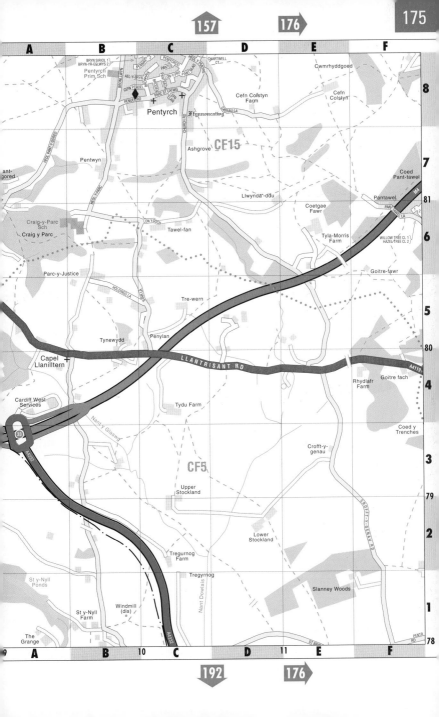

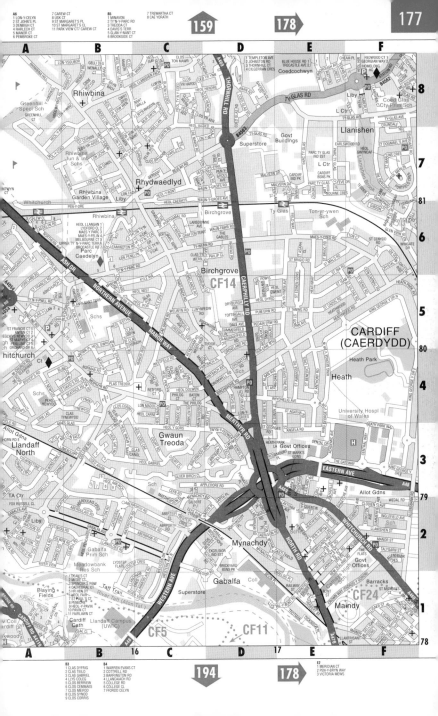

CF14

TY-GLAS AVE
NORDALE CT

Llanishen Resr

Rhyd-y-Penau
Jun & Inf Sch

Rhyd-
y-Penau
Libv

Cyncoed

Cardiff
High Sch

Heath High &
Low Level

Heath
Park

CF14

Heath

The Lake

Memi

Roath
Park

Cemy

CF24

Cemy

Archive

Cathays   Liby

Pentwyn

Glyncoed
Jun & Inf
Sch

Wern-goch

Llanedeyrn

Springwood
Jun & Inf
Sch

Lakeside
Ctv Jun &
Inf Sch

Llanedeyrn
High Sch

Chapel
Wood

Motel

CF23

Univ of Wales
Inst Cardiff

Llanedeyrn
Jun & Inf Sch

CARDIFF
(CAERDYDD)

Ty
Gwyn Sch

Univ
Hall

W Tower

St Teilo's
CW High Sch

Obsy

Nature
Reserve

EASTERN AVE

Allot
Gdns

Tennis
Ctr

Coll

Pen-y-lan

Roath Brook

Sch

Liby

Univ of Wales
Inst Cardiff

Colchester
Est

Superstore

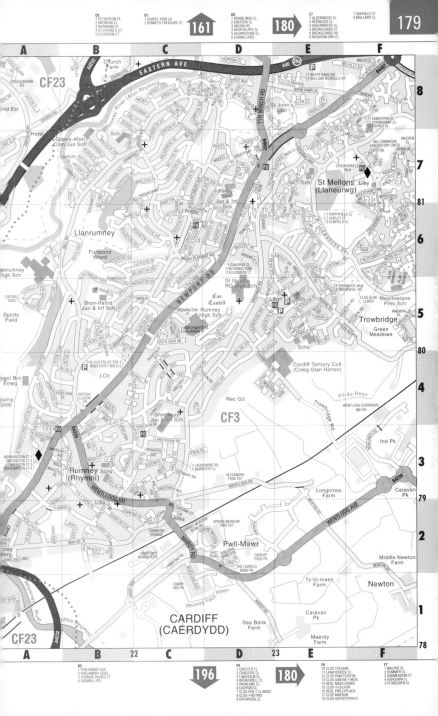

C6
1 PETHERTON PL
2 BRENDON CL
3 BURNHAM CT
4 ST DYFRIG'S CT
5 CLEVEDON CT

D7
1 CHAPEL ROW LA
2 KENNETH TREASURE CT

161

D8
1 DRAWLINGS CL
2 EASTERN CL
3 ARCON HO
4 HEATHCLIFFE CL
5 SILVERSTONE CL
6 EURWG CRES

180

E7
1 ALDERWOOD CL
2 REDWOOD CL
3 SHEERWATER CL
4 BROADLANDS CT
5 BROADLANDS HO
6 MEADOWLARK CL

7 ASHFIELD CT
8 MALLARD CL

179

B3
1 TRELAWNEY AVE
2 TRELAWNEY CRES
3 THOMAS DAVIES CT
4 CASWELL RD

196

F6
1 CHESTER CL
2 CRAGSIDE CL
3 LINGHOLM CL
4 BROADWELL CL
5 PAVALAND CL
6 CASPIAN CL
7 CLOS PEN Y CLAWDD
8 CLOS-Y-BETWS
9 DRYBROOK CL

180

F6
10 CLOS TREGARE
11 LANHYDROCK CL
12 CLOS PANTYCOSYN
13 CLOS GWERIN-Y-MOR
14 HEOL MAES EIRWG
15 CLOS-Y-CULFOR
16 HEOL PWLLYPLACA
17 CLOS MAERUN
18 CLOS HAFODYRYNYS

F7
1 MALPAS CL
2 DUMMER CL
3 OAKMEADOW CT
4 ASHDOWN CL
5 PITMEDDEN CL

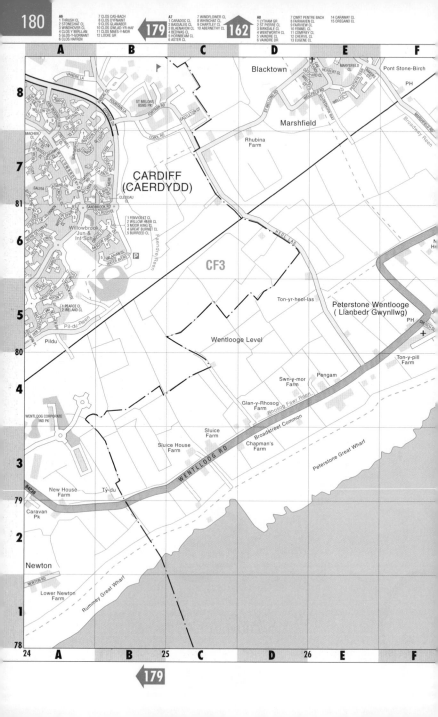

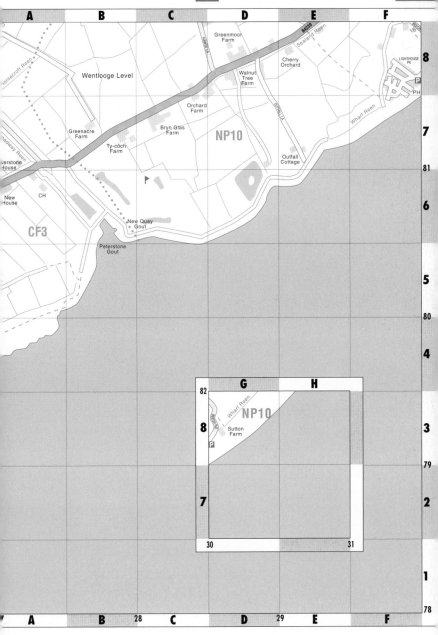

A B C D E F

8

7

81

6

5

80

4

3

79

2

1

78

G H

82

8

79

7

30 31

A B C D E F
28 29

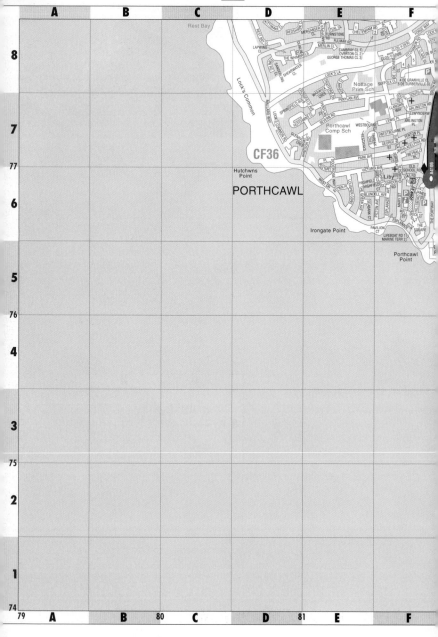

Rest Bay

Lock's Common

Hutchwns Point

CF36

PORTHCAWL

Irongate Point

Porthcawl Point

Nottage Prim Sch

Porthcawl Comp Sch

Liby

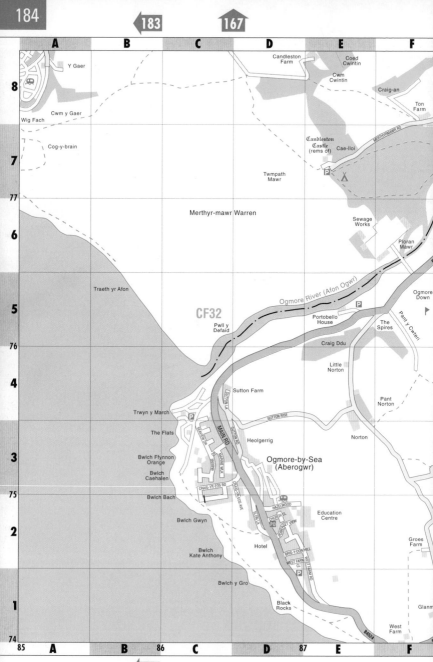

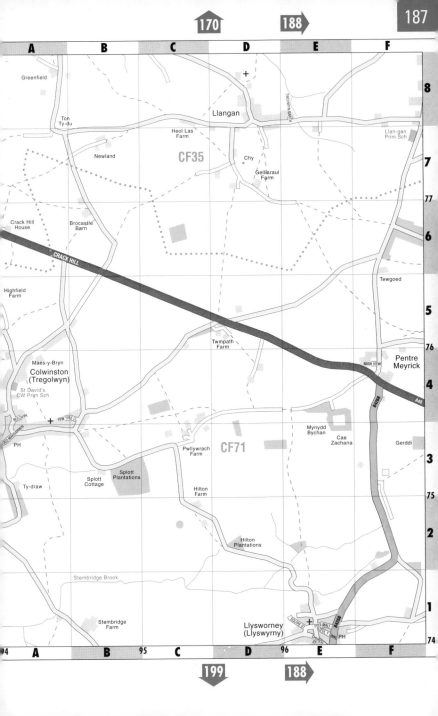

170
188
199
188

A B C D E F

8
7
77
6
5
76
4
3
75
2
1
74

Greenfield

Ton Ty-du

Heol Las Farm

Llangan

TWICWYN BACH

Llan-gan Prim Sch

Newland

CF35

Chy

Gelliaraul Farm

Crack Hill House

Brocastle Barn

CRACK HILL

Tewgoed

Highfield Farm

Twmpath Farm

Maes-y-Bryn

Colwinston (Tregolwyn)

St David's CW Prim Sch

NASH VIEW

Pentre Meyrick

A48

B4268

BEILI PK

YEW TREE CL

HEOL MAESHOWEL

PH

Mynydd Bychan

Cae Zacharia

Gerddi

Pwllywrach Farm

CF71

Splott Cottage

Splott Plantations

Hilton Farm

Ty-draw

Hilton Plantations

Stembridge Brook

Stembridge Farm

Llysworney (Llyswyrny)

SQUIRE ST

TYLE MALL

HEOL Y MAEN

CHURCH ST

PH

B4268

94 A B 95 C D 96 E F

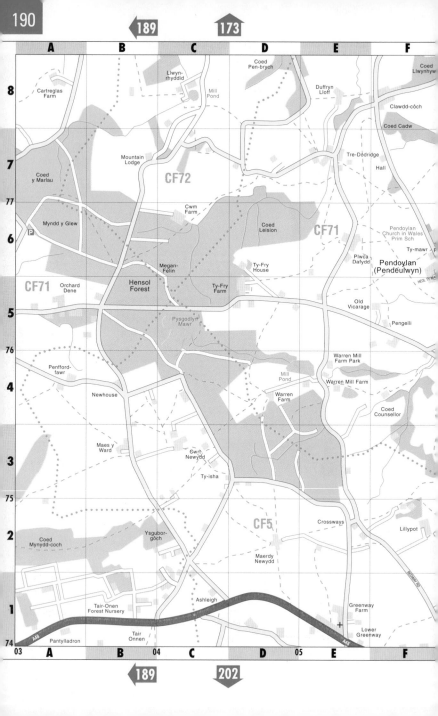

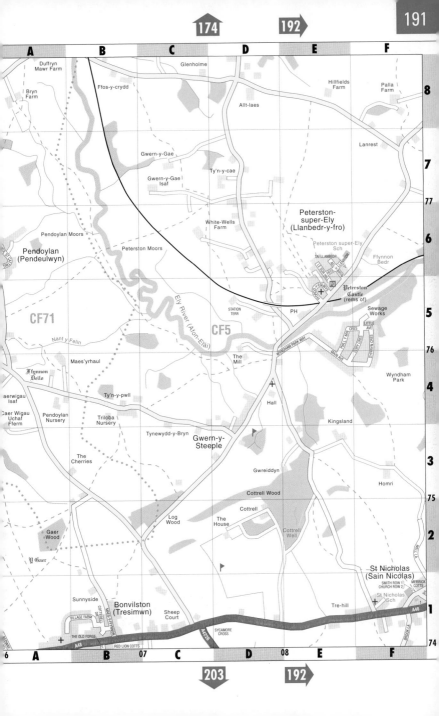

191
175
191
204

Willows Farm

ST BRIDES RD

Tregochas

Tynewydd

Pwll Arthur

Forty Farm

ST BRIDES PL

St Bride's-super-Ely
(Llansanffraid-ar-Elai)

Nant Rhych

Welsh Folk Mus

Cast

Morlanga

Llwyn-yr-eos

LC

Gwern Rhyd

LC

St Georges

Ely River

Ely Valley

Ty-fry

PH

(Afon Elái)

NANT Y-DOWLAIS 1
NANT-YR-ELY 2
NANT YR ARTHUR 3
SWAGLOWFOREST CL 4
LONGREACH CL 5

CF5

Drope

Ffordd Cottages

Drope Farm

Nant y Plác

Glan Ely High Sch

MICHAELSTON CT 1
GREEN FARM RD 2

Nant y Drope

DROPE RD

DROPE TERR

Haelfraes

Coedarhydyglyn

Superstore

COWBRIDGE RD W

A48

Coedarhydyglyn Park

Tumbledown

Hotel

The Caia

Old Coedarhydyglyn

Downs

PH

VALEGATE RET PK.

PORT RD

A48

A4050

A48

TV Studios

St Nicholas
(Sain Nicolas)

THE LANE

GRANT'S FIELD

Tychwith Farm

Penrhiw Farm

TV Transmitting Sta

TV

Rhiwa

Vianshill

Mast

DUFFRYN LA

BROADWAY GN

NANT FAWR

09

10

11

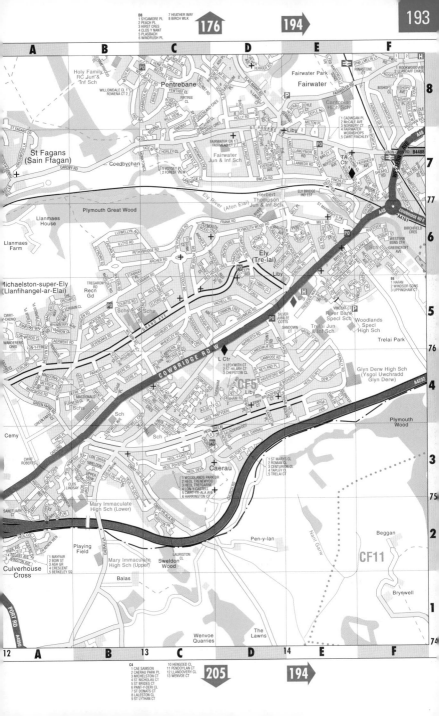

193
177
193
206

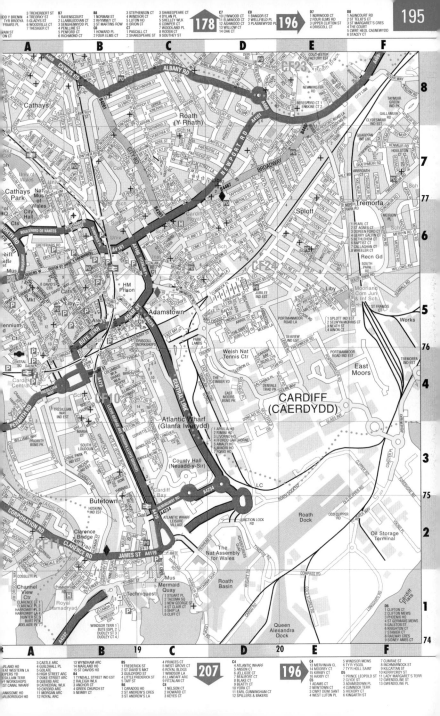

CF23
Allot Gdns

CARDIFF
(CAERDYDD)

Lamby

CF3

Maerdy Farm

Rumney
Great Whar

Little
Wharf

Rhymney River (Afon Rhymni)

AVONMUIR
RD

STORRAR
PL

BRONWYDD
RD

GALLAMUIR
RD
Tremorfa
Park

St Albans
RC Prim Sch

RUNWAY RD

CF24

Pengam Moors

ROVER WAY

Willows
Com High Sch

WILLOWS
AVE

SEAWALL RD

Works

LC

Wks

PEN-Y-BRYN RD

TREMORFA
IND EST

Cardiff Flats

Orchard Ledges

FOXGLOVE RD

8

7

77

6

5

76

4

3

75

2

1

74

21   A   B   22   C   D   23   E   F

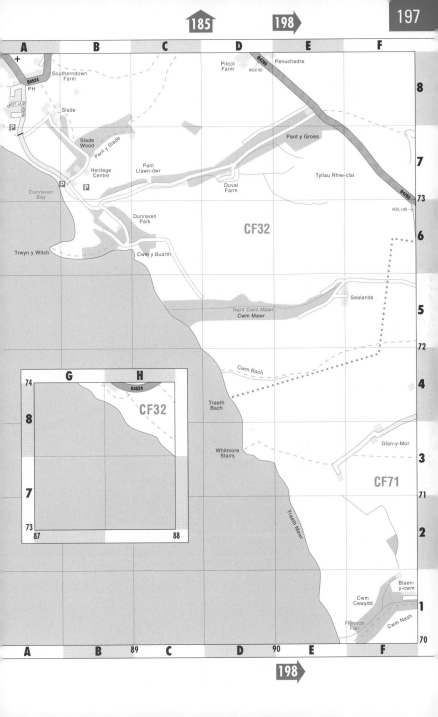

A   B   C   D   E   F

8

Pitcot Farm
Penuchadre
B4265
WICK RD

Southerndown Farm
B4524
PH

Slade

Slade Wood
Pant y Slade

Pant y Groes

7

Pant Llawn-dwr

Heritage Centre

Duval Farm

Tyllau Rhiw-clai

B4265

Dunraven Bay

73

CF32

HEOL LAS

Dunraven Park

6

Trwyn y Witch

Cwm y Buarth

Sealands

5

Nant Cwm Mawr
Cwm Mawr

72

Cwm Bach

4

G   H

74   B4524

CF32

Traeth Bach

8

Whitmore Stairs

Glan-y-Mor

3

7

CF71

71

73
87   88

2

Traeth Mawr

Blaen-y-cwm

Cwm Cewydd

1

Ffynnon Fair

Cwm Nash

70

A   B   89   C   D   90   E   F

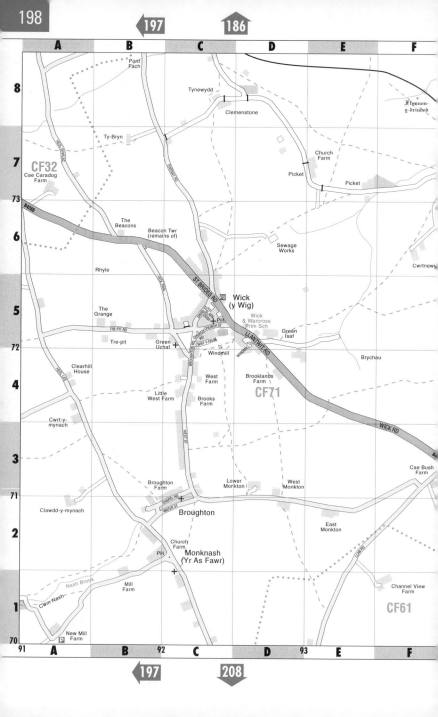

197
186

A   B   C   D   E   F

8

Pont Fach

Tynewydd

Clemenstone

Ffynnon-y-drindod

7   CF32

Ty-Bryn

Church Farm

Cae Caradog Farm

Picket

Picket

73

The Beacons

Beacon Twr (remains of)

Cwrtnewy

6

Rhyle

Sewage Works

Wick (y Wig)

Wick & Warcross Prim Sch

5   The Grange

Green Isaf

TRE-PIT RD

Tre-pit

Green Uchaf

Windmill

Brychau

72   Clearhill House

West Farm

Brooklands Farm

CF71

4   Little West Farm

Brooks Farm

Cwrt-y-mynach

Cae Bush Farm

3

Broughton Farm

Lower Monkton

West Monkton

71   Clawdd-y-mynach

CHAPEL RD

WATER ST

Broughton

East Monkton

2

Church Farm

PH

Monknash (Yr As Fawr)

Nash Brook

Mill Farm

Channel View Farm

1   Cwm Nash

CF61

New Mill Farm

70

91   A   B   92   C   D   93   E   F

197
208

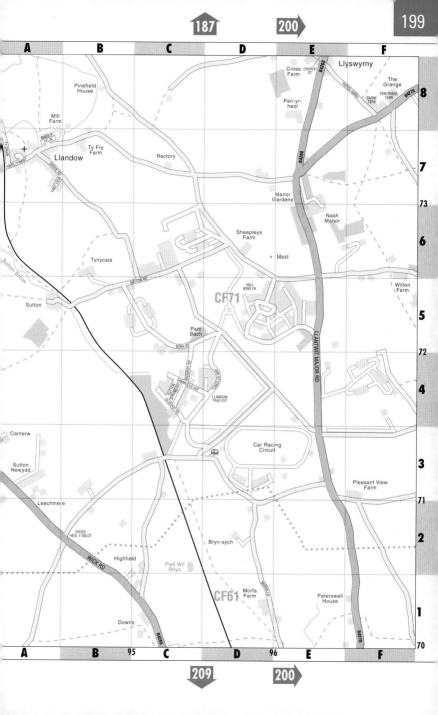

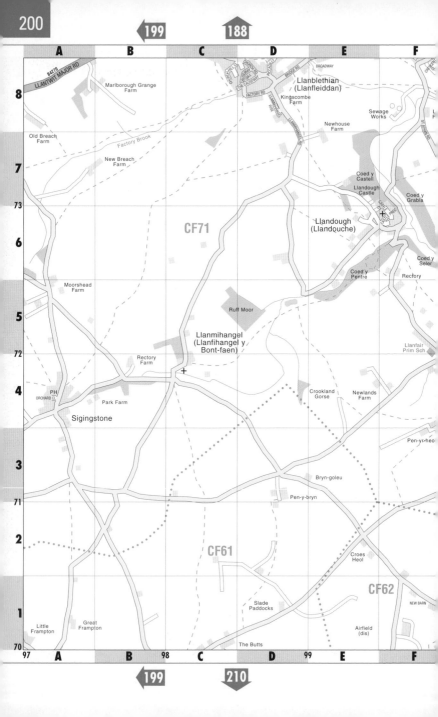

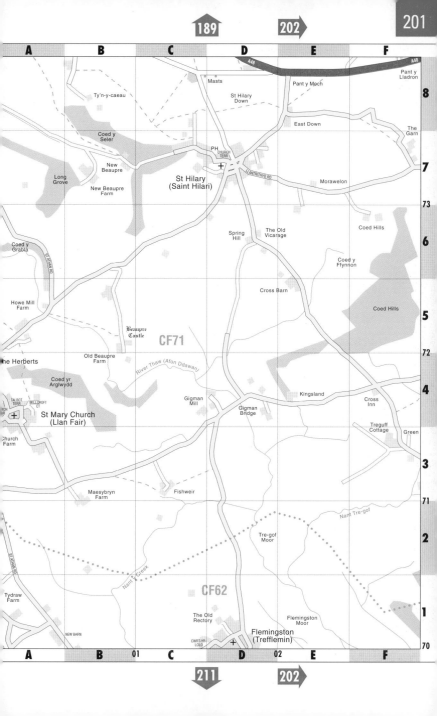

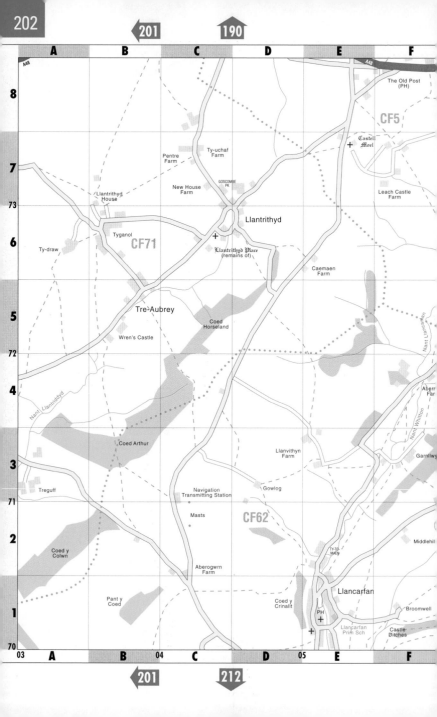

201
190
201
212

A   B   C   D   E   F

A48

The Old Post
(PH)

CF5

8

Castell
Moel

Ty-uchaf
Farm

7

Pentre
Farm

Leach Castle
Farm

New House
Farm

GOSCOMBE
PK

73

Llantrithyd
House

Llantrithyd

Tyganol

6

CF71

Ty-draw

Llantrithyd Place
(remains of)

Caemaen
Farm

5

Tre-Aubrey

Coed
Horseland

Wren's Castle

Nant Llancarfan

72

Nant Llantriddyd

4

Aberr
Far

Nant Whitton

Coed Arthur

Llanvithyn
Farm

Garnllwy

3

Treguff

Gowlog

71

Navigation
Transmitting Station

Masts

CF62

Middlehil

2

Coed y
Colwn

TY-TO-
MAEN

Aberogwrn
Farm

Llancarfan

Pant y
Coed

1

Coed y
Crinallt

Broomwell

PH

Llancarfan
Prim Sch

Castle
Ditches

70

03   04   05

A   B   C   D   E   F

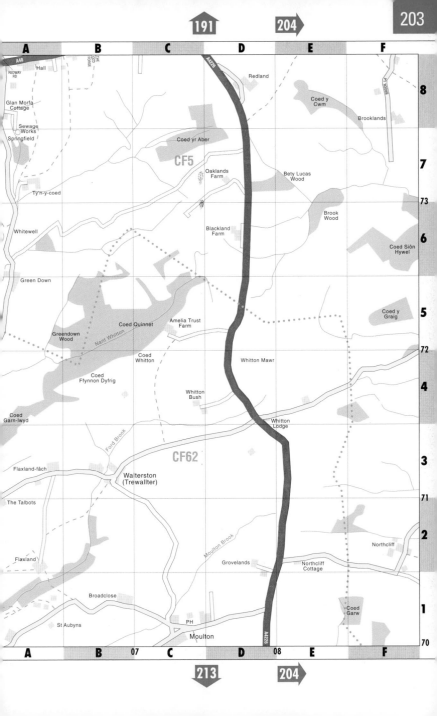

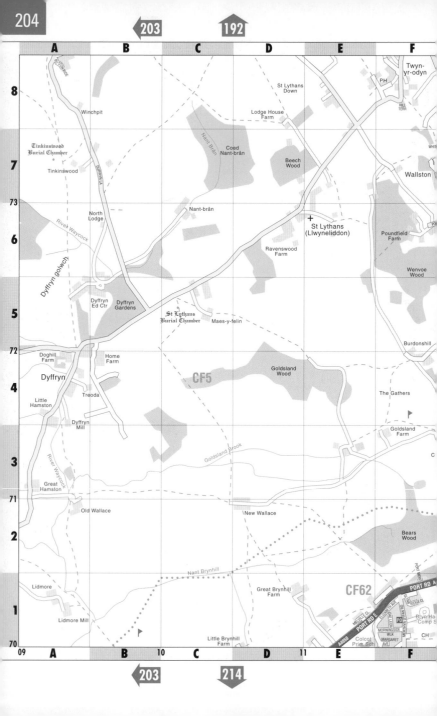

A B C D E F

8
Langcross Wood
Cwm Cydfin
Meadowvale Farm
CF11
LECKWITH RD
LLANDOUGH TRAD EST
GRANGETOWN LINK
Ely River (Afon Elai)
CHATTERTON SQ 1
HARRISON WAY 2
MOREL CT 3
Penarth Moors
CF11
CARDIFF BAY RET PK
WEST POINT IND EST

7
Coed Twm-lw
Langcross Farm
Coed yr Eglwys
Michaelston-le-Pit
(Llanfihangel-y-pwll)
Home Farm
Midfield
Llandough
(Llandochau)
GREENWAY CT
Cross
Llandough Prim Sch
TUSCAN CT
1 GRASSMERE CL
2 DOWNFIELD CL
3 GREEN HAVEN RISE
4 PINE WOOD CL
5 ASH CL
6 OAKWOOD CL
7 SYCAMORE CL
8 ELIZABETHAN CT

73
NORMAN COTTS
LEWIS RD
PENLAN RD
COGAN

6
Holms Farm
Llandough
St Mary's Day
CWRT LLANDOUGH 1
SUMMERLAND CL 2
PENLAN RISE 3
BARRY RD
Cogan
A4160
A4055
MARCONI

5
Case Hill Wood
Hill Farm
FOXGLOVE RISE
PH
ANDREW RD
PARKVIEW CT
L Ctr
Cogan
Cogan Prim Sch
ROCKROSE WAY
GWYN JAMES CT
Superstore
WINDSOR RD

72
TURNPIKE RD
MATTHEW TERR
RAILWAY TERR
HIGHFIELD
SUNNYBANK
Ysgol Pen-y-Garth
BYRON CT
LING CL
TENNYSON CL
Prim Sch

4
Dinas Powis
(Dinas Powys)
Dinas Powis Castle
(Remains of)
GEORGES ROW
PORTS RD
MILLBROOK HTS
ST DAVID AVE
CELTIC
CEC CL
Eastbrook
CHAMBERLAIN ROW
CONWAY
MEURIGLAN WAY
St Cyres Sch
Erw y Delyn
Ysgol Erw y Delyn
Ashgrove Specl Sch
MASEFIELD RD
SHAKESPEARE RD
WORDSWORTH AVE
HASTINGS PL
MOUNTJOY AVE
COWPER CL
CORNERSWELL
BYRON PL

3
CH
HIGHWALLS END
COTTONS WAY
HIGHWALLS AVE
BRITWAY RD
BRITWAY CT
FELM GRN CL
PH
THE ELMS
MOUNT RD
OLD MALT HO
Murch Jun Sch
Libvw
SUNNYCROFT CL 1
YOULDON HO 2
PEN-Y-WAUN 3
ST GWYNNOS
Murch
CASTLE RD
TEMP
MURCH RD
CHERRY
Morristown
St Joseph's RC Prim Sch
OAK CT
HAZEL RD
Comp Sch

71
CARDIFF RD
Dinas Powis
OLD MALT HO
ST CYRES RD
ST DYFRIG RD
CF64
MOUNTJOY CL
BEDWAS PL
MACHEN ST
Recn Gd
MONKSTONE

2
Southra
THE GABLES
CAE GARW
HEOL
CHESTNUT CL
ASHGROVE
St Cyres Sch
Glascoed Farm
Old Cogan Hall Farm
ELGAR RD
LAVERNOCK RD

1
Cadoxton River
A4055
Cross Common
The Breeches
Pop Hill
The Oxhams
CROSS COMMON RD
SULLY RD
CASTLE AVE
Cem

70

15   A   B   16   C   D   17   E   F

CF71

8

7

69

6

CF61

5

68

4

3

67

2

1

66

91   A   B   92   C   D   93   E   F

A   B   C   D   E   F

Pen-y-Cae Farm

Lan-Farm

Marcross (Marcroes)

CHANNEL VIEW

PH

Village Farm

Cwm Marcroes

Ty'n-y-caeau

Cwm Bach

Marcross Brook

CHURCH VIEW

Windmill Covert

Parc Farm

Perllan yr Afal

St Donat's (Sain Dunwyd)

Cwm Hancorne

WEST DR

KEMPS COVERT

EAST DR

PARC WOOD

Marcross Farm

Nature Trail

Cae'r Eglwys

Nash Point

Castell y Dryw

Nash Lighthouse (West) (disused)

Nash Lighthouse (East)

Tower

St Donat's Castle

United World Co of the Atlantic

Barracks Wood

IRB Sta

St Donat's Bay

St Donat's Point

70   G   H   CF71

8

67

7

69

90   91

B   92   C

A B C D E F

8

Ty Newydd Farm
NEW BARN

Flemingstone Court Farm

Greenfield

Llanbydderi Moor

Picketston

Mast

Eglwys-Brewis

CEDAR RD

ELM GR
PINEWOOD

ASH

SYCAMORE AVE

CRESCHESTNUT AVE

OAK GR

LIME

WALNUT GR 1
YEWTREE GR 2
ROWAN GR 3

Mast

MARGAM CL 1
CRYNANT CL 2
TALYBONT CL 3

EBBW

SCOTT

ELOISE RD

BURLEY PK

Sports Gd

7

69

6

RAF Station St Athan

Airfield

Beggars Pound

Pant-yn-Awel Farm

Castleton

Oxmoor Wood

BINGLE LA

ST DAVIDS CRES

CASTLETON RD

Rills Valley

Castleton Wood

St John's Valley

CF62

Higher End

West Farm

Briarbank

Batslays

JOHN'S MS

ROGERS CL

ST TATHAN CL

ST MICHAELS CL

RECTORY DR

LLANTWIT GARDENS CL

LLANTWIT RD

Lidy PH

ST ANDREW AVE

PANT-Y-CELYN

ST ILLTYD AVE

ROSS

PANT-Y-CELYN

LOUGHER PL

Rock Farm

St Athan Prim Sch

1 OWAIN CT
2 THE WILLOWS
3 FFRAM-Y-GRAIG

St Athan (Sain Tathan)

East Orchard Wood

5

68

4

B4265

Baronswell

Seaview

Gileston Farm

Gileston Manor

Cemy

ORCHARD

GILESTON RD

St Athan Boys Village

West Lodge

3

67

CF61

Gileston (Silstwn)

West Aberthaw Farm

West Aberthaw

2

Walls Pool

The Walls

Limpert

P

Penry Bay

Limpert Bay

Power Station

NORTH RD

PUMP HOUSE RD

SOUTH RD

ASH PLANT RD

Chy

The Leys

1

66

A B 01 C D 02

ADMINISTRATION

NORTH WALL

GARAGE CIRCULAR

212

Breaksea Point

Leys Beach

River Thaw (Afon Ddawan)

211
202

A B C D E F

8
7
69
6
68
5
4
67
3
2
66
1

Downs
Pant y Coed
Llanbethery Farm
PANT-Y-COED
The Wild Goose (PH)
CATTWG COTTS
Crosstown
Pancross
Ford Farm
Cwm y Breach
Redholme
Llanbethêry (Llanbydderi)
Pen Onn Farm
Pen-onn
Cliff House
Penmark (Pèn-marc)
Barrenhill
PO
The Six Bell (PH)
Cwm
Llancadle (Llancatal)
The Green Dragon (PH)
Llancadle Gorse
Kenson Wood
New Wood
Penmark Place
Kenson
Lower Llancadle Farm
Coed Llancadle
Kenson River
Castle Wood
Ffontygwyn Brook
Fonmon Castle
Woodhouse
Kenson River
CF62
Cardiff-Wales Airport
CASTLE RD
Rocks Head
B4265
Burton
Chy
Wks
LC
Home Farm
Fonmon (Ffwl-y-mwn)
Fonmon Farm
Highwayman Inn (PH)
Nurston
PORT RD
BURTON TERR
BELL RD
Upper House Farm
Blue Anchor Inn (PH)
STATION TERR
East Aberthaw
Font-y-gary (Ffont-y-gari)
BUNKER PARK RD
DRUIDS RD
MA TREW RD
NURSTON CL
ST JOHN'S PL
CELTIC WAY
WHITLA WY
SPEEDWELL DR 1
MAYFLOWER WAY 2
PICTON RD 3
GREAT THOMAS CL 4
CROWN E ACRE
CHANNEL DR
BURDENS CL
PARADE
MILL RD
LOS COTS PARK
FONTYGARY RD
PO
RAILWAY HOS
Fontygary Inn (PH)
P
Fontygari Holiday & L Pk
PH
KENSON CL
SEATON
SOUTH
Andrew's Pant
Watch House Point
Ffontygari Bay

211

03 04 05

A B C D E F

CF5

8
Little Brynhill Farm
Highlight Farm
GRIFFIN CL
Highbight Farm
CH
Merthyr Dyfan
Gibbonsdown

7
Welsh Hawking Ctr
Coed Mawr
Barry Coll of F Ed
Whitmore Park Dr
Colcot
Barry Comp Sch
CAERNARVON GDNS 1
ST MICHAELS GDNS 2
DOROTHY CL 3
DOROTHY AVE 4
WINIFRED AVE 5
CHAUCER RD 6.

69
The Barry
H
Recn Gd
RADNOR GN 1
CARMARTHEN CL 2
DENBIGH WAY 3
MERIONETH PL 4.
Cemy

6
Middleton Plantation
Walters Farm
WAYCOCK CROSS
CF62
Barry C of E Nursery

5
Motel
Green Farm
PONTYPRIDD RD
PORT RD
1 PLAS CLEDDAU
2 GWENOG CT
Allot Gdns
Cwm Talwg
WINCHESTER
RUTHEN TERR

68
Cwm-cidy Farm
Cwm Cidi
Nant Talwg
Mill Wood
PARKLAND WLK
GOWER ST
Civic Offs
L Ctr
GREENWOOD
DSPREY CL 1
CWRT TREM YR YNYS 2.

4
Mill Wood
1 LLYS Y COED
2 MILLWOOD RISE 2
DAEN ST
Schs
GLADSTONE GARDEN CT
CF63
CFFORDD Y MILENIWM
Y RHODFA

3
Nature Trail
Porthkerry Country Park
Barry Brook
Cwm Barri
COED YN YNYS
1 EAST VIEW TERR
2 ROMILLY CT
3 ROMILLY BLDGS
BARRY (BARRI)
1 FFORDD SEALAND
2 RHODFA SWELDON
3 HEOL BROADLAND
4 HEOL GWENDOLINE
5 GERDDI MARGARET
Docks
Oil Storage Terminal
CHARLES DARWIN WAY

67
WESTWAY RISE
BRON AFALLON
TAN Y FRON
Romilly Park
YEW TREE CT 1
MULBERRY CT 2
ROWAN CT 3
ST NICHOLAS CT 4
HOLLY CT 5
PYRA CT 6
LAUREL CT 7.
Barry Island Prim Sch
PHYLLIS ST
CLIVE RD

2
Bull Cliff
BRYN BARRWG
Storehouse Point
Barry Island
Mus
Barry Island
PLYMOUTH RD

FRIARS RD
A4055
Barry Island

1
The Knap
Pebble Beach
SEALAWNS
Little Island
Watch House Bay
Barry Island Pleasure Park
Whitmore Bay
ANGHER CT 1
ST BARUCHS CT 2
TRIANGLE 3
SOUTHBOURNE CT 4
GWENNOL Y MOR 5
ADAR Y MOR 6
HEOL GYLFINIA 7
HEOL PAL 8
BREAKSEA CT 9.
Nell's Poi

66
09 A B 10 C D 11 E Friars Point F

F5
1 COPPERFIELD CT
2 HANOVER ST
3 BYRON ST
4 WOODLANDS CT
5 GLADSTONE CT
6 SPENCER ST
7 THE MEWS
8 BELVEDERE CRES
9 DUNLIN CT

A6
MOUNTBATTEN RD
BEATTY CL
CWRT PENCOEDTRE
BROUGHTON PL
GIBBONSDOWN CL
GWILYM PL

B6
1 BLACKWELL CL
2 LLANOVER ST
3 COURT NEWTON
4 COURT MEWS
5 DAVINC CL
6 FOSTER ST

7 WESTON ST
8 RECTORY RD
9 COURTENAY RD
10 WESTERN CT
11 TENSING TERR
12 HUNT PL
13 HILLARY MEWS

B7
1 PADDOCK PL
2 JENKIN ST
3 COWBRIDGE ST
4 NEW HOUSE CT
5 TY CERRIG

C8
1 FFORDD GWYNETH
2 PARC CLWYD
3 EASTBOURNE CT
4 HATHAWAY PL
5 STRATFORD GN

CF62 Playing Field
1 CRWYS LA
2 AR Y NANT
3 HOLLAND WAY

St Richard Gwyn RC High Sch

1 LONGACRE CL
2 MEADOW VIEW
3 ST CADOCS RISE
4 GREENWAY CT
5 SHIRLEY CL
6 PALMERSTOWN RD

Biglis Farm

BARRY DOCKS LINK RD

Pymbylu Moors

Cadoxton River

Palmerstown
1 PHILADELPHIA CL
Palmerston Prim Sch

PALMERSTON WORKSHOPS
Superstore

Cadoxton   Schs
Pol HQ

PRIORITY ENT PK
PRIORITY WORKSHOPS
TY-VERLON IND EST

NORTHC...
BRYNSTON RD
FURNACE...
COLUMB...
TWEET WAY
ELEVEN...
HORTON WAY

GLADSTONE RD

Barry Dock

CARDIFF RD

1 GRANGE ST
1 TERMINUS GN

1 LOWER HOLMES ST
2 LODDICOAT CT
3 ST THOMAS CT
4 ST AIDAN'S RISE
5 MENDIP VIEW
6 TY GWENT
7 NORDALE RISE
8 CHURCHILL TERR

Works

CF63

SULLY MOORS RD

CF64
B4267

VALE ENT CTR
SOUTH RD

1 CAMBRIAN CT
2 BELVEDERE CRES
3 AVOCET CT
4 LOWER GUTHRIE ST

Reservoir

Works

WINDMILL IND AREA
Windmill
HAYES RD

Barry Docks

1 WAVERLEY CT
2 WYATT ST
3 PHILIPPA FREETH CT
4 CAMBEL CT

ATLANTIC CRES

Docks

QUEENS WAY

ATLANTIC TRAD EST

Coed-yr-Hayes

Sully Bay

Hayes Point

Black Rocks

CF62
LB Sta
Entrance Channel

East Breakwater

Jackson's Bay

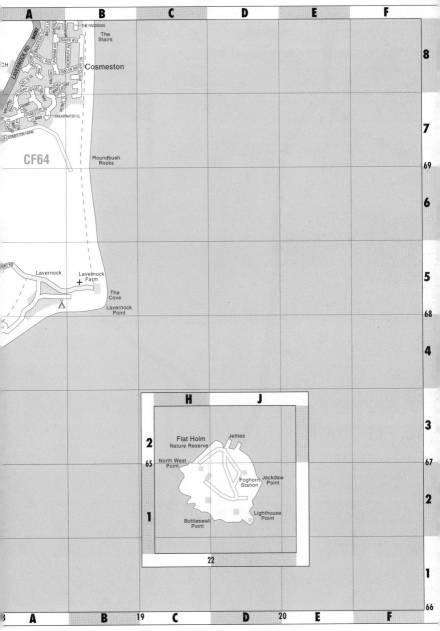

A   B   C   D   E   F

8

Cosmeston

The Stairs

THE PADDOCKS

7

CF64

Roundbush Rocks

69

6

Lavernock
Lavernock Farm
The Cove
Lavernock Point

5

68

4

H   J

3

Flat Holm
Nature Reserve

Jetties

2

North West Point

65

67

Foghorn Station

Jackdaw Point

2

1

Bottleswell Point

Lighthouse Point

22

1

66

A   B   19   C   D   20   E   F

Scale: 1¼ inches to 1 m
0   ¼   ½ mile
0 250m 500m 750m 1 k

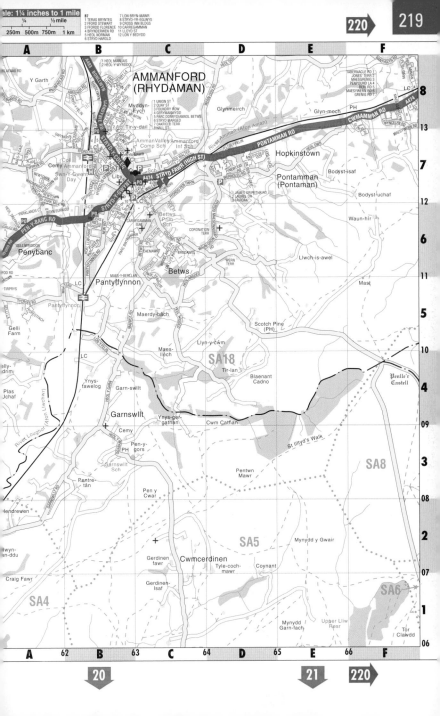

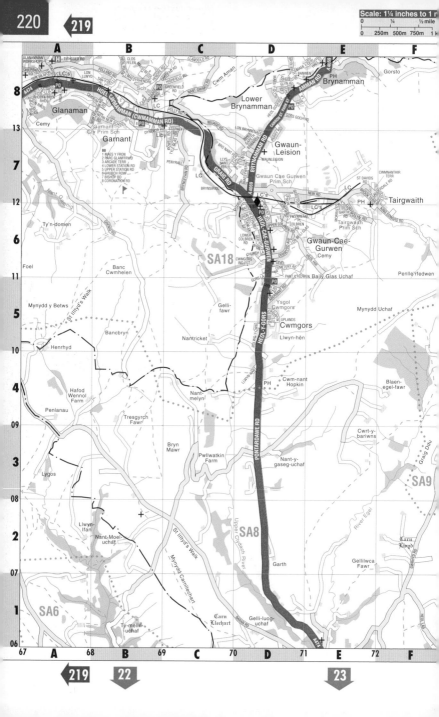

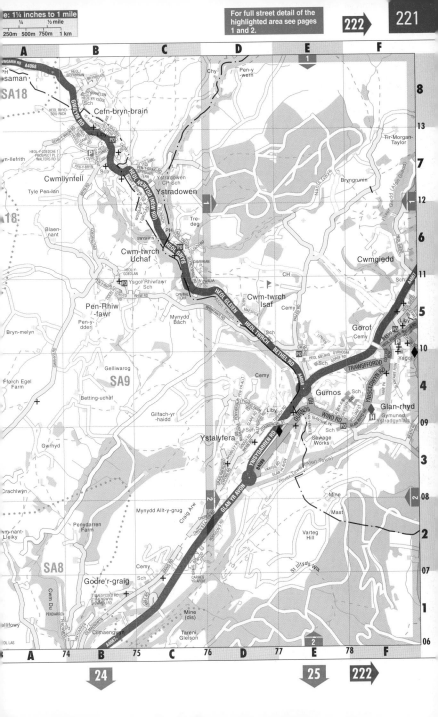

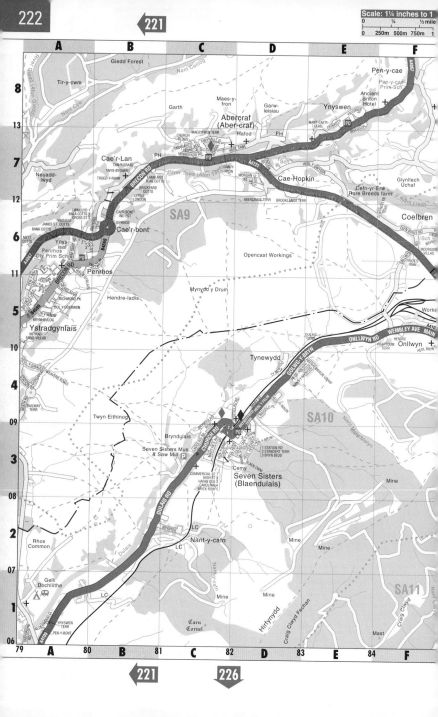

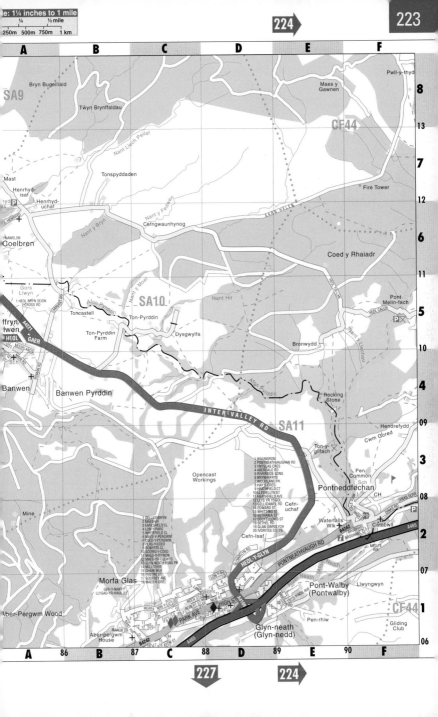

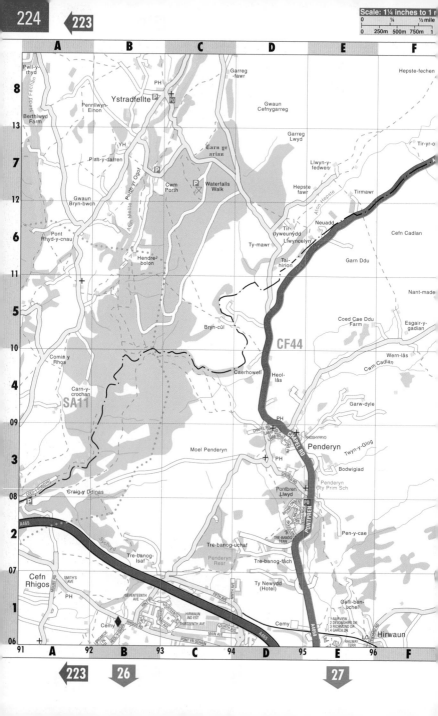

Scale: 1¼ inches to 1 r

| 0 | ¼ | ½ mile |
| 0 | 250m | 500m 750m 1 |

A B C D E F

Pwll-y-rhyd
Nedd Fechan
Berthlwyd Farm
Penrllwyn Einon
Ystradfellte
PH
P
PO
Garreg -fawr
Gwaun Cefnygarreg
Hepste-fechan

YH
Plas-y-darren
Carn yr arian
Garreg Lwyd
Llwyn-y-fedwery
Tir-yr-o

Porth yr Ogof
Cwm Porth
P
Waterfalls Walk
Hepste fawr
Afon Hepste
Tirmawr

Gwaun Bryn-bwch
Afon Mellte
Tir-dyweunydd
Neuadd
Cefn Cadlan

Pont Rhyd-y-cnau
Hendre-bolon
Ty-mawr
Llwyncelyn
Tai-hirion
Garn Ddu

Nant-made

Bryn-cûl
CF44
Coed Cae Ddu Farm
Esgair-y-gadian

Comin y Rhos
Caerhowell
Heol-lâs
Wern-lâs
Cwm Cadlan

Carn-y-crochan
SA11
Garw-dyle

PH
RHOSHYFRYD
Penderyn
Twyn-y-Glog

COED-Y-PWLL
Craig-y Ddinas
P
Moel Penderyn
CHAPEL ROW
LLANFAIR RD
LAMB ROW RD
CHAPEL RD
PH
Bodwigiad

A465
Sychryd
Pontbren Llwyd
CHURCH RD
Penderyn Cty Prim Sch
PO
PONTPREN

Tre-banog-uchaf
Tre-banog-fâch
Pen-y-cae

Cefn Rhigos
SMITH'S AVE
Tre-banog-Isaf
Penderyn Rest
Ty Newydd (Hotel)
Gelli-ban-bchel

PH
SEVENTEENTH AVE
HIRWAUN IND EST
THIRTEENTH AVE
FIFTH AVE
Cemy
RAILWAY TERR
Hirwaun

MAIN AVE
PONT YR OCHAIN
A465
Cemy

91 A 92 B 93 C 94 D 95 E 96 F

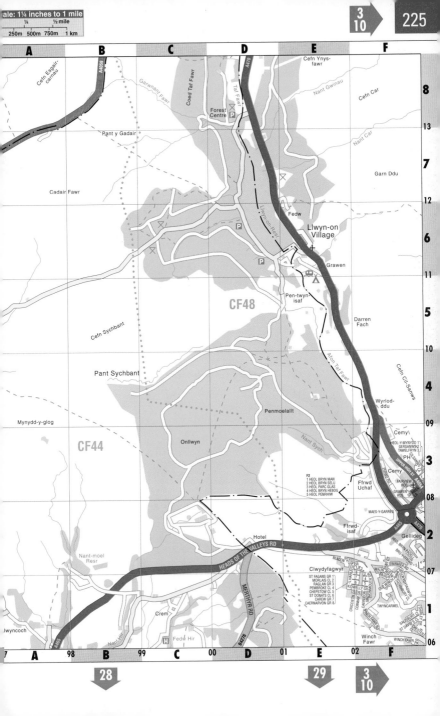

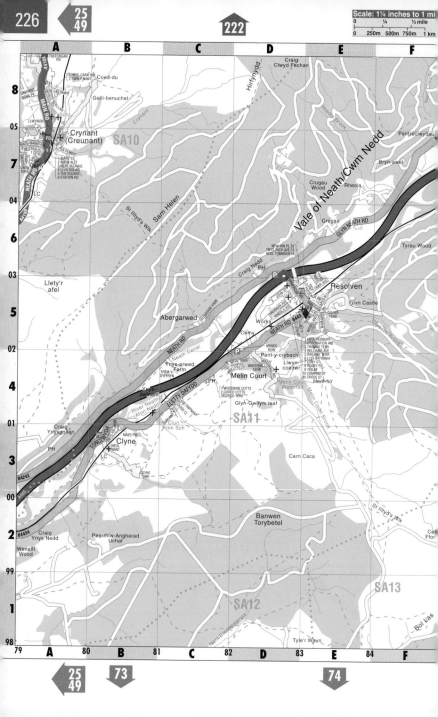

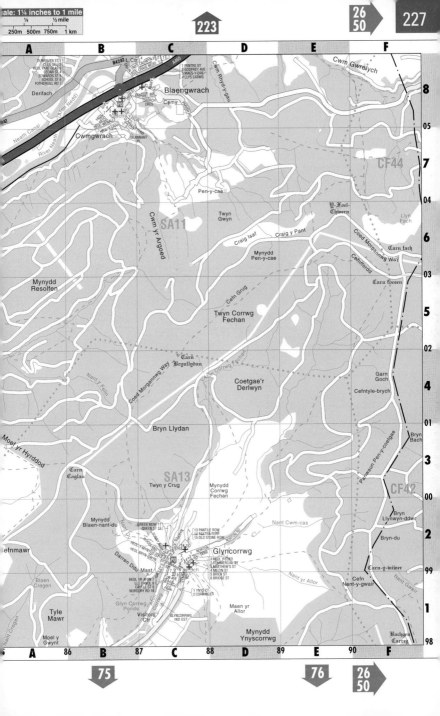

Scale: 1¼ inches to 1 n

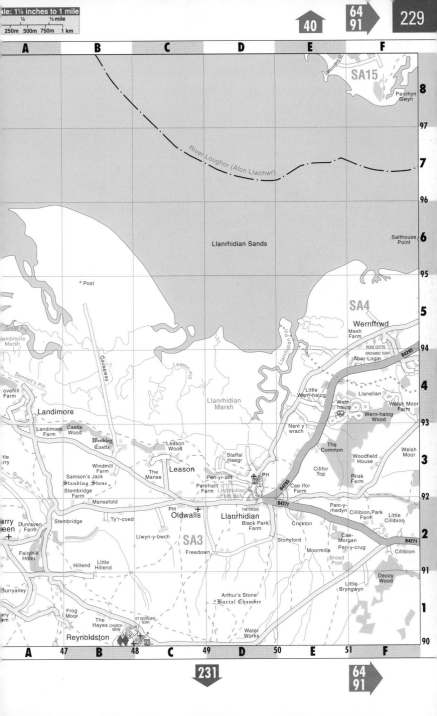

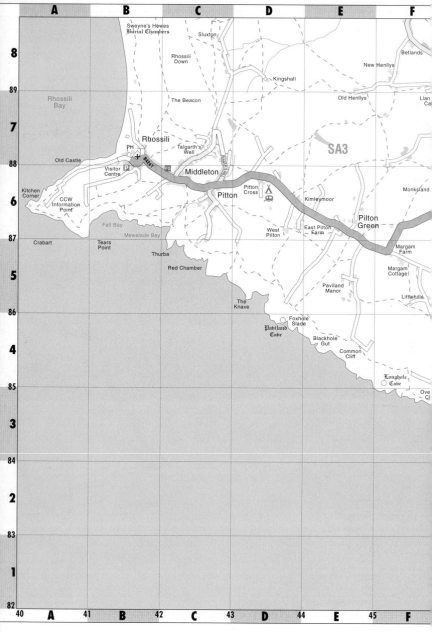

Sweyne's Howes
Burial Chambers

Sluxton

Rhossili
Down

The Beacon

Kingshall

Betlands

New Henllys

Old Henllys

Llan
Ca

Rhossili
Bay

SA3

Rhossili

Talgarth's
Well

PH

Old Castle

Visitor
Centre

Middleton

Kitchen
Corner

CCW
Information
Point

Pitton

Pitton
Cross

Kimleymoor

Monksland

Pilton
Green

Fall Bay

Mewslade Bay

West
Pilton

East Pilton
Farm

Margam
Farm

Crabart

Tears
Point

Thurba

Red Chamber

Margam
Cottage

Littlehills

Paviland
Manor

The
Knave

Foxhole
Slade

Paviland
Cave

Blackhole
Gut

Common
Cliff

Longhole
Cave

Ove
Cl

A   B   C   D   E   F

8

Reynoldston

King Arthur Hotel (PH)

Ty Bryn

The Cross

Little Reynoldston

Great Walterston

Little Walterston

Cefn Bryn

Lake Farm

Llanddewi

Stout Hall

Knelston Prim Sch

Knelston

Kittle Top

Home Farm

Perriswood

Nicholaston

89

7

A4118

Scurlage

Berry

Forest Walks P

Penrice Castle

Penrice

Nicholaston Woods

88

Sanctuary Farmhouse

SA3

Pitt

Oxwich Burrows

6

Moor Corner Farm

HANGMAN'S CROSS

Oxwich

Nature Reserve

87

PH

WER HOLIDAY VILLAGE

Norton

OXWICH LEISURE PK

Oxwich Castle

Oxwich Bay

5

Port-Eynon

Horton

ROCK LA

UNDERHILL LA

HIGHFIELDS HOLIDAY PK

SPRINGFIELD

Slade

Oxwich Green

86

NEW PARK HOLIDAY PK

PH

PO

Overton

The Cove

The Sands

Holy's Wash

Oxwich Point

85

Overton Mere

Culver Hole

Port-Eynon YH

The Salt House (rems of)

Port-Eynon Point

Port-Eynon Bay

4

3

84

2

83

1

82

A   47   B   48   C   49   D   50   E   51   F

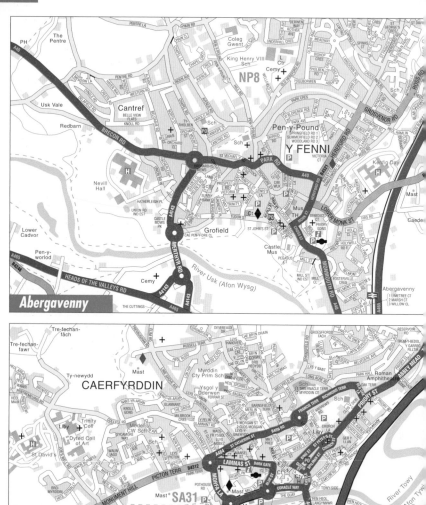

Abergavenny

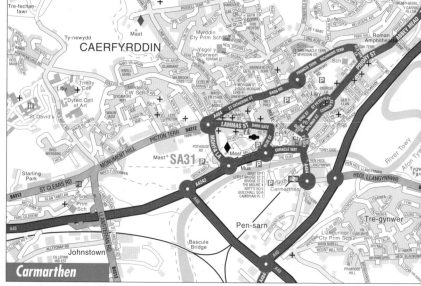

Carmarthen

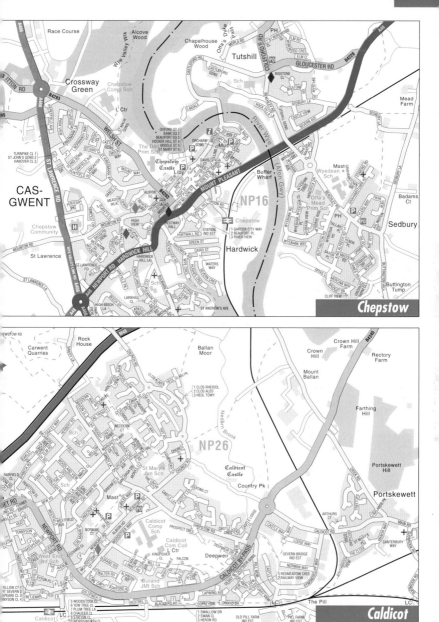

Chepstow

Caldicot

Index

Street names are listed alphabetically and show the locality, the Postcode District, the page number and a reference to the square in which the name falls on the map page

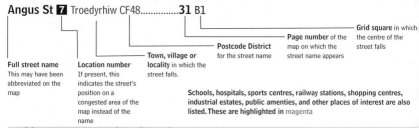

Angus St **7** Troedyrhiw CF48............**31** B1

Grid square in which the centre of the street falls

Page number of the map on which the street name appears

Postcode District for the street name

Town, village or locality in which the street falls.

Full street name
This may have been abbreviated on the map

Location number
If present, this indicates the street's position on a congested area of the map instead of the name

Schools, hospitals, sports centres, railway stations, shopping centres, industrial estates, public amenties, and other places of interest are also listed. These are highlighted in magenta

Abbreviations used in the index

App **Approach**	Cl **Close**	Espl **Esplanade**	N **North**	S **South**
Arc **Arcade**	Comm **Common**	Est **Estate**	Orch **Orchard**	Sq **Square**
Ave **Avenue**	Cnr **Corner**	Gdns **Gardens**	Par **Parade**	Strs **Stairs**
Bvd **Boulevard**	Cotts **Cottages**	Gn **Green**	Pk **Park**	Stps **Steps**
Bldgs **Buildings**	Ct **Court**	Gr **Grove**	Pas **Passage**	St **Street, Saint**
Bsns Pk **Business Park**	Ctyd **Courtyard**	Hts **Heights**	Pl **Place**	Terr **Terrace**
Bsns Ctr **Business Centre**	Cres **Crescent**	Ind Est **Industrial**	Prec **Precinct**	Trad **Trading Est**
Bglws **Bungalows**	Dr **Drive**	**Estate**	Prom **Promenade**	Wlk **Walk**
Cswy **Causeway**	Dro **Drove**	Intc **Interchange**	Ret Pk **Retail Park**	W **West**
Ctr **Centre**	E **East**	Junc **Junction**	Rd **Road**	Yd **Yard**
Cir **Circus**	Emb **Embankment**	La **Lane**	Rdbt **Roundabout**	

Town and village index

Aberavon	124 F8	Cilfynydd	109 E5	Gwaun-Cae-Gurwen	220 E6	Neath	71 B7	Risca	115 A3
Aberbargoed	58 B4	Cimla	72 C6	Hawthorn	136 B3	Neath Abbey	71 A8	Rogerstone	141 F6
Abercanaid	30 E4	Clydach(Bryn-mawr)	9 E6	Hendreforgan	132 C6	Nelson	83 E4	Rudry	139 C2
Abercarn	87 B2	Clydach(Swansea)	46 D7	Hendy	19 A5	New Tredegar	33 F3	St Athan	211 D4
Abercraf	222 C8	Clyne	226 B3	Hengoed	85 A3	Newbridge	87 B7	St Brides Major	185 D2
Abercwmboi	53 E4	Coedely	154 E8	Heol-y-Cyw	152 A5	Newport	143 F2	St Brides Wentlooge	163 E1
Abercynon	82 D3	Coedkernew	163 B3	Heolgerrig	10 A1	North Cornelly	165 E7	St Donat's	208 B5
Aberdare	29 C2	Coelbren	222 F6	Hirwaun	27 C8	Ogmore	185 A6	St Fagans	193 A7
Aberdulais	49 C4	Coity	169 C8	Hollybush	34 C3	Ogmore Vale	104 D1	St Hilary	201 C7
Aberfan	55 B5	Colwinston	187 A4	Horton	231 B4	Ogmore-By-Sea	184 D3	St Mary Church	201 A4
Abergarw	151 A7	Corntown	186 B2	Killay	93 B7	Oxwich	231 D5	St Nicholas	192 A1
Abergwynfi	76 C5	Cowbridge	188 C2	Knelston	231 A7	Pantyrawel	130 E4	Sarn	150 F4
Aberkenfig	150 C4	Coytrahen	150 B8	Laleston	167 F5	Parkmill	120 F7	Scurlage	231 A6
Abersychan	37 E3	Craig-Cefn-Parc	22 A2	Langstone	119 D1	Pen-clawdd	64 E3	Senghenydd	110 E2
Aberthin	189 B3	Creigiau	174 D8	Llandeilo Ferwallt	91 C4	Pen-Rhiw-fawr	221 B5	Seven Sisters	222 D3
Abertillery	36 C5	Croescyceiliog	90 B5	Llanelli	41 B5	Pen-y-fai	150 D1	Sigingstone	200 A4
Abertridwr	137 B8	Crofty	64 B3	Llanelli Hill	9 C4	Penarth	207 B3	Sirhowy	6 F1
Abertysswg	33 C8	Cross Hands	218 A7	Llanfrechfa	117 D7	Pencoed	170 C7	Skewen	70 D7
Ammanford	219 C8	Crynant	226 A7	Llangan	187 D8	Penderyn	224 E3	South Cornelly	165 F8
Argoed	58 F5	Cwm	35 B7	Llanbethëry	212 B8	Pendoylan	190 F6	Southerndown	185 A1
Baglan	98 E7	Cwm-twrch Isaf	1 B1	Llanblethian	200 D8	Pengam	85 B7	Southgate	121 A5
Banwen	223 A4	Cwm-twrch Uchaf	221 C6	Llanbradach	111 F1	Penllergaer	44 A2	Sully	216 B5
Bargoed	58 A3	Cwmaman	53 A4	Llancarfan	202 E1	Penllyn	188 A5	Swansea	95 B5
Barry	214 E3	Cwmavon(Blaenavon)	17 F1	Llandough	200 D6	Penmaen	120 B6	Taffs Well	158 A5
Bassaleg	142 A2	Cwmavon(Neath)	99 C5	Llandow	199 A2	Penpedairheol	84 D8	Talbot Green	155 B3
Beddau	156 B6	Cwmbran	89 D3	Llangstone	119 D1	Penperlleni	39 F6	Thomastown	133 A2
Bedlinog	56 B7	Cwmbrwla	28 C3	Llanelli Hill	9 C4	Pen-rhiwtyn	71 C5	Three Crosses	65 E1
Bedwas	138 D7	Cwmfelin	128 C8	Llangan	187 D8	Penrhys	80 B2	Tir-y-Berth	84 F6
Bettws(Bridgend)	129 E2	Cwmfelinfach	113 B4	Llangeinor	130 B3	Pentre	78 A5	Ton Pentre	79 A3
Bettws(Newport)	116 E2	Cwmllynfell	221 B3	Llangennech	42 B8	Pentre Meyrick	187 F4	Tondu	150 C5
Birchgrove	47 B2	Cwmparc	78 C5	Llangennith	228 C2	Pentrebach	31 B4	Tongwynlais	158 D2
Bishopston	121 F7	Cymmer	75 C4	Llangynwyd	128 B6	Pentyrch	175 C8	Tonmawr	73 C6
Bishton	145 F3	Cynonville	74 C1	Llanharan	154 A3	Penybryn	84 C5	Tonna	49 D2
Blackmill	130 E2	Deri	57 B8	Llanharry	172 A5	Penycoedcae	135 A4	Tonypandy	106 D5
Blackwood	85 D8	Dinas Powys	206 B8	Llanmadoc	228 E4	Penygraes	218 D8	Tonyrefail	133 C4
Blaenavon	17 E6	Dowlais	11 B4	Llanmaes	210 C8	Penywaun	28 A5	Tredegar	13 E7
Blaencwm	50 C2	Duffryn	74 D4	Llanmihangel	200 B1	Peterston-Super-Ely	191 E6	Tredomen	84 D1
Blaengarw	103 B6	Dunvant	93 B8	Llanrhidian	229 D2	Peterstone Wentlooge	180 E5	Trefechan	10 A6
Blaengwrach	227 C8	Dyffryn Cellwen	223 A5	Llansamlet	69 D8	Pitton	230 C6	Trehafod	108 D3
Blaengwynfi	76 C6	East Aberthaw	212 B2	Llansanor	188 E7	Pont Rhyd-y-cyff	128 C7	Treharris	83 B8
Blaenrhondda	50 D4	Ebbw Vale	14 F8	Llantarnam	117 A7	Pontardawe	23 D4	Treherbert	50 E1
Blaina	15 F5	Efail Isaf	156 F5	Llantrisant	155 C4	Pontarddulais	19 E5	Trelewis	83 D7
Bonvilston	191 B1	Evanstown	132 B8	Llantrithyd	202 D6	Ponthir	117 E6	Treoes	170 B1
Boverton	210 C7	Ewenny	185 F7	Llantwit Fardre	156 E7	Pontllanfraith	86 B5	Treorchy	78 E7
Bridgend	168 C7	Fairwood	92 D7	Llantwit Major	209 E5	Pontlliw	44 A7	Troedyrhiw	31 B2
Briton Ferry	71 B2	Felindre	20 F2	Llanwern	145 B5	Pontllyfni	12 E1	Tycroes	218 F5
Bryn(Caerphilly)	85 D4	Ferndale	79 F6	Llwydcoed	28 F6	Quakers Yard	83 B5	Tylorstown	80 C3
Bryn(Llanelli)	41 F6	Fforest	19 A6	Llysworney	187 D1	Pyle	148 A2	Upper Boat	136 E2
Bryn(Maesteg)	100 F5	Fleur De Lis	85 B6	Loughor	42 E2	Radyr	176 B6	Upper Killay	93 B5
Bryn-côch	48 D5	Fochriw	32 C7	Machen	140 A7	Rassau	7 B4	Varteg	17 E1
Brynamman	220 E8	Forge Side	17 A5	Maerdy	52 B1	Reduin	173 B6	Wattstown	107 E8
Bryncae	153 E1	Garnswllt	219 B4	Maesteg	102 B1	Resolven	226 E5	Waunarlwydd	66 E4
Bryncethin	151 B5	Gelligaer	84 D6	Maesycwmmer	85 B1	Reynoldston	229 B1	Wenvoe	205 A6
Brynmawr	8 A4	Gelligroes	85 E2	Maesygwartha	9 D8	Rhigos	26 C8	Wern-olau	65 D4
Brynmenyn	151 A6	Georgetown	13 F6	Marcross	208 D7	Rhiwderin	141 C6	Wick	198 D5
Brynna	153 C3	Gileston	211 E3	Margam	125 E4	Rhoose	213 B1	Wyllie	85 E1
Bynea	41 F3	Gilfach Goch	132 C7	Markham	58 D6	Rhydfelin	136 C5	Ynysddu	113 B5
Caerleon	118 C4	Glais	47 B6	Marshfield	162 D1	Rhydri	139 C1	Ynysforgan	46 C4
Caerphilly	138 D3	Glan y Nant	85 A7	Merthyr Mawr	185 A8	Rhydyfro	23 D8	Ynysmaerdy	155 A5
Capel Hendre	218 E6	Glanaman	220 A8	Merthyr Tydfil	11 A3	Rhymney	12 F4	Ynysmeudwy	24 B8
Cardiff	201 C7	Glyncorrwg	227 D2	Merthyr Vale	55 D4			Ynyswen	50 C2
Castle-upon-Alun	186 A2	Glynneath	223 D1	Michaelston-y-Fedw	162 A5			Ynyshir	81 F1
Castleton	162 C3	Godregraig	221 B1	Miskin	173 B6			Ystalyfera	2 A6
Cefn Cribwr	149 A2	Gorseinon	43 C3	Monknash	198 C2			Ystrad	79 D3
Cefn Hengoed	84 E4	Gorslas	218 C8	Morganstown	176 A8			Ystrad Mynach	84 F1
Cefn-bryn-brain	221 B8	Govilon	66 B4	Mountain Ash	54 F3			Ystradgynlais	222 A5
Cefneithin	218 E6	Gowerton	125 F7	Mumbles	123 B4			Ystradowen	189 D8
Cheltenham	9 C6	Graig Penllyn	188 B8	Nant-y-Moel	104 C6			Ystradowen	221 C7
Church Village	135 F1	Groesfaen	174 B7	Nantgarw	158 A8			
Cilfrew	49 B5	Grovesend	43 C6	Nantyglo	8 D2			

1
132kv Switch House Rd
CF62 .....211 E1

2
275kv Switch House Rd
CF62 .....211 E1

A

A R D Bsns Pk NP4 ....62 F4
Abbey Cl CF15 ....158 B3
Abbey Cotts NP44 ....117 B7
Abbey Ct CF38 ....135 E1
Abbey Gn NP44 ....116 F8
Abbey Gr NP44 ....117 B6
Abbey Rd
　Cwmbran NP44 ....89 E2
　Ewenny CF35 ....185 F8
　Newport NP19 ....144 D6
　Port Talbot SA13 ....125 C7
　Pyle CF33 ....148 C2
Abbey Road Ind Est
　SA10 ....71 C7
Abbeyfield Ho CF31 169 A5
Abbeyville Ave
　Port Talbot SA11 ....124 D8
　8 Port Talbot SA12 ..98 D1
Abbeyville Ct SA11 ....98 D1
Abbeyville Ho **9**
　SA10 ....98 D1
Abbot's Wlk SA10 ....71 C8
Abbots Mews NP20 143 B3
Abbott's Cl SA13 ....125 F3
Abbott's Mews SA13 125 F3
Aber Cl SA6 ....69 B7
Aber Halt CF83 ....137 F2
Aber Inf Sch CF32 ....104 F4
Aber Inf Sch CF32 ....130 E8
Aber Rd CF32 ....104 E3
Aber St CF71 ....195 A2
Aber-Fawr Terr
　CF83 ....137 A7
Aber-Ffrwd Rd CF45 ..54 D4
Aber-nant Cty Prim Sch
　CF44 ....29 C3
Aber-Rhondda Rd
　CF39 ....107 E4
Aberaeron Cl CF62 215 A8
Aberafan Rd SA12 ....98 E2
Aberaman Enterprise Pk
　CF44 ....53 E7
Aberaman Hos **5**
　SA44 ....53 D7
Aberaman Ind Est
　CF44 ....53 E6
Aberaman Park Ind Est
　CF44 ....53 D6
Aberavon Cl **12** SA12 ..98 F1
Aberbargoed & District
　Hospl CF81 ....58 B5
Aberbargoed District
　Hospl CF81 ....58 A5
Aberbargoed Inf Sch
　CF81 ....58 A5
Aberbargoed Jun Sch
　(Ysgol Iau Aberbargoed)
　CF81 ....58 A5
Aberbeeg Day Hospl
　NP13 ....59 F8
Aberbeeg Rd NP13 ....36 B2
Aberbran Rd CF14 ....177 C2
Abercanaid Ind Est
　CF48 ....30 E6
Abercanaid Prim Sch
　CF48 ....30 D6
Abercarn Fach NP11 114 C8
Abercarn Jun & Inf Sch
　NP11 ....87 B4
Abercedy SA4 ....65 A4
Abercerdin Prim Sch
　CF39 ....132 B7
Abercerdin Rd CF39 132 B8
Aberclydach Pl SA6 ...46 D7
Aberconway Pl NP12 ..59 B1
Abercrave Cty Prim Sch
　SA9 ....222 C7
Abercrave Terr SA9 ...222 D7
Abercregan Rd SA13 ..74 F6
Abercwmboi-Isaf Rd
　CF45 ....54 B3
Abercynon Ct
　CF45 ....82 E3
Abercynon North Sta
　CF45 ....82 C5
Abercynon Rd
　Abercynon CF45 ....82 C5
　Mountain Ash CF45 ...82 A6
　Pontypridd CF37 ....109 D7
Abercynon South Sta
　CF45 ....82 E2
Abercynon St CF11 ..195 A2
Aberdale Rd SA11 ..124 B2
Aberdare Boys Comp Sch
　CF44 ....28 D4
Aberdare Coll CF44 ...28 D4
Aberdare General Hospl
　CF44 ....28 D3
Aberdare Girls Comp Sch
　(Upper) CF44 ....29 B2
Aberdare Girls Lower
　Comp Sch CF44 ....28 D7
Aberdare Rd
　Abercynon CF11 ....82 D2
　Ferndale CF43 ....79 F8
　Glynneath SA11 ....223 D1
　Merthyr Tydfil CF48 ..10 C1
　Mountain Ash CF45 ...54 B3

Aberdare Sta CF44 ....29 A2
Aberdare Town CW Prim
　Sch CF44 ....29 B1
Aberdaron Rd CF3 ..179 E5
Aberdore Rd CF14 ..177 C2
Aberdovey Cl CF64 ..206 C3
Aberdovey St CF24 ..195 C5
Aberdulais Cres
　CF14 ....177 B2
Aberdulais Falls SA10 49 C4
Aberdulais Rd CF14 ..177 B2
Aberdyberthi La St 68 D2
Aberfan Cres CF48 ....55 C4
Aberfan Fawr CF48 ....55 C3
Aberfan Rd CF48 ....55 C3
Aberfawr Rd CF83 ..137 A7
Aberffrwd NP22 ....13 D5
Aberfields View
　CF32 ....104 F4
Abergarw Rd CF32 ..150 F6
Abergarw Trad Est
　CF32 ....151 A6
Abergavenny Rd NP4 ..17 D8
Abergele Cl CF3 ..179 E6
Abergele Rd CF3 ..179 E5
Abergelly Rd SA5 ....67 C5
Abergorki Ind Est
　CF42 ....73 C5
Abergwawr Pl CF44 ...53 B8
Abergwawr St CF44 ...53 B8
Abergwernffrwd Row
　SA13 ....73 C5
Abergwynfi Inf Sch
　SA13 ....76 C5
Abergwynfi Jun Sch
　SA13 ....76 C5
Aberhenwaun Uchaf
　SA13 ....222 E4
Aberlash Rd SA18 ..219 B8
Aberllechau Cty Prim Sch
　CF39 ....107 D8
Aberllefenni St
　CF39 ....107 D8
Abermorlais Terr
　CF47 ....10 D1
Abernant Cres CF48 ...58 E7
Abernant Rd
　Aberdare CF44 ....29 B3
　Gwaun-Cae-Gurwen
　SA18 ....220 D5
　Markham NP12 ....58 E7
Abernethy Cl **10** CF3 180 A7
Abernethy Quay **10**
　SA1 ....95 D6
Abernethy Sq **15** SA1 ..95 E6
Aberpennar St CF45 ...54 D2
Aberporth Rd CF14 ..177 B2
Aberskynan Comp Sch
　NP4 ....37 F4
Abertaf CF45 ....82 E3
Abertaf Prim Sch
　CF45 ....82 E3
Aberteifi Cl CF14 ....177 C2
Aberteifi Rd CF14 ....177 C2
Aberthaw Ave NP19 144 C5
Aberthaw Circ NP19 144 C5
Aberthaw Cl NP19 ..144 C5
Aberthaw Dr NP19 ..144 B4
Aberthaw Rd
　Cardiff CF5 ....193 D5
　Newport NP19 ....144 C4
Aberthin La CF71 ....189 B2
Aberthin Rd CF71 ....189 A2
Abertillery Comp Sch
　NP13 ....36 B6
Abertillery Prim & Inf
　Schs NP13 ....36 B6
Abertillery Rd NP13 ...15 E3
Abertonlwyd St CF42 ..50 F2
Abertysswg Cty Prim Sch
　NP22 ....33 B8
Aberystwith Cl CF62 195 E5
Aberystwyth Cres
　CF62 ....214 E4
Abingdon St CF63 ..215 B7

Acacia Ave
　Hengoed CF82 ....84 F3
　Merthyr Tydfil CF47 ..10 F8
　Newport NP19 ....144 B5
　Port Talbot SA12 ....98 D2
　Porthcawl CF36 ....183 D7
Acacia Cl SA12 ....98 C2
Acacia Rd SA3 ....123 A8
Acacia Sq NP19 ....144 B5
Acacia Terr NP11 ....87 B4
Academic Way
　(Coedlan y Coleg)
　CF14 ....177 E3
Acer Ave CF38 ....156 C5
Acer Ct CF72 ....172 C6
Acland Rd CF31 ....168 F5
Acorn Cl
　Michaelston-y-Fedw CF3 ..161 D4
　Ebbw Vale NP23 ....7 C5
　Port Talbot SA6 ....46 B1
Acorn Gr Cardiff CF23 161 A1
　Llantwit Fardre CF38 156 E8
Acorn Pl SA12 ....98 D7
Acorns The
　Cardiff CF14 ....159 E3
　Llanmartin NP18 ....145 E2
Acre Cl NP11 ....60 C2
Adam St
　Abertillery NP13 ....36 C5
　Cardiff CF24 ....195 B5
Adam Wlk SA10 ....71 C8
Adams Ave CF32 ..150 F4
Adams Ct **11** CF24 ..195 C5
Adams Sq NP23 ....14 E8

Adams St CF40 ....106 B7
Adamscroft Pl CF10 195 C3
Adamsdown La
　CF24 ....195 C5
Adamsdown Pl **3**
　CF24 ....195 C5
Adamsdown Sq
　CF24 ....195 C5
Adare St
　8 Bridgend CF31 ..168 F4
　Evanstown CF39 ....132 B8
　Ogmore Vale CF32 ..104 E3
　Port Talbot SA12 ....124 E8
Adare Terr CF32 ....78 C7
Addison Ave CF72 ....172 A5
Addison Cres CF5 ..193 C5
Addison La SA12 ....124 E8
Addison St
　Neath SA11 ....71 D4
　Port Talbot SA12 ....124 E8
Addison Ind Est NP12 35 D8
Addison Way CF83 ..139 C6
Addoldy Rd SA11 ....223 C1
Adelaide Cl NP12 ....85 C6
Adelaide Pl CF10 ..195 B2
Adelaide St
　Cardiff CF10 ....195 B2
　Swansea SA1 ....95 D6
Adeline St
　Cardiff CF24 ....195 C6
　Newport NP20 ....143 C2
Adenfield Way **14** CF62 212 E2
Adey r Mor CF62 ....214 F2
Adit Wlk NP44 ....89 C5
Administration Rd
　CF24 ....211 E1
Admirals Wlk SA2 ....94 C6
Adrian Bolt Gn NP19 144 C4
Adrian Cl CF36 ....182 E8
Adrian Stephens Ho
　CF48 ....10 A3
Adventurers Quay
　CF10 ....195 D2
Ael y Bryn CF42 ....85 A2
Ael-y-Bryn CF31 ..168 B5
Ael-y-Bryn
　Beddau CF38 ....156 A7
　Bedwas CF83 ....136 B3
　Blaenavon NP4 ....11 D7
　Caerphilly CF83 ....137 F5
　Cardiff CF23 ....178 D4
　Cwmdare CF44 ....28 D3
　Maesteg CF34 ....75 A2
　Mumbles SA3 ....123 C1
　North Cornelly CF33 ..166 A8
　Pen-clawdd SA4 ....64 F4
　Pentyrch CF15 ....175 E6
　Peterston-Super-Ely
　CF5 ....171 G6

Ael-y-Bryn Rd SA5 ....66 B4
Aelfryn CF72 ....172 B5
Aelfryn Terr SA12 ....99 D6
Aelybryn CF37 ....109 A2
Aelybryn Cl SA15 ....40 E8
Aelybryn Dr SA15 ....40 E8
Aeron Cl CF81 ....58 A2
Aeron Ct CF81 ....58 A2
Aeron Pl Bargoed CF81 58 A2
Aeron Terr CF47 ....30 F8
Aerons Ho NP44 ....116 E8
Afan Argoed Ctry Prk
　SA13 ....73 F1
Afan Cl CF62 ....214 D5
Afan Coll SA13 ....125 F3
Afan Fach SA13 ....74 D4
Afan Terr SA13 ....99 F6
Afan Valley Rd
　Cimla SA11 ....72 B5
　Cwmavon SA12 ....99 E4
　Pontrhydyfen SA12,
　SA13 ....73 D2
Afan Way
　Aberavon SA12 ....124 F8
　Port Talbot SA12 ....98 D2
Afandale SA12 ....98 C4
Afon Cl
　Michaelston-y-Fedw
　CF3 ....161 D4
Afon Ct NP4 ....38 A3
Afon Fach CF33 ....148 A1
Afon Llwyd Terr NP4 ..38 A1
Afon Llwyd Cl NP18 ..118 C3
Afon Mead NP10 ....141 D7
Afon Rd SA14 ....42 C8
Afon St CF37 ....108 D2
Afon Taf High Sch
　CF48 ....31 C1
Afon Terr NP44 ....89 F5
Afon Villas SA13 ....100 A7
Afon-Llan Gdns SA4 ..67 D6
Afon-y-Felin CF61 ....49 C4
Afon-y-Felin Prim Sch
　CF33 ....147 F1

Africa Gdns CF14 ....177 E2
Agate St CF24 ....195 D6
Agent's Row CF44 ....29 C3
Agincourt Rd **1**
　CF23 ....195 D8
Agincourt St NP20 ..143 B7
Agnes St CF64 ....206 E5
Ailesbury St NP20 ..143 C2
Ainon Ct CF24 ....195 C7
Aintree Dr CF5 ....160 F1
Airport Bsns Pk
　CF24 ....213 C4
Alamein Rd SA1 ....68 E3
Alan Cl NP10 ....142 B4
Alan Terr CF38 ....156 F4
Alanbrooke Ave
　NP20 ....117 A4
Alandale Rd NP23 ....7 A4
Alaw Prim Sch CF40 107 B5
Alaw Rd CF40 ....107 B5
Alban Rd SA13 ....40 E6
Alban Terr SA13 ....74 F6
Albany Cl SA5 ....68 C4
Albany Com Jun & Inf Sch
　CF24 ....195 B8
Albany La NP20 ....143 C1
Albany Pl
　Abercynon CF45 ....82 F3
　Maesteg CF34 ....75 C2
　Newbridge NP11 ....86 F7
　Rhymney NP22 ....12 E5
　Tredegar NP22 ....13 E8
Albany Rd
　Abertillery NP13 ....36 C5
　Cardiff CF5 ....194 C5
　Gorseinon SA4 ....43 A2
　Hengoed CF82 ....45 B3
　Merthyr Tydfil CF47 ..10 E3
　New Tredegar NP24 ...33 F2
　Pontycymer CF32 ....103 F3
　Pontypridd CF37 ....125 A8
　Swansea SA2 ....94 F6
　Tredegar NP22 ....13 E6
Albany St CF37 ....125 D7
Albert Ave NP19 ....143 E6
Albert Cres CF64 ..207 B4
Albert Ct
　Newport NP19 ....143 E5
　8 Penarth CF64 ....207 B4
Albert Cty Prim Sch
　CF64 ....207 B5
Albert Pl SA3 ....123 A5
Albert Rd
　Aberbychan NP4 ....99 A1
　Blaina NP13 ....15 E4
　Pontypridd CF37 ....135 B8
　Swansea SA1 ....95 D6
Albert Row SA1 ....95 D6
Albert Sq CF48 ....11 B5
Albert St
　Abertridwr CF83 ....29 A1
　Barry CF63 ....215 D6
　Cardiff CF11 ....194 D1
　Cwmdare CF44 ....28 D3
　Ferndale CF43 ....80 A1
　17 Merthyr Tydfil CF47 30 E8
　Mountain Ash CF45 ...54 D1
　Newport NP20 ....143 C2
　Pentyrch CF15 ....78 F5
Albert Terr
　Maesteg CF34 ....101 F3
　Newport NP19 ....143 B4
Albert Wlk **9** CF11 ..194 D5
Alberta Pl CF64 ....207 A2
Alberta Rd CF64 ....207 B2
Alberto Rd SA6 ....69 A6
Albion Cl
　Ebbw Vale NP23 ....7 C5
　Llantwit Fardre CF38 156 C5
　Merthyr Tydfil CF47 ...10 D1
　Neath SA11 ....71 E7
Albion Ct CF24 ....178 B1
Albion Flats CF15 ..109 F5
Albion Ind Est CF14 109 F5
Albion Pl
　Pontypool NP4 ....62 A8
　Pyle CF33 ....148 C1
Albion Rd Baglan SA12 98 D7
Albion Rd App SA12 ..98 C7
Albion St
　Ebbw Vale NP23 ....7 C5
　Llantwit Fardre CF38 156 C5
Albion Terr NP12 ....85 F6
Alcock Cl NP19 ....144 B3
Alden Dr SA2 ....67 D1
Aldenham Rd CF36 ..183 C7
Alder Ave SA9 ....2 D7
Alder Cl NP4 ....63 B5
Alder Cl CF44 ....28 E2
Alder Gr
　Ebbw Vale NP23 ....7 C5
　Llantwit Fardre CF38 156 C5
　Merthyr Tydfil CF47 ...10 F8
Alderbrook CF23 ..160 D1
Aldergrove Cl SA12 ...98 C4
Aldergrove Rd CF39 107 E5
Alderman Cl NP23 ....7 C5
Alderman Davies Prim
　Sch SA11 ....71 E7
Alderney St NP20 ..143 C7
Alders The
　Blackwood NP12 ....59 C1
　Llanrumney NP44 ....90 B1
Alderwood Cl
　1 Cardiff CF23 ....179 E7
　Cwmbran NP44 ....89 A3
Alderwood Rd SA3 ..123 A7

Aldsworth Rd CF5 ...193 F7
Aldwych Cl CF14 ..159 E2
Aldwyn Rd SA5 ....67 D2
Aled Way CF62 ..211 C7
Alexander Cres SA10 48 E2
Alexander Ct CF83 138 C3
Alexander Pl CF48 ...30 F4
Alexander Rd
　Briton Ferry SA11 ....71 C3
　Neath SA10 ....48 E2
Alexandra Ave
　Cardiff CF5 ....194 B8
　2 Cardiff CF5 ....194 D6
　Newport NP20 ....143 D2
　Penarth CF64 ....207 B3
　Ynysddu NP11 ....112 F6
Alexandra La NP20 ..143 C1
Alexandra Pl
　Abercynon CF45 ....82 F3
　Maesteg CF34 ....75 C2
　Newbridge NP11 ....86 F7
　Rhymney NP22 ....12 E5
　Tredegar NP22 ....13 E8
Alexandra Rd
　Abertillery NP13 ....36 C3
　Cardiff CF5 ....194 C5
　Gorseinon SA4 ....43 A2
　Hengoed CF82 ....45 B3
　Llantwit Fardre CF38 156 C6
　7 Merthyr Tydfil CF47 30 E8
　Mountain Ash CF45 ...54 C2
　Senghenydd CF83 ....110 F3
　Swansea SA2 ....94 F6
　Tredegar NP22 ....13 E6
Alexandra Trad Est
　CF5 ....179 D3
Alexandra St **8**
　NP23 ....8 C4
Alford Cl CF14 ....71 E7
Alfred Rd SA6 ....68 E6
Alfred St
　Aberavon SA12 ....98 F1
　Abertysswg NP22 ....33 C8
　Bargoed CF81 ....58 A2
　Cardiff CF24 ....178 B1
　Ebbw Vale NP23 ....7 C1
　Hendreforgan CF39 ..132 C5
　Maesteg CF34 ....102 A3
　Merthyr Tydfil CF47 ...10 F4
　Neath SA11 ....71 E7
　Newport NP20 ....143 D1
　Swansea SA4 ....65 A2
Alfred's Terr CF15 ..158 A3
Alfreda Rd CF14 ....176 F4
Alfreds Ct CF14 ....176 F4
Alice Pl CF44 ....53 A3
Alice St Cardiff CF10 195 B2
　Neath SA11 ....71 D6
　Newport NP20 ....143 C1
　Swansea SA4 ....68 A2
Alison Ct CF36 ....183 C7
All Saints CW Prim Sch
　CF63 ....214 C5
All Saints Cl NP23 ....7 C5
All Saints RC Jun & Inf
　Sch NP23 ....14 B8
All Saints Way CF31 ..150 D1
Allan Durst Cl CF5 ..176 D3
Allaway Ct **5** SA1 ....68 C2
Allen Cl Bettws NP20 116 C1
　Cardiff CF3 ....179 E8
Allen Ct CF61 ....210 B6
Allen St CF45 ....54 D3
Allensbank Cres
　CF14 ....177 F2
Allensbank Jun & Inf Schs
　CF14 ....177 F2
Allensbank Rd CF14 177 F2
Allerton St CF11 ..194 F4
Alleyn Ho NP44 ....90 A4
Allgood Ave NP44 ....17 B6
Allister St SA11 ....71 E7
Allotment Rd CF72 ...44 C4
Alloy Ct Est SA8 ....23 F5
Allt Cl CF14 ....176 F8
Allt y Grug SA11 ....70 C1
Allt-iago Rd SA4 ....19 D4
Allt-y-Graban Rd
　SA4 ....43 B8
Allt-y-Waun SA8 ....23 D7
Allt-yr-Yn Ave NP20 143 A6
Allt-yr-Yn Cres
　NP20 ....143 A7
Allt-yr-Yn Ct NP20 ..143 A7

Allt-yr-Yn Hts NP20 .142 F6
Allt-yr-Yn Rd NP20 143 A6
Allt-yr-Yn View
　NP20 ....142 F6
Allt-yr-Yn Way
　NP20 ....143 A7
Alltacham Dr SA8 ....23 E5
Alltmawr Rd CF23 ..178 C6
Alltwen Hill SA8 ....23 F3
Alltwen Inf Sch SA8 ...24 A5
Alltwen Prim Sch SA8 24 A5
Alltygrug Farm Rd SA9 2 B7
Alltygrug Rd SA9 ....2 B7
Alltywerin SA8 ....23 D6
Alma Cl NP20 ....143 C3
Alma Pl Pentre CF41 ..78 F5
　Pontypridd CF37 ....62 E1
Alma Rd Cardiff CF23 178 C1
　Maesteg CF34 ....102 B2
Alma St Aberdare CF44 28 F4
　Ammanford SA18 ....23 B6
　8 Blaenavon NP4 ....17 C7
　Brynmawr NP23 ....8 C4
　Dowlais CF48 ....11 A5
　Machen CF83 ....140 A5
　Merthyr Tydfil CF47 ...30 E8
　Newport NP20 ....143 C3
　Treherbert CF42 ....50 E2
Alma Terr
　Cardiff CF23 ....150 C3
　Brynmawr NP23 ....8 D5
　Dowlais CF48 ....11 A5
　Maesteg CF34 ....102 B2
　Ogmore Vale CF32 ..130 E8
　Port Talbot SA13 ....125 D6
Almond Ave NP11 ..115 B2
Almond Cl CF36 ..156 C6
Almond Ct SA12 ....98 D7
Almond Dr
　Cardiff CF23 ....160 F1
　Newport NP20 ....117 B3
Almond Wlk SA10 ....71 C8
Alpha Ho CF10 ....195 C3
Alpha Cl CF14 ....157 E8
Alpha Pl Baglan SA12 ..98 D2
　Ebbw Vale NP23 ....7 B6
Alpha St CF37 ....109 D2
Als St SA15 ....40 E5
Althorp Dr CF64 ....217 A8
Alton Terr NP4 ....62 B7
Alun Rd SA1 ....68 B1
Alway Cl NP19 ....144 D5
Alway Cres NP19 ....144 D5
Alway Inf Sch NP19 144 C4
Alway Jun Sch NP19 144 C4
Alway Par NP19 ....144 D4
Alwen Dr Barry CF62 214 C6
　Cardiff CF14 ....159 F3
Alwyn Cl NP10 ....142 A7
Alyson Way CF35 ....170 C8
Amalfi Ho CF10 ....195 C3
Aman Ct CF44 ....53 A3
Aman St CF44 ....53 A3
Amanwy SA14 ....41 D5
Amber Cl Cardiff CF23 160 F1
　Port Talbot SA12 ....98 B2
Ambergate Dr CF23 160 F1
Amberheart Dr CF14 159 F7
Amberley Cl CF23 ..178 F8
Amberley Ct CF23 ..178 F8
Amberton Pl **4** CF14 160 F1
Amberwood Cl CF23 160 F1
Amblecote Cl CF23 ..160 F1
Ambleside NP4 ....37 E5
Ambleside Ave CF23 178 A2
Ambleside Ct CF82 ...84 E8
Ambleside Pl SA3 ..123 A8
Ambrooke Cl CF23 ..160 F1
Ambrose Way NP4 ....63 A4
Amelia Trust Farm
　CF62 ....203 C5
America Pl CF39 ....107 F4
Amesbury Rd CF23 ..178 D1
Amethyst Rd CF5 ..176 D1
Amherst Cres CF62 ..214 F2
Amherst St CF11 ....194 F2
Amman Rd SA18 ....220 E8
Amman Valley Comp Sch
　SA18 ....219 C7
Amman Valley Hospl
　SA18 ....220 A8
Ammanford Cty Prim Sch
　SA18 ....219 C7
Ammanford Rd
　Betws SA18 ....219 A6
　Tycroes SA18 ....218 F6
Ammanford Sta
　SA18 ....219 B7
Amos Hill CF40 ....107 A3
Amos St SA15 ....40 C4
Amroth Ct CF62 ....214 F7
Amroth Rd CF5 ....193 D5
Amroth Wlk NP44 ....89 C2
Amry St CF41 ....79 D3
Amy Johnson Cl
　NP19 ....144 B3
Amyas Cl CF11 ....194 E3
Anchor Ct
　3 Cardiff CF10 ....195 B4
　8 Swansea SA1 ....95 D6
Anchor Ind Est CF15 158 A3

236 Anc – Bar

Anchor Way CF64 ... 206 F6
Anderson La SA3 ... 121 A5
Anderson Pl
Cardiff CF24 ... 195 D6
Newport NP20 ... 117 A4
Andover Cl CF62 ... 214 B7
Andrew Cres SA6 ... 46 B4
Andrew Rd CF64 ... 206 E5
Andrew St SA15 ... 40 E6
Andrew's Rd CF14 ... 176 F2
Andrews Bldgs 2 CF64 ... 207 B4
Andrews Cl
Bargoed CF81 ... 58 A2
Merthyr Tydfil CF48 ... 30 A8
Andrews Ct
Boverton CF61 ... 210 A6
Ebbw Vale NP23 ... 7 B1
Pontypridd CF37 ... 135 C8
Andrews Terr NP11 ... 60 C4
Androven Ct CF23 ... 178 D6
Aneddfan SA12 ... 99 F6
Aneurin Ave
Newbridge NP11 ... 60 B3
Pengam NP12 ... 85 B6
Aneurin Bevan Ave
Brynmenyn CF32 ... 150 F6
Gelligaer CF82 ... 84 C6
Aneurin Bevan Ct
Newport NP10 ... 163 E7
Pontypool NP4 ... 62 C6
Aneurin Bevan's Way CF34 ... 102 D2
Aneurin Cl
Swansea SA2 ... 94 A6
Tredegar NP22 ... 13 E7
Aneurin Cres CF47 ... 30 F7
Aneurin Pl NP23 ... 8 C5
Aneurin Rd CF63 ... 215 A6
Aneurin Terr NP22 ... 12 E6
Aneurin Way SA2 ... 94 A6
Angel La Bargoed CF81 58 A3
Blackwood NP12 ... 58 B2
Angel Pl SA11 ... 71 E8
Angel Sq NP23 ... 14 D6
Angel St
Aberavon SA12 ... 98 F1
Bridgend CF31 ... 168 E4
Neath SA11 ... 71 E8
Angelica Way CF14 . 159 D3
Angelina St CF10 ... 195 B3
Angelsey Ct NP18 ... 117 F3
Angelton Gn CF31 ... 150 D1
Angelton Rd CF31 ... 168 D8
Angle Cl CF62 ... 214 F8
Angle Pl CF14 ... 159 D1
Anglesey Cl
Boverton CF61 ... 210 B7
Church Village CF38 ... 136 A2
Anglesey St 10 CF5 ... 194 C6
Anglesey Way CF36 . 165 E1
Angleton Rd CF31 ... 168 D8
Anglia Cl CF31 ... 150 F1
Angus St Aberfan CF48 55 C5
Cardiff CF24 ... 178 C1
7 Troedyrhiw CF48 ... 31 B1
Ann St Abercynon CF45 82 D2
Aberdare CF44 ... 28 F3
Cardiff CF11 ... 194 D5
Llanelli SA15 ... 40 D4
Pontypridd CF37 ... 109 F5
Ann's Cl CF47 ... 30 E7
Anne St 6 NP4 ... 17 C6
Annes Ct NP23 ... 7 C1
Annesley Rd NP19 ... 143 E6
Annesley St SA15 ... 40 C5
Anson Ct 5 CF10 ... 195 C4
Anson Gn NP19 ... 144 E7
Anstee Ct 7 CF5 ... 194 D5
Anthony Dr NP18 ... 117 F4
Anthony Gr CF48 ... 30 E4
Anton Ct CF14 ... 177 A5
Antwerp Pl NP13 ... 36 A6
Anwyll Cl NP18 ... 118 A4
Apollo Cl CF14 ... 159 E2
Apollo Way NP12 ... 85 D7
Appledore Pl SA3 ... 122 E6
Appledore Rd CF14 . 177 D3
Applegrove SA3 ... 229 B1
Appletree Ave CF40 . 107 C4
Appletree Rd CF40 ... 107 C4
Applewood Cl CF24 . 195 D5
Approach Rd SA5 ... 68 C2
Aprilia Ho CF10 ... 195 C3
Aqueduct Terr SA12 ... 73 B1
Ar y Nant CF63 ... 215 A7
Arabella St CF24 ... 178 B1
Arael Jun & Inf Sch NP13 ... 36 B2
Arael View NP13 ... 35 F8
Aragon Ho NP20 ... 143 A5
Aragon St NP20 ... 143 C7
Arail St NP13 ... 36 C3
Aran Ct NP44 ... 89 B5
Aran St SA6 ... 68 F7
Arbroath Ct CF24 ... 195 F7
Arbutus Cl CF47 ... 10 D5
Arcade Abertillery NP13 36 B5
1 Llanelli SA15 ... 40 D5
Arcade Terr 3 SA18 . 220 B8
Arcade The
Cwmbran NP44 ... 89 F3
10 Merthyr Tydfil CF47 . 10 D1
Arcadia Way NP4 ... 38 B2
Arch Hill NP11 ... 114 C6
Archbishop Mcgrath RC Sch CF32 ... 150 E5
Archdeacon John Lewis CW Prim Sch CF31 . 169 C5
Archer Cres CF5 ... 193 D6
Archer Ct CF62 ... 214 F2
Archer Pl Cardiff CF5 . 193 C6
Penarth CF64 ... 207 A3
Archer Rd Barry CF62 214 F2
Cardiff CF5 ... 193 C6
Cwmbran NP44 ... 89 B3
Penarth CF64 ... 207 A3
Archer St
Troedyrhiw CF48 ... 31 C2
Ynysybwl CF37 ... 81 F1
Archer Terr CF64 ... 207 A2
Arches The 23 CF47 ... 30 E8
Archibald St NP19 ... 143 E5
Archview Ct CF24 ... 178 A2
Arcon Ho 3 CF3 ... 179 D8
Arcot La CF64 ... 207 A4
Arcot Lane N 4 CF64 ... 207 A5
Arcot St CF64 ... 207 A4
Arden Way CF63 ... 215 C7
Ardmore Ave 3 CF40 ... 106 F4
Ardwyn CF14 ... 176 F8
Ardwyn Pl CF32 ... 104 E2
Ardwyn Terr
Ton Pentre CF41 ... 79 A2
Tonypandy CF40 ... 106 E6
Arennig Rd SA5 ... 68 B5
Arethusa Ct SA2 ... 93 C6
Arfonfab Cres CF37 . 136 B4
Arfryn CF44 ... 28 A6
Arfryn Ave SA15 ... 40 E7
Arfryn Pl CF47 ... 30 E8
Arfryn Prim Sch SA5 . 68 B5
Arfryn Rd SA2 ... 94 E8
Arfryn Terr
Ebbw Vale NP23 ... 7 D4
7 Merthyr Tydfil CF47 . 30 F8
Tylorstown CF43 ... 80 B4
Argae La CF63 ... 205 D2
Argoed Ave CF72 ... 154 A3
Argoed Prim Sch NP12 ... 58 F5
Argoed Terr CF48 ... 55 D5
Argyle St
Abercynon CF45 ... 82 F3
Abertillery NP13 ... 36 B5
Merthyr Tydfil CF47 ... 10 F1
Newport NP20 ... 143 C7
Pentre CF41 ... 78 F5
Porth CF39 ... 107 E2
Swansea SA1 ... 95 B6
Argyle Terr CF40 ... 106 E8
Argyle Way CF5 ... 193 E4
Argyll Ave SA4 ... 43 B2
Argyll Ct 4 CF15 ... 176 B6
Arlan Gwilli SA4 ... 19 A4
Arles Rd CF5 ... 193 E5
Arlington Cl NP20 ... 117 A4
Arlington Cres CF3 ... 179 C6
Arlington Pl CF36 ... 182 F7
Arlington Rd
Porthcawl CF36 ... 182 F7
Sully CF64 ... 216 B5
Armine Rd SA5 ... 67 E3
Armoury Terr NP23 ... 14 D7
Armstrong Cl NP19 ... 144 B4
Arnant Villas CF32 ... 104 E5
Arne Cl NP19 ... 144 E5
Arno Rd CF63 ... 215 C7
Arnold Ave CF3 ... 179 C8
Arnold Cl NP20 ... 142 F2
Arnold Ct SA9 ... 2 B6
Arnold Pl NP22 ... 6 D1
Arnold St CF45 ... 54 E3
Arnott's Pl CF44 ... 28 F1
Arnside Rd CF23 ... 178 C2
Arosfa Ave CF36 ... 183 D8
Arosfa Ct NP22 ... 13 E6
Arran Cl
Penycoedcae CF37 ... 135 B6
Risca NP11 ... 115 C1
Arran Pl CF24 ... 195 C8
Arran St CF24 ... 195 C8
Arrol St CF24 ... 195 D5
Arthur Bliss Rd NP19 ... 144 C4
Arthur Cl NP20 ... 143 C2
Arthur St
Aberavon SA12 ... 99 A1
Abertysswg NP22 ... 33 C8
Barry CF63 ... 215 D6
Blaengwynfi SA13 ... 76 B6
Caerleon NP18 ... 118 C2
Cardiff CF24 ... 195 E7
Cwmfelinfach NP11 ... 113 B4
Llanelli SA15 ... 40 D5
Mountain Ash CF45 ... 54 D1
Neath SA11 ... 71 E7
Newport NP20 ... 143 C2
Pentrebach CF48 ... 31 A3
Tonypandy CF40 ... 107 A2
Ystrad CF41 ... 79 C3
Arthur Terr SA8 ... 23 E5
Artillery Pl NP19 ... 143 C5
Arundel Cl NP44 ... 89 A3
Arundel Pl CF11 ... 194 D2
Arundel Rd NP19 ... 143 F5
Arvonia Terr NP12 ... 85 B6
Arwelfa SA6 ... 45 D1
Ascot Cl CF5 ... 193 F5
Ascot Dr SA12 ... 98 E6
Asgog St CF24 ... 195 D5
Ash Cres CF47 ... 10 E4
Ash Ct Caerphilly NP12 . 85 F6
Pontllanfraith NP12 ... 86 A6
Ash Gn NP44 ... 116 F8
Ash Gr
Ammanford SA18 ... 219 D7
Barry CF63 ... 215 C7
Bridgend CF31 ... 168 A5
Cardiff CF14 ... 177 B6
Cardiff CF5 ... 193 A2
Cimla SA11 ... 72 B5
Ebbw Vale NP23 ... 14 E6
Gorseinon SA4 ... 43 A3
Killay SA2 ... 93 D7
Llandough CF64 ... 206 E6
Llanharry CF72 ... 172 B5
Llanmartin NP18 ... 145 E6
Mountain Ash CF45 ... 81 E8
Pentre CF41 ... 78 F5
Pontyclun CF72 ... 172 F8
Pontypool NP4 ... 38 D1
Porthcawl CF36 ... 183 E8
Trefechan CF48 ... 10 B6
Waunarlwydd SA5 ... 66 D4
Ystradowen CF71 ... 189 C8
Ash La CF62 ... 211 B7
Ash Pk CF71 ... 189 C8
Ash Pl Bargoed CF81 ... 57 F2
Cardiff CF5 ... 176 D1
Ash Plant Rd CF62 ... 211 E1
Ash Rd CF48 ... 31 B1
Ash Sq CF37 ... 136 A5
Ash St
Abercwmboi CF44 ... 53 E4
Cwm NP23 ... 35 A8
Gilfach Goch CF39 ... 132 B5
Swansea SA6 ... 69 A7
Ash Tree Cl CF15 ... 176 A6
Ash Villas 8 CF48 ... 31 C1
Ash Wlk CF72 ... 155 C2
Ashbourne Ct CF44 ... 28 D2
Ashbrook CF31 ... 169 B5
Ashburnham Dr SA3 ... 93 E2
Ashburton Ave CF3 ... 179 C7
Ashby Rd CF64 ... 216 A6
Ashchurch Cl CF14 ... 177 A5
Ashcroft Cres CF5 ... 176 C1
Ashdale Rd CF40 ... 107 A1
Ashdene Cl CF5 ... 176 D2
Ashdown Cl 4 CF3 ... 179 F7
Ashfield Cl CF39 ... 107 D4
Ashfield Ct 7 CF3 ... 179 E7
Ashfield Rd
Abertillery NP13 ... 36 B5
Newbridge NP11 ... 86 F7
Ashford CF14 ... 160 A2
Ashford Cl
Croesyceiliog NP44 ... 90 B5
Pontypridd CF37 ... 109 C5
Ashford Cl N NP44 ... 90 B5
Ashford Cl S NP44 ... 90 B4
Ashgrove
Aberdare CF44 ... 28 F3
Baglan SA12 ... 98 D7
Bedwas CF83 ... 138 F6
Bryn NP12 ... 85 E5
Dinas Powys CF64 ... 206 B2
Llantwit Major CF61 ... 209 F6
Pontypridd CF37 ... 109 D6
Treharris CF46 ... 82 F6
Ystrad Mynach CF82 ... 84 F2
Ashgrove Cl NP4 ... 62 D1
Ashgrove Specl Sch CF64 ... 206 D3
Ashgrove Terr CF46 ... 83 E3
Ashgrove Villas CF46 . 56 A7
Ashlea Dr CF47 ... 10 F1
Ashleigh Cl SA2 ... 94 C3
Ashleigh Ct
Cwmbran NP44 ... 89 A1
Tredegar NP22 ... 13 E8
Ashleigh Rd SA2 ... 94 C3
Ashleigh Terr SA10 ... 97 C8
Ashley Rd NP19 ... 144 B5
Ashman Cl CF83 ... 137 D1
Ashmount Bsns Parc SA6 ... 46 B1
Ashton Ho NP44 ... 89 D2
Ashvale NP22 ... 6 C1
Ashville
Blackwood NP12 ... 59 A1
Tredegar NP22 ... 13 F5
Ashwell Cotts NP18 . 144 C8
Ashwood Cl NP12 ... 85 E5
Ashwood Ct 12 CF24 195 C7
Ashwood Dr SA8 ... 24 B5
Aspen Ave NP12 ... 85 E5
Aspen Cl CF3 ... 179 E7
Aspen Way Cimla SA11 72 C6
Llantwit Fardre CF38 . 156 C6
Newport NP20 ... 117 A3
Asquith Ct SA1 ... 95 A6
Asquith St
Pontypool NP4 ... 62 E3
Tir-y-Berth CF82 ... 85 A6
Assembly Rooms 3 SA1 ... 95 E6
Aster Cl
6 Cardiff CF3 ... 180 A7
Risca NP11 ... 115 A2
Aster View SA12 ... 98 C3
Aston Cres NP20 ... 143 B8
Aston Pl CF3 ... 180 A5
Astoria Cl CF14 ... 159 E2
Atfield Cl CF23 ... 178 E1
Athelstan Rd CF14 ... 176 F4
Atlantic Cl SA7 ... 69 A5
Atlantic Cres CF63 ... 215 C3
Atlantic Pl CF63 ... 215 C7
Atlantic Trad Est CF63 ... 215 C3
Atlantic Way CF63 ... 215 B3
Atlantic Wharf 4 CF10 ... 195 C4
Atlantic Wharf Leisure Village CF10 ... 195 C2
Atlas Pl 5 CF5 ... 194 D5
Atlas Rd CF5 ... 194 D5
Atlee Terr CF34 ... 75 A2
Attlee Ave
Abertillery NP13 ... 36 A7
Port Talbot SA12 ... 124 E8
Attlee Cl
Ebbw Vale NP23 ... 7 D6
Tredegar NP22 ... 13 D6
Attlee Ct CF83 ... 138 C3
Attlee Ho 3 CF47 ... 30 D8
Attlee Rd
Blackwood NP12 ... 85 E7
Nantyglo NP23 ... 15 E7
Attlee St CF32 ... 150 F5
Attlee Way NP22 ... 13 D5
Aubrey Ave CF5 ... 194 A7
Aubrey Hames Cl NP20 ... 143 A2
Aubrey Rd Porth CF39 107 F2
Tonypandy CF40 ... 107 A4
Aubrey Terr
Cowbridge CF71 ... 188 F1
Cwm NP23 ... 35 B7
Auburn Ave SA12 ... 98 B2
Auckland Cl NP12 ... 86 A8
Auckland Rd NP20 ... 142 D3
Augusta Cres CF64 ... 207 A1
Augusta Pk NP23 ... 14 F2
Augusta Rd CF64 ... 207 A1
Augusta St
Cardiff CF24 ... 195 C6
Ebbw Vale NP23 ... 14 E3
Treorchy CF41 ... 79 A3
Augustan Cl NP18 ... 117 F3
Augustan Dr NP18 ... 117 F3
Augustan Way NP18 . 117 F3
Augustus John Cl NP19 ... 144 A8
Augustus St CF37 ... 81 F1
Austen Cl CF3 ... 179 D8
Austin Ave
Bridgend CF31 ... 168 F6
Laleston CF32 ... 167 F4
Porthcawl CF36 ... 183 C8
Austin Cl CF36 ... 183 D8
Austin Friars 5 NP20 ... 143 C5
Austin Rd NP4 ... 62 F1
Austin St CF45 ... 54 D3
Australia Rd CF14 ... 177 E2
Australian Terr CF31 . 168 F6
Auxilliary Boiler House Rd CF62 ... 211 E1
Avalon Ct
Newport NP19 ... 143 F7
Pontypool NP4 ... 62 B6
Avalon Dr NP19 ... 143 F7
Avalon Terr NP22 ... 6 E1
Avan St SA13 ... 99 B1
Avenue Cilfig The SA15 ... 40 D6
Avenue Cl CF82 ... 84 F2
Avenue De Clichy CF47 ... 10 D1
Avenue Ind Est CF23 160 F1
Avenue Ind Pk CF23 . 179 A8
Avenue The
Abersychan NP4 ... 37 E6
Bargoed CF81 ... 58 A1
Bedwas CF83 ... 139 A6
Cardiff CF14 ... 176 F4
Cardiff CF3 ... 179 C2
Cardiff CF5 ... 177 A1
Cwmavon SA12 ... 99 D6
Llanbradach CF83 ... 111 F1
Llanelli SA14 ... 41 C5
Llanelli SA15 ... 40 E2
Merthyr Tydfil CF47 ... 10 E2
Mountain Ash CF45 ... 54 B5
Neath SA11 ... 71 D4
Pontycymer CF32 ... 103 E5
Pontypool NP4 ... 62 D1
Pontypool NP4 ... 62 F5
Pontypridd CF37 ... 109 D2
Tonyrefail CF39 ... 133 D5
Treharris CF46 ... 82 F6
Tylorstown CF43 ... 107 C8
Wyllie NP12 ... 85 F1
Ystrad Mynach CF82 ... 85 A2
Averil Vivian Gr SA2 ... 94 E6
Avis Terr SA15 ... 40 E5
Avoca Pl CF11 ... 194 E3
Avocet Ct CF63 ... 215 A5
Avon Cl Barry CF63 ... 215 C7
Bettws NP20 ... 116 E2
Bryn NP12 ... 85 D3
Avon Ct NP23 ... 7 C5
Avon Pl NP44 ... 90 A3
Avon Rd NP4 ... 17 C5
Avon St Cymmer SA13 . 75 C5
Ferndale CF43 ... 79 F7
Glynneath SA11 ... 223 C1
Avon Terr CF39 ... 107 F7
Avondale NP4 ... 17 C6
Avondale Cl
Abercynon CF45 ... 82 C5
Cwmbran NP44 ... 89 F6
Avondale Cres
Cardiff CF11 ... 195 A2
Cwmbran NP44 ... 89 F7
Avondale Dr NP44 ... 89 F7
Avondale Gdns CF11 195 A2
Avondale Gdns S CF11 ... 195 A2
Avondale Ind Est NP44 ... 89 F6
Avondale Rd
Cardiff CF11 ... 195 A2
Cwmbran NP44 ... 89 F7
Pontypool NP4 ... 62 F1
Porth CF39 ... 108 A2
Ton Pentre CF41 ... 79 B2
Avondale Sq SA13 ... 75 C5
Avondale St CF45 ... 82 C5
Avondale Terr SA13 ... 75 C5
Avondale Way NP44 ... 89 F6
Avonmuir Rd CF24 ... 196 A8
Avonridge CF14 ... 159 D2
Awbery Ho CF62 ... 214 D6
Awel Mor CF23 ... 178 D3
Awelfryn
Penycoedcae CF37 ... 135 A3
Penywaun CF44 ... 28 B6
Awelfryn Cl NP23 ... 7 E4
Awelfryn Terr 7 CF47 10 F4
Axbridge Cres CF3 ... 179 D6
Axminster Rd CF23 ... 195 E8
Aylesbury Mans 2 CF14 ... 176 F6
Aylesbury Rd SA2 ... 94 F5
Aynho Pl NP23 ... 14 D8
Ayron St CF43 ... 79 F5
Ayton Terr CF40 ... 106 E7
Azalea Cl CF23 ... 178 D7
Azalea Pk CF48 ... 11 C4

B

B Sta Access Rd CF62 ... 211 E1
Baber Cl CF23 ... 178 E1
Bach Rd SA12 ... 98 B3
Back Dr SA10 ... 70 B7
Backhall St NP18 ... 118 C2
Bacon Pl NP20 ... 117 A3
Bacton Rd CF14 ... 177 B2
Baden Powell Com Jun & Inf Sch CF24 ... 195 F6
Baden Rd CF24 ... 196 A6
Baden Terr CF47 ... 10 F2
Bader Cl CF14 ... 177 F6
Badgers Brook CF31 169 A6
Badgers Brook Cl CF71 ... 189 C8
Badgers Brook Dr CF71 ... 189 C8
Badgers Brook Rise CF71 ... 189 D8
Badgers Mdw NP18 . 117 F7
Badgers Mead CF31 . 169 A6
Badgers Mede 4 NP44 ... 89 B3
Badgers Wood NP10 141 F2
Badham Cl CF83 ... 137 D1
Badminton Gdns SA5 . 67 E5
Badminton Gr NP23 ... 7 D3
Badminton Rd NP19 . 143 F8
Baglan Cotts CF32 ... 150 C7
Baglan Hts SA12 ... 98 F7
Baglan Ind Pk SA12 ... 98 E2
Baglan Prim Sch SA12 ... 98 D6
Baglan St Pentre CF41 . 78 F5
Swansea SA1 ... 96 A7
Treherbert CF42 ... 78 A8
Tylorstown CF43 ... 80 C1
Baglan Sta SA12 ... 98 D5
Baglan Way SA12 ... 98 E3
Bagle Ct SA12 ... 98 E5
Bagley Ct NP44 ... 89 B5
Bagot St CF45 ... 82 B6
Baiden Ave CF33 ... 148 C2
Bailey Cl CF5 ... 193 E7
Bailey Cres NP4 ... 37 E6
Bailey St
Aberavon SA12 ... 99 A1
Abersychan NP4 ... 37 E6
Brynmawr NP23 ... 8 B4
Cwm NP23 ... 35 B8
Deri CF81 ... 33 B1
Mountain Ash CF45 ... 54 D2
Newport NP20 ... 143 B4
Ton Pentre CF41 ... 78 F4
Treorchy CF41 ... 79 A3
Wattstown CF39 ... 107 E8
Bailey's Hos NP4 ... 61 F8
Bailey's Terr NP4 ... 61 F8
Baillie Smith Ave NP11 ... 60 B2
Baird Cl NP20 ... 116 F3
Baird Rise CF62 ... 214 D5
Baker Street Ho 11 NP4 ... 17 C6
Baker's La CF61 ... 209 E7
Bakers Ct
5 Cardiff CF5 ... 194 B7
Marshfield CF3 ... 180 E8
Bakers Row CF10 ... 195 A5
Bakers Way CF32 ... 150 F4
Bakers Wharf 8 CF37 ... 109 D2
Bakery La CF3 ... 162 D2
Bala Cl NP23 ... 7 A5
Bala Cotts SA9 ... 222 A6
Bala Dr NP10 ... 142 B7
Bala Rd CF14 ... 177 A2
Balaclava Ct CF40 ... 106 F3
Balaclava Rd
Cardiff CF23 ... 178 C1
Dowlais CF48 ... 11 A4
Glais SA7 ... 47 B5
Balaclava St SA1 ... 95 E7
Balance Mdws NP4 ... 37 C7
Balance Rd NP4 ... 37 E7
Baldwin Cl
Cardiff CF5 ... 176 D3
Baldwin Cl *continued*
Newport NP20 ... 143 C2
Baldwin St
Bargoed CF81 ... 57 F4
Bryn SA13 ... 100 E5
Newport NP20 ... 143 C2
Baldwin's Cres SA1 ... 96 E7
Balfe Rd NP19 ... 144 D4
Ball Cl CF3 ... 179 B7
Ball La CF3 ... 179 A6
Ball Rd CF3 ... 179 B6
Ballarat CF35 ... 152 E2
Ballards Ct SA10 ... 70 F8
Ballas Cl CF33 ... 166 A7
Balmond Terr NP4 ... 62 B8
Balmoral Cl
Cardiff CF14 ... 160 B2
Penycoedcae CF37 ... 135 B6
Balmoral Ct CF62 ... 214 C8
Balmoral La 1 NP19 144 A4
Balmoral Rd NP19 ... 144 A4
Baltic Terr NP44 ... 116 E7
Baltimore Cl CF23 ... 161 A2
Bamber Ho NP44 ... 90 B4
Bampton Rd CF3 ... 179 C7
Bananlog Terr NP12 ... 34 C2
Banastre Ave CF14 ... 177 E2
Banc Bach SA4 ... 64 E4
Banc Gelli Las CF31 . 168 B2
Banc Gwyn CF31 ... 168 B2
Banc y Ddraenen SA18 ... 218 D6
Banc-yr-Allt CF31 ... 168 B6
Banc-Yr-eithin SA4 ... 43 A3
Bancyffynnon SA14 . 218 B7
Baneswell Ctyd 6 NP20 ... 143 B4
Baneswell Rd 6 NP20 ... 143 B5
Banfield Terr SA4 ... 42 E2
Bangor Ct 3 CF24 ... 178 C1
Bangor La 2 CF24 ... 178 C1
Bangor Rd NP23 ... 7 E4
Bangor St
Cardiff CF24 ... 178 C1
Maesteg CF34 ... 102 A6
Bangor Terr CF34 ... 102 A6
Bank Bldgs CF31 ... 169 E3
Bank Cotts SA9 ... 222 A6
Bank La
3 Newport NP19 ... 143 E8
Tredegar NP22 ... 13 E7
Bank Rd SA14 ... 42 C8
Bank Side SA11 ... 71 E8
Bank St
Maesteg CF34 ... 102 B3
Newport NP19 ... 143 D8
Tonypandy CF40 ... 107 A3
Bank Terr CF48 ... 10 A4
Bankers Hill CF32 ... 149 D3
Bankes St 2 CF44 ... 29 A2
Bankside NP19 ... 143 D4
Bankside Cl CF14 ... 159 F3
Banna Bglws NP23 ... 8 C2
Bantock Cl NP19 ... 144 E5
Banwell Ct
Cwmbran NP44 ... 89 B5
Swansea SA6 ... 68 F8
Banwell Pl CF3 ... 179 C6
Banwell St SA6 ... 68 F8
Banwen La SA8 ... 23 F4
Banwen Pl SA18 ... 220 D8
Banwy Rd SA6 ... 45 D1
Baptist Ct CF24 ... 195 E6
Baptist Pl NP23 ... 7 D4
Baptist Row CF43 ... 79 F8
Baptist Sq CF43 ... 79 F8
Baptist Well Pl SA1 ... 68 C1
Baptist Well St SA1 ... 68 C1
Baran Rd
Pontardawe SA8 ... 220 D1
Rhydyfro SA8 ... 23 B8
Barberry Rise CF64 ... 206 E5
Barbirolli Gn NP19 ... 144 D4
Barbrook Cl CF14 ... 160 A2
Bardsey Ave SA5 ... 67 E7
Bardsey Cl CF36 ... 165 E2
Bardsey Cres CF14 ... 159 E1
Bardsy Cl NP19 ... 143 F7
Bargoed Cl CF46 ... 83 B7
Bargoed Inf Sch CF81 57 F5
Bargoed St CF11 ... 195 A3
Bargoed Sta CF81 ... 58 A5
Bargoed Terr CF46 ... 83 B7
Barker Ave NP13 ... 36 A6
Barkley St NP22 ... 33 C8
Barley Field Rd NP23 ... 8 C3
Barmouth Rd CF3 ... 179 B3
Barn Cl NP4 ... 38 B2
Barn Cotts SA11 ... 71 C2
Barnabas Cl SA5 ... 66 F3
Barnard Ave CF5 ... 193 E6
Barnard St NP19 ... 143 D6
Barnardo St CF34 ... 102 A6
Barnes Ave CF31 ... 168 B6
Barnes Cl NP23 ... 7 A4
Barnets NP44 ... 89 B3
Barnfield
Caerleon NP18 ... 117 F5
Ponthir NP18 ... 117 F5
Barnfield Cl CF23 ... 161 B1
Barnfield Pl NP44 ... 89 C5
Barnfield Terr NP4 ... 17 B6
Barnstaple Rd CF3 ... 179 C6
Barnwood CF14 ... 160 A2
Barnwood Cres CF5 . 192 F4
Baron Cl CF64 ... 206 F3
Baron Rd CF64 ... 206 E3
Baron's Cl CF61 ... 210 A6

Baron's Court Rd CF23 ....178 D1
Baroness PI CF44 ...206 F3
Barquentine PI CF10 195 C3
Barrack Hill NP20 ...143 B7
Barrack St CF83 ......91 A5
Barrack Row CF48 ...11 B5
Barrett St CF42 ....94 B1
Barrians Way CF62 ..214 E5
Barrie Gdns NP20 ...142 E2
Barrington Rd 3 CF14 ....177 B4
Barrington St CF48 ..55 C5
Barry Cl CF82 ....84 E7
Barry Coll (Annexe) CF62 ....213 C4
Barry Coll of F Ed Barry CF62 ......214 A7
Barry CF62 ......214 D6
Barry Comp Sch CF62 ....214 D7
Barry Docks Link Rd CF63 ....215 D8
Barry Docks Sta CF63 ....215 A4
Barry Ho SA12 ......98 A2
Barry Hospl The CF62 ....214 E3
Barry Island Pleasure Pk CF62 ....214 F3
Barry Island Prim Sch Annexe CF62 .....214 F2
Barry Island Sta CF62 ....214 F2
Barry Rd Barry CF63 .215 A6
Gwaun-Cae-Gurwen SA18 ....220 D7
Penarth CF64 .....206 E6
Pontypridd CF37 ...109 A1
Barry Sidings Countryside Pk CF37 ....108 E2
Barry Sta CF62 ....214 D3
Barry View CF37 ....136 A6
Barry Wlk NP10 ....142 A6
Barthenwydd Ct 18 CF47 ....10 D2
Barthrop St NP19 ..144 A3
Bartlett St CF83 ....138 B2
Bartley Terr SA6 ....68 E5
Basil PI CF24 ....195 A8
Bassaleg Cl 2 CF3 ..180 A7
Bassaleg Comp Sch NP10 ....142 A2
Bassaleg Rd NP20 ..142 E3
Bassett Ho 11 SA12 ..98 F1
Bassett St CF44 ....216 A5
Bassett Rd Abercynon CF45 .....82 E3
Barry CF63 ......215 B5
Cardiff CF5 ......194 C5
Newport CF62 .....109 D2
Bastian Cl CF63 ....215 C7
Batchelor Rd Cardiff CF14 ......177 D2
2 Newport NP19 ..143 F5
Bath Ave SA6 ....45 F1
Bath Gn NP44 ....90 B2
Bath La Brynmawr NP23 .8 A4
Swansea SA1 .....95 D6
Bath Rd SA6 ....45 F1
Bath Row NP7 ....9 E7
Bath St Newport NP19 ....143 D6
Port Talbot SA13 ...99 B1
Bath Villas SA6 .....68 F8
Bathurst St Swansea SA1 ......95 C5
3 Swansea SA1 ...95 C6
Baton Ct CF14 .....177 C4
Batten Way CF37 ...109 F4
Battenberg St CF45 ..82 C5
Baxter Terr SA13 ...227 C2
Bay St SA1 ....96 A7
Bay Tree Ave SA4 ...94 B6
Bay Tree Cl NP18 ...117 E2
Bay View Port Talbot SA13 ...99 C2
Swansea SA1 .....95 E8
Bay View Cl SA10 ...70 F5
Bay View Cres SA1 ..95 E8
Bay View Gdns SA10 .70 E5
Bay View Hts SA13 ..99 C2
Bay View Rd Llanelli SA14 ....41 A6
Porthcawl CF36 ...183 D6
Bay View Terr SA1 ...95 A6
Baylis Ct CF5 ......193 E6
Bayliss Rd CF32 ....54 C3
Baynton Cl CF5 ....176 E2
Bayside Rd CF14 ...195 D5
Bayswater Ct SA3 ...94 C3
Baywood Ave SA3 ..123 A8
BBC Cymru Wales CF5 ....176 F1
Beach La CF64 .....207 B4
Beach Rd Llanelli SA15 .40 A6
Penarth CF64 .....207 B4
Porthcawl CF36 ...183 D7
Pyle CF33 ....148 A1
Southerndown CF32 .197 A8
Sully CF64 ......216 D4
Beachcroft St Aberavon SA12 ...124 F8
Swansea SA1 ......95 B5
Beachway CF62 ....214 B1
Beacon Hts CF48 ...225 E2

Beacon St CF11 ....194 C7
Beacon View NP23 ...8 D1
Beacons Cl NP10 ...142 A7
Beacons Pk CF44 ...224 D3
Beacons The CF44 ...27 D7
Beacons View SA11 ..72 A5
Beacons View Rd SA6 .68 D8
Beaconsfield Cl SA2 ..94 B7
Beaconsfield Ho CF62 ....214 D4
Beaconsfield Rd SA10 418 C2
Beaconsfield Way SA2 ....94 B7
Beadon St CF45 .....54 D2
Beale Cl CF5 ......176 E2
Beatrice Rd Barry CF63 ......215 B6
Cardiff CF14 ......177 B4
Beatrice St SA13 ....76 C6
Beattie St SA5 ....68 B2
Beatty Ave CF23 ...178 A5
Beatty Cl CF62 ....215 A8
Beatty Ct CF10 ....195 C4
Beatty Rd NP19 ...144 F7
Beatty St CF62 .....85 A6
Beauchamp St CF11 194 F5
Beaufort Ave SA3 ..123 A3
Beaufort Cl Cwmbran NP44 .....89 C1
Mumbles SA3 .....123 A3
Tredegar NP22 ......6 F1
Beaufort Ct 7 Cardiff CF10 ...195 C4
Llantrisant CF72 ..155 E2
Swansea SA15 .....67 E5
Swansea SA6 ......68 F6
Beaufort Gdns 1 SA7 ....63 B1
Beaufort Gdns SA3 121 E7
Beaufort Hill NP23 ...7 F4
Beaufort Hill Jun & Inf Sch NP23 ......143 F8
Beaufort Rd Ebbw Vale NP23 .....7 D2
Newport NP19 ....144 A7
Swansea SA6 ......68 F5
Tredegar NP22 ......6 F1
Beaufort Rise NP23 ...7 D4
Beaufort St NP23 ....8 A1
Beaufort Terr Ebbw Vale NP23 .....7 D3
4 Newport NP20 ..143 B4
Beaufort Way CF62 212 E2
Beaumaris Cl Bassaleg NP10 ....141 E3
Church Village CF38 135 F2
Beaumaris Dr NP44 ..90 B1
Beaumaris Ho 5 NP44 ....90 B2
Beaumaris Rd CF3 ..179 B3
Beaumaris Way SA6 58 E1
Beaumont Cl Barry CF62 ......214 C7
Newport NP19 .....15 D8
Beaumont Cres SA1 ..95 D4
Beaumont Ct CF64 .206 F3
Beaupre Castle CF71 201 B5
Beavers Wlk NP10 ..142 B4
Beck Ho SA2 ....94 F6
Beckett St CF45 .....54 D4
Beckgrove Cl CF24 ..196 A7
Beda Rd CF5 ......194 C5
Bedavere Cl CF14 ..159 E2
Beddick NP44 ....90 A3
Beddoe St CF44 ......53 C8
Beddoe Terr CF46 ...83 A5
Bedford Cl Cefn Cribwr CF32 ..149 A2
Cwmbran NP44 .....89 A3
Bedford Ho 11 SA6 ..68 F8
Bedford Pl CF64 ...195 C7
Bedford Rd Cefn Cribwr CF32 ..149 A3
Newport NP19 ....143 D5
Bedford Rice CF61 ..210 B6
Bedford St Aberdare CF44 ......53 D7
Cardiff CF24 ......195 B7
Swansea SA6 ......69 A8
Bedlington Terr CF46 ....214 D5
Bedlinog Cty Inf Sch CF46 ....56 A7
Bedlinog Cty Jun Sch CF46 ....56 A7
Bedlinog Rd NP24 ...56 A7
Bedwas Arian CF31 ..168 B6
Bedw Cl CF39 ......107 F2
Bedw Farm Est CF37 107 F2
Bedw Rd Bedlinog CF46 ......56 A7
Pontypridd CF37 ...109 F4
Bedw St Maesteg CF34 ....102 A8
Porth CF39 ....107 F2
Bedwas Cl 4 CF3 ..180 A7
Bedwas Comp Sch CF83 ....138 E6
Bedwas House Ind Est CF83 ....138 D6
Bedwas Inf Sch CF83 ....138 D6
Bedwas Jun Sch CF83 ....138 D6
Bedwas Pl 2 CF64 ..206 F4
Bedwas Rd Caerphilly CF83 ...138 C4
Caerphilly CF83 ...138 D5
Bedwas St CF11 ....194 E3

Bedwdellty Rd CF81, NP12 ....58 C5
Bedwellty Comp Sch NP12 ....58 B2
Bedwellty Pits NP22 ..14 B1
Bedwellty Rd Aberbargoed CF81 ..58 B5
Blackwood NP12 .....85 C8
New Tredegar NP24 ..33 F2
Bedwlwyn Cl CF82 ..84 F2
Bedwlwyn Rd CF82 ..84 F2
Bedwlwyn St CF82 ..84 F2
Beech Ave NP19 ....85 E4
Llantwit Major CF61 210 A4
Beech Bargoed CF81 57 E2
Beech Cl Caerphilly CF83 ...137 D1
Cwmbran NP44 .....89 D6
Llanmartin NP18 ..145 E6
Beech Cres SA4 ....43 A4
Beech Ct CF15 ....158 D2
Beech Dr CF82 .....84 F3
Beech Emb CF82 ....84 F2
Beech Gr Blackwood NP12 .....59 B1
Ebbw Vale NP23 .....14 E2
Merthyr Tydfil CF47 ..10 E8
Newport NP10 ....163 F8
Porthcawl CF36 ...183 D8
Beech Ho CF14 ....176 E7
Beech Pk CF71 ....187 A4
Beech Rd Cardiff CF5 193 B8
Beech Tree La SA4 ..94 C5
Beech Tree Terr NP4 ..61 F8
Beech Tree Way CF46 83 F3
Beecham St NP19 ..144 D5
Beechcroft Bryn NP12 85 E3
Beechdale Rd NP19 144 A5
Beecher Ave CF11 ..194 F1
Beecher Terr NP11 ..114 C5
Beeches Cl The SA2 ..94 A8
Beeches Ind Est The CF72 ....155 A1
Beeches The CF77 ....82 E3
Beeches La CF44 ....94 C5
Beechfield Ave Hengoed CF82 .....85 A3
Bridgend CF31 ....168 E6
Cwmbran NP44 .....89 D2
Pontypool NP4 .....38 A2
Beechfield Ave Aberdare CF44 .....28 E2
Bridgend CF31 ....168 C5
Cwmfelinfach NP11 ..113 F4
Neath SA11 ....71 F7
Trefechan CF48 .....10 B6
Beechwood Cl NP11 ..86 C6
Beechwood Cres NP19 ....144 A5
Beechwood Dr Llantwit Fardre CF38 156 D1
Merthyr Tydfil CF48 ..29 F8
Penarth CF64 .....206 E2
Tonyrefail CF39 ...132 E5
Beechwood Gr CF35 152 D1
Beechwood Rd Margam SA13 .....125 F3
Newport NP44 ....144 A5
Swansea SA2 ......94 F6
Taffs Well CF15 ...158 B4
Beechwood St CF37 136 B5
Beechwood Wln NP4 ..38 B2
Began Rd CF3 ......163 D4
Beignon Cl CF24 ...195 D4
Beili Glas SA14 ......42 B6
Beili Glas Rd NP12 ..85 B5
Bela Ho 2 NP44 .....89 C2
Belgrave Cl Cardiff CF14 ......159 E3
Gorseinon SA4 .....43 A1
Belgrave Ct Cardiff CF11 ......194 F5
4 Pontypool NP4 .....38 A1
Swansea SA1 ......95 A6
Belgrave Gdns 2 SA1 95 A6
Belgrave La SA1 .....95 A6
Belgrave Rd SA4 ....43 A1
Belgrave St CF37 ....79 A2
Belgrave Terr CF37 ..136 A6
Bell La NP4 ....37 F3
Bell St Aberdare CF44 ..28 F4
Barry CF62 ......214 C4
Bell Vue Terr NP20 ..143 C2
Belle View 2 NP4 ....107 A4
Belle Vue Cl 12 NP4 ..38 A1
Belle Vue

Belle Vue *continued* Pen-clawdd SA4 ....64 F4
Belle Vue Cl Penarth CF44 .....207 B4
Pontypool NP4 .....38 A1
Belle Vue Cres CF14 176 F3
Belle Vue La NP20 ..143 B3
Belle Vue Terr Barry CF63 ......215 C7
Penarth CF64 .....207 B5
Cwmbran NP44 .....89 E2
Belle Vue Way 1 SA1 95 C7
Bellevue Gdns NP44 ..89 E2
Bellevue Rd Cwmbran NP44 .....89 E2
Mumbles SA3 .....122 F6
Bellevue Terr Merthyr Vale CF48 ..55 D4
Mountain Ash CF45 ..81 F8
Bellin Cl NP18 .....118 A3
Bellis Hill CF48 ......55 D4
Bellvue Rd SA14 .....89 E2
Bellvue St SA14 ......41 E3
Belmont Cl CF34 ...102 B3
Belmont Hill NP18 144 D8
Belmont Rd CF63 ...215 A6
Belmont Terr Aberdare CF44 .....53 C8
Porth CF39 ....107 F2
Belmont Wlk CF10 ..195 B2
Belvedere Cl Abertillery NP11 .....59 F6
Bishopston SA3 ...121 E7
Belvedere Cres CF63 215 A5
Belvedere Rd SA15 ..40 C6
Belvedere Terr Newport NP20 ....143 B7
6 Risca NP11 .....114 F3
Belvoir Ct CF72 ....155 E2
Ben Jonson Way NP20 ....142 E2
Bembow Cl SA7 .....94 C6
Benbow Rd NP19 ..144 E7
Bendrick Dr SA3 ...120 F5
Bendrick Rd CF63 ..215 C4
Benediction NP10 ...80 F8
Benjamin Cl NP22 ...13 A2
Bennett Ave CF31 ...169 D3
Bennett St Blaina NP13 15 E4
Bridgend CF31 ....169 D3
Swansea SA1 ......68 D3
Benson Ave NP10 ..142 B4
Benson Rd SA4 ......64 F4
Benson St SA4 ......64 F4
Benthall Pl SA1 .....95 E7
Bentley Rd NP10 ..142 A7
Beresford Ct CF24 ..195 E7
Beresford Rd Cardiff CF24 ......195 E7
Newport NP19 ....143 D5
Beresford Road La CF24 ....195 E7
Berkeley Cl SA7 .....47 A2
Berkeley Cres SA4 ..89 E8
Berkeley Ct NP44 ...89 A2
Berkeley Sq CF5 ...193 A2
Berkley Cl NP10 ...141 F3
Berkley Dr CF64 ...206 E4
Berkley Rd NP10 ..141 F3
Berkrolles Ave CF62 211 D4
Berllan Deg SA15 ...41 A6
Berllanwyd Ave NP18 58 F1
Berllanwyd St CF82 ..84 E8
Berma CF32 ....123 C3
Bernard Ave CF5 ...194 A6
Bernard St Abercarn NP11 ....114 C7
Swansea SA2 ......94 F6
Bernays Row SA1 ....96 B7
Berry St CF37 ......69 E5
Berwick La NP10 ...142 D5
Berryfields SA12 ...124 D8
Berthin PI SA13 ....125 A5
Berthin St CF37 ....135 E5
Berthin NP44 ....89 B3
Berthin Rd NP4 .....39 D2
Berthlwyd CF15 ....157 C1
Berthon Rd NP4 .....39 D2
Berthwin St CF11 ..194 D7
Bertram St CF24 ...195 E7
Berw Rd Pontypridd CF37 ...109 D2
Tonypandy CF40 ..106 E6
Berwedd-dy-Cotts CF37 ....109 E4
Berwick Rd SA14 ....41 F3
Berwick Terr SA1 ....95 C8
Berwyn Pl SA5 ......68 A4
Beryl Pl CF62 ......214 F5
Beryl Rd CF62 .....214 F5
Bessant Cl CF71 ....188 F1
Bessborough Dr CF11 ....194 E3
Bessemer Cl Cardiff CF11 ......194 D2
Newport NP20 ....116 F4
Bessemer Close Workshops CF11 ...194 C2
Bessemer Rd CF11 ..194 D3
Bethania SA14 ......82 E3
Bethania Hill CF39 ..133 C2

Bethania PI CF44 ....53 E8
Bethania Rd Clydach SA6 ....46 D7
Cross Hands SA14 ..218 A7
Bethania Row Cardiff CF3 ....179 D7
Ogmore Vale CF32 ..104 E1
Bethania St Glynneath SA11 ...223 D1
Maesteg CF34 ....102 B2
Bethania Terr 1 Cwmavon SA12 ...99 F6
Llanelli SA15 ....40 E2
Bethany Cl CF82 .....84 E1
Bethany Ct CF44 .....50 F2
Bethany La SA3 ....123 A1
Bethania Sq 6 SA13 ..99 B1
Bethcar St NP23 ....14 D7
Bethel Ave NP22 ....13 E6
Bethel Cl Aberystwyth NP4 ...37 E6
Swansea SA5 ......68 C3
Trehafod CF37 ....108 C2
Bethel La NP44 ......89 B6
Bethel PI Cardiff CF14 ......159 D1
Merthyr Tydfil CF47 ..10 D5
Bethel Rd Glynneath SA11 ...223 D1
Pen-clawdd SA4 ....64 E4
Swansea SA7 ....69 E7
Ystradgynlais SA9 ...2 C8
Bethel St Briton Ferry SA11 ...98 C8
Pontypridd CF37 ...135 B8
Bethesda Cl NP10 ..142 A6
Bethesda Ct 4 SA1 ..95 D8
Bethesda Pl Ebbw Vale NP23 ....14 D6
Rogerstone NP10 ..142 A6
Bethesda Rd SA8 ....24 B8
Bethesda St Ebbw Vale NP23 ....14 C6
Merthyr Tydfil CF47 ..10 D1
Betthws SA14 ......219 C6
Bettws High Sch NP20 ....116 F1
Bettws Cl NP20 ....116 F1
Bettws La NP20 ....116 F1
Bettws Rd SA5 ......68 A4
Bettws-y-Coed Rd CF23 ....178 B7
Betws Prim Sch CF32 ....129 E2
Betws Rd CF32 ....129 D1
Betws Road SA18 ..219 C6
Betwyns 2 NP44 ....89 A2
Beulah Cl CF14 ....177 C7
Beulah St NP22 .....12 F3
Bevan Ave NP22 .....6 C1
Bevan Cl CF34 .....138 F6
Bevan Cres Blackwood NP12 ....85 D8
Ebbw Vale NP23 .....7 C3
Newport NP20 ....143 F6
Bevan Pl CF14 ....177 D2
Bevan St SA12 .....124 F8
Bevan Way SA5 .....66 E3
Bevan's La NP4,NP44 89 D8
Bevans Terr SA12 ...73 A2
Bevans Row SA1 ....96 B7
Bevans Terr SA7 ....69 E5
Beverley Gdns SA4 ..67 E4
Beverley St Barry CF63 ......215 B7
Port Talbot SA13 ..125 B8
Bevin Ave SA12 ...124 D8
Bevin Ho SA12 ....124 C8
Bevin Pl CF14 .....177 D2
Bible Coll of Wales The SA2 ....94 B3
Bicester Rd CF64 ..215 E6
Biddulph SA15 ......40 E2
Bideford Cl NP20 ..143 A1
Bideford Rd Cardiff CF3 ....179 C5
Newport NP20 ....143 A1
Big La NP23 ....7 F4
Big Pit Mining Mus NP4 ....16 F6
Bigyn Cty Prim Sch SA15 ....40 D4
Bigyn La SA15 ......40 D4
Bigyn Park Terr SA15 40 D4
Bigyn Rd SA15 ......40 D4
Bilberry Dr NP16 ..111 A5
Billingham Cres CF47 10 E3
Bilston St NP19 ....143 F4
Bilton Rd NP19 ....143 F5
Bingle La CF62 .....211 D6
Birch Cres Cefn Hengoed CF82 ..85 B3
Llanelli Fardre CF38 156 C5
Birch Ct CF15 .....158 D2
Birch Gr Barry CF62 ..214 C2
Bridgend CF31 ....168 A5
Brynmawr NP23 ......8 B5

Birch Gr *continued* Caerphilly CF83 ...138 C5
Church Village CF38 135 F1
Cwmbran NP44 ....116 A8
Llanharry CF72 ....172 B5
Merthyr Tydfil CF47 ..10 D5
Risca NP11 ....115 A2
Waunarlwydd SA5 ...66 D4
Birch Hill Cardiff CF15 ......158 C1
Newport NP20 ....117 B3
Birch La CF64 ......207 A1
Birch Rd Baglan SA12 ..98 D7
Cardiff CF5 ......193 D8
Llanmartin NP18 ..145 F7
Birch Tree Cl SA2 ...94 C6
Birch Trees NP10 ..142 B2
Birch Wlk Cardiff CF5 ......193 D8
Porthcawl CF36 ...183 D8
Birches The NP44 ...89 C5
Birchfield Cl CF38 ..136 A1
Birchfield Cres CF5 193 F7
Birchfield Rd Mumbles SA3 .....122 F8
Pontardawe SA8 ....23 F6
Birchgrove Aberdare CF44 .....28 E2
Bedwas CF83 .....138 F6
New Tredegar NP24 ..33 D3
Pontypridd CF37 ...135 C8
Rogerstone NP10 ..141 F6
Treharris CF46 .....82 F6
Birchgrove Comp Sch SA7 ....47 B2
Birchgrove Jun & Inf Sch Birchgrove SA7 ....47 A1
Cardiff CF14 ......177 D4
Birchgrove Rd Cardiff CF14 ......177 D4
Glais SA7 ....47 A4
Swansea SA7 ....70 A8
Birchgrove St CF37 ..82 E2
Birchgrove Sta CF14 177 D6
Birchley CF37 .....135 D6
Birchway The CF48 135 E6
Birchwood Ave CF14 135 C6
Birchwood Cl Baglan SA12 ......98 E5
Bryn NP12 ....85 E5
Bryn-côch SA10 .....48 A5
Birchwood Dr CF39 132 C4
Birchwood Gdns Bedwas CF83 .....138 D6
Cardiff CF14 ......177 C3
Birchwood La CF23 178 C3
Birchwood Rd CF23 ..178 C3
Birkdale Cl 3 Cardiff CF23 ...180 A8
Mumbles SA3 ......93 F2
Bishop Childs CW Jun & Inf Sch CF3 ......179 F7
Bishop Gore Comp Sch SA2 ....94 C6
Bishop Hedley RC High Sch CF47 ......10 E3
Bishop Hannon Dr CF5 ....176 E3
Bishop of Llandaff CW High Sch CF5 .....176 F1
Bishop Rd Ammanford SA18 ..219 B6
7 Glanaman SA18 ..220 B8
Bishops Cl Abertillery NP13 ....36 C5
Cardiff CF11 ......194 C3
Newport NP19 ....143 D6
Bishop Vaughan RC Comp Sch SA6 ....68 B8
Bishop's Gr SA2 ....94 B5
Bishop's Pl NP23 ...14 D8
Bishop's Rd CF14 ..177 A4
Bishop's Wlk SA6 ...45 F2
Bishop's Wood Nature Reserve SA3 ....122 C4
Bishops Ct CF14 ...177 A4
Bishops Ct CF11 ...177 A4
Bishops Gr CF47 ....10 C3
Bishops Pl CF47 ....10 C3
Bishops' Ave CF5 ..193 F8
Bishops' Cl CF5 ...193 F8
Bishops' Pl CF5 ...193 F8
Bishops' Wlk CF5 ..193 F8
Bishopston Comp Sch SA3 ....122 A7
Bishopston Prim Sch SA3 ....122 A7
Bishopston Rd Bishopston SA3 ...121 F6
Cardiff CF5 ......193 A2
Bishopswood Ct SA3 169 C4
Bishpool Est NP19 ..144 D6
Bishpool La NP19 ..144 D6
Bishton Rd NP18 ..145 B5
Bishton St NP19 ...143 E5
Bishwell Pk SA4 ....64 C4
Bishwell Rd SA4 ....64 C4
Bisley Cl CF24 .....196 B7
Bittern Cl SA14 ....217 A8
Bittern Way SA12 ...98 A2
Bitterton No SA12 ...98 A2
Black Lion Rd SA14 ..218 C7
Black Oak Rd CF23 ..178 C8
Black Rd Church Village CF38 135 C1

Black Rd *continued*
Pontypridd CF37 135 B4
Blackberry Dr CF62 214 C6
Blackberry Pl CF45 54 B6
Blackbird Cl NP10 142 C3
Blackbird Rd CF62 210 D6
Blackbirds Cl NP44 117 A5
Blackbirds Way CF3 179 D8
Blackbrook Rd CF83 158 E8
Blackett Ave NP20 117 A3
Blackfield Row CF32 149 F2
Blackhall Rd CF32 185 E3
Blackhill Rd SA4 43 A3
Blackhills La
Fairwood SA2 92 F3
Upper Killay SA2 93 B3
Blackmill Rd
Bryncethin CF32 151 B5
Lewistown CF32 130 E5
Blackmoor Pl CF3 179 C6
Blacksmiths Way
NP10 163 A6
Blackstone St 9
CF11 194 E5
Blackthorn Ave CF47 10 D5
Blackthorn Gr NP18 117 E2
Blackthorn Pl SA2 67 B1
Blackvein Rd NP11 114 C3
Blackwater Cl NP20 116 D2
Blackweir Terr CF10 194 F8
Blackwell Cl 1 CF63 215 B6
Blackwood Comp Sch
NP12 85 D8
Blackwood Inf Sch
NP12 85 D7
Blackwood Jun Sch
NP12 85 E8
Blackwood Rd NP12 85 F4
Blaen Baglan Prim Sch
SA12 98 F6
Blaen Cefn SA1 69 D5
Blaen Cendl NP23 7 E4
Blaen Cwm SA10 222 D3
Blaen Dewi CF71 198 C5
Blaen Dowlais St
CF48 11 D4
Blaen Ogwr Ct CF32 104 F5
Blaen Wern
Cwmdare CF44 28 D3
Ebbw Vale NP23 14 B8
Blaen y Cwm CF31 168 B4
Blaen y Ddol CF31 168 B4
Blaen-Afon Rd NP7,
NP23 8 F3
Blaen-Blodau St
NP11 86 F6
Blaen-Cyffin Rd NP13 60 B6
Blaen-gwawr Prim Sch
CF44 53 B8
Blaen-Nant Rd NP23 8 C2
Blaen-y-Coed
Cardiff CF14 177 C8
Radyr CF15 176 A6
Blaen-y-Cwm CF81 58 A5
Blaen-y-Cwm Rd
Abertillery NP11 60 F6
Pontypool NP4 61 A4
Treherbert CF42 50 D3
Blaen-y-Cwm Terr
CF42 50 E3
Blaen-y-Cwm View
NP44 88 F1
Blaen-y-Fro CF35 152 F1
Blaen-y-Maes Dr SA5 67 E6
Blaen-y-Morfa SA15 40 F2
Blaen-y-Pant Ave
NP20 143 A8
Blaen-y-Pant Cres
NP20 143 A8
Blaen-y-Pant Pl
NP20 143 A8
Blaenant St SA13 74 D4
Blaenau Cty Prim Sch
SA18 218 F8
Blaenau Gwent Inf Sch
NP13 36 A6
Blaenau Gwent Rows
NP13 36 A6
Blaenau Rd SA18 219 A8
Blaenavon Cl 3 CF3 180 A7
Blaenavon Hospl NP4 17 B7
Blaenavon Ironworks
NP4 17 B7
Blaenavon Terr SA12 73 C6
Blaencaerau Est CF34 75 C2
Blaencaerau Jun Sch
CF34 75 C2
Blaencaerau Rd CF34 75 C2
Blaencedi SA4 64 F3
Blaenclydach Pl 3
CF11 194 F3
Blaenclydach St
CF11 194 F3
Blaencoed Rd SA7 69 F7
Blaencwm Rd SA7 70 A7
Blaendare Farm La
NP4 62 A4
Blaendare Rd NP4 62 C5
Blaendulais Prim Sch
SA10 222 D3
Blaengarw Prim Sch
CF32 103 E6
Blaengarw Rd CF32 103 D7
Blaengwawr Cl CF44 53 B8
Blaengwawr Comp Sch
CF44 53 B8
Blaengwrach Prim Sch
SA11 227 B8
Blaenhonddan Prim Sch
SA10 48 D3
Blaenlau St 1 CF40 106 F4
Blaenllechau Cty Inf Sch
CF43 79 F8
Blaenllechau Rd CF43 80 A7
Blaenllynfi Inf Sch
CF34 75 B1
Blaenmorfa SA4 19 C3
Blaennantygroes Rd
CF44 29 E1
Blaenogwr Terr
CF32 104 F6
Blaenrhondda Rd
CF42 50 D3
Blaenrhondda Waterfalls
Wlk CF42 26 C1
Blaenwern
Cwmbran NP44 89 F6
Neath SA10 48 E2
Blaenycwm Jun & Inf Sch
NP23 8 C3
Blaenymaes Prim Sch
SA5 67 E7
Blagdon Cl CF3 179 B5
Blaina & District Hospl
NP23 15 D8
Blaina Cl CF3 179 F7
Blaina Inf Sch NP13 15 E4
Blaina Jun Sch NP13 15 E5
Blaina Rd
Abertillery NP13 35 E7
Brynmawr NP23 8 C3
Blair Way SA12 98 F2
Blaise Pl CF11 194 E2
Blake Ct 8 CF10 195 C4
Blake Rd NP19 144 B3
Blake St CF43 52 B1
Blanch St CF40 107 A2
Blanche Cl NP10 163 F6
Blanche St
Cardiff CF24 195 E7
Dowlais CF48 11 C4
Pontypridd CF37 109 C2
Blandings Ct CF23 178 C6
Blandon Way CF14 177 B4
Blandy Terr
Gilfach Goch CF39 106 C1
Nant-y-Moel CF32 104 F6
Ogmore Vale CF32 104 E1
Pontycymer CF32 103 F3
Blanthorn Ct 1
CF14 176 F6
Blenheim Cl CF62 214 C7
Blenheim Ct NP44 89 C2
Blenheim Rd
Abertillery NP13 36 C3
Cardiff CF23 178 D1
Cwmbran NP44 89 C2
Newport NP19 144 A5
Blenheim Sq NP44 89 C2
Bleriot Cl NP19 144 A3
Blethin Cl CF5 176 E3
Blewitt St NP20 143 B4
Blodwen Rd NP4 63 A4
Blodwen St SA12 98 F1
Blodwen Terr SA4 64 F4
Blodwen Way NP4 63 A4
Bloom St CF11 194 C7
Bloomfield Rd NP12 85 D7
Blorenge Terr 1 NP4 17 D7
Bloss Terr CF39 107 F2
Blosse Rd CF14 177 A2
Blosse St CF34 102 A6
Blossom Cl NP18 145 B8
Blossom Dr CF14 160 A4
Blue Anchor Rd SA4 64 F3
Blue House Rd CF14 177 E8
Bluebell Ct NP44 88 F2
Bluebell Dr CF3 179 D8
Bluebell Way
Rogerstone NP10 141 D7
Swansea SA5 68 A5
Bluett's Rd NP4 37 E5
Blundell Ave CF36 182 F6
Blyth Cl CF62 205 A1
Blythe St NP13 36 B5
Board St CF81 12 F1
Boarlands The SA3 231 A4
Bodalaw CF48 11 B4
Bodnant Cl CF3 179 F6
Bodringallt Ct CF41 79 D3
Bodringallt Prim Sch
CF41 79 D3
Bodringallt Terr CF41 79 C3
Bodwenarth Rd
CF37 109 F4
Bog Rd SA7,SA10 69 E4
Bogey Rd CF48 31 B8
Bohun St SA5 68 C3
Boi Cl CF45 54 B3
Boiler House Rd
CF62 211 E1
Boleyn Wlk CF23 178 C1
Bolgoed Rd SA4 19 E2
Bolt Cl NP20 143 D3
Bolt St NP20 143 D3
Bolton Rd NP20 143 A4
Bolts Row NP19 144 B5
Bon-y-Maen Rd SA1 69 A3
Bona Rd CF71 199 C5
Boncath Rd CF14 177 A2
Bond Ave SA15 40 E4
Bond St Aberdare CF44 29 A1
Newport NP19 143 C6
Swansea SA1 95 B5
Bondfield Ho 5 SA12 98 F1
Bonllwyn SA18 219 B8
Bont Cl NP12 85 B7
Bontnewydd Terr
CF46 83 C7
Bonville Terr SA1 95 A6
Bonvilston Rd CF37 109 D2
Bonvilston Terr 2
CF37 109 D2
Booker St CF24 195 E7
Boon Cl CF63 215 A7
Boot La 5 NP4 17 C6
Boot The CF82 85 A1
Booth Ho SA12 98 A2
Borage Cl CF23 160 E1
Border Rd SA12 98 C3
Borfa Pl NP12 85 C7
Borough Ave CF62 214 E8
Borough Cl CF71 188 F1
Borough Rd SA4 42 F2
Borough St SA12 124 F8
Borrowdale Cl CF23 178 C2
Borth Rd CF3 179 D5
Bosco La SA3 121 B3
Boswell Cl
Cardiff CF3 179 B8
Newport NP20 142 F2
Bosworth Dr NP20 143 A7
Bosworth Rd SA10 70 F7
Boulevard De Nantes
CF10 195 A6
Boulevard The NP23 14 E3
Boundary St NP23 8 B4
Bournville Rd NP13 15 E1
Bournville Terr NP22 13 D7
Boverton Brook
CF61 210 C5
Boverton Ct CF61 210 C6
Boverton Park Dr
CF61 210 C5
Boverton Pk CF61 210 C5
Boverton Rd CF61 209 F6
Boverton St CF23 178 B1
Bovil Cl CF83 140 A7
Bow St CF5 193 A2
Bowden Rd SA11 71 E6
Bowen Cl NP4 17 C7
Bowen Ind Est NP12 58 C2
Bowen Pl 23 NP20 143 C3
Bowen St Neath SA11 71 D6
Swansea SA1 68 D2
Bowen Terr SA15 40 F3
Bower St CF33 148 C1
Bowham Ave CF31 168 E2
Bowleaze NP44 89 B3
Bowls La CF83 137 D7
Bowls Terr CF83 137 E5
Bowman's Way CF71 188 D2
Bowman's Well
CF71 188 D2
Box Cotts CF32 150 C7
Box Rd SA4 43 B7
Box Terr
Coytrahen CF32 150 C7
3 Llanelli SA15 40 F6
Boxer Ind Est NP18 118 A4
Boxtree Cl NP18 117 E2
Boyle Cl NP20 116 F2
Brace Ave NP13 35 F7
Brachdy Cl CF3 179 B2
Brachdy La CF3 179 B2
Brachdy Rd CF3 179 B2
Bracken Pl CF14 176 D1
Bracken Rd
Margam SA13 125 E4
Neath SA11 71 F8
Bracken Rise CF44 29 D1
Bracken Way CF31 150 F1
Brackla Ind Est CF31 169 C7
Brackla Inf Sch CF31 169 B5
Brackla Jun Sch
CF31 169 B5
Brackla St CF31 168 F4
Brackla Street Ctr 7
CF31 168 F4
Brackla Way CF31 169 C5
Bradenham Pl 5
CF64 207 A4
Brades The NP18 118 B3
Bradfield Ave CF31 168 D5
Bradfield Rd CF31 168 D4
Bradford Pl CF64 207 B4
Bradford St
Caerphilly CF83 138 A2
Cardiff CF11 195 A2
1 Llanelli SA15 40 F6
Bradley Cl CF47 10 F6
Bradley St
Abercynon CF45 82 D2
Cardiff CF24 195 E7
Braeval St CF24 195 B8
Bragdu CF35 170 B8
Brahms Ave SA12 98 B3
Braichycymer Rd
CF32 103 E3
Brain Cl NP19 145 A6
Bramble Ave CF62 214 D6
Bramble Cl
Bridgend CF31 169 C4
Cardiff CF5 176 B1
Merthyr Tydfil CF47 10 C4
Bramble Rise CF64 206 E5
Bramblewood Cl
Baglan SA12 98 E5
Cardiff CF14 159 F2
Brambling Dr CF14 159 E3
Bramley Cl NP18 145 C8
Bramley Dr SA3 122 F6
Bramshill Dr CF23 161 B1
Bran Cl SA7 69 C7
Bran-y-Garth NP44 90 B4
Brandon Cres SA1 69 D5
Brandreth Rd CF23 178 B2
Brandy Cove Cl SA3 123 B4
Brandy Cove Rd SA3 122 A5
Brangwyn Ave NP44 117 A8
Brangwyn Cl
4 Penarth CF64 206 F5
Swansea SA6 45 E2
Brangwyn Cres NP19 143 F7
Brangwyn Rd NP22 13 D5
Branksome Ho 1
CF10 195 A5
Bransby Rd CF40 107 A4
Branwen Cl CF5 193 A2
Branwen Gdns SA1 68 B1
Braunton Ave CF3 179 C6
Braunton Cres CF3 179 B6
Brayford Pl CF3 179 C8
Brayley Rd SA6 45 F2
Breaksea Cl CF64 216 B4
Breaksea Ct CF62 214 F2
Breaksea Dr CF62 214 F2
Brean Cl CF64 216 C5
Brechfa Cl NP18 117 E7
Brecon Cl CF44 27 D8
Brecon Ct Barry CF62 215 A6
Caerleon NP18 117 F3
8 Cardiff CF5 194 C6
Brecon Ho
7 Penarth CF64 206 F2
Port Talbot SA12 124 D8
5 Swansea SA1 95 E6
Brecon Hts NP23 14 E2
Brecon Park Cotts NP7 9 C5
Brecon Pl CF44 53 D7
Brecon Rd
Abercraf SA9 222 B7
Hirwaun CF44 27 D7
Merthyr Tydfil CF47 10 B3
Merthyr Tydfil CF47 10 D2
Newport NP19 143 F7
Pontardawe SA8 23 F6
Ystradgynlais SA9 1 F1
Ystradgynlais SA9 222 A6
Brecon Rise CF48 11 B7
Brecon Road Infants Sch
8 CF47 10 D2
Brecon St
3 Aberdare CF44 53 D7
Boverton CF61 210 B7
Cardiff CF5 194 C6
Brecon Terr Deri CF81 57 B8
Tredegar NP22 5 F1
Brecon Way CF38 135 F2
Brecon Wlk NP44 89 F3
Bredenbury Gdns
CF36 165 E1
Bredon Cl NP11 115 C1
Brendon Cl 2 CF3 179 C6
Brendon View Cl
CF62 213 A2
Brenig Cl Barry CF62 214 C6
Cardiff CF14 159 F3
Brenig Rd SA5 68 A4
Brenroy Rd CF71 199 C4
Brentwood Ct CF14 159 F1
Brentwood Pl NP23 7 C1
Breon Rd CF64 215 E6
Bres Rd SA15 40 D5
Brett Rd NP11 87 C3
Brettenham St SA15 40 C6
Brewer St CF81 32 F8
Brewery Ct NP13 36 A1
Brewery La
Bridgend CF31 168 E5
Cefn Coed CF48 10 A4
Brewery Terr
Abertillery NP13 35 F1
Tylorstown CF43 107 C8
Brian Cres CF36 182 F7
Brianne Dr CF14 159 F3
Briar Cl Cardiff CF5 193 C8
Ebbw Vale NP23 7 C5
Briar Dene SA2 94 B6
Briar Rd Aberdare CF44 53 F7
Port Talbot SA12 98 C1
Briar Way
Church Village CF38 136 A1
Hirwaun CF44 27 C8
Briar's Ct SA5 67 F6
Briarmeadow Dr
CF14 159 E3
Briarwood Cl SA10 48 D4
Briarwood Dr CF23 178 D7
Briarwood Gdns
SA3 122 D5
Briary Way CF31 169 C4
Brick Row
Maesteg CF34 102 C1
Seven Sisters SA10 222 C3
Brick St SA13 227 C2
Brickfield Cres CF47 30 E8
Brickyard Bsns Pk
CF14 177 D2
Brickyard Cotts
Abercraf SA9 222 B7
Neath SA11 71 E8
Brickyard Rd SA5 67 F3
Brickyard The CF36 183 C7
Bridesvale Gdns
NP10 163 E1
Bridge Rd
Aberdare CF44 53 E8
Cardiff CF3 161 C1
Cardiff CF5,CF14 176 F2
Llanblethian CF71 200 D8
Upper Boat CF37 136 D2
Waunarlwydd SA5 66 E4
Bridge St
Abercarn NP11 87 A3
Aberdare CF44 29 A3
Bridge St *continued*
Aberfan CF48 55 C5
Abertillery NP13 36 A5
Abertillery NP13 36 C2
Bargoed CF81 58 A5
Barry CF63 215 B7
18 Blaenavon NP4 17 C6
Blaengarw CF32 103 E6
Caerphilly NP12 85 F6
Cardiff CF10 195 B5
Cardiff CF5 177 A1
Cwm-twrch Isaf SA9 1 B1
Ebbw Vale NP23 7 D1
Glais SA7 47 A6
Glyncorrwg SA13 227 C2
Llanelli SA15 40 D6
Llangennech SA14 42 C8
Maesteg CF34 102 B3
Neath SA11 71 E8
Newbridge NP11 87 A6
Newport NP20 143 B5
Ogmore Vale CF32 130 E8
Penarth CF64 206 F5
Penygroes SA14 218 D8
Pontypool NP4 62 E3
Pontypridd CF37 109 C1
3 Pontypridd CF37 135 E7
3 Port Talbot SA13 125 C8
Pyle CF33 148 C2
Risca NP11 114 F2
Swansea SA1 68 D1
Tonypandy CF40 106 F5
Tredegar NP22 13 E6
Trehafod CF37 108 C3
Troedyrhiw CF48 31 C1
Ynysddu NP11 112 F6
Bridge Street Ind Est
NP22 13 E6
Bridge Terr
Michaelston-y-Fedw
CF3 162 A7
2 Port Talbot SA13 125 C8
Bridgefield St CF83 137 A8
Bridgeman Ct CF64 207 B3
Bridgeman Rd CF64 207 B3
Bridgend Bsns Ctr
CF31 169 E3
Bridgend Coll CF31 168 F3
Bridgend Ind Est
Bridgend CF31 169 B7
Bridgend CF31 169 C3
Bridgend PRU CF32 150 D4
Bridgend Rd
Aberkenfig CF32 150 C4
Bryncae CF72 153 F2
Laleston CF32,CF36 167 B2
Maesteg CF34 102 C2
Pen-y-fai CF32 150 D2
Pont Rhyd-y-cyff CF34 128 D6
Pontycymer CF32 103 E2
Porthcawl CF36 183 D8
Bridgend Sta CF31 168 F4
Bridgewater Rd
CF64 216 B6
Bridgwater Rd CF3 179 D6
Bridle Mews SA3 123 C3
Brierley Cl NP11 115 C1
Brierley La CF31 168 F2
Brierly Pl NP11 114 B8
Briers Gate NP44 115 E8
Briery Ct NP23 14 D6
Briery Hill Jun & Inf Sch
NP23 14 D6
Brig-y-Don Hill
CF32 184 D2
Brigantine Pl CF10 195 C4
Brigham Ct CF83 137 C4
Bright St NP11 114 C4
Brighton Rd SA4 43 C2
Brights La 6 NP4 17 D6
Brin Williams Ho 1
NP20 143 A4
Brindley Rd CF11 194 D1
Brisbane Ct NP12 85 C6
Bristol Ho NP4 62 A8
Bristol St
Aberkenfig CF32 150 C4
Newport NP19 143 E6
Bristol Terr
Bargoed CF81 58 A5
New Tredegar NP24 58 A8
Taffs Well CF15 157 F4
Bristol View Cl NP44 89 A4
Britannia Ctr for
Enterprise NP12 58 B1
Britannia Quay CF10 195 C2
Britannia Rd SA6 68 E5
Britannia St CF39 108 A2
Britannia Terr NP12 58 B1
Britannia Villas NP12 58 B1
Britannia Wlk NP12 58 B2
Brithdir St CF24 177 F1
Brithdir Sta NP24 58 A8
Brithwen Rd SA5 66 D3
Brithweunydd Rd
CF40 107 A5
British Legion Dr
CF3 179 B4
British Rd NP4 37 C4
British School Cl NP4 37 E4
Briton Ferry Ind Est
SA12 98 B8
Briton Ferry Rd SA11 71 E6
Briton Ferry Specl Sch
SA11 71 D3
Briton Ferry Sta SA11 71 C2
Briton Ferry Workshops
Ind Est SA11 98 A8
Briton Ho 6 SA12 98 C3
Brittania Cl NP11 115 A1
Brittania Pl CF43 80 A5
Britten Cl NP19 144 D4
Britten Rd CF64 206 F1
Britway Ct CF64 206 A3
Britway Rd CF64 206 A3
Brixham CF33 166 A8
Bro Athro CF3 179 D4
Bro Dawel
Dunvant SA2 93 D7
Pontyclun CF72 173 A6
Swansea SA6 45 C2
Bro Dedwydd SA2 93 D8
Bro Deg CF44 53 F8
Bro Dirion
Bridgend CF31 168 B4
Dunvant SA2 93 D8
Bro Nant Fer SA18 220 D7
Bro Ryan SA18 220 A8
Bro-Deg CF35 170 D8
Bro-Wen SA14 41 C5
Bro-y-Fan CF83 138 D5
Bro-y-Ffrwd CF48 225 F2
Broad Cl CF62 214 B5
Broad Oak Way
CF31 168 B5
Broad Pl CF11 194 C5
Broad Quay Rd NP19 164 E8
Broad Shoard The
CF71 188 E2
Broad St
Abersychan NP4 37 F3
Barry CF62 214 D4
Blaenavon NP4 17 C6
Cardiff CF11 194 C5
Dowlais CF48 11 A4
12 Merthyr Tydfil CF47 30 D8
Newport NP20 143 D3
Pontypool NP4 62 E3
Port Talbot SA13 125 C8
Broad Street Par
CF62 214 D3
Broad View
Cwmbran NP44 89 C5
Tondu CF32 150 C6
Broadacre SA2 93 C7
Broadacres CF11 194 C5
Broadcommon Cl
NP19 144 C3
Broadfield Cl CF40 107 A4
Broadfield Ct CF5 193 D4
Broadhaven CF11 194 C4
Broadlands Ct 4
CF3 179 E7
Broadlands Ho 5
CF3 179 E7
Broadmead Bryn NP12 85 D4
Killay SA2 93 D7
Broadmead Cres
SA3 122 B6
Broadmead Pk NP19 144 D3
Broadoak Ct SA4 42 E1
Broadparks SA3 122 F8
Broadstairs Rd CF11 194 C5
Broadview Cl SA3 123 B4
Broadview La SA3 123 B4
Broadwalk NP18 118 B2
Broadwater Rd
NP19 144 C1
Broadway
Cardiff CF24 195 D7
Llanblethian CF71 188 E1
Pontypool NP4 62 B6
Pontypridd CF37 135 D8
Swansea SA2 94 D7
Broadway Ct SA2 94 D7
Broadway Gn CF5 192 A1
Broadweir Rd NP44 89 E2
Broadwell Cl 4 CF3 179 F6
Broadwell Ct NP18 118 B2
Broadwood Cl NP19 144 E5
Brocastle Ave CF31 169 F2
Brocastle Rd CF14 177 B6
Brock St CF63 215 B7
Brockhampton Rd
CF3 179 F7
Brockhill Rise CF64 217 A8
Brockhill Way CF64 217 A8
Brodawel
Ammanford SA18 219 C6
Cimla SA11 72 B6
Maesteg CF34 102 B3
Merthyr Tydfil CF47 30 F7
Penywaun CF44 28 B6
Pontneddfechan SA11 223 F2
Brodawel Cl SA11 223 F2
Brodeg CF15 175 C8
Brodorion Dr SA6 45 E3
Brohedydd CF43 52 A2
Brokesby Cl SA1 69 A3
Brokesby Rd SA1 69 A3
Brombil SA13 125 F4
Brombil Ct SA13 125 F4
Brombil Gdns SA13 125 F4
Brombil St SA13 125 D5
Bromfield Pl CF64 207 B5
Bromfield Rd CF62 214 E2
Bromfield St CF11 194 F2
Bromley Dr CF5 193 E5
Brompton Pl NP22 14 A3
Bromsgrove St CF11 194 F2
Bron Afon SA4 44 B5
Bron Afon Uchaf SA4 44 B5
Bron Allt SA10 226 A7
Bron Awelon CF62 214 B3
Bron Deg CF46 56 D1
Bron Felen CF14 159 D2
Bron Hafod CF31 168 B2
Bron Haul CF44 53 F8
Bron Las CF82 84 F6
Bron Rhiw CF83 139 F7

Bron Yr Allt SA9 .....2 A8
Bron-y-Bryn SA2 ....93 E8
Bron-y-De NP23 ....14 C7
Bron-y-Deri CF45 ...54 E3
Bron-y-Garth CF82 ..84 E7
Bron-y-Mer CF62 ...214 C2
Bron-y-Waun CF44 ..102 D2
Bron-y-Wawr CF33 ..148 A1
Bronallt Terr CF44 ...52 F4
Bronawenion NP11 ...60 B2
Broncynon Terr CF44 .28 D3
Brondeg
  Heolgerrig CF48 .....10 B1
  Swansea SA5 ....68 B3
Brondeg Cres SA5 ...68 B3
Brondeg La SA8 ......23 F3
Brondeg St CF83 .....80 B2
Brondeg Terr CF44 ...28 F1
Bronhafod NP23 ....8 C5
Bronhall CF72 ....155 C2
Bronhaul CF15 ......175 C8
Bronheulwen CF39 ..107 D4
Broniestyn Terr
  Aberdare CF44 ......28 F3
  Aberfan CF44 ....27 D8
Bronllan SA1 ....69 D5
Bronllwyn CF15 .....175 B8
Bronllwyn Rd CF41 ...79 B2
Bronllys CF44 ....28 B6
Bronllys Pl NP44 .....90 A5
Bronmynydd CF83 ..137 A6
Bronrhiw Ave CF83 ..138 B1
Bronrhiw Fach CF83 138 B1
Bronte Cl CF73 .....179 C8
Bronte Cres CF73 ...179 C8
Bronte Gr NP20 .....21 C4
Bronte Ho 7 SA12 ...98 F1
Bronwydd SA7 ....70 C8
Bronwydd Ave CF73 178 C2
Bronwydd Cl CF73 ..178 D2
Bronwydd Rd CF24 ..96 A6
Bronywawr SA8 ......23 E5
Brook Cl CF5 ....193 F7
Brook La
  Pontllanfraith NP12 ..86 A4
  St Nicholas CF5 ....203 F8
Brook Pl Cwm NP22 ..35 A7
  Treorchy CF41 ......78 F5
Brook Rd
  Cardiff CF14 ....177 B4
  Cardiff CF5 ....193 F7
Brook Row
  Bryncethin CF32 ...151 A5
  Fochriw CF81 ....32 C7
Brook St
  Aberaman NP11 ......87 B4
  Aberdare CF44 ......53 C7
  Abertridwr CF83 ...137 A8
  Barry CF63 ....215 A5
  Blaenrhondda CF42 ..50 D4
  Bridgend CF31 .....125 F2
  8 Bridgend CF31 ....8 B4
  Cardiff CF11 ......194 E5
  Cwmbran NP44 ......89 E7
  Ferndale CF43 ......79 F6
  Maerdy CF43 ....52 B1
  Mountain Ash CF45 ..54 D2
  Neath SA10 ....70 F7
  Pontypridd CF37 ...135 E6
  Port Talbot SA13 ..125 C7
  Porth CF39 ....107 E2
  Tonypandy CF40 ...108 A2
  Tonypandy CF40 ...107 A3
  Treorchy CF42 ......78 E6
  Ystrad CF41 ....79 D2
Brook Terr
  Cwmaman-Cae-Gurwen
    SA18 ....220 E7
  Llanharan CF72 ....153 F3
Brookbank Cl CF44 ..29 D1
Brookdale Cl CF38 ..156 F8
Brookdale La SA11 ..71 E6
Brookfield Neath SA10 48 B1
  Neath Abbey SA10 ..71 B8
  Ynysybwl CF37 .....109 A6
Brookfield Ave
  Barry CF63 ....215 C8
  Rhymney NP22 ......13 A2
Brookfield Cl
  Gorseinon SA4 ......42 F3
  Newport NP19 ......144 B3
Brookfield Dr CF73 .179 E6
Brookfield La CF37 .109 E3
Brookfield Park Rd
  CF71 ....188 F1
Brookfield Pl SA15 ..67 E6
Brookfield Prim Sch
  NP44 ....89 E3
Brookfield Rd
  Maerdy CF43 ....79 C8
  Maesteg CF34 .....102 D2
  Pontllanfraith NP12 .86 A4
Brookfield Terr CF48 .31 C2
Brookland Ho 8
  NP44 ....89 E2
Brookland Rd NP11 115 A1
Brookland Terr
  Cwmbran NP44 .....89 F4
  Nant-y-Moel CF32 ..104 F5
Brookland View NP24 33 F3
Brooklands
  Nelson CF46 ....83 D5
  Tredegar NP22 ....6 C2
Brooklands Cl
  Dunvant SA2 ....66 B1
  Maesycwmmer CF82 .82 B2
  Merthyr Tydfil CF47 ..10 D3
Brooklands Cotts
  CF46 ....83 D5

Brooklands Terr
  Abercarn NP11 .....114 C7
  Abercraf SA9 ....222 D7
  Cardiff CF5 ....192 D2
  Swansea SA1 ....95 B7
Brooklands The NP13 36 C6
Brooklea NP18 ......118 B4
Brooklyn Cl CF14 ...159 A1
Brooklyn Gdns
  Baglan SA12 ....98 C4
  Mumbles SA3 ......123 A6
Brooklyn Terr
  Abertillery NP13 .....60 B6
  Mumbles SA3 ......122 F5
Brookside
  Bettws NP20 ....116 C2
  Church Village CF38 136 A1
  Cwmbran NP44 ......89 C2
  Dinas Powys CF64 ..206 B4
  Gowerton SA4 ......66 D3
  Treoes CF35 ....170 A1
Brookside Cl
  Baglan SA12 ....98 E5
  Caerphilly CF83 ...137 D4
  Cardiff CF14 ....177 D5
  Pontypridd CF37 ...109 F4
Brookside Cres
  CF83 ....138 C3
Brookside Ct 6
  CF14 ....177 B5
Brookside Row NP13 .36 B8
Brookvale Dr CF14 .159 E3
Brookvale Rd SA3 ..122 F7
Brookview Cl CF14 .159 F2
Brookville Terr SA10 .70 E7
Brookway CF38 .....136 A1
Brookway Cl SA12 ..98 E5
Broom Pl CF5 ......193 D8
Broome Path NP44 ..89 C2
Broomfield Cl
  Church Village CF38 136 A1
  Newport NP19 ......144 D6
Broomfield St CF83 138 B2
Broomhill SA13 ....125 D8
Brotalwg CF46 ....83 B7
Broughton Ave SA5 ..67 E6
Broughton Pl 4
  CF63 ....215 A8
Broughton Rd CF71 198 C4
Brown Ave SA15 .....40 F2
Brown St NP19 .....144 A3
Brown St
  Ferndale CF43 ......80 A6
  Maesteg CF34 .....101 F5
Browning Cl
  Bridgend CF31 .....168 D6
  Cardiff CF3 ....179 B7
  Newport NP20 .....142 F2
Browns Dr SA3 .....121 A5
Bruce Knight Cl CF5 176 E2
Bruce Rd SA5 ....67 B4
Bruce St Cardiff CF24 178 A1
  4 Mountain Ash CF45 .54 D3
Brummell Dr CF15 ..174 F6
Brunant Rd Clydach NP7 9 E8
  Gorseinon SA4 ......43 E3
Brundall Cres CF5 ..193 A3
Brunel Ave NP10 ...142 B6
Brunel Cl Barry CF63 215 D8
  Penpedairheol CF82 .84 E7
  Tonna SA11 ....49 D3
Brunel Ct 1 SA1 ...95 B7
Brunel Ind Est SA12 ..99 D4
Brunel Rd NP44 ....29 D2
Brunel St
  Cardiff CF11 ......194 E5
  Newport NP20 .....143 D1
Brunel Way SA1 .....68 F3
Brunner Dr SA6 .....22 E1
Brunswick Mews
  CF5 ....194 C5
Brunswick St
  Cardiff CF5 ....194 C6
  6 Merthyr Tydfil CF47 .10 D2
  Swansea SA1 ....95 B6
Bruton Pl CF5 ......177 A1
Brwyna Ave SA12 ...98 F1
Brwynen Las SA10 ..48 C2
Bryanston Rd CF64 215 E6
Brychan 1 SA5 ....40 F1
Brychan Pl 7 CF47 ..10 D2
Brydges Pl CF24 ...195 A8
Brymbo Ave SA13 ..125 D4
Bryn Awel SA9 ......26 C7
Bryn Aber CF83 ....137 A8
Bryn Adar CF14 ....176 F8
Bryn Amlwg
  Hengoed CF82 ......84 F3
  North Cornelly CF33 .165 F8
Bryn Aur CF37 .....109 D6
Bryn Awel
  Bedwas CF83 ......138 F6
  Bettws CF32 ....129 E3
  Bridgend CF31 .....168 B5
  Hengoed CF82 ......85 A4
  Neath SA11 ....71 F5
  Pontypridd CF37 ...109 D6
Bryn Awelon
  Aberdare SA4 ....53 F7
  Bridgend CF31 .....168 C5
  Ebbw Vale NP23 .....7 D4
  Ebbw Vale NP23 .....7 D4
  Penpedairheol CF82 .84 E7
Bryn Bach
  Cardiff CF14 ....177 B8
  Pontlliw SA4 ....44 C5
Bryn Bach Cotts
  CF32 ....129 D2
Bryn Bach Rd
  Brynammman SA18 ...220 D8

Bryn Bach Rd continued
  Pontlliw SA4 ....20 B2
Bryn Barrwg CF62 ..214 D2
Bryn Bedd SA10 ....222 D3
Bryn Bedw CF39 ...107 E1
Bryn Bedw NP20 ...143 B8
Bryn Brithdir NP11 ..59 C3
Bryn Calch CF15 ...176 A8
Bryn Caed
  Bedwas CF83 ......138 E6
  Cefn Hengoed CF82 ..84 F5
  Llanelli SA14 ....41 A6
Bryn Carno NP22 ...12 E8
Bryn Carwyn CF48 ..11 B4
Bryn Castell CF15 ..176 B7
Bryn Catwg SA10 ...48 F2
Bryn Celyn
  Cardiff CF23 ......178 F7
  Maesteg CF34 .....102 A1
  Swansea SA4 ....23 D5
  Swansea SA7 ....70 A6
Bryn Celyn Jun & Inf Sch
  CF23 ....178 F7
Bryn Celyn Pl NP44 .89 D5
Bryn Celyn Rd
  Cardiff CF23 ......178 F6
  Cwmbran NP44 ......89 C5
  CF38 ....155 F7
Bryn Celyn Cl Bedwas CF83 138 F6
  Gorseinon SA4 ......43 B3
  Gowerton SA4 ......66 D4
Bryn Coch NP23 ......7 D4
Bryn Coed SA13 ....75 E3
Bryn Cotts Bryn SA13 100 F5
  Pontyrhyl CF32 .....127 F7
Bryn Creigiau CF72 174 C7
Bryn Cres
  Abertillery SA13 ....60 A7
  Hengoed SA12 ......58 E7
Bryn Crydd CF39 ..107 D1
Bryn Cly Prim Sch
  SA14 ....41 E6
Bryn Deri
  Bridgend CF31 .....168 B5
  Ebbw Vale NP23 ....14 C7
Bryn Deri City Prim Sch
  CF15 ....176 B7
Bryn Derw
  Beddau CF38 ......156 A7
  Hengoed CF82 ......85 D6
Bryn Derw Gdns SA6 .45 E2
Bryn Derwen
  Cwmdare CF44 .....28 C3
  Pontardawe SA8 ....23 D5
  Radyr CF15 ....176 A1
Bryn Eithin
  Cwmdare CF44 ......28 D3
  Swansea SA6 ....66 B5
Bryn Elli SA14 ....40 A7
Bryn Euraidd SA18 219 A6
Bryn Ffynon CF39 ..107 D2
Bryn Garw NP44 ....90 A5
Bryn Glas
  Aberdare CF44 ......53 E8
  Bedwas CF83 ......138 E7
  Cardiff CF14 ....159 D2
  Cefn Cribwr CF32 ..149 C2
  Neath SA10 ....48 F3
  Swansea SA6 ....46 E5
Bryn Goleu CF83 ...138 E7
Bryn Goleu Rd SA6 .67 F3
Bryn Golwg CF15 ..176 B7
Bryn Gomer NP44 ..90 A6
Bryn Gorof SA9 .....2 D8
Bryn Gors CF32 ....150 E6
Bryn Gorsedd CF31 168 F7
Bryn Gors Cf44 ... 28 A6
Bryn Hafren Comp Sch
  CF62 ....204 F1
Bryn Haidd CF23 ..179 F7
Bryn Hawddgar SA4 .68 D4
Bryn Hedydd
  Bassaleg NP10 .....141 E3
  Swansea SA6 ....45 C1
Bryn Helyg SA1 ......69 D5
Bryn Henllan
  Brynna CF72 ....153 C3
  Treherbert CF42 .....50 D4
Bryn Heol CF83 ....138 E6
Bryn Heulog
  Brynmenyn CF32 ...150 E6
  Caerphilly CF83 ...137 E5
  Heol-y-Cyw CF35 ..152 B6
  Neath SA10 ....48 C1
  Pontypool NP4 ......62 D4
  Treherbert CF42 ....51 A1
Bryn Heulog Terr
  CF83 ....139 F7
Bryn Hir CF44 ....53 F8
Bryn Hyfryd CF32 ..150 F3
Bryn Ifor
  Caerphilly CF83 ...137 D5
  Mountain Ash CF45 ..54 D2
Bryn Ilan CF37 .....135 F8
Bryn Isaf SA14 .....41 D4
Bryn Ivor CF40 .....106 F8
Bryn Kendall NP23 ..14 C7

Bryn La NP12 ....85 D3
Bryn Llawen CF33 ..148 C2
Bryn Llewelyn SA8 ..23 E3
Bryn Llidiard CF31 ..168 F8
Bryn Mair CF48 .....11 B4
Bryn Melys CF31 ...168 B2
Bryn Milwr NP44 ...116 C8
Bryn Morcia CF44 ..28 E6
Bryn Morfa
  Bridgend CF31 .....168 F5
  Swansea SA1 ....69 D5
Bryn Morlais CF44 ..41 F6
Bryn Nant
  Caerphilly CF83 ...137 D6
  Fochriw CF81 ....32 D8
Bryn Nedd SA11 .....71 F5
Bryn Olwg CF37 ....109 E2
Bryn Onnen
  Penderyn CF44 .....224 D2
  Pontardawe SA8 ....23 D5
  Pyle CF33 ....148 D2
Bryn Owain CF83 ..137 E6
Bryn Parc SA6 ......68 F7
Bryn Pica NP22 ......6 F1
Bryn Pinwydden
  CF23 ....178 E8
Bryn Pl 6 SA15 .....40 C4
Bryn Pobydd CF35 .170 D8
Bryn Sch
  Bryn NP23 ....85 D3
  Bryn SA13 ....100 E5
Bryn Rd Abercarn NP11 87 B3
  Blackwood NP12 ....85 D7
  Bridgend CF35 .....169 F4
  Bryn NP32 ....85 D3
  Bryn NP12 ....85 E3
  Brynmenyn CF32 ...150 D6
  Caerphilly NP12 ....85 D6
  Clydach SA6 ....46 D8
  Cwmllynfell SA9 ....221 B7
  Glyncorrwg SA13 ..227 C2
  Llanelli SA15 ....40 C4
  Loughor SA4 ....42 F1
  Markham NP22 .....58 D7
  Neath SA11 ....71 F6
  Ogmore Vale CF32 .130 E8
  Pengraes SA14 ....218 D8
  Pontardulais SA4 ...19 B4
  Pontllliw SA4 ....44 A8
  Swansea SA2 ....94 C5
  Swansea SA6 ....67 F3
  Ynysmeudwy SA8 ...23 D5
Bryn Rhedyn
  Church Village CF38 135 F2
  Llanyraron NP44 ...117 B8
  Pencoed CF35 .....170 C8
  Pontypridd CF37 ...109 D6
  Tonyrefail CF39 ...133 B5
Bryn Rhedyn
  Caerphilly CF83 ...137 E5
  Llanelli SA14 ......41 C6
  Penywaun CF44 ....28 A6
Bryn Rhosog SA4 ..65 E8
Bryn Rhosyn
  Radyr CF15 ....176 A7
  Swansea SA4 ....45 C2
  Tredegar NP22 ......6 C1
Bryn Seion Ct CF41 .79 B2
Bryn Seion St NP22 .12 D5
Bryn Siriol
  Bedwas CF83 ......138 E7
  Cardiff CF14 ....159 D2
  Cymmer SA13 ......75 D5
  Penpedairheol CF82 .84 F7
  Pentyrch CF15 .....175 C8
  Swansea SA4 ....67 E3
Bryn St
  Merthyr Tydfil CF47 ..30 F8
  Swansea SA4 ....68 C4
Bryn Teg Bargoed CF81 57 F2
  Bedwas CF83 ......138 E7
  Briton Ferry SA11 ..71 B3
  Caerphilly CF83 ...137 E5
  Hengoed CF82 ......85 A3
  Swansea SA7 ....70 A7
Bryn Terr
  Abertillery NP13 ....36 B8
  Abertillery NP13 ....36 C2
  Abertillery NP13 ....60 A7
  Cefn Cribwr CF32 ..149 B2
  Clyne SA11 ....226 C4
  Cwmdare CF44 .....28 C4
  Ebbw Vale NP23 ....14 F3
  Gorseinon SA4 ......43 A2
  Hengoed CF82 ......85 A3
  Llanelli SA15 ....40 C4
  Llangynwyd CF34 ..129 A6
  Liantwit Fardre CF38 156 D7
  Maesteg CF34 .....101 F5
  Merthyr Tydfil CF47 ..11 A1
  Mumbles SA3 ......123 B4
  Pontsticill CF48 ......3 F3
  Pontyclun CF72 ....172 F6
  Porth CF39 ....107 D3
  Swansea SA1 ....68 D3
  Tonypandy CF40 ...106 D6
  Tonyrefail CF40 ...107 A4
  Wattstown CF39 ...107 D8
  Ystrad CF41 ....79 D2

Bryn Vernel SA4 .....42 E1
Bryn View NP23 ......8 D1
Bryn View Cl SA3 ..231 C8
Bryn Villas
  Blaina NP13 ....15 D5
  Pontyrhyl CF32 .....129 F7
Bryn Wyndham Terr
  CF42 ....50 E3
Bryn Yr Gors SA6 ...45 B2
Bryn Yr Ysgol CF83 137 D6
Bryn-Amlwg Rd SA5 .67 E3
Bryn-Awelon Rd
  CF23 ....178 C8
Bryn-Bedw SA4 .....44 A8
Bryn-Bedw St CF32 103 E7
Bryn-Dedwydd SA11 .72 E5
Bryn-Deri Terr NP11 .86 F8
Bryn-Derwen CF83 138 C7
Bryn-Eirw CF37 .....108 C2
Bryn-Gaer SA4 .....41 A7
Bryn-Gaer Terr NP13 .60 A7
Bryn-Garreg NP44 ..37 F5
Bryn-Glas Rd SA5 ...67 E3
Bryn-Glas Terr CF33 .148 B1
Bryn-Gwyn Rd
  Abertillery NP13 ....36 C3
  Cardiff CF23 ......178 C7
Bryn-Gwyn St CF83 138 C2
Bryn-Hafod Jun & Inf Sch
  SA6 ....45 B3
Bryn-Hedd CF39 ...132 D5
Bryn-Heulog NP13 ..60 A7
Bryn-Howard Terr
  NP12 ....59 C2
Bryn-Hyfryd Terr
  NP11 ....114 F2
Bryn-Ithel Terr NP13 .60 A7
Bryn-Llöi Rd SA18 ..220 A8
Bryn-Melyn St SA1 ..68 D2
Bryn-Mor Rd SA15 ..40 B4
Bryn-onen Terr
  CF47 ....10 F4
Bryn-Rhedyn
  Caerphilly CF83 ...138 D4
  Swansea SA10 .....85 D6
Bryn-Serth Rd NP23 .8 A3
Bryn-Seton St CF48 .11 A4
Bryn-Syfi Terr SA1 ..95 C6
Bryn-Teg Cres NP22 .12 F3
Bryn-teg Terr 9
  CF47 ....10 E1
Bryn-tywod SA4 ....45 A3
Bryn-Welon Cl NP4 ..17 E6
Bryn-y-Don Rd SA1 .95 C8
Bryn-y-Fran Ave
  CF83 ....138 F6
Bryn-y-Gnwg SA4 ...2 A7
Bryn-y-Gwynt NP23 .2 B8
Bryn-y-Mor SA4 ....65 D1
Bryn-y-Mor Rd
  Gowerton SA4 ......65 F6
  Swansea SA1 ....95 A6
Bryn-y-Nant CF23 ..178 F5
Bryn-y-Pwll CF81 ...58 B4
Bryn-yr-cegin
  Hendrefgaran CF39 132 C5
Bryn-yr-Orsaf CF35 166 A8
Brynaeron SA2 ......66 C1
Brynaeron Ct SA2 ..66 C1
Brynaldon Rd SA4 ..43 A3
Brynallt Terr SA15 ..40 F5
Brynamlwg
  Clydach SA6 ....22 F1
  Llanelli SA15 ....40 F6
  Pontyclun CF72 ...173 C8
  7 Tonypandy CF40 106 C6
  Ynysybwl CF37 ....109 C6
Brynamman Rd
  Brynamman SA18 ..218 F8
  Cefn-bryn-brain SA9 .222 F6
  Coelbren SA10 ....222 F6
  Llanelli SA14 ....41 C6
  Nantyglo NP23 ......8 E3
  Tonna SA11 ....49 E3
Brynbach SY NP22 ....6 C6
Brynbala Way CF3 ..179 E5
Brynbedw Rd CF43 .80 B3
Brynbraen SA4 ....21 B8
Brynbryddan SA12 ..99 D5
Bryncae Isaf SA14 .41 D4
Bryncae Rd CF72 ...153 E2
Bryncelyn Blaina NP13 .15 E6
  Nelson CF46 ....83 D3
  Swansea SA7 ....70 A6
Bryncelyn Rd SA4 ..43 A2

Bryncerdin Rd SA3 ..122 E5
Bryncethin Jun & Inf Scls
  CF32 ....151 A4
Bryncethin Rd SA18 220 C7
Bryncoch Llanelli SA14 41 C6
  Taffs Well CF15 ....158 A4
Bryncoch CW Prim Sch
  SA10 ....48 C5
Bryncoch Rd CF32 .150 E3
Bryncoed
  Penywaun CF44 ....28 A6
  Radyr CF15 ....176 A6
Bryncoed Terr
  Abertridwr CF83 ...137 A8
  Penpedairheol CF82 .84 E8
Bryncwar Rd SA14 ..218 D8
Bryncyn CF83 ....173 E8
Bryncynon CF44 ....27 E8
Bryndedwyddfa
  SA14 ....218 D8
Brynderi SA18 ......218 E8
Brynderi Cl SA4 .....44 B2
Brynderi Clos CF14 177 C7
Brynderi Ct CF31 ..168 B5
Brynderwen CF37 ..109 F5
Bryncderwen Gr
  Ferndale CF43 ......79 F7
  1 Newport NP19 ...143 E6
  NP12 ....143 E6
Bryndderwen Rd
  1 Ammanford SA18 219 B7
  Newport NP19 .....143 E6
  Pontypridd CF37 ...109 F5
  Tonypandy CF40 ...106 F4
Brynddolau SA2 .....93 B8
Bryndu Rd CF33 ....148 C3
Bryndulais Ave
  Llanelli SA14 ....40 F7
  Seven Sisters SA10 222 C3
Bryndulais Row
  SA10 ....222 C4
Brynegiwys Ave
  CF36 ....183 D7
Brynegiwys Gdns
  CF36 ....183 D7
Bryneinon Rd SA4 ..43 A3
Bryneithin Rd SA4 ..43 A2
Bryneithyn SA4 .....1 C1
Bryneithin Terr SA6 ..45 F1
Brynfa Terr SA4 .....64 E4
Brynfab Rd CF37 ...136 B5
Brynfedw
  Bedwas CF83 ......138 E6
  Cardiff CF23 ......178 E6
Bryndfedwen Cl CF42 ..51 A1
Bryntfed CF35 .....169 F3
Brynffynnon Rd SA4 43 A3
Bryntffynnon Cl CF44 .29 A1
Brynfield Ct SA3 ...122 F4
Brynfield Rd SA3 ..122 E4
Bryngarn Rd CF35 .152 E3
Bryngarw Ctry Pk
  CF32 ....150 E7
Bryngelli Dr SA5 ....68 C7
Bryngelli Est CF44 ..27 C7
Bryngelli Pk SA5 ...68 C7
Bryngelli Rd SA5 ...68 C7
Bryngelli Terr CF83 137 A8
Bryngerwn Ave CF83 83 B5
Bryngerwn Cotts
  CF83 ....83 B5
Brynglas
  Bridgend CF31 .....168 B4
  Bryn-cöch SA10 ....48 C3
  Caerphilly CF83 ...137 E5
  Cwmbran NP44 .....116 D3
  Pengroes SA14 ....218 D7
  Pontlottyn CF81 .....32 E8
Brynglas Ave
  Cwmavon SA12 .....99 D5
  Newport NP20 .....143 C8
  Pontllanfraith NP12 .86 A5
Brynglas Cl NP20 ..143 C8
Brynglas Cres NP20 143 B8
Brynglas Dr NP20 ..117 B1
Brynglas Jun & Inf Schs
  NP20 ....143 B8
Brynglas Rd NP20 ..117 B1
Brynglas St CF24 ...95 C2
Brynglas Terr CF42 .75 C2
Brynglas
  Bridgend CF31 .....168 B5
  Gorseinon SA4 ......43 A2
  Llanelli SA14 ......41 A7
  Rudry CF83 ....139 B3
  Tonyrefail CF39 ...133 A5
Bryngolau CF15 .....55 C3
Bryngolau Cres CF37 79 F7
Bryngolau Terr
  2 Pontllanfraith NP12 .85 F4
  Swansea SA2 ....94 D7
Bryngolwg CF44 ....53 F8
Bryngwastad Rd SA4 43 A2
Bryngwenllli CF44 ..112 A5
Bryngwili Rd SA4 ...18 B3
Bryngwyn
  Caerphilly CF83 ...137 F1
  Neath SA10 ....70 C6
Bryngwyn Ave SA4 ..66 D8
Bryngwyn Bach SA14 .41 C6
Bryngwyn Cotts NP11 86 E6
Bryngwyn Pl NP22 ..62 B6

Bryngwyn Prim Sch
NP13 . . . . 36 C4
Bryngwyn Rd
Ebbw Vale NP23 . . . . . . 7 D4
Llanelli SA14 . . . . A1 B7
Newbridge NP11 . . . . . 86 E6
Newport NP20 . . . . . . 143 A4
Pontypool NP4 . . . . . . 62 B6
Bryngwyn St
Fleur De Lis NP12 . . . . 85 B5
Fleur De Lis NP12 . . . . 85 B5
Perth CF39 . . . . 107 E4
Bryngwynmawr Comp Sch
SA14 . . . . 41 A8
Bryngyrnos St SA13 100 E5
Brynhafod Bryn SA13 100 E5
Tycroes SA18 . . . . . . 218 F5
Brynhafod Rd CF83 137 A7
Brynhaulog Terr CF44 53 C6
Brynhenwysg CF37 108 F2
Brynheulog
Blaina NP13 . . . . 15 E5
Brynmenyn CF32 . . . . 150 C6
Cardiff CF14 . . . . 176 F5
Cardiff CF23 . . . . 178 F7
Llanelli SA14 . . . . 40 F8
Mountain Ash CF45 . . . 81 J8
Ystradgynlais SA9 . . . 222 A5
Brynheulog Ct CF32 150 D6
Brynheulog Pl
SA13 . . . . 125 C8
Brynheulog Rd
Cymmer SA13 . . . . . . 75 C6
Newbridge NP11 . . . . . 86 F7
Brynheulog St
Ebbw Vale NP23 . . . . . 14 C8
Merthyr Tydfil CF47 . . . 10 F3
Penybryn CF82 . . . . . . 84 D5
Port Talbot SA13 . . . . 125 C8
Brynheulog Terr
Cwmavon SA12 . . . . . . 99 D5
Porth CF39 . . . . 107 F4
Tonypandy CF40 . . . . 106 C6
Treharris CF46 . . . . . . 83 A5
Tylorstown CF43 . . . . . 80 B3
Brynhill CF23 . . . . . . 178 C6
Brynhill Cl CF62 . . . . 214 D8
Brynhill Terr CF38 . . 135 E2
Brynhy Fryd CF39 . . . 132 D2
Brynhyfryd NP22 . . . . 13 A2

Brynhyfryd
Aberdare CF44 . . . . . . 52 F4
Beddau CF38 . . . . . . 156 A7
Bedwas CF83 . . . . . . 138 D7
Bettws CF32 . . . . 129 D3
Caerphilly CF83 . . . . . 137 F4
Croesyceiliog NP44 . . . 90 A5
Glynneath SA11 . . . . 223 D1
Llangennech SA14 . . . 42 B6
Pontllïw SA4 . . . . 44 C5
Pontlottyn CF81 . . . . . 12 E1
Pontycymer CF32 . . . 103 F3
Radyr CF15 . . . . 176 B7
Tonypandy CF40 . . . . 106 E6
Tylorstown CF43 . . . . . 80 B3
Brynhyfryd Ave
Nantyglo NP23 . . . . . . 2 D1
Newport NP20 . . . . . . 143 B4
Tonypandy CF40 . . . . 107 A4
Brynhyfryd Inf Sch
SA5 . . . . 68 C4
Brynhyfryd Jun Sch
SA5 . . . . 68 C4
Brynhyfryd Prim Sch
Abertillery NP13 . . . . . 60 B6
Briton Ferry SA11 . . . . 71 B2
Brynhyfryd Rd
Briton Ferry SA11 . . . . 71 B2
Garnant SA4 . . . . 43 A3
Llanelli SA15 . . . . 40 D6
Margam SA13 . . . . . . 125 E3
Newport NP20 . . . . . . 143 A4
Brynhyfryd Sq CF45 68 C4
Brynhyfryd St
Merthyr Tydfil CF47 . . . 10 F4
Pontllanfraith NP12 . . . 85 F4
Swansea SA5 . . . . . . 68 C4
Tonypandy CF40 . . . . 106 C7
Treorchy CF42 . . . . . . 78 B8
Brynhyfryd Terr
Cefn Coed CF48 . . . . . 10 A4
Ebbw Vale NP23 . . . . . 14 F2
Ferndale CF43 . . . . . . 79 F6
Machen CF83 . . . . . . 140 A7
Penpedairheol CF82 . . 84 E8
Seven Sisters SA10 . . 222 D4
Brynhyfryd Villas
New Tredegar NP24 . . . 33 F2
Troedyrhiw CF48 . . . . 59 C8
Bryniago SA4 . . . . . . 15 E4
Bryniau Rd CF48 . . . . 10 F6
Brynllian SA14 . . . . . 218 B8
Brynllwchwr Rd SA4 65 E8
Brynllywarch CF34 . . 101 F1
Brynmair Cl CF44 . . . 53 D1
Brynmair Rd CF44 . . . 101 F1
Brynmair Terr 5
CF47 . . . . 10 F4
Brynmawr Cl CF33 . . 129 D3
Brynmawr Cl CF3 . . . 180 A7
Brynmawr Comp Sch
NP23 . . . . D6
Brynmawr Cres
SA18 . . . . 219 B7
Brynmawr Pl CF34 . 102 A3

Brynmawr RC Jun & Inf
Sch NP23 . . . . 8 C4
Brynmawr Rd NP23 . . . 7 F1
Brynmead SA14 . . . . . 41 E6
Brynmead Cl SA2 . . . . 94 C8
Brynmelyn Ave SA15 . 40 E6
Brynmenyns Bsns Ctr
CF32 . . . . 150 F5
Brynmenyn Ind Est
CF32 . . . . 150 E6
Brynmenyn Prim Sch
CF32 . . . . 150 E6
Brynmill Ave SA2 . . . . 94 F5
Brynmill Cres SA2 . . . 94 F5
Brynmill La SA2 . . . . . 94 E5
Brynmill Primary Sch
SA2 . . . . 94 F5
Brynmill Terr SA2 . . . 94 E5
Brynmoor SA15 . . . . . 40 C4
Brynmorgrug SA8 . . . 24 A5
Brynmorlais St 1
CF47 . . . . 10 B1
Brynna Ave
CF82 . . . . 84 E1
Brynna Rd
Brynna CF72 . . . . 153 E3
Cwmavon SA12 . . . . . . 99 D5
Pencoed CF35 . . . . . . 153 B2
Brynnewydd Gdns
SA2 . . . . 94 C6
Brynnyfryd NP13 . . . . 60 B7
Brynogwy Terr CF32 104 F5
Brynonnen Ct NP44 115 F8
Brynrhos Cres SA4 . . 44 B2
Brynsierfel SA14 . . . . 41 C5
Brynsierfel Sch SA14 41 D5
Brynsiriol Cimla SA11 72 C5
Gwaun-Cae-Gurwen
SA18 . . . . 220 D7
Hirwaun CF44 . . . . . . 208 A2
Llanelli SA14 . . . . 40 F7
Pontrhydyfen SA12 . . . 78 F3
Bryntaf Aberfan CF48 55 C4
Cefn Coed CF48 . . . . . 10 A4
Bryntawe Hall Cl SA6 46 C5
Bryntawe Rd SA6 . . . 46 B5
Bryntawel Terr CF40 106 C6
Brynteg
Aberyschan NP4 . . . . . 37 F3
Capel Hendre SA18 . . 218 E6
Cardiff CF14 . . . . 159 A1
Clydach SA6 . . . . 46 D7
Maesteg CF34 . . . . . . 101 F2
Seven Sisters SA10 . . 222 C2
Treharris CF46 . . . . . . 83 B7
Brynteg (Lower) Sch
CF31 . . . . 168 E2
Brynteg (Upper) Sch
CF31 . . . . 168 F2
Brynteg Ave
Bridgend CF31 . . . . . . 168 F3
Pontllanfraith NP12 . . . 85 F4
Pyle CF33 . . . . 148 A1
Brynteg Cl CF23 . . . . 178 C4
Brynteg Ct CF38 . . . . 156 A5
Brynteg Gdns CF31 . 168 F2
Brynteg Ho NP13 . . . 36 B6
Brynteg La CF38 . . . . 156 A5
Brynteg Pl NP4 . . . . . 39 E3
Brynteg Rd
Blaina NP13 . . . . 15 E4
Gorseinon SA4 . . . . . . 43 B3
Brynteg St SA11 . . . . 100 E5
Brynteg Terr
Ebbw Vale NP23 . . . . . 14 C8
Ferndale CF43 . . . . . . 80 A4
Fochriw CF81 . . . . 32 D7
Merthyr Vale CF48 . . . 55 D4
New Tredegar NP24 . . . 33 F2
Tonypandy CF40 . . . . 107 B4
Bryntirion
Bedwas CF83 . . . . . . 138 E7
Caerphilly CF83 . . . . . 137 E5
Cardiff CF14 . . . . 177 C8
Mountain Ash CF45 . . . 82 B6
Bryntirion (Evangelical
Theological Coll of
Wales) CF31 . . . . 168 B4
Bryntirion Cl CF31 . . 168 C4
Bryntirion Hill CF31 168 C4
Bryntirion Hospl SA15 68 C6
Bryntirion Inf Sch
CF31 . . . . 168 B5
Bryntirion Jun Sch
CF31 . . . . 168 C5
Bryntirion Rd
Merthyr Tydfil CF47 . . . 10 F1
Pontarddulais SA4 . . . 19 F1
Pontllïw SA4 . . . . 44 A8
Bryntirion St CF48 . . 11 A5
Bryntirion Terr SA15 40 F6
Brynview Ave CF82 . . 84 E1
Brynwern NP4 . . . . . . 62 B6
Brynwern St CF48 . . . 11 B5
Brynygroes Cotts SA9 1 F2
Brynymor Rd SA4 . . . 42 E2
Bryony Cl 3 CF47 . . 30 F8
Brython Dr CF3 . . . . . 180 A7
Brytwn Rd SA13 . . . . 125 A5
Buarth y Capel CF37 81 E2
Buchan Cl NP20 . . . . 124 F2
Buckingham Cl CF14 160 B2
Buckingham Cres
NP19 . . . . 143 F6
Buckingham Pl
Barry CF62 . . . . 214 C8
Newport NP20 . . . . . . 143 F6
Buckingham Rd SA4 . 44 C6
Buckland Dr SA4 . . . . 79 E2

Buckland Ho 5 CF47 30 D8
Buckley Cl
Cardiff CF5 . . . . 176 D3
Tonypandy CF40 . . . . 106 F7
Buckley Rd CF40 . . . . 106 F7
Bude Haven Terr
SA3 . . . . 123 A6
Bude Terr NP12 . . . . . 63 B6
Bull Cliff Wlk CF62 . . 214 A2
Bull Hill CF37 . . . . . . 185 C2
Buller St NP4 . . . . 61 E8
Bullfinch Rd CF62 . . . 210 E6
Bullin's La SA1 . . . . . 155 C6
Bullring CF72 . . . . . . 155 D4
Bulmore Rd NP18 . . . 118 C2
Bulrush Cl CF31 . . . . 180 B6
Bungalow Ave CF36 183 A7
Bungalows The
Aberysychan NP4 . . . . . 37 C7
Abertillery NP13 . . . . . 36 C4
Blaina NP13 . . . . 15 E4
Bridgend CF31 . . . . . . 168 F6
Bridgend CF31 . . . . . . 168 A3
Cwmfelinfach NP11 . . 113 E3
Evanstown CF39 . . . . . 132 B8
Ogmore Vale CF32 . . . 130 B6
Pontyrhyl CF32 . . . . . 130 A6
1 Ystrad Mynach CF82 84 F2
Bunker's Hill SA3 . . . 230 C6
Bunyan Cl CF3 . . . . . 170 C6
BUPA Hospl Cardiff
CF23 . . . . 178 F8
Burford St 3 NP4 . . 62 A7
Burgess Pl CF11 . . . . 194 E3
Burgesse Cres CF72 155 D2
Burgley Ct SA5 . . . . . 67 E5
Burial La CF61 . . . . . 209 F6
Burke Ave SA12 . . . . . 96 A3
Burleigh Rd 2 NP20 143 A4
Burley Pl CF62 . . . . . 211 D7
Burlington St CF63 . . 215 B5
Burlington Terr CF5 194 B7
Burman St SA1 . . . . . 193 A6
Burn's Way CF37 . . . . 135 B6
Burnaby St CF24 . . . . 195 B6
Burne Jones Cl CF5 176 E2
Burnet Dr CF82 . . . . . 84 E6
Burnfort Rd NP20 . . . 142 F3
Burnham Ave
Cardiff CF3 . . . . 179 C7
Sully CF64 . . . . 216 B5
Burnham Cl 3 CF3 179 C6
Burnham Dr SA3 . . . . 122 E6
Burns Cl
Machen CF83 . . . . . . 139 C6
Newport NP20 . . . . . . 142 E1
Burns Cres
Barry CF62 . . . . 214 F8
Bridgend CF31 . . . . . . 168 C6
Burns La NP44 . . . . . . 89 D2
Burns Rd SA12 . . . . . 124 E7
Burnside SA11 . . . . . . 71 E5
Burreed Cl CF3 . . . . . 180 B6
Burrows Chambers 1
SA1 . . . . 95 D6
Burrows Cl SA3 . . . . . 121 A5
Burrows La SA3 . . . . . 228 C3
Burrows Pl SA1 . . . . . 95 C6
Burrows Rd
Baglan SA12 . . . . 98 D6
Neath SA10 . . . . 70 E6
11 Neath SA11 . . . . . 71 E6
Swansea SA1 . . . . . . 95 B5
Burrows The CF36 . . 183 E7
Burry Rd SA15 . . . . . . 40 D1
Burry St SA15 . . . . . . 40 D1
Burt Pl CF10 . . . . 195 B2
Burt St CF10 . . . . 195 B1
Burton Homes NP20 143 F8
Burton Rd NP19 . . . . 143 F8
Burton Terr CF62 . . . . 212 B2
Burwell Cl CF23 . . . . 161 B1
Bush Bach NP27 . . . . 6 C2
Bush Rd Morriston SA6 46 A5
Bush Row SA11 . . . . . 71 D5
Bush Terr NP4 . . . . . . 61 C4
Bushy Pk NP4 . . . . . . 62 A7
Bute Cres CF10 . . . . . 195 C2
Bute Espl CF10 . . . . . 195 B1
Bute La CF64 . . . . 207 A4
Bute Pl
Abertillery NP13 . . . . . 59 E6
Cardiff CF10 . . . . 195 C1
Bute St Aberdare CF44 29 A1
Cardiff CF10 . . . . 195 B3
Cardiff CF15 . . . . 158 C1
Treherbert CF42 . . . . . 78 D1
Bute (Stryd Bute)
CF10 . . . . 195 B3
Bute Terr
Cardiff CF10 . . . . 195 B5
Hirwaun CF44 . . . . . . 27 C8
New Tredegar NP24 . . . 33 F2
Buteleigh Ave CF5 . . . 194 A7
Butleigh Terr NP22 . . . 6 E1
Butler's Ct NP4 . . . . . 37 D6
Butt Lee Ct CF62 . . . . 214 E5
Butterbur Pl CF5 . . . . 193 A5
Buttercup Ct NP44 . . 88 F1
Butterfield Dr CF23 . . 160 A4
Buttermere Way 3
NP19 . . . . 143 F8
Butterslade Gr SA4 . . 64 C4
Butterworth Cl NP19 144 E5
Button Ride CF5 . . . . 204 A8
Buttrills Cl CF62 . . . . 214 E6
Buttrills Rd CF62 . . . . 214 E6
Buttrills Wlk CF62 . . . 214 E6

Buttry Terr NP12 . . . . 85 B5
Butts The CF71 . . . . . 188 E2
Buxton Cl NP20 . . . . 142 F1
Buxton Ct CF83 . . . . . 135 C2
Bwl Rd CF46 . . . . 83 D4
Bwlch Cres SA11 . . . . 72 A4
Bwlch Rd Cardiff CF5 193 D7
Loughor SA4 . . . . 42 A1
Neath SA11 . . . . 72 A4
Bwlch y Gwyn SA5 . . 20 E2
Bwlch-y-Clawdd Rd
CF2,CF42 . . . . 77 F2
Bwlch-y-Garn Rd NP23 7 F1
Bwllfa Cotts CF41 . . . 79 A2
Bwllfa Rd
Cwmdare CF44 . . . . . . 28 B3
Ynysmaw SA6 . . . . . . 46 C5
Bwrw Rd SA4 . . . . 65 D8
By Pass Rd CF31,
CF33 . . . . 168 D2
By-Ways Ct CF35 . . . 169 F3
Byass St SA13 . . . . . . 125 E3
Bynea Cty Prim Sch
SA14 . . . . 41 F3
Bynea Sta SA14 . . . . . 41 F3
Byng Morris Cl SA2 . . 94 B5
Byng St SA1 . . . . 68 D4
Byrd Cres CF44 . . . . . 206 E1
Byrde Cl NP19 . . . . . . 144 C5
Byron Ave
Beddau CF38 . . . . . . 156 A5
Bridgend CF31 . . . . . . 168 C6
Byron Ct
Llantwit Major CF61 . . 210 B5
Penarth CF64 . . . . . . 206 F5
Byron Ho SA12 . . . . . 124 D7
Byron Pl
Blackwood NP11 . . . . . 59 D1
Cwmbran NP44 . . . . . 89 D2
Penarth CF64 . . . . . . 206 F4
Byron Rd
Aberbargoed CF81 . . . 58 B3
Newport NP20 . . . . . . 142 F2
Byron St
5 Barry CF63 . . . . 214 F5
Cardiff CF24 . . . . 195 C7
Cwmaman CF44 . . . . . 53 A4
Byron Way SA2 . . . . . 93 A3
Bythway Rd NP4 . . . . 38 B1
Bywater Row NP13 . . 36 B5
Byways NP44 . . . . . . 89 B3

C

C Row NP4 . . . . 17 A6
Cae Pentre CF32 . . . . 149 A2
Cabin Cl NP10 . . . . . 142 B7
Caban Isaac Rd SA4 . 64 F3
Caddick's Row NP13 15 C6
Cader Idris Cl NP11 115 C2
Cadfan Rd SA6 . . . . . 46 A8
Cadlan Bethel CF48 . 10 C1
Cadlc Cl SA5 . . . . 67 E6
Cadle Cres SA5 . . . . . 67 D5
Cadle Dell Pl SA5 . . . 67 D6
Cadle Mill SA5 . . . . . 67 C7
Cadle Pl SA5 . . . . 67 E6
Cadle Prim Sch SA5 . 67 D5
Cadlewood Rd SA5 . . 67 D6
Cadman Cl CF24 . . . . 196 A7
Cadnant Cl CF14 . . . . 159 D1
Cadnant Rd SA5 . . . . 68 A5
Cadoc Cres CF63 . . . . 215 D6
Cadoc Rd 5 NP44 . . 29 D6
Cadogan Cl CF41 . . . 79 D3
Cadogan St CF32 . . . 104 F5
Cadoxton Rd SA10 . . 71 D8
Cadoxton Sta CF63 . . 215 C6
Cadoxton Terr SA10 . 49 A2
Cadraed Rd SA1 . . . . 64 B1
Cadvan Rd CF5 . . . . . 193 B6
Cadwaladr Cir 4 SA1 95 B8
Cadwaladr St CF45 . . 54 C3
Cadwgan CF37 . . . . . 135 E1
Cadwgan Rd
Craig-Cefn-Parc SA6 . . 22 B2
Treorchy CF42 . . . . . . 78 E6
Cadwgan Terr CF37 108 C2
Cae Bach
Llangeinor CF32 . . . . . 130 A3
Machen CF83 . . . . . . 139 E7
Cae Banc SA2 . . . . . . 94 D7
Cae Bedw CF83 . . . . . 137 F2
Cae Bracla CF31 . . . . 169 B5
Cae Brandi CF83 . . . . 180 E8
Cae Bron CF83 . . . . . 169 B4
Cae Bryn CF31 . . . . . 168 C4

Cae Ffynnon
Bridgend CF31 . . . . . . 169 B5
Caerphilly CF83 . . . . . 137 F6
Church Village CF38 . . 135 E2
Penybryn CF82 . . . . . 84 D5
Cae Folland SA4 . . . . 64 E4
Cae Forgan Cotts
CF32 . . . . 130 B4
Cae Ganol CF36 . . . . 165 E2
Cae Gar SA14 . . . . . . 41 C5
Cae Garn CF35 . . . . . 152 B6
Cae Garw
Cardiff CF14 . . . . 159 D2
Dinas Powys CF64 . . . 206 A2
Cae Gethin CF83 . . . 137 F6
Cae Glas Barry CF63 215 B7
Caerphilly CF83 . . . . . 137 E5
Ewenny CF35 . . . . . . 185 E7
Fochriw CF81 . . . . 32 C8
Gorseinon SA4 . . . . . . 64 C3
Nantyglo NP23 . . . . . . 15 D8
Pencoed CF35 . . . . . . 170 E7
Tonypandy CF40 . . . . 107 A4
Cae Gorlan St NP11 87 A3
Cae Gorlan St NP11 87 B3
Cae Grawn SA4 . . . . . 66 B5
Cae Gwyn Rd CF14 . . 177 C5
Cae Leon CF62 . . . . . 204 F1
Cae Lewis CF15 . . . . . 158 C1
Cae Llwyd CF83 . . . . 138 B5
Cae lLwydd CF46 . . . . 83 E3
Cae Lynch SA10 . . . . 70 F6
Cae Maen CF11 . . . . 177 D6
Cae Maen Lloyd CF82 84 E5
Cae Mansel Rd
Gowerton SA4 . . . . . . 65 A4
Three Crosses SA4 . . . 65 F3
Cae Marchog CF83 . . 137 F6
Cae Mari Dwn CF47 . 10 E1
Cae Mawr Cl CF61 . . 210 B6
Cae Mawr Ind Est
CF83 . . . . 137 D3
Cae Mawr Rd CF14 . . 177 C7
Cae Melln NP4 . . . . . 39 E3
Cae Melyn NP23 . . . . 7 C2
Cae Morfa Rd SA12 . . 98 C2
Cae Nant Coch CF83 137 D5
Cae Nant Gledyr
CF83 . . . . 137 D3
Cae Odin CF83 . . . . . 169 B5
Cae Pandy CF83 . . . . 138 B5
Cae Pant CF83 . . . . . 137 E5
Cae Pen-y-Graig
CF83 . . . . 137 E7
Cae Pentice CF32 . . . 149 A2
Cae Perllan CF31 . . . 169 B5
Cae Perllan Rd NP20 143 A3
Cae Rex CF71 . . . . . . 188 E1
Cae Rhedyn
Croesyceiliog NP44 . . . 90 B4
Pontardawe SA8 . . . . . 24 C3
Cae Rhos CF83 . . . . . 138 B5
Cae Rhys Ddu SA1 . . 72 A5
Cae Rowland St SA5 . 68 B3
Cae Samson 1 CF5 193 C4
Cae Siriol CF39 . . . . . 107 E6
Cae Siwsan CF31 . . . 169 B5
Cae Stumpie CF71 . . 188 F1
Cae Syr Dafydd
CF11 . . . . 194 C2
Cae Talcen CF35 . . . . 152 F1
Cae Terr SA15 . . . . . . 40 F5
Cae Ty Mawr CF14 . . 159 C1
Cae Uwchllyn CF83 . 137 E1
Cae Yorath 8 CF14 177 B5
Cae Ysgubor
Bridgend CF31 . . . . . . 169 B4
Caerphilly CF83 . . . . . 137 E5
Cefn Hengoed CF82 . . 84 E5
Cae'r Berllan CF35 . . 152 F1
Cae'r Cynffig CF33 . . 166 A8
Cae'r Efail CF38 . . . . 152 E1
Cae'r Ffcrm CF83 . . . 137 E8
Cae'r Gerddi CF38 . . 135 E1
Cae'r Graig CF15 . . . 176 B7
Cae'r Hen Eglwys
CF33 . . . . 168 C6
Cae'r Odyn CF64 . . . 206 A2
Cae'r Wern CF48 . . . . 30 D8
Cae'r Ysgol SA10 . . . 49 B4
Cae'r- Llwyn Terr
NP11 . . . . 112 F7
Cae'r-bryn Terr
SA18 . . . . 218 E8
Cae'r-Odyn NP13 . . . 15 C5
Cae'rgwigau CF39 . . . 133 A5
Cae-Bricks Rd SA5 . . 68 B2
Cae-Bryn CF83 . . . . . 137 A7
Cae-Bryn Ave SA2 . . 94 D6
Cae-Coed-Erw CF31 169 B5
Cae-Du-Bach 1
SA15 . . . . 40 E6
Cae-gross Terr SA10 . 48 F2
Cae-Gwyn Rd SA4 . . 19 D3
Cae-Is-Maen SA8 . . . 23 C3
Cae-Nan SA6 . . . . . . 46 B3
Cae-Pys Rd SA5 . . . . 68 B2
Cae-Yr-Ebol NP44 . . . 89 C5
Caeau Duon CF35 . . . 152 E1
Caebach Cl CF5 . . . . 192 F3
Caecerrig Rd SA14 . . 19 D4
Caeconna Rd SA5 . . . 67 E7
Caedegar Rd SA9 . . . 1 F2
Caedelyn Rd CF14 . . 177 C6
Caedenw Rd CF43 . . . 71 C5
Caederwen Rd SA11 . 71 F5
Caedraw Prim Sch
CF47 . . . . 30 D8
Caedraw Rd CF47 . . . 30 D8
Caedu Rd
Cwmllynfell SA9 . . . . . 221 B7

Caedu Rd continued
Ogmore Vale CF32 . . . 104 E1
Caegarw Cty Prim Sch
CF45 . . . . 54 D3
Caeglas
Cross Hands SA14 . . . 218 B7
Cwmavon SA12 . . . . . . 99 D4
Llanelli SA14 . . . . 40 F8
Caeglas Ave CF3 . . . 179 B3
Caeglas Rd CF3 . . . . 179 C3
Caegwenith Clos
SA11 . . . . 49 B1
Caehopkin Cty Prim Sch
SA9 . . . . 222 D7
Caelbryn Terr CF32 . . 150 D6
Caemaen St CF45 . . . 82 C5
Caemawr SA11 . . . . . 82 A4
Caemawr SA18 . . . . . 219 C7
Caemawr Gdns CF39 107 E3
Caemawr Rd
Porth CF39 . . . . 107 E3
Swansea SA6 . . . . . . 68 E8
Caemawr Terr CF40 . 107 A1
Caenant Terr CF37 . . 135 F6
Caenant CF83 . . . . . . 138 A4
Caenant Terr SA10 . . 70 F7
Caenewydd Cl CF5 . . 192 F3
Caepalish Pl NP44 . . 62 A8
Caepistyll St SA1 . . . 68 D1
Caer Bont Ind Est
SA9 . . . . 222 B6
Caer Bryn Rd SA14,
SA18 . . . . 218 E8
Caer Cady Cl CF23 . . 178 C4
Caer Castell Pl CF3 . 179 D5
Caer Ffynnon CF62 . . 214 C3
Caer Gynnig CF34 . . 102 A2
Caer Mead Cl CF61 . . 210 B6
Caer Newydd CF3 . . . 179 D5
Caer Odyn CF64 . . . . 206 A2
Caer Salem Newydd
CF39 . . . . 107 E2
Caer St SA1 . . . . 195 D7
Caer Ty Clwyd CF61 . 209 F7
Caer Wenallt CF14 . . 158 F1
Caer Wetral CF33 . . . 148 C2
Caer Worgan CF61 . . 209 F7
Caer-Gynydd Rd SA5 66 F3
Caeracca Villas CF48 11 A5
Caerau Cm Inf Sch
CF5 . . . . 193 C3
Caerau Court Rd
CF5 . . . . 193 C3
Caerau Cres NP20 . . 143 A4
Caerau Ct CF72 . . . . 155 F3
Caerau La Cardiff CF5 193 B2
Cardiff CF5 . . . . 193 C4
Pentyrch CF15 . . . . . . 175 D8
Wenvoe CF5 . . . . 205 A8
Caerau Park Cres
CF5 . . . . 193 C4
Caerau Park Pl 2
CF5 . . . . 193 C4
Caerau Park Rd CF5 193 C4
Caerau Rd
Cardiff CF5 . . . . 193 C4
Maesteg CF34 . . . . . . 75 B1
Newport NP20 . . . . . . 143 A4
Caerbragdy CF83 . . . 138 B3
Caerbryn NP11 . . . . . 86 D5
Caerhendy St CF47 . . 10 F4
Caerleon (Lodge Hill) Inf
Sch NP18 . . . . 118 A3
Caerleon (Lodge Hill) Jun
Sch NP18 . . . . 118 F3
Caerleon Cl CF3 . . . . 180 A7
Caerleon Comp Sch
NP18 . . . . 118 A4
Caerleon Ct CF83 . . . 137 C4
Caerleon Endowed Jun
Sch NP18 . . . . 118 A2
Caerleon Gr CF83 . . . 225 F1
Caerleon Rd
Caerleon NP18 . . . . . . 118 A5
Cardiff CF14 . . . . 177 D2
Dinas Powys CF64 . . . 206 C4
Newport NP19 . . . . . . 143 F8
Ponthir NP18,NP44 . . 117 E7
Caerlicken La NP18 . 119 F5
Caerllysi CF35 . . . . . 170 E8
Caernarfon Cl 1
CF64 . . . . 206 C3
Caernarvon Cres
NP44 . . . . 90 A3
Caernarvon Ct CF83 137 D4
Caernarvon Dr NP10 141 F3
Caernarvon Gdns
CF62 . . . . 214 E8
Caernarvon Gr CF3 . . 225 F1
Caernarvon Pl NP13 58 D1
Caernarvon Rd NP13 141 E3
Caernarvon Way
Cardiff CF3 . . . . 179 D5
Swansea SA1 . . . . . . 69 B4
Caerphilly Ave SA1 . . 69 C4
Caerphilly Bsns Pk
CF83 . . . . 138 C2
Caerphilly Castle
CF83 . . . . 138 B3
Caerphilly Cl
Bassaleg NP10 . . . . . . 141 E3
Dinas Powys CF64 . . . 206 C4
Caerphilly District Miners
Hospl CF83 . . . . 137 F1
Caerphilly Ent Ctr
CF83 . . . . 138 D6
Caerphilly Rd
Bassaleg NP10 . . . . . . 141 E3
Cardiff CF14 . . . . 177 D5
Nantgarw CF15 . . . . . 158 B8
Nelson CF46 . . . . 83 F3

Caerphilly Rd continued
Senghenydd CF83 . . . . .110 F1
Tredomen CF46 . . . . .46 A5
Treharris CF46 . . . . .83 B5
Ystrad Mynach CF82 . . . . . . .111 F8
Caerphilly Sta CF83 . . . . .138 B2
Caersalem Terr 2
SA15 . . . . .40 D3
Caerwent Rd
Cardiff CF5 . . . . .193 A5
Croesyceiliog NP44 . . . . .90 A6
Pontypool NP4 . . . . .38 D1
Caesar Cres NP18 . . . . .118 A4
Caetyla Heol CF35 . . . . .169 F4
Caewal CF5 . . . . .194 A8
Caewallis St CF31 . . . . .168 F3
Caiach Terr CF46 . . . . .83 D6
Cairn Ct CF43 . . . . .52 B1
Cairnmuir Rd CF24 . . . . .197 C2
Calcot Rd CF40 . . . . .107 B5
Calcot Ho NP44 . . . . .90 B4
Calderton Rd CF38 . . . . .156 A6
Caldy CF71 . . . . .67 E7
Caldicot Cl
Blackwood NP12 . . . . .58 D1
Swansea SA1 . . . . .69 C4
Caldicot CF83 . . . . .137 D4
Caldicot Rd
Cardiff CF5 . . . . .193 D4
Swansea SA1 . . . . .69 C4
Caldicot St NP19 . . . . .143 F4
Caldicot Way NP44 . . . . .89 F6
Caldicot Cl CF38 . . . . .156 A5
Caldwell Cl CF38 . . . . .156 A6
Caldy Cl Barry CF62 . . . . .214 F8
Newport NP23 . . . . .143 F7
Porthcawl CF36 . . . . .165 E1
Caldy Ct CF14 . . . . .177 A3
Caldy Rd CF14 . . . . .177 A3
Calfaria Chapel Ho
CF39 . . . . .107 D8
Calfaria Flats CF45 . . . . .82 E3
Callaghan Ct CF24 . . . . .195 E6
Calland St SA6 . . . . .60 E5
Calvert Terr 3 SA1 . . . . .95 B7
Calyn CF44 . . . . .89 C6
Cam Ct NP44 . . . . .89 A5
Camarthen Rd SA1 . . . . .67 E4
Cambell Ct CF43 . . . . .215 A4
Camberwell Ave
CF14 . . . . .168 C6
Cambourne Ave
CF14 . . . . .176 F5
Cambourne Cl CF62 . . . . .214 C7
Cambray Cl CF36 . . . . .182 E8
Cambria Cl NP18 . . . . .118 C2
Cambria Rd CF5 . . . . .193 B4
Cambria St NP4 . . . . .62 E2
Cambrian Ave
Brynna CF72 . . . . .132 C5
Llantwit Major CF61 . . . . .210 A5
Cambrian Ct
Barry CF63 . . . . .215 A5
Swansea SA2 . . . . .69 A7
Cambrian Ind Est
CF72 . . . . .173 A8
Cambrian Ind Pk
CF40 . . . . .106 C6
Cambrian Pl
Cwm-twrch Uchaf SA9 . . . . . .221 C6
5 Llanelli SA15 . . . . .40 C4
Pontarddulais SA4 . . . . .19 C4
1 Pontypridd CF37 . . . . .135 E7
Port Talbot SA13 . . . . .125 C7
Swansea SA1 . . . . .95 E6
Cambrian Ret Ctr 4
NP20 . . . . .143 B5
Cambrian St Deri CF81 . . . . . .57 B8
Llanelli SA15 . . . . .40 C4
14 Merthyr Tydfil CF47 . . . . .10 D2
Rhymney NP22 . . . . .12 E5
Cambrian Terr
Merthyr Tydfil CF47 . . . . .10 D3
Tonypandy CF40 . . . . .106 E7
Cambridge Cl SA3 . . . . .123 A4
Cambridge Ct NP18 . . . . . . .117 F3
Cambridge Gdns
Ebbw Vale NP23 . . . . .7 D3
Mumbles SA3 . . . . .123 B4
Cambridge Rd
Mumbles SA3 . . . . .123 A4
Newport NP19 . . . . .143 D5
Cambridge St
Barry CF62 . . . . .214 C3
Cardiff CF11 . . . . .195 A2
Swansea SA2 . . . . .94 E1
Camelia Cl CF44 . . . . .28 D3
Camelia Dr SA4 . . . . .45 F3
Camelot Cl NP18 . . . . .118 D1
Camelot Pl **5** NP19 . . . . . . .143 D6
Camelot Way CF14 . . . . .159 D2
Cameron Pl SA4 . . . . .42 D4
Cameron St CF24 . . . . .195 E7
Camffrwd Way SA6 . . . . .46 C1
Camm's Cnr **8** CF63 . . . . . .206 C3
Camnant CF81 . . . . .111 E7
Camnant Rd SA10 . . . . .223 A5
Camona Dr **11** SA1 . . . . .95 D5
Campbell Dr CF11 . . . . .207 A8
Campbell St
Llanelli SA15 . . . . .40 E2
Pontypool NP4 . . . . .62 A7
2 Swansea SA1 . . . . .95 G5
Campbell Terr
Mountain Ash CF45 . . . . .54 D3
Tonypandy CF40 . . . . .106 E7
Camperdown Rd
NP19 . . . . .144 B3
Camperly Cl 7 CF38 . . . . . .156 A5

Campion Cl
Cwmbran NP44 . . . . .116 A8
Campion Pl CF5 . . . . .176 D2
Campion Pl CF38 . . . . .156 B5
Camrose Ct CF62 . . . . .214 F8
Camrose Dr SA5 . . . . .66 E3
Camrose Rd CF5 . . . . .193 D4
Camrose Wlk NP44 . . . . .89 C2
Can-Yr-Aderyn SA6 . . . . .45 D2
Can-Yr-Eos SA6 . . . . .45 E2
Canada Rd CF14 . . . . .177 E2
Canal Cl NP44 . . . . .62 E2
Canal Lock Cl CF48 . . . . .55 C3
Canal Par
Cardiff CF10 . . . . .195 B3
Newport NP20 . . . . .143 D4
Canal Park Ind Est
CF10 . . . . .195 B3
Canal Row CF48 . . . . .30 F4
Canal Side SA1 . . . . .49 C3
Canal St NP20 . . . . .143 B7
Canal Terr
Abercarn NP11 . . . . .87 A2
Newport NP20 . . . . .143 D3
Ystalyfera SA9 . . . . .2 B6
Canaston Cl SA15 . . . . .67 F7
Canaston Pl CF5 . . . . .193 D4
Canberra Cl
Blackwood NP12 . . . . .85 F8
Cwmbran NP44 . . . . .89 D2
Canberra Cres NP20 . . . . . . .142 E4
Canberra Rd CF31 . . . . .168 F5
Candleston Castle (rems
of) CF32 . . . . .188 E7
Candleston Cl CF36 . . . . .165 E2
Candleston Pl SA1 . . . . .69 C3
Candor Pl NP18 . . . . .117 F7
Candwr Pk NP18 . . . . .118 A6
Candwr Rd NP18 . . . . .118 A6
Canford St NP4 . . . . .38 B2
Canning St Cwm NP23 . . . . . .35 A8
Ton Pentre CF41 . . . . .78 F3
Cannington Ave CF3 . . . . .179 C5
Cannington Cl CF64 . . . . .216 B5
Cannisland Pk SA3 . . . . .92 D1
Cannon St SA18 . . . . .220 D8
Canolfan
Bridgend CF31 . . . . .169 B4
Seven Sisters SA10 . . . . .222 C3
Canon St
Aberdare SA4 . . . . .29 A2
Barry CF62 . . . . .214 D3
Newport NP19 . . . . .143 D6
Canonbie Cres CF48 . . . . .55 C3
Canopus Cl CF3 . . . . .179 D6
Canterbury Cl 9
NP20 . . . . .143 C6
Canterbury Rd
Ebbw Vale NP23 . . . . .7 F3
Swansea SA2 . . . . .94 E5
Canton Cl 12 CF11 . . . . .194 D5
Cantonian High Sch
CF5 . . . . .193 E8
Cantref Cl
Cardiff CF14 . . . . .159 F3
Rogerstone NP10 . . . . .142 B7
Cantref St SA5 . . . . .67 E5
Capcoch Prim Sch
CF44 . . . . .53 E5
Capel Cres NP20 . . . . .143 C2
Capel Ct **15** NP4 . . . . .38 A1
Capel Ed La NP4 . . . . .39 E7
Capel Gwilym Rd
CF14 . . . . .159 D4
Capel Hendre Ind Est
SA18 . . . . .218 E5
Capel Ifan CF39 . . . . .133 D5
Capel Isaf Rd SA15 . . . . .41 A6
Capel Newydd Ave
NP4 . . . . .17 D5
Capel Newydd La 3
SA15 . . . . .40 F6
Capel-Newydd La
SA15 . . . . .40 F6
Capital Bldgs SA9 . . . . .2 C7
Capital Valley Ind Pk
NP22 . . . . .13 D5
Caple Rd CF62 . . . . .214 C3
Captains Hill CF46 . . . . .83 C7
Caradoc Ave CF62,
CF63 . . . . .215 A7
Caradoc Cl **1** CF63 . . . . .180 A7
Caradoc Rd
Cwmbran NP44 . . . . .89 E4
Mountain Ash CF45 . . . . .54 D2
Caradoc St
Abercarn NP11 . . . . .114 C7
Aberycwan NP4 . . . . .37 F3
Merthyr Tydfil CF47 . . . . .10 D2
Mountain Ash CF45 . . . . .54 D2
Caradoc Wlk **19** NP4 . . . . . . .17 D7
Caradog Cl
Bridgend CF31 . . . . .169 A5
Caerleon NP18 . . . . .118 A3
Caradog City Prim Sch
CF44 . . . . .29 A1
Caradog Ho 10 CF43 . . . . . .195 B6
Caradog Pl SA1 . . . . .95 A8
Caradog Rd
Bridgend CF31 . . . . .169 D3
Tylorstown CF43 . . . . .80 B3

Caradog St SA13 . . . . .125 D7
Caraway Cl 14 CF37 . . . . . . .180 A8
Cardiff Arms Pk
CF10 . . . . .194 C5
Cardiff Bsns Ctr
CF24 . . . . .196 B3
Cardiff Bay Ret Pk
CF11 . . . . .206 F8
Cardiff Bay Ret Pk (Parc
Manwerthu Bae
Caerdydd) CF11 . . . . .194 C2
Cardiff Bsns Pk
CF14 . . . . .177 E7
Cardiff Castle CF10 . . . . . . .195 A6
Cardiff Central Sta
CF10 . . . . .195 A4
Cardiff Centre Trad Est
CF10 . . . . .195 B4
Cardiff City Farm (Fferm
Dinas Caerdydd)
CF11 . . . . .194 C3
Cardiff Food Pk CF3 . . . . . .179 D2
Cardiff Gate Ret Pk
CF23 . . . . .161 B2
Cardiff Gate Services
CF23 . . . . .161 A2
Cardiff High Sch
CF23 . . . . .178 B6
Cardiff Ind Pk CF14 . . . . . .177 E7
Cardiff International
Arena CF10 . . . . .195 B5
Cardiff PI CF62 . . . . .214 D4
Cardiff Queen Street Sta
CF10 . . . . .195 B6
Cardiff Rd
Abercynon CF45 . . . . .53 C7
Aberdare CF44 . . . . .53 C7
Bargoed CF81 . . . . .36 A5
Barry CF63 . . . . .215 E6
Caerphilly CF83 . . . . .138 B2
Cowbridge CF71 . . . . .189 A1
Creigiau CF15 . . . . .174 A6
Dinas Powys CF64 . . . . .206 A3
Glan y Nant NP12 . . . . .85 A7
Llantrisant CF72 . . . . .155 D2
Merthyr Vale CF48 . . . . .55 D5
Mountain Ash CF45 . . . . .54 D2
Pontypridd CF37 . . . . .135 F6
Quakers Yard CF46 . . . . .83 B5
Rhydyfelin CF37 . . . . .136 B4
St Fagans CF5 . . . . .174 D7
Taffs Well CF15 . . . . .157 F5
Treharris CF46 . . . . .83 A6
Trelewis CF46 . . . . .83 C7
Cardiff Rd Infmy
CF24 . . . . .195 C6
Cardiff St
Abercanaid CF48 . . . . .30 F4
Aberdare CF44 . . . . .29 A2
Ogmore Vale CF32 . . . . .104 E2
Treorchy CF42 . . . . .78 D6
Cardiff Tertiary Coll
(Coleg Glan Hafren)
CF3 . . . . .179 E4
Cardiff-Wales Airport
(Maes-Awyr
Caerdydd-Cymru)
CF62 . . . . .213 B3
Cardigan Cl
Church Village CF38 . . . . .135 F1
Croesyceiliog NP44 . . . . .89 F6
Dinas Powys CF64 . . . . .206 C3
Porthcawl CF36 . . . . .165 E2
Cardigan Ct
Boverton CF61 . . . . .210 C6
Croesyceiliog NP44 . . . . .89 F6
Swansea SA1 . . . . .69 C5
Cardigan Ho
2 Penarth CF64 . . . . .206 F2
Port Talbot SA12 . . . . .124 D8
Cardigan Pl 11 NP19 . . . . . .143 F6
Cardigan Rd 10
CF64 . . . . .206 C3
Cardigan St CF5 . . . . .194 D4
Cardigan Terr CF32 . . . . .104 F6
Cardigan Way NP12 . . . . .58 E1
Cardinal Dr CF14 . . . . .160 A4
Cardinal Newman RC Sch
CF37 . . . . .136 B5
Cardonnel Rd SA10 . . . . .70 F6
Carew Cl CF62 . . . . .214 F7
Carew Gr **17** CF14 . . . . .177 A6
Carew Gr CF48 . . . . .225 F1
Carew Pl SA1 . . . . .69 C5
Carey Rd NP19 . . . . .144 A5
Carey Wlk SA10 . . . . .71 C8
Carfax Path NP4 . . . . .89 A1
Cargill Cl CF38 . . . . .156 B5
Cargo Rd CF10 . . . . .195 D1
Caridwen Terr
6 Llantrisant CF72 . . . . .155 D3
Llantrisant CF72 . . . . .155 D3
Carig Cres SA1 . . . . .68 B1
Carig Gdns SA1 . . . . .68 B1
Carisbrooke Rd
NP19 . . . . .143 F5
Carisbrooke Way
CF23 . . . . .178 D3
Carlin Rd CF23 . . . . .15 C8
Carling Ct CF5 . . . . .193 A3

Carlisle St
Cardiff CF24 . . . . .195 E6
Newport NP20 . . . . .143 D2
Carlos St 2 SA13 . . . . .290 F5
Carlton Cl CF14 . . . . .159 E3
Carlton Cres CF38 . . . . .156 B5
Carlton Ct NP4 . . . . .62 A8
Carlton Dr NP11 . . . . .59 D3
Carlton Pl
Abercarn NP11 . . . . .114 C5
Clydach SA6 . . . . .22 E1
Newport NP19 . . . . .143 E7
Carlton Rd
Clydach SA6 . . . . .22 E1
Newport NP19 . . . . .143 E7
Carlton Terr
Abercarn NP11 . . . . .114 C5
Swansea SA1 . . . . .95 C7
Troedyrhiw CF48 . . . . .31 B1
Carlyle St
Abertillery NP13 . . . . .36 B5
Briton Ferry SA11 . . . . .71 C3
Carlyon Rd NP11 . . . . .87 B8
Carmarthen Cl
Barry CF62 . . . . .214 F7
Swansea SA1 . . . . .210 B6
Carmarthen Cres
CF83 . . . . .137 D4
7 CF85 . . . . .194 C6
Carmarthen Dr CF38 . . . . .139 E2
Carmarthen Ho CF38,
4 Penarth CF64 . . . . .206 F2
Port Talbot SA12 . . . . .124 D8
Carmarthen Rd
Cross Hands SA14 . . . . .218 A8
8 Dinas Powys CF64 . . . . . . .206 C3
Florest SA4 . . . . .18 F6
Swansea SA1,SA5 . . . . .68 B2
Carmarthen St CF5 . . . . .194 B4
Carmarthenshire Coll of
Tech & Art SA18 . . . . .219 B7
Carmel Cl NP23 . . . . .7 C5
Carmel Ct CF24 . . . . .178 C1
Carmel Flats CF40 . . . . .107 A5
Carmel St
Pontlliw SA4 . . . . .43 F7
Swansea SA1 . . . . .69 D5
Carmel
Abertillery NP13 . . . . .36 B5
Tredegar NP22 . . . . .6 E1
Treherbert CF42 . . . . .78 A8
Carn Celyn CF38 . . . . .156 A5
Carn Celyn CF38 . . . . .156 A5
Carn-y-Celyn CF40 . . . . .106 F3
Carn-y-Tyla Terr
Abertysswg NP22 . . . . .33 A8
Rhymney NP22 . . . . .13 A1
Carne Ct CF61 . . . . .210 B6
Carne St Cwm NP23 . . . . .35 A8
Pentre CF41 . . . . .78 F3
Carne Terr CF71 . . . . .199 F8
Carnegie Dr CF23 . . . . .178 B5

Castell Morlais CF48 . . . . .3 F3
Castell Tal-y-van
CF71 . . . . .189 E7
Castell y Fan CF83 . . . . .138 C5
Castell-y-Mynach Rd
CF38 . . . . .155 F7
Castella Rd CF38,
CF72 . . . . .155 E7
Castle Arc **3** CF10 . . . . .195 A5
Castle Ave
Cardiff CF3 . . . . .178 F2
Mumbles SA3 . . . . .123 A5
Penarth CF64 . . . . .206 F1
Castle Bailey St SA1 . . . . .95 D7
Castle Bldgs CF37 . . . . .133 E6
Castle Cl
Abercarn NP11 . . . . .114 C6
Boverton CF61 . . . . .210 C5
Creigiau CF15 . . . . .174 B6
3 Dinas Powys CF64 . . . . . . .206 B3
Rogerstone NP10 . . . . .142 B4
Castle Cotts CF82 . . . . .36 C4
Castle Cres
Cardiff CF3 . . . . .178 F2
Mumbles SA3 . . . . .123 A5
Castle Ct
Church Village CF38 . . . . .135 F1
Llanelli SA15 . . . . .40 C3
5 Pontypridd CF37 . . . . .135 E7
Castle Dr Cimla SA11 . . . . . .72 B6
Dinas Powys CF64 . . . . .206 C3
Castle Fields NP22 . . . . .12 E4
Castle Gdns **2** SA1 . . . . .95 D7
Castle Graig Rd SA6 . . . . .60 D5
Castle Graig Rd SA6 . . . . .60 D5
Castle Hill
Llanblethian CF71 . . . . .188 D1
Penpedairheol CF82 . . . . .84 D6
St Fagans CF5 . . . . .174 A7
Castle Ivor St CF37 . . . . .109 A1
Castle La
Abercarn NP11 . . . . .114 C6
Cardiff CF24 . . . . .195 D7
1 Swansea SA1 . . . . .95 D7
Castle Mdws CF35 . . . . .169 C7
Castle Mews NP18 . . . . .118 C1
Castle Park Ind Est SA11 . .167 B3
Castle Park Rd NP20 . . . . .142 D3
Castle Prec CF71 . . . . .200 F6
Castle Rd
3 East Aberthaw CF62 . . . . . .212 C4
Mumbles SA3 . . . . .123 A5
Rhoose CF62 . . . . .213 A1
Castle Rise CF37 . . . . .179 A2
Castle Sq
Mumbles SA3 . . . . .123 A5
Castle St
Abercarn SA12 . . . . .124 D8
Abertillery NP13 . . . . .36 B4
Barry CF62 . . . . .214 C1
Blaenavon NP4 . . . . .17 C7
Bridgend CF31 . . . . .169 B2
Caerleon NP18 . . . . .118 C2
6 Cardiff CF83 . . . . .138 B3
Fleur De Lis NP12 . . . . .85 B3
Glyncorrwg SA13 . . . . .227 C2
1 Llantrisant CF72 . . . . .155 D3
Llantwit Major CF61 . . . . .209 F7
Loughor SA4 . . . . .42 D1
Maesteg CF34 . . . . .102 B3
Merthyr Tydfil CF47 . . . . .10 D1
Mumbles SA3 . . . . .123 A5
Neath SA11 . . . . .70 F7
Neath SA11 . . . . .71 E8
Newport NP20 . . . . .143 D2
Pentrebach CF48 . . . . .31 A4
1 Pontypridd CF37 . . . . .135 E7
Swansea SA1 . . . . .95 D7
Taffs Well CF15 . . . . .158 A3
Tredegar NP22 . . . . .13 E6
Treorchy CF42 . . . . .78 C5
Castle St (Heol y Castell)
CF10 . . . . .194 C5
Castle View
Caerphilly CF83 . . . . .137 F6
Heolgerrig CF48 . . . . .10 B1
Neath SA11 . . . . .71 E8
Tongwynlais CF15 . . . . .176 D8
Castle Wood NP4 . . . . .37 D5
Castle Yd CF47 . . . . .10 D1
Castleland PI CF11 . . . . .177 E2
Castleland CF63 . . . . .215 A5
Castleton Ave CF42 . . . . .195 E7
Castleton Ct CF3 . . . . .180 C8
Castleton Rd CF3 . . . . .162 C3
Caswell Ave SA3 . . . . .122 E4
Caswell Bay Rd SA3 . . . . . . .122 A5
Caswell Ct SA7 . . . . .48 A1
Caswell Dr SA3 . . . . .122 A6
Caswell Rd
Bishopston SA3 . . . . .122 B4
4 Cardiff CF3 . . . . .179 B3
Mumbles SA3 . . . . .122 E4
Caswell St
Llanelli SA15 . . . . .40 E3
Swansea SA1 . . . . .95 B6
Caswell Way SA1 . . . . .144 A5
Catalpa Cl NP20 . . . . .117 B3

Cath Cob Cl CF3 . . . . .179 E7
Cathan Cl SA5 . . . . .67 E6
Cathan Cres SA5 . . . . .67 E6
Cathays High Sch
CF14 . . . . .177 E1
Cathays Sta CF10 . . . . .195 A7
Cathays Terr CF24 . . . . .195 A8
Cathedral Church of SS
Peter & Paul with SS
Dyfrri, Teild & Euddogwy
CF14 . . . . .177 B1
Cathedral Cl CF5 . . . . .177 B1
Cathedral Ct
5 Newport NP20 . . . . .143 B4
Cathedral Gn The
CF5 . . . . .177 B1
Cathedral Rd
Cardiff CF11 . . . . .194 D7
Cardiff CF11 . . . . .194 D8
Cathedral Sch The
CF5 . . . . .194 B8
Cathedral View CF14 . . . . . . .177 B2
Cathedral Way SA12 . . . . .98 D3
Cathedral Wlk 8
CF10 . . . . .195 A5
Catherine Cl
Abercanaid CF48 . . . . .30 F4
Newport NP20 . . . . .163 F5
Catherine Dr
Cardiff CF15 . . . . .158 D2
Marshfield CF3 . . . . .180 E8
Catherine Meazey Flats 6
CF64 . . . . .207 A5
Catherine St
5 Aberavon SA12 . . . . .98 E1
5 Aberdare CF44 . . . . .29 A1
Cardiff CF24 . . . . .195 A8
Llanelli SA15 . . . . .40 C3
5 Pontypridd CF37 . . . . .109 A1
Swansea SA1 . . . . .95 B6
Treorchy CF41 . . . . .79 A5
Catherine Terr CF39 . . . . . . .107 E2
Catholic Rd NP23 . . . . .8 C4
Catkin Dr CF64 . . . . .206 B5
Catsash Rd NP18 . . . . .118 F1
Cattle St SA11 . . . . .71 E8
Cattwg Cl CF61 . . . . .209 F7
Cattwg Cotts CF62 . . . . .212 B8
Cattybrook Terr 2
SA12 . . . . .99 F6
Cattwg Prim Sch SA10 . . . . . . .48 F2
Causeway Hill CF71 . . . . . . .200 D8
Causeway The
Clanbrook CF38 . . . . .170 D8
Swansea SA2 . . . . .94 E7
Causeway View
Gwaun Row CF34 . . . . .102 A4
Cave St SA5 . . . . .68 A2
Cavell Ho SA12 . . . . .98 F2
Cavell St SA13 . . . . .227 C1
Cavendish Cl CF14 . . . . .159 E2
Cavendish Pl CF38 . . . . .156 B6
Cawdor Pl SA1 . . . . .40 D6
Cawley Pl CF63 . . . . .215 B7
Cawnpore St CF64 . . . . .206 E5
Caxton Pl
Cardiff CF23 . . . . .179 A8
6 Newport NP20 . . . . .143 B5
Caynham Ave CF64 . . . . .217 A8
Cecil Rd Gorseinon SA4 . . . .43 C2
Gorseinon SA4 . . . . .66 C4
Cecil Sharp Rd NP19 . . . . . .144 F5
Cecil St Cardiff CF24 . . . . .195 D7
Neath SA11 . . . . .71 D6
Cedar Ave SA5 . . . . .43 A4
Cedar Cl
Aberdare CF44 . . . . .28 E2
Bryn NP23 . . . . .85 D3
Ebbw Vale NP23 . . . . .7 C5
Gowerton SA4 . . . . .66 D4
Cedar Ct
Church Village CF38 . . . . .136 A1
Mumbles SA3 . . . . .122 F8
Cedar Gdns
Baglan SA12 . . . . .98 D5
Pontypool NP4 . . . . .62 A4
Cedar Gr CF14 . . . . .176 C1
Cedar La CF37 . . . . .136 B5
Cedar Rd
Abertillery NP13 . . . . .59 F5
Neath SA11 . . . . .71 F7
Newport NP19 . . . . .143 D5
St Athan SA12 . . . . .211 B7
Cedar Way
Merthyr Tydfil CF47 . . . . .10 D4
Penarth CF64 . . . . .206 E3
Ystrad Mynach CF82 . . . . .84 E1
Cedar Wlk NP44 . . . . .89 B5
Cedar Wood Dr
CF39 . . . . .132 C5
Cedars The NP18 . . . . .145 F7
Cedor y Wrach CF63 . . . . . . .205 B1
Cedric Cl SA3 . . . . .94 B5
Cedric St SA15 . . . . .40 C5
Cefn Brith SA14 . . . . .46 B6
Cefn Bryn CF39 . . . . .107 D1
Cefn Byrle Rd SA10 . . . . .222 F6
Cefn Carfan Cotts
CF35 . . . . .151 D6
Cefn Carfan Rd
CF35 . . . . .151 D6
Cefn Carnau Rd
CF14 . . . . .177 F5

Cefn Celyn SA2 ....66 B1
Cefn Cl
Croescyceiliog NP44 .....90 B6
Pontypridd CF37 ....109 C6
Rogerstone NP10 ....142 B5
Cefn Coch CF15 ....176 A7
Cefn Coed CF31 ....168 D5
Cefn Coed Ave CF23 .178 C6
Cefn Coed Colliery Mus
SA10 ....25 E3
Cefn Coed Cres SA2 ..67 D1
Cefn Coed Hospl SA2 .67 C1
Cefn Coed La CF15 ...168 D5
Cefn Cres NP13 ....36 B6
Cefn Cribwr Prim Sch
CF32 ....149 B2
Cefn Ct
Blackwood NP12 ....155 E7
Newbridge NP11 ....87 B8
Newport NP20 ....143 A3
Rogerstone NP10 ....142 B5
Cefn Dr NP10 ....142 B5
Cefn Fforest Jun Sch
NP12 ....85 C8
Cefn Fforest Jun Sch
NP12 ....85 C8
Cefn Ffynon SA13 ....125 F3
Cefn Gelli SA11 ......227 B8
Cefn Glas Inf Sch
CF31 ....168 D6
Cefn Graig CF14 ......177 B8
Cefn Gwrgan Rd
SA13 ....125 E3
Cefn Helyg SA2 ....67 B1
Cefn Hengoed Comp Sch
SA1 ....69 D4
Cefn Hengoed Rd
SA1 ....69 D4
Cefn Ilan CF83 ....137 A6
Cefn Isaf CF48 ....10 A4
Cefn La CF37 ....109 C5
Cefn Llan CF15 ......178 A8
Cefn Llwyn SA1 ....69 C5
Cefn Llynwau St CF82 .94 D4
Cefn Mably Farm Pk
CF3 ....161 E5
Cefn Mably Rd CF14 ..162 A7
Cefn Milwr NP44 .....116 D8
Cefn Mount CF64 .....206 A3
Cefn Nant
Cardiff CF14 ....159 B1
Pencoed CF35 ....152 C1
Cefn Onn Cl CF14 ....159 F1
Cefn Onn Mdws
CF14 ....159 F4
Cefn Onn Prim Sch
CF14 ....143 D7
Cefn Parc NP22 ....13 E5
Cefn Penuel CF15 ....178 C3
Cefn Prim Sch CF37 .109 C5
Cefn Rd
Blackwood NP12 ....155 A1
Blackwood NP12 ....85 C8
Newbridge NP11 ....87 A6
Newport NP19 ....144 D2
Pontypool NP4 ....39 B1
Cefn Rhos NP22 ......143 D7
Cefn Rise NP10 ......142 A6
Cefn Saeson Comp Sch
SA11 ....227 A8
Cefn Stylle Rd SA4 ...65 D4
Cefn N NP16 ....147 D8
Cefn Wood Jun Sch
NP10 ....142 A5
Cefn y Mynydd CF37 .109 B5
Cefn-Coed Cres
CF23 ....178 C3
Cefn-Coed Gdns
CF23 ....178 B3
Cefn-Coed Rd CF23 ..178 B4
Cefn-Crib Rd
Newbridge NP11 ....60 E3
Pontypool NP4 ....63 B4
Cefn-Draw SA4 ....65 D1
Cefn-Fforest Ave
Blackwood NP12 ....85 C7
Blackwood NP12 ....85 C8
Cefn-Glas Rd CF31 ...168 D6
Cefn-Parc SA10 ....49 C6
Cefn-Pennar Rd CF14 .160 F6
Cefn-Porth Rd CF14 ..160 F6
Cefn-Rhychdir Rd
NP24 ....33 E4
Cefn-Saeson Cl SA11 .72 A6
Cefn-y-Lon CF83 .....137 D6
Cefn-y-Maes SA5 .....67 A6
Cefn-yr-Allt SA10 ....49 C4
Cefn-yr-Erw Rare Breeds
farm SA9 ....222 E7
Cefnbrynbrain Cty Prim
Sch SA9 ....221 B8
Cefncoed Rd SA12 ....99 C5
Cefncrug SA18 ....218 E7
Cefndon Terr
Cwmavon SA12 ....99 D5
Hirwaun CF44 ....136 D8

Cefneithin Cty Prim Sch
SA14 ....218 A8
Cefneithin Rd SA14 ..218 B8
Cefnllan Rd SA8 ....23 D6
Cefnpennar Rd
Aberdare CF44 ....97 A1
Mountain Ash CF45 .....54 B7
Cefnsaeson Rd SA7 ....70 A8
Ceidrim Rd SA18 .....220 B8
Ceiriog Cl Barry CF63 215 A8
Penarth CF64 ....206 F4
Ceiriog Cres CF37 ...135 F6
Ceiriog Dr
Caerphilly CF83 ....138 A4
Cardiff CF14 ....176 F8
Ceiriog Rd SA1 ....98 B2
Celandine Cl N P44 ...88 F2
Celandine Rd CF5 .....193 A5
Celerity Dr CF10 .....203 A8
Celtic Gn CF64 ......206 B4
Celtic Rd
Cardiff CF14 ....177 D3
Maesteg CF34 ....102 D1
Celtic View CF31 .....150 F1
Celtic Way
Bedwas CF83 ....138 E6
Newport NP10 ....163 C5
Rhoose CF62 ....212 E1
Celyn Ave
Caerphilly CF83 ....138 A4
Cardiff CF23 ....178 B5
Celyn Cl CF62 ....211 C7
Celyn Gr
Caerphilly CF83 ....138 A4
Cardiff CF23 ....178 C7
Celyn Isaf CF39 ......193 A4
Celynen Rd NP11 ......87 B4
Cemaes Cres CF3 .....179 E5
Cemaes Rd NP11 ....59 D2
Cemetery Rd
Abercarn NP11 ....87 B3
Abercynon CF45 ....82 C4
Aberdare CF44 ....28 E4
Abertillery NP13 ....60 A6
Barry CF62 ....214 F6
Bridgend CF31 ....168 E6
Ebbw Vale NP23 ....15 A1
Ebbw Vale NP23 ....7 D1
Gwaun-Cae-Gurwen
SA18 ....220 D6
Maesteg CF34 ....102 C3
Ogmore Vale CF32 .....130 E7
Porth CF39 ....135 F7
Swansea SA5 ....68 D6
Taffs Well CF15 ....158 B3
Taffs Well CF15 ....158 B4
Treorchy CF42 ....78 D7
Cemetery Rd W NP23 .3 B4
Cenarth Dr CF44 ......29 E2
Cendl Cres NP23 ....7 C4
Cendl Terr NP23 ......35 B8
Cenfedd St SA1 ....196 B2
Cennin Pede CF63 ....205 B1
Centenary CF38 ......156 B6
Central Ave
Blackwood NP12 ....59 A1
Blackwood NP12 ....85 C8
Newbridge NP11 ....87 A6
Newport NP19 ....144 D2
Pontypool NP4 ....39 B1
Central Bldgs
Bedwas CF83 ....139 A6
Blackwood NP12 ....59 B1
Cardiff Dr NP4 ....38 B1
Central Hos CF83 ....138 F6
Central Inf Sch SA13 128 C7
Central Jun Sch
SA13 ....125 B8
Central Link CF10 ...195 C4
Central Rd SA13 .....125 D3
Central Sq
Cardiff CF10 ....195 A4
Pontypridd CF37 ....109 D2
Central St
Caerphilly CF83 ....137 F6
Ystrad Mynach CF82 ....84 E1
Central Way
Barry CF63 ....215 E6
Cwmbran NP44 ....89 C5
**Central Way (Ffordd
Ganolog)** CF14 ....177 F3
Centre Ct CF15 ....157 E8
Centurion Ct CF15 ...193 D3
Centurion Gate
NP18 ....118 C2
Century Pk SA6 ....69 A6
Cenydd Terr CF83 ....110 F4
Cerdin Ave CF27 .....173 B7
Ceredig Ct NP44 ......90 B2
Ceredig St CF48 ....11 A3
Ceri Ave CF42 ....213 B2
Ceri Rd Rhoose CF62 .213 B2
Swansea SA1 ....67 F1
Ceridwen St
Maerdy CF43 ....52 A1
Mountain Ash CF45 ....54 B7
Cerise Cl SA12 ....98 B3
Chaddesley Terr
SA1 ....95 B7
Chadwick Cl NP20 ...117 A2
Chaffinch Cl CF31 ...116 C1
Chaffinch Way NP10 .163 F7
Chain Rd SA11 ....227 B8
Chain Wlk SA11 ......223 C1
Chalfont Cl CF38 ....156 B6
Chalice Cl SA11 ......98 D3
Challacombe Pl SA3 .122 E6
Chalvington Cl CF38 .156 B6

Chamberlain Rd
Cardiff CF14 ....177 A3
Neath SA11 ....71 D4
Chamberlain Row
CF64 ....206 C4
Chancery La
Cardiff CF11 ....194 D5
Chandlers Ct NP19 ...214 F3
Chandlers Ct [B]
CF37 ....109 D2
Chandlers Rd NP23 ...7 E4
Chandlers Reach
Llantwit Fardre CF38 ..156 C5
Mumbles SA3 ....123 C4
Chandlers Way CF40 .207 A6
Chandlery The CF40 .107 A7
Channel Ave CF39 ...133 E8
Channel Cl CF62 .....212 F1
Channel Hts CF33 ....148 E1
Channel View
Bassaley NP10 ....141 F3
Bridgend CF31 ....169 D4
Bryn-côch SA10 ....48 D4
Castleton CF3 ....162 B3
Cwmbran NP44 ....89 C5
Marcross CF61 ....208 D7
Penarth CF64 ....207 B1
Pontypool NP4 ....62 D7
Port Talbot SA12 .....124 D8
Risca NP11 ....115 B1
Swansea SA2 ....94 B5
Channel View Ct
NP11 ....115 B1
Channel View Rd
CF11 ....194 F1
Chantal Ave CF31 ....150 D1
Chantry Ct SA5 ....67 F5
Chantry Rise CF64 ...207 A1
Chantry The CF5 .....176 E1
Chapel Banks CF48 ...10 C2
Chapel Cl
Aberystchan NP4 ....37 E6
Abertrin CF71 ....189 B3
Baglan SA12 ....98 D3
Dinas Powys CF64 .....206 C4
[2] Newport NP20 .....143 C3
Pentrebach CF48 ....31 A4
Pontllanfraith NP12 ...85 A1
Chapel Farm Terr
NP11 ....114 B8
Chapel Hill CF72 .....153 F3
Chapel Hill CF72 .....153 F3
Chapel La
Croescyceiliog NP44 ...90 A7
Penarth CF64 ....207 A5
Chapel Mead NP44 ...89 C3
Chapel Rd
[B] Aberdare CF44 .....29 A2
Cardiff CF23 ....179 D7
Dinas Powys CF64 .....206 C4
Llanharan CF72 ....154 A3
Monknash CF71 ....198 C2
Morganstown CF15 ....176 B8
Nantyglo NP23 ....8 C2
New Tredegar NP24 .....33 B5
Penderyn CF44 ....224 D3
Pontypool NP4 ....61 F8
Three Crosses SA4 ....65 E1
Chapel Row
[B] Aberdare CF44 .....29 A2
Cardiff CF23 ....179 D7
Dinas Powys CF64 .....206 C4
Pontypool NP4 ....38 B1
Pontypridd CF37 ....53 E8
Chapel Row La [1]
CF3 ....179 D7
Chapel Sq CF48 ....30 E5
Chapel St
Abergarwed CF32 ....58 A5
Abercanaid CF48 ....30 E4
Abercarn NP11 ....87 B4
Aberdare CF44 ....53 C7
Abergwynfi SA13 ....76 C5
Bedling CF46 ....56 A7
Blaencwm CF42 ....50 D4
Blaenrhondda CF42 ....50 D4
Bridgend CF31 ....168 F3
Brynmawr NP23 ....8 A4
Brynmenyn CF32 ......150 F6
Cardiff CF5 ....194 B8
Cwmbran NP44 ....89 C5
Deri CF81 ....57 B8
Gorseinon SA4 ....43 D2
Mumbles SA3 ....123 A5
Nant-y-Moel CF32 .....104 F6
New Tredegar NP24 .....33 E3
Pontllotyn CF81 ....12 F1
Pontycymer CF32 .....103 E3
Pontypridd CF37 ....109 C1
Pontypridd CF37 ....135 F5
Ton Pentre CF41 ....79 A3
[B] Tonypandy CF40 ..106 C6
Tonypandy CF40 ....107 A3
Treorchy CF42 ....78 D6
Tredyrhiw CF48 ....31 C1
Ystrad CF41 ....79 D3
Chapel Terr
Bryn SA13 ....100 E5
Hengoed CF82 ....84 F3
[B] Port Talbot SA13 .125 C6
Wattstown CF39 ....107 E8
Chapel Wood CF23 ...178 C7
Chapman Cl NP20 ....117 A3
Chapman Ct [8] NP20 142 F4
Chapman St SA15 .....28 E6
Chard Ave CF5 ....179 B5
Chargot Rd CF5 ....194 B7

Charles Ave CF35 ....152 D1
Charles Ct
Ebbw Vale NP23 ....7 B1
Gorseinon SA4 ....43 A1
Charles Darwin Way
SA2 ....94 D3
Charles Pl CF62 .....214 F3
Charles Row CF34 ...102 A4
Charles St
Abertillery NP11 ....59 E6
Abertysswg NP22 ....33 C8
Blaenavon NP4 ....17 D6
Bridgend CF31 ....168 F5
Caerphilly CF83 ....118 B3
Cardiff CF14 ....168 B3
Croescyceiliog NP44 ...90 B5
Langstone NP18 ......145 B8
Newport NP20 ....117 B3
Trefechan CF48 ....100 B4
Cherry Tree Rd NP12 .85 E3
Cherry Tree Way
CF46 ....83 C2
Cherry Tree Wlk
CF72 ....55 C2
Cherry Trees NP12 ...58 D7
Cherrydale Rd CF5 ...193 E6
Cherrydown Cl CF14 .159 F2
Cherrywood Cl CF14 .159 F2
Chervil Cl [12] CF3 ..180 A8
Cherwell Cl CF5 .....176 D1
Cherwell Rd CF64 ....206 F2
Cherwell Wlk NP20 ..116 C2
Cheshire Cl CF14 ....177 F6
Chesnut Gr NP18 .....117 E2
Chesshyre St SA2 ....94 E5
Chester Cl
[1] Cardiff CF3 ....179 F6
Merthyr Tydfil CF48 ...225 F1
Pontypool NP4 ....63 B5
Chester Dr CF3 ......137 D4
Chester Pl CF11 .....194 F3
Chester St CF11 .....194 F3
Chesterfield St CF63 215 B7
Chesterholme NP20 .143 A3
Chesterton Rd CF3 ..179 B7
Chestnut Ave
Gorseinon SA4 ....43 A4
Mumbles SA3 ....122 E8
St Athan CF62 ....211 B7
Chestnut Cl
Aberdare CF44 ....28 E2
Dinas Powys CF64 .....206 B2
Ebbw Vale NP23 ....7 C5
Machen CF83 ....140 A7
Neath SA10 ....48 D2
Pontypridd NP4 ....63 B5
Chestnut Dr CF36 ...183 E8
Chestnut Gn NP44 ...89 B6
Chestnut Gr Bryn NP22 85 E1
Maesteg CF34 ....102 C3
Chestnut Rd
Baglan SA12 ....98 D3
Cardiff CF5 ....193 D8
Neath SA11 ....72 A6
Chestnut St CF37 ....136 A5
Chestnut Tree Cl
CF15 ....176 A6
Chestnut Way
Bridgend CF31 ....168 B3
Merthyr Tydfil CF47 ...10 D5
Penarth CF64 ....206 F3
Chestnuts The CF72 .173 D6
Cheviot Cl
Cardiff CF14 ....177 E7
Risca NP11 ....115 C2
Swansea SA5 ....67 B3
Chevron St CF39 .....107 E4
Chichester Cl NP19 .117 F1
Chichester Rd CF64 .206 C4
Chichester Way CF5 193 E6
Chick La NP20 ....142 F4
Chilcote St CF63 .....215 B6
Chilcott Ave CF3 ....178 E5
Childrens Orthopaedic
Hospl SA1 ....95 B6
Chiltern Cl
Cardiff CF14 ....177 E7
Newport NP19 ....144 C6
Risca NP11 ....115 D1
Swansea SA5 ....67 E3
Chimney Rd CF62 ....211 E1
Chirk Gdns SA1 ....69 C4
Chiswick Cl CF31 ...168 C6
Chopin Rd SA12 ......98 B3
Chorley Cl CF5 ....193 C7
Chorleywood Cl
CF31 ....169 A4
Christ Church Prim Sch
SA11 ....95 B5
Christ The King RC Prim
Sch CF14 ....160 A1
Christchurch Hill
NP18 ....147 D7
Christchurch Rd
Baglan SA12 ....98 D3
Blackwood NP12 ....85 F8
Newport NP19 ....144 B6
Christina Cres NP10 142 C4
Christina St
Cardiff CF10 ....195 B3
[7] Swansea SA1 ......95 C7
Christopher Cl SA6 ..69 A6
Christopher Rd
Maesteg CF34 ....102 C3
Neath SA10 ....70 E7
Ynysforgan SA6 ....46 A4
Christopher Rise SA4 .45 A5
Christopher St SA10 .64 B8
Christopher Terr
CF47 ....30 F7
Chrome Ave SA12 ....98 B2

Chumleigh Cl CF3 .....179 A
Church Acre CF31 .....169 D
Church Ave
Ebbw Vale NP23 ....7 F
Llwydcoed CF44 ....28 E
[B] Penarth CF64 .....207 B
Pontypool NP4 ....38 C
Church Bldgs SA9 ...222 C
Church Cl
Bryn-côch SA10 ....48 D
Cardiff CF14 ....160 C
Croescyceiliog NP44 ...90 A
Llantwit Fardre CF38 ..184 D
Ogmore-By-Sea CF32 ..184 D
Peterstone Wentlooge
CF3 ....188 A
Pontypool NP4 ....63 A
Rogerstone NP10 ......142 A
Swansea SA7 ....69 D
Church Cotts SA5 .....45 B
Church Cres
Bassaley NP10 ....142 A
Blaengwrach SA11 ....227 C
Coedkernew NP10 .....163 A
Ebbw Vale NP23 ....7 C
Ebbw Vale NP23 ....7 C
Church Ct
Newport NP19 ....144 E
Newport NP19 ....144 A
Church Farm Cl
NP20 ....116 E
Church Hill Cl CF71 .200 C
Church La Baglan SA12 98 E
Bishopston SA3 ....121 F
Brynmawr NP23 ....8 C
Cardiff CF23 ....179 D
Coedkernew NP10 .....163 A
Gwaun-Cae-Gurwen
SA18 ....220 D
Llantwit Major CF61 ..209 F
Marshfield CF3 ....162 D
Nantgarw CF15 ....158 A
Nelson CF46 ....83 E
Pen-clawdd SA4 ....64 F
Pontypool NP4 ....62 B
Pontypool NP4 ....63 B
St Athan CF62 ....211 B
Church Mdw
Boverton CF61 ....210 D
Gelligaer CF82 ....84 D
Reynoldston SA3 .....229 B
Church Mews NP4 ....62 C
Church Park La SA3 .123 A
Church Pk SA3 ....123 A
Church Pl
Bargoed CF81 ....58 A
Blaengarw CF32 ....103 E
Maesteg CF34 ....102 A
Neath SA11 ....71 E
Porthcawl CF36 ....182 F
Church Pl S CF64 ....207 B
Church Rd
Abersychan NP4 ....37 E
Abertillery NP13 ....60 A
Abertridwr CF83 ......136 F
Baglan SA12 ....98 E
Barry CF63 ....215 E
Blaenavon NP4 ....17 C
Bridgend CF31 ....168 B
Cardiff CF14 ....160 C
Cardiff CF3 ....177 A
Cardiff CF3 ....161 C
Cardiff CF83 ....179 B
Cardiff CF5 ....193 C
Cardiff CF5 ....194 D
Church Village CF38 ..135 F
Cwmbran NP44 ....89 C
Gelligaer CF82 ....84 C
Gorslas SA14 ....218 B
Llanbiethian CF71 ....188 C
Llanedi SA4 ....218 D
Llanfrechfa NP44 .....102 D
Maesycwmmer NP7 ......9 D
Neath SA10 ....48 D
Newbridge NP11 ....86 F
Newport NP19 ....143 D
Penarth CF64 ....207 B
Penderyn CF44 ....224 D
Penllyn CF15 ....175 C
Pontardawe SA8 ....24 A
Pontardawe SA8 ....24 D
Pontarddulais SA4 ....19 D
[1] Pontypridd CF37 ..109 E
Rhoose CF62 ....213 A
Risca NP11 ....114 F
Seven Sisters SA10 ...222 C
St Brides Wentlooge
NP10 ....163 E
Swansea SA7 ....69 D
Ton Pentre CF41 ....79 A
Tonypandy CF40 ....107 A
Wick CF71 ....198 C
Ynysmeudwy SA8 ......23 F
Ystalyfera SA9 ....24 A
Church Rise CF5 .....205 A
Church St
[7] Aberavon SA12 .....99 A
Aberbargoed CF81 .....58 A
Aberbeeg NP13 ....29 A
Aberkenfig CF32 ......150 C
Abertillery NP13 ....36 B
Bargoed CF81 ....57 F
Bedwas CF83 ....138 E
Blaengarw CF32 ....103 E
Blaina NP13 ....15 E

Church St continued
Briton Ferry SA11 . . . . .71 B1
Bryncae CF72 . . . . .153 D3
Caerleon NP18 . . . . .36 D8
Cardiff CF10 . . . . .195 A5
Cowbridge CF71 . . . . .188 E2
Cymmer SA13 . . . . .75 D3
Dowlais CF48 . . . . .11 B4
Ebbw Vale NP23 . . . . .14 D6
Ferndale CF43 . . . . .79 F7
Gowerton SA4 . . . . .66 B5
Llanbradach CF83 . . . . . . .111 A1
Llanelli SA15 . . . . .40 D5
Llantrisant CF72 . . . . .155 D3
Llantwit Major CF61 . . . . .209 F6
Llyswenny CF71 . . . . .187 E1
Machen CF83 . . . . .140 A7
Maerdy CF43 . . . . .52 A1
Maesteg CF34 . . . . .102 A3
Maesteg CF34 . . . . .75 B2
Merthyr Tydfil CF47 . . . . . .10 D2
Merthyr Tydfil CF47 . . . . . .10 B4
Mountain Ash CF45 . . . . . . .81 F8
Newport NP20 . . . . .143 D2
Pontardawe SA8 . . . . .23 E5
Pontlottyn CF81 . . . . .12 F1
Pontycymer CF32 . . . . . . .103 F3
Porthcawl CF36 . . . . .183 D8
Rhymney NP22 . . . . .12 E5
Rogerstone NP10 . . . . . . .141 F6
Taffs Well CF15 . . . . .158 A3
Ton Pentre CF41 . . . . .79 A3
Tonypandy CF40 . . . . .106 A8
Tonypandy CF40 . . . . .106 F8
Tredegar NP22 . . . . .13 E8
Treherbert CF42 . . . . .51 A1
Treorchy CF42 . . . . .78 B5
Troedyrhiw CF48 . . . . .31 B1
Wick CF71 . . . . .198 C5
Ynysybwl CF37 . . . . .81 F1
Ystrad Mynach CF82 . . . . . .84 E1
Church Terr
Blaengarw CF32 . . . . .103 E6
Cardiff CF23 . . . . .195 D8
Llanharan CF72 . . . . .154 A3
Nant-y-Moel CF32 . . . . . . .104 E6
New Tredegar NP24 . . . . . . .33 E3
Pontypool NP4 . . . . .38 A1
St Hilary CF71 . . . . .201 D7
St Mary Church CF71 . . . .201 A4
Tonypandy CF40 . . . . .107 A1
Tylorstown CF43 . . . . .80 C3
Church View
Baglan SA12 . . . . .98 E5
Blaenavon NP4 . . . . .17 C6
Brynna CF72 . . . . .153 D3
Ebbw Vale NP23 . . . . .7 D3
Laleston CF32 . . . . .167 E4
Llanblethian CF71 . . . . . . .188 C1
Marcross CF61 . . . . .208 C7
Pontllanfraith NP12 . . . . . .86 A6
Abercanaid CF48 . . . . .30 F4
Church View Cl
Brynna CF72 . . . . .153 D3
Llandough CF64 . . . . .206 D7
Church Wlk CF39 . . . . . . .108 A3
Church Wood Rd
NP44 . . . . .89 D5
Churchfield Cl CF82 . . . . .84 F6
Churchfield Row
CF41 . . . . .79 A4
Churchfields CF63 . . . . . .215 B8
Churchill Cl
Bridgend CF31 . . . . .168 D4
Cardiff CF14 . . . . .160 A4
Churchill Terr CF63 . . . . .215 C6
Churchill Way CF10 . . . . .195 B5
Churchmead NP10 . . . . . .142 B2
Churchward Dr
NP19 . . . . .144 B4
Cil Heol Hendy CF72 . . . . . .62 C7
Cil-Hendy CF72 . . . . .73 C7
Cil-Sanws La CF48 . . . . . . .10 A5
Cil-y-Coed SA5 . . . . .67 A3
Cila City Prim Sch
SA2 . . . . .93 D5
Cilddu Rd CF32 . . . . . . .150 B7
Cilfedw CF15 . . . . .176 B7
Cilfrew Prim Sch
SA10 . . . . .49 B4
Cilfrow Ct SA1 . . . . .68 C2
Cilfynydd Prim Sch
CF37 . . . . .109 F5
Cilfynydd Rd CF37 . . . . . .109 F5
Cilgerran Ct NP44 . . . . .90 B3
Cilgerran Cres CF38 . . . . .177 D8
Cilgerran Pl SA4 . . . . .64 C6
Cilgerran Way NP12 . . . . . .58 E1
Cilhall CF46 . . . . .83 B8
Cilhaul Terr CF45 . . . . .54 D1
Cilmaengwyn
Godregraig SA8 . . . . .221 B1
Pontardawe SA8 . . . . .24 C8
Cilonen Rd SA4 . . . . .65 D1
Cilparc CF26 . . . . .183 A8
Cilsaig Rd SA14 . . . . .41 B8
Cilsanws Ho CF48 . . . . . . .10 A3
Cilsanws La CF48 . . . . . . .225 F3
Cimla Cl SA11 . . . . .76 D1
Cimla Cres SA11 . . . . .72 A6
Cimla Hospl SA11 . . . . .72 A5
Cimla Rd SA11 . . . . .71 F6
Cinema Bldgs
SA15 . . . . .40 D3
Circle The Bryn NP12 . . . . .89 E3
Cwmbran NP44 . . . . .89 D1
Tredegar NP22 . . . . .13 E6

Circle Way E CF23 . . . . .178 F5
Circle Way W CF23 . . . . .178 D4
Citadel Cl CF62 . . . . .13 D7
Citrine Ave SA12 . . . . .98 B2
Citrine Cl SA12 . . . . .198 B2
City Hall CF10 . . . . .195 A4
City Hall Rd CF10 . . . . . . .195 A4
City Link CF24 . . . . .195 E8
City Rd Bethes CF32 . . . . .129 C1
Cardiff CF24 . . . . .195 B7
Claerwen CF82 . . . . .84 D6
Claerwen Cl CF44 . . . . .29 E2
Claerwen Dr CF23 . . . . . . .178 B5
Clairwain NP4 . . . . .63 A3
Clan-yr-Afon CF72 . . . . . .173 B7
Clapham Terr NP4 . . . . .17 B5
Clara St CF41 . . . . .7 C2
Clarbeston Rd CF14 . . . . .177 A3
Clare Ct SA4 . . . . .42 C2
Clare Dr CF71 . . . . .188 F1
Clare Drew Way NP44 . . . . .94 B3
Clare Gdns CF11 . . . . .194 F5
Clare Pl CF11 . . . . .194 F5
Clare Rd Cardiff CF11 . . . .194 F4
Treorchy CF42 . . . . .78 C5
Ystalyfera SA9 . . . . .2 B7
Clare St Cardiff CF11 . . . . .194 F5
Merthyr Tydfil CF47 . . . . . . .10 B4
Swansea SA5 . . . . .68 C3
Claremont NP20 . . . . . . .178 F6
Claremont Ave CF23 . . . . .179 B4
Claremont Cres CF23 . . . .179 B4
Claremont Ct CF46 . . . . . . .83 C5
Claremont Rd NP44 . . . . . .87 B8
Claremont Cnr NP4 . . . . . .62 C6
Clarence Ct
Cardiff CF24 . . . . .195 B1
Maesteg CF34 . . . . .102 A3
Clarence Emb CF10 . . . . .195 B1
Clarence Pl
Newport NP19 . . . . .143 C5
Pontypool NP4 . . . . .62 D6
Clarence Rd
Cardiff CF10 . . . . .195 B2
Pontypool NP4 . . . . .62 D6
Clarence Terr
Aberdare CF44 . . . . .53 D6
Swansea SA1 . . . . .67 A6
Clarendon CF23 . . . . .178 D3
Clarendon Rd
Cardiff CF23 . . . . .178 D3
Swansea SA2 . . . . .94 D7
Clarice St SA12 . . . . .98 E1
Clarion Cl
Cardiff CF24 . . . . .46 B1
Swansea SA6 . . . . .69 C8
Swansea SA6 . . . . .69 C8
Clark Ave NP44 . . . . .89 E6
Clark St CF42 . . . . .78 B6
Clarke St CF5 . . . . .193 F6
Clarke Way SA1 . . . . .69 C6
-y-Dderwen
CF45 . . . . .54 E3
Clas Ael-y-Bryn CF37 . . . .83 D3
Clas Dyffryn CF14 . . . . . .109 D6
Clas Dyfrig CF14 . . . . . .177 B3
Clas Gabriel CF14 . . . . . .177 B3
Clas Gwenllior CF45 . . . . . .54 E2
Clas Heulog CF14 . . . . . . .177 C4
Clas Illtyd CF14 . . . . .177 C4
Clas Isan CF14 . . . . .177 C4
Clas Odyn CF14 . . . . .177 B5
Clas Teilo CF14 . . . . .177 B5
Clas Ty Nwrn
CF14 . . . . .177 C6
Clas Ty'n-y-Cae
CF14 . . . . .177 C6
Clas Tynewydd CF14 . . . . .177 B4
Clas Yorath CF14 . . . . . . .177 B5
Clas-Ty-Gelli CF37 . . . . . .109 D6
Clas-y-Bedw SA6 . . . . .60 F7
Clas-y-Deri SA14 . . . . .42 A4
Clas-y-Onnen SA6 . . . . . . .67 A3
Clase Dr SA6 . . . . .45 D1
Clas Isan CF14 . . . . .177 C4
Clase Prim Sch SA6 . . . . .68 D8
Clase Rd Morriston SA6 . .46 A1
Swansea SA6 . . . . .69 B8
Clasemont Rd SA6 . . . . . . .45 D2
Claude Pl CF24 . . . . .195 C8
Claude Rd
Barry CF62 . . . . .214 D5
Caerphilly CF83 . . . . .138 A2
Cardiff CF24 . . . . .195 C8
Claude Rd W CF24 . . . . . .214 D4
Claverton Cl CF38 . . . . . . .156 B6
Claymore Pl CF11 . . . . . . .207 A8
Clayton Cres CF37 . . . . . .109 C5
Clayton Rd SA4 . . . . .19 A4
Clayton St
Newport NP19 . . . . .143 D6
Swansea SA1 . . . . .68 D4
Clear Water CF72 . . . . . .155 D7
Clearwater Rd NP19 . . . . .144 D1
Clearway Ct CF14 . . . . . . .177 A4
Cleddau Ct CF83 . . . . .133 C3
Cleddau Cl CF62 . . . . .180 B7
Cledwen Terr CF44 . . . . . . .28 E4
Clees La SA9 . . . . .2 A5
Cleeve Dr CF14 . . . . .177 E7

Cleeves Terr NP4 . . . . .61 E1
Clement St SA10 . . . . .48 F2
Clement Attlee Dr
NP19 . . . . .144 D2
Clement Pl CF62 . . . . .214 C2
Cleppa Park Ind Est
NP10 . . . . .142 A8
Clevedon Ave CF64 . . . . . .216 B4
Clevedon Cl 7 NP19 . . . .143 F6
Clevedon Ct
Cardiff CF37 . . . . .179 C6
Swansea SA2 . . . . .94 F7
Clevedon Rd
Newport NP19 . . . . .144 A6
Tynewydd CF42 . . . . .78 D7
Cleveland Ave SA13 . . . . . .83 A1
Cleveland Dr NP11 . . . . . .115 C1
Clevis Cl CF36 . . . . .183 D8
Clevis Ct CF33 . . . . .165 F6
Clevis Hill CF36 . . . . .183 D8
Clevis La CF36 . . . . .183 D8
Clevisfield Ave CF36 . . . . .183 D8
Cleviston Gdns CF36 . . . .183 C8
Cleviston Pk SA14 . . . . . . .42 A6
Clewer Court Mews 7
NP20 . . . . .142 F4
Clewer Ct 6 NP20 . . . . . .142 F4
Cliff Hill CF64 . . . . .195 C2
Cliff Hill CF64 . . . . .207 B2
Cliff Par CF64 . . . . .207 B2
Cliff Pl CF5 . . . . .194 B6
Cliff Rd
Mountain Ash CF45 . . . . . . .54 D2
Penarth CF64 . . . . .207 B1
Cliff Terr CF37 . . . . .135 D8
Cliff St
Aberdare CF44 . . . . .28 F2
1 Cardiff CF24 . . . . .195 D6
Swansea SA5 . . . . .68 C6
Clifton Cl
CF24 . . . . .195 D6
Clifton Mews 2
CF24 . . . . .195 D6
Clifton Pl NP20 . . . . .143 B4
Clifton Rd NP20 . . . . .143 B4
Clifton Row
CF24 . . . . .108 A2
Clifton Sq NP4 . . . . .62 E3
Clifton St
Aberdare CF44 . . . . .28 F2
Barry CF62 . . . . .214 D3
Cardiff CF24 . . . . .195 D6
Risca NP11 . . . . .141 D8
Treorchy CF42 . . . . .78 D5
Clifton Terr
Aberavon SA12 . . . . .99 B1
1 Blaenavon NP4 . . . . .17 C7
2 Llanelli SA15 . . . . .40 F6
Mumbles SA3 . . . . .123 C4
Clinton Rd CF64 . . . . .207 A2
Clipper Cl NP19 . . . . .117 F1
Clipper Rd CF10 . . . . .195 F3
Clist Rd NP20 . . . . .143 E4
Clive Cres CF64 . . . . .207 B4
Clive La Cardiff CF11 . . . .194 F2
1 Penarth CF64 . . . . .206 F5
Clive Mews CF11 . . . . . . .194 B6
Clive Pl Aberdare CF44 . . . .28 E4
Barry CF62 . . . . .214 F2
Penarth CF64 . . . . .207 B4
Clive Rd Barry CF62 . . . . .214 F3
Cardiff CF5 . . . . .194 B6
St Athan CF62 . . . . .211 D6
Clive St Aberavon SA12 . . .99 B1
Caerphilly CF83 . . . . .138 A2
Cardiff CF11 . . . . .194 F2
Senghenydd CF83 . . . . . . .110 F2
Clive Terr CF37 . . . . .81 F1
Cloda Ave SA10 . . . . .48 C2
Clodien Ave CF14 . . . . . . .177 B4
Cloister Ct CF5 . . . . .193 E4
Cloisters The SA1 . . . . .95 A6
Clomendy Rd NP44 . . . . . .89 E2
Clonakilty Way CF23 . . . . .161 A2
Clordir Rd SA4 . . . . .44 D7
Clos Aderyn Du SA6 . . . . .67 F3
Clos Afon Llan SA4 . . . . . .66 C6
Clos Afon Tywi NP12 . . . . .59 D5
Clos Alaw SA7 . . . . .69 E6
Clos Allt-y-Gog SA4 . . . . .119 C3
Clos Alun CF72 . . . . .153 C3
Clos Alyn CF23 . . . . .160 F1
Clos Aneira SA4 . . . . .67 D3
Clos Aneurin CF37 . . . . . .136 B4
Clos Ar Ddafen SA14 . . . . .41 C5
Clos Avro CF24 . . . . .196 B2
Clos Banc y Berllan
SA4 . . . . .19 D3
Clos Berriew 5
CF14 . . . . .177 B3
Clos Bevan SA4 . . . . .66 A5
Clos Blean Crymlyn
SA7 . . . . .69 F6
Clos Bron Iestyn
CF37 . . . . .109 A1
Clos Bryn Dafydd SA4 . . . .42 F3
Clos Bryn Isaf SA4 . . . . . . .41 D4
Clos Brynafon SA4 . . . . . . .42 F3

Clos Bryngwyn
Garden Village SA4 . . . . . . .43 D1
Gorseinon SA4 . . . . .66 D8
Clos Brynmellyn 1
CF15 . . . . .176 B6
Clos Bwlch SA4 . . . . .66 B6
Clos Bychan CF44 . . . . . . .28 C3
Clos Cadno SA6 . . . . .45 F5
Clos Cadwgan 4
CF38 . . . . .156 A5
Clos Cae Dafydd SA4 . . . .66 A5
Clos Cae Fain SA14 . . . . . .42 B7
Clos Cae Mawr CF82 . . . . .84 F7
Clos Cae Pwll CF46 . . . . . .83 D4
Clos Cae Wal CF15 . . . . . .158 C1
Clos Cae'r Wern
CF38 . . . . .156 E8
Clos Caer Elms SA15 . . . .40 B6
Clos Caersalem SA6 . . . . . .68 C7
Clos Caewal CF5 . . . . .157 C1
Clos Camlas CF37 . . . . . . .109 F2
Clos Caradog CF38 . . . . . .156 D8
Clos Carolyn NP12 . . . . . . .85 C6
Clos Cas-Bach 7
CF3 . . . . .180 A1
Clos Castell Coity
CF31 . . . . .168 C3
Clos Castell Newydd
CF31 . . . . .168 C3
Clos Cefn Bychan
CF15 . . . . .176 B6
Clos Cefn-y-Maes
SA14 . . . . .41 C5
Clos Cefni CF62 . . . . .214 C6
Clos Ceirw NP12 . . . . .35 C6
Clos Celyn SA7 . . . . .69 D6
Clos Cemmaes 6
CF14 . . . . .177 B3
Clos Cenawon SA4 . . . . . . .46 A3
Clos Cerdinen SA4 . . . . . . .43 D3
Clos Cilfwnwr SA4 . . . . . . .44 B3
Clos Cilsaig SA14 . . . . . . .41 C8
Clos Claerwen NP22 . . . . .85 C6
Clos Coed Arian SA12 . . .98 D1
Clos Coed Duon SA12 . . . .86 B8
Clos Coedydafarn
CF14 . . . . .160 C2
Clos Cornel CF14 . . . . .177 B4
Clos Corris 4 CF14 . . . . .177 B3
Clos Crepy CF38 . . . . .135 D1
Clos Cromwell CF14 . . . . .159 C1
Clos Crucywel SA6 . . . . . . .46 A4
Clos Culver CF5 . . . . .193 B3
Clos Cwm Barri
CF62 . . . . .214 B4
Clos Cwm Creunant
CF23 . . . . .160 F1
Clos Cwm Du CF23 . . . . . .160 F1
Clos Cwm Garw
CF83 . . . . .137 D3
Clos Cwm Golau SA4 . . . . .43 A4
Clos Cwningen SA7 . . . . . .47 B1
Clos Cwrt y Carne
SA4 . . . . .43 A4
Clos Cynan SA2 . . . . .93 F8
Clos Cyncoed CF23 . . . . .160 F1
Clos Darran Las
CF15 . . . . .174 E7
Clos Ddu SA5 . . . . .68 B7
Clos Delyth SA4 . . . . .43 C2
Clos Derwen
Cardiff CF23 . . . . .178 B2
Swansea SA2 . . . . .94 F6
Clos Dewi Medi SA15 . . . . .40 E2
Clos Dwerw CF37 . . . . . . .137 C1
Clos Dyfnaint 8
CF3 . . . . .180 A6
Clos Ebol SA5 . . . . .45 F4
Clos Edno CF23 . . . . .178 C3
Clos Eileen Chilcott
SA6 . . . . .69 E6
Clos Enfys CF83 . . . . .137 E1
Clos Eran CF14 . . . . .159 B1
Clos Fach CF14 . . . . .177 C8
Clos Felen SA14 . . . . .220 B8
Clos Ffawydden
CF71 . . . . .189 C8
Clos Gathen SA15 . . . . . . .40 D4
Clos George Morgan
SA6 . . . . .45 E4
Clos Glanllwyn SA4 . . . . . .44 A6
Clos Glanmor SA15 . . . . . .40 C4
Clos Glas Llwch CF38 . . . .77 B5
Clos Golwyg Yr Hafod
NP23 . . . . .8 D4
Clos Gors Fawr SA4 . . . . . .43 C6
Clos Graddfa CF72 . . . . . .111 F7
Clos Granby SA15 . . . . . . .40 E2
Clos Gronw NP23 . . . . .35 C6
Clos Gwili CF83 . . . . .138 D4
Clos Gwastir CF37 . . . . . .137 C1
Clos Gwaun Gledyr
CF83 . . . . .137 D3
Clos Gwendraeth
NP12 . . . . .85 C6
Clos Gwent CF38 . . . . .155 F5
Clos Gwern-y-Mor 15
CF3 . . . . .179 F6
Clos Gwernen SA4 . . . . . . .66 C6
Clos Gwernydd CF83 . . . . .137 D8
Clos Gwlad-Yr-Haf 10
CF3 . . . . .180 A6
Clos Gwy CF23 . . . . .160 F1

Clos Gwylne CF83 . . . . . .137 D1
Clos Gwynedd CF38 . . . .155 F5
Clos Hafodyrynys 18
CF15 . . . . .176 B6
Clos Hafren 6 CF3 . . . . . .180 A6
Clos Healy SA4 . . . . .66 B6
Clos Hector CF24 . . . . . . .196 B7
Clos Helyg SA4 . . . . .66 B5
Clos Hendra SA6 . . . . .22 B2
Clos Hendre CF14 . . . . . . .177 D8
Clos Henfaes CF35 . . . . . .168 B6
Clos Hereford CF72 . . . . .155 D2
Clos Islwyn SA2 . . . . .93 E8
Clos Lancaster CF72 . . . . .155 D2
Clos Leighton Davies
CF38 . . . . .156 A5
Clos Leland CF72 . . . . . . .155 D2
Clos Lindsay CF5 . . . . .193 A3
Clos Llandyfan SA4 . . . . . .42 C2
Clos Llanfair CF5 . . . . . . .205 A6
Clos Llanfihangel
SA14 . . . . .41 B6
Clos Llangefni CF38 . . . . .155 F6
Clos Llanwydden SA4 . . . . .44 A6
Clos Llawhaden
CF62 . . . . .215 A8
Clos Llewellyn CF15 . . . . .174 E6
Clos Llwyn Cwm SA6 . . . . .69 A6
Clos Llwyn y Pwll
NP23 . . . . .8 C4
Clos Llyg SA7 . . . . .70 B8
Clos Madlen SA3 . . . . .67 D4
Clos Maenar 1 CF3 . . . . .179 F6
Clos Maes Isaf SA14 . . . . .42 C7
Clos Maes Yr Ysgol
CF83 . . . . .137 D8
Clos Maes-y-mor 11
CF3 . . . . .180 A6
Clos Mair CF23 . . . . .178 B3
Clos Mancheldowne
CF62 . . . . .214 E4
Clos Marina SA4 . . . . .66 B6
Clos Meifod 1 CF14 . . . .177 B3
Clos Melin Ddwr
CF14 . . . . .160 C2
Clos Melin Mynach
SA4 . . . . .66 C8
Clos Menter CF24 . . . . . . .177 D2
Clos Mynd Yr Afon SA4 . . .42 F7
Clos Morgan Gruffydd
CF83 . . . . .136 F7
Clos Morgan Owen
SA4 . . . . .66 A5
Clos Morganwg SA1 . . . . .95 A8
Clos Myddlyn CF38 . . . . . .155 F5
Clos Nant Bran SA7 . . . . . .47 B1
Clos Nant Coslech
CF23 . . . . .160 E1
Clos Nant Ddu CF23 . . . . .160 E1
Clos Nant Glaswg
CF23 . . . . .160 E1
Clos Nant Mwlan
CF23 . . . . .160 F1
Clos Nant y Cor
CF23 . . . . .160 F1
Clos Nant y Cwm
CF23 . . . . .160 F1
Clos Nant yr Aber
CF83 . . . . .137 F4
Clos Nantydd SA14 . . . . . .41 F5
Clos Newydd CF14 . . . . . .176 D3
Clos Ogney CF61 . . . . . . .209 F7
Clos Onnen SA13 . . . . . . .143 A5
Clos Pandy CF83 . . . . .136 D6
Clos Pant Glas CF83 . . . . .138 D6
Clos Pantycosyn 1
CF3 . . . . .179 F6
Clos Pen y Banc SA4 . . . . .68 C8
Clos Pen y Clawdd 7
CF3 . . . . .179 F6
Clos Penbwl SA4 . . . . .44 C2
Clos Pendderi SA14 . . . . . .41 F5
Clos Penderri SA4 . . . . . . .44 C2
Clos Pengelli SA4 . . . . . . .42 F3
Clos Penglyn CF23 . . . . . .152 E2
Clos Pentyle SA4 . . . . .23 B2
Clos Penyfai SA15 . . . . . . .40 B7
Clos Plas Isaf SA14 . . . . . .42 C7
Clos Powys CF38 . . . . .155 F6
Clos Rhandir SA4 . . . . .65 E8
Clos Rhedyn SA6 . . . . .46 A4
Clos Rhymni SA6 . . . . .46 A4
Clos San Pedr 5
SA15 . . . . .40 D4
Clos Sant Paul SA15 . . . . .40 D4
Clos Sant Teilo SA5 . . . . . .45 B1
Clos Saron SA5 . . . . .67 F3
Clos Sirhowy NP22 . . . . . .84 E8
Clos St Cenydd SA3 . . . . . .228 C2
Clos Synod CF14 . . . . .177 B3
Clos Taf CF5 . . . . .176 F2
Clos Tan-y-cefn
CF31 . . . . .169 B3
Clos Tan-'y-fron
CF31 . . . . .169 B3
Clos Tawe CF62 . . . . .214 C6
Clos Tecwyn CF23 . . . . . . .178 B3
Clos Tir Rwyn CF82 . . . . .111 F7
Clos Tir-y-Pwll NP11 . . . . .87 B2
Clos Tirfferdd SA4 . . . . . . .44 C2
Clos Ton Mawr CF14 . . . .159 C1
Clos Trafle SA4 . . . . .66 C6
Clos Trefin NP12 . . . . .85 F3
Clos Tregare 18 CF3 . . . .179 F6
Clos Ty Bronna CF5 . . . . .193 C7
Clos Ty Clyd CF14 . . . . . .176 E4
Clos Ty Mawr SA4 . . . . . . .44 B2
Clos Ty-Gwyn SA4 . . . . . . .18 F4

Clos Tygwyn
Clydach SA4 . . . . .46 E8
Clos Tyla Bach CF3 . . . . . .66 B6
Clos Tyla Bach CF3 . . . . . .180 B7
Clos Vernon Watkins
SA4 . . . . .43 A4
Clos Waun Ceffyl
CF83 . . . . .83 D4
Clos Waun Fach
CF83 . . . . .137 D1
Clos Waun Wen SA4 . . . . . .45 B1
Clos William CF14 . . . . . . .159 C1
Clos y Banc-yr-Eithin
SA4 . . . . .43 A3
Clos y Berllan 4
CF3 . . . . .180 A6
Clos y Bont Faen
Cwmrhydyceirw SA6 . . . . . .46 A5
Swansea SA6 . . . . .45 F5
Clos y Bryn CF14 . . . . . . .159 A1
Clos y Coed
Llantwit Fardre CF38 . . . . .156 E8
Pen-y-Fai CF31 . . . . .168 D8
Clos y Craig CF14 . . . . . . .159 B1
Clos y Cyrdd NP23 . . . . . . .8 C4
Clos y Deri SA14 . . . . .41 B8
Clos y Dolydd CF38 . . . . . .156 A5
Clos y Dryw CF14 . . . . . . .159 B1
Clos y Ffynnon CF23 . . . . .160 F1
Clos y Gelyn CF23 . . . . . . .179 A7
Clos y Gwadd CF14 . . . . . .159 C1
Clos y Gwalch CF14 . . . . .159 E4
Clos y Gwyddfid
CF15 . . . . .176 A8
Clos y Hebog CF14 . . . . . .159 E4
Clos y Morfa SA4 . . . . .42 F3
Clos y Mynydd
Gorseinon SA4 . . . . .42 F2
Morganstown CF15 . . . . . .176 A7
Clos y Nant
1 Cardiff CF5 . . . . .193 D8
Gorseinon SA4 . . . . .42 F2
Clos y Waun
Cross Hands SA14 . . . . . . .218 A3
Thomastown CF39 . . . . . . .133 A3
Clos Yr Aer CF14 . . . . .177 C8
Clos Yr Aer CF14 . . . . .177 C8
Clos Yr Alarch CF14 . . . . .159 E4
Clos Yr Arad CF83 . . . . . . .137 D1
Clos Yr Efail SA4 . . . . .66 C6
Clos Yr Hafod CF14 . . . . . .177 C8
Clos yr Harbwr CF62 . . . . .214 D2
Clos Yr Onnen SA7 . . . . . . .46 D1
Clos Yr Orsaf SA4 . . . . .69 A8
Clos Yr Wenallt
CF14 . . . . .159 B1
Clos Yr Ysgol SA4 . . . . .70 A7
Clos Ysbyty
Caerphilly CF83 . . . . .137 F3
Neath SA11 . . . . .72 A4
Clos Ysgallen SA4 . . . . . . .69 D6
Clos Ysgol Gymraeg
SA5 . . . . .66 B2
Clos Ystum Taf CF14 . . . .176 E4
Clos-Mabon CF14 . . . . . . .177 B8
Clos-y-Dyfrisi CF14 . . . . . .159 D3
Clos-y-Berllan SA14 . . . . . .41 F5
Clos-y-Betws 8
CF3 . . . . .179 F6
Clos-y-Blaidd CF14 . . . . . .159 E4
Clos-y-Broch CF14 . . . . . .159 E4
Clos-y-Carlwm
CF14 . . . . .159 D3
Clos-y-Cedr CF83 . . . . . . .138 A2
Clos-y-Ceinach
CF14 . . . . .159 E4
Clos-y-Culfor CF3 . . . . . . .121 B7
Clos-y-Cwm SA14 . . . . . . .218 D2
Clos-y-Deri
Llanelli SA14 . . . . .218 D2
Porthcawl CF36 . . . . .182 F8
Clos-y-Derwen
SA14 . . . . .218 B8
Clos-y-Draenog
CF14 . . . . .159 E4
Clos-y-Felin SA18 . . . . . . .219 D7
Clos-y-Gof CF5 . . . . .192 F5
Clos-y-Grug CF36 . . . . . . .182 F8
Clos-y-Gweydd SA4 . . . . . .66 A5
Clos-y-Maerdy SA4 . . . . . .66 C8
Clos-y-pant CF43 . . . . .158 E8
Clos-y-Rhiw CF5 . . . . .193 B3
Clos-y-Talcen CF31 . . . . . .168 D8
Clos-y-Wern CF83 . . . . . . .138 D8
Clos-y-Wiwer CF14 . . . . . .159 E4
Clos-yr- Eirin CF31 . . . . . .168 B6
Clos-yr-Ardd CF14 . . . . . . .159 A1
Clos-yr-Eos CF33 . . . . .165 F6
Clos-yr-Gornant 8
CF3 . . . . .180 A6
Clos-yr-Hendre
SA18 . . . . .218 C6
Clos-yr-Onnen
CF3 . . . . .180 A6
Close The
Aberdare CF44 . . . . .29 A1
Bargoed CF81 . . . . .58 A1
Cardiff CF14 . . . . .177 D2
Cefn Neigcoed CF82 . . . . . .84 F4
Cwmbran NP44 . . . . .116 F8
Gorseinon SA4 . . . . .43 A1
Rhydyfelin CF37 . . . . .136 A6

Close The continued
Sarn CF32 . . . . . . 150 D4
Swansea SA5 . . . . . 45 C2
Cloth Reoda CF14 . . 17 B5
Cloth Hall La CF48 . . 10 A5
Clovelly Ave NP23 . . 14 E5
Clovelly Cres CF3 . . 179 A5
Clovelly Pl SA3 . . . . 122 E6
Clover Ct NP44 . . . . 88 F1
Clover Gr CF5 . . . . 176 C1
Clover Rd CF47 . . . . 10 C4
Club La SA9 . . . . . . 1 F1
Club Rd NP4 . . . . . 62 A6
Club Row Blaina NP13 . 18 E5
 Clydach NP7 . . . . . 9 D6
 Ystrad CF41 . . . . . 79 D3
Club St CF44 . . . . . 53 B8
Clun Ave CF72 . . . . 173 B8
Clun Cres CF72 . . . . 173 B8
Clun Prim Sch SA11 . 226 C4
Clun Terr CF24 . . . . 178 A2
Clwyd CF64 . . . . . . 207 C5
Clwyd -Wen SA4 . . . 66 A5
Clwyd Ave CF24 . . . . 29 E2
Clwyd Com Prim Sch
 SA5 . . . . 68 A4
Clwyd Ho ⑧ CF23 . . 178 C2
Clwyd Rd
 Gwaun-Cae-Gurwen
 SA18 . . . . 220 D6
 Swansea SA5 . . . . 68 B4
Clwyd Way CF62 . . . 211 D7
Clwyd-y-Clap La NP4 39 C4
Clwydyfagwyr CF48 . 225 F1
Clydach Ave
 Ebbw Vale NP23 . . . 7 C5
 Resolven SA11 . . . . 226 E5
Clydach Cl
 Bettws NP20 . . . . 116 C1
 Pontypridd CF37 . . 109 D5
Clydach Inf Sch SA6 . 46 D7
Clydach Jun Sch SA6 46 D8
Clydach Rd
 Craig-Cefn-Parc SA6 22 B2
 Tonypandy CF40 . . 106 C7
 Ynysforgan SA6 . . 46 A2
 Ynystawe SA6 . . . 46 C5
 Ynysybwl CF37 . . . 81 F2
Clydach NP7 . . . . . . 9 D6
Clydach St
 Brynmawr NP23 . . . 8 C5
 Cardiff CF11 . . . . 195 A3
Clydach Terr CF37 . . 81 F2
Clydach War Meml Hospl
 SA6 . . . . 46 D7
Clyde Cl NP12 . . . . 85 D4
Clyde St
 ② Cardiff CF24 . . 195 D5
 Risca NP11 . . . . . 115 A1
Clydesmuir Ind Est
 CF24 . . . . 195 F8
Clydesmuir Rd CF24 195 F7
Clyffard Cres NP20 . 143 B4
Clyffes NP44 . . . . . 89 B3
Clyndu St SA6 . . . . 68 F8
Clyne Cl SA3 . . . . . 93 F1
Clyne Cres SA3 . . . . 93 F1
Clyne Dr SA2 . . . . . 94 A4
Clyne Farm Activties Ctr
 SA3 . . . . 93 F2
Clyne Rd CF82 . . . . 84 F5
Clyne Terr SA11 . . . 226 B3
Clyne Valley Cotts
 SA2 . . . . 94 A4
Clyne Valley Ctry Pk
 SA2 . . . . 94 A4
Clyne Valley La SA2 . 93 E6
Clyne Valley Rd SA2 . 93 E5
Clyne View SA2 . . . . 93 E6
Clyngwyn Rd
 Treherbert CF42 . . . 50 D3
 Ystrad CF41 . . . . . 50 D3
Clynmaes Pl SA5 . . . 67 E6
Clynmawr St NP13 . . 36 A5
Clyro Ct SA1 . . . . . 69 C4
Clyro Pl CF14 . . . . 177 A3
Clytha Cres ⑱ NP20 143 C3
Clytha Inf & Jun Sch
 NP20 . . . . 142 F4
Clytha Park Rd NP20 143 A5
Clytha Sq NP20 . . . . 143 C3
Cnap Llwyd Rd SA6 . 68 D6
Co-operative Cotts
 CF42 . . . . 78 C5
Co-operative St CF41 78 F3
Coach Bach NP22 . . . 6 D1
Coal Pit La CF3 . . . . 162 B4
Coal Plant Control Rd
 CF62 . . . . 211 F1
Coalbrook Rd SA4 . . 43 C5
Coalbrook Valecourt
 NP21 . . . . 15 C7
Coalbrookvale Terr
 NP23 . . . . 115 E6
Coaster Pl CF10 . . . 195 F3
Coates Pl CF37 . . . . 179 D7
Coates Rd CF64 . . . 206 F1
Cobblers Ct ⑪ SA15 40 C7
Cobden Pl
 Abercarn NP11 . . . 114 C4
 ④ Merthyr Tydfil CF47 30 E8
Cobden St
 Abercarn NP11 . . . 114 C4
 Aberdare CF44 . . . 53 C6
Cobham Cl SA4 . . . 43 A5
Cobham Dr SA11 . . . 72 C5

Cobner Cl NP4 . . . . 38 C1
Cobol Rd CF3 . . . . 180 B7
Coburn St CF24 . . . 195 B8
Coch-y-Cwm Rd SA1 . 69 C2
Coch-y-North Rd
 NP4 . . . . 61 E5
Cocker Ave NP44 . . 61 D5
Cockett Rd SA2 . . . 67 D2
Codgers Cnr CF38 . . 156 B7
Coed Arhyd CF5 . . . 192 E4
Coed Arian CF14 . . . 177 B3
Coed Bach
 Barry CF62 . . . . . 214 C7
 Pencoed CF35 . . . 170 C8
Coed Bychan Cres
 CF72 . . . . 153 F3
Coed Cae
 Caerphilly CF83 . . 138 C4
 Cwmbran NP44 . . . 89 C5
 New Tredegar NP24 . 33 E2
Coed Cae Jun Sch
 NP13 . . . . 15 D7
Coed Cae Rd
 Llanelli SA15 . . . . 40 F5
 Llanelli SA15 . . . . 41 A5
Coed Cae Uchaf SA15 40 F5
Coed Cae'r Odyn
 CF35 . . . . 168 B6
Coed Camlas NP4 . . 62 F5
Coed Ceirios
 Cardiff CF14 . . . . 177 B7
 Llansamlet SA7 . . . 46 D1
Coed Celyn Rd SA2 . 94 B4
Coed Cochwyn Ave
 CF14 . . . . 159 E1
Coed Duon View
 NP11 . . . . 86 D5
Coed Edeyrn CF23 . . 178 D4
Coed Eithen ⑤ NP4 . 17 D5
Coed Eva Jun & Inf Schs
 NP44 . . . . 89 B1
Coed Garw NP44 . . . 90 A6
Coed Gelli Parc NP12 58 E4
Coed Gethin CF83 . . 137 E7
Coed Glas NP44 . . . 89 D1
Coed Glas Cty Prim Sch
 CF14 . . . . 177 E8
Coed Glas Rd CF14 . 177 D8
Coed Helyg CF31 . . . 168 B5
Coed Isaf Rd CF37 . 135 A8
Coed Lan SA4 . . . . 65 D1
Coed Leddyn CF83 . . 168 C8
Coed Lee NP44 . . . . 89 C1
Coed Lee Ct NP44 . . 89 C1
Coed Llwyd NP44 . . 17 D6
Coed Main CF83 . . . 138 D4
Coed Marsarnen
 CF71 . . . . 187 A3
Coed Mawr
 Barry CF62 . . . . . 214 C7
 Ystrad Mynach CF82 . 111 E7
Coed Moelfa Rd NP11 87 B3
Coed Mor SA2 . . . . 94 B5
Coed Nant Ho SA6 . . 68 D2
Coed Parc SA12 . . . . 99 D5
Coed Parc Ct CF31 . . 168 E4
Coed Pwll CF83 . . . 138 D4
Coed Terr
 Aberaychan NP4 . . 37 E4
 ⑪ Blaenavon NP4 . . 17 D6
Coed Tymaen CF31 . . 168 C6
Coed y Bronallt SA4 . 19 A5
Coed y Bryn NP12 . . 85 D6
Coed y Cadno CF31 . 168 D8
Coed y Capel CF62 . 214 C7
Coed y Gog CF31 . . . 168 E4
Coed y Llinos CF83 . 137 E1
Coed y Pergwm
 SA11 . . . . 223 C1
Coed-y-Pia CF83 . . . 137 F1
Coed-y-pica CF83 . . 137 A6
Coed-y-Rhaidyr
 SA11 . . . . 224 A3
Coed-yr-Esgob Prim Sch
 CF72 . . . . 155 C4
Coed-yr-Haf CF83 . . 137 E1
Coed-yr-Onen CF83 . 137 E1

Coedbach SA4 . . . . 19 C3
Coedcae
 Ebbw Vale NP23 . . . 7 B4
 Pontardawe SA8 . . . 23 F6
 Ystrad Mynach CF82 . 111 E8
Coedcae Back CF48 . 11 D5
Coedcae Comp Sch
 SA15 . . . . 40 F5
Coedcae Ind Est
 CF21 . . . . 154 F1
Coedcae La
 Pontyclun CF72 . . 172 F8
 Talbot Green CF72 . 155 A1
Coedcae Pl NP4 . . . 62 B6
Coedcae Rd
 Aberthaw CF83 . . . 137 A7
 Porth CF39 . . . . . 108 A2
 Trehafod CF37 . . . 108 B3
Coedcae Row CF48 . 11 D5
Coedcae St CF11 . . . 194 F3
Coedcae Terr NP4 . . 62 B6
Coedcae Wlk NP12 . . 85 D7
Coedcae'r Cwrt ⑫
 CF47 . . . . 30 E8
Coeden Dal CF23 . . . 178 E8
Coedeva Mill NP44 . 116 C8
Coedffaldau SA9 . . . 221 B6
Coedffranc Inf Sch
 SA10 . . . . 70 F7
Coedffranc Prim Sch
 SA10 . . . . 70 F7
Coedglas CF44 . . . . 28 B6
Coedlan Sav 28 B6
Coedpenmaen Rd
 Pontypridd CF37 . . 109 D1
 Pontypridd CF37 . . 109 E2
Coedriglan Dr CF5 . 192 E3
Coedwig Pl SA5 . . . 68 A3
Coedygric Rd NP4 . . 17 D5
Coedygric Rd NP4 . . 62 E3
Coedylan Comp Sch The
 CF37 . . . . 109 F6
Coedymoeth Rd CF81 58 B6
Coegnant CF31 . . . . 169 B7
Coegnant Cotts
 CF34 . . . . 102 A7
Coegnant Rd
 Maesteg CF34 . . . 102 A6
 Maesteg CF34 . . . 102 B7
Coelbren Cty Prim Sch
 SA10 . . . . 222 F6
Coety Prim Sch
 CF35 . . . . 169 D8
Coffins Row CF48 . . 10 D1
Cog Rd CF64 . . . . . 216 B6
Cogan Ct CF64 . . . . 206 E6
Cogan Hill CF64 . . . 206 F6
Cogan Pill Rd CF64 206 E6
Cogan Prim Sch
 CF64 . . . . 206 E5
Cogan Sta CF64 . . . 206 D6
Cogan Terr CF24 . . . 195 A7
Coggins Cl CF83 . . . 137 D1
Coigne Terr CF63 . . 215 B5
Coity Cl CF3 . . . . . 180 A7
Coity Cres CF31 . . . 169 C3
Coity Rd CF31 . . . . 168 F4
Coity Terr NP4 . . . . 17 C6
Colbourne Rd CF38 156 A6
Colbourne Terr SA1 . 68 C4
Colbourne Wlk ⑧
 CF11 . . . . 194 D5
Colbren Sq SA10 . . . 70 D5
Colchester Ave CF23 178 E1
Colchester Ct CF23 178 D1
Colchester Factory Est
 CF23 . . . . 195 E8
Colcot Prim Sch
 CF62 . . . . 204 E1
Colcot Rd CF62 . . . 214 D7
Cold Bath Rd NP18 118 B2
Cold Knap Way CF62 214 C1
Cold Store The NP44 90 A1
Cold Stores Rd CF10 195 C1
Coldbrook Rd E
 CF63 . . . . 215 C8
Coldbrook Rd W
 CF63 . . . . 215 C8
Coldra Est NP18 . . . 144 F7
Coldra Rd
 Blaenrhondda CF42 . 50 D4
 Newport NP20 . . . 143 A3
 Treherbert CF42 . . 50 D4
Coldra The NP18 . . . 144 F7
Coldra Wood Dr
 NP18 . . . . 144 E8
Coldstream Cl NP44 . 90 A5
Coldstream St SA15 . 40 C6
Coldstream Terr
 CF11 . . . . 194 F5
Cole Ct CF83 . . . . . 138 D4
Coleford Dr CF3 . . . 180 A6
Colenso Terr
 Rhymney NP22 . . . 12 E5
 ③ Aberdare CF44 . . 53 A7
Coleridge Ave CF64 206 F4
Coleridge Cl CF31 . . 168 C6
Coleridge Cres
 Barry CF62 . . . . . 214 E8
 Swansea SA2 . . . . 93 F8
Coleridge Gdns
 CF83 . . . . 139 C6
Coleridge Gn NP44 . 89 C2
Coleridge Rd
 Aberbargoed CF81 . 58 B4
 ⑬ Aberdare CF44 . 52 A3
 Abergwili SA13 . . . 76 C5
 Abertillery NP13 . . 64 F3
 Bargoed CF81 . . . 58 A1
 Bedlau CF38 . . . . 156 A2
 Newport NP19 . . . 37 E5
Colesliil Terr SA15 . 40 C5
Colhugh Cl CF61 . . . 209 F6
Colhugh Pk CF61 . . 209 F5
Colhugh St CF61 . . . 209 F5

Colin Way CF5 . . . . 193 E6
Collard Cres CF62 . 214 F7
College Cl
 Bridgend CF31 . . . 169 A3
 ⑥ Cardiff CF14 . . 177 B4
 Pontypridd CF37 . . 135 F5
College Cres NP18 . 118 B3
College Fields Cl
 CF62 . . . . 214 E5
College Gdns CF81 . 209 F6
College Glade NP18 118 A4
College Gn SA13 . . . 125 F3
College Hill SA15 . . 40 E5
College Pl CF62 . . . 214 E5
College Rd
 Barry CF64 . . . . . 214 E5
 Caerleon NP18 . . . 118 B3
 Ogmore Vale CF32 104 E2
 Pengam NP12 . . . 85 B7
 Pontllanfraith NP12 . 85 F4
 Pontypool NP4 . . . 62 C6
 Pontypool NP4 . . . 62 E3
College Sq SA9 . . . 2 F8
College St
 Aberdare CF44 . . . 29 B2
 Llantwit Major CF61 209 F6
 Seven Sisters SA10 . 222 C3
 Tredegar NP22 . . . 13 E7
College Terr ⑨ NP4 . 38 A1
College Way Cardiff Rd
 CF37 . . . . 135 F5
Collenna Rd CF39 . 133 C6
Collier Row NP19 . . 143 D6
Colliers Row NP24 . . 33 D3
Colliers Way (Ffordd y
 Glowyr) CF40 . . . 106 E7
Colliers' Row NP23 . 7 D1
Colliery Rd
 Bedwas CF83 . . . 138 E7
 Llanbradach CF83 . 111 F4
Colliery St CF37 . . . 108 D2
Collingwood Ave ⑪
 NP19 . . . . 144 B4
Collingwood Cl
 NP19 . . . . 144 A4
Collingwood Cres ⑧
 NP19 . . . . 144 A4
Collins Cl
 Newport NP20 . . . 142 E2
 Treherbert CF42 . . 50 F1
Collins Row NP22 . . 12 C7
Collins St SA11 . . . 71 C4
Collins Terr CF37 . . 109 E3
Colliwaul Pl CF24 . 195 D4
Collwyn Rd CF33 . . 148 B1
Collwyn St CF39 . . . 154 D8
Colne St NP19 . . . . 143 D5
Colonel Road SA18 219 C6
Colston Ave SA1 . . . 69 B1
Colston Ct NP19 . . . 144 A3
Colston Pl NP19 . . . 144 A3
Colts Foot Cl NP20 143 A6
Coltshill Dr SA3 . . . 122 F5
Colum Ct CF10 . . . 194 F8
Colum Dr CF10 . . . 194 F8
Colum Pl CF10 . . . 194 F8
Colum Rd CF10 . . . 194 F8
Colum Terr CF10 . . 194 F7
Columbia Row ⑫
 SA15 . . . . 40 D5
Columbus Cl CF62 215 A8
Columbus Wlk CF10 195 B4
Column St
 Barry CF64 . . . . . 215 E6
 Treorchy CF42 . . . 78 D6
Colwill Rd CF14 . . . 177 B2
Colwinstone Cl CF14 177 A3
Colwinstone St CF14 177 A3
Colwyn Ave SA1 . . . 65 C5
Colwyn Rd
 Ton Pentre CF41 . . 79 A2
Coly Row CF46 . . . 55 F8
Comet St CF24 . . . 195 C6
Comfrey Cl
 ⑪ Cardiff CF3 . . 180 A8
 Newport NP20 . . . 143 A6
Comin Cty Jun Mix Sch
 CF44 . . . . 28 F3
Comin Inf Sch CF44 . 28 F3
Commerce Pl CF44 . 53 C7
Commercial Bldgs
 Blackwood NP12 . . 59 B2
 Port Talbot SA13 . . 125 B7
Commercial Cl NP47 . 10 C3
Commercial Pl
 ⑤ Cwmbran NP44 . 89 E5
 Mountain Ash CF45 . 22 B6
 Pontycymer CF32 . 103 E3
Commercial Rd
 Abercarn NP11 . . . 37 E1
 Aberycynon NP4 . . 37 E5
 Abertillery NP13 . . 40 A4
 Barry CF63 . . . . . 215 A6
 Cwmfelinfach NP11 113 A4
 Machen CF83 . . . 140 B6
 Newbridge NP11 . . 60 A1
 Newport NP20 . . . 143 C3
 Port Talbot SA13 . . 125 C6
 Resolven SA11 . . . 226 D5
 Rhydyfro SA8 . . . 23 C8
Commercial St
 Aberbargoed CF81 . 58 B4
 ④ Aberdare CF44 . 29 B2
 Abergwynfi SA13 . . 76 C5
 Bargoed CF81 . . . 58 A1
 Bedlinog CF46 . . . 56 A7
 ⑧ Blaenavon NP4 . . 17 C6
 Cwmbran NP44 . . . 89 E2

Commercial St continued
 Cwmbran NP44 . . . 89 E5
 Cwmfelinfach NP11 113 A6
 Ebbw Vale NP23 . . 14 D6
 Ferndale CF43 . . . 80 A7
 Gelligaer CF82 . . . 84 D7
 Glyncorrwg SA13 . 227 C2
 Llantrisant CF72 . . 155 D3
 Llanhilleth NP13 . . 209 F6
 Maesteg CF34 . . . 102 A3
 Mountain Ash CF45 . 54 D3
 Nant-y-Moel CF32 104 E6
 Neath SA11 . . . . . 71 E8
 Nelson CF46 . . . . 83 E3
 Newbridge NP24 . . 33 E3
 Newport NP20 . . . 143 C4
 Ogmore Vale CF32 104 E2
 Pengam NP12 . . . 85 B7
 Pontllanfraith NP12 . 85 F4
 Pontypool NP4 . . . 62 C6
 Pontypridd NP4 . . 62 E3
 Pyle CF33 . . . . . 148 D2
 Risca NP11 . . . . . 115 A1
 Senghenydd CF83 . 110 F2
 Seven Sisters SA10 . 222 C3
 Tredegar NP22 . . . 13 E7
 Ystalyfera SA9 . . . 2 B6
 Ystrad Mynach CF82 . 84 F1
 Ystradgynlais SA9 . 1 F1
Commercial Terr
 CF44 . . . . 83 B6
Commerical St CF48 . 11 A4
Commercial La NP12 . 58 D7
Commin Rd CF81 . . 58 B6
Commin Rd CF81 . . 58 B6
Common App ⑪
 SA18 . . . . 156 A6
Common Rd CF37 . 109 D1
Commonwealth Rd
 NP23 . . . . 7 D6
Compass Cl SA10 . 195 E1
Compass Row SA8 . 23 D5
Compass St SA1 . . . 68 C3
Compton Ave SA10 . 70 C3
Compton Cl NP10 . 142 B6
Compton Rd
 Skewen SA10 . . . 71 A7
 Tonypandy CF40 . . 106 E5
Compton St CF11 . . 194 E4
Concorde Dr CF29 . 133 E5
Conduit Pl SA13 . . 125 C5
Conduit St SA13 . . 125 D7
Coney Beach Amusement
 Pk CF36 . . . . . . 183 A6
Conifer Cl NP18 . . . 117 E2
Coniston Cl ⑪ NP19 143 F8
Coniston Ho SA2 . . 89 B3
Coniston Rise CF44 29 E1
Coniston Wlk SA2 . . 94 D7
Connaught Cl CF36 165 F2
Connaught Ho CF11 194 E6
Connaught Rd CF24 195 C8
Connaught St SA13 125 C8
Consort St SA45 . . . 54 B1
Constable Dr NP19 144 A8
Constable Ho ⑧ SA12 98 D1
Constance St NP19 143 D7
Constant Cl CF11 . . 207 A8
Constant Rd SA13 . 125 C6
Constant Row NP11 115 A2
Constantine Cl CF40 107 A3
Constantine St CF40 107 A3
Constellation St
 CF24 . . . . 195 D6
Constitution Hill
 Cowbridge CF71 . . 188 E1
 Swansea SA1 . . . 95 B7
Convent St SA1 . . . 68 C1
Conway Cl CF38 . . 103 E6
Conway Ct
 Cwmbran NP44 . . . 89 E4
 Dinas Powys CF64 . 206 C3
 Pontypridd CF37 . . 109 C5
 Swansea SA5 . . . 68 A4
Conway Cres CF38 . 135 F2
Conway Croft NP19 144 A4
Conway Ct
 Blackwood NP12 . . 58 D1
 Caerphilly CF83 . . 137 D4
 Swansea SA5 . . . 68 A4
Conway Dr
 Aberdare CF44 . . . 29 E1
 Barry CF62 . . . . . 214 C6
Conway Gr CF48 . . 225 F1
Conway Rd
 Abertillery NP11 . . 194 D7
 Cardiff CF11 . . . . 194 D7
 Newport NP19 . . . 144 A4
 Pontypool NP4 . . . 62 E3
 Swansea SA5 . . . 68 A4
 Treorchy CF42 . . . 78 D6
Conway Sac ②
 NP19 . . . . 144 A4
Conway Terr NP44 . 89 F5
Conybeare Rd
 Cardiff CF5 . . . . 194 B7
 Sully CF64 . . . . . 216 B5
Cook Cl CF62 . . . . 54 D2
Cook Rd CF62 . . . 205 A1
Cook Rees Ave SA11 . 71 A6
Coolgreany Cl NP20 117 A1
Coolgreany Cres
 NP20 . . . . 117 A1
Cools Cl NP23 . . . 33 B6
Comassie St NP20 . 143 D1
Coombe-Tennant Ave
 SA10 . . . . 70 D7
Coombes Rd SA10 . 70 E7
Coopers SA18 . . . . 218 E5
Coopers Cl NP18 . . 119 E1
Coopers La CF71 . . 188 C2

Coopers Pl CF83 . . . 137 E6
Coopers Rd SA18 . . 218 E5
Coopers Way CF72 . 155 C3
Coopers Yd ⑬ CF10 195 A2
Copleston Rd CF14 . 177 A4
Copplestone St CF45 54 F
Copley Cl SA3 . . . . 122 C
Copley Lodge SA3 . 122 C
Copley St CF45 . . . . 54 F
Copper Beech Cl
 NP18 . . . . 117 —
Copper St CF24 . . . 195 D
Copperfield Ct ❶ . . .
Copperfield Dr CF14 159 F
Copperworks Prim Sch
 SA15 . . . . 40 D
Copperworks Rd
 SA15 . . . . 40 D
Coppice The CF38 . 136 A
Coppins The
 Cardiff CF14 . . . . 160 —
 Newport NP20 . . . 117 —
Copse Cl CF48 . . . 10 E
Copse Wlk CF23 . . . 161 A
Copthorne Way CF5 192 F
Cora St CF63 . . . . 215 A
Coral Ct SA12 . . . . 98 E
Corban Ct NP13 . . . 36 F
Corbett Cres CF83 138 A
Corbett Gr CF83 . . . 137 F
Corbett Rd
 Cardiff CF10 . . . . 194 —
 Llandough CF64 . . 206 —
Corbett St
 Ogmore Vale CF32 104 —
 Treherbert CF42 . . 51 A
Corbetts La CF83 . . 138 A
Corelli St NP19 . . . 143 C
Coriander Cl NP20 . 143 A
Corinthian Cl CF64 206 —
Cork Dr CF23 . . . . 161 A
Cork Ho ❶ SA1 . . . 95 —
Cormorant Cl
 Cardiff CF3 . . . . 179 —
 Llanelli SA15 . . . . 40 —
Cormorant Way
 Mumbles SA3 . . . 122 —
 Newport NP10 . . . 163 —
Corn St NP20 . . . . 143 —
Cornbrook Rd NP20 116 —
Corneli Jun Sch
 CF33 . . . . 165 —
Cornelly Cl CF14 . . 177 —
Cornelly St CF14 . . 177 —
Corner House St CF44 28 —
Cornerswell La ❸
 CF64 . . . . 206 —
Cornerswell Pl CF64 206 —
Cornerswell Rd CF64 206 —
Cornfield Cl CF14 . . 159 —
Cornfield Rise CF83 138 —
Cornflower Cl CF14 160 —
Cornish Cl CF11 . . 195 A
Cornish Pl SA15 . . . 40 —
Corntown Rd CF35 . 186 —
Cornwall Cl CF11 . . 194 —
Cornwall Ho ❹ SA12 98 —
Cornwall Pl SA1 . . . 123 —
Cornwall Rd
 Barry CF62 . . . . . 214 —
 Newport NP19 . . . 143 —
 Rhoose CF62 . . . . 214 —
 Tonypandy CF40 . . 107 —
Cornwall St CF44 . . 194 —
Cornwall Terr CF62 214 —
Cornwall St CF11 . . 194 —
Cornwood Cl CF5 . . 179 —
Coronation Ave
 Cymmer SA13 . . . 75 —
 Resolven SA11 . . . 226 —
Coronation Cres
 Fochriw CF81 . . . . 32 —
 Newbridge NP11 . . 87 —
Coronation Ho SA12 124 —
Coronation Pl
 Abercarn NP11 . . . 114 —
 Aberfan CF48 . . . 55 —
Coronation Rd
 Caerphilly NP12 . . 85 —
 Cardiff CF14 . . . . 177 —
 Evanstown CF39 . . 132 —
 ⑬ Glanaman SA18 220 —
 Llanelli SA15 . . . . 40 —
 Pont Rhyd-y-cyff CF34 128 —
Coronation St
 Aberkenfig CF32 . . 150 —
 Merthyr Vale SA13 . 36 —
 Barry CF63 . . . . . 215 —
 Bedwas CF83 . . . 139 —
 Blaina NP13 . . . . 115 —
 Bryn SA13 . . . . . 100 —
 Ogmore Vale CF32 104 —
 Pontlottyn CF81 . . 109 —
 Porth CF39 . . . . . 107 —
 Rhymney NP22 . . . 12 —
 Senghenydd CF83 . 110 —
Coronet Way SA6 . . 69 —
Corporation Ave SA15 40 —
Corporation Cl SA15 40 —
Corporation Rd
 Aberavon SA12 . . . 98 F1

Corporation Rd continued
Cardiff CF11 ....195 A2
Loughor SA4 ....42 E1
Newport NP19 .....143 E4
Newport NP20 .....164 F8
Swansea SA5 ....67 C4
Corporation St CF47 .10 F2
Corpus Christi RC High Sch CF23 ....116 B6
Corris NP44 ....89 F6
Corrwg Ct SA13 ....227 C1
Corrymore Ho SA2 .94 F6
Corvette Ct CF10 ..195 C3
Corwen Cres CF14 .177 A3
Cory Cres CF5 .....191 F5
Cory Pk NP44 ......117 B6
Cory Pl CF11 ....207 A8
Cory St
Resolven SA11 ....226 D5
Swansea SA2 .....94 D6
Cory Way CF63 .....215 A3
Coryton Cl CF14 ...176 F7
Coryton Cres CF14 .176 F7
Coryton Ct CF14 ...176 E7
Coryton Halt CF14 .176 F6
Coryton Prim Sch CF14 ....176 E7
Coryton Rise CF14 .176 E7
Cosheston Rd CF5 .176 D1
Cosmeston Dr CF64 .217 A7
Cosmeston Lakes Ctry Pk CF64 ....216 F7
Cosmeston Medieval Village CF64 ......216 F6
Cosmeston St CF24 .177 F1
Cosslett Pl CF11 ...195 A2
Cosy Pl 2 NP23 ....8 B4
Cot Farm Circ NP19 .144 F6
Cot Farm Cl NP19 ..144 F6
Cot Farm Wlk NP19 .144 F6
Cot Hill NP18 ......145 A6
Cotfarm Gdns NP19 .144 F6
Cotman Cl NP19 ....144 F6
Cotswold Ave CF14 .160 B3
Cotswold Cl
Newport NP19 ....144 C6
Swansea SA5 .....67 E3
Cotswold Ct CF23 ..116 B6
Cotswold Rise CF63 .215 B6
Cotswold Way
Newport NP19 ....144 C6
Risca NP11 ....115 D2
Cottage Cl CF14 ...159 F2
Cottage Gdns CF32 .167 F4
Cotterells Hos NP44 .17 D6
Cottesmore Way CF72 ....155 E2
Cotton Ct SA11 ....71 D5
Cottrell Rd
2 Cardiff CF14 ...177 B4
Cardiff CF24 .....195 C8
Cottrell Sq CF63 ..215 A8
Cottrell St CF48 ...55 D2
Coulson Cl 27 NP20 .143 C3
Council Hos
Boverton CF61 ....210 C6
Cwmbran NP44 ...89 E2
Council St
Ebbw Vale NP23 ..7 C1
Merthyr Tydfil CF47 .10 D1
Countess Terr SA13 .125 C7
Coundley Cl NP12 ..85 B5
Countess Pl CF44 ..206 F3
Countisbury Ave CF3 ....179 C7
Country View CF37 .136 C4
County Hospl NP4 ..62 E4
Court Cl Cardiff CF14 .177 C3
Llantwit Major CF61 .209 F7
Court Colman Flats CF32 ....104 E7
Court Colman St CF32 ....104 E7
Court Cres
Aberthin CF71 ....189 C3
Bassaleg NP10 ...142 B2
Court Dr CF71 .....188 C7
Court Farm Cl NP44 .117 A8
Court Farm Rd NP44 .117 A8
Court Gdns NP10 ..141 F6
Court House St CF37 .135 C8
Court Isha CF32 ...167 B2
Court La SA6 ....213 B5
Court Mdw NP18 ...145 C8
Court Mews 4 CF63 .215 B6
Court Newton 3 CF63 ....215 B6
Court Pl 3 CF40 ...106 E6
Court Rd Barry CF63 .215 A5
Barry CF63 ....215 B8
Bridgend CF31 ....168 F4
Caerphilly CF83 ..137 F4
Caerphilly CF83 ..137 F5
Cardiff CF11 ......194 F4
Cardiff CF14 ......177 C3
Cwmbran NP44 ...90 A1
Court Rise 8 NP4 ..17 D7
Court Sch The CF14 .160 A1
Court St
Maesteg CF34 ....149 C3
1 Merthyr Tydfil CF47 .30 E8
Tonypandy CF40 ..106 D6
Court Terr
Cefn Cribwr CF32 .149 C3
11 Merthyr Tydfil CF47 .30 E8
Court The
Bridgend CF35 ....169 F4
Cardiff CF14 ......160 B4
4 Cardiff CF24 ...195 C8
Corntown CF35 ...186 C7

Court The continued
Llanvravon NP44 ...117 B8
Cramic Way SA13 ..125 B8
Court Vale NP18 ...145 C8
Court Wlk SA10 ....71 C8
Courtenay Cl CF3 ..179 D7
Courtenay Rd
8 Barry CF63 .....215 B6
Cardiff CF24 ......195 C6
Llanelli SA15 .....40 C6
Courtenay St SA1 ..68 C2
Courtfield Cl NP10 .141 E6
Courtis Rd CF3 ....193 B5
Courtland Bldgs SA13 ....125 B8
Courtland Pl SA13 .125 B8
Courtland Terr 8 CF47 ....10 E1
Courtlands CF62 ...214 C3
Courtlands The 7 NP44 ....89 B3
Courtlands Way SA5 .67 E5
Courtney St NP19 ..143 D6
Courtyard The
Cardiff CF10 .....163 D6
Porthcawl CF36 ..165 D3
Courtyard Units SA10 .70 D5
Courtybella Gdns NP20 ....143 D2
Courtybella Terr
Newport NP20 ....143 B2
Newport NP20 ....143 D2
Cove Ho 4 SA12 ...98 D1
Cove Rd SA12 .....98 D1
Covney St CF24 ....96 B6
Coverack Rd NP19 .143 E4
Covert Wlk NP44 ..89 B1
Cowbridge By-Pass CF71 ....174 D8
Cowbridge Comp Sch
Cowbridge CF71 ..188 E2
Cowbridge CF71 ..189 A2
Cowbridge Rd
Bridgend CF31 ....169 A2
Pontyclun CF72 ..172 E4
St Athan CF62 ....211 D7
Talbot Green CF72 .155 B1
Talbot Green CF72 .155 B2
Cowbridge Rd E
Cardiff CF11 ......194 F5
Cardiff CF5 ....194 A6
Cardiff CF5 ....193 C4
Cowbridge Rd W CF5 ....193 C4
Cowbridge St 8 SA13 ....215 B7
Cowell Prec 8 SA15 .40 D5
Cowell Rd SA18 ...220 C2
Cowell St SA15 ....40 D5
Cowper Cl
Newport NP20 ....142 E2
Penarth CF64 .....206 F4
Swansea SA2 .....93 F7
Cowper Ct 6 CF24 .195 C7
Cowper Pl CF24 ...195 C7
Cowshed La NP10 .142 A2
Cowslip Cl CF23 ..161 A1
Cowslip Dr CF64 ..206 E5
Coychurch Rd
Bridgend CF31 ....169 B3
Pencoed CF35 ...170 B5
Coychurch Rise CF63 ....215 A8
Coychurch Road Gdns CF31 ....168 F3
Coytrahen Cl CF31 .169 B6
Crabapple Cl CF47 .10 D5
Crabtree Rd CF40 .107 A5
Crabtree Wlk CF48 .10 A6
Crack Hill CF31, CF35 .186 E7
Craddock St CF11 .194 E5
Cradoc Rd CF14 ...177 C4
Cradock St
Llanelli SA15 .....40 D4
Swansea SA1 .....95 C7
Cragside Cl 2 CF3 .179 F6
Craig Castell CF15 .158 F2
Craig Cres CF39 ...107 D2
Craig Nedd SA11 ..227 C8
Craig Rd
Briton Ferry SA11 .71 C1
Cwmbran NP44 ...89 A3
Craig Rhymni NP24 .33 D4
Craig View Terr NP4 .37 D6
Craig y Darren CF44 .28 C3
Craig y Fan Terr SA13 .75 C5
Craig y Mynydd CF39 ....133 A3
Craig y Nos NP22 ..6 F1
Craig Yr Allt CF14 .159 B1
Craig-cefn-parc Cty Prim Sch SA6 ....22 B4
Craig-fryn Terr CF32 ....104 E7
Craig-y-Bwldan SA2 .93 E8
Craig-y-Haul Dr CF3 ....162 C3
Craig-y-Hendre CF46 .56 B7
Craig-y-Llyn Cres CF44 ....29 E2
Craig-y-Parc Sch CF15 ....175 B6
Craig-yr-Eos Ave CF32 ....184 D3
Craig-yr-Eos Rd CF37 ....109 D5
Craiglas CF72 ......83 D3
Craiglas Cres NP12 .85 C8
Craiglee Dr CF10 ..195 B4

Craigmuir Rd CF24 .195 F7
Craigwen SA14 ....41 E4
Craig-y Terr SA13 .125 B8
Cranbourne Way CF23 ....160 E1
Cranbrook St CF24 .195 B7
Crane St NP4 ......62 C6
Cranfield Ct SA5 ..67 E5
Cranford CF14 .....160 A2
Cranham Ho NP44 .89 C2
Cranleigh Rise CF3 .179 A4
Cranmer Ct
Cardiff CF5 ....194 A8
Swansea SA5 .....67 E5
Cranwell Cl 4 CF5 .176 E2
Craven Wlk CF44 ..217 B8
Crawford Cl CF38 .156 B6
Crawford Dr CF23 .161 A1
Crawford Gn SA12 .98 D7
Crawford Rd SA12 .98 C7
Crawley St NP19 ..143 D6
Crawley Trad Est
Crawley Cl CF14 ..159 E3
Crawshay Ct
Llantwit Major CF61 .210 B7
Mumbles SA3 ....122 F3
Crawshay Dr CF61 .210 B7
Crawshay Ho CF48 .10 A3
Crawshay Rd CF40 .107 A4
Crawshay St
Cardiff CF10 .....195 A4
Hirwaun CF44 ....27 D8
Treorchy CF41 ....79 A4
Ynysybwl CF37 ..109 A8
Crediton Rd CF3 ..179 C6
Creidiol Rd SA1 ...95 C8
Creigiau Prim Sch CF15 ....174 D8
Cres The CF44 .....28 C4
Crescent CF5 ......193 A2
Crescent Cl CF71 .188 F1
Crescent Ct
Cardiff CF23 .....178 D6
4 Newport NP19 .143 F6
Crescent Rd NP20 .142 E1
Crescent Rd
Caerphilly CF83 .138 A3
Gwaun-Cae-Gurwen SA18 ....220 D6
Newport NP19 ...143 F6
Risca NP11 ....114 E3
Sarn CF32 ....150 E4
Crescent St CF48 ..55 D4
Crescent The
Aberkenfig CF32 .150 C4
Barry CF62 ....214 B5
Bedwas CF83 ....138 E6
Bridgend CF31 ...169 A4
Caerphilly CF83 ..137 E4
Cardiff CF5 ....193 D7
Cardiff CF5 ....194 B8
Crynant SA10 ....226 A7
Cwmbran NP44 ..89 D1
Ebbw Vale NP23 .14 C8
Gorslas SA14 ....218 C8
Machen CF83 ....139 F7
Maesycwmmer CF82 .85 B1
Nantyglo NP23 ..15 D7
Swansea SA5 .....67 F5
Tredegar NP22 ...6 C1
Cresselly Villas CF5 .54 E3
Cressfield Dr CF23 .161 B1
Cresswell Cl CF3 ..180 A7
Cresswell Ct CF62 .214 D4
Cressy Rd CF23 ...178 C1
Crest Acre Cl SA3 .122 E5
Creswell Ct SA6 ...68 D8
Creswell Rd
Neath SA11 ....71 E7
Swansea SA6 ....68 D8
Creunant Prim Sch SA10 ....226 A8
Cribarth SA9 ......222 E8
Cribb's Row SA11 ..71 E8
Cribbwr Sq CF33 ..148 C1
Cribyn-Du St CF37 .109 A8
Criccieth Cl NP12 ..58 D1
Criccieth Ct CF64 .206 C4
Criccieth Gr CF48 .225 E1
Criccieth Pl SA1 ..69 C5
Criccieth Rd CF3 ..179 C3
Crichton St
Treherbert CF42 ..51 A1
Treorchy CF42 ...78 C7
Crickhowell Pl SA1 .69 C5
Crickhowell Rd CF3 .179 F6
Crickhowell Wlk CF3 .179 F7
Cricklewood Cl CF31 ....168 C6
Crimson Ave SA12 .98 B2
Crimson Cl SA12 ..98 B2
Crimson Ct SA12 ..98 B2
Crindau Jun & Inf Sch NP20 ....143 C7
Crindau Rd NP20 ..143 B8
Cripps Ave NP22 ..13 D5
Crockett Pl CF37 ..109 A2
Crockherbtown La CF10 ....195 A6
Croes-y-Pant La NP4 .39 C5
Croescadarn Rd CF23 ....161 A1
Croescadarn Rd CF23 ....160 F1
Croescade Rd CF38 .156 B8
Croeserw Inf Sch SA13 ....75 D3
Croeserw Prim Sch
New Tredegar NP24 .33 F2

Croesffyrdd SA9 ...2 D7
Croespenmaen Ind Est NP11 ....59 D1
Croesty Prim Sch CF35 ....170 D7
Croeswen NP44 ...116 F8
Croesyceiliog By-Pass NP44 ....90 B5
Croesyceiliog Comp Sch NP44 ....90 A4
Croesyceiliog Jun Sch NP44 ....90 A5
Croesyceiliog North Road Inf Sch NP44 .....90 A5
Croft-y-Genau Rd CF5 ....175 F2
Croffta CF64 ....206 A2
Croft Gdn CF71 ...37 A5
Croft Gdns CF64 ..216 A5
Croft Goch Gdns CF35 ....148 C2
Croft Goch Rd CF35 .148 C2
Croft La CF32 .....197 A8
Croft Rd SA11 ....71 E8
Croft St
Cowbridge CF71 .188 F1
New Tredegar NP24 .33 E4
Swansea SA1 .....95 D8
Croft Terr
Cowbridge CF71 .188 F1
2 Swansea SA5 ..68 C4
Croft The
Bettws CF32 .....129 D3
Llangeinor CF32 .130 B4
Loughor SA4 .....42 D1
Neath Abbey SA10 .71 B8
Crofta CF14 ....160 B1
Croften Mede NP44 .89 B1
Croftfield Cres SA3 .122 E5
Crofton Dr SA12 ..98 E6
Crofts Cnr 3 NP44 .89 B3
Crofts St CF24 ....195 C7
Crofty Ind Est SA4 .64 B3
Crole St SA1 ......95 B7
Cromer St CF24 ...53 E4
Cromwell Ave SA10 .48 E2
Cromwell Ct 6 NP19 ....144 A4
Cromwell Pl 8 NP44 .89 E5
Cromwell Rd
Cardiff CF14 .....177 D4
Neath SA10 ......48 E2
Newport NP19 ...143 F4
Risca NP11 ....114 E3
Cromwell St
Aberdare CF44 ...36 B5
Merthyr Tydfil CF47 .10 D2
Swansea SA1 .....95 B7
Cromwell Street Bnglws NP11 ....114 D4
Cronin Ave SA12 ..124 E7
Crook Hill (lower) NP13 ....36 B7
Crosby Yd CF31 ...168 E6
Cross Acre SA3 ...122 E7
Cross Blanche St CF48 ....11 C5
Cross Brook St CF42 .50 D5
Cross Common Rd CF64 ....206 C1
Cross Francis St CF48 .11 A5
Cross Hands Bsns Pk SA14 ....218 B7
Cross Hands Cty Prim Sch CF48 ....218 A8
Cross Houlson St CF48 ....11 B5
Cross Inn Rd CF72 .83 D3
Cross Inn Bldgs 9 SA18 ....219 B7
Cross Inn Rd CF72 .155 E3
Cross King St CF48 .11 A7
Cross Mardy St CF47 .11 A1
Cross Margaret St CF47 ....10 C2
Cross Morgan St 5 CF47 ....10 D2
Cross Morlais St CF48 .11 A5
Cross Pl CF24 .....177 E1
Cross Rd
Dyffryn Cellwen SA10 .223 A5
Llanelli SA15 ....40 D6
Cross Row 1 CF40 .106 F3
Cross St
Aberaman CF44 ..82 C5
14 Aberdare CF44 .29 A1
Aberfan CF48 ....55 C4
Aberystwan NP4 .37 E6
Abertillery NP13 .36 B5
Abertridwr CF83 .137 A7
Bargoed CF81 ....58 A2
Bargoed CF81 ....58 A4
Barry CF63 ....215 A5
Bedwas CF83 ....138 E6
Blaenavon NP4 ..17 C6
Blaengarw CF32 .103 D7
Blaina NP13 .....15 E5
4 Briton Ferry SA11 .71 E8
Caerleon NP18 ..118 C2
Cardiff CF15 .....175 B5
Cilfynydd CF37 ..109 F5
Deri CF81 ....57 B8
Ferndale CF43 ...79 F6
Gorseinon SA4 ..43 C2
Maesteg CF34 ...168 B2
Mountain Ash CF45 .81 F8
New Tredegar NP24 .33 F2

Cross St continued
Pontarddulais SA4 .19 D4
Port Talbot SA13 .99 B1
Porth CF39 ......107 F2
4 Porth CF39 ....107 F3
Porth CF39 ......107 F7
Resolven SA11 ...226 D5
Rhymney NP22 ..12 E4
Senghenydd CF83 .110 F2
Swansea SA5 ....68 C4
Tondu CF32 ......150 C5
Tonypandy CF40 .106 F4
Tonypandy CF40 .106 F4
3 Trallwn CF37 ..109 D2
Trehafod CF37 ..108 D2
Treharris CF46 ..83 B7
Ystrad CF41 .....79 D2
Ystradgynlais SA9 .222 A6
Cross The
Llanrhidian SA3 .229 D2
Morriston SA6 ...46 A1
Cross Thomas St 5 CF47 ....30 E8
Cross Way NP22 ...6 D1
Crossbrook St CF37 .109 C1
Crosscombe Terr NP23 ....35 B7
Crossfield Ave CF36 .182 E7
Crossfield Rd CF62 .214 C4
Crossfields NP11 ..59 D1
Crosshill CF22 ....214 C1
Crosskeys Coll NP11 .114 C4
Crossways NP11 ..87 B7
Crossways Rd CF5 .193 C5
Crossways St
Barry CF63 ....215 A5
1 Pontypridd CF37 .109 D2
Crosswells Way CF5 .193 A5
Crosswood St CF42 .78 E6
Crouch Cl NP20 ..116 D1
Crown Ave
Tredegar NP22 ...6 D2
Treorchy CF42 ...78 C8
Crown Bsns Pk NP22 .6 E3
Crown Cl
Caerleon NP18 ..118 C2
Cwmbran NP44 ..89 D6
Crown Cotts SA9 ..1 F2
Crown Hill NP22 ..85 D3
Crown Hill CF38 ..156 C6
Crown Hill Dr CF38 .156 C6
Crown La NP12 ...85 D3
Crown Rd
Llanrayon NP44 ..90 B1
Maesteg CF34 ...102 C3
Pyle CF33 ....148 F5
Crown Rise
Llanrayon NP44 ..90 A1
Maesteg CF34 ...102 C3
Crown Row
Aberdare CF44 ...53 E7
Maesteg CF34 ...102 B3
Crown St
Abertillery NP13 .36 A6
Newbridge NP11 .60 A1
Newport NP19 ...143 E6
Port Talbot SA13 .99 B1
Swansea SA6 ....69 B8
Crown Terr CF42 ..78 C8
Crown Way (Ffordd y Goron) CF14 .....90 B1
Crown Wlk CF83 ..140 B7
Crownbridge Specl Sch NP4 ....62 E1
Croyde Ave CF3 ..179 C6
Croydon Cl NP19 .143 E8
Croydon Ct 6 NP19 .143 E8
Crud-yr-Awel
Gorseinon SA4 ..66 B8
Maesteg CF34 ...101 B1
Crumlin Dr CF3 ..180 A7
Crumlin High Level Jun Sch NP11 ....60 A1
Crumlin Rd
Newbridge NP11 .60 A2
Newbridge NP11 .60 B3
Pontypool NP4 ..61 C4
Crumlin St NP4 ...62 B6
Crundale Cres CF14 .177 F8
Crwys La CF63 ...215 B8
Crwys Pl CF24 ....195 B8
Crwys Prim Sch (Ysgol Gynradd y Crwys) SA4 ....65 E1
Crwys Rd CF24 ...195 B8
Crwys Terr SA5 ...68 A6
Crydian Rd SA11 ..71 E6
Crymlyn Bog Visitor Ctr SA1 ....69 D1
Crymlyn Parc SA10 .70 B8
Crymlyn Rd SA7,SA10 .70 B6
Crymlyn St SA1 ...96 B7
Crynallt Inf Sch SA11 .72 B5
Crynallt Jun Sch SA11 .72 B5
Crynallt Rd SA11 ..72 B5
Crynant Bsns Pk SA10 ....226 A8
Crynant Cl CF62 ..211 D7
Crystal Ave CF23 .178 A5
Crystal Glen CF14 .177 F6
Crystal Ct CF15 ..158 C6
Crystal Rise CF14 .177 F6
Crystal Wood Rd CF14 ....177 F6
Cty Fire Hq CF22 ..155 A2
Cty H CF10 ....195 A6
Cty H (Neuadd-y-Sir) CF10 ....195 B4
Cty Prim Sch SA18 .220 D6
Cuckoo St CF32 ..103 F1

Cules Terr CF15 ...157 F5
Culfor Rd SA4 .....65 E8
Culver Cl CF64 ....206 E1
Cumslie Cres NP12 .86 A3
Cumberland Rd NP19 ....143 E8
Cumberland St CF5 .194 C5
Cumnock Pl CF24 .195 C5
Cumnock Terr 4 CF24 ....195 C5
Cumrae St 7 CF24 .195 C5
Cunard Row 1 SA12 .99 F5
Cunard Terr SA12 .99 F5
Cunningham Cl
Cardiff CF23 .....178 A4
Swansea SA2 .....94 C6
Cunningham Rd NP19 ....144 F7
Curie Cl NP20 ....117 A3
Curlew Cl
Cardiff CF14 .....177 A6
Llanelli SA15 ....40 A6
Mumbles SA3 ....93 E1
Neath SA10 ......48 E2
Newport NP19 ...144 E1
Porthcawl CF36 .165 D1
Curlew Cres CF62 .210 D6
Curll Ave CF14 ...177 E3
Curran Emb CF10 .195 A3
Curran Rd CF10 ..195 A3
Curre St
Aberdare CF44 ...53 C8
Cwm NP23 ....35 A8
Currie Ho SA12 ..98 F2
Curry Cl SA2 .....93 E8
Curtis St SA11 ....71 E5
Curwen Cl SA12 ..72 F3
Curwen Terr
North Cornelly CF33 .165 F7
Pontrhydyfen SA12 .72 F4
Curwood NP44 ....17 C6
Curzon St 8 CF11 .195 A3
Custom House Pl 1 CF64 ....207 B5
Customhouse St CF10 ....195 A4
Cuthbert St CF32 .104 E2
Cuthbertson St SA11 .71 C4
Cutter Cl NP19 ...117 F1
Cwat Pen y Twyn NP22 .6 D2
Cwm Alarch CF45 .54 B3
Cwm Alarch Cl CF45 .54 B3
Cwm Arian SA6 ...46 A2
Cwm Barry Way CF62 ....214 C4
Cwm Bath Rd SA4 .45 F1
Cwm Cadle SA5 ...67 E6
Cwm Cadno SA13 .148 A6
Cwm Chapel Rd SA1 .69 B4
Cwm Clyd SA5 ....67 A3
Cwm Cotts CF32 .130 B4
Cwm Crachen NP23 .8 C2
Cwm Cwddy Dr NP10 ....141 E2
Cwm Cynon Bsns Ctr CF45 ....81 F8
Cwm Cynon Bsns Pk CF45 ....54 F1
Cwm Ddu Ho CF48 .10 A3
Cwm Draw Cl NP12 .86 A3
Cwm Draw Ind Est NP23 ....14 E8
Cwm Du Cl SA5 ..67 F3
Cwm Dylan Cl NP10 .141 E2
Cwm Eithin CF46 .83 D3
Cwm Farm La NP4 .62 D5
Cwm Farm Rd NP13 .36 C4
Cwm Farteg SA13 .100 F4
Cwm Fedw CF83 ..140 A8
Cwm Ffoes CF22 ..149 C2
Cwm Glas NP22 ...13 D8
Cwm Glas Prim Sch SA4 ....69 C4
Cwm Graig Bglws CF14 ....11 A4
Cwm Gwynlais CF15 .158 D6
Cwm Hir NP23 .....7 D3
Cwm Hyfryd CF39 .133 A3
Cwm Ifor Prim Sch CF83 ....137 D5
Cwm Isaac CF44 ..26 C8
Cwm La NP10 .....142 B6
Cwm Level Rd SA6 .68 D5
Cwm Mwyn SA14 .218 B8
Cwm Nant SA11 ..72 A4
Cwm Nant-Llwyd Rd SA13 ....24 C5
Cwm Nedd Prim Sch SA11 ....223 D1
Cwm Nofydd CF14 .177 B8
Cwm Parc CF42 ..214 C5
Cwm Pennar SA11 .69 B4
Cwm Rd
Abergarged CF81 .58 A5
Argoed NP12 ....58 F4
Ebbw Vale NP23 .13 D8
Neath SA10 ......48 A8
Pontardawe SA8 .68 B1
Cwm Rhos View NP23 .13 D6
Cwm Sor Cl NP44 .63 A8
Cwm Tawe RG SA9 .222 A6
2 Llanelli SA15 ...40 C7
Cwm y Dwr SA11 ..71 C1
Cwm-bach Inf Sch CF44 ....53 E8

246 Cwm – Den

Cwm-Celyn Rd NP13 15 E6
Cwm-Cidy La CF62 214 A4
Cwm-Iai Jun & Inf Schs CF39 133 C2
Cwm-y-Nant NP11 141 A7
Cwm-y-Nant Fields NP44 89 D2
Cwm-Yr-Wch SA2 93 B8
Cwmaber Inf Sch CF83 137 A8
Cwmaber Jun Sch CF83 137 A8
Cwmafan Inf Sch SA12 99 E5
Cwmafan Jun Sch SA12 99 E5
Cwmaman Inf Sch CF44 53 A4
Cwmaman Rd CF44 53 C6
Cwmamman Rd SA18 219 F8
Cwmavon Rd
Abersychan NP4 37 F7
Blaenavon NP4 17 F4
Cwmavon SA12 99 C3
Cwmbach CW Prim Sch CF44 53 F7
Cwmbach Ind Est CF44 53 E7
Cwmbach Jun Sch CF44 29 E1
Cwmbach Rd
Aberdare CF44 29 C2
Aberdare CF44 29 D1
Llanelli SA15 40 A8
Neath SA10 48 F3
Swansea SA5 67 C3
Cwmbach Sta CF44 53 E7
Cwmbran Dr NP44 89 E4
Cwmbran Sta NP44 89 F4
Cwmbwrla Prim Sch SA5 68 B2
CwMCarn Cl CF3 179 F7
Cwmcarn Forest Dr NP11 114 E7
Cwmcarn High Sch NP11 114 B8
Cwmcarn Jun & Inf Sch NP11 114 C7
Cwmcelyn Inf Sch NP13 15 E6
Cwmcelyn Newydd NP13 15 F6
Cwmclais Rd SA12 99 D5
Cwmclyd SA9 222 A6
Cwmclydach Inf & Jun Mix Schs CF40 106 B7
CwMCottage Rd NP13 36 C4
Cwmdar Cty Prim Sch CF44 28 C3
Cwmdare Rd CF44 28 C4
Cwmdare St CF24 177 F1
Cwmdonkin Dr SA2 95 A7
Cwmdonkin Terr SA2 94 F7
Cwmdows Terr NP11 86 E6
Cwmdu Ind Est SA5 67 F2
Cwmdu Rd
Godrergraig SA8 221 B1
Maesteg CF34 102 D3
Pontardawe SA8 24 C8
Troedyrhiw CF48 31 B1
Cwmdu St CF34 102 B3
Cwmfelin SA10 71 B8
Cwmfelin Prim Sch CF34 128 C8
Cwmfelin Rd SA14 41 F3
Cwmfelin Way SA1 68 C2
Cwmfelinfach Jun & Inf Sch NP11 113 A4
Cwmffrwdoer Prim Sch NP4 61 E8
Cwmgarw Rd SA18 221 A8
Cwmgelli Cl SA5 68 D6
Cwmgelli Dr SA5 68 C6
Cwmgelli Rd SA6 68 C7
Cwmgelli Villas NP12 58 F1
Cwmglas Inf Sch CF83 112 A3
Cwmglo Rd CF48 10 A1
Cwmgors Ind Est SA18 220 D6
Cwmgwili Cty Prim Sch SA14 218 C5
Cwmhir Rd NP4 63 D7
Cwmlan Terr SA1 68 D4
Cwmlas Flats CF83 112 A3
Cwmllynfell Prim Sch SA9 221 B7
Cwmnanthir Terr SA18 220 E7
Cwmneol Pl CF44 53 A4
Cwmneol St CF44 53 A4
Cwmparc Forest Wlk CF42 78 D5
Cwmphil Rd SA9 1 C1
Cwmrhydyceirw Prim Sch SA6 45 F4
Cwmrhydyceirw Rd SA6 45 F3
Cwmsaerbren Flats CF42 50 F1
Cwmsaerbren St CF42 50 F1
Cwmsyfiog Prim Sch NP24 34 A1
Cwmsyfiog Rd CF81 58 B7
Cwmtawe Bsns Pk SA8 23 F5
Cwmtawe Comp Sch (Ysgol Gyfun Cwmtawe) SA8 23 E3
Cwmtawe Cty Comp (upper) Sch SA8 23 E6
Cwmtillery Ind Est NP13 36 B7
Cwmtillery Jun Sch NP13 36 A7
Cwmtorlais Rd NP11 86 E6
Cwmynyscoy Rd NP4 62 C4
Cwmynysmintan Rd CF44 28 D7
Cwndonkin Cl SA2 95 A7
Cwrdy Cl NP4 62 D2
Cwrdy La NP4 62 C2
Cwrdy Rd NP4 62 D2
Cwrdy Wlk NP4 62 D2
Cwrt Alexandre NP13 36 C4
Cwrt Alun Lewis CF44 53 A3
Cwrt Anghorfa CF33 148 B2
Cwrt Bethel CF37 109 F5
Cwrt Bethell CF72 173 B8
Cwrt Bleddyn NP44 89 D1
Cwrt Bryn Cynon CF45 82 C5
Cwrt Bryn Isaf CF44 26 C8
Cwrt Cefn CF14 160 B2
Cwrt Cilmeri SA6 46 A2
Cwrt Coed Parc CF34 102 B2
Cwrt Deri CF14 177 B8
Cwrt Dewi Sant 3 CF24 195 C5
Cwrt Dowlas NP44 116 E8
Cwrt Draw Llyn CF83 158 F8
Cwrt Eglwys Newydd CF14 177 A5
Cwrt Elusendy 4 SA15 40 E5
Cwrt Emily SA7 46 F1
Cwrt Faenor CF38 155 F5
Cwrt Fforest CF45 54 E2
Cwrt Finchley CF5 193 E7
Cwrt Glanhowy NP12 85 E8
Cwrt Glanrhyd CF44 26 C8
Cwrt Glanwern 4 CF44 53 E8
Cwrt Glyn CF37 109 A8
Cwrt Hendre NP12 85 C7
Cwrt Heol Casnewydd 5 CF24 195 D8
Cwrt Hocys SA7 69 D6
Cwrt Hydd SA6 45 F5
Cwrt Isaf SA7 47 B1
Cwrt Ivor Sims SA6 46 A2
Cwrt Llandough CF64 206 D6
Cwrt Llanwonno CF45 54 D1
Cwrt Llechau CF72 172 D6
Cwrt Llwyn Fedwen SA6 46 A1
Cwrt Llwynog SA6 45 F4
Cwrt Maes Cynon CF44 27 E8
Cwrt Merlyn SA6 45 F5
Cwrt Nant y Felin CF83 137 D1
Cwrt Neuadd Wen CF81 58 C5
Cwrt Neville 2 SA15 40 D4
Cwrt Olwyn Ddwr SA7 47 A1
Cwrt Pencoedtre 3 CF62 215 A8
Cwrt Pentre Bach 7 CF3 180 A8
Cwrt Pentwyn CF38 156 B7
Cwrt Rhian SA4 43 C2
Cwrt Rhosyn SA7 69 D6
Cwrt Rhyd NP23 7 C4
Cwrt Roberts CF5 193 A3
Cwrt Saron CF40 107 A2
Cwrt Sart SA11 71 C3
Cwrt Sart Comp Sch SA11 71 C3
Cwrt St Cyres CF64 206 E4
Cwrt Swalia CF32 104 E2
Cwrt Syr Dafydd CF61 209 F7
Cwrt Tr Eos SA13 148 A6
Cwrt Tre-aman CF44 53 D6
Cwrt Trem yr Ynys CF63 214 F4
Cwrt Twyn-Rhyd CF44 26 C8
Cwrt Ty Mawr CF83 138 D2
Cwrt Ty-Fferm CF83 137 F8
Cwrt Waddl 3 SA15 40 D4
Cwrt y Carw SA13 147 F6
Cwrt y Castell (Castle Court Sh Ctr) CF83 138 B3
Cwrt y Coed NP12 85 D6
Cwrt y Fedwen SA7 46 D1
Cwrt y Garth 5 CF38 156 A5
Cwrt y Mwnws CF34 102 A4
Cwrt y Waun
3 Beddau CF38 156 A5
Caerphilly NP12 85 C7
Rhydyfro SA8 23 D7
Cwrt Ynysmeurig CF45 82 E2
Cwrt Yr Aeron SA6 46 A4
Cwrt Yr Gollen NP23 14 D6
Cwrt Yr Ysgol 1 NP11 114 F3
Cwrt-Coch St CF81 58 B4
Cwrt-Ty-Mynydd CF15 176 B6
Cwrt-Ucha Terr 7 SA13 125 C7
Cwrt-y- Goedwig CF38 156 B7
Cwrt-y-Cadno
Cardiff CF5 192 F5
Llantwit Major CF61 210 A7
Cwrt-y-Clafdy SA10 70 F8
Cwrt-y-Clafdy Rd SA10 70 F8
Cwrt-y-Coed CF31 169 B4
Cwrt-y-Farchnad 1 CF5 194 D6
Cwrt-y-Felin CF71 198 C5
Cwrt-y-Vil Rd CF64 207 A3
Cwrt-y-Vil Road (Lower) CF64 207 A2
Cwrt-y-Ysgol SA11 49 C2
Cwrt-yr-Ala Ave CF5 193 B3
Cwrt-yr-Ala Com Jun Sch CF5 193 B4
Cwrt-yr-Ala Rd CF5 193 C2
Cwrt-y-Lolo CF62 201 C1
Cwrt-yy-Fedw SA7 47 B1
Cwrtglas NP44 90 A4
Cyfartha Jun Sch CF47 10 C3
Cyfartha Mus & Art Gall CF47 10 C3
Cyfarthfa Gdns CF48 10 B4
Cyfarthfa High (Lower) Comp Sch CF47 10 C3
Cyfarthfa High (Upper) Comp Sch CF47 10 F1
Cyfarthfa Ho CF48 10 A3
Cyfarthfa Ind Est CF47 10 C2
Cyfarthfa Rd CF48 10 C2
Cyfarthfa St CF24 195 C7
Cyfyng Rd SA9 2 A5
Cygnet Cl SA2 93 E6
Cylla St CF82 84 D5
Cymdda CF32 150 E3
Cymer Rd CF34 75 B2
Cymmer Afan Comp Sch SA13 75 C4
Cymmer Afan Prim Sch SA13 75 B5
Cymmer Cty Inf Sch CF39 107 E2
Cymmer Jun Sch CF39 107 E2
Cymmer Rd
Glyncorrwg SA13 227 C1
Porth CF39 107 D4
Cymmer St CF11 194 F3
Cymric Cl Cardiff CF5 193 D5
Hirwaun CF44 27 F6
Cymtawe Coll SA8 23 E6
Cyn-Coed Ave CF23 178 D6
Cyn-Coed Cres CF23 178 D6
Cynan Cl Barry CF63 215 B8
Beddau CF38 156 A5
Ebbw Vale NP23 7 D5
Cyncoed CF37 81 E3
Cyncoed Ave CF23 178 C6
Cyncoed Cl SA2 93 C8
Cyncoed Pl CF23 178 C6
Cyncoed Rd
Cardiff CF23 178 C5
Margam SA13 125 E3
Cyncoed Rise CF23 178 C6
Cynffig Comp Sch CF33 148 D1
Cynlais Cty Prim Jun & Inf Sch SA9 1 F2
Cynllwyndu Rd CF43 80 B3
Cynon Cl SA6 69 A7
Cynon Inf Sch CF45 54 C3
Cynon St
1 Aberdare CF44 28 F4
Aberdare CF44 53 D6
Cynon Terr
Abercynon CF45 82 E2
Hirwaun CF44 27 E7
Mountain Ash CF45 82 A7
Cynon Valley Mus CF44 29 A3
Cynon View CF37 109 F3
Cyntwell Ave CF5 193 B3
Cyntwell Cres CF5 193 B4
Cyntwell Pl CF5 193 B4
Cynwal Terr SA9 221 C5
Cypress Ave SA3 122 F8
Cypress Cl
Caerleon NP18 117 E2
Merthyr Tydfil CF47 10 D5
Cypress Ct CF44 28 E2
Cypress Dr CF3 180 B8
Cypress Gdns CF36 183 E7
Cypress Pl CF5 176 D2
Cypress St CF37 136 A5
Cyrch-y-Gwas Rd CF37 135 E7
Cyres St CF47 10 F3
Cyril Pl NP13 35 F6
Cyril St Barry CF63 215 B5
Cardiff CF24 195 D7
Newport NP19 143 D4
Cysgod-y-Fro SA8 23 D7

D

D C Griffiths Way SA11 71 D6
D Row NP4 17 A6
D'arcy Bsns Ctr SA10 70 D5
Dafen Inn Row SA14 41 C7
Dafen Rd Llanelli SA14 41 A8
Llanelli SA14 41 B7
Dafen Row SA15 40 E2
Daffodil Cl SA12 98 C3
Daffodil Ct NP44 88 F2
Daffyn Ct NP4 37 E6
Dafolog Terr NP24 33 F4
Dafydd Pl CF63 215 A8
Dahlia Cl 2 SA12 98 C2
Daisy St CF5 194 B6
Daisy View NP4 62 D5
Dalcross St CF24 178 B1
Dale Ave CF14 177 D5
Dale Cl SA5 67 B4
Dale Ct CF62 214 F8
Dale Path NP44 89 B2
Dale Rd NP19 144 D6
Dale View
Cefn Cribwr CF32 149 C2
Nantyglo NP23 15 D8
Daleside CF32 151 A5
Dalmuir Rd CF24 195 F7
Dalrymple St 3 SA12 99 A1
Dalton Cl
8 Merthyr Tydfil CF47 30 F8
Port Talbot SA12 124 D8
Dalton Ct 2 CF24 195 A8
Dalton Ho 6 SA12 98 D1
Dalton Rd Neath SA11 71 E6
Port Talbot SA12 98 D1
Dalton St CF24 195 A8
Dan Caerlan CF72 155 E3
Dan y Bryn CF39 132 B7
Dan y Coed CF35 170 D7
Dan y Cribyn CF37 109 A7
Dan y Graig
Cardiff CF14 176 F8
Pontlottyn CF81 33 A7
Risca NP11 114 F2
Dan y Graig Rd NP11 114 F2
Dan y Mynydd CF14 159 C3
Dan Yr Allt SA4 66 A5
Dan Yr Ardd CF83 137 E1
Dan Yr Heol CF32 130 E4
Dan-y-Bryn
Maesteg CF34 75 A1
Tonna SA11 49 D3
Dan-y-Bryn Ave CF15 176 A6
Dan-y-bryn Bglws NP13 15 E4
Dan-y-Bryn Cl CF15 176 B6
Dan-y-Bryn Rd SA13 125 C8
Dan-y-Coed
Aberkenfig CF32 150 C3
Blackmill CF35 130 E1
Cefn Hengoed CF82 84 F4
Cwmavon SA12 99 E5
Mountain Ash CF45 54 E3
Pontrhydyfen SA12 73 B5
Pontsticill CF48 3 F3
Dan-y-Coed Cl CF23 178 B6
Dan-y-Coed Rd
Cardiff CF23 178 B6
Swansea SA7 70 A8
Dan-y-Coed Rise
Bridgend CF31 169 A5
Cardiff CF23 178 B6
Dan-y-Coedcae Rd CF37 135 B7
Dan-y-Craig Rd SA11 71 E6
Dan-y-darren CF83 112 A5
Dan-y-Deri
Bedwas CF83 138 C7
Bridgend CF31 168 B4
Dan-y-Deri La CF48 10 A4
Dan-y-Felin CF72 155 D3
Dan-y-fron SA9 222 C7
Dan-y-Gaer Rd CF82 84 C6
Dan-y-Graig CF83 137 A7
Dan-y-Graig Rd SA10 71 B8
Dan-y-Lan CF32 150 C3
Dan-y-Parc SA6 45 E1
Dan-y-Rhiw CF44 53 A3
Dan-y-Rhiw Terr NP11 87 A3
Dan-y-twyn CF46 83 B5
Dan-yr-Allt Cl CF37 136 B5
Dan-Yr-Heol
Cardiff CF23 178 B6
Penywaun CF44 28 B6
Dana Dr SA2 94 C6
Dane St CF47 10 D2
Dane Terr CF47 10 D2
Danescourt Halt CF5 176 E2
Danescourt Jun & Inf Sch CF5 176 E2
Danescourt Way CF5 176 E3
Daniel Hopkin Cl CF61 209 F5
Daniel Pl 11 NP20 143 C3
Daniel St
Aberdare CF44 29 F1
Barry CF63 215 B7
Cardiff CF24 178 A1
Daniell Cl CF64 216 A5
Danton Ho NP44 90 B4
Dantwyn Rd SA4 19 E5
Danybanc SA15 40 E8
Danybryn CF72 172 F6
Danybryn Rd SA4 43 A1
Danycoed
Caerphilly CF83 138 B1
Clydach NP7 9 D6
Tonypandy CF41 79 E2
Danycoed Terr CF40 106 D7
Danycwm SA14 40 F8
Danyderi St CF44 53 C6
Danyderi Terr CF48 55 C5
Danyffynon SA13 99 C2
Danygraig
Aberavon SA12 99 A2
Clydach SA6 46 C8
Croesyceiliog NP44 90 A7
Cwm-twrch Isaf SA9 1 A2
Lewistown CF32 130 E5
Machen CF83 139 B6
Ystrad CF41 79 E3
Danygraig Ave CF36 183 E8
Danygraig Bglws NP11 114 E1
Danygraig Cres CF72 155 C3
Danygraig Dr CF72 155 C3
Danygraig Prim Sch SA1 96 A7
Danygraig Rd
Llanharan CF72 154 A3
Pontardawe SA8 23 C2
Swansea SA1 96 B7
Danygraig St CF37 135 B7
Danygraig Terr CF72 154 A3
Danylan Rd CF37 109 A1
Danyparc CF47 10 E2
Danyrallt SA14 40 F8
Danywern Terr CF41 79 D3
Daphne Cl SA10 48 E2
Daphne Rd SA10 48 E2
Darby Cres NP23 14 B8
Darby Rd CF24 196 A4
Dare Ct CF44 28 C3
Dare Rd CF44 28 C3
Dare Valley Ctry Pk CF44 28 B2
Dare Valley Visitor Ctr CF44 28 C2
Dare Villas CF44 28 F2
Daren Cl CF34 102 D2
Daren Ddu Rd CF37 109 C4
Darren-Felen Rd NP23 8 C4
Darent Cl NP20 116 C1
Darent Rd NP20 116 C1
Darent Wlk NP20 116 D1
Darlington Ct NP19 143 D8
Darran Park Prim Sch CF43 79 F6
Darran Pk
Neath Abbey SA10 47 F1
Pontypridd CF37 109 D3
Darran Rd
Mountain Ash CF45 54 D2
Risca NP11 114 E4
Darran St CF24 194 F8
Darran Terr
Ferndale CF43 79 F6
Pontardawe SA8 23 B3
Darren Bglws CF32 103 E6
Darren Cl
Caerphilly CF83 138 D5
Cowbridge CF71 188 D2
Neath Abbey SA10 47 F1
Darren Ct
Blackwood NP12 59 B1
Pontypridd CF37 109 D5
Darren Dr NP11 87 A1
Darren Hill CF71 188 D2
Darren Las CF48 55 D2
Darren Rd
Abertillery NP13 36 C5
Briton Ferry SA11 71 C3
Ystalyfera SA9 2 B6
Darren View
Merthyr Tydfil CF47 10 F2
Pont Rhyd-y-cyff CF34 128 D7
Darren Wen SA12 98 F7
Darrenfelen Jun & Inf Sch NP7 9 B5
Darrenlas Prim Sch CF45 54 D2
Dart Rd NP20 116 E1
Dartford Dr SA1 69 A3
Dartford Pl SA1 69 A2
Dartford Rd SA1 69 A3
Dartington Dr CF23 160 E1
Darwin Dr NP20 117 A2
Darwin Rd SA12 124 E7
David Cl NP20 143 C1
David Davies Rd CF63 215 B4
David Dower Cl CF45 82 E2
David Issac Cl SA1 68 D3
David Price St 11 CF44 29 A1
David St Aberdare CF44 28 E3
Barry CF63 215 C8
Blaengarw CF32 103 E7
Blaenrhondda CF42 50 D4
Caerphilly NP12 85 F6
Cardiff CF10 195 B5
Cwmdare CF44 28 C3
Ebbw Vale NP23 14 C8
14 Merthyr Tydfil CF47 10 D2
Merthyr Tydfil CF47 30 E7
Swansea SA5 68 B2
Tonypandy CF40 106 D7
Tonypandy CF40 107 A3
Treherbert CF42 50 F1
Treorchy CF42 78 B4
Wick CF71 198 C5
David Williams Terr SA1 96 C7
David's Ct CF72 173 B8
Davies Andrews Heol SA11 49 B1
Davies Andrews Rd SA11 49 B1
Davies Ave
Bridgend CF31 168 F7
Porthcawl CF36 165 F1
Davies Cl CF40 107 C5
Davies Dr CF83 137 F5
Davies Pl Cardiff CF5 193 F7
Porth CF39 107 E6
Davies Rd Neath SA11 71 E7
Ynysmeudwy SA8 23 F6
Davies Row
Hirwaun CF44 27 D8
Swansea SA5 68 D5
Davies Sq 3 SA15 40 E5
Davies St
Abercraf SA9 222 D7
Barry CF63 215 A6
Blackwood NP12 85 C7
5 Brynmawr NP23 8 C4
Dowlais CF48 11 B5
Porth CF39 107 E4
2 Swansea SA6 69 A8
Tonypandy CF40 106 D6
Ystrad Mynach CF82 84 F2
Davies Ter 13 CF47 30 E8
Davies Terr CF34 101 F6
Daviot Ct CF24 178 B1
Daviot St CF24 178 B1
Davis Ave CF32 151 A6
Davis Cl NP4 62 C7
Davis Sq 14 NP20 143 C3
Davis St Aberdare CF44 53 C8
Cardiff CF24 195 C5
Swansea SA6 68 E5
Davis's Terr 4 CF14 177 B5
Davnic Cl 5 CF63 215 B6
Davy Cl NP20 117 A3
Davy Evans Ct NP13 36 B4
Dawan Cl CF62 214 D5
Dawlish Cl SA3 122 E6
Dawson Cl NP19 144 F6
Dderi Rd SA9 221 B5
Ddol Rd SA2 93 B7
De Berclos CF36 182 F8
De Braose Cl CF5 176 D3
De Breos Dr CF36 183 A8
De Burgh Pl 8 CF11 194 E5
De Burgh St CF11 194 E5
De Clare Cl CF36 182 F8
De Clare Ct CF61 210 B6
De Croche Pl CF11 194 E5
De Granville Cl CF36 182 F8
De Haviland Rd CF24 196 A7
De La Beche Terr SA6 45 F1
De Londres Cl CF36 182 F8
De Turberville Cl CF36 182 F8
De Winton St 7 CF40 106 E6
De Winton Terr
Caerphilly CF83 137 F8
Tonypandy CF40 106 E7
De-Barri St CF37 135 F4
De-Breos St SA2 94 F5
De-La Beche St SA1 95 C7
De-La-Beche Rd SA2 94 D6
Dean Ct NP44 115 F8
Dean St Aberdare CF44 29 A2
Newport NP19 143 E6
Dean's Ct CF5 177 A1
Deanery Gdns 13 NP20 143 B4
Deans Cl CF5 194 B8
Deans Ct CF62 213 A2
Dee Pl SA6 46 A4
Deeley Rd SA9 2 B6
Deemuir Rd CF24 195 F7
Deepdale Cl CF23 178 B3
Deepdene Cl CF5 192 F5
Deepfield Cl CF5 192 F5
Deepslade Cl SA3 121 A4
Deepwood Cl CF5 192 F5
Deerbrook NP44 89 B2
Deere Cl CF5 193 B4
Deere Pl CF5 193 B4
Deere Rd Cardiff CF5 193 B4
Llantwit Fardre CF38 156 C6
Deganwy Cl CF14 159 E1
Dehewydd Isaf CF38 156 D8
Dehewydd La CF38 156 D7
Deighton Cl NP22 13 D8
Delabeche St SA15 40 D4
Delfan Swansea SA6 45 C2
Swansea SA7 69 F5
Delffordd SA8 24 B2
Delfryn
Capel Hendre SA18 218 D6
Llanelli SA14 41 D6
Llwydcoed CF44 28 F6
Delhi St SA1 95 E7
Delius Cl
Newport NP19 144 C5
Rogerstone NP10 142 A6
Dell The Baglan SA12 98 E5
Bryncethin CF32 151 A4
Cardiff CF3 179 D8
Church Village CF38 135 F3
Laleston CF32 167 E4
Llanelli SA15 40 C8
Pontlliw SA4 43 F6
Swansea SA2 93 E6
Delta St 3 CF11 194 D5
Delwen Terr CF42 50 B2
Den-y-bryn CF32 104 F6
Denbigh Cl
Blackwood NP12 58 E1
Church Village CF38 135 F2
Denbigh Cres SA6 46 B5
Denbigh Ct
Caerphilly CF83 137 C4

Denbigh Ct continued
3 Cardiff CF14 .... **177** A6
3 Penarth CF64 .... **206** F2
Denbigh Dr CF61 .... **210** C6
Denbigh Rd
Dinas Powys CF64 .... **206** C4
Newport NP19 .... **143** E8
Denbigh St CF11 .... **194** D7
Denbigh Way CF62 .. **201** F6
Denbury Ave SA15 .... **40** A7
Denison Way CF5 .... **192** F5
Denleigh Cl CF81 .... **57** F3
Dennis Pl CF32 .... **151** B5
Dennithorne Cl CF48 **11** C4
Dental Drive (Rhodfa'r
Dintyddion) CF14 .. **177** E3
Denton Rd CF5 ...... **194** D5
Dents Cl NP19 ...... **144** D5
Dents Hill NP19 .... **144** D5
Denvale Trad Pk
CF24 .... **195** D4
Denver Rd SA5 .... **67** B5
Denys Cl CF64 ...... **206** B4
Depot Rd
Aberdare CF44 .... **28** F2
Cwmavon SA12 .... **99** E5
Derby Cl NP19 ...... **144** B2
Deri Ave CF35 ...... **170** C8
Deri Cl Cardiff CF23 .. **178** F1
Pencoed CF35 .... **152** C1
Deri Farm SA18 .... **57** B8
Deri Rd Cardiff CF23 **178** D1
Glanaman SA18 ...... **219** F8
Deri St CF43 .... **80** B2
Dering Rd CF23 .... **161** B1
Derlin Pk SA18 .... **218** F5
Derllwyn Cl CF32 .. **150** C6
Derllwyn Rd CF32 .. **150** C6
Derwen Ave SA10 .. **93** D8
Neath SA10 .... **48** C1
Penywaun CF44 ...... **28** A6
Perlwyn St NP24 .... **33** E3
Derw Rd SA8 .... **23** D3
Derwen Aur CF39 .. **107** F5
Derwen Cl
Blackwood NP12 .... **85** E8
Bridgend CF31 ...... **168** F8
Tredomen CF82 ...... **84** D1
Waunarlwydd SA5 .. **66** D4
Derwen Deg
Neath SA10 .... **48** C3
Swansea SA8 .... **23** D6
Derwen Fawr SA10 .. **49** C6
Derwen Fawr Rd SA2 **94** B4
Derwen Las CF31 .. **168** B2
Derwen Cl
Bridgend CF31 ...... **168** F4
Cardiff CF23 .... **178** C8
Pontardawe SA8 ...... **23** D2
Pontyclun CF72 ...... **173** B7
Ystradgynlais SA9 .. **79** C3
Derwendeg Ave
Blackwood NP12 .... **85** C8
Cefn Hengoed CF82 .. **84** F4
Pontypridd CF37 .... **109** D5
Derwendeg Prim Sch
CF82 .... **84** F5
Derwent Cl CF14 .... **159** E2
Derwent Ct NP20 .... **116** C1
Derwent Dr SA12 .. **96** F2
Derwent Ho **5** NP44 **89** C2
Derwent St SA15 .... **40** C6
Derwlas SA4 .... **44** B5
Derwydd Ave SA18 .. **220** D6
Derwydd Rd CF40 .. **106** E5
Despenser Gdns **11**
CF11 .... **194** F5
Despenser Pl **12**
CF11 .... **194** F5
Despenser Rd CF64 **216** A5
Despenser St CF11 .. **194** F5
Dessmuir Rd SA15 .. **195** F7
Devon Ave CF63 .... **214** F6
Devon Ct NP18 ...... **118** A3
Devon Pl NP20 ...... **143** B5
Devon Pl Cardiff CF11 **194** F3
Mumbles SA3 .... **123** B4
Newport NP20 .... **143** B5
Devon St CF11 .... **194** E3
Devon View SA2 .... **94** B7
Devonshire Dr CF44 **224** E1
Devonshire Pl SA13 **125** C7
Dew Cres CF5 .... **193** E4
Dew La SA12 .... **98** C2
Dewi Cl CF5 .... **194** A8
Dewi Sant Hospl
CF37 .... **135** C8
Dewi St CF37 .... **109** E3
Dewi Terr SA1 .... **68** A1
Dewsbury Ct 2 SA4 **95** D6
Dewsland Park Rd
NP20 .... **143** B3
Dewstow St NP19 .. **143** F4
Diagonal Rd CF62 .. **211** E1
Diamond Ct CF83 .. **137** F4
Diamond Jubilee Terr
NP13 .... **36** B5
Diamond St CF24 .. **195** D6
Diana La CF24 ...... **178** B1
Diana St CF24 ...... **178** B1
Troedyrhiw CF48 .... **55** B8
Dibdin Cl NP19 .... **144** F5
Dickens Ave
Cardiff CF3 .... **179** B7
Port Talbot SA12 .... **124** C7
Dickens Ct CF83 .. **139** C6
Dickens Dr NP20 .. **142** E2

Dickinson Cl SA12 .. **98** E6
Dickslade SA3 .... **123** C4
Digby Cl SA3 .... **128** F1
Digby Rd SA11 ...... **72** A8
Digby St CF63 ...... **215** A5
Dillington Terr CF45 **81** F7
Dillwyn Ct Pontlliw SA4 **43** F6
Swansea SA2 .... **66** F5
Dillwyn Llewelyn Com Sch
SA2 .... **67** D2
Dillwyn Rd SA2 .... **94** C6
Dillwyn St
Llanelli SA15 .... **40** D4
Swansea SA1 .... **95** C6
Dilwyn Ave CF82 .. **84** F2
Dilwyn Gdns CF31 .. **168** E2
Dilwyn Rd SA4 ...... **43** F2
Dilwyn St CF45 ...... **81** F8
Dilys St CF42 .... **50** D2
Dimbath Ave CF35 .. **131** A3
Dimbath St SA3 .... **131** B5
Dimlands Rd CF61 .. **209** D5
Dimpath Terr SA15 .. **40** E7
Dinam Cl CF32 ...... **104** F6
Dinam Park Ave CF32 **78** F3
Dinam Pk CF41 ...... **78** F3
Dinam Rd SA11 .... **84** D3
Dinam St CF32 ...... **104** E6
Dinas Baglan Rd 2 SA12 **98** F3
Dinas Ent Cctr CF39 **107** E4
Dinas Isaf Cotts
CF40 .... **107** A1
Dinas Isaf Ind Est
CF40 .... **133** B8
Dinas Isaf Ind Est (east)
CF40 .... **107** B1
Dinas Jun Sch CF40 **107** A3
Dinas Path NP44 .. **89** B2
Dinas Pl CF11 ...... **194** F3
Dinas Powis Inf Sch
CF64 .... **206** B3
Dinas Powis Sta
CF64 .... **206** A2
Dinas Rd
Penarth CF64 .... **206** F2
Pontneddfechan SA11 **223** F2
Tonypandy CF40 .... **107** A4
Dinas St CF11 ...... **194** F4
Swansea SA6 .... **68** C5
Dinas Terr SA11 .... **223** F2
Dingle Cl CF62 ...... **214** B2
Dingle Dr CF64 ...... **207** A4
Dingle Rd
Penarth CF64 .... **207** A4
Pontypool NP4 ...... **62** D5
Dingle The NP23 .. **14** D8
Distillery Road La
CF37 .... **108** F2
District St CF47 .... **10** F3
Ditchling Ct CF64 .. **207** A2
Division St NP13 .... **36** B5
Dixon St CF47 .... **10** D1
Dixon's Pl NP11 .... **115** A2
Dobbins Rd CF63 .. **215** D7
Dochdwy Rd CF64 .. **206** E6
Dock Rd Barry CF62 **214** E2
Port Talbot SA13 .... **125** A7
Dock St Loughor SA4 **45** C8
Penarth CF64 .... **206** F5
Porthcawl CF36 ...... **182** F6
Dock View Rd CF63 **215** A4
Docks Way NP20 .. **164** A8
Dockwell Terr NP18 **145** B4
Doddridge Way
CF38 .... **182** E6
Dodington Pl **2**
CF37 .... **109** E2
Dogfield St CF24 .. **178** C1
Dogo St CF11 .... **194** D7
Dol Afon CF35 ...... **170** E7
Dol Coed Pl SA12 .. **49** C2
Dol Fach CF31 ...... **169** B4
Dol Fran CF83 ...... **138** D4
Dol Henrhyd SA12 .. **223** A6
Dol Las SA12 .... **98** E6
Dol Nant Dderwen
SA11 .... **168** B4
Dol y Dderwen SA9 **222** A5
Dol y Pandy CF83 .. **138** C7
Dol y Paun CF37 .. **137** E2
Dol yr Eos CF83 .. **138** C4
Dol-Wen CF35 ...... **152** F1
Dol-y-Coed SA12 .. **93** B8
Dol-y-Felin CF15 .. **174** D7
Dol-y-Felin St CF83 **138** C4
Dol-y-Garn Terr
SA11 .... **15** E6
Dol-y-Llan CF72 .. **173** D8
Dolafon SA14 .... **41** E3
Dolau Cl SA15 ...... **40** E2
Dolau Fach SA15 .. **40** E2
Dolau Fawr SA15 .. **40** E3
Dolau Ifan Ddu Terr
CF35 .... **130** F2
Dolau Prim Sch
CF72 .... **153** E2
Dolau Rd SA15 ...... **40** E3
Dolawel SA9 .... **221** C7
Dolcoed CF48 .... **28** D6
Dolcoed Terr SA11 **49** C2
Dolfain SA9 .... **222** A5
Dolgellau Ave CF38 **135** F2
Dolgoch Cl CF3 .... **179** D5
Dolgoy Cl SA3 ...... **123** A7
Dolgwilym St SA14 **80** C1
Dolphin St SA12 .... **98** C3

Dolphin St NP20 .... **143** D3
Dolwar Fach SA14 .. **41** C5
Dolwen Rd CF14 .... **177** A2
Dolwerdd SA14 ...... **40** B4
Dolwyddelan Cl NP12 **58** E1
Dombey Cl CF14 .... **159** F2
Domen Ct NP23 .... **14** F6
Dominion Way CF24 **195** E8
Dominion Way Ind Est
CF24 .... **195** E8
Don Cl NP20 .... **116** D1
Donald St
Abercanaid CF48 .... **30** F4
Cardiff CF24 .... **178** B1
Nelson CF46 .... **83** E4
Doniford Cl CF64 .. **216** B6
Donnen St SA13 .... **125** C5
Donnington Rd CF64 **215** C6
Dorallt Cl NP44 ...... **88** B1
Dorallt Way NP44 .. **9** F5
Dorchester Ave
CF23 .... **178** D2
Dorchester Mans 5
CF24 .... **176** F6
Dorleigh Ct NP44 .. **89** B5
Dorothy Ave CF62 .. **214** E8
Dorothy Cl CF62 .. **214** E8
Dorothy St
Pontypridd CF37 .... **109** D2
Ton Pentre CF41 .... **79** B3
Dorset Ave CF63 .. **214** F6
Dorset Cl NP19 .... **144** B2
Dorset Ho **6** SA12 **98** C3
Dorset St CF11 .... **194** F3
Dorstone Wlk NP44 **90** A3
Dos Cotts NP20 .... **143** B6
Dos Rd NP20 ...... **143** B7
Douglas Cl CF5 .... **176** E2
Douglas Ct
Bishopston SA3 .... **122** A5
Cardiff CF14 .... **159** E1
Dove Rd SA5 .... **67** E7
Dovedale Cl CF23 .. **178** D5
Dovedale St CF43 **215** B6
Dover St
Mountain Ash CF45 **54** D2
Ton Pentre CF41 .... **79** B2
Dovey Cl Barry CF62 **214** C6
Ton Pentre CF41 .... **79** B2
Dowlais Inf Sch CF48 **11** B4
Dowlais Rd CF24 .. **195** D4
Dowland Cl NP19 .. **144** B5
Dowlands Cl CF64 .. **206** E1
Dowlands Way CF3 **179** A2
Down Leaze SA3 .... **67** D1
Down St SA6 .... **46** F7
Downey Gr CF82 .... **84** E6
Downfield Cl CF64 .. **206** E6
Downs St
Llanelli SA15 .... **40** C4
Newport NP19 ...... **144** A3
Downs Cl SA5 ...... **67** A2
Downs The SA3 .... **231** C8
Downs View CF71 .. **189** B3
Downs View CF71 .. **189** B3
Downs Grange
CF3 .... **179** C2
Downton Rd CF3 .. **179** B2
Downton Rise CF3 **179** B2
Doyle Ave CF5 ...... **193** E8
Doyle Ct CF5 .... **193** E8
Dr William Price Bsns Ctr
CF37 .... **10** C3
Dragon Auto Ctr SA7 **69** B7
Dragonfly Dr CF62 **213** A5
Drake Cl
Newport NP19 ...... **144** E6
St Athan CF62 ...... **221** D7
Drake Wlk CF10 .... **195** B4
Drangway CF61 .... **209** F6
Dranllwyn Cl CF38 **139** F7
Dranllwyn La CF82 **139** F7
Drawlings Cl 1 CF3 **179** D6
Drayton Cl NP44 .... **89** C3
Drefelin SA9 .... **112** B8
Drefan SA9 .... **222** A5
Dreweyndd Mus NP22 **12** C7
Dring St SA1 .... **95** B8
Drinkwater Gdns
NP20 .... **142** F2
Driscoll Cl **4** CF24 **195** D7
Driscoll Workshops
CF10 .... **195** C5
Drive The
Bargoed CF81 .... **58** A1
Cardiff CF5 .... **193** D7
Dinas Powys CF64 .. **206** C3
Miskin CF72 .... **173** D6
Neath Abbey SA10 .. **71** B8
Pontardawe SA8 .... **23** D2
Southgate SA3 ...... **121** A4
Drope Rd CF5 ...... **192** E4
Drope Terr CF5 .... **192** E4
Dros Col CF72 ...... **172** B5
Dros y Mor CF64 .. **207** B2
Dros-y-Morfa CF3 **179** C2
Drovers Mews 8
NP20 .... **143** C3
Druce St SA14 ...... **40** C3
Druids Cl
Mumbles SA3 ...... **123** A6
Treorchy CF42 ...... **78** D5
Druids Gn CF71 .... **188** F2
Druidstone Rd CF3 **161** F3
Druidstone Way SA4 **44** B2
Drumau Cl SA10 .... **70** F8
Drumau Pk SA10 .. **70** F8

Drumau Rd
Birchgrove SA7 ...... **47** B1
Neath SA10 .... **70** D8
Drumfields SA10 .. **70** F8
Drury Cl CF14 ...... **159** E2
Druslyn Rd SA3 .... **122** F7
Drybrook Cl
3 Cardiff CF23 .... **179** F6
Cwmbran NP44 ...... **89** F3
Dryburgh Ave CF14 **177** D5
Dryden Cl CF3 ...... **179** B7
Dryden Rd CF64 .. **206** F4
Dryden Terr CF62 **214** F8
Drylla CF64 .... **206** A2
Drymau Rd SA11 .. **71** A7
Drysgol Rd CF15 .. **176** B5
Drysio Cl NP23 .... **14** D6
Drysiog St NP23 .. **14** D6
Dryslwyn Cl SA4 .. **44** B2
Duckpool Rd NP19 **143** E6
Dudley Cl CF10 ...... **195** B1
Dudley Pl CF62 .... **214** D4
Dudley St
Cardiff CF10 .... **195** B1
Neath SA11 .... **71** E7
Newport NP19 ...... **143** E4
Duffryn CF35 ...... **170** B8
Duffryn Cres CF72 **153** E2
Duffryn Cty Prim Sch
SA13 .... **74** C4
Duffryn Dr CF64 .. **206** E7
Three Crosses SA4 **65** F1
Duffryn Fawr SA4 **31** B4
Duffryn High Sch
NP10 .... **163** F7
Duffryn Ho 5 CF64 **206** C3
Duffryn Jun Sch
NP10 .... **163** F7
Duffryn La
Abertillery NP13 .... **36** B6
St Brides Major CF32 **128** A2
Wick CF71 .... **188** D4
Duffryn Rd
Aberbargoed CF81 .. **58** B4
Caerphilly CF83 .... **137** F3
Cardiff CF23 .... **178** C2
Pentwyn CF82 ...... **59** C2
Pontypridd CF37 .. **135** E7
Port Talbot SA13 .. **125** D5
Swansea SA1 .... **95** B6
Tredegar NP22 ...... **13** C6
Duffryn St (Heol y Dug)
CF10 .... **195** A5
Duffryn Ave CF37 **136** A6
Duffryn Bach Terr
CF38 .... **156** F7
Duffryn Cl
St Nicholas CF5 .... **192** A1
Swansea SA6 .... **69** A8
Duffryn Comp Sch
CF37 .... **125** C3
Duffryn Cres
Peterston-Super-Ely
CF5 .... **191** F4
Rhydyfelin CF37 .. **136** A6
Duffryn Gdns
Rhiwderin CF37 .... **204** B5
Wenvoe CF5 .... **204** B5
Duffryn La
Coedkernew NP10 .. **163** C4
Rhydyfelin CF37 .. **136** A6
Duffryn Link
Abertillery NP13 .... **36** C4
Barry CF63 .... **215** D3
Bridgend CF31 ...... **169** B2
Port Talbot SA13 .. **125** D5
Duffryn Pl Barry CF62 **214** D7
Cwm NP23 .... **35** B6
Maesteg CF34 ...... **102** A8
Duffryn Rd
Aberdare CF44 ...... **53** F7
Ammanford SA18 .. **219** A7
Neath SA10 .... **48** C3
Ebbw Vale NP23 .... **14** F3
Maesteg CF34 ...... **75** A1
Mountain Ash CF45 **54** D4
Neath SA11 .... **72** C8
Pentrebach CF48 .. **31** A4
Pontardawe SA8 .... **23** F4
Pontypridd CF37 .. **136** A5
Rhydyfelin CF37 .. **136** A6
Duffryn Terr
Abergoed CF81 ...... **58** B4
Aberdare CF44 ...... **53** C6
Ferndale CF43 ...... **80** A5
Duffryn Way
Morriston SA6 ...... **46** A1
New Tredegar NP24 **33** E3

Dunraven Arc 10
CF40 .... **106** E6
Dunraven Bsns Pk
CF31 .... **169** A3
Dunraven Cl
Dinas Powys CF64 .. **206** C3
Pen-clawdd SA4 .... **64** B8
Dunraven Cres CF72 **155** A2
Dunraven Ct CF33 **137** C4
Dunraven Ho 5
CF11 .... **194** D3
Dunraven Pl
Bridgend CF31 ...... **168** E4
Evanstown CF39 .. **132** B8
Ogmore Vale CF32 **104** E3
Dunraven Rd
Cardiff CF11 .... **194** D4
Llanyrafon NP44 .. **90** B2
Swansea SA2 .... **94** B7
Dunraven St
Aberavon SA12 .... **42** H1
Aberkenfig CF32 .. **150** C4
Barry CF62 .... **214** C3
Blaengwrach SA11 **227** B8
Bridgend CF31 ...... **169** B2
Glyncorrwg SA13 .. **227** D8
Tonypandy CF40 .. **106** C5
Treherbert CF42 .... **50** F1
Dunraven Terr CF42 **78** C7
Dunsmuir Rd CF24 **195** F6
Dunstable Rd NP19 **144** E5
Dunster Cl SA3 .... **123** C6
Dunster Dr CF64 .. **216** A5
Dunster Rd CF3 .. **179** D7
Dunvant Ave SA4 .. **226** C4
Dunvant Pl SA1 .. **95** C5
Dunvant Prim Sch
SA2 .... **93** B8
Dunvant Rd
Dunvant SA2 .... **93** D8
Three Crosses SA4 **65** F1
Dunvant Sq SA2 .. **98** C2
Dupre Rd SA1 ...... **95** F8
Durell St CF62 .... **209** F6
Durham Cl CF48 .. **10** A1
Durham St NP19 .. **143** E2
Durham Road Jun & Inf
Sch NP19 .... **143** D7
Durham St CF11 .. **194** F3
Durleigh Cl CF3 .. **179** C7
Durlston Cl **4** CF14 **176** F3
Duxford CF15 ...... **176** D2
Dwr-y-Felin Comp Sch
SA10 .... **48** A1
Neath SA10 .... **48** D1
Neath SA10 .... **71** A8
Dwr-y-Felin Rd
Neath SA10 .... **48** B1
Neath SA10 .... **48** D1
Dwr-y-Felin Comp Sch
SA10 .... **71** B8
Dwyer Terr
Abertillery NP13 .... **36** B6
Cwmfelinfach NP11 **113** D3
Duffryn View NP22 **12** F3
Dwyfor SA14 ...... **41** D5
Dwyfor Rd SA13 .. **125** D3
Dyfatty St SA1 ...... **95** D8
Dyfed CF64 .... **207** B5
Dyfed Ave SA1 .... **95** A8
Dyfed Cl SA1 ...... **94** F8
Dyfed Dr **1** CF23 .. **178** C2
Dyfed Rd SA1 ...... **71** F7
Dyffryn
Bryn-côch SA10 .. **48** B4
Penperlleni CF37 .. **84** D7
Penrhiwfer CF37 .. **136** A6
Dyffryn La
Coedkernew NP10 .. **163** C4
Rhydyfelin CF37 .. **136** A6
Dyfrig Cl CF5 ...... **195** C4
Dyffryn Cres
Peterston-Super-Ely
CF5 .... **191** F4
Rhydyfelin CF37 .. **136** A6
Dumfries Pl
Brynmawr NP23 .... **8** C5
Cardiff CF10 .... **195** B6
Newport NP20 ...... **143** C4
Ystradgynlais SA9 **2** E7
Dumfries Sq
Aberdare CF44 ...... **29** A1
Treherbert CF42 .... **50** F2
Treorchy CF42 ...... **78** D8
Dummer Cl 2 CF23 **178** F7
Duncan Ct CF11 .. **178** C1
Duncan Cl CF3 ...... **179** D6
Dungarvan Dr CF23 **161** A1
Dunkery Cl CF3 .... **179** B5
Dunkeay Dr CF64 **206** E7
Dunlin Cl CF36 .. **182** D8
Dunlin Ct CF63 ...... **214** F5
Dunn Sq **20** NP20 **143** C3
Dunnet Gdns NP4 **63** B3
Dunns Cl SA3 ...... **123** B5
Dunns La SA3 ...... **123** B5
Dunns The SA3 .... **123** B5

Dyffryn Terr continued
Tonyrefail CF39 ...... **133** B5
Dyffryn View SA10 **48** C5
Dyffryn-Aur Rd SA7 **69** E6
Dyfnallt Rd CF63 .. **215** A6
Dyfodwg St CF42 .. **78** D6
Dyfrig Cl CF5 ...... **193** F6
Dyfrig Ct CF61 .... **210** B7
Dyfrig Rd CF5 ...... **193** F6
Dyfrig St Barry CF62 **214** F8
Cardiff CF11 .... **194** E7
Dyke St **11** CF47 .... **30** E8
Dylan SA14 .... **41** D5
Dylan Ave
1 Beddau CF38 .... **156** A5
Blackwood NP12 .. **85** C7
Dylan Cres
Barry CF63 .... **215** B8
Port Talbot SA12 .. **124** B7
Dylan Dr CF83 ...... **138** A5
Dylan Pl **4** CF24 .. **195** C7
Dylan Rd SA2 ...... **93** F7
Dylan Thomas Sq 3
SA1 .... **195** D6
Dyllas Ct CF39 .... **107** F2
Dyllas Rd CF39 .... **107** F3
Dynea Cl CF37 .... **136** B5
Dynea Rd CF37 .... **136** B5
Dynevor Cl
Llanyrafon NP44 .. **90** B3
Neath SA10 .... **70** D8
Dynevor Comp Sch
SA1 .... **95** C7
Dynevor PL
Neath SA10 .... **70** D7
Swansea SA1 .... **95** C7
Dynevor Rd
Cardiff CF23 .... **178** D3
Glanaman SA18 .. **220** B7
Neath SA10 .... **70** F8
Dynevor Terr
Fochriw CF81 .... **32** C7
Merthyr Tydfil CF48 **10** D1
Dynevor Terr
Port Talbot SA12 .. **124** C7
Dynevor Terr
Neath CF46 .... **83** E3
Pontardawe SA8 .. **23** E5
Dyrus Rd SA6 ...... **68** E5
Dyserth Rd CF64 .. **206** F5
Dysgwylfa SA2 .... **94** C6

E

E Row NP4 .... **17** A6
Eagle La CF71 ...... **188** E2
Eagle Mews SA13 **125** B8
Eagle Rd CF62 .. **210** D6
Eagle St SA15 ...... **40** E4
Eagle View CF31 **169** D6
Eaglebush Cl SA11 **71** D4
Eagles CF5 .... **67** E6
Eagleswell Prim Sch
CF61 .... **210** B7
Eagleswell Rd CF61 **210** B6
Earl Cl NP4 .... **37** E6
Earl Cres CF62 .... **214** F2
Earl Cunningham Ct
CF10 .... **195** C4
Earl La
Cardiff CF11 .... **194** F1
Margam SA13 ...... **125** E5
Penarth CF64 ...... **206** F3
Earl St Abersychan NP4 **37** E5
Abertillery NP13 .... **36** C4
Cardiff CF11 .... **194** F1
Swansea SA1 .... **68** B1
Tredegar NP22 ...... **13** D7
Earl's Court Rd CF23 **178** D1
Earle Pl CF5 .... **194** D5
Earls Rd CF61 ...... **194** D5
Earlsfield Cl SA11 **223** C1
Earlsmede 5 NP44 **89** B3
Earlswood Rd CF14 **177** E7
East Ave
Aberdare CF44 ...... **28** F2
Bedwas CF83 ...... **138** C6
Caerphilly CF83 .... **137** F4
Cefn Cribwr CF32 .. **149** B2
Pontypool NP4 .... **62** E1
East Bank 1 SA3 .. **36** B8
East Bank Rd NP19 **164** F8
East Bank Way (Ffordd
Glan y Dwyrain) SA1 **95** E7
East Bay Cl CF10 **195** C4
East Burrows Rd SA1 **95** C6
East Cliff SA3 ...... **121** B3
East Crossways SA8 **23** D6
East Ct CF43 .... **80** C4
East Dock Rd
Newport NP20 ...... **143** D2
Newport NP20 ...... **143** E3
East Dr CF61 .... **208** F5
East Gr CF24 .... **195** C6
East Grove La CF24 **195** C6
East Grove Rd NP19 **144** C5
East Lynne Gdns
NP18 .... **118** C3
East Market St NP20 **143** D3
East Moors Bsns Pk
CF24 .... **195** E4
East Moors Rd CF24 **195** D4
East Pen-Twyn NP15 **15** E4

East Pen-Twyn Bglws NP13 ....15 E4
East Pentwyn Rd NP13 ....15 E5
East Point CF3 ....179 D2
East Rd Barry CF64 ....215 F6
Cefn Hengoed CF82 ....84 E5
Cwmbran NP44 ....116 F8
Port Talbot SA13 ....125 D3
Treorchy CF43 ....80 B2
Tylorstown CF43 ....80 C4
East Rise CF14 ....178 A8
East Roedin NP44 ....116 C8
East St
Aberkenfig CF32 ....150 C4
Barry CF62 ....214 D4
Bridgend CF31 ....169 E3
Dowlais CF48 ....11 B4
Goytre SA13 ....125 F8
Llantwit Major CF61 ....209 F6
Newport NP20 ....143 B5
Pontypridd CF37 ....109 D2
Tonypandy CF40 ....106 D6
Tylorstown CF43 ....80 C4
East Tyndall St CF24 ....195 D5
East Usk Rd NP19 ....143 C6
East View Blaina NP13 ....15 D5
Caerphilly CF83 ....138 B2
Llandow CF71 ....199 A7
New Tredegar NP24 ....34 A1
Pontypool NP4 ....62 B6
Pontypool NP4 ....62 E2
East View Terr CF62 ....214 D3
East Way Rd NP20 ....143 D1
East Wlk CF62 ....214 E6
Eastbourne Ct 3 CF63 ....215 C8
Eastbourne Gr SA2 ....94 C7
Eastbourne Pl CF47 ....30 E7
Eastbrook Cl CF64 ....206 B4
Eastbrook Sta CF64 ....206 C4
Easterfield Dr SA3 ....121 A4
Easterly Cl CF31 ....169 D5
Eastern Ave
Cardiff CF23 ....178 E2
Cymmer SA13 ....75 D4
Eastern Cl 2 CF3 ....179 D8
Eastern Prim Sch SA13 ....125 D6
Eastern Prom CF36 ....183 A6
Eastfield Cl NP18 ....118 A4
Eastfield Ct CF72 ....155 E2
Eastfield Dr NP18 ....118 A4
Eastfield Mews NP18 ....118 A4
Eastfield Rd NP18 ....118 A4
Eastfield Terr CF47 ....30 E7
Eastfield View NP18 ....118 A4
Eastfield Way NP18 ....118 A4
Eastgate CF71 ....188 F1
Eastgate Mews CF71 ....188 F1
Eastland Cl SA3 ....122 E7
Eastland Pl SA11 ....71 E6
Eastland Rd SA11 ....71 E7
Eastlands Pk SA3 ....122 A7
Eastmoor Park Cres SA3 ....122 E7
Eastmoor Rd NP19 ....144 C3
Eastview Terr CF81 ....58 A3
Eastville Rd
Abertillery NP13 ....36 C3
Ebbw Vale NP23 ....14 F5
Eastway NP4 ....39 B2
Eaton Cres SA1 ....95 A6
Eaton Ct SA5 ....68 D3
Eaton Rd SA5 ....68 C3
Ebbw Cl CF62 ....211 C7
Ebbw St NP11 ....114 F2
Ebbw Vale Coll of F Ed NP23 ....7 C2
Ebbw Vale Comp Sch NP23 ....7 C2
Ebbw Vale Row SA12 ....99 E5
Ebbw View NP23 ....7 D3
Ebbw View Terr NP11 ....86 F6
Ebenezer Cl CF46 ....83 D7
Ebenezer Ct
Blackmill CF35 ....130 F2
Tredegar NP22 ....6 E1
Ebenezer Dr NP10 ....142 B4
Ebenezer Rd CF40 ....106 F5
Ebenezer St
2 Aberdare CF44 ....28 E4
Pontypridd CF37 ....135 F6
7 Swansea SA1 ....95 D8
Tredegar NP22 ....6 E1
Ebenezer Terr
Blackmill CF35 ....130 F3
14 Newport NP20 ....143 C4
Ebury Ho NP44 ....90 B4
Ebwy Ct CF5 ....193 D4
Eckley Rd CF64 ....216 A5
Eclipse St CF24 ....195 C6
Eddystone Cl CF11 ....194 E3
Eden Ave SA2 ....94 F7
Edgar St CF47 ....10 F4
Edgcort NP44 ....89 B1
Edgehill Bryn NP12 ....85 D5
Llanyravon NP44 ....90 B1
Edgehill Ave CF14 ....159 C1
Edgehill Cl SA12 ....98 E4
Edgehill Ct CF14 ....159 D1
Edgemoor Cl SA2 ....93 B5
Edgemoor Dr SA2 ....93 B6
Edgeware Rd SA2 ....94 E7
Edinburgh Cl NP44 ....89 A3
Edinburgh Ct 10 CF11 ....194 E5
Edington Ave CF14 ....177 F2
Edison Cres SA6 ....22 D1
Edison Ridge NP20 ....117 A3
Edith Rd CF64 ....206 B3
Edlogan Sq NP44 ....90 A6
Edlogan Way NP44 ....90 A5
Edmond's Ct CF24 ....178 B1
Edmondes St CF43 ....80 C3
Edmondstown Rd CF40 ....107 C1
Edmonton Ct NP4 ....62 C7
Edmund Pl
Barry CF63 ....215 D6
Newbridge NP11 ....86 C5
Edmund St
Pontlottyn CF81 ....32 F8
Porth CF39 ....108 A3
Edmunds Cl NP13 ....15 D5
Edward Cl CF47 ....10 F1
Edward Clarke Cl CF5 ....176 E2
Edward German Cres NP19 ....144 E5
Edward Ho 13 CF11 ....194 F5
Edward Jarvis Ct SA11 ....71 E6
Edward Nicholl Ct CF23 ....178 D2
Edward St
Abercarn NP11 ....114 C8
Abercynon CF45 ....82 E2
Aberdare CF44 ....28 E4
Abertillery NP13 ....36 B6
Barry CF63 ....215 B7
Bridgend CF31 ....168 F3
Cardiff CF10 ....195 B6
Glynneath SA11 ....223 D1
Maerdy CF43 ....52 A1
Neath SA11 ....71 E6
Pant CF48 ....11 B7
Pengam NP12 ....85 B6
Pontardawe SA8 ....23 F4
Pontypool NP4 ....62 B7
Pontypool NP4 ....62 E3
Port Talbot SA13 ....99 B1
5 Porth CF39 ....107 F3
5 Treharris CF46 ....83 B6
Ystrad Mynach CF82 ....111 E7
Edward Stephens Terr CF48 ....55 C8
Edward Terr
Abertridwr CF83 ....137 A8
Tredegar NP22 ....13 F6
Edward Thomas Cl CF83 ....139 B3
Edward Vii Ave NP20 ....142 F4
Edward VII Cres NP20 ....143 A5
Edward VII La NP20 ....143 A5
Edwardian Way CF72 ....173 D7
Edwards Ct NP23 ....7 C1
Edwards St
Blaengwrach SA11 ....227 B8
7 Mountain Ash CF45 ....54 E1
Tonypandy CF40 ....106 F6
Edwards Terr
Bedlinog CF46 ....56 A7
Treharris CF46 ....83 B5
Trelewis CF46 ....83 C8
Edwardsville
Abercarn NP11 ....114 B8
Treharris CF46 ....82 F6
Edwin Ind Est NP20 ....143 C7
Edwin St NP20 ....143 C7
EFI Ind Est CF47 ....10 B3
Egerton St CF5 ....194 C6
Egham St CF5 ....194 C6
Eglwys Ave CF37 ....136 A5
Eglwys Newydd Jun & Inf Sch CF14 ....177 B5
Eglwysilan Rd
Abertridwr CF37, CF83 ....136 D7
Rhydyfelin CF37 ....136 E5
Eglwysilan Way CF83 ....136 F7
Egremont Rd CF23 ....178 B2
Egypt St
Pontypridd CF37 ....135 E8
Tonypandy CF40 ....107 B5
Eiddil SA14 ....41 D6
Eiddwen Rd SA5 ....68 B4
Eider Cl CF3 ....179 E8
Eifion Cl CF63 ....215 A8
Eigen Cres SA1 ....95 B8
Eighth Ave
Merthyr Tydfil CF47 ....10 E5
Swansea SA6 ....45 D1
Eileen Pl CF42 ....50 E2
Eileen Rd SA7 ....69 F7
Eileen Terr CF42 ....50 E2
Einon Ct SA4 ....43 D2
Eirw Rd CF39 ....108 A2
Eisteddfa Rd CF40 ....79 F2
Eisteddford Wlk NP19 ....144 D6
Eithen Pl CF36 ....182 E6
Elaine Cl CF14 ....159 E2
Elaine Cres NP19 ....143 F7
Elan Ave SA6 ....45 D1
Elan Cl Aberdare CF44 ....29 E2
Barry CF62 ....214 C6
Bettws NP20 ....116 E1
Elan Rd CF14 ....178 A7
Elan Wlk NP44 ....89 C2
Elba Ave SA13 ....125 D5
Elba Cres SA1 ....97 A7
Elba St SA4 ....66 C6
Elder Cl NP18 ....117 F2
Elder Dr CF36 ....166 D1
Elder Rd SA12 ....98 D7
Elder St CF31 ....168 F4
Elder Wood Cl CF23 ....178 E3
Elderberry Rd CF5 ....176 B1
Eldon Ct 12 CF11 ....194 E5
Eleanor Cl CF35 ....170 B8
Eleanor Pl CF10 ....195 B1
Eleanor St
Tonypandy CF40 ....106 E5
Treherbert CF42 ....78 A8
Eleven St CF64 ....215 E6
Eleventh Ave CF47 ....10 F5
Elfed Ave
Penarth CF64 ....206 E3
Port Talbot SA12 ....124 D7
Elfed Gn CF5 ....176 E1
Elfed Rd SA1 ....95 B8
Elfed Way CF63 ....215 B7
Elford Rd CF5 ....193 C5
Elgam Gn 4 NP4 ....17 C7
Elgar Ave
Newport NP19 ....144 D5
Port Talbot SA12 ....98 A2
Elgar Circ NP19 ....144 D5
Elgar Cl
Caerphilly NP12 ....85 C7
Newport NP19 ....144 D5
Elgar Cres CF3 ....179 D7
Elgar Rd CF64 ....206 F1
Elgin St SA5 ....68 B3
Elias Dr SA10 ....48 D4
Elias Rd SA10 ....48 C4
Elias St SA11 ....71 E7
Elidyr Cres NP11 ....86 F8
Elidyr Rd NP11 ....86 F8
Elim St CF47 ....10 F3
Elim Way NP12 ....86 A5
Eliot Cl SA2 ....93 F8
Elizabeth Ave CF62 ....204 F1
Elizabeth Cl
Pentre CF41 ....78 F4
Ynysforgan SA6 ....46 B4
Elizabeth Maisonettes CF11 ....194 E4
Elizabeth Rd CF31 ....168 C5
Elizabeth Row NP4 ....37 C3
Elizabeth St
Abercynon CF45 ....82 D2
Aberdare CF44 ....29 A1
Llanelli SA15 ....40 D5
Pentre CF41 ....78 F5
Thomastown CF39 ....133 B2
Elizabeth Way NP23 ....7 C1
Elizabethian Ct CF64 ....206 E6
Elled Rd NP4 ....62 A8
Ellen St CF10 ....195 B5
Ellen's Rd SA10 ....70 D8
Ellesmere Ct
Cardiff CF3 ....179 D6
Newbridge NP11 ....87 B8
Ellick St NP4 ....17 C7
Elliot St NP24 ....33 F2
Elliot's Colliery Winding House Mus NP24 ....33 F2
Elliotstown Prim Sch NP24 ....33 F2
Ellipse The NP4 ....62 D1
Ellis CF72 ....155 A5
Ellwood Cl CF3 ....179 F6
Ellwood Path NP44 ....89 B2
Elm Cl
Llanmartin NP18 ....145 E6
Pontypool NP4 ....38 B2
Sully CF64 ....216 C4
Waunarlwydd SA5 ....66 D4
Elm Cotts CF32 ....167 F4
Elm Cres
Bridgend CF31 ....168 B5
Penllergaer SA4 ....44 C2
Elm Ct Caerphilly NP12 ....85 F6
Gorseinon SA4 ....43 A3
Newbridge NP11 ....60 C1
Elm Dr NP11 ....115 C1
Elm Gr Aberdare CF44 ....28 F2
Barry CF63 ....215 C8
Caerphilly CF83 ....138 C5
Gorseinon SA4 ....43 A3
Hirwaun CF44 ....27 E8
Merthyr Tydfil CF47 ....10 D3
Newport NP20 ....117 B2
Pontypool NP4 ....62 E1
St Athan CF62 ....211 B7
Elm Grove La CF64 ....206 A3
Elm Grove Pl CF64 ....206 B3
Elm Grove Rd CF64 ....206 A3
Elm Ho CF14 ....176 E6
Elm Rd
Briton Ferry SA11 ....71 B2
Llanharry CF72 ....172 B5
Porthcawl CF36 ....183 D8
Elm Rise CF32 ....150 F4
Elm St
Aberbargoed CF81 ....58 B4
Abercwmboi CF44 ....53 E4
Cardiff CF24 ....195 C7
Cwm NP23 ....35 A8
Ferndale CF43 ....79 F7
Gilfach Goch CF39 ....132 B5
Rhydyfelin CF37 ....136 B5
Troedyrhiw CF48 ....31 B1
Elm Street La CF24 ....195 C7
Elm Terr CF32 ....104 E1
Elm Tree House Sch CF5 ....194 B7
Elmfield Cl CF3 ....179 E6
Elmgrove CF83 ....138 F6
Elmgrove Cl CF37 ....109 C5
Elmgrove Rd
Cardiff CF14 ....176 E4
Mumbles SA3 ....122 F8
Elmhurst Cl NP4 ....38 B1
Elmhurst Cres SA1 ....95 E8
Elms Pk CF72 ....173 D6
Elms The NP12 ....59 C2
Elmwood NP22 ....13 F5
Elmwood Ct 11 CF24 ....195 C7
Elmwood Dr
Briton Ferry SA11 ....71 C2
Tonyrefail CF39 ....132 E4
Elmwood Gr NP22 ....13 F5
Elmwood Rd SA12 ....98 D6
Elmwood Terr NP22 ....13 F5
Elphin Cres SA1 ....67 E1
Elphin Gdns SA1 ....68 A1
Elphin Rd SA1 ....67 F1
Elworthy Cl CF64 ....216 B5
Elwy Cres SA2 ....67 F1
Elwy Gdns SA2 ....67 F1
Elwyn Dr CF47 ....30 F8
Elwyn St CF39 ....154 D8
Ely Bridge Ind Est CF5 ....193 E7
Ely Hospl CF5 ....193 E5
Ely Ind Est CF40 ....107 A2
Ely Rd CF5 ....194 A8
Ely St Pontyclun CF72 ....173 B8
Tonypandy CF40 ....106 E5
Ely Valley Ind Est CF72 ....173 A8
Ely Valley Rd
Coedely CF39 ....133 D1
Llantrisant CF72 ....155 B5
Talbot Green CF72 ....155 C3
Ynysmaerdy CF72 ....154 F7
Elysia St NP19 ....143 D7
Emanuel Cl CF83 ....137 D1
Embankment Rd SA15 ....40 E2
Emblem Cl CF5 ....193 E4
Emerald St CF24 ....195 D7
Emlyn Ave NP23 ....7 C2
Emlyn Dr CF83 ....138 A4
Emlyn Gdns SA1 ....68 B1
Emlyn Rd
Abersychan NP4 ....37 E6
Cwm NP23 ....35 B8
Swansea SA1 ....68 B1
Emlyn Sq 20 NP20 ....143 C4
Emlyn St 19 NP20 ....143 C4
Emlyn Terr
Merthyr Tydfil CF47 ....10 C2
Swansea SA6 ....68 E6
Tonypandy CF40 ....106 B6
Emma St SA15 ....40 D4
Emmanuel Cl CF42 ....50 F1
Emmanuel Gdns SA2 ....94 B3
Empire Ave SA11 ....227 C8
Empire Terr NP4 ....37 E6
Emroch St SA13 ....125 E8
Emsworth Ct CF23 ....178 C6
Ena Ave SA11 ....71 F7
Endeavour Cl
Bridgend CF31 ....169 C6
Port Talbot SA12 ....98 A3
Endyngs NP44 ....89 B1
Energlyn Cl CF83 ....137 F4
Energlyn Cres 1 CF83 ....137 F5
Energlyn Terr CF83 ....137 E5
Enfield Cl SA6 ....45 E4
Enfield Dr CF62 ....214 C7
Enfield St SA12 ....124 F8
Engine Row NP4 ....17 B7
Enid Rd SA6 ....46 F8
Enid St CF40 ....107 B5
Ennerdale Cl CF23 ....178 B2
Ennerdale Ct 2 NP19 ....143 F8
Enoch Morrell Cl CF48 ....31 B1
Enterprise Ctr NP13 ....15 D6
Enterprise Park Ind Est NP20 ....143 D3
Enterprise Way NP20 ....143 D3
Enville Cl NP20 ....142 E4
Enville Rd NP20 ....142 E4
Eppynt Cl NP11 ....115 C2
Eppynt Rd SA5 ....68 A4
Epsom Cl CF5 ....193 F5
Epstein Cl CF5 ....176 D2
Erasmus Terr CF82 ....85 B2
Eric Coates Cl NP19 ....144 D4
Eric Coates Wlk NP19 ....144 E4
Eridge Rd NP4 ....37 F5
Ernald Pl SA2 ....94 F6
Ernest St CF47 ....30 E7
Erskine Ct CF24 ....195 E7
Erw Deg CF31 ....168 B5
Erw Fach CF38 ....135 D1
Erw Hir CF72 ....155 E3
Erw Hydref SA9 ....2 D8
Erw Ifan CF35 ....170 D8
Erw Las Cardiff CF14 ....177 A4
Merthyr Tydfil CF48 ....10 A2
Penywaun CF44 ....28 C6
Erw Rd SA15 ....40 C5
Erw Wen Cardiff CF14 ....177 B8
North Cornelly CF33 ....165 F7
Pencoed CF35 ....170 D8
Erw'r-Delyn Cl CF64 ....206 D4
Erwlas SA14 ....41 D3
Eschol Cl NP19 ....144 B3
Eschol Ct NP19 ....144 B3
Esgair-y-llys CF31 ....168 B4
Esgid Mair CF63 ....205 C1
Eskdale Cl CF23 ....178 B3
Espalone SA3 ....122 C6
Esplanade
Penarth CF64 ....207 B3
Porthcawl CF36 ....182 F6
Esplanade Ave CF36 ....182 F6
Esplanade Bldgs CF62 ....214 E2
Essex Ct NP18 ....118 A3
Essex St NP19 ....143 E4
Essex Terr SA6 ....68 E6
Essich St 5 CF24 ....178 C1
Estate Rd
Blaenavon NP4 ....17 B7
Pontypool NP4 ....62 A8
Esterling Dr CF36 ....182 F8
Estuary Pk SA14 ....42 C7
Estuary Rd NP19 ....144 D1
Ethel St Cardiff CF5 ....194 B6
Neath SA11 ....71 D6
Etna Terr CF39 ....132 C7
Eton Ct CF14 ....177 F6
Eton Pl 1 CF5 ....194 D5
Eton Rd NP19 ....143 D5
Eton St CF62 ....214 C3
Eugene Cl 13 CF3 ....180 A8
Eureka Pl NP23 ....14 D7
Eurgan Cl CF61 ....209 F5
Eurocast Trad Est CF14 ....176 E6
Eurwg Cres 6 CF3 ....179 D8
Eustace Dr CF32 ....150 F4
Eva St
Mountain Ash CF45 ....54 D2
Neath SA11 ....71 E6
Evan St CF46 ....83 B8
Evan's Rd SA11 ....71 D5
Evan's Terr NP22 ....6 D2
Evans Hos CF48 ....3 F3
Evans Sq CF37 ....109 E3
Evans St Barry CF62 ....214 F5
Newport NP20 ....143 C6
8 Port Talbot SA13 ....99 C1
Pyle CF33 ....148 D3
Evans Terr
Maesteg CF34 ....102 B8
6 Merthyr Tydfil CF47 ....30 F8
North Cornelly CF33 ....165 F7
Swansea SA1 ....95 C8
Tonypandy CF40 ....107 B5
Evans' Terr SA15 ....40 F6
Evans's Terr CF40 ....106 C7
Evansfield Rd CF14 ....176 F3
Eve's Well Ct NP19 ....143 E5
Eveline Terr SA13 ....125 B8
Evelyn Rd SA10 ....70 E7
Evelyn St
Abertillery NP13 ....36 B5
Barry CF63 ....215 A5
Evenlode Ave CF64 ....206 F2
Evenlode Prim Sch CF64 ....206 E2
Evenwood Cl CF23 ....160 F1
Everard St CF63 ....215 B6
Everard Way CF23 ....178 B4
Everest Ave CF14 ....159 F1
Everest Wlk CF14 ....159 F1
Evergreen NP20 ....143 A3
Evergreen Cotts CF33 ....165 D8
Evergreen Ct CF39 ....133 E6
Eversley Rd SA2 ....94 D6
Everswell Ave CF5 ....193 D7
Everswell Rd CF5 ....193 D7
Evesham Ct NP20 ....143 A7
Eveswell Jun & Inf Sch NP19 ....143 F5
Eveswell La 1 NP19 ....143 F5
Eveswell Park Rd NP19 ....143 F5
Eveswell St NP19 ....143 F5
Evtol Ind Est NP20 ....143 D2
Ewanni Fach CF72 ....154 A3
Ewart Pl SA5 ....68 C4
Ewbank Cl CF63 ....215 C8
Ewenny Cl
Barry CF63 ....215 A8
Porthcawl CF36 ....165 E2
Ewenny Cross CF35 ....185 E7
Ewenny Ind Est CF31 ....169 C1
Ewenny Pl SA6 ....68 D8
Ewenny Priory CF35 ....186 A8
Ewenny Rd
Bridgend CF31,CF35 ....168 F2
Cardiff CF14 ....178 A7
Castle-upon-Alun CF32 ....198 C7
Maesteg CF34 ....102 B2
St Brides Major CF32 ....185 D2
Wick CF71 ....198 C7
Ewenny Road Sta CF34 ....102 B2
Excalibur Dr CF14 ....159 E2
Excelsior Ind Est CF14 ....177 D2
Excelsior Rd CF14 ....177 C2
Excelsior St NP23 ....14 F2
Excelsior Terr CF43 ....79 C8
Exchange Ct 3 NP11 ....114 F3
Exchange Rd
Neath SA11 ....71 D6
2 Risca NP11 ....114 F3
Exchange Row SA14 ....41 C7
Exchange St CF34 ....101 F3
Exe Rd NP20 ....116 D2
Exeter Cl
Cwmbran NP44 ....89 A3
Heolgerrig CF48 ....10 A1
Exeter Mans 6 CF14 ....176 F6
Exeter Pl NP4 ....37 F3
Exeter Rd 6 NP19 ....143 E4
Exeter St NP19 ....143 E5
Exford Cres CF3 ....179 A5
Exhibition Row CF44 ....28 E7
Eynon St SA4 ....43 D4
Eyre St CF24 ....195 E6

F

Faber Way CF11 ....194 D3
Fabian Way SA1,SA10 ....96 C7
Factory La
Abersychan NP4 ....37 F4
Pontypridd CF37 ....135 B8
Factory Rd
Bargoed CF81 ....57 F5
Brynmawr NP23 ....8 C4
Clydach SA6 ....46 D7
Llanblethian CF71 ....200 D8
Newport NP20 ....143 B6
Factory Terr CF32 ....150 C3
Fagwr Isaf SA6 ....22 B2
Fagwr Pl SA6 ....46 A1
Fagwr Rd SA6 ....22 B2
Fair View
Gilfach Goch CF39 ....106 C1
Neath SA10 ....48 C1
Pengam NP12 ....85 C7
Pontlottyn CF81 ....32 F8
Tredegar NP22 ....6 C1
Treharris CF46 ....83 B5
Fair View Cl
Pontyclun CF72 ....173 B7
Swansea SA7 ....69 F6
Fair View Terr NP23 ....8 C1
Fairacre Cl CF14 ....159 E2
Fairbrook Cl CF14 ....177 B8
Fairfax Cres CF36 ....182 E7
Fairfax Rd
Cardiff CF14 ....177 D6
Newport NP19 ....144 A4
Fairfield
Aberavon SA12 ....98 F1
Abersychan NP4 ....37 F4
North Cornelly CF33 ....166 A8
Penperlleni NP4 ....39 E6
Pontypool NP4 ....62 A7
Tredegar NP22 ....13 F8
Fairfield Ave
Cardiff CF5 ....194 A6
Maesteg CF34 ....102 A2
Fairfield Cl
Aberdare CF44 ....29 D1
Caerleon NP18 ....117 F3
Caerphilly NP12 ....85 E6
Cardiff CF5 ....193 F7
Hawthorn CF37 ....136 A4
Llantwit Major CF61 ....210 A6
Fairfield Cres CF61 ....210 A6
Fairfield Ind Est CF15 ....158 A2
Fairfield La CF37 ....136 A4
Fairfield Prim Sch CF64 ....206 F4
Fairfield Rd
Bridgend CF31 ....169 A2
Caerleon NP18 ....117 F3
Cymmer SA13 ....75 D3
Penarth CF64 ....206 F4
Fairfield Rise CF61 ....210 A6
Fairfield Terr SA1 ....95 B7
Fairfield Way SA11 ....71 E8
Fairford St CF63 ....215 B7
Fairhaven Cl 8 CF3 ....180 A8
Fairhaven Cl SA3 ....123 A3
Fairhill NP44 ....89 B2
Fairhill Dr Baglan SA12 ....98 E4
Church Village CF38 ....136 B1
Fairhill Wlk NP44 ....89 B2
Fairland Cl CF72 ....155 E3
Fairlawn Ct CF5 ....177 A1
Fairlawn Terr CF35 ....170 D8
Fairlawns SA11 ....71 B3
Fairleigh CF5 ....205 F7
Fairleigh Ct CF11 ....194 D8
Fairleigh Rd CF11 ....194 D7
Fairmead Ct CF5 ....193 D7
Fairmeadow CF15 ....157 C1
Fairmeadows CF34 ....128 C8
Fairmound Pl CF38 ....136 B1
Fairoak SA18 ....219 D7
Fairoak Ave NP19 ....143 E6
Fairoak Chase CF31 ....169 C4
Fairoak Cres CF44 ....28 E2
Fairoak Ct
Cardiff CF23 ....178 B2
4 Newport NP19 ....143 E6
Fairoak Gdns 8 NP19 ....143 E6
Fairoak Gr NP10 ....141 F2
Fairoak La NP44 ....90 B4
Fairoak Mews CF24 ....178 A2
Fairoak Rd CF24 ....178 A1
Fairoak Terr NP19 ....143 E5
Fairoaks CF64 ....206 B3
Fairthorn Cl CF14 ....159 E3
Fairview Beddau CF38 ....156 B7
Ebbw Vale NP23 ....14 C8
Hirwaun CF44 ....224 E1
Tonypandy CF40 ....107 B1
Fairview Ave
Aberavon SA12 ....98 F1
Risca NP11 ....115 A2
Fairview Cl 9 CF3 ....180 A8
Fairview Ct
Cardiff CF23 ....178 E7
Pontypool NP4 ....62 A8
Fairview Est CF48 ....225 F1
Fairview Hos CF48 ....225 F3
Fairview Rd SA5 ....45 C2

Fairview Terr
Abercynon CF45 .82 F3
Abersychan NP4 .37 E5
Abertillery NP13 .36 B7
Merthyr Tydfil CF47 .30 E8
Fairwater (Tyllgoed) Halt CF5 .193 E8
Fairwater Ave CF5 .193 F7
Fairwater Cl
Cwmbran NP44 .89 B2
Michaelston-y-Fedw CF3 .162 A5
Fairwater Gn CF5 .193 D7
Fairwater Gr E CF5 .193 F8
Fairwater Gr W CF5 .193 F8
Fairwater Jun & Inf Sch CF5 .193 D7
Fairwater Jun & Inf Schs NP44 .89 C2
Fairwater Rd CF5 .193 E8
Fairwater Square Shops NP44 .89 B1
Fairwater Way NP44 .89 B1
Fairwater Workshops CF5 .193 E7
Fairway SA12 .98 C2
Fairway Cl NP10 .142 A7
Fairway Dr
Caerphilly CF83 .137 F6
Pontardawe SA8 .23 D6
Fairway The
Cardiff CF23 .160 C1
Pontypool NP4 .63 B4
Fairways Bargoed CF81 57 E5
North Cornelly CF33 .165 E8
Fairways Cres CF5 .193 C7
Fairways The NP12 .85 E8
Fairways View CF72 .155 A3
Fairwood Cl CF5 .176 E1
Fairwood Dr SA12 .98 E6
Fairwood Hospl SA2 .93 A6
Fairwood Rd
Cardiff CF5 .176 E1
Dunvant SA2 .93 C8
Mumbles SA3 .123 A8
Fairwood Terr SA4 .66 C6
Fairy Glen CF32 .104 E4
Fairy Gr SA2 .93 E7
Fairyland SA11 .72 A8
Fairyland Rd SA11 .49 B1
Falcon Chambers 4 SA15 .40 D6
Falcon Dr SA11 .72 B4
Falcon Gr CF64 .217 A7
Falcon Pl SA5 .67 E7
Falcon Rd CF63 .215 D7
Falcon Terr NP23 .35 B7
Falconwood Dr CF5 .192 F5
Falfield Cl CF14 .160 A2
Fallowfield 11 NP44 .89 B1
Fallowfield Dr NP19 .144 C3
Fan Heulog CF37 .109 D6
Fanheulog CF72 .155 B2
Fanny St Cardiff CF24 178 A1
Cardiff CF24 .195 A8
Faraday Cl NP20 .116 F2
Faraday Rd SA6 .22 E1
Fardre Cres CF38 .135 F1
Fardre Ct CF38 .135 E1
Farlays NP44 .89 A1
Farlington Ct CF3 .179 A3
Farlow Wlk NP44 .89 D2
Farm Cl
Abertridwr CF83 .137 A7
Blackwood NP12 .59 A1
Farm Dr Cardiff CF23 .178 B4
Port Talbot SA12 .98 C1
Farm Fields Rd NP23 .14 D6
Farm La
Cwmbran NP44 .89 F4
Newport NP19 .143 E7
Farm Rd
Aberdare CF44 .53 D6
Abersychan NP4 .37 D5
Briton Ferry SA11 .71 C3
Caerphilly CF83 .138 C3
Cefn Cribwr CF32 .149 E2
Ebbw Vale NP23 .14 D5
Nantyglo NP23 .15 C8
Newbridge NP11 .60 B2
Pontardawe SA8 .23 B1
Pontlottyn CF81 .12 F1
Pontypool NP4 .62 C5
Ton Pentre CF41 .79 A2
Farm Terr NP24 .33 F4
Farm View NP12 .58 B2
Farmers Rd SA10 .48 C5
Farmfield Ave SA12 .98 D2
Farmhouse Way CF5 193 B3
Farmleigh CF3 .179 B3
Farmville Rd CF24 .195 E6
Farmwood Cl NP19 .144 B5
Farnaby Cl NP19 .144 E5
Farraday Dr CF82 .84 E7
Farteg Rd SA13 .100 F5
Farthings The CF23 .160 F1
Faulkner Rd NP20 .143 B5
Faull St SA6 .45 E1
Fedw Hir Hospl CF44 .225 C1
Feeder Bank NP22 .6 D1
Feeder Row NP11 .114 C7
Feering St NP19 .143 E4
Felbridge Cl CF10 .195 C4
Felbrigg Cres CF23 .160 E1
Felin Fach CF14 .177 B3
Felin Fran SA7 .46 E2
Felin Wen CF14 .177 C7
Felindre Ave CF35 .170 E7
Felindre Rd CF35 .170 F7
Felinfach SA9 .221 C6
Felinfoel Jun Sch SA14 .41 A8
Felinfoel Rd SA15 .40 E7
Fell St CF46 .83 B7
Felnex Ind Est NP19 .164 E8
Felsted Cl CF23 .160 F1
Fenbrook Cl SA12 .98 D5
Fendrod Bsns Pk SA6 69 A6
Fendrod Way SA7 .69 C7
Fennel Cl
10 Cardiff CF3 .180 A8
Penarth CF64 .206 E5
Fenner Brockway Cl 1 NP19 .144 D7
Fenton Pl
Pontycymer CF32 .103 F2
Porthcawl CF36 .182 F7
Fenviolet Cl CF3 .180 B6
Fenwick Dr CF31 .169 C5
Fenwick St CF43 .107 C8
Fermoy Ct SA5 .67 F6
Fern Cl NP11 .59 D3
Fern Cres CF44 .28 D2
Fern Ct SA5 .67 F5
Fern Dr CF62 .214 D5
Fern Hill CF41 .79 B2
Fern Pl CF5 .193 D8
Fern Rise NP20 .117 B3
Fern St Cardiff CF5 .194 B6
Hendreforgan CF39 .132 C5
Ogmore Vale CF32 .130 E8
Swansea SA5 .68 B2
Fern Terr CF40 .106 D6
Fernbank NP44 .89 B2
Fernbrook Cl NP23 .7 D6
Ferncroft Way NP4 .38 B2
Ferndale Cl NP23 .7 B5
Ferndale Comp Sch CF43 .79 C8
Ferndale Ct CF43 .79 F7
Ferndale Ind Est CF43 79 D8
Ferndale Inf Sch CF43 79 F7
Ferndale Rd CF43 .80 B2
Ferndale St CF11 .194 F3
Fernfield SA12 .98 E4
Fernfield Terr NP13 .36 B5
Fernhill CF45 .54 A3
Fernhill Cl
Merthyr Tydfil CF47 .10 D5
Mumbles SA2 .94 B1
Troedyrhiw CF48 .31 C1
Fernhill Rd SA4 .43 A3
Fernhill Sta CF45 .54 B4
Fernhill Terr
New Tredegar NP24 .33 F3
Treharris CF46 .83 A7
Fernlea NP11 .114 F3
Ferns The
4 Penarth CF64 .207 B5
Quakers Yard CF46 .83 C6
Fernside NP19 .144 B3
Ferntree Dr CF3 .179 E7
Ferny Ct CF23 .178 D2
Ferrara Sq SA1 .95 D5
Ferrier Ave CF5 .176 D1
Ferrier's Row CF34 .102 B3
Ferry La 7 CF64 .207 B5
Ferry Rd Cardiff CF11 .206 F8
Loughor SA4 .42 C1
Ferry Side SA1 .95 E6
Ferryboat Cl SA6 .69 A7
Fescue Pl CF5 .193 A5
Festiniog Rd CF14 .177 A2
Festival Cres NP4 .63 B4
Festival Dr NP23 .14 E4
Festival Pk NP23 .14 F1
Fetty Pl NP44 .89 D1
Ffald Rd CF33 .148 B2
Ffaldau Ind Est CF32 103 E5
Ffaldau Prim Sch CF32 .103 F3
Ffaldau Terr CF43 .79 D7
Ffeam-y-Graig CF62 211 D4
Fferm Goch CF35 .170 F1
Fferm-y-Bryn CF82 .84 E1
Ffferws Rd SA18 .218 F6
Fflorens Rd NP11 .59 F1
Fforch Cl CF42 .78 D7
Fforch-Dwm Rd SA12 73 E6
Fforchaman Rd CF44 .53 B4
Fforchneol Row CF44 .53 B5
Fford Llanbad CF39 .132 D5
Fford Rhaglan CF35 .152 B6
Fford-yr-Orsaf SA18 219 B7
Fford-yr-Ywen CF38 136 A2
Ffordd -yr-Afon CF31 .168 B6
Ffordd Abiah SA6 .46 E8
Ffordd Afan SA12 .99 D5
Ffordd Alltwen SA4 .66 A5
Ffordd Aneurin Bevan SA2 .94 C8
Ffordd Beck SA4 .66 B6
Ffordd Bodlyn CF23 .178 C3
Ffordd Briallu SA7 .69 D6
Ffordd Bryngwyn SA4 66 D8
Ffordd Brynheulog SA8 .23 D5
Ffordd Butler SA4 .66 B6
Ffordd Candleston CF31 .168 C3
Ffordd Catraeth CF37 .109 F3
Ffordd Celyn 7 CF14 .177 B4
Ffordd Cwell Yn CF23 .178 C3
Ffordd Cwellyn CF23 178 B3
Ffordd Cwm Cidi CF62 .214 B5
Ffordd Cwm Tawe
Swansea SA6 .68 F6
Ynysforgan SA6,SA7 .46 D5
Ffordd Cynghordy SA7 .69 D7
Ffordd Cynore SA5 .67 C6
Ffordd Dafydd SA14 .218 D7
Ffordd Dawel SA7 .69 E6
Ffordd Ddu CF33 .148 B2
Ffordd Derwen SA13 148 A6
Ffordd Dewi SA6 .45 B1
Ffordd Dillwyn-Llewellyn SA4 .44 C2
Ffordd Dinas SA12 .99 D5
Ffordd Dinefwr CF15 .174 D7
Ffordd Draenen Ddu SA3 .122 E6
Ffordd Dryden SA2 .93 E8
Ffordd Eira SA4 .43 C2
Ffordd Elin CF63 .215 D7
Ffordd Ellen SA6 .22 B2
Ffordd Emlyn SA9 .2 B5
Ffordd Erw CF83 .158 E8
Ffordd Eynon Evans CF83 .137 D6
Ffordd Florence 3 SA18 .219 B7
Ffordd Ganol CF31 .169 A4
Ffordd Garthorne CF10 .195 C3
Ffordd Gerdinan CF38 .136 A1
Ffordd Glandwr SA9 .2 B6
Ffordd Gower Davies CF37 .109 A7
Ffordd Gwyn SA7 .69 D7
Ffordd Gwyneth 1 CF63 .215 C8
Ffordd Is-Cennen SA18 .219 B7
Ffordd Las
Abertridwr CF83 .137 A8
Radyr CF15 .176 A6
Ffordd Llundain SA7 .69 D7
Ffordd Llyffant SA7 .70 B8
Ffordd Maescwarrau SA18 .219 D6
Ffordd Newydd CF33 .166 A8
Ffordd Parc Ynysderw SA8 .23 E4
Ffordd Pen Twyn SA18 .219 C7
Ffordd Pengam CF24 .196 A8
Ffordd Penrhos CF83 .137 D3
Ffordd Priordy CF32 150 D4
Ffordd Scott
Birchgrove SA7 .46 F1
Swansea SA7 .70 A8
Ffordd Sealand CF62 .214 E4
Ffordd Silkin SA8 .23 E5
Ffordd Stewart 2 SA18 .219 B7
Ffordd Talbot SA18 .219 B7
Ffordd Talfan SA4 .66 D8
Ffordd Taliesin
Pontypridd CF37 .109 F4
Swansea SA2 .93 F8
Ffordd Talygarn CF72 .173 A7
Ffordd Tollborth SA7 .69 D7
Ffordd Traws Cwm CF83 .137 E1
Ffordd Trecastell CF72 .172 D6
Ffordd Treforgan CF15 .176 A8
Ffordd Tryweryn CF37 .109 F3
Ffordd Walter SA18 .219 C7
Ffordd y Bedol CF37 109 D6
Ffordd y Brain SA5 .67 E5
Ffordd y Brenin 1 CF10 .195 A6
Ffordd y Dderwen CF71 .189 C8
Ffordd y Faenor SA18 .219 B7
Ffordd y Frenhines CF34,SA13 .126 E6
Ffordd y Gamlas SA4 .66 B6
Ffordd y Goedwig CF33 .148 C3
Ffordd y Mileniwm CF62,CF63 .214 F4
Ffordd y Morfa SA14 218 C7
Ffordd y Mynach CF33 .148 B2
Ffordd y Rhyd SA18 .219 B6
Ffordd yr Eglwys CF33 .166 A8
Ffordd Ysgol SA12 .98 D1
Ffordd-y-Barcer CF5 .192 F5
Ffordd-y-Berllan CF15 .176 A7
Ffordd-y-Bryn
Birchgrove SA7 .47 B1
Swansea SA7 .70 B8
Ffordd-y-Capel CF38 .156 F6
Ffordd-y-Dderwyn CF31 .168 C6
Ffordd-y-Derwen CF45 .54 B6
Ffordd-y-Eglwys CF5 .191 E5
Ffordd-y-Gollen CF38 .135 F2
Ffordd-y-Gyfraith CF32 .149 E6
Ffordd-y-Mynach SA10 .71 A7
Ffordd-y-Mynydd
Birchgrove SA7 .47 B1
Swansea SA7 .70 B8
Ffordd-y-Parc
Bridgend CF31 .169 A8
Swansea SA6 .45 E1
Ffordd-yr-Afon SA18 .219 B8
Fforde Cae Duke SA4 .66 A8
Fforde Kilby SA4 .66 A8
Fforest Dr CF62 .214 B4
Fforest Glade NP19 .143 F6
Fforest Hill SA10 .49 C4
Fforest Rd
Llanharry CF72 .172 C4
Mountain Ash CF45 .54 E3
Fforestfach SA18 .219 A5
Ffos Cl CF46 .83 E4
Ffos Felen SA4 .66 B5
Ffos y Cerridden CF46 .83 D3
Ffos y Fran Cl NP10 .141 F2
Ffos-y-Fran NP10 .141 F2
Ffos-Yr-Efail Terr SA4 .19 C4
Ffos-yr-Hebog CF83 112 A5
Ffosmaen Rd NP23 .8 D1
Ffridd Las CF31 .168 B4
Ffrwd Cres CF45 .54 D3
Ffrwd Rd
Abersychan NP4 .38 A4
Merthyr Tydfil CF48 .225 F3
Ffrwd St CF44 .53 C6
Ffrwd Terr
Hirwaun CF44 .27 E7
Llanbradach CF83 .111 F2
Ffrwd Vale SA10 .48 D1
Ffrwd-Wyllt St SA13 125 C6
Ffrwd-y-Felin SA18 .219 B8
Ffrwdwyllt Cotts 4 SA13 .125 C6
Ffwrwm Rd CF83 .139 F7
Ffynnon Ct 3 NP23 .8 B4
Ffynnon Deilo CF71 .191 A4
Ffynnon Samlet SA7 .69 D7
Ffynnon Taf Prim Sch CF15 .157 F4
Ffynnon Tudful CF47 .10 D2
Ffynnon Wen
Clydach SA6 .46 C7
North Cornelly CF33 .148 A1
Ffynnon-Las CF41 .79 F2
Ffynnon-wen Terr NP12 .58 B1
Ffynnonbwla Rd CF37 .136 E4
Ffynon y Maen CF33 148 A2
Ffynone Cl SA1 .95 A7
Ffynone Dr SA1 .95 A7
Ffynone Rd SA1 .95 A7
Ffynonn Las SA18 .219 B6
Fiddlers Elbow CF46 .83 A4
Fidlas Ave CF14 .178 A7
Fidlas Rd CF14 .178 A7
Field Cl SA6 .46 A2
Field St Swansea SA1 .68 D3
Tonypandy CF40 .106 F4
Trelewis CF46 .83 C7
Field Terr
New Tredegar NP24 .33 E4
Pentyrch CF15 .157 C1
Port Talbot SA13 .125 D8
Field View NP44 .90 A5
Field View Rd CF63 .215 A7
Field Way CF14 .177 E6
Field's Park Rd NP11 .86 E7
Fieldfare Dr CF3 .180 A6
Fielding Cl CF3 .179 B7
Fieldings 7 NP44 .89 B1
Fields Ave NP44 .89 D6
Fields Ct CF11 .194 C7
Fields Park Ave NP20 .142 F5
Fields Park Cres NP20 .143 A5
Fields Park Ct NP20 .143 A5
Fields Park Gdns NP20 .142 F5
Fields Park La NP20 .142 F5
Fields Park Rd
Cardiff CF11 .194 D8
Newport NP20 .142 F5
Fields Park Terr NP11 .114 B5
Fields Rd
Cwmbran NP44 .116 F8
Newport NP20 .143 A5
Risca NP11 .141 B8
Tredegar NP22 .13 F5
Fieldview Cl CF64 .206 E5
Fife St CF45 .82 E3
Fifth Ave
Hirwaun CF44 .224 C1
Merthyr Tydfil CF47 .10 E5
Swansea SA6 .45 D1
Filey Rd NP19 .143 D7
Finchley Rd CF5 .193 E7
Finchway Ct NP4 .37 E7
Finsbury Terr SA2 .94 F5
Fir Grove St CF41 .78 F5
Fir St CF43 .79 F7
Fir Tree Cl CF47 .10 D5
Fir Tree Cotts CF33 .165 D8
Fir Tree Dr CF46 .83 A6
Firbank Ave NP19 .144 A7
Firbank Cres NP19 .144 A6
Firbank Terr NP11 .113 A5
Firbanks Way CF72 .155 A3
Firemans Ct 2 NP23 .8 C4
Firm St SA1 .95 C8
Firs Ave CF5 .193 B8
Firs The Blaenavon NP4 17 E6
Newport NP20 .117 C2
Porthcawl CF36 .183 E7
First Ave
Caerphilly CF83 .137 F3
Merthyr Tydfil CF47 .10 E5
Swansea SA6 .68 C8
Firth Rd
Ebbw Vale NP23 .14 B8
Llanelli SA15 .40 E4
Firtree Cl
Caerleon NP18 .117 E2
Cardiff CF5 .193 C8
Firwood Cl
Bryn-côch SA10 .48 C5
Cardiff CF14 .176 F4
Fisher Cl NP19 .144 F7
Fishguard Cl CF14 .178 A7
Fishguard Rd CF14 .177 F7
Fishmarket Quay 11 SA1 .95 E6
Fishpond Rd CF3 .179 B6
Fitzalan Com High Sch CF11 .194 B5
Fitzalan Ct 9 CF24 .195 B6
Fitzalan Pl CF24 .195 C6
Fitzalan Rd
Cardiff CF24 .195 B6
Cardiff CF24 .195 C6
Fitzhamon Ave CF61 210 A5
Fitzhamon Emb CF11 .194 F5
Fitzhamon La CF11 .194 F5
Fitzhamon Rd CF36 .182 F8
Fitzroy Ave NP23 .7 D2
Fitzroy Lodge NP12 .85 C7
Fitzroy St
Brynmawr NP23 .8 B5
Cardiff CF24 .195 A8
Fitzwilliam Cl CF72 .155 E2
Five Bells Rd CF31 .168 F3
Five Hos NP23 .7 E4
Five Locks Cl NP44 .89 D7
Five Locks Rd NP44 .89 D6
Five Oaks La NP44 .90 A5
Flanders Mdw CF61 .209 F5
Flanders Rd CF61 .209 F5
Flatholm Pl SA5 .67 E7
Flatholm Way CF36 .165 E1
Flats The CF14 .177 F2
Flax Ct CF64 .206 E5
Flaxland Ave CF14 .177 E3
Fleet St SA1 .95 B5
Fleet Way CF11 .194 E2
Fleetwood Cl NP19 .143 F4
Fleming Cl NP20 .117 A2
Flemingston Rd CF62 .211 D7
Fleur-de-lis Prim Sch NP12 .85 B5
Fleur-De-Lys Ave NP12 .85 E4
Flint Ave CF61 .210 B7
Flint Cl NP19 .144 A7
Flint Ct NP18 .118 A3
Flint Ho SA12 .124 D8
Flint St CF14 .177 E1
Flora St CF24 .195 A8
Floral Ave NP12 .85 B7
Florence Ave CF62 .214 E8
Florence Cl NP13 .36 C5
Florence Gr CF83 .138 A2
Florence Pl NP4 .62 E2
Florence St
Cardiff CF24 .195 E7
Llanelli SA15 .40 E3
Neath SA11 .71 E6
Porthcawl CF36 .165 F1
Florentia St CF24 .178 A1
Fochriw Prim Sch CF81 .32 D8
Fochriw Rd CF81 .32 E8
Foel View Cl CF38 .156 B7
Foley Ho NP44 .90 B4
Folland Ct SA2 .94 B1
Folland Rd SA18 .220 B8
Folly La
Penperlleni NP4 .39 A3
Pontypool NP4 .38 D2
Folly Rd NP4 .38 C1
Folly View NP4 .62 D7
Fonmon Cres CF5 .193 D5
Fonmon Park Rd CF62 .212 E2
Fonmon Rd CF62 .212 D2
Fonthill Pl CF11 .194 E3
Fontigary Rd CF3 .179 C3
Fontygari Holiday & L Pk CF62 .212 E1
Fontygary Rd CF62 .212 F1
Forbes St SA6 .68 E5
Ford Farm La NP18 .119 E1
Ford Rd
Fleur De Lis NP12 .85 A6
Pontypridd CF37 .109 A1
Port Talbot SA13 .99 B1
Upper Boat CF37 .136 D2
Ford St NP20 .143 B5
Fordwell CF5 .177 A1
Foreland Rd CF14 .177 A5
Foreshore Rd CF10 .195 F2
Forest Ave CF82 .84 F5
Forest Cl
Cwmbran NP44 .116 B8
Newport NP19 .143 F6
Sarn CF32 .150 E3
Forest Farm Nature Trail CF14 .176 D6
Forest Farm Rd
Cardiff CF14 .176 E5
Radyr CF14 .176 D6
Forest Fawr Wlks CF83 .158 E4
Forest Gr
Pontypridd CF37 .135 E5
Treharris CF46 .82 F6
Forest Hill NP12 .85 E3
Forest Hills Dr CF72 .155 A2
Forest Level CF45 .54 E2
Forest Lodge La SA12 99 F4
Forest Oak Cl CF23 .160 C1
Forest Rd
Beddau CF38 .156 A6
Pontypridd CF37 .135 E6
Treharris CF46 .83 B7
Forest Veiw NP11 .114 D8
Forest View
Cardiff CF5 .193 C7
Mountain Ash CF45 .54 A3
Neath SA11 .72 B4
Pontypridd CF37 .109 C6
Pyle CF33 .148 A2
Talbot Green CF72 .155 C2
Forest Wlk CF72 .155 A2
Forge Cl NP18 .118 B4
Forge Cres NP22 .12 F2
Forge Fach SA6 .46 D7
Forge Factory Est CF34 .101 F4
Forge Hammer Ind Est NP44 .89 D4
Forge La NP10 .142 B2
Forge Mews NP10 .142 B3
Forge Pl
Aberdare CF44 .29 B3
Cardiff CF5 .193 B4
Forge Rd
Blaenavon NP4 .17 B6
Crofty SA4 .64 B2
Machen CF83 .140 A7
Newport NP10 .142 C1
Port Talbot SA13 .99 B1
Forge Row
Aberdare CF44 .53 D6
Maesygwartha NP7 .9 E8
Pontypool NP4 .61 F8
Forge Side Rd NP4 .17 B5
Forge St CF41 .79 A4
Forge Trip CF44 .29 B3
Forge View CF44 .53 C5
Forge Way CF36 .182 F8
Forgeside NP44 .89 E4
Forio Ho CF10 .195 C2
Forrest Rd
Cardiff CF5 .194 B6
Penarth CF64 .207 A1
Forrest St CF11 .194 F2
Forster Rd SA11 .71 F7
Forsythia Cl
Merthyr Tydfil CF47 .10 C5
Risca NP11 .115 C1
Forsythia Dr CF23 .178 D7
Fort Rd CF64 .217 A5
Fort St CF24 .195 E7
Fort View NP10 .142 A3
Fortlee NP20 .142 E3
Fortran Rd CF3 .180 B8
Fosse Cl NP19 .144 C2
Fosse Rd NP19 .144 C2
Foster Dr CF23 .178 E1
Foster St 6 CF63 .215 B6
Fothergill Cres CF47 .10 F2
Fothergill Rd SA11 .227 B8
Fothergill St
Aberdare CF44 .29 B3
Merthyr Tydfil CF47 .10 F2
Pontypridd CF37 .135 E7
Fothergills Rd NP24 .33 E3
Founders Row CF44 .28 E5
Foundry Bridge NP13 .36 B5
Foundry Pl
Pontypridd CF37 .109 D2
6 Porth CF39 .107 F3
Foundry Rd
Abersychan NP4 .37 E3
Hirwaun CF44 .27 D8
Morriston SA6 .46 A1
Neath SA11 .71 E5
Pontypridd CF37 .109 A1
Tonypandy CF40 .106 F6
Foundry Row
Ammanford SA18 .219 C7
Neath SA10 .70 E8
Foundry View CF44 .53 C5
Fountain Ct NP13 .36 B7
Fountain La CF3 .180 B8
Fountain Rd
Aberkenfig CF32 .150 B3
Pontypool NP4 .62 E5
Fountain St
Ferndale CF43 .80 A6
3 Mountain Ash CF45 .54 D3
Trehafod CF37 .108 D2
Fountain Terr CF32 .129 D2
Four Acre CF61 .210 A7

Four Elms Ct 2
CF24 ....195 C6
Four Elms Rd 2
CF24 ....195 D2
Fouracres Cl CF43 ....215 C7
Fourteen Locks Canal Ctr
NP10 ....142 B6
Fourteenth Ave
CF44 ....224 C1
Fourth Ave
Hirwaun CF44 ....224 C1
Merthyr Tydfil CF47 ......10 E5
Swansea SA6 ....45 D1
Fowler St NP4 ....62 A8
Fowler's Pl CF34 ......102 A8
Fox Ave NP11 ....86 D5
Fox Gr SA11 ....67 A4
Fox Hollows CF71 ......189 C5
Fox Russell Cl CF14 ...177 C2
Fox St Llandaff CF5 ....54 D3
Mountain Ash CF45 ....54 D3
Treharris CF46 ....83 B7
Foxberry Cl CF23 ....161 B1
Foxfields CF31 ....169 D4
Foxglove Cl CF5 ....193 A6
Foxglove Rise CF64 ...206 E5
Foxgrove SA4 ....66 B8
Foxhole Dr SA1 ....122 A4
Foxhole Rd SA1 ....68 E1
Foxhollows CF14 ....169 D5
Foxwood Cl NP10 ......141 F3
Foxwood Ct NP10 ......141 F3
Foyer The 7 SA1 ....95 D7
Frampton Ct SA4 ....42 F2
Frampton Rd SA4 ....43 A3
Francis Cl NP20 ....143 C3
Francis Ct SA8 ....24 C4
Francis Dr NP20 ....143 C3
Francis Morris Est 5
NP4 ....17 D6
Francis Rd
Barry CF62 ....205 A1
Swansea SA6 ....45 E1
Francis St
Abertridwr CF83 ....136 F7
Bargoed CF81 ....58 A4
Dowlais CF48 ....11 A5
Fleur De Lis NP12 ....85 E6
Hawthorn CF37 ....136 A4
Neath SA10 ....77 B7
3 Newport NP20 ....143 C3
Pontarbawe SA8 ....23 E4
Risca NP11 ....145 A1
Swansea SA1 ....95 A5
Thomastown CF39 ....133 B4
Tonypandy CF40 ....106 B7
Francis Terr
Pont CF48 ....11 A7
Pontypridd CF37 ....109 E3
Frank Rd CF5 ....193 D6
Frank St NP19 ....143 C6
Franklen Rd CF14 .....177 C4
Franklen St 4 CF11 ...194 F3
Fransham St 3 SA15 ...40 E6
Fraternal Par 2
CF37 ....109 C1
Frederick Ct SA11 ......71 E6
Frederick Mews
NP20 ....143 D3
Frederick Pl SA7 ....69 F7
Frederick St
Aberdare CF44 ....28 E4
Cardiff CF10 ....195 B3
1 Cardiff CF10 ....195 A6
Ferndale CF43 ....79 F6
2 Llanelli SA15 ....40 D5
Newport NP20 ....143 D3
1 Port Talbot SA12 ...124 F8
Swansea SA5 ....68 C3
Free School Ct CF31 ..195 D6
Freehold Land Rd
NP4 ....38 A1
Freeman St SA5 ....68 A7
Fremington Pl CF3 .....179 C5
Freshmoor Rd CF24 ...196 C3
Freshwater Rd NP19 ..144 D1
Frewer Ave CF5 ....176 D1
Friars Cl SA10 ....71 B8
Friars Ct NP20 ....143 B3
Friars Field NP20 ......143 B3
Friars Gdn NP44 ....90 B1
Friars Rd Barry CF62 ..214 E2
Barry CF62 ....214 F2
Friars St 3 NP20 ....143 C4
Friary The NP20 ....143 B3
Friary The CF10 ....195 A6
Frigate Rd CF10 ....195 D1
Frobisher Rd NP19 ....144 B3
Frogiane SA3 ....228 E4
Frogmore Ave SA2 .....94 D6
Frome Wlk NP20 ....116 C2
Fron Heulog CF31 ......168 D5
Fron Terr Llanelli SA15 ..40 D5
4 Pontypridd CF37 ...109 C2
Fron Wen NP12 ....85 C6
Fron-Wen Terr CF32 ..104 E3
Frondeg
Penperlleni NP4 ....39 E5
Tredegar NP22 ....29 B4
Frondeg Terr SA15 .....40 D6
Fronheulog CF37 ....109 A2
Fronwen Rd CF31 ....169 C4
Fronwen Terr CF47 ......10 F3
Frost Pl NP12 ....85 C4
Frost Rd NP23 ....7 E4

Fryatt St CF63 ....215 A4
Full Moon Visitor Ctr
NP11 ....114 A3
Fuller St SA8 ....23 E5
Fullers Row SA1 ....95 C7
Fulmar Cl Cardiff CF3 .179 F8
Mumbles SA3 ....122 E7
Penarth CF64 ....217 B4
Furnace Dr SA12 ....182 E8
Furnace Prim Sch
SA15 ....108 D7
Furnace Rd CF43 ....80 C1
Furnace Row CF48 ......31 B2
Furnace St
Barry CF64 ....215 E6
Ebbw Vale NP23 ....3 F7
Furnace Terr SA11 .....71 C5
Furness Cl CF5 ....193 B4
Furze Cres SA6 ....45 D2
Furzeland Dr
Bryn-côch SA10 ....48 C4
Swansea SA2 ....94 B6
Fynnon Caeonna
SA5 ....67 E6

G

Gabalal Wookshops
CF14 ....177 A2
Gaballfa Ave CF14 .....177 A2
Gaballfa Prim Sch
CF14 ....177 B2
Gaballfa Rd
Cardiff CF14 ....177 A2
Swansea SA2 ....94 B5
Gables The
Cardiff CF14 ....177 D6
Dinas Powys CF64 ....206 A2
Gadley's Terr SA13 ....227 C2
Gadlys Rd CF44 ....29 A2
Gadlys Rd E CF62 ....214 E5
Gadlys Rd W CF62 .....214 D5
Gadlys St CF44 ....28 E4
Gadlys Terr CF44 ....28 E4
Gaen St Abertillery NP13 .36 B6
Barry CF62 ....214 C4
Gaer Inf Sch NP20 ....142 F3
Gaer Jun Sch NP20 ...142 F2
Gaer La NP20 ....143 A3
Gaer Park Ave NP20 ..142 F3
Gaer Park Dr NP20 ....142 F3
Gaer Park Hill NP20 ..142 E3
Gaer Park La NP20 ....142 E2
Gaer Park Par NP20 ..142 E2
Gaer Park Rd NP20 ....142 F3
Gaer Pl CF82 ....84 C6
Gaer Rd
Newport NP20 ....142 F3
Newport NP20 ....142 F3
Gaer St NP20 ....143 A2
Gaer Vale NP20 ....142 F1
Gaerwen Cl CF14 ......177 D8
Gainsborough Cl
NP44 ....117 A8
Gainsborough Ct 2
CF64 ....206 F5
Gainsborough Dr
NP19 ....144 A8
Gainsborough Ho 1
SA12 ....133 A1
Gainsborough Rd
6 Penarth CF64 ....206 F5
Tredegar NP22 ....13 C6
Galahad Cl CF14 ....159 D2
Galames CF24 ....195 F7
Gallamuir Rd CF24 ....195 F7
Gallidawel Flats
CF39 ....133 B5
Galipoli Row SA13 ....125 D6
Gallewm Terr SA13 ...100 F4
Galon Uchaf Rd CF47 ..10 F4
Galston St 5 CF24 .....195 D6
Gamlyn Terr CF44 ....27 F6
Gantre Cl NP23 ....7 C5
Gantref Way NP23 ....7 D3
Gar-y-nant CF31 ....168 F5
Gar-yr-adon 5 CF44 ...53 D7
Garage Circular Rd
CF62 ....211 E1
Gardd Jolyon NP12 .....85 C6
Gardde SA14 ....93 E6
Garden City
Merthyr Tydfil CF47 ......10 F4
Rhymney NP22 ....12 E2
Garden Cl CF83 ....112 A2
Garden Cres SA4 ....66 D8
Garden Ct CF31 ....169 D5
Garden St
Dowlais CF48 ....11 B4
Ebbw Vale NP23 ....14 D8
Llandrabach CF83 ....112 A2
Swansea SA1 ....95 C6
Garden Suburbs
NP11 ....114 C6
Gardenia Cl CF23 ......178 D7
Gardens The
Ynysddu NP11 ....112 F6
Ystalyfera SA9 ....2 B6
Gardner Cl CF37 ....109 D5
Gardners La SA11 ....71 D4
Garesfield St CF24 .....196 C3
Gareth Cl CF14 ....159 D2
Garfield Ave CF5 ....168 F8
Garfield St NP12 ....85 E6
Garfield Terr NP23 .....3 D6
Garn Cross NP23 ....15 D8

Garn Dyrus Mount 3
NP4 ....17 D7
Garn Rd Blaenavon NP4 .16 B8
Maesteg CF34 ....102 B2
Nantyglo NP23 ....8 C1
Garn St NP11 ....87 B3
Garn Terr NP23 ....14 F3
Garn-yr-erw NP4 ....16 F8
Garnant Cty Prim Sch
SA18 ....220 B8
Garnfach Inf Sch NP23 .8 D1
Garnfoel SA14 ....218 D7
Garngoch Hospl SA4 ..67 F6
Garngoch Ind Est SA4 .68 E8
Garngoch Terr SA4 .....66 D8
Garnllwyd Cl SA6 ....68 C7
Garnlydan Jun & Inf Sch
NP23 ....8 C6
Garnswllt Rd SA4 ......218 F1
Garnswllt Sch SA18 ..219 B3
Garnteg Prim Sch
NP4 ....37 F6
Garnwen Rd SA14 .....101 F6
Garnwen Terr CF34 ...101 F6
Garon Terr CF32 ....104 E7
Garreg Hollt SA14 .....218 A8
Garreg Rd CF32 ....103 E3
Garreg Side CF32 ......103 E5
Garreg-Wen CF82 ....84 D8
Garrick Ho 3 SA12 ....198 B3
Garrod Ave CF22 ....66 C2
Garth Ave
Maesteg CF34 ....102 D2
Pontypridd CF37 ....109 D5
Garth Cl
Bassaleg NP10 ....142 A3
Morganstown CF15 .....176 B8
Pontypool NP4 ....38 B2
Rudry CF83 ....93 B5
Garth Cotts CF47 ....10 E2
Garth Dan-y-Bryn
NP23 ....7 D4
Garth Dr CF31 ....169 B7
Garth La CF83 ....136 C7
Garth Gr CF44 ....224 E1
Garth La CF83 ....139 B3
Garth Lwyd CF83 ....139 D1
Garth Olwg CF15 ....157 F5
Garth Pl CF14 ....177 D2
Garth Prim Sch
CF34 ....102 D1
Garth Rd
Cwmbran NP44 ....116 D8
Glais SA7 ....46 E6
Gwaun-Cae-Gurwen
SA18 ....220 E6
Tonypandy CF40 ....107 B5
Ynystawe SA6 ....46 D4
Garth St Cardiff CF24 .195 B5
Coedely CF39 ....154 D8
6 Merthyr Tydfil CF47 .10 D2
Pontlottyn CF81 ....32 F8
Pyle CF33 ....148 C2
Taffs Well CF15 ....158 A3
Garth Sta CF34 ....128 C8
Garth Terr
Bassaleg NP10 ....141 F2
Bedlinog CF46 ....56 A6
Merthyr Tydfil CF47 ......10 F2
Garth View
Beddau CF38 ....156 A6
Bedwas CF83 ....138 D7
Merthyr Tydfil CF47 .....11 A8
Ynysforgan SA6 ....46 B4
Ynysybwl CF37 ....154 F8
Church Village CF38 ....156 F8
Garth Villas
Taffs Well CF15 ....157 F4
Garth Wen CF40 ....107 A5
Garth-Fechan Woodland
Park) Forest Walks
CF32 ....103 D1
Garw Fechan Woodland
Park) Forest Walks
CF32 ....103 D1
Garw Row NP44 ....90 B5
Garw The NP44 ....90 B5
Garw Wd NP44 ....90 B5
Garwell CF44 ....28 A6
Garwfechan Rd
CF32 ....129 E8
Gas Rd CF32 ....109 C1
Gaskell Cl CF61 ....109 C6
Gaskell St NP19 ....143 F3
Gaspard Pl CF62 ....214 C2
Gasworks Rd CF44 .....53 D7
Gasworks Terr CF32 ...150 D6
Gate Rd
Bridgend CF31 ....169 D2
Pengroes SA14 ....218 D8
Gateholm Cl CF62 .....214 F8
Gateside Cl CF23 ......161 A2
Gateway (Y Porth) The
CF14 ....177 E3
Gathen Terr 5 SA15 ...39 E3
Gaudi Wlk NP10 ....142 A6
Gaulden Gr CF23 ....160 E1
Gawain Cl CF14 ....159 D2
Gaynors NP44 ....89 B5
Geifr Rd SA13 ....125 E5
Geiriol Gdns SA1 ....67 F1
Geiriol Rd SA1 ....67 F1
Gelert St SA5 ....68 A8
Gelli Arael Rd CF39 ..132 B6
Gelli Aur
Cwmdare CF44 ....28 C3
Neath SA10 ....48 D2
Gelli Ave NP11 ....115 A2
Gelli Cl NP11 ....115 A2
Gelli Crescent CF31 ...79 C3
Gelli Crug NP23 ....19 C6

Gelli Dawel
Caerphilly CF83 ....137 F4
Neath SA10 ....48 D2
Gelli Deg
Caerphilly CF83 ....137 F5
Cardiff CF14 ....177 B8
Llanelli SA14 ....41 A6
Neath SA10 ....48 D2
Rhydyfelin CF37 ....161 C6
Gelli Fawr Ct NP44 ...115 F8
Gelli Feld Rise CF72 ..153 D4
Gelli Fron CF41 ....79 A2
Gelli Gdns SA7 ....70 B8
Gelli Hirion Ind Est
CF37 ....136 C4
Gelli Hos SA13 ....125 E5
Gelli Ind Est CF41 .....79 C2
Gelli Isaf
Ammanford SA18 ....219 A5
Pontllanfraith NP12 .....85 F3
Gelli Llwynog Cres
NP11 ....115 A2
Gelli Prim Sch CF41 ...79 C2
Gelli-Groes Rd NP12 ..85 F3
Gelli-Gynore SA4 ......41 C3
Gelli-Onn SA15 ....40 D6
Gelli-Ron CF83 ....39 B4
Gelli-siriol Cotts
CF34 ....128 E6
Gelli-Unig Pl NP11 ....114 C6
Gelli-Unig Rd NP11 ...114 C6
Gelli-unig Terr
NP11 ....114 C5
Gelligaerdd Rd CF82 ..84 D5
Gelliair CF35 ....152 C1
Gellicebryn SA11 ....223 C1
Gellidawel Rd
Glynneath SA11 ....223 D1
3 Pontypridd CF37 ...135 F6
Rhydyfelin CF37 ....136 A6
Gellidoren SA8 ....23 D6
Gelliddeg SA6 ....23 C6
Gelliddeg Hts CF83 ....85 C2
Gelliddeg Inf & Jun Sch
CF48 ....10 A3
Gelliddeg Rd CF37 ....135 B8
Gellifaich Cres SA6 ...68 D7
Gellifaelog Old Rd
CF47 ....11 A4
Gellifaelog Prim Sch
CF47 ....11 A4
Gellifaelog Terr CF47 ..11 A4
Gellifawr Rd SA6 ....68 D7
Gellifedi Rd CF72 ......153 D3
Gellifedi Terr CF72 .....153 D3
Gelligaer Gdns CF24 ..177 F1
Gelligaer La CF24 ......177 F1
Gelligaer St CF24 ......177 F1
Gelligaer SA14 ....93 C6
Gelligaer St CF24 ......177 F1
Gelligalog Rd CF24 ....177 F1
Gelligwr Cl CF37 ....136 A6
Gelligwr Rd CF37 ......136 A6
Gelliguy Rd 1 NP12 ....85 D5
Gellinos Ave CF82 ......84 B7
Gellinudd Rd SA8 ......24 B5
Gellionnen Cl SA6 ......46 D8
Gellionnen Rd
Clydach SA6,SA8 ....24 A1
Pontardawe SA8 ....23 B5
Gellionnen Cl SA6 ......46 D8
Gelliwastad Ct CF37 ..109 E1
Gelliwastad Gr CF37 ..109 E1
Gelliwen St CF82 ....84 D5
Gelliwion Rd CF37 .....134 F1
Gelliwion Rd SA18 ....219 A6
Gellyfelyn NP7 ....9 B5
Gelynis Terr CF15 ......176 B8
Gelynis Terr N CF15 ...176 B8
Gelynog Cl CF38 ....155 F8
Gelynos Ave NP12 ......13 A6
Gendros Ave E SA5 .....68 A3
Gendros Ave W SA5 ...67 F4
Gendros Cl SA5 ....68 A3
Gendros Cres SA5 ......68 A3
Gendros Dr SA5 ....67 F3
Gendros Prim Sch
SA5 ....67 F3
General Hospl CF64 ...101 E4
General Rees Sq 5
NP44 ....89 E4

Genwen Rd SA14 ....41 F4
Geoffrey Ashe Ct
CF71 ....188 F1
Geoffrey St SA11 ....67 F7
George Bank SA3 ......123 C4
George Cl CF15 ....157 F3
George Daggar's Ave
NP13 ....35 F7
George Lansbury Dr 2
NP19 ....144 D6
George Manning Way
SA4 ....66 B4
George St
Aberbargoed CF81 ....58 B4
Abercarn NP11 ....114 C8
Aberdare CF44 ....53 D7
Abertillery NP13 ....36 B6
Argoed NP12 ....58 F5
Barry CF63 ....215 A5
Bedling CF46 ....56 A7
Blackwood NP12 ....85 F7
7 Blaenavon NP4 ......17 C6
Bridgend CF31 ....169 C3
Brynmawr NP23 ....8 A4
Cwmbran NP44 ....89 C4
Cwmfelinfach NP11 .....113 F4
Ferndale CF43 ....80 A7
Llanelli SA15 ....40 D3
Llantrisant CF72 ....155 D3
Maesteg CF34 ....75 B2
Neath SA11 ....72 C6
New Tredegar NP24 ......33 E3
Newport NP19,NP20 ...143 D4
Pontardawe SA8 ....23 D6
Pontypool NP4 ....62 A8
Pontypridd NP4 ....62 A8
Port Talbot SA13 ....125 C7
Porthcawl CF36 ....182 F7
Swansea SA1 ....95 B6
Tonypandy CF40 ....106 A8
Treherbert CF42 ....78 A8
Ystrad Mynach CF82 ....84 E7
George Street Bridge
NP19 ....143 E5
George Street Est
CF31 ....169 C3
George Street Prim Sch
NP4 ....62 A8
George Terr CF45 ....81 F8
George Thomas Ave
CF32 ....150 F6
George Thomas Cl
CF36 ....182 F8
George Thomas Hosp
CF42 ....182 F8
George's Row SA11 ...71 B1
George's Terr CF46 ....106 D7
Georges Row CF64 ....206 C4
Georgetown CF15 .....157 F3
Georgetown Hill NP22 .13 F6
Georgetown Villas
NP23 ....13 F5
Georgian Cl
Llantwit Major CF61 .....210 B7
Porthcawl CF36 ....183 A8
Georgian Way
Bridgend CF31 ....169 A4
Cardiff CF14 ....177 F8
Miskin CF72 ....173 D7
Geotre Bellaf Rd CF32 ..57 A7
Ger Nant CF82 ....111 E7
Ger y Afon CF37 ....109 D6
Ger y Llan SA15 ....40 D4
Ger y Nant SA14 ....42 B8
Ger y Pant SA4 ....19 C4
Ger Yr Afon SA18 ......220 A8
Ger-y-Bont CF44 ....28 A6
Ger-y-Coed CF31 ......169 E5
Ger-y-Ffrwd SA11 ......71 C6
Ger-y-Llan CF5 ....192 A1
Ger-y-Mais SA14 ....41 A7
Ger-y-Nant SA11 ....223 B1
Ger-y-Parc SA4 ....45 E1
Ger-y-Sedd CF35 ......169 C5
Ger-yr-Afon
Aberdulais SA10 ....49 C4
Cwm-twrch Isaf SA9 ......1 A1
Gwaun-Cae-Gurwen
SA18 ....220 D6
Gilar St 1 CF24 ....177 C1
Gildas Cl 1 CF61 ......209 F7
Giles Rd NP4 ....17 E6
Gileston Rd
Cardiff CF11 ....194 D7
St Athan CF62 ....211 D3
Gileston Wlk 6 NP44 ..89 C2
Gilfach SA4 ....44 A2
Gilfach Bargoed Sta
CF81 ....58 A1
Gilfach Fargoed Sta
CF81 ....58 A3
Gilfach Goch Inf Sch
CF39 ....106 C3
Gilfach Hos CF34 ......127 F5
Gilfach Rd
Cwm-twrch Uchaf SA9 ..222 C4
Neath SA10 ....48 E4
Tonypandy CF40 ....106 B6
Tonypandy CF40 ....106 F4
Tonyrefail CF39 ....133 A5
Gilfach St CF81 ....58 A3
Gilmour Ct SA10 ....71 C6
Gilmour St CF40 ....106 E6
Gilsea Bsns Pk SA6 ....69 A5
Gilwern Cres CF14 .....159 E1
Gilwern Farm Cl
NP18 ....117 F7
Gilwern Pl
Cardiff CF14 ....159 E1
Cwmbran NP44 ....89 D5
Glade Cl NP44 ....116 A8
Glade The
Brynceithin CF32 ....151 A4
Cardiff CF14 ....160 A1
Mumbles SA3 ....122 F8
Porthcawl CF36 ....165 F1
Gladeside CF14 ....160 B1
Gladeside Cl CF14 .....159 E3
Gladstone Bldgs NP13 .36 B8
Gladstone Bridge
CF62 ....214 E6
Gladstone Ct 5
CF62 ....214 E4
Gladstone Garden Ct
CF62 ....214 E4
Gladstone Jun & Inf Sch
CF24 ....177 F1
Gladstone Pl
Pontypool NP4 ....62 E2
Tredegar NP22 ....13 F5
Gladstone Prim Sch
CF62 ....214 E5
Gladstone Rd
Barry CF62 ....215 A6
Newbridge NP11 ....60 B2
Gladstone St
Abercarn NP11 ....114 B4
Aberdare CF44 ....53 D6
Abertillery NP13 ....36 A5
Blaina NP13 ....15 E4
10 Brynmawr NP23 .....8 A4
Maesteg CF34 ....102 A3
Mountain Ash CF45 ......54 E1
Gladstone Terr
Abercynon NP4 ....37 E8
1 Blaenavon NP4 ......17 D6
Merthyr Tydfil CF47 ......30 E7
Merthyr Tydfil NP47 ......30 E7
Rhymney NP22 ....12 D5
Gladys St
Aberavon SA12 ....98 F1
5 Aberdare CF44 ......195 A8
Coedely CF39 ....154 D8
Glais Prim Sch SA7 .....47 A6
Glais Rd SA7 ....23 D1

Glamorgan Cl CF61 210 B7
Glamorgan Ct 4
CF44 53 D7
Glamorgan St
Aberdare CF44 53 C7
Aberdare CF44 53 D7
Barry CF62 214 C3
Brynmawr NP23 8 B4
Cardiff CF5 194 C6
Mountain Ash CF45 81 F7
Swansea SA1 95 C6
Glamorgan Street Mews
11 CF5 194 C6
Glamorgan Terr
Gilfach Goch CF39 132 C7
Tonypandy CF40 106 E7
Tonypandy CF40 107 A1
Glamorgan Vale Ret Pk
CF72 155 D1
Glan Creigiau CF72 174 C7
Glan Dulais SA2 93 C7
Glan Ebbw NP13 15 D4
Glan Ebbw Terr
Abertillery NP13 36 B5
Ebbw Vale NP23 14 E3
Glan Ely Cl CF5 193 C7
Glan Ely High Sch
CF5 192 F4
Glan Ffrwd
Caerphilly CF83 137 E6
Porth CF39 107 D1
Glan Gwrelych SA11 223 D1
Glan Hafren
Baglan SA12 98 D6
Barry CF62 214 B2
Glan Islwyn NP12 85 E4
Glan Llwyd SA4 19 C6
Glan Nant Rd CF31 168 D5
Glan Rd Aberdare CF44 28 E2
Porthcawl CF36 183 A7
Glan Rhyd
Caerphilly CF83 137 F4
Cwmbran NP44 116 A8
Glan y Lli SA4 65 A4
Glan y Nant CF37 136 C4
Glan yr Afon
Ammanford SA18 219 B8
Llanelli SA15 40 F8
Machen CF83 140 A6
Glan Yr Afon Rd
Pyle CF33 148 C4
Swansea SA2 94 C7
Glan Yr Avon SA9 2 C5
Glan-Ddu Rd NP12 85 A6
Glan-Ddu Terr CF82 85 A6
Glan-Ffrwd Inf Sch
CF37 81 E2
Glan-Nant Row CF32 129 C2
Glan-Nant St 8 CF44 29 A1
Glan-Pelenna SA12 72 F3
Glan-Rhyd Rd
Pontardawe SA8 23 D5
Ystradgynlais SA9 2 E7
Glan-taf Cty Inf Sch
CF37 135 F6
Glan-y-Afon Com Jun Sch
CF3 179 B7
Glan-y-Ffordd CF15 158 A5
Glan-y-Gors SA14 218 D8
Glan-y-Llyn
North Cornelly CF33 166 A7
Tonypandy CF40 106 C6
Glan-y-Mor CF62 214 B2
Glan-y-Mor Ave
SA13 125 E4
Glan-y-mor Prim Sch
SA12 98 D1
Glan-y-Mor Rd CF3 179 E5
Glan-y-Nant
Fochriw CF81 32 D7
Pencoed CF35 170 D7
Rhymney NP22 12 E8
Tondu CF32 150 D5
Treoes CF35 170 A2
Glan-y-Nant Cl NP44 89 D1
Glan-y-nant Ct 5
CF14 177 B5
Glan-y-nant Inf Sch
NP12 85 A7
Glan-y-Nant Rd
CF14 177 B5
Glan-y-Nant Terr
CF14 177 B5
Glan-y-Parc CF31 168 E4
Glan-y-Wern Rd SA7 69 E7
Glan-yr- Afon CF42 78 C7
Glan-Yr-Afon
Aberfan CF48 55 C3
Cwmfelin CF34 128 C8
Rhymney NP22 12 D5
Glan-Yr-Afon Ct
CF34 75 A1
Glan-Yr-Afon Gdns
SA2 94 C6
Glan-yr-avon NP24 33 E3
Glan-Yr-Ely CF72 155 A5
Glan-Yr-Ysgol SA9 2 B6
Glanafan Comp (Lower)
Sch SA13 99 C1
Glanafan Comp Sch
SA13 125 B8
Glanafon Terr CF34 102 A8
Glanaman Cty Prim Sch
SA18 220 A8
Glanaman Rd
Aberdare CF44 52 F4
Cwmaman CF44 53 A4
Glanamman Workshops
SA18 220 A8
Glanberis Terr CF32 103 D7
Glanbran Rd SA7 70 A8
Glanbrydan Ave SA2 94 F6
Glancynon St CF45 54 E1
Glancynon Terr
Abercynon CF45 82 E3
1 Aberdare CF44 53 D7
Glandafen Rd SA15 40 F2
Glandovery Terr
NP22 13 D7
Glandovey Gr CF3 179 E6
Glandwr Cres SA1 68 D4
Glandwr Ind Est NP13 60 A7
Glandwr Pl CF14 177 B4
Glandwr St
Abertillery NP13 36 A5
Abertillery NP13 59 F7
Glandwr Terr CF40 106 E7
Glandyffryn Cl SA13 125 D7
Glanfelin CF37 136 A4
Glanffornwg CF31 168 E7
Glanffrwd Ave NP23 7 C2
Glanffrwd Rd SA4 19 D6
Glanffrwd Terr
Ebbw Vale NP23 7 D2
Ynysybwl CF37 81 F2
Glanheulog NP23 8 B5
Glanhowy Jun & Inf Sch
NP22 6 E1
Glanhowy Rd NP12 112 F8
Glanhowy St NP22 6 D1
Glanlay St CF45 81 F7
Glanllyn Rd SA7 47 A5
Glanmor Cres
Newport NP19 144 B5
Swansea SA2 94 F7
Glanmor Ct SA2 94 F7
Glanmor La SA2 94 F7
Glanmor Mews SA2 94 E7
Glanmor Park Ave
NP19 144 B5
Glanmor Park Rd SA2 94 E7
Glanmor Pl 3 SA15 40 C4
Glanmor Rd
Llanelli SA15 40 D4
Swansea SA2 94 E7
Glanmor Terr
2 Llanelli SA15 40 C4
Pen-clawdd SA4 19 E4
Glanmore Cres CF62 214 D5
Glanmorfa SA4 66 B5
Glanmorlais CF48 11 B7
Glanmuir Rd CF24 196 A8
Glannant Pl SA11 227 B8
Glannant Rd
Evanstown CF39 132 B7
Pontarddulais SA4 19 E5
Glannant Rise SA11 72 C6
Glannant St
Cwmfelinfach NP11 113 A4
Tonypandy CF40 106 F4
Glannant Terr
Blaengwrach SA11 227 B8
Ystradgynlais SA9 2 E7
Glannant Way SA11 72 B6
Glanogwr Rd CF31 168 E3
Glanrhyd CF14 177 C7
Glanrhyd Cl NP22 6 D1
Glanrhyd CP Sch SA9 2 D6
Glanrhyd Hospl
CF31 168 E8
Glanrhyd St CF44 52 E4
Glanrhyd Terr SA4 66 C8
Glanselsig Terr CF42 50 B2
Glanshon Ct NP11 60 C1
Glansychan Hos NP4 37 E4
Glantaff Rd CF48 31 B1
Glantawe Pk SA9 2 D7
Glantawe Row SA9 2 F8
Glantawe St
4 Morriston SA6 46 A1
Swansea SA6 69 A8
Glantorvaen Rd NP4 62 C6
Glantorvaen Terr Upper
NP4 17 B6
Glantwrch SA9 2 C7
Glanville Terr CF43 79 C8
Glanwern Ave NP19 144 C6
Glanwern Cl NP19 144 C6
Glanwern Dr NP18 144 C5
Glanwern Ho NP4 62 B6
Glanwern Rise NP19 144 C6
Glanymor CF61 210 C6
Glanymor La SA4 42 E1
Glanymor Park Dr
SA4 42 D1
Glanymor Rd SA4 42 E1
Glanymor St SA11 71 B3
Glanynys Ho CF44 29 B2
Glanyrafon
Ebbw Vale NP23 7 D3
Taffs Well CF15 157 F4
Glanyrafon Cl SA4 44 B2
Glanyrafon Jun Comp Sch
NP23 7 D2
Glanyrafon Rd
Pencoed CF35 170 E8
Pontarddulais SA4 19 D4
Glanyrafon Terr NP13 15 E2
Glanystruth NP13 15 F5
Glas Canol CF14 177 B3
Glas Efail CF14 177 D7
Glas Fryn CF82 84 E7
Glas Ifor CF14 177 C5
Glas y Llwyn CF63 205 C1
Glas-y-Pant CF14 176 F7
Glasbrook Pl SA5 67 E5
Glasbrook Terr CF45 82 A7
Glasbury Rd SA6 68 D7
Glascoed La NP4 63 E6
Glascoed Rd NP4 63 B4
Glasfryn
Bridgend CF31 169 D4
Caerphilly NP12 85 D6
Cwmdare CF44 28 D3
Llanelli SA14 41 A7
Glasfryn Cl SA2 67 E2
Glasfryn Rd SA4 19 C3
Glasfryn Sq CF33 148 B1
Glasfryn Terr SA15 40 E7
Glasier Rd CF47 30 F8
Glasllwch Cres NP10,
NP20 142 C4
Glasllwch Jun & Inf Sch
NP20 142 D4
Glasllwch La NP20 142 D3
Glasllwch View
NP20 142 C3
Glaslyn Cl CF62 214 C5
Glaslyn Ct NP44 90 A6
Glaslyn Dr CF44 29 E2
Glaslyn Pl SA6 45 D1
Glass Ave CF24 195 E4
Glass Works Cotts
NP20 143 C8
Glastonbury Cl 4
NP20 143 C6
Glastonbury Rd
CF64 216 B5
Glastonbury Terr
CF3 179 B6
Glebe Pl CF14 177 F8
Glebe Rd SA4 42 F1
Glebe St Barry CF63 215 A7
Bedwas CF83 138 E6
Newport NP19 143 E5
Penarth CF64 207 A4
Glebe The SA3 122 A7
Glebeland Cl CF35 169 F4
Glebeland Pl CF62 211 D4
Glebeland St
4 Merthyr Tydfil CF47 10 D1
Neath SA10 48 F2
Glen Afric Cl CF62 214 D6
Glen Cl CF45 54 B3
Glen Coed CF82 85 A1
Glen Garw CF32 103 E6
Glen Mavis Way
CF62 214 D6
Glen Rd Mumbles SA3 122 F6
Neath SA11 72 A8
Glen The
Langstone NP18 119 D1
Sarn CF32 150 F4
Glen View
Blackmill CF35 131 A3
Bridgend CF31 168 F8
Cardiff CF14 177 F6
Cwmbran NP44 89 D4
Hollybush NP12 34 C2
Maesycwmmer CF82 85 A1
Ystrad Mynach CF82 84 E2
Glen View Bglws NP23 8 B2
Glen View Ct NP11 86 D5
Glen View Rd NP4 38 B2
Glen View St CF40 106 D7
Glen View Terr
Aberavon SA12 99 A2
Fochriw CF81 32 C6
Glen-Usk View
NP18 118 A4
Glenalla Rd SA15 40 E5
Glenavon Cres CF36 182 D7
Glenavon St
12 Aberavon SA12 124 F8
Cymmer SA13 75 B5
Glenavon Terr
Gilfach Goch CF39 132 C7
Nant-y-Moel CF32 104 E7
Glenboi CF45 54 B3
Glenboi Prim Sch
CF45 54 B3
Glenbrook CF45 54 B3
Glenbrook Dr CF63 215 D8
Glencoe St CF63 215 A6
Glencourt NP4 62 E1
Glendale SA10 48 C3
Glendale Ave CF14 159 E1
Glendale Ct SA10 48 C3
Glendale Gdns NP12 85 A5
Glendower Cl CF31 169 A5
Glendower Ct CF14 176 F5
Glendower St CF48 11 A5
Glenfield Cl SA2 94 A7
Glengariff Ct NP4 62 E2
Glengower Cl SA3 123 A5
Glenmount Way
CF14 159 D2
Glenrhondda Ct CF42 50 F2
Glenrise Cl CF3 180 B7
Glenroy Ave SA1 95 E8
Glenroy St CF24 195 C8
Glenside NP44 89 D6
Glenside Ct CF24 178 C1
Glenside Rd SA5 67 E6
Glenview
Newbridge NP11 60 A1
Pen-y-fai CF31 150 C1
Glenview Terr
Llanbradach CF83 112 A2
Ynysddu NP11 112 F6
Glenview Villas 4
CF46 83 B6
Glenville Rd SA3 123 A6
Glenwern Terr NP4 62 B5
Glenwood CF23 178 D6
Glenwood Cl CF35 169 F4
Glevering St SA15 40 E5
Globe Hill NP23 14 D6
Globe Row SA14 41 B8
Globe St 1 SA6 69 A8
Globe Works CF24 195 D4
Glossop Ct CF35 170 E7
Glossop Rd CF24 195 C6
Glossop Terr CF35 170 D7
Gloster Pl 1 NP19 143 D6
Gloster St 3 NP19 143 D6
Gloster's Par NP4 63 B3
Gloucester Bldgs
CF32 103 F2
Gloucester Cl
Barry CF62 214 F6
Llanyravon NP44 90 B3
Gloucester Ct NP18 118 A3
Gloucester Ho 5
SA12 98 C3
Gloucester Pl
Mumbles SA3 123 B4
Swansea SA1 95 E6
Gloucester St
Aberdare CF44 29 A2
Cardiff CF11 194 F5
Gloucester Terr CF45 82 C5
Gluepot Rd CF71 199 C4
Glyn Bargoed Rd
CF46 83 C7
Glyn Bedw CF83 112 A4
Glyn Coed CF43 79 B8
Glyn Coed Rd CF23 178 E7
Glyn Collen CF83 112 A4
Glyn Cres SA3 94 C2
Glyn Derwen CF83 112 A3
Glyn Eiddew
Cardiff CF23 178 F8
Llanbradach CF83 112 A4
Glyn Hirnant SA6 46 A3
Glyn Llwyfen CF83 112 A4
Glyn Neath Rd SA11 226 E6
Glyn Rd SA18 220 D8
Glyn Rhosyn CF23 178 E8
Glyn Simon Cl CF5 176 E2
Glyn St
Aberavon SA12 124 F8
Abertysswg NP22 33 B8
Ogmore Vale CF32 104 E1
Porth CF39 107 F2
Swansea SA1 68 D2
Ynysybwl CF37 109 A8
Glyn Teg CF32 129 D1
Glyn Terr Fochriw CF81 32 C7
Tonypandy CF40 106 C7
Tredegar NP22 13 F4
Glyn View CF39 133 E6
Glyn-Deri SA18 219 F8
Glyn-Dwr Ave CF37 135 F6
Glyn-Gaer Rd CF82 84 E7
Glyn-Llwchwr Rd SA4 19 C4
Glyn-Meirch Rd SA8 23 C3
Glyn-Mynach St
CF37 109 A8
Glyn-neath Bsns Pk
SA11 223 C1
Glyn-y-Coed Rd SA11 71 F7
Glyn-y-Mel CF35 170 D8
Glynbargoed Cl CF46 83 C7
Glynbridge Cl CF62 204 F1
Glynbridge Gdns
CF31 168 F6
Glyncoch Terr CF37 109 E5
Glyncoed Comp Sch
NP23 7 C3
Glyncoed Jun & Inf Sch
Cardiff CF23 178 E7
Ebbw Vale NP23 7 D3
Glyncoed Terr
Llanelli SA15 41 A5
Merthyr Tydfil CF47 30 E7
Glyncoli Cl CF42 78 D7
Glyncoli Rd CF42 78 D6
Glyncollen Cres SA6 46 A3
Glyncollen Dr SA6 46 B3
Glyncollen Prim Sch
SA6 46 A4
Glyncornel Cl CF40 106 E8
Glyncorrwg Ind Est
SA13 227 C1
Glyncorrwg Prim Sch
SA13 227 C2
Glyncrug Cotts NP13 36 B5
Glyncynwal Rd SA9 221 C6
Glynderw CF83 138 A4
Glynderwen Cl SA2 94 B3
Glynderwen Cres SA2 94 B3
Glynderwen Rd SA14 41 D4
Glyndwr Ave CF62 211 D4
Glyndwr Ct CF41 79 A4
Glyndwr Ho
Baglan SA12 98 C7
Cwmbran NP44 89 F3
7 Merthyr Tydfil CF47 30 D8
Glyndwr Pl SA1 95 A8
Glyndwr Rd
Barry CF62 214 E5
Cardiff CF5 193 B6
Cwmbran NP44 89 F3
Ebbw Vale NP23 7 B5
Penarth CF64 206 E3
Glyndwr St
Merthyr Vale CF48 55 D5
Port Talbot SA13 99 B1
Glyndyrus Cl CF48 30 E5
Glynfach Rd CF39 107 F2
Glyngwyn St CF45 54 E1
Glynhafod Jun Sch
CF44 52 F4
Glynhafod St CF44 52 E4
Glynhir Rd SA4 19 D5
Glynleiros Gdns SA10 71 D8
Glynmarch St CF81 57 B8
Glynmelyn Rd SA11 223 D2
Glynn Vivian Art Gal
SA1 95 C7
Glynne St CF11 194 D6
Glynne Twr CF64 207 B3
Glynrhondda St
Cardiff CF24 195 B7
Treorchy CF42 78 C7
Glynrhosyn SA4 43 B1
Glynstell Cl CF11 194 D2
Glynstell Rd CF36 165 F1
Glynsyfi NP24 33 F2
Glyntaf Ct 5 CF48 31 B1
Glyntaff Cl CF37 136 A6
Glyntaff Rd CF37 135 F8
Glynteg Rd SA4 19 D5
Glyntirion NP44 89 D1
Gnoll Ave SA11 71 F7
Gnoll Bank SA11 72 A8
Gnoll Cres SA11 71 F7
Gnoll Dr SA11 71 F7
Gnoll Gdns SA11 72 A8
Gnoll Park Rd SA11 71 F8
Gnoll Rd SA9 221 C1
Gnoll View SA11 72 A7
Goat Mill Rd
Dowlais CF48 11 A3
Merthyr Tydfil CF47 11 A1
Gobaith Row 2 CF44 28 C3
Godfrey Ave SA11 223 C1
Godfrey Rd
Cwmbran NP44 89 D5
Newport NP20 143 B5
Godre'r Coed SA6 45 D2
Godre'r Coed Rd CF48 10 A4
Godre'r Fro SA8 23 D7
Godre'Rgraig CP Sch
SA9 221 C1
Godreaman St CF44 53 C5
Godrer Coed CF82 84 F7
Godwin Cl CF15 176 D4
Goetre Bellaf Rd SA2 93 C7
Goetre Fach Rd SA2 93 E7
Goetre Fawr Rd SA2 93 D7
Goetre Inf & Jun Sch
CF47 10 C4
Goitre Coed Isaf CF45 82 F4
Goitre La CF47 10 D5
Goitre-Coed Rd CF46 83 A5
Golate 5 CF10 195 A5
Gold St CF24 195 D6
Gold Tops NP20 143 B5
Goldcliff Ct NP44 89 F3
Goldcliff Ho NP44 89 F3
Goldcrest Dr CF23 178 D7
Goldcroft Ct NP18 118 B2
Golden Ave SA12 98 B2
Golden Cl SA3 122 F7
Golden Gr SA5 68 D6
Golden Terr CF34 102 B3
Goldsland Pl CF62 214 C5
Goldsmith Cl
Bridgend CF31 168 C5
Cardiff CF3 179 B7
Newport NP20 142 E2
Goleg-y-Fro CF31 169 B4
Golf Rd Pontypool NP4 63 B4
Port Talbot SA12 98 D1
Golf View NP23 8 C2
Golwg Hafren SA2 94 C4
Golwg y Coed CF83 137 D5
Golwg y Craig SA10 226 A7
Golwg y Mynydd
Craig-Cefn-Parc SA6 22 B1
Godrergraig SA9 2 A3
Golwg-y-Bryn SA10 222 D4
Golwg-y-coed SA11 223 C1
Golwg-y-Cwm SA18 220 D5
Golwg-y-Gamlas
SA10 48 E1
Golwg-y-Mynydd
Neath SA10 48 C2
Rhymney NP22 12 E5
Golwg-Yr -Afon SA14 42 B7
Golwg-yr-Afon SA10 49 C4
Golwyg yr Eglwys
CF83 138 D6
Golwyg-y-mynydd
NP22 6 C3
Golygafar Eglwys
CF37 109 A1
Golygfor SA15 40 F4
Gomer Gdns SA1 68 A1
Gomer Rd SA1 67 F1
Gonhill SA3 122 E8
Goodrich Ave CF83 138 C2
Goodrich Cres NP20 143 B7
Goodrich Ct 1 NP44 90 B2
Goodrich Gr NP10 163 E5
Goodrich La NP20 143 B7
Goodrich St CF83 138 B2
Goodwick Cl CF62 214 F8
Goodwick Rd CF3 179 C3
Goodwin St CF34 102 B3
Goodwood Cl CF5 192 F4
Goole Rd SA5 67 D5
Goose Island SA1 95 D5
Goossens Cl NP19 144 F6
Goppa Rd SA4 19 E3
Gordings NP44 89 B3
Gordon Ave NP11 60 B3
Gordon Cl NP12 85 D6
Gordon Cres SA12 98 C2
Gordon Rd
Abersychan NP4 37 E4
Caerphilly NP12 85 E6
Cardiff CF24 195 B7
Llanelli SA14 41 B7
Port Talbot SA12 98 C2
Porthcawl CF36 182 F6
Gordon St
Aberdare CF44 53 B5
Newport NP19 143 E5
Ton Pentre CF41 78 F3
Gordon Thomas Cl 4
SA1 68 C2
Gordon Villas CF44 29 B2
Gore St NP19 143 D7
Gore Terr 2 SA1 95 C7
Gored Cotts SA11 226 C4
Gored Terr SA11 226 C4
Gorge Terr NP24 33 F3
Goring Rd SA15 40 D6
Gorof Rd SA9 2 D8
Goronwy Rd SA2 67 E1
Gors Ave SA1 68 B1
Gors Com Jun & Inf Schs
SA1 67 E1
Gors Goch Rd SA18 220 D8
Gors La SA18 220 D6
Gors Rd SA4 44 A3
Gors-Fach SA14 41 C6
Gorsafle SA9 222 A4
Gorsddu Rd SA14 218 D8
Gorsddu Terr SA14 218 C8
Gorse La SA1 95 A5
Gorse Pl CF5 193 D8
Gorsedd SA15 40 F4
Gorsedd Cl NP23 7 D5
Gorsedd Gardens Rd
CF10 195 A6
Gorsedd St CF45 54 D2
Gorsedd Terr CF47 10 E2
Gorseinon Bsns Pk
SA4 43 C1
Gorseinon Coll
Gorseinon SA4 43 A1
Loughor SA4 42 F1
Gorseinon Inf Sch
SA4 43 C2
Gorseinon Jun Sch
SA4 43 B2
Gorseinon Rd SA4 43 E1
Gorslas CF33 147 F1
Gorslas Cty Prim Sch
SA14 218 B8
Gorslwyn Terr SA18 220 D5
Gorsto Rd
Gwaun-Cae-Gurwen
SA18 220 D7
Pen-Rhiw-fawr SA9 221 B5
Gorwydd Rd SA4 66 C4
Gorwyl Rd CF32 104 E2
Goscombe Dr CF64 206 F5
Goscombe Pk CF71 202 C7
Goshen Cl NP22 12 E4
Goshen Pk SA10 70 F8
Goshen St NP22 12 E4
Gospel Hall Terr CF44 28 F3
Gough Ave SA9 2 D7
Gough Rd Cardiff CF5 193 C5
Ystalyfera SA9 2 B6
Gould Cl CF3 179 E8
Govilion Pl NP44 89 D5
Gowan Ct CF14 159 D3
Gower Cres SA12 98 C7
Gower Ct CF62 214 D5
Gower Davies Ct
CF37 109 A7
Gower Gn NP44 90 A6
Gower Holiday Village
SA3 231 A6
Gower Pl SA3 123 A5
Gower Rd
Aberdare CF44 29 E1
Killay SA2 93 D5
Swansea SA2 94 C7
Gower Rise SA4 66 C4
Gower St
Briton Ferry SA11 71 C3
Cardiff CF24 178 A1
Port Talbot SA13 125 C7
Gower Terr SA4 64 F4
Gower View SA15 40 E8
Gower View Rd SA4 43 A4
Gower's Bldgs SA11 71 B1
Gowerton SA4 66 C8
Gowerton Comp Sch
SA4 66 C4
Gowerton Rd
Pen-clawdd SA4 65 A4
Three Crosses SA4 65 F2
Gowerton Sta SA4 66 C5
Goya Cl NP19 144 A7
Goya Pl SA12 124 D8
Goytre Cl SA13 125 F8
Goytre Cres SA13 125 E8
Goytre Fawr Jun & Inf Sch
NP4 39 E5
Goytre Rd SA13 125 F8
Graddfa Ind Est
CF83 111 F2
Gradon Cl CF63 215 C6
Grafog St SA1 96 B7
Grafton Cl CF23 178 D3
Grafton Dr CF72 155 E2
Grafton La NP19 143 D5
Grafton Rd NP19 143 C5
Grafton Terr CF14 177 C6
Graham Ave CF31 150 D2
Graham Bell Cl NP20 116 F4
Graham Berry Ct SA5 68 A5
Graham Cl CF23 178 E2
Graham Ct CF83 138 C3
Graham St
6 Merthyr Tydfil CF47 10 D1
Newport NP20 143 B4

Graham St *continued*
Swansea SA1 68 D2
Graham Terr SA10 70 E7
Graham Way 7 CF47 10 D1
Graham Wlk 10
CF11 194 D5
Graham's Yd NP22 6 E1
Graig Ave
Abercwmboi CF44 53 E5
Llanelli SA15 40 E4
3 Margam SA13 125 E4
Pontypridd CF37 135 B7
Graig Cl
Abercanaid CF48 30 E4
Bassaleg NP10 142 A3
Graig Cotts CF72 173 D6
Graig Cres CF44 53 E5
Graig Ddu CF43 79 B8
Graig Ddu Pl CF40 107 C4
Graig Ebbw NP23 7 B4
Graig Fach CF37 135 F7
Graig Gellinudd SA8 24 B5
Graig Hir CF15 176 B7
Graig Inf Sch SA6 68 F8
Graig Jun Sch The (Ysgol Iau y Graig) CF81 57 F4
Graig Llwyn Rd
CF14 160 D4
Graig Lwyd CF15 176 B7
Graig Newydd SA9 221 C2
Graig Parc Neath SA10 48 B1
Neath Abbey SA10 71 B8
Graig Park Ave NP20 117 B1
Graig Park Circ
NP20 117 A1
Graig Park Hill NP20 117 B1
Graig Park La NP20 117 B1
Graig Park Par NP20 117 B1
Graig Park Rd NP20 117 B1
Graig Park Villas
NP20 117 A1
Graig Pl Aberdare CF44 28 F1
Swansea SA1 95 D8
Graig Rd
Abercanaid CF48 30 E4
Abergwynfi SA13 76 B6
Abertillery NP13 36 C2
Cardiff CF14 160 A5
Cwmbran NP44 89 A5
Glais SA7 47 A6
Glanaman SA18 220 C7
Godrergraig SA9 221 C2
Neath SA10 70 D7
Newbridge NP11 87 A6
Pontardawe SA8 23 C3
Pontardawe SA8 24 A5
Porth CF39 107 E7
Swansea SA6 68 F7
Ystrad Mynach CF82 84 F2
Graig St Aberdare CF44 28 F1
4 Mountain Ash CF45 54 D3
Pontypridd CF37 135 C8
9 Swansea SA1 95 D8
Tylorstown CF40 80 B1
Graig Terr
Abercwmboi CF44 53 E5
Abergwynfi SA13 76 B5
Bargoed CF81 57 F5
Bedlinog CF46 56 A7
Blackmill CF35 130 F2
Cwm NP23 35 B6
Dowlais CF48 11 A5
Ferndale CF43 80 A5
Pontypridd CF37 135 C8
Senghenydd CF83 110 F4
Swansea SA1 95 C8
Graig The
Bridgend CF31 168 E4
Cefn Cribwr CF32 149 C2
Graig Twrch SA9 1 A1
Graig View
Abertillery NP13 60 A7
Cardiff CF14 160 B3
Cwmfelinfach NP11 113 A5
Machen CF83 140 B7
Nantgarw CF15 158 B8
Risca NP11 114 F1
Graig Wen
Maerdy CF43 79 B8
Morganstown CF15 176 B8
Graig Wood Cl NP20 117 B1
Graig y Darren SA9 2 A3
Graig y Pal SA7 47 A5
Graig Yr Wylan CF83 137 E2
Graig Ysguthan
CF83 112 A5
Graig-Llwyn Rd
CF14 160 E4
Graig-Wen Hos NP11 87 C3
Graig-y-Bedw NP24 33 F3
Graig-y-Coed SA4 64 D4
Graig-y-Ddelw CF42 50 D3
Graig-y-Dderi SA7 47 A6
Graig-y-Rhacca Prim Sch
CF83 139 C6
Graig-y-Wion Cty Prim
Sch CF37 135 B6
Graig-Yr-Eos Terr
CF40 107 A3
Graig-Yr-Helfa Rd
CF37 135 E8
Graigddu Rd CF40 107 B4
Graigfelen Co Prim Sch
SA6 46 C8
Graiglas CF32 130 A2
Graiglwyd CF44 28 C4
Graiglwyd Rd SA2 94 E8
Graiglwyd Sq SA1 94 F8
Graigola Rd SA7 47 B6
Graigwen Cres CF83 137 B7
Graigwen Parc CF37 109 A3
Graigwen Pl CF37 109 B1
Graigwen Rd
Pontypridd CF37 109 B2
Porth CF39 107 E2
Graigymerched SA9 2 A5
Graigyrhesg Pl CF37 109 D3
Graigyrhesg Rd
CF37 109 D3
Grampian Way SA5 67 E3
Grand Ave CF5 193 C5
Grand View Terr
CF40 107 A3
Grandison St
Briton Ferry SA11 71 C2
2 Swansea SA1 68 D1
Grange Ave CF5 205 A7
Grange Cl
Caerphilly CF83 137 F3
Wenvoe CF5 205 A7
Grange Cres
Bridgend CF35 169 F4
Mumbles SA3 123 A7
Grange Ct
Barry CF63 215 D6
Newport NP20 143 A4
Grange Gdns
Cardiff CF11 194 F2
Llantwit Major CF61 210 A6
Grange Hill NP12 85 C6
Grange Ind Site NP44 89 F2
Grange La
4 Cwmbran NP44 89 E4
Mumbles SA3 123 A8
Grange Pl CF11 195 A2
Grange Prim Sch
SA3 123 A7
Grange Rd
Cwmbran NP44 89 F3
Mumbles SA3 123 A7
Grange St SA13 125 C8
Grange Terr CF40 106 E7
Grange The
Caerphilly CF83 137 F3
Cardiff CF5 194 A8
Miskin CF72 173 D7
4 Penarth CF64 206 F3
Grangemoor Ct
CF11 206 E7
Grangetown Jun & Inf Sch
CF11 194 F2
Grangetown Link
Cardiff CF11 194 C2
Penarth CF11 206 D8
Grangetown Sta
CF11 194 E2
Grangewood Cl
CF23 161 B1
Granogwen Rd SA1 68 C1
Granston Ho NP44 89 B2
Granston Sq NP44 89 B2
Grant St SA15 40 E4
Grant's Cl CF15 176 C8
Grant's Field CF5 192 D2
Grantham Cl CF5 176 E2
Granville Ave CF5 194 A7
Granville Cl NP10 142 C4
Granville La NP20 143 D4
Granville Rd SA1 95 E8
Granville St
Abertillery NP13 36 A6
Newport NP20 143 D4
Granville Terr
Llanelli SA14 41 C6
Mountain Ash CF45 54 D4
Grasmere Ave CF23 178 A3
Grasmere Dr CF44 29 E1
Grassholm Gdns SA5 67 E7
Grassholm Way
CF36 165 D1
Grassmere Cl CF64 206 E6
Grawen CF47 10 C2
Grawen Hos CF48 225 F3
Grawen La CF48 225 F3
Grawen St CF39 107 E4
Grawen Terr CF47 10 D2
Gray La CF11 194 D6
Gray St
Abertillery NP13 36 B5
Cardiff CF11 194 D6
Gray's Pl CF48 55 D4
Graylands The CF14 177 C6
Grays Gdns CF83 139 D6
Grays Wlk CF71 188 F2
Great Burnet Cl CF3 180 B6
Great House Mdws
CF61 209 F7
Great Oaks Pk NP10 141 F7
Great St CF37 108 D2
Great Thomas Cl
CF62 212 F2
Great Western Ave
CF31 168 F6
Great Western Cres
SA15 40 D3
Great Western Ct
CF5 194 C5
Great Western La 2
CF10 195 A4
Great Western Terr
Cwmavon SA12 99 F6
1 Llanelli SA15 40 D3
Talbot Green CF72 155 B1
Greave Cl CF5 205 A7
Greek Church St 4
CF10 195 B4
Green Acre
Creigiau CF15 174 E7
Cwmbran NP44 89 D1
Green Acre Dr CF40 106 E5
Green Ave The CF36 182 E6
Green Bank Rd SA3 122 F7
Green Circ CF33 148 A1
Green Cl SA2 94 A1
Green Dragon La SA1 95 D6
Green Farm Cl CF5 193 A4
Green Farm Rd CF5 193 A4
Green Field Terr
CF32 129 C2
Green Hill
Pontycymer CF32 103 E3
5 Swansea SA1 68 D1
Ton Pentre CF41 79 B3
Green La Barry CF63 215 C8
Llantwit Major CF61 209 D6
St Brides Wentlooge
NP10 163 E3
Green Lawn Jun Sch
NP4 63 B4
Green Lawns CF62 215 A7
Green Mdw
Glyncorrwg SA13 227 C2
Tredegar NP22 6 F1
Green Mdws CF3 179 E5
Green Meadow Terr
CF32 130 B4
Green Park St SA12 125 A8
Green Pk
Pontyclun CF72 154 F1
Talbot Green CF72 155 C2
Green Row CF83 139 F6
Green St
7 Aberavon SA12 124 F8
Bridgend CF31 168 F5
Cardiff CF11 194 F5
Ebbw Vale NP23 14 F1
Neath SA11 71 E8
Swansea SA6 69 A8
Green The
Abertysswg NP22 33 C8
Bryn NP12 85 D4
Leckwith CF11 194 B1
Neath SA11 71 D7
Pencoed CF35 170 E8
Radyr CF15 176 C5
Sarn CF32 150 E3
Trefechan CF48 10 B6
Green Villas NP13 36 B6
Green Way NP4 37 E5
Green Willows NP44 116 F8
Green Wood Dr
CF38 156 B7
Greenacre Dr
Bedwas CF83 138 D6
Cardiff CF23 161 B2
Glais SA7 47 A5
Pencoed CF35 170 C8
Greenacre Gdns
CF83 138 F6
Greenacres
Barry CF63 215 D7
Pen-clawdd SA4 64 D4
Port Talbot SA13 126 A1
South Cornelly CF33 165 F5
Greenbanks Dr CF62 214 D6
Greenbay Rd CF24 196 A6
Greenclose Rd CF14 177 C4
Greencourt NP44 90 A6
Greencroft Ave CF5 193 F6
Greene Cl NP19 144 F5
Greenfield
Caerleon NP18 117 F3
New Tredegar NP24 33 D4
Newbridge NP11 87 A7
Greenfield Ave
Cardiff CF11 194 C7
Cardiff CF14 177 C5
Dinas Powys CF64 206 B3
2 Margam SA13 125 E4
Newbridge NP11 87 A7
Pontypridd CF37 109 C5
Greenfield Cl
Cwmbran NP44 89 D6
Swansea SA7 69 F7
Greenfield Cotts NP22 6 D2
Greenfield Cres
Ebbw Vale NP23 7 C4
Swansea SA7 69 F7
Greenfield Gdns CF48 31 A4
Greenfield Pl
Abertridwr CF83 136 E7
Blaenavon NP4 17 D6
Loughor SA4 65 F8
Greenfield Rd
Barry CF62 214 D7
Cardiff CF14 177 C5
Glanaman SA18 220 B8
Rogerstone NP10 142 B4
Greenfield Sch CF48 31 A4
Greenfield St
Bargoed CF81 58 A4
Pontlottyn CF81 32 F8
Tonypandy CF40 107 A3
Greenfield Stores
NP10 142 C4
Greenfield Terr
Abercynon CF45 82 E4
Aberdare CF44 53 F7
Abersychan NP4 37 E7
Argoed NP12 58 F4
Blaengarw CF32 103 E7
Bryncethin CF32 151 E6
Cwmparc CF42 78 A4
Ebbw Vale NP23 14 E6
Maesteg CF34 102 B3
Maesteg CF34 75 B1
Greenfield Terr *continued*
Merthyr Tydfil CF47 11 A4
Mountain Ash CF45 54 B6
North Cornelly CF33 165 F8
Ogmore Vale CF32 104 E1
Pont Rhyd-y-cyff CF34 128 E6
Swansea SA1 68 D4
Swansea SA7 69 D8
Tredegar NP22 13 F6
Troedyrhiw CF48 31 C2
Ynysddu NP11 112 F6
Pentrebach CF48 31 A4
Greenfield Way
Llanblethian CF71 188 D1
Porthcawl CF36 165 F2
Greenfields Ave
CF31 168 C4
Greenfields Terr SA2 94 C7
Greenforge Way
NP44 89 C4
Greenhaven Rise
CF64 206 E6
Greenhill Ct CF14 177 A8
Greenhill Dr CF44 53 C7
Greenhill Pl CF82 84 C6
Greenhill Prim Sch
CF82 84 C7
Greenhill Rd
Cwmbran NP44 89 D4
Pontypool NP4 62 E2
Greenhill Specl Sch
CF14 177 A8
Greenhill St 6 SA1 68 D1
Greenland Cres CF5 193 C8
Greenland Rd
Brynmawr NP23 8 C4
Pontypool NP4 62 C8
Greenlands
Blackwood NP11 59 D1
Newbridge NP11 87 A7
Greenlands Rd CF72 155 E3
Greenlawns CF23 178 D2
Greenmeadow
Bettws CF32 129 C2
Cefn Cribwr CF32 149 B2
Machen CF83 139 D5
Greenmeadow Ave
NP19 144 C3
Greenmeadow Bglws
NP12 85 A7
Greenmeadow Cl
Cwmbran NP44 89 D2
5 Dinas Powys CF64 206 B2
Pontypridd CF37 109 D5
Greenmeadow Community
Farm NP44 89 B4
Greenmeadow Cres
NP4 39 E3
Greenmeadow Ct
CF72 155 E2
Greenmeadow Dr
Cardiff CF15 176 D8
Risca NP11 114 D4
Greenmeadow Ho
NP44 89 D2
Greenmeadow Prim Sch
NP44 89 A3
Greenmeadow Rd
Cwmfelinfach NP11 113 C3
Newport NP19 144 C3
Greenmeadow Terr
Abertillery NP13 36 B7
Tonypandy CF40 107 A2
Greenmeadow Way
NP44 89 D2
Greenmeadows
CF31 168 F5
Greenock Rd CF3 179 D6
Greenside CF71 188 F1
Greensway NP22 33 C8
Greenway CF83 138 C6
Greenway Ave CF3 179 C3
Greenway Cl
Llandough CF64 206 D7
Pontypool NP4 62 D2
Greenway Ct CF63 215 D8
Greenway Dr NP4 62 D2
Greenway Jun & Inf Sch
CF3 179 C4
Greenway Rd
Cardiff CF3 179 D5
Neath SA11 71 E7
Greenway St SA15 40 C6
Greenway The SA10 70 C3
Greenway Wlk NP4 62 D3
Greenway Workshops
CF83 138 D6
Greenways
Aberdare CF44 29 D3
Ebbw Vale NP23 14 B8
Porthcawl CF36 183 B8
Waunarlwydd SA5 66 D3
Greenways The
CF34 102 A2
Greenwich Rd
Cardiff CF5 194 B7
Newport NP20 143 B1
Greenwillows NP44 116 F8
Greenwood NP18 144 A8
Greenwood Ave
Cwmbran NP44 89 C5
Maesteg CF34 102 A1
Tredegar NP22 6 C1
Greenwood Cl
Bridgend CF31 168 F7
Cardiff CF23 161 B2
Swansea SA2 94 C6
Merthyr Tydfil CF47 30 F7
Greenwood Ct
Caerphilly CF83 138 C3
Greenwood Ct *continued*
New Tredegar NP24 33 D3
Greenwood Dr
Cimla SA11 72 C5
Cwmbran NP44 115 E8
Hirwaun CF44 27 F7
Greenwood La CF5 193 A7
Greenwood Pl SA5 67 D6
Greenwood Rd
Abersychan NP4 37 F5
Baglan SA12 98 D7
Blackwood NP12 58 D1
Cardiff CF5 176 F2
Neath SA11 71 D4
Greenwood St CF63 214 F4
Gregory Cl CF35 170 B8
Greig Cl SA12 98 B3
Greig Ct 7 SA12 98 B3
Grenadier Dr NP18 145 C8
Grenfell Ave SA4 43 A3
Grenfell Park Rd SA1 95 F7
Grenfell Town SA1 68 F3
Grenig Rd SA18 220 B6
Grenville Rd CF23 195 D8
Gresford Cl CF3 179 D6
Gresham Pl CF46 83 A6
Grey Cres CF82 85 A6
Grey St SA1 68 D3
Grey Waters NP44 90 A3
Grey's Dr CF61 210 B6
Grey's Pl CF44 28 F7
Greyfriars CF31 168 F5
Greyfriars Ct CF36 183 D8
Greyfriars Pl 3
CF10 195 A6
Greyfriars Rd CF10 195 A6
Greys Rd NP4 62 C5
Greys Terr SA7 47 B1
Griffin Ave NP4 17 D6
Griffin Cl CF62 214 C8
Griffin Ct NP4 62 B7
Griffin Park Ct CF36 183 A7
Griffin St
Abertillery NP13 36 C3
3 Newport NP20 143 C5
Griffin The NP10 142 A2
Griffith John St SA1 68 D1
Griffith St
1 Aberdare CF44 29 A1
Maerdy CF43 52 A2
Pentre CF41 78 F4
Griffith Terr CF48 55 C4
Griffiths Ct NP4 17 A6
Griffiths Gdns NP22 6 C1
Griffiths Sq NP22 6 C1
Griffiths St CF82 84 E2
Griffiths Terr CF34 75 A2
Griffiths Way NP4 37 E5
Griffithstown Inf Sch
NP4 62 E3
Griffithstown Jun Sch
NP4 62 E2
Grimson Cl CF64 216 B5
Grindle Wlk NP10 142 A6
Gripoly Mills CF11 194 E3
Grisedale Cl CF23 178 B2
Groes Cl NP10 142 A7
Groes Lon CF14 177 B8
Groes Prim Sch
SA13 125 F3
Groes Rd
Rogerstone NP10 142 A6
Rogerstone NP10 142 A7
Groes-Faen Terr
CF81 57 D5
Groes-Wen La 1
SA13 125 D5
Groeswen CF61 209 F7
Groeswen Dr CF83 137 D4
Groeswen Hospl
SA13 125 E5
Groeswen Rd
Caerphilly CF15, CF83 137 C3
Caerphilly CF83 137 D4
Gron Ffordd CF14 159 B1
Gron Rd SA18 220 D6
Grongaer Terr CF37 135 C8
Grosmont Cl NP12 58 E1
Grosmont Pl NP44 90 A6
Grosmont Rd NP4 63 B5
Grosmont Way NP10 163 E5
Grosvenor Pl NP4 62 E1
Grosvenor Rd
Abertillery NP13 36 B6
Swansea SA2 94 D7
Grosvenor St CF5 194 B6
Grosvenor Terr CF34 75 A1
Grouse St CF24 195 C7
Grove Cres NP4 38 B1
Grove Est
Bedwas CF83 139 A7
Pontypool NP4 38 A1
Grove Farm Rd SA4 43 C7
Grove Hill Pk SA14 218 C8
Grove House Ct CF43 80 C1
Grove La Neath SA10 70 E7
1 Newport NP20 143 C3
Penrhiwtyn SA11 71 C5
Grove Park Ave NP44 89 E6
Grove Park Dr NP20 117 B1
Grove Pk
Cwmbran NP44 89 E6
Merthyr Tydfil CF47 10 D3
Grove Pl Cardiff CF14 177 D5
Penarth CF64 207 A4
Pontypool NP4 62 E2
Port Talbot SA13 125 B8
Swansea SA1 95 C7
Grove Place La 4
CF64 207 A4
Grove Rd
Bridgend CF31 168 F3
Clydach SA6 22 D1
Llandow CF71 199 A7
Pontardawe SA8 23 F5
Pontypool NP4 62 A8
Risca NP11 114 F3
Grove St
Gorseinon SA4 43 B3
Llanbradach CF83 111 F1
Maesteg CF34 102 A6
Newbridge NP11 86 F6
Grove Terr
Abercwmboi CF44 53 E5
Bedlinog CF46 56 A7
Llanharan CF72 153 F3
Penarth CF64 207 A4
10 Pontypool NP4 38 A1
Senghenydd CF83 110 E2
Ynysybwl CF37 109 A8
Grove The
Aberdare CF44 29 A1
Aberfan CF48 55 C6
Barry CF62 214 C2
Bryn NP12 85 E4
Cardiff CF3 179 C3
Fochriw CF81 32 D7
Merthyr Tydfil CF47 10 D2
Mumbles SA3 123 A5
Pontypridd CF37 109 D6
Swansea SA2 94 F6
Grove Way CF3 179 C3
Grove Wlk NP11 59 D1
Grovefield Ho 9
CF40 106 F4
Grovefield Terr 8
CF40 106 F4
Groveland Rd CF14 177 D5
Grovenor Rd NP10 141 F3
Grover St CF37 135 B8
Grovers Cl CF37 109 D6
Grovers Field CF45 109 D8
Groves Ave SA3 122 F4
Groves Rd Neath SA11 71 F5
Newport NP20 142 D4
Groveside Rd NP12 86 A8
Groveside Villas 8
NP4 38 A1
Gruffyd Dr CF83 138 A5
Grwyne Terr NP12 58 F4
Guardian Ind Est
CF24 195 F7
Guenever Cl CF14 159 D2
Guest Cotts CF48 11 B5
Guest Rd CF24 195 E4
Guest St CF81 32 C7
Guildford Cres CF10 195 B5
Guildford St 3 CF10 195 B5
Guildhall Pl 4 CF10 195 A5
Guildhall Rd N SA1 95 A5
Guildhall Rd S SA1 95 A5
Gulf Ind Area CF11 194 E2
Gulliver's Cl SA3 123 B8
Gurnos CP Jun Sch
SA9 2 D8
Gurnos Est NP23 8 A5
Gurnos Rd
Gowerton SA4 66 B5
Merthyr Tydfil CF47 10 C4
Ystradgynlais SA9 2 C7
Guthrie St CF63 215 A5
Guy's Rd CF63 215 B6
Gwaelod y Foel
CF38 156 D8
Gwaelod-y-Garth Ind Est
CF15 158 A2
Gwaelod-y-Garth Rd
CF37 136 C2
Gwaelodygarth Cl
CF47 10 D3
Gwaelodygarth Rd
CF47 10 D3
Gwaelodywaun Villas
CF81 58 B3
Gwaila Gr 5 CF37 135 F6
Gwalch y Penwaig
CF62 214 F2
Gwalia Cl
Bridgend CF31 150 F1
Gorseinon SA4 43 D2
Gwalia Cres SA4 43 D2
Gwalia Ct Clydach SA6 46 D7
Swansea SA1 95 B5
Gwalia Rd CF35 170 E8
Gwalia Terr
Aberdare CF44 53 C8
Blaina NP13 15 E6
Gorseinon SA4 43 D2
Gwalin y Cwrt CF83 137 D1
Gwan-y-garw CF32 103 F3
Gwar-y-Caeau SA13 125 C8
Gwaun Bedw CF39 107 E2
Gwaun Cae Gurwen Prim
Sch SA18 220 D7
Gwaun Cl CF14 176 E4
Gwaun Coed CF31 169 A4
Gwaun Cotts CF72 172 A8
Gwaun Delyn Cl NP23 15 D7
Gwaun Helyg NP23 14 B8
Gwaun Helyg Rd NP23 7 B1
Gwaun Newydd
CF83 138 D4
Gwaun Rd CF37 135 F6
Gwaun-Bant CF32 103 E4
Gwaun-Fro CF82 84 D7
Gwaun-Hyfryd CF83 138 D4
Gwaun-Ruperra Cl
CF72 155 D4
Gwaun-y-groes
CF72 155 F2

Gwauncelyn Jun & Inf Sch CF38 ..... 135 F1
Gwaunfarren Cl CF47 10 E4
Gwaunfarren Gr CF47 10 E3
Gwaunfarren Prim Sch CF47 ..... 10 E3
Gwaunfarren Rd CF47 ..... 10 E3
Gwaunfelin Wlk 8 NP4 ..... 17 D7
Gwaunmisgyn Jun & Inf Sch CF38 ..... 156 A6
Gwaunmiskin Rd CF38 ..... 156 A6
Gwaunrhydd 2 CF38 ..... 156 A6
Gwaunrparra Rd CF72 ..... 155 D4
Gwawr St CF44 ..... 53 B8
Gwbert Cl CF3 ..... 179 E5
Gwelfor
Cefn Cribwr CF32 ..... 149 A2
Dunvant SA2 ..... 93 E8
Llanelli SA14 ..... 41 E4
Gwendoline Pl 3 CF24 ..... 195 D5
Gwendoline Rd NP11 ..... 114 F1
Gwendoline St
4 Aberavon SA12 ..... 99 A1
Blaengarw CF32 ..... 103 E6
2 Cardiff CF24 ..... 195 D5
Merthyr Tydfil CF47 10 E3
Nant-y-Moel CF32 ..... 104 F5
Treherbert CF42 ..... 50 E2
Gwendoline Terr
Abercynon CF45 ..... 82 E3
Cwmfelin CF34 ..... 128 B8
Gwendraeth Pl SA1 ..... 69 B2
Gwenfo CH in W Prim Sch CF5 ..... 205 A6
Gwenfo Ct CF5 ..... 205 A7
Gwenlais Rd SA4 ..... 43 E7
Gwenllian St CF63 ..... 215 D6
Gwenllian Terr CF37 135 F4
Gwennol y Mor CF62 214 F2
Gwennyth St CF24 ..... 178 A1
Gwenog Ct CF62 ..... 214 C5
Gwent CF64 ..... 207 C5
Gwent Ct
Ebbw Vale NP23 ..... 14 E3
Fleur De Lis NP12 ..... 85 A6
Gwent Gdns SA1 ..... 67 F1
Gwent Gr SA2 ..... 94 A6
Gwent Ho
4 Cardiff CF23 ..... 178 C2
Port Talbot SA12 ..... 124 D8
Gwent Rd Cardiff CF5 193 B4
Swansea SA1 ..... 68 A1
Upper Boat CF37 ..... 136 D1
Gwent Sh Ctr NP22 ..... 13 E7
Gwent Sq NP44 ..... 89 E3
Gwent St NP4 ..... 62 B6
Gwent Terr
Blaina NP13 ..... 15 E6
Nantyglo NP23 ..... 8 D1
Porth CF39 ..... 107 E4
Gwent Way NP22 ..... 13 D8
Gwern Ave CF81 ..... 110 F2
Gwern Einon Rd SA2 94 B3
Gwern Fadog Rd SA6 46 A3
Gwern Las NP13 ..... 36 B6
Gwern Rhuddi Rd CF23 ..... 160 D1
Gwern-Berthi Rd NP13 .....
Gwern-Rhuddi Rd CF23 ..... 178 C8
Gwerna Cres CF82 ..... 85 A1
Gwernant SA9 ..... 221 B7
Gwernifor St CF47 ..... 10 E2
Gwernllwyn Cl CF48 ..... 11 A4
Gwernllwyn Jun Sch CF48 ..... 11 C4
Gwernllwyn Terr CF43 ..... 80 B4
Gwernllwynchwyth Rd
Llansamlet SA7 ..... 46 F1
Swansea SA7 ..... 69 F8
Gwernllyn Rd CF48 ..... 11 B4
Gwernos SA6 ..... 46 A2
Gwerthonor La
Bargoed CF81 ..... 58 A1
Gilfach CF81 ..... 85 A8
Gwerthonor Rd
Bargoed CF81 ..... 58 A1
Gilfach CF81 ..... 85 A8
Gwerthonor Pl CF81 ..... 58 A1
Gwili Ave SA14 ..... 218 C6
Gwili Terr SA1 ..... 68 B1
Gwilym Pl 6 CF63 ..... 215 A8
Gwilym Rd SA9 ..... 221 B8
Gwilym St CF37 ..... 135 F4
Gwlad Du Gwyrdd CF39 ..... 132 B5
Gwlad-y-Gan SA6 ..... 45 D1
Gwladys Pl NP10 ..... 118 A3
Gwladys St
Merthyr Tydfil CF47 ..... 10 F3
Pant CF48 ..... 11 B7
Penywaun CF44 ..... 28 B6
Gwrhyd Rd
Pen-Rhiw-fawr SA9 ..221 A4
Pontardawe SA8,SA9 .220 F2
Rhydyfro SA8 ..... 220 D8
Gwrangon Cl NP11 ..... 87 B2
Gwyddon Rd NP11 ..... 87 C3
Gwydr Cres SA2 ..... 94 F6
Gwydr Mews SA2 ..... 94 F6
Gwydr Pl SA1 ..... 42 D1
Gwydr Sq SA2 ..... 94 F6

Gwylfa SA14 ..... 41 D6
Gwylfa Rd SA1 ..... 67 F1
Gwylym St SA5 ..... 68 A2
Gwyn Cres NP4 ..... 37 E7
Gwyn Ct 8 SA12 ..... 125 A8
Gwyn Dr CF83 ..... 138 A4
Gwyn James Ct
Cardiff CF24 ..... 206 E5
Gwyn Rd CF40 ..... 107 A4
Gwyn St
Pontardawe SA8 ..... 23 E3
Pontypridd CF37 ..... 135 E5
Gwyn Terr
2 Aberavon SA12 ..... 125 A8
Crynant SA10 ..... 26 A7
Gwyn's Pl SA8 ..... 23 F3
Gwynant Cres CF37 178 B5
Gwyndy Rd SA1 ..... 69 A2
Gwynedd Ave
Cymmer SA13 ..... 75 D3
Swansea SA1 ..... 67 F1
Gwynedd Gdns SA1 ..... 68 A1
Gwynedd Ho 5 CF23 ..... 178 C2
Gwynfan Pl CF47 ..... 30 E7
Gwynfe Rd SA14 ..... 42 E3
Gwynfi St
Blaengwynfi SA13 ..... 76 B6
Swansea SA5 ..... 68 C5
Gwynfi Terr CF72 ..... 154 A3
Gwynfor Rd SA2 ..... 67 E1
Gwynfryn Bd SA4 ..... 219 B7
Gwynfryn Rd SA4 ..... 19 C3
Gwynfryn Terr CF38 156 D7
Gwynllyw 3 NP44 ..... 89 C6
Gwynne Terr SA1 ..... 96 A8
Gwynnes Ct CF47 ..... 10 E2
Gwyrddgoed SA8 ..... 23 E6
Gwyrosydd Jun & Inf Sch SA5 ..... 68 C5
Gwysfa Rd SA6 ..... 46 A5
Gwysfryn SA9 ..... 221 C6
Gyfeillon Rd CF37 ..... 108 E2
Gynol Rd SA4 ..... 221 B7
Gynor Ave CF39 ..... 107 E5
Gynor Pl CF39 ..... 107 E6
Gypsy La
Caerphilly CF15 ..... 137 C2
Pontypool NP4 ..... 37 E1
Gyrnosfa SA9 ..... 2 D8

Habershon St CF24 .195 E6
Hackerford Rd CF3 178 C8
Haden St NP4 ..... 62 B6
Hadfield Cl CF11 ..... 194 C7
Hadfield Rd CF11 ..... 194 D2
Hadland Terr SA3 ..... 123 A6
Hadrian Cl NP18 ..... 118 A3
Hadrian's Ct CF82 ..... 84 C7
Hael La SA3 ..... 121 B4
Hafan Cardiff CF5 ..... 193 E6
4 Llanelli SA15 ..... 40 C4
Hafan Deg
Aberkenfig CF32 ..... 150 C3
Cwmfelin CF34 ..... 128 C8
Pencoed CF35 ..... 170 D8
Seven Sisters SA10 ..... 222 C3
Hafan Elim CF47 ..... 10 F3
Hafan Glyd SA6 ..... 46 E8
Hafan Heulog CF37 .109 D7
Hafan y Don SA2 ..... 93 E8
Hafan-Werdd CF83 .138 A2
Hafan-y-Bryn CF31 .168 C4
Hafan-y-morfa SA15 40 F2
Hafandeg CF44 ..... 28 F6
Hafnant SA1 ..... 69 D5
Hafod Bryan SA14 ..... 41 C4
Hafod Cl
Fleur De Lis NP12 ..... 85 A6
Ponthir NP18 ..... 117 F6
Hafod Cotts CF48 ..... 11 B6
Hafod Court Rd NP44 89 A5
Hafod Decaf CF33 ..... 148 B2
Hafod Gdns CF48 ..... 117 F6
Hafod La
Bargoed CF81 ..... 58 A4
Swansea SA1 ..... 68 D2
Hafod Pk SA1 ..... 68 D2
Hafod Prim Sch
Swansea SA1 ..... 68 D2
Trehafod CF37 ..... 108 C2
Hafod Rd
Ammanford SA18 ..219 A6
Ponthir NP18 ..... 117 F6
Tycroes SA18 ..... 218 F6
Hafod St Cardiff CF11 194 F4
Pentrebach CF48 ..... 31 B3
Swansea SA1 ..... 68 D1
Hafod The CF48 ..... 11 B6
Hafod Tudor Terr NP11 ..... 113 E3
Hafod Wen
Cwmdare CF44 ..... 28 C3
Tonyrefail CF39 ..... 133 D6
Hafod-Arthen Rd NP13 ..... 60 B7
Hafod-fan Rd NP13 ..... 36 C3
Hafod-fan Terr NP13 36 C3
Hafod-y-Bryn SA14 ..... 40 B5
Hafod-y-Mynydd NP22 ..... 12 F3
Hafod-Yr-Ynys Rd NP11 ..... 60 C2
Hafodyrynys Clos CF3 ..... 179 F6
Hafon Mews NP18 .117 F6
Haford St SA13 ..... 125 C8

Haforarethen NP13 ...60 B7
Hafren Ct CF11 ..... 194 D7
Hafren Rd Barry CF62 215 A5
Cwmbran NP44 ..... 89 A4
Haircourt Pl NP22 ....12 D5
Haircourt Rd
Swansea SA5 ..... 67 F4
Hailey Ct CF14 ..... 176 F3
Haines Cl CF83 ..... 137 E1
HaisbrO' Ave NP19 .143 E8
Halcyon Rd CF5 ..... 194 B6
Haldane Cl CF83 ..... 138 D3
Haldane Pl NP20 ..... 117 A2
Haldens The NP44 ..... 89 B1
Halfway Cty Prim Sch SA14 ..... 41 A6
Halifax Cl CF14 ..... 196 A7
Halifax Terr CF42 ..... 50 E3
Hall Cl CF33 ..... 166 A8
Hall Cl CF33 ..... 166 A8
Hall La SA4 ..... 64 D4
Hall St Aberdare CF44 29 A2
Ammanford SA18 ..... 219 C7
Blackwood NP12 ..... 85 F7
Ebbw Vale NP23 ..... 220 E8
Llanelli SA15 ..... 40 D6
Swansea SA1 ..... 68 D1
Nd Cl NP11 ..... 114 C5
Hall's Road Terr SA11 ..... 221 A6
Hallam Ho SA12 ..... 98 A2
Hallbank SA3 ..... 123 B4
Halliard Terr SA3 ..... 123 B4
Halle Cl NP19 ..... 145 A5
Halliard Ct CF10 ..... 195 C3
Halls Rd NP11 ..... 86 E6
Halsbury Rd CF5 ..... 194 B7
Halstead St NP19 ..... 143 E4
Halswell St CF45 ..... 82 B6
Halt Cl CF44 ..... 224 B1
Halt Rd CF44 ..... 224 B1
Halton Cl CF64 ..... 217 A8
Halton St NP11 ..... 86 E6
Ham La S CF61 ..... 210 A5
Ham La CF61 ..... 210 A5
Ham Manor CF61 ..... 210 A5
Ham Manor Caravan Pk CF61 ..... 210 A4
Ham Mews CF61 ..... 210 A4
Hamadryad Rd CF10 195 A1
Haman Pl CF82 ..... 84 C6
Hamilton St
Cardiff CF11 ..... 194 E6
Pentrebach CF48 ..... 54 C3
Newport NP19 ..... 143 F3
Swansea SA1 ..... 68 D4
Hamilton Terr CF47 ..... 75 C2
Hammond Dr NP19 .143 F4
Hammond Way CF23 178 E1
Hampden Ct NP19 .143 A3
Hampden Rd NP19 .143 A3
Hampshire Ave NP19 ..... 144 B2
Hampshire Cl NP19 .144 B2
Hampshire Cres NP19 ..... 144 B2
Hampstead Wlk CF5 192 F4
Hampton Court Rd CF23 ..... 178 E2
Hampton Cres E CF23 ..... 160 C1
Hampton Rd CF14 .177 D4
Hampton St CF47 ..... 30 E8
Hanbury Cl
Caerleon NP18 ..... 118 C1
Cardiff CF14 ..... 176 E5
Cwmbran NP44 ..... 89 E4
Hanbury Gdns NP44 .62 A8
Hanbury Rd
Bargoed NP12 ..... 58 A4
Pontypool NP4 ..... 62 A8
Hanbury Sq CF81 ..... 58 A4
Hand Farm Rd NP4 ..... 62 F5
Handel Ave SA12 ..... 98 B3
Handel Cl
Newport NP19 ..... 145 A5
Penarth CF64 ..... 206 F1
Handley Rd CF24 ..... 196 A7
Handsworth St NP19 143 F4
Hanfield Pk NP44 ..... 90 A4
Hangmanstone La SA3 ..... 231 C5
Hankey Pl CF47 ..... 30 E7
Hankey Terr CF47 ..... 30 E7
Hanley Path 8 NP44 .89 C2
Hannah Cl CF14 ..... 177 F6
Hannah St
Barry CF63 ..... 215 A6
Cardiff CF10 ..... 195 B3
Porth CF39 ..... 107 F3
Hannants The SA10 ..71 C8
Hanover Cl SA3 ..... 123 A6
Hanover Ct
Barry CF63 ..... 215 D7
Bridgend CF31 ..... 168 E5
4 Cardiff CF14 ..... 176 C6
Swansea SA2 ..... 94 D7
Hanover St
2 Barry CF62 ..... 214 F5
Cardiff CF5 ..... 194 C6
Merthyr Tydfil CF47 ..... 10 D2
Swansea SA1 ..... 95 B7

Harbour View Rd
Penarth CF64 ..... 207 A5
Swansea SA1 ..... 96 A8
Harcombe Rd CF44 107 A8
Harcourt Pl NP22 ....12 D5
Harcourt Rd
Brynmawr NP23 ..... 8 B5
Mountain Ash CF45 ..... 54 C3
Harcourt St
Ebbw Vale NP23 ..... 7 D1
Swansea SA1 ..... 95 B7
Harcourt Terr
Abertillery NP13 ..... 36 A6
Mountain Ash CF45 ..... 81 F8
Nantyglo NP23 ..... 8 A1
Tredegar NP22 ..... 13 E6
Harddian SA14 ..... 41 F6
Harding Ave NP20 ..... 117 A3
Harding Cl CF61 ..... 210 C6
Hardingsdown La SA3 ..... 228 E2
Hardwicke Ct CF5 ..... 194 A8
Hardy Cl Barry CF62 215 A8
Newport NP20 ..... 142 E1
Hardy Ct 19 NP4 ..... 38 A1
Hardy Pl CF24 ..... 195 C7
Harebell Cl SA6 ..... 46 B4
Harefield Cl CF23 ..... 161 B1
Harford Cl CF14 ..... 176 E5
Harford Ct SA2 ..... 94 C5
Harford Gdns NP12 ..... 23 F6
Harford St NP22 ..... 13 F8
Hargreaves Dr NP20 117 A3
Harle St SA11 ..... 71 F8
Harlech Cl
Blackwood NP12 ..... 58 D1
Croesyceiliog NP44 ..... 90 A6
Dinas Powys CF64 ..... 206 C3
Swansea SA2 ..... 94 B7
Harlech Cres SA2 ..... 94 B7
Harlech Ct
Caerphilly CF83 ..... 137 D4
4 Cardiff CF14 ..... 177 A6
Harlech Dr
Bassaleg NP10 ..... 141 E3
Dinas Powys CF64 ..... 206 C3
Merthyr Tydfil CF48 225 E1
Harlech Gdns CF62 .214 E8
Harlech Ho CF15 ..... 176 C6
Harlech Pl CF14 ..... 28 E1
Harlech Rd CF3 ..... 179 C3
Harlech Ret Pk NP20 ..... 143 A1
Harlequin Ct
Cardiff CF23 ..... 195 E8
Newport NP20 ..... 143 B6
Harlequin Dr NP20 .143 B6
Harlequin Rd SA12 ..... 98 F1
Harlequin Rdbt 3 NP20 ..... 143 C6
Harlequin Way CF23 178 D1
Harlington SA5 ..... 68 A2
Harold St
Cardiff CF24 ..... 195 E7
6 Cwmbran NP44 ..... 89 C2
Llanharan CF72 ..... 153 F2
Harper's Rd NP4 ..... 37 F5
Harpur St CF10 ..... 195 A4
Harries Ave SA15 ..... 40 C6
Harries St SA1 ..... 95 B8
Harris Ave SA3 ..... 179 D4
Harris Rd SA9 ..... 221 B7
Harris St Hirwaun CF44 27 D7
Swansea SA6 ..... 68 F8
Harris View CF63 ..... 215 B6
Harris's Lea SA3 ..... 181 C1
Harrison Dr CF3 ..... 180 A5
Harrison St CF47 ..... 10 F4
Harrison Way CF11 .206 B8
Harrogate Rd 2 NP19 ..... 143 E8
Harrow Cl NP18 ..... 117 F4
Harrow Rd NP19 ..... 143 D5
Harrowby La CF10 195 B2
Harrowby Pl CF10 .195 B1
Harrowby St CF10 .195 B1
Harry St SA6 ..... 45 E1
Hart Gdns 10 NP20 .142 A3
Hartland Cl CF3 ..... 179 A5
Hartland Rd CF3 ..... 179 A5
Hartley Pl CF11 ..... 194 E3
Hartridge Farm Rd NP18,NP19 ..... 143 E5
Hartridge High Sch NP18 ..... 144 E4
Hartshorn Ct CF83 .138 D3
Hartshorn Terr CF83 75 A2
Harvey Cl NP20 ..... 117 A2
Harvey Cres SA12 .124 D8
Harvey St Barry CF63 215 C6
2 Cardiff CF5 ..... 194 C6
Maesteg CF34 ..... 102 B3
Harwy Wlk NP23 ..... 116 C1
Hascocks Lea 5 SA3 ..... 231 F5
Hassock Rd CF5 ..... 89 B1
Hastings Ave CF44 206 E4
Hastings Cl CF44 ..... 206 E4
Hastings Cres CF3 179 D8
Hastings Pl CF10 ..... 206 E4
Hatfield Cl SA5 ..... 67 E5

Hathaway Ho SA12 ..98 F2
Hathaway Pl CF63 .215 C8
Hathaway St NP19 .144 B6
Hatherleigh NP19 ..144 B6
Hatherleigh Dr SA3 122 E5
Hatherleigh Rd CF3 179 A3
Hatter St 4 NP23 ..... 8 B4
Haul Bryn CF32 ..... 104 F6
Haul Fron CF40 ..... 107 A2
Haul Fryn
Cardiff CF14 ..... 176 F8
Pyle CF33 ..... 148 E3
Haulfryn
Birchgrove SA7 ..... 47 A2
Mountain Ash CF45 ..... 54 A3
Brynmenyn CF32 ..... 150 E6
Clydach NP7 ..... 9 D6
Penywaun CF44 ..... 28 B6
Pontardawe SA8 ..... 23 E5
Swansea SA1 ..... 28 D3
Haulwen Rd
Pengelairheol CF82 ..... 84 E8
Swansea SA2 ..... 67 D1
Haulwen Terr SA1 ..... 40 E7
Havannah St CF10 .195 B1
Havant Cl CF62 ..... 213 A1
Havard Rd
Abertridwr CF83 ..... 136 F7
Llanelli SA14 ..... 41 A6
Havard's Row NP22 12 F3
Havelock Pl CF11 ..... 194 F3
Havelock St
Cardiff CF10 ..... 195 A5
Llanelli SA15 ..... 40 E2
Newport NP20 ..... 143 B4
Haven Cl CF48 ..... 31 B1
Haven The
Hirwaun CF44 ..... 27 D7
Penperllenni NP4 ..... 39 E6
Havenwood Dr CF14 159 D3
Haverford Way CF5 193 D4
Havergal Cl SA3 ..... 122 D4
Hawarden La NP22 ..90 B2
Hawarden Pl 6 CF48 31 B1
Hawarden Rd NP19 144 A5
Hawfinch Cl CF23 ..... 178 D7
Hawke Cl NP19 ..... 144 E7
Hawker Cl CF24 ..... 196 B3
Hawkes Ridge NP44 .88 F2
Hawkhurst St CF36 .165 E1
Hawkins Cres NP44 144 E6
Hawks Moor Cl NP10 ..... 142 B6
Hawkstone Cl SA3 .122 E7
Hawksworth Gr NP19 ..... 144 B4
Hawkwood Cl CF5 176 B1
Hawse La NP10 ..... 163 C2
Hawthorn Ave
Baglan SA12 ..... 98 D6
Gorseinon SA4 ..... 43 A2
Merthyr Tydfil CF47 ..... 10 D4
Neath SA11 ..... 71 F6
Newport NP19 ..... 144 B4
Penarth CF64 ..... 206 E3
Hawthorn Cl
Cwmavon SA12 ..... 99 E4
Dinas Powys CF64 ..... 206 B2
Llanharry SA18 ..... 153 F2
Hawthorn Cres CF37 136 B4
Hawthorn Hill CF83 .10 B7
Hawthorn Inf Sch CF14 ..... 136 B4
Hawthorn Jun Sch CF14 ..... 176 F3
Hawthorn Pk
CF4B,CF47 ..... 225 D2
Rhymney NP22 ..... 12 C7
Tredegar NP22 ..... 6 D2
Hawthorn Pl CF62 .213 A2
Hawthorn Prim Sch CF37 ..... 136 B3
Hawthorn Rd
Barry CF62 ..... 214 C4
Ebbw Vale NP23 ..... 7 D4
Llanharry CF72 ..... 172 C5
Pontypool NP4 ..... 62 D1
Rhydyfelin CF37 ..... 136 B4
Hawthorn Rd E CF14 176 F3
Hawthorn Rd W CF14 ..... 176 F3
Hawthorn Rise CF44 .81 F8
Hawthorn St NP19 .144 B6
Hawthorn Way CF5 169 D4
Hawthorne Ave SA2 .94 F7
Hawthorne Cl NP13 .15 F5
Hawthorne Fosse NP19 ..... 144 B4
Hawthorne Rd CF44 .83 F2
Hawthorne Sq 7 NP19 ..... 144 B4
Hawthorne Terr 12 SA12 ..... 29 A1
Hawthorns The
Caerleon NP18 ..... 118 B3
Cardiff CF23 ..... 178 E6
Cwmbran NP44 ..... 89 B6
Pant CF48 ..... 11 A7

Hayes Bridge Rd CF10 ..... 195 B5
Hayes La Barry CF64 .215 D3
Barry CF64 ..... 215 D4
Hayes The CF10 ..... 195 B5
Hayling Cl NP19 ..... 143 F7
Hayman Rd NP20 ..... 143 D2
Hayswayn 2 NP44 ..... 89 B1
Haywain Ct CF31 ..... 169 A3
Hazel Cl Pontypool NP4 63 B5
Porthcawl CF36 ..... 183 D8
Hazel Ct Ebbw Vale NP23 7 C5
Swansea SA2 ..... 94 B6
Tonyrefail CF39 ..... 133 D6
Hazel Dr CF44 ..... 28 D2
Hazel Gr
Bedwas CF83 ..... 138 F6
Caerphilly CF83 ..... 138 C5
Dinas Powys CF64 ..... 206 B2
Hazel Mead CF32 ..... 150 E6
Hazel Rd
Llanmartin NP18 ..... 145 F7
Penarth CF64 ..... 206 F2
Swansea SA2 ..... 94 F7
Hazel Terr
Mountain Ash CF45 ..... 81 F8
Tredegar NP22 ..... 6 B4
Hazel Tree Cl CF15 .176 A6
Hazel Tree Ho SA10 ..... 48 C2
Hazel Tree Way CF23 161 C1
Hazel Wlk
Caerleon NP18 ..... 117 F2
Croesyceiliog NP44 ..... 90 A6
Hazeldene CF72 ..... 172 B5
Hazeldene Ave
Bridgend CF31 ..... 169 D4
Cardiff CF24 ..... 178 A1
Hazelhurst Ct CF14 176 F3
Hazelhurst Rd CF14 176 F3
Hazelmere Rd SA2 ..94 D7
Hazelmere Copse SA4 .64 B2
Hazelwell Rd CF36 .182 F8
Hazelwood Cl CF23 184 D2
Hazelwood Dr CF3 .179 E7
Hazelwood Rd
Neath SA11 ..... 71 F8
Newbridge NP11 ..... 87 B8
Hazelwood Row 3 SA12 ..... 99 F5
Hazelwood Terr 2 SA12 ..... 99 F5
Hazledene Cl CF63 .215 A7
Hazlitt Cl Cardiff CF3 .179 C8
Newport NP20 ..... 142 E1
Headland Cl SA3 ..... 122 A5
Headland Rd
Bishopston SA3 ..... 122 A5
Swansea SA1 ..... 95 F8
Heads Of The Valleys Ind Est NP22 ..... 12 D5
Heads Of The Valleys Rd
Aberdare CF44 ..... 26 A2
Brynmawr NP23 ..... 8 D5
Clydach NP7 ..... 9 D6
Dowlais CF48 ..... 11 E6
Ebbw Vale NP23 ..... 7 C4
Merthyr Tydfil CF48,CF47 ..... 225 D2
Rhymney NP22 ..... 12 C7
Tredegar NP22 ..... 6 D2
Heath Bsns Pk CF14 ..... 178 A5
Heath Cl CF23 ..... 178 A5
Heath Cres CF37 ..... 109 B1
Heath Cl CF23 ..... 178 A5
Heath Halt Rd CF23 178 A5
Heath High Level Sta CF14 ..... 178 A5
Heath Low Level Sta CF14 ..... 178 A4
Heath Mead CF14 .178 A4
Heath Park Ave CF14 ..... 178 A4
Heath Park Cres CF14 ..... 178 A4
Heath Park Ct CF14 178 A4
Heath Park La
Cardiff CF14 ..... 177 D3
Cardiff CF14 ..... 178 A4
Heath Park Way (Ffordd Parc y Mynydd Bychan) CF14 ..... 177 F3
Heath Rd NP22 ..... 85 D4
Heath St CF11 ..... 194 E5
Heath St CF11 ..... 194 E5
Heather Ave CF5 ..... 193 F6
Heather Cl Sarn CF32 150 E2
Tonpandy CF40 ..... 106 F6
Tredegar NP22 ..... 6 F1
Heather Cres SA2 ..... 94 B6
Heather Ct NP44 ..... 88 F1

Heather Rd
Merthyr Tydfil CF47 10 C5
Newport NP19 143 F7
Heather Way
[7] Cardiff CF5 193 D8
Porth CF39 108 A3
Heathers The CF62 214 D5
Heatherslade Cl
Mumbles SA3 123 B4
Southgate SA3 121 A3
Heatherslade Rd
SA3 121 A4
Heatherview Rd
CF37 109 E2
Heathfield
Gorseinon SA4 43 A1
Swansea SA1 95 C7
Tredegar NP22 14 A3
Heathfield Ave SA11 223 D1
Heathfield Cl NP23 7 D5
Heathfield Cres
CF72 153 E2
Heathfield Ct SA11 223 D1
Heathfield Dr CF62 214 E7
Heathfield Ind Pk
SA14 218 C6
Heathfield Pl CF14 177 E2
Heathfield Rd
Cardiff CF14 177 E2
Pontardawe SA8 23 F6
Heathfield Villas [4]
CF37 135 E7
Heathfield Wlk CF81 58 A5
Heathlands CF82 84 E2
Heathlands The
CF39 132 C6
Heathway CF14 177 E5
Heathwood Ct CF14 177 E5
Heathwood Gr CF14 178 A4
Heathwood Rd
Cardiff CF14 177 E5
Mumbles SA3 123 A8
Hebbles La CF63 215 B7
Hebron Rd SA6 46 D7
Hebron Villas CF45 82 C6
Hector Ave NP11 60 B2
Hedd Aberth SA10 222 D4
Heddfaen N CF23 178 F7
Heddfaen S CF23 178 F7
Heddfan NP23 8 C5
Heddwch Cl CF48 11 A6
Hedel Rd CF11 194 A6
Hedgemoor CF31 169 D4
Hedl-y Delyn Du
CF31 168 B5
Hedley Terr SA15 40 D6
Hedreladus SA9 222 A5
Hefod CF72 155 A5
Heilbronn Way SA12 99 A1
Hel Ton CF33 165 C7
Helen Pl CF24 195 D7
Helen St CF24 195 D7
Helen's Rd SA11 71 D5
Helford Sq NP20 116 D2
Helig Fan CF33 148 B1
Hellas Dr CF62 214 C8
Helpstone Terr NP4 62 A7
Helwick Cl SA3 123 A5
Hemingway Rd CF10 195 C2
Hen Felin
Pontardawe SA8 24 B5
Ystradgynlais SA9 2 C7
Hen Parc Ave SA2 93 B5
Hen Parc La SA2 93 C4
Henderson Rd NP23 8 A4
Hendre
Caerphilly CF83 137 F6
Dunvant SA2 93 D8
Dyffryn Cellwen SA10 222 F5
Ebbw Vale NP23 7 E1
Hendre Ave CF32 104 E4
Hendre Cl Cardiff CF5 194 A8
Llangennech SA14 42 A7
Hendre Cres SA14 42 B7
Hendre Ct NP44 115 F8
Hendre Farm Ct
NP19 144 F6
Hendre Farm Dr
NP19 144 F5
Hendre Farm Gdns
NP19 144 E5
Hendre Gdns CF5 194 A8
Hendre Isaf SA14 41 D4
Hendre Owain SA2 94 C8
Hendre Owen Rd
SA13 74 D4
Hendre Pk SA14 42 A7
Hendre Rd
Abertridwr CF83 136 E7
Capel Hendre SA18 218 E5
Cardiff CF3 179 E5
Glanaman SA18 220 B8
Llanelli SA14 41 D4
Llangennech SA14 42 B7
Pencoed CF35 170 B8
Tycroes SA18 218 F6
Hendre Selaig CF42 50 D3
Hendre Terr [3] CF40 107 A4
Hendre-Foilan Rd
SA2 94 B8
Hendrecafn Rd CF40 106 F4
Hendredenny Dr
CF83 137 D4
Hendredenny Inf Sch
CF83 137 E4
Hendredenny Jun Sch
CF83 137 E4
Hendredenny Park Prim
Sch CF83 137 D4
Hendrefadog St CF43 80 C4
Hendrefoilan Ave SA2 94 B7
Hendrefoilan Cl SA2 94 A7
Hendrefoilan Ct SA2 94 B8
Hendrefoilan Dr SA2 94 A7
Hendrefoilan Prim Sch
SA2 93 F7
Hendrefoilan Student
Village SA2 94 A7
Hendreforgan Cres
CF39 132 C5
Hendreforgan Jun & Inf
Schs CF39 132 C5
Hendregwilym CF40 106 F3
Hendremawr Cl SA2 94 C8
Hendrewen Rd CF42 50 C2
Hendy Cl SA2 94 B4
Hendy Ind Est SA4 19 A4
Hendy Prim Sch SA4 19 A4
Hendy Rd SA4 64 F4
Hendy St CF23 178 B1
Heneage Dr SA2 94 B1
Henfaes Rd SA11 49 C2
Henfaes Terr SA11 49 C2
Hengoed Ave CF82 85 A4
Hengoed Cl [10] CF5 193 C4
Hengoed Cres CF82 84 F4
Hengoed Hall Cl CF82 84 F3
Hengoed Hall Dr CF82 84 F4
Hengoed Parc CF82 85 A3
Hengoed Prim Sch
CF82 84 F3
Hengoed Rd
Hengoed CF82 84 F3
Penpedairheol CF82 84 E6
Hengoed Sta CF82 85 A2
Henke Ct CF10 195 C3
Henllys CF39 133 E8
Henllys CW Sch NP44 88 F1
Henllys La NP44 115 F7
Henllys Rd CF23 178 C7
Henllys Village Rd
NP44 115 F8
Henllys Way
Cwmbran NP44 115 F8
Cwmbran NP44 89 E1
Henneuadd SA9 222 C7
Hennoyadd Rd SA9 222 C7
Henrhyd Falls SA10 223 A6
Henrietta St SA1 95 B6
Henry Morgan Cl
NP10 163 F6
Henry Richard St
CF48 55 C8
Henry St
Aberdare CF44 53 C8
Bargoed CF81 57 F4
Barry CF63 215 D6
Cardiff CF10 195 B3
Mountain Ash CF45 54 D3
Neath SA11 71 E6
Pontypridd CF37 109 A2
Henry Wood Cl
NP19 144 C4
Henry Wood Wlk
NP19 144 C4
Henshaw St SA12 124 F8
Hensol Cl
Llanyravon NP44 90 A3
Rogerstone NP10 142 B6
Hensol Hospl CF72 173 D2
Hensol Rd CF72 173 C5
Hensol Villas CF72 173 E3
Henson St NP19 143 F4
Henwaun Bglws NP13 15 E3
Henwaun St NP13 15 E3
Henwysg Cl CF37 109 A2
Heol Aaron SA9 2 D8
Heol Abram SA9 2 D8
Heol Adam CF82 84 B8
Heol Adare CF32 150 D5
Heol Aer CF14 177 C8
Heol Alfred CF43 79 B8
Heol Amlwch CF14 177 B3
Heol Amman SA18 219 F8
Heol Aneurin
Caerphilly CF83 137 E6
Tonyrefail CF39 133 D5
Heol Ansurin Bevan
NP22 12 E5
Heol Ap Gethin NP23 15 E7
Heol Ap Pryce CF38 156 A6
Heol Aradur CF5 176 D3
Heol Arfryn CF32 129 E2
Heol Argoed SA18 219 C5
Heol Arthur Fear
NP13 15 E5
Heol Aur SA14 41 C8
Heol Awstin SA5 67 E5
Heol Barcud SA7 70 B8
Heol Barri CF83 137 F5
Heol Bedw CF39 107 E2
Heol Bedwas SA7 47 A1
Heol Berllan
Caerphilly CF83 138 B5
Crynant SA10 226 A8
Heol Berry CF15 158 A3
Heol Beulah CF83 137 F8
Heol Beuno NP4 63 A5
Heol Billingsley
CF15 157 F8
Heol Blakemore
CF14 176 F5
Heol Bonymaen CF48 11 A6
Heol Booker CF14 176 F5
Heol Bradford CF32 129 E2
Heol Briallu SA6 45 F2
Heol Brithdir SA7 70 B8
Heol Briwnant CF14 159 B1
Heol Bro Wen CF83 138 B5
Heol Broadland
CF62 214 E4
Heol Broch SA7 70 B8
Heol Brofiscin CF72 174 B7
Heol Bronallt SA4 19 A5
Heol Bronwen SA12 98 E1
Heol Broom CF33 165 E7
Heol Brown
Ammanford SA18 219 A5
Tycroes SA18 218 F5
Heol Brychan
Bargoed CF81 57 E3
Merthyr Tydfil CF48 10 A3
Heol Bryn CF33 165 E8
Heol Bryn Fab CF46 83 D3
Heol Bryn Glas CF38 156 D7
Heol Bryn Gwyn CF44 28 A6
Heol Bryn Hebog [4]
CF48 225 F2
Heol Bryn Heulog
CF38 156 D8
Heol Bryn Man [1]
CF48 225 F2
Heol Bryn Padell
CF48 225 F2
Heol Bryn Seion
SA10 222 F5
Heol Bryn Selu [2]
CF48 225 F2
Heol Bryn-gwyn
SA13 227 C2
Heol Bryn-y-Gwyddyl
CF48 10 A3
Heol Brynbrain SA9 221 B8
Heol Bryncelyn SA14 41 C8
Heol Bryncwils CF32 150 E3
Heol Bryncwtyn
CF35 170 D6
Heol Bryncyn SA7 47 A1
Heol Brynglas
Bridgend CF31 169 A5
Cardiff CF14 177 A8
Gorseinon SA4 66 B8
Heol Bryngwili SA14 218 A7
Heol Brynhyfryd
CF38 156 B7
Heol Brynmor John
CF38 135 E1
Heol Brynna SA11 72 C5
Heol Brynnau CF44 28 C3
Heol Brynteg
Tonyrefail CF39 133 B4
Ystrad Mynach CF82 111 E8
Heol Brython SA2 93 B8
Heol Buckley SA15 40 E8
Heol Cadifor SA5 68 B6
Heol Cadnawes SA6 45 F4
Heol Cadrawd CF34 128 D6
Heol Cae Bach CF83 138 B5
Heol Cae Celynnen
CF83 138 B5
Heol Cae Copyn SA4 42 E1
Heol Cae Fan Heulog
CF83 138 B5
Heol Cae Glas CF32 150 F3
Heol Cae Gwyn CF83 137 E1
Heol Cae Maen CF83 138 B5
Heol Cae Rhosyn SA7 47 A1
Heol Cae Tynewydd
SA4 42 F1
Heol Cae-Defaid
CF34 102 C3
Heol Cae-Derwen
CF81 57 E3
Heol Cae-Glas SA7 69 F6
Heol Caeglas CF32 150 D5
Heol Caer Bont
Margam SA13 146 E7
Port Talbot SA13 147 A8
Heol Caerhys CF14 177 C7
Heol Caerlan CF38 155 F6
Heol Caerllion SA6 46 B5
Heol Calfin SA5 67 E4
Heol Cambrensis
CF33 148 A2
Heol Camddwr CF23 161 B1
Heol Camlan SA7 47 A1
Heol Camlas SA12 99 E6
Heol Canola CF32 150 F4
Heol Capel CF39 133 C6
Heol Cara Hir SA10 226 A8
Heol Caradoc
Bargoed CF81 57 E3
Penywaun CF44 28 C6
Heol Caredig SA11 49 D3
Heol Carnau CF5 193 D3
Heol Carne CF14 177 C4
Heol Carodog SA13 125 D7
Heol Castell CF32 149 A2
Heol Castell Coety
CF31 169 A8
Heol Cattwg
Cardiff CF14 177 B3
Gelligaer CF82 84 D6
Heol Catwg SA10 48 D2
Heol Cawrdaf CF38 156 A6
Heol Cefn On CF14 160 A3
Heol Cefn Ydfa
Coytrahen CF32 150 B8
Maesteg CF34 101 F1
Heol Cefn-yr Hendy
CF72 173 C7
Heol Cefni SA6 68 E8
Heol Ceiriog CF39 80 D1
Heol Celyn
Church Village CF38 135 F1
Cimla SA11 72 B6
Hengoed CF82 85 A3
Heol Celynen CF37 109 D6
Heol Cerdin CF34 128 D8
Heol Ceri SA5 66 D3
Heol Ceulanydd CF34 75 A2
Heol Chappell CF14 176 F5
Heol Claerwen NP23 7 B5
Heol Cleddau SA5 66 D3
Heol Cledwyn SA7 47 A1
Heol Clwyddau CF38 156 A5
Heol Clyd CF83 137 D5
Heol Coch CF31 169 D5
Heol Coed Cae CF14 177 C3
Heol Coed Leyshon
CF32 150 B8
Heol Coedcae CF81 57 E3
Heol Coflorna CF46 83 C6
Heol Collen CF5 193 A2
Heol Coroniad CF38 156 A7
Heol Creigiau CF38,
CF15 156 D3
Heol Crochendy
CF15, CF37 136 E1
Heol Croes Faen
CF36 165 F1
Heol Cronfa CF37 109 F4
Heol Cropin SA14 41 C8
Heol Crwys SA4 43 B4
Heol Cumfferws
SA18 218 F6
Heol Cwarrel Clark
CF83 137 E7
Heol Cwm Ifor CF83 137 D6
Heol Cwm Mawr
SA12 99 D6
Heol Cwrdy CF32 150 E4
Heol Cynan
Gorseinon SA4 43 B4
Pont Rhyd-y-cyff CF34 128 D6
Heol Cynllan CF72 154 A2
Heol Cynwyd CF34 128 D6
Heol Dafydd CF72 173 A7
Heol Dalycopa SA7 69 E6
Heol Daniel
Cwmllynfell SA9 221 B7
Llanelli SA14, SA15 40 F8
Heol Danyrodyn
CF15 157 C1
Heol Dderwen
Church Village CF38 136 A2
Llanelli SA15 40 F4
Heol Ddeusant CF38 155 F6
Heol Ddu
Ammanford SA18 219 D8
Beddau CF72 134 C1
Swansea SA5 68 B7
Tycroes SA18 218 F5
Heol Ddwr SA4 19 E7
Heol Deg CF38 136 A1
Heol Degwm CF33 165 E8
Heol Deiniol NP4 63 A5
Heol Dennant CF5 193 E8
Heol Deri CF39 133 B4
Heol Derlwyn CF14 177 B8
Heol Derw
Brynmawr NP23 8 A5
Hengoed CF82 84 F3
Heol Derwen
Cimla SA11 72 B5
Pontypool NP4 63 A5
Heol Deva CF5 193 C3
Heol Dewi
Brynna CF72 153 C3
Hengoed CF82 85 A2
Heol Dewi Sant
Barry CF62 214 E5
Bettws CF32 129 D3
Penllergaer SA4 44 A2
Heol Dinbych SA15 40 F4
Heol Dolfain SA6 46 A4
Heol Dolwen CF14 177 C4
Heol Don CF14 176 F4
Heol Don Ct CF14 176 F4
Heol Dowlais CF38 156 E5
Heol Dowr SA4 19 E6
Heol Draenen Wen
CF5 193 A2
Heol Drewi CF33,
CF36 165 E4
Heol Dulais SA7 47 A1
Heol Dwr SA18 219 E7
Heol Dwyrain CF31 169 A4
Heol Dyddwr SA11 49 D3
Heol Dyfan SA6 45 F3
Heol Dyfed
Beddau CF38 155 F5
Cardiff CF14 177 D5
Gorseinon SA4 43 B4
Maesteg CF34 102 D2
Penrhys CF43 80 A2
Penywaun CF44 28 C6
Heol Dyfodwg CF72 155 D4
Heol Dyhewydd
CF38 156 B7
Heol Dylan
Gorseinon SA4 43 B4
North Cornelly CF33 165 F8
Heol Dynys SA5 67 E5
Heol Dywyll SA6 46 C7
Heol Ebwy CF5 193 D4
Heol Edward Lewis
CF82 84 C6
Heol Edwards CF15 158 A8
Heol Eglwys
Cardiff CF5 193 E4
Coelbren SA10 222 F6
Pen-y-fai CF31 150 C1
Ystradgynlais SA9 1 F1
Heol Eifion SA4 43 C2
Heol Eifion Wyn SA7 69 E6
Heol Eirlys SA6 45 F2
Heol Eithrim SA6 46 D8
Heol Elan NP23 7 B5
Heol Elfed
Gorseinon SA4 43 B4
Llanelli SA14 41 C5
Maesteg CF34 102 D2
Swansea SA7 69 E6
Heol Elli SA15 40 F5
Heol Emrys SA5 68 A5
Heol Erw-y-Rhos
CF83 138 B5
Heol Erwin CF14 159 C1
Heol Esgyn
Cardiff CF23 178 A6
Neath SA10 48 B1
Rhigos CF44 26 C8
Heol Evan Wynne
CF81 12 F1
Heol Ewenny CF35 170 D6
Heol Fach
Ammanford SA18 218 E8
Bargoed CF81 57 F2
Caerphilly CF83 137 E4
Nantgarw CF15 158 A8
North Cornelly CF33 165 F8
Pencoed CF35 170 D8
Sarn CF32 150 F4
Swansea SA5 45 B3
Swansea SA5 68 C6
Heol Faen CF34 102 D2
Heol Faenor CF38 155 F5
Heol Fain Sarn CF32 150 E3
Wick CF71 198 B5
Heol Fair CF5 194 A8
Heol Fargoed CF81 57 F2
Heol Fawr
Caerphilly CF83 137 D6
Nelson CF46 83 F2
North Cornelly CF33 166 A7
Tredomen CF46 84 A1
Heol Fechan CF31 168 B6
Heol Fedw
Cwmrhydyceirw SA6 46 A3
Swansea SA6 45 F3
Heol Felen SA18 220 B8
Heol Felyn Fach
CF32 150 C5
Heol Fer CF83 137 E6
Heol Ffaldau CF31 169 B6
Heol Ffion SA4 43 C2
Heol Fforest (Fforest
Road) SA4 19 B5
Heol Ffranc SA10 70 C6
Heol Ffrwd Philip
CF38 156 F5
Heol Ffynnon
Llanelli SA15 40 F4
Loughor SA4 42 E1
Heol Ffynnon Wen
CF14 176 F8
Heol Frank SA5 68 B5
Heol Gabriel CF14 177 C3
Heol Gadlys CF31 169 A7
Heol Gaer SA10 223 A5
Heol Gam
Bridgend CF31 168 E2
Pentyrch CF15 157 B1
Heol Ganol
Brynmawr NP23 8 B4
Caerphilly CF83 137 F3
Nant-y-Moel CF32 104 F6
Heol Gelli Lenor
CF34 101 F1
Heol Gelynen CF44 28 A6
Heol Gelynog [4]
CF38 156 A6
Heol Ger-y-Felin
CF61 210 A7
Heol Gerrig SA5 68 C6
Heol Gethin CF82 85 A4
Heol Giedd SA9 1 F3
Heol Glan Elai CF72 173 A6
Heol Glan-Nant SA6 46 A4
Heol Glan-Yr-Afon
NP11 113 C3
Heol Glandulais
CF23 160 F1
Heol Glanllechau SA8 23 E3
Heol Glannant
Bettws CF32 129 D3
Tonypandy CF40 107 B1
Heol Glaslyn CF23 161 B1
Heol Glasnant SA2 93 F7
Heol Gledyr CF83 138 A2
Heol Gleien SA9 1 A2
Heol Glyn CF83 137 F5
Heol Glyn Derwen
SA10 48 C1
Heol Glyn-Dyfal SA5 20 F4
Heol Glyncoch CF39 132 D5
Heol Glyndernwen
SA8 23 E3
Heol Glynderwen
SA10 48 C1
Heol Glyndwr CF31 169 D6
Heol Goch CF15 157 E2
Heol Godfrey SA18 220 D8
Heol Goedog CF32 149 B2
Heol Goffa SA15 40 E7
Heol Goronwy CF39 80 D1
Heol Graig Wen
CF83 137 E6
Heol Graig-Felen
SA6 46 D8
Heol Groeswen
CF37 136 D3
Heol Gron SA9 2 D8
Heol Gruffydd SA5 67 F5
Heol Grug SA6 45 E2
Heol Gwalia SA14 41 C5
Heol Gwanwyn SA7 69 F7
Heol Gwaun Rhos
CF83 138 B5
Heol Gwell SA5 68 D5
Heol Gwenallt SA4 43 B4
Heol Gwendoline
CF62 214 E4
Heol Gwent CF14 177 D5
Heol Gwernen
Cwmrhydyceirw SA6 46 A3
Swansea SA6 45 F3
Heol Gwili
Gorseinon SA4 43 B4
Llanelli SA14 41 D5
Swansea SA7 69 E6
Heol Gwilym CF5 176 D1
Heol Gwrangfryn
CF44 26 C8
Heol Gwrgan
Beddau CF38 155 F6
Cardiff CF14 177 B5
Heol Gwyn Lliw NP23 7 F3
Heol Gwyndaf CF14 177 F7
Heol Gwynedd CF14 177 D5
Heol Gwynno CF72 155 D4
Heol Gwyr SA15 40 F4
Heol Gwyrosydd SA5 68 B5
Heol Gwys SA9 221 C6
Heol Gylfinia CF62 214 F2
Heol Hafdy SA7 69 F7
Heol Harlech CF5 194 A8
Heol Harri Lewis
CF46 83 D3
Heol Haulfryn CF39 133 B4
Heol Haydn SA18 219 B7
Heol Heddwch
Neath SA10 48 A1
Seven Sisters SA10 222 D3
Heol Helig NP23 8 A4
Heol Hen Llanelli SA14 41 C4
Seven Sisters SA10 222 C3
Heol Hendre
Bryn-côch SA10 48 C5
Cardiff CF14 177 D8
Heol Hensol CF38 156 A6
Heol Herbert SA11 226 D5
Heol Hermas SA5 68 B6
Heol Heulog CF39 132 B7
Heol Hir Cardiff CF14 159 F1
Gwaun-Cae-Gurwen
SA18 220 E6
Heol Homfray CF5 193 A3
Heol Hopcyn John
CF35 151 B2
Heol Horeb CF39 107 E2
Heol Iago CF81 32 D7
Heol Ida CF38 156 A7
Heol Iestyn CF14 177 B5
Heol Ifor CF14 177 C5
Heol Illtyd
Llantrisant CF72 155 D4
Neath SA10 48 D1
Heol Innes SA15 40 E8
Heol Ioan CF43 80 A2
Heol Isaf
Brynmawr NP23 8 B4
Cardiff CF14 159 C1
Cimla SA11 72 C5
[4] Cwmavon SA12 99 D5
Nelson CF46 83 F3
Pontypool NP4 63 A5
Radyr CF15 176 C5
Tonyrefail CF39 133 C2
Trelewis CF46 83 C8
Heol Isaf Hendy
CF72 173 C7
Heol Iscoed
Cardiff CF14 177 C8
Efail Isaf CF38 156 E5
Heol Iscoed (Iscoed Road)
SA4 19 A4
Heol Islwyn
Gorseinon SA4 43 B4
Nelson CF46 83 D3
Tonyrefail CF39 133 C6
Heol Johnson CF72 155 C2
Heol Keir Hardie
CF44 28 B5
Heol Klockner NP22 12 D4
Heol Laethog CF32 151 E5
Heol Las
Caerphilly CF83 137 E7
Coity CF35 169 D8
Cross Hands SA14 218 B8
Godregraig SA8 221 A1
Llantrisant CF72 155 C4
Marshfield CF3 180 D6
North Cornelly CF33 165 D8
North Cornelly CF33 165 E8
Pencoed CF35 170 D8
Pontardawe SA8 24 A8
Tredomen CF46 111 B8
Wick CF71 198 A4
Heol Las Fawr SA10 226 A8
Heol Las Villas CF33 165 D8
Heol Lewis
Caerphilly CF83 138 D5
Cardiff CF14 159 C1
Heol Llan Coity CF35 151 F3
North Cornelly CF33 165 E8
Heol Llanbedr CF5 191 E6
Heol Llangan CF14 177 B6
Heol Llangeinor
CF32 130 A3
Heol Llanishen Fach
CF14 177 C8
Heol Llansantffraid
CF32 150 E4
Heol Llechau CF39 80 D1
Heol Llidiard CF35 170 F1

Heol Llinos CF14 .... 159 E4
Heol Llwyd
  Ammanford SA18 .... 219 B8
  Ebbw Vale NP23 ..... 7 B5
Heol Llwyn Bedw SA4 18 F4
Heol Llwyn Brain
  CF48 .... 10 A3
Heol Llwyn Celyn
  SA10 .... 48 D2
Heol Llwyn Deri CF48 10 A3
Heol Llwyn Drysi
  CF48 .... 10 A3
Heol Llwyn Gollen
  CF48 .... 10 A3
Heol Llwyn Onnen
  CF48 .... 10 A3
Heol Llwyndyrus
  CF34 .... 128 C6
Heol Llwynonn SA10 .. 48 D2
Heol Llwynyffynnon
  CF32 .... 130 A3
Heol Llynfi NP23 ..... 7 B5
Heol Llyswen CF46 ... 83 E4
Heol Lotwen SA18 .... 218 D6
Heol Mabon
  Cardiff CF14 .... 177 C8
  Cwmavon SA12 ...... 99 E6
  Nelson CF46 .... 83 D3
Heol Madoc
  Cardiff CF14 .... 177 C4
  Pontypool NP4 ...... 63 A5
Heol Maendy
  North Cornelly CF33 .165 E8
  Sarn CF32 .... 150 F3
Heol Maes Eglwys
  SA6 .... 45 E4
Heol Maes Eirwg 14
  CF3 .... 179 F6
Heol Maes Eiwrg
  SA4 .... 180 A6
Heol Maes y Cerrig
  SA4 .... 42 E1
Heol Maes-y-Dre SA9 .1 F3
Heol Maes-y-Gelynen
  SA6 .... 45 F2
Heol Maes-yr-Haf
  CF35 .... 170 D6
Heol Maesbryn SA4 ...42 F1
Heol Maespica SA9 ...1 B2
Heol Morfa
  Bridgend CF31 ...... 150 F1
  Penrhys CF43 .... 80 A2
Heol Marsais SA18 ...219 B8
Heol Mathew CF14 ...176 F5
Heol Merioneth
  CF61 .... 210 C6
Heol Merlin CF14 ....177 F7
Heol Meurig SA9 .....2 D8
Heol Miaren
  Barry CF63 .... 215 C8
  Swansea SA4 .... 45 F2
Heol Miles CF72 .....155 B2
Heol Miskin CF72 ....173 B7
Heol Moor CF62 .....214 B4
Heol Morfa
  Llanelli SA15 .... 40 F3
  Pyle CF33 .... 166 C8
Heol Morlan CF46 ....18 F3
Heol Morlais SA4 ....18 F3
Heol Mostyn CF33 ...148 C1
Heol Muston CF5 ....193 D6
Heol Mwrwg SA4 ....18 E2
Heol Mwyrdy CF38 ..155 F6
Heol Mynydd
  Church Village CF38 .136 A1
  Cowbridge CF71 ..... 189 F5
  Pontypridd CF37 .... 110 A4
Heol Nant
  Church Village CF38 .135 F1
  Clyne SA11 .... 226 B3
  Cwmdare CF44 ...... 28 C4
  North Cornelly CF33 .165 E8
  Pontypridd CF37 .... 109 F4
Heol Nant Bran CF47 .47 A2
Heol Nant Caiach
  CF46 .... 83 C6
Heol Nant Castan
  CF14 .... 177 C2
Heol Nant Gelli SA5 ..68 D5
Heol Nant-y-Felin
  SA15 .... 40 E2
Heol Nantgae CF48 ..10 A3
Heol Nedd SA11 .....227 B8
Heol Nest CF14 .....177 C5
Heol Neuadd CF33 ..166 A7
Heol Neuadd Domos
  CF34 .... 128 C8
Heol Newydd
  Cardiff CF3 .... 179 D4
  Cefn Cribwr CF32 ...149 B2
  Swansea SA4 .... 67 F5
Heol Newydd (New Rd)
  SA9 .... 221 C2
Heol Norman 3
  SA18 .... 219 B7
Heol Onen NP23 .....8 A4
Heol Onnen CF43 ....165 E8
Heol Orchwy CF42 ...78 F7
Heol Padarn NP4 ....43 B6
Heol Pal CF62 ......214 F2
Heol Pandy CF32 ....129 F2
Heol Pant Glas SA11 .227 B8
Heol Pant Gwyn
  CF72 .... 155 C5
Heol Pant Ruthin
  CF35 .... 170 D6
Heol Pant y Dwr SA4 42 F2
Heol Pant y Rhyn
  CF14 .... 176 F7

Heol Pant-y-Gored
  Creigiau CF15 ...... 175 A7
  Pentyrch CF15 ..... 175 A4
Heol Pant-y-Liw SA4 44 A7
Heol Pant-yr-Awel
  CF32 .... 130 D4
Heol Pantglas SA8 ..48 C5
Heol Pantycelyn
  Barry CF62 .... 214 D4
  Cardiff CF14 .... 176 F7
  Porth CF5 .... 193 D4
Heol Parc Glas 8
  CF48 .... 225 F2
Heol Parc Maen CF48 10 A2
Heol Parc Mawr
  SA14 .... 218 C7
Heol Parc-y-Lan
  CF48 .... 10 A3
Heol Pen y Cae SA4 ..42 F2
Heol Pen-Nant SA6 ..46 A4
Heol Pen-Rhiw'r Eglwys
  NP12 .... 58 E6
Heol Pen-Rhiw'r-Eglwys
  NP12 .... 58 E6
Heol Pen-Tir-Garw
  SA5 .... 67 F6
Heol Pen-y-Beili SA4 42 E1
Heol Pen-y-Bryn
  SA4 .... 80 A2
Heol Pen-y-Coed
  SA11 .... 72 B5
Heol Pen-y-Foel
  CF37 .... 109 D6
Heol Pen-y-Parc
  Llantrisant CF72 .... 155 D3
  Pontypridd CF37 .... 109 D7
Heol Pen-y-Scallen
  SA4 .... 42 E1
Heol Penalita CF82 ..84 D6
Heol Penar SA5 .....68 B6
Heol Pencarreg
  Bargoed CF81 ...... 57 E3
  Cardiff CF14 .... 177 B2
Heol Pencastell
  CF33 .... 148 D2
Heol Pendarren CF44 26 C8
Heol Penderyn
  Bridgend CF31 ...... 169 D6
  Neath SA10 .... 48 A1
Heol Pendrylus CF43 .80 B3
Heol Penhydd SA13 .100 E5
Heol Penlan
  Cardiff CF14 .... 176 F5
  Neath Abbey SA10 ...48 A1
  Swansea SA7 .... 71 A8
Heol Penllwyn CF15 .175 A7
Heol Penmaen 3
  3 Merthyr Tydfil
  CF48 .... 225 F2
  Mountain Ash CF45 ..54 B5
Heol Pentre CF34 ...101 F1
Heol Pentre Bach SA4 42 F2
Heol Pentre Felin
  SA6 .... 45 F2
Heol Pentre'r Cwrt
  CF61 .... 210 A7
Heol Pentre'r Felin
  CF61 .... 210 B7
Heol Pentwyn
  Cardiff CF14 .... 176 F7
  Neath SA10 .... 70 C6
  Tonyrefail CF37 .... 133 B4
Heol Pentyla
  Sarn CF32 .... 150 D3
  Swansea SA7 .... 69 F6
Heol Penyfai CF14 ...59 C6
Heol Peredur CF14 ..159 D2
Heol Persondy
  Aberkenfig CF32 ....150 D3
  Aberkenfig CF32 ....150 D4
  Bettws CF32 .... 129 D2
Heol Philip SA9 .....1 D1
Heol Phillip SA8 ....23 E3
Heol Pit-y-Ceiliogod
  NP12 .... 58 E2
Heol Plas Isaf SA14 ..42 B7
Heol Pont George
  CF33 .... 148 B2
Heol Pont y Seison
  CF46 .... 84 C2
Heol Pont-y-Cwcw
  NP10 .... 164 A5
Heol Pontprennau
  CF23 .... 160 F1
Heol Powis CF14 ....177 D5
Heol Poyston CF5 ...193 C3
Heol Pwllpant CF83 137 F6
Heol Pwllpilaca 10
  CF3 .... 179 F6
Heol Pymmer CF39 ..133 B4
Heol Rees CF82 .....85 A2
Heol Rhayader CF14 176 E4
Heol Rheidol NP23 ..7 B5
Heol Rhos CF83 .....137 D3
Heol Rhos Las CF48 .10 A3
Heol Rhosyn SA6 ....45 F2
Heol Rhuddos SA7 ..70 A7
Heol Rhyd SA6 .....22 E4
Heol Rhyd-Ddu-Fach
  SA9 .... 221 B8
Heol Rhyd-y-Bedd
  CF48 .... 11 A6
Heol Rhys CF44 ....53 F8

Heol Richard Price
  CF32 .... 129 E3
Heol Robart CF72 ...127 B7
Heol S D Davies CF48 10 C1
Heol Saffrwm SA6 ...45 F2
Heol Salem CF38 ....135 F1
Heol Sant Bridget
  CF32 .... 185 C2
Heol Scwrfa CF48 ...10 A3
Heol Seddon CF5 ....176 D2
Heol Seion SA14 ....42 B7
Heol Serth CF83 ....137 D5
Heol Seward CF38 ...155 F6
Heol Shon CF32 ....149 A2
Heol Shwrac CF32 ...198 A7
Heol Siloam NP23 ...7 E4
Heol Siloh SA15 ....40 C4
Heol Silyn CF44 ....28 C6
Heol Simonston
  CF35 .... 169 D7
Heol Sirhwi CF62 ...214 C6
Heol Solva CF5 .....193 E4
Heol Spencer CF32,
  CF35 .... 151 B3
Heol St Cattwg CF37 191 A6
Heol St Denys CF14 .160 A3
Heol Stanllyd SA14 .218 B7
Heol Stradling CF14 .177 B4
Heol Syr Lewis CF15 176 B8
Heol Syr William
  SA13 .... 75 D3
Heol Tai Mawr CF41 .53 C6
Heol Taliesin SA12 ..99 F6
Heol Tasker CF46 ...83 D3
Heol Tawe SA4 .....222 D7
Heol Tegfryn CF33 .148 B2
Heol Teifi NP23 .....7 B5
Heol Teifionydd CF43 .80 A2
Heol Teilo NP4 .....63 A5
Heol Tewgood SA12 .99 E6
Heol Tir Coch CF38 .156 E5
Heol Tir Du
  Cwmrhydyceirw SA6 .46 A3
  Swansea SA6 ...... 45 F3
Heol Tir Gibbon
  CF83 .... 137 E5
Heol Tir Gwaidd CF43 80 B3
Heol Tir Ton NP11 ...113 B3
Heol Tir-Lan SA11 ..223 E5
Heol Tirbach CF83 ..137 D6
Heol Tircoed SA4 ...44 B5
Heol Ton
  North Cornelly CF33 .165 D6
  Sarn CF32 .... 150 F3
  Tonyrefail CF39 .... 133 B4
Heol Tonmaen SA11 226 E5
Heol Tranne CF39 ...133 B4
Heol Tre Dwr CF31 ..169 B2
Heol Trecastell CF83 138 A2
Heol Tredeg SA9 ....221 C6
Heol Treferig CF38 ..156 A6
Heol Treffynnon SA6 46 B5
Heol Tregare CF5 ...193 C3
Heol Trefor SA5 ....68 B6
Heol Trefrhiw SA18 .219 A6
Heol Tregoning SA5 .40 F2
Heol Treharne
  Abergwynfi SA13 ....76 A6
  Coytrahen CF32 ....150 B7
Heol Trelai CF5 .....193 C3
Heol Trelales CF32 ..167 F4
Heol Trenewydd
  CF35 .... 193 C3
Heol Treth SA13 ....148 C1
Heol Trewilliam
  CF40 .... 107 B1
Heol Troeon Bach
  SA4 .... 218 D2
Heol Trostre CF3 ...179 F6
Heol Trubshaw SA15 .40 E8
Heol Twrch SA4 ....1 B1
Heol Twyn Du CF48 .10 A3
Heol Ty Aberaman
  CF44 .... 53 D6
Heol Ty Crwn CF83 .138 B5
Heol Ty Ffynnon
  CF23 .... 160 F1
Heol Ty Gwyn
  Bryn-co SA10 ...... 48 C4
  Margam SA13 ...... 101 F4
Heol Ty Gwyn Ind Est
  CF34 .... 101 F4
Heol Ty Maen CF34 .136 D2
Heol Ty Mawr CF71 .190 F6
Heol Ty Merchant
  CF83 .... 138 B5
Heol Ty Nant CF32 .130 B4
Heol Ty'n y Coed
  CF14 .... 177 C8
Heol Ty'n-y-Cae
  CF14 .... 177 C8
Heol Ty-Gwyn CF83 .112 A3
Heol Tyddyn CF83 ..137 D1
Heol Tydraw CF33 ..166 B8
Heol Tyle-Du CF42 ..78 F7
Heol Tylluan SA7 ...70 B8
Heol Tyllwyd CF39 ..133 D6
Heol Tyn-y-Waun
  CF14 .... 128 D6
Heol Tynewydd NP12 58 E4
Heol Tynygarn CF31 150 D2
Heol Tyr Brodya 2
  CF10 .... 195 A6
Heol Tysant CF31 ...169 A7

Heol Tywith CF34 ...102 A6
Heol Uchaf
  Cardiff CF14 .... 159 B1
  Cimla SA11 .... 72 C5
  Hengoed CF82 ..... 84 F3
  Hirwaun CF44 ...... 27 D7
  Nelson CF46 .... 83 F3
  8 Penywaun CF44 ...28 A6
Heol Undeb
  Beddau CF38 ...... 155 F6
  Cwmavon SA12 .... 99 F5
Heol Urban CF14 ...176 E2
Heol Valentine SA6 ..46 D8
Heol Waen NP23 ....7 B4
Heol Wallaseg SA18 .219 C7
Heol Wastadwaun
  CF35 .... 170 C8
Heol Waun
  Aberystwyn NP4 ....37 E4
  Tonyrefail CF39 .... 133 A4
Heol Waun Fawr
  CF14 .... 133 F1
Heol Waun Waelod
  SA13 .... 137 F1
Heol Waun Wen SA6 .45 B1
Heol Waun y Nant
  CF14 .... 177 B3
Heol Wen CF14 .....177 B7
Heol Wernlas CF14 .177 C4
Heol West Plas CF31,
  CF35 .... 169 B7
Heol Westfa SA14 ...40 F8
Heol Wil Hopcyn
  SA5 .... 41 B8
Heol Will George SA5 66 E3
Heol William Trigg
  CF32 .... 103 E6
Heol Wyllt SA4 .....19 E4
Heol y Barcud CF14 159 A4
Heol y Barcud SA4 ..19 F2
Heol y Beddau CF83 138 A2
Heol y Bedw-Hirion
  NP12 .... 58 D4
Heol y Berllan CF33 148 B2
Heol y Bwlch SA12 ..99 F6
Heol y Cacan-Meinion
  SA4 .... 58 D4
Heol y Carnau CF83 138 B5
Heol y Cawl CF14 ...187 E1
Heol y Cefn NP12 ...58 D4
Heol y Celyn SA12 ..46 D1
Heol y Clun CF34 ...155 F6
Heol y Cnap SA5 ....68 D5
Heol y Coed
  Beddau CF38 ...... 155 F6
  Glyncorrwg SA13 ...227 C2
Heol y Cwm CF15 ..176 A7
Heol y Cyw SA7 ....70 B8
Heol y Dderwen NP12 85 C7
Heol y Delyn CF14 ..160 A2
Heol y Derw CF32 ..132 B7
Heol y Drudwen SA6 45 F5
Heol y Felin
  Bettws CF72 .... 129 E1
  Fforest SA4 .... 18 F5
  Seven Sisters SA10 .222 D4
Heol y Ffynnon SA11 .72 C5
Heol y Fran SA4 ....45 F5
Heol y Frenhines
  CF64 .... 206 A2
Heol y Gamlas CF15,
  CF37 .... 136 E1
Heol y Garn SA18 ..219 B4
Heol y Garth CF83 ..139 B3
Heol y Glyn
  Tonyrefail CF39 .... 133 C5
  Treherbert CF41,
  Treherbert CF41 ....83 C6
Heol y Gors CF14 ...177 C3
Heol y Gwydde SA4 .222 E7
Heol y Gyfraith CF72 155 C2
Heol y Moch CF34 ..101 C3
Heol y Mynydd
  Ammanford SA18 ...219 B3
  Bargoed CF81 ...... 57 E2
  Gorseinon SA4 ..... 43 D3
Heol y Nant
  Gorseinon SA4 ..... 42 F3
  Heol-y-Cyw CF35 ...152 B5
Heol y Nantlais SA4 .43 B4
Heol y Onnen CF72 .172 D5
Heol y Parc Hendy SA4 18 C7
  Llangennech SA4 ...42 C7
  Pontardawe SA8 ...23 F3
Heol y Pentre CF15 .157 C1
Heol y Pia CF83 .....137 A8
Heol y Pwca NP44 ..89 C6
Heol y Pwll CF15 ...157 F8
Heol y Rhosog CF3 ..179 F2
Heol y Stepsau CF35 186 A4
Heol y Twyn CF39 ...80 D1
Heol y Waun
  Pontllyw SA4 ...... 43 F7
  Pontlliw SA14 ..... 33 A8
  SA14 .... 41 C8
Heol y Wern CF14 ..177 C8
Heol Ynys Ddu CF83 137 E1
Heol Ysgwydde
  CF32 .... 150 E4
Heol Yr Afon
  Bridgend CF31 ..... 168 E7
  Glyncorrwg SA13 ...227 C2
Heol Yr Eglwys
  Brynceinon CF32 ...151 A5
  Coity CF35 .... 169 C7
Heol Yr Eithen SA6 ..46 A3
Heol Yr Eryr
  Cwmrhydyceirw SA6 46 A5
  Swansea SA6 ...... 45 F5
Heol Yr Odyn CF15 .157 F8

Heol yr Orsaf CF72 ..173 A7
Heol Yr Wylan SA6 ..45 F5
Heol yr Ysgol
  Bedwas CF83 ...... 139 A6
  Cardiff CF15 .... 168 C5
  Cefn-bryn-brain SA9 .221 B8
Heol Ysgawen SA2 ..94 C8
Heol Ysgubor CF63 .158 C8
Heol Ysgyfarnog SA7 .70 B8
Heol Ystwyth NP23 ..7 B5
Heol-Ael-y-Bryn NP23 7 C3
Heol-Cae-Globe SA4 .65 F8
Heol-Cae-Gurwen
  SA18 .... 220 D6
Heol-Croeserw SA13 75 D4
Heol-Croesty CF35 .170 D6
Heol-Crwys SA12 ...99 E6
Heol-Fair CF36 .....183 A7
Heol-Jirbilli SA12 ...99 E5
Heol-Las
  Ammanford SA18 ...219 B6
  Birchgrove SA7 .... 46 F2
  Heol-Las CI SA7 .... 46 F1
Heol-Pen-y-Bryn
  CF83 .... 158 E5
Heol-Pen-y-Cae NP23 7 C2
Heol-Tewdwr SA13 ..75 C4
Heol-Treventy SA14 .218 A8
Heol-Ty-Cribwr
  CF31 .... 168 B6
Heol-Ty-Maen CF31 .168 B6
Heol-Uchaf NP22 ...12 E6
Heol-y-Bryn CF37 ...136 B6
Heol-y-Coed CF15 ...158 B8
Heol-y-Dail CF31 ...168 B6
Heol-y-Deiliaid
  SA13 .... 126 A1
Heol-y-Bardd CF31 .168 B6
Heol-y-Beddau
  CF38 .... 136 A7
Heol-y-Beiliau 5
  CF72 .... 155 D3
Heol-y-Berllan CF5 .193 C2
Heol-y-Berth CF83 ..158 E8
Heol-y-Blodau CF83 158 B5
Heol-y-Bont
  Cardiff CF14 .... 177 C7
  Tondu CF32 .... 150 E4
Heol-y-Bryn
  Barry CF62 .... 214 C2
  Cardiff CF14 .... 177 A7
  Fochriw CF81 ...... 32 D8
  Hendreforgan CF39 .132 D5
  Pentyrch CF15 ..... 157 B1
  Pont Rhyd-y-cyff CF34 128 D6
  Pontyclun CF72 .... 173 C7
  Rhigos CF44 ...... 26 C8
  Sarn CF32 .... 150 F3
Heol-y-Bryniau CF48 11 A7
Heol-y-Bwlch SA14 ..42 A2
Heol-y-Bwnsi CF14 ..136 F2
Heol-y-Cadno CF14 .159 E3
Heol-y-Cae
  Cefn Coed CF48 ....10 B4
  Clydach SA6 .... 46 D7
  Pontarddulais SA4 ..19 E5
Heol-y-Capel
  Bridgend CF31 ..... 169 F4
  Porthcawl CF36 .... 165 F1
  Tonna SA11 .... 109 B4
Heol-y-Carw CF14 ..159 E3
Heol-y-Castell
  Cardiff CF5 .... 193 C3
  Duffryn SA13 ...... 74 D4
  Pant CF48 .... 11 A7
Heol-y-Cawl
  Cwmtown CF35 .... 186 C7
  Dinas Powys CF64 ..206 A3
Heol-y-Coed
  Cardiff CF14 .... 177 A7
  Llantwit Major CF61 .210 A5
  Pontardduais SA4 ..19 E5
  Pontyclun CF72 .... 173 C8
  Wyllie NP12 .... 85 F1
Heol-y-Coedcae
  SA9 .... 221 B7
Heol-y-Craig SA13 ..226 A7
Heol-y-Cwm CF83 ..137 C2
Heol-y-Cyw Prim Sch
  CF35 .... 152 B5
Heol-y-Dderwen
  CF15 .... 158 B8
Heol-y-Ddol CF83 ..158 B5
Heol-y-De CF44 ....26 C8
Heol-y-Delyn CF31 .160 B3
Heol-y-Deri
  Capel Hendre SA18 .218 C5
  Cardiff CF14 .... 177 B7
  Cwmrhydyceirw SA6 .46 A3
  Pontypridd CF37 ....109 A2
  Swansea SA6 ...... 45 F3
Heol-y-Deryn SA13 .227 C2
Heol-y-Derw SA14 ..218 A8
Heol-y-Dre CF31 ...168 B6
Heol-y-Dreflan
  CF83 .... 138 B5
Heol-y-Fagwr SA6 ..227 D2
Heol-y-Fedw SA13 ..75 D4
Heol-y-Felin
  Church Village CF38 .136 A2
  Nant-y-Moel CF32 ..104 F6

Heol-y-Felin continued
  Cardiff CF15 .... 193 E6
  Cardiff CF5 .... 193 E6
  Pencoed Feolgas CF82 84 E5
  Cardiff CF5 .... 152 B6
  Llantwit Major CF61 .210 A5
  Neath SA10 .... 48 D2
  Penllergaer SA4 .... 44 B2
  Pontyclun CF72 .... 173 A7
Heol-y-Ffin CF31 ...168 C4
Heol-y-Fforest CF14,
  CF15, cf83 .... 158 E3
Heol-y-Flowndri
  SA18 .... 219 C7
Heol-y-Ffynnon
  CF36 .... 156 F6
Heol-y-Foel
  Cwmavon SA12 .... 99 D5
  Llantwit Fardre CF38 156 D8
Heol-y-Foelas CF31 .168 C5
Heol-y-Forlan CF14 .177 A6
Heol-y-Frenhines
  CF31 .... 168 C5
Heol-y-Fro
  Church Village CF38 .135 E1
  Llantwit Major CF61 .210 A7
Heol-y-Gadarn SA13 74 E4
Heol-y-Gaer
  Penllergaer SA4 .... 43 F2
  Cardiff CF5 .... 193 C3
Heol-y-Gelli
  Aberdare CF44 ..... 53 B5
  Penllergaer SA4 .... 43 F2
Heol-y-Gerddi CF35 152 D1
Heol-y-Glo
  Pyle CF33 .... 148 C5
  Tonna SA11 .... 49 E3
Heol-y-glyn
  Cymmer SA13 ..... 75 C7
  Glynneath SA11 ....223 D1
Heol-y-Goedlan
  SA9 .... 221 B6
Heol-y-Goedwig
  CF36 .... 183 A8
Heol-y-Gog SA4 ....66 B5
Heol-y-Gogledd
  CF83 .... 137 E6
Heol-y-Gors
  Caerphilly CF83 .... 138 B5
  Gwaun-Cae-Gurwen
  SA18 .... 220 D5
  Nantgarw CF15 .... 158 B8
  Pyle SA13 .... 147 C6
Heol-y-Graig
  Blaengwrach SA13 ..227 B8
  Clydach SA6 .... 46 D7
  Llanelli SA14 ...... 41 E4
  Llantrisant CF72 .... 155 D3
  Penrhys CF43 ..... 80 A3
  Porthcawl CF36 .... 183 D8
  Rhigos CF44 ...... 224 B1
  Tonna SA11 .... 49 D3
  Ystrad Mynach CF82 .111 E8
Heol-y-Groes
  Bridgend CF31 ..... 150 F1
  Pencoed CF35 .... 170 E8
Heol-y-Grug CF39 ..132 D5
Heol-y-Gwaudd SA9 222 A4
Heol-y-Gwrgan
  SA13 .... 125 C3
Heol-y-Llan SA4 ....65 E8
Heol-y-Llwynan SA4 .23 B1
Heol-y-Llwyni CF34 .102 C2
Heol-y-Lyfrail CF32 .150 C4
Heol-y-Maes
  Llantwit Fardre CF38 156 D7
  Pontardulais SA4 ..19 D4
Heol-y-Mynach NP37 .81 C7
Heol-y-Mynydd
  Aberdare CF44 ..... 28 F1
  Bryn SA14 .... 41 F6
  Cefn Coed CF48 ...10 A5
  Glyncorrwg SA13 ...227 C2
  Hendreforgan CF39 .132 D5
  Sarn CF32 .... 150 F3
  Ystrad CF41 ...... 79 C3
Heol-y-Nant
  Baglan SA12 ...... 98 E4
  Barry CF63 .... 215 A7
  Blaengwrach SA13 ..76 B6
  Bridgend CF31 .... 168 D5
  Caerphilly CF83 .... 137 F3
  Cardiff CF14 ...... 177 B6
  Clydach SA6 .... 46 E8
  Llanelli SA13 ...... 199 A7
  Maesteg CF34 ..... 102 D2
  Neath SA10 .... 48 D2
  Pontardawe SA8 ...24 B3
  Sarn CF32 .... 150 F4
  Talbot Green CF72 ..157 A3
Heol-y-Parc
  Aberdare CF44 ..... 29 C3
  Caerphilly CF83 .... 138 A3
  Celfneithon SA14 ..161 A4
  Cwmavon SA12 .... 99 D5
  Efail Isaf CF38 .... 156 F6
  Evanstown CF39 ...132 B7
  North Cornelly CF33 .166 A8
  Pentyrch CF15 ..... 175 A7
  Pontllw SA4 ...... 44 A7
Heol-y-Pavin CF5 ...177 A1
Heol-y-Plas SA4 ....18 F6

Heol-y-Plwyf CF37 ....81 F2
Heol-y-Rhedyn SA6 ...45 E2
Heol-y-Rhos CF31 ....169 A5
Heol-y-Sarn CF72 ....155 D5
Heol-y-Sheet
 North Cornelly CF33 ..166 A7
 North Cornelly CF33 ..166 C6
Heol-y-Slough CF32 185 B2
Heol-y-Splot CF33 ...166 C5
Heol-y-Twyn
 Cwmdare CF44 ......28 C4
 Pontlliw SA4 ....43 F7
 Rhymney NP22 ......12 E6
Heol-y-Tyla SA13 ....74 E4
Heol-y-Waun
 Cardiff CF14 ....177 B3
 Gelligaer CF82 ......84 C6
 Penrhys CF43 ....80 A3
 Pontarddulais SA4 ..19 D5
 Seven Sisters SA10 222 D4
Heol-y-Worm
 Caerphilly CF83 .....138 B5
 Loughor SA4 ....65 E8
 Neath SA10 ....48 D1
 Neath CF44 ....83 F4
Heol-y-Wyrddol
SA18 ....219 B8
Heol-Yr-Afael SA13 ..74 E4
Heol-Yr-Afon CF32 ..150 D5
Heol-Yr-Efail CF41 ..177 D7
Heol-yr-Enfys CF31 .168 B6
Heol-Yr-Eos SA4 .....43 F2
Heol-yr-Haul CF72 ..174 C7
Heol-yr-Odyn CF5 ..193 B3
Heol-yr-Onen CF81 ..166 C5
Heol-yr-Onnen
 Bridgend CF31 ......168 B4
 Pencoed CF35 ....170 E7
Heol-Yr-Orsaf 148 D3
Heol-Yr-Orsedd
 ....125 D6
Heol-yr-Ynys CF15 .158 B2
Heol-yr-Ysbyty
 CF83 ....137 E1
Heol-yr-Ysgol
 Cefneithin SA14 ....218 A8
 Ebbw Vale NP23 ....14 B7
 Pont Rhyd-y-cyff CF34 128 D6
 St Brides Major CF32 185 C2
 Tondu CF32 ....150 D5
Heolaelfryn CF32 ....130 E4
Heolddu Ave CF81 ...57 F4
 Heolddu Comp Sch (Ysgol
 Gyfun Heol-ddu)
 CF81 ....57 F4
Heolddu Cres CF81 ..57 F4
Heolddu Ct CF81 ....57 E4
Heolddu Gdns CF81 .57 F4
Heolddu Gr CF81 ....57 F4
Heolddu Rd
 Bargoed CF81 ....57 F4
 Gelligroes NP12 .....85 F2
Heolganol CF32 .....150 E4
Heolgerrig
 Abertillery NP13 .....36 B5
 Heolgerrig CF48 .....10 A1
 Merthyr Tydfil CF48 ..29 F8
 Heolgerrig Sch CF48 30 A8
Heoltynton CF32 ....130 A3
Heolyffin SA18 ......23 B7
Herbert Ave NP11 ...141 C8
Herbert Ct CF31 .....180 E8
Herbert Dr CF14 ....137 F5
Herbert March Cl
 CF5 ....176 D3
Herbert Rd
 Neath SA11 ....71 D5
 Newport NP19 ......143 D6
Herbert St
 Abercynon CF45 .....82 E2
 Aberdare CF44 ......29 A1
 Barry CF62 ....215 A7
 Blaengarw CF32 .....63 D7
 Bridgend CF31 ......169 A5
 Cardiff CF10 ....195 B4
 Cardiff CF14 ....177 E1
 New Tredegar NP24 ..34 A1
 Newbridge NP11 ....160 D2
 Newport NP20 ......143 C3
 Pontardawe SA8 ....23 E4
 Treherbert CF42 ....51 B1
 Treorchy CF42 ......78 D6
Herbert Terr
 Newbridge NP11 .....60 D2
 Penarth CF64 ....207 A4
Herbert Thompson Jun &
 Inf Sch CF5 ....193 D6
Herbert Wlk NP20 ..143 C3
Herbert's Cl NP11 ...61 A3
Herbert's Rd NP4 ....37 E6
Hereford Ct NP18 ...118 A3
Hereford Rd NP23 ....7 F2
Hereford St
 Cardiff CF11 ....194 E4
 Newport NP19 ......143 D6
Heritage Ct CF14 ....10 E2
Heritage Dr CF42 ...214 D5
Heritage Pk CF3 ....179 F8
Hermon Cl CF44 .....11 A4
Hermon Hill CF15 ...158 C1
Hermon Rd CF34 ...102 A8
Hermon St CF42 .....78 E6
Herne St SA11 ....81 B1
Hernston La CF31 ..168 F1
Heron Ave SA15 .....30 B5
Heron Rd CF3 ....179 C3
Heron Way NP10 ...143 F7

Herons Way
 Caerphilly CF83 ....137 E1
 Newport NP20 ....48 E2
Heronsbridge Sch
 CF31 ....168 F2
Herrick Pl CF83 .....139 A5
Hertford Pl NP19 ...143 F6
Heulwen Cl CF48 ....11 A6
Heulwen Clos CF15 158 A6
Hewell Ct CF11 .....194 F2
Hewell St
 Cardiff CF11 ....194 F2
 Penarth CF64 ....206 F5
Hewson St SA1 ......96 B3
Hibbert Rd SA11 .....71 F8
Hibiscus Ct CF38 ...156 C5
Hick St SA15 ....40 D4
Hickman Rd CF64 ...207 A4
Hickman St CF48 .....31 A4
Hickory Cl 🗓 CF24 ...195 D5
High Bank CF23 .....161 B2
High Banks NP19 ...143 E8
High Cl
 Llanyrnewn NP44 ...90 B1
 Nelson CF46 ....83 E3
High Cnr CF15 ......157 C1
High Croft Wlk CF3 .179 B4
High Cross Cl NP10 142 C4
High Cross Dr NP10 142 C4
High Cross Jun & Inf Sch
 NP10 ....142 C4
High Cross La NP10 142 C4
High Mdw CF61 .....209 F5
High Mdws CF64 .....54 C5
High St
 Abercarn NP11 ......114 C5
 Abercarn NP11 ......87 B2
 Aberdare CF44 ......29 A2
 Abergwynfi SA13 ....76 E1
 Abersychan NP4 ....37 E6
 Abersychan NP4 ....37 F3
 Abertillery NP13 .....36 B5
 Abertillery CF83 ....137 A8
 Argoed NP12 ....58 F5
 Bargoed CF81 ....58 A4
 Barry CF62 ....214 D4
 Bedlinog CF46 ......56 A7
 Blackwood NP12 ....58 F1
 Blackwood NP12 ....83 E7
 Blaenavon NP4 .....17 C6
 Blaengwrach SA11 ..227 B8
 Blaina NP13 ....15 D5
 Caerleon NP18 .....108 B7
 Cardiff CF10 ....195 A5
 Cardiff CF5 ....194 A8
 Cefn Coed CF48 .....10 A4
 Clydach SA6 ....46 E7
 Cowbridge CF71 ...188 E2
 Cwmavon SA12 .....99 D5
 Cwmfelinfach NP11 .113 A5
 Dowlais CF48 ....11 C4
 Ebbw Vale NP23 ....14 D6
 Ferndale CF43 ......79 F6
 Fleur De Lis NP12 ...83 B6
 Gilfach Goch CF39 ..132 C7
 Glanaman SA18 ....220 A8
 Glynneath SA11 ....223 D1
 Gorseinon SA4 .....43 C2
 Groveseend SA4 ....43 C6
 Heol-y-Cyw CF35 ..152 B5
 Hirwaun CF32 ......167 F4
 Llanbradach CF83 ..111 F1
 Llanelli SA15 ....40 D4
 🔟 Llantrisant CF72 ...155 D3
 Llantwit Major CF61 209 F7
 Maesteg CF34 ......102 A5
 Merthyr Tydfil CF47 ..10 D5
 Merthyr Tydfil CF47 ..10 F3
 Mountain Ash CF45 ..50 B4
 Mountain Ash CF45 ..54 D2
 Neath SA10 ....70 F7
 Neath SA11 ....71 E8
 Nelson CF46 ....83 E3
 New Tredegar NP24 ..33 C5
 Newbridge NP11 ....86 C5
 Newbridge NP11 ....86 F6
 Newport NP20 ......143 C5
 Ogmore Vale CF32 ..104 E1
 Penarth CF64 ....207 A5
 Pengam NP12 ....85 B8
 Penydarren CF47 ...10 E2
 Pontardawe SA8 ....23 E5
 Pontardawe SA8 ....23 E3
 Pontlottyn CF81 .....12 F1
 Pontneddfechan SA11 223 F2
 Pontyclun CF72 ....172 F6
 Pontycymer CF32 ...103 F3
 Pontypool NP4 ......62 B6
 Pontypool NP4 ......62 E3
 Pontypridd CF37 ...135 C8
 Port Talbot SA13 ....99 B1
 CF39 ....107 E2
 Port Talbot SA12 ....96 C3
 Rhymney NP22 ....12 E4
 Senghenydd CF83 ..110 F2
 Seven Sisters SA10 222 C3
 Tonypandy CF40 ...106 B6
 Tonyrefail CF39 ...133 C5
 Trelewis CF46 ......83 D7
 Treorchy CF42 ......78 E6
 Ynysddu NP11 ......112 F6
 Ynysybwl CF37 .....81 F1
High St
 CF10 ....195 A5
High Street Arc 🖂
 CF10 ....195 A5

High Street Jun & Inf Sch
 CF62 ....214 E4
High Street Prim Sch
 CF62 ....214 E4
High Street Sta SA1 .95 D8
High Trees CF48 .....10 B7
High View
 Bridgend CF31 ......168 F5
 Swansea SA1 ....68 A3
High View Gdns SA2 .94 B2
High View Way CF47 .63 A4
High Way The NP4 ...63 A4
Highbridge Ct CF64 .216 C4
Highbury Cl SA5 .....68 B2
Highbury Cres CF31 168 C6
Highbury Dr NP12 ...85 E6
Highbury Pl CF25 ...193 B4
Highbury Rd CF64 ...207 B5
Highcliffe CF SA3 ...122 E4
Highcroft Rd NP20 .143 A6
Highcross Rd NP10 143 A6
Highdale Cl CF72 ...155 E2
Highfield
 Ferndale CF43 ......79 D8
 Gorseinon SA4 ......66 A8
 🎇 Penarth CF64 .....207 B4
 Penperlleni NP4 .....39 E7
Highfield Ave
 Bridgend CF31 ......168 F8
 Porthcawl CF36 ....182 F6
Highfield Cl
 Caerleon NP18 .....117 F4
 Church Village CF38 136 A1
 Dinas Powys CF64 ..206 C4
 Neath SA10 ....48 E2
 Pontypool NP4 ......37 F1
 Porthcawl CF36 ....182 F6
 Risca NP11 ....114 F2
 Sarn CF32 ....150 E3
 Tredegar NP22 ....6 C2
Highfield Cres
 Aberbargoed CF81 ..58 B6
 Bryn NP12 ....85 E3
Highfield Ct
 Bassaleg NP10 .....141 F3
 Porthcawl CF36 ....182 F6
Highfield Gdns NP10 141 F3
Highfield Ind Est
 CF5 ....79 D7
Highfield La NP10 ..141 F3
Highfield Pl CF32 ...150 E3
Highfield Rd
 Barry CF62 ....214 D7
 Bassaleg NP10 .....142 A3
 Briton Ferry SA11 ...71 B2
 Bryn NP12 ....85 E3
 Caerleon NP18 .....117 F4
 Cardiff CF14 CF23 ..178 A4
 Glanaman SA18 ....220 C8
 Newport NP20 ......142 E3
Highfield Terr
 Llanelli SA15 ....40 E4
 🗓 Porthcawl CF36 ..182 F6
Highfield Way NP18 117 F4
Highfields
 Bridgend CF31 ......169 B5
 Cardiff CF5 ....176 F2
Highfields Holiday Pk
 SA3 ....231 A4
Highfields Way NP12 .85 D5
Highgrove CF71 .....189 D8
Highland Ave CF31 ..151 A6
Highland Cl
 Merthyr Tydfil CF47 ..30 E8
 Neath SA10 ....70 F8
 Sarn CF32 ....150 E3
Highland Cres
 Dyffryn Cellwen SA10 223 A5
 Pontllanfraith NP12 ..86 B4
Highland Ct CF32 ...151 A6
Highland Gdns SA10 .48 A1
Highland Gr NP44 ...89 E6
Highland Pl
 Aberdare CF44 ......28 F1
 Bridgend CF31 ......168 F5
 Ogmore Vale CF32 ..104 E1
Highland View CF47 .30 E8
Highlands Cardiff CF23 179 A2
Highlands Dr CF39 ...133 D6
Highlands Cl CF39 ...133 C6
Highlands Cres NP23 ..7 F2
Highlands Rd SA15 ..53 F1
Highlands The SA10 ..71 A8
Highlight La
 Barry CF62 ....214 C7
 Barry CF62 ....214 C8
Highmead NP12 .....85 D4
Highmead Ave
 Llanelli SA15 ....40 E8
 Mumbles SA3 ....122 E6
Highmead Cl SA3 ...122 E5
Highmead Rd CF5 ..193 D5
Highmoor SA1 ......95 D5
Highpool Cl SA3 ....122 C5
Highpool La SA3 ....122 C5
Hightree Rise NP12 ..86 A8
Highview Cl CF64 ...206 A3
Highwalls Ave CF64 .206 A3
Highwalls End CF64 .206 A3
Highwalls Rd CF64 ..206 A3
Highway The
 Croesyceiliog NP44 ..90 B5
 Cwmbran NP44 .....116 F8
 Nelson CF46 ....83 E8
Highway Rd CF31 ...151 A6
Hilary Cl NP11 ....87 B8
Hilary Way SA13 ....214 E4
Hilda St Barry CF62 .214 E4
 Pontypridd CF37 ...135 E5

Hiles Rd CF5 ....193 C5
Hileys Row NP7 ......9 E7
Hill Cres NP23 ....8 B4
Hill Crest
 Brynmawr NP23 .....8 B4
 Mumbles SA3 ....123 B4
Hill Dr CF38 ....156 D7
Hill Head CF61 ......62 B6
Hill Head CF61 .....209 F6
Hill Ho 📁 CF5 ....54 E1
Hill House Hospl SA2 94 D8
Hill Rd
 Abertysswg NP22 ...33 C8
 Neath Abbey SA10 ..71 A8
 Pontlottyn CF81 .....12 E1
Hill Side CF45 ....61 B4
Hill Side Rd NP4 ....62 D3
Hill Side St CF41 ....78 F5
Hill St Abercarn NP11 87 B4
 Abercynon CF45 .....82 E2
 Aberdare CF44 ......53 C7
 Abertillery NP13 .....36 B4
 Bargoed CF81 ....57 F5
 Barry CF63 ....215 B5
 Blaenavon NP4 .....17 C6
 Briton Ferry SA11 ...71 C1
 Brynmawr NP23 .....8 B4
 Deri CF81 ....57 C8
 Ebbw Vale NP23 ....14 F2
 Gowerton SA4 ......66 B5
 Hendreforgan CF39 132 C5
 Maerdy CF43 ....52 A1
 Maesteg CF34 ......102 A6
 Mumbles SA3 ....123 C4
 Nant-y-Moel CF32 ..104 F5
 Newbridge NP11 ....86 F6
 Newport NP20 ......143 C4
 Ogmore Vale CF32 ..104 E2
 🗓 Penarth CF64 .....207 B5
 Pontypool NP4 ......62 A8
 Pontypool NP4 ......62 E3
 Resolven SA11 .....226 C4
 Rhymney NP22 ....12 F3
 Risca NP11 ....115 A3
 Swansea SA1 ....95 C8
 Tonypandy CF40 ...106 F4
 Treherbert CF42 ....50 F2
 Troedyrhiw CF48 ....31 B1
 Ystrad Mynach CF82 84 E2
Hill Terr
 Aberavon SA12 ......99 B2
 Penarth CF64 ....206 F5
 Wenvoe CF5 ....204 F8
Hill Top NP44 ....89 D2
Hill View
 Beddau CF38 ....156 A6
 Bridgend CF31 ......168 A5
 Bryn NP12 ....85 E3
 Cardiff CF5 ....193 C8
 Cwmfelinfach NP11 .113 A4
Hengoed CF82 ....85 A2
Maesycwmmer CF82 ..85 B1
Pencoed CF35 ......170 B8
Pontycymer CF32 ...103 E4
Pyle CF33 ....148 C2
Swansea SA10 .....70 F7
Tredegar NP22 ......12 C5
Hill View Cres SA6 ..68 D8
Hill View Rd CF10 ..195 A3
Hilla Rd NP20 ......143 A4
Hilland Dr SA3 ......122 B6
Hillary Cl CF14 .....159 F1
Hillary Ho SA11 .....71 B4
Hillary Mews 🗓
 CF63 ....215 B6
Hillary Rise
 Abercarn NP11 .....114 C6
 Barry CF63 ....215 B6
Hillbrook Cl
 Aberdare CF44 ......53 B7
 Waunarlwydd SA5 ..66 D3
Hillcot CF14 ....160 A2
Hillcrest
 Abersychan NP4 ....37 E6
 Brynna CF72 ....153 E3
 Caerleon NP18 .....117 F4
 Merthyr Tydfil CF47 ..10 F4
 Pen-y-fai CF31 .....150 D1
 Pontypool NP4 ......63 B4
Hillcrest Ave CF44 ..53 C8
 Cefn Coed CF48 .....10 A4
Hillcrest Cl CF14 ...159 F3
Hillcrest Dr CF39 ...107 F2
Hillcrest Rd NP4 ....62 F5
Hillcrest View
 Abertillery NP13 .....36 B7
 Maerdy CF43 ....79 C8
Hillcroft Cres SA13 .75 D1
Hillfort Cl CF5 ....193 D3
Hillgrove SA3 ....122 E4
Hillrise Abersychan NP4 37 F5
 Cardiff CF23 ....178 F7
Hillrise Pk SA6 ......46 C7
Hillsboro CF31 .....168 C5
Hillsboro Pl CF36 ...182 F6
Hillside
 Caerphilly CF83 ....138 B1
 Cwmdare CF44 ......28 D3
 Fochriw CF81 ....56 A8
 Llanelli SA15 ....40 C7
 Loughor SA4 ....42 E1
 Neath SA11 ....71 B6
 Newbridge NP11 .....60 A1
 Pantywaed CF32 ...130 D4
 Pen-y-fai CF31 .....150 D1
 Risca NP11 ....115 A1
Hillside Ave
 Abertridwr CF83 ....136 E7
 Blaenavon NP4 .....17 D7

Hillside Ave continued
 Llanharan CF72 ....154 A3
 Markham NP12 ......58 D8
Hillside Cl
 Aberfan CF48 ....55 C5
 Barry CF63 ....215 C6
Hillside Cres
 Rogerstone NP10 ...142 B4
 Swansea SA2 ....95 A7
Hillside Ct
 Cardiff CF24 ....178 C1
 Cwmbran NP44 ......89 D5
 Llantwit Fardre CF38 136 E6
 Llanhilleth Day Hospl
 NP22 ....13 E6
Hillside Dr
 Cowbridge CF71 ...188 F1
 Pontypool NP4 ......62 C4
Hillside Gdns CF81 ..57 F2
Hillside Gn CF31 ...150 D1
Hillside Pk CF81 ....57 F2
Hillside Prim Sch
 NP4 ....89 C1
Hillside Rd CF39 ...133 D5
Hillside Terr
 Abertillery NP13 .....60 C6
 Bedwas CF83 ....138 E6
 Blackwood NP12 ....85 E7
 Deri CF81 ....33 A2
 Ebbw Vale NP23 ....14 F2
 Pantyrawel CF32 ...130 D4
 Pontypridd CF37 ...109 C2
 Ton Pentre CF41 ....79 B2
 Tonypandy CF40 ...106 F7
 Tredomen CF82 ....84 D1
 Wattstown CF39 ...107 D8
Hillside View
 Bargoed CF81 ....57 F2
 Pontypridd CF37 ...109 B2
Hilltop Ave CF37 ...109 F3
Hilltop Cl Baglan SA12 98 F6
 Trefrannis CF46 .....83 A6
Hilltop Cres
 Newbridge NP11 .....87 A7
 Pontypridd CF37 ...109 E1
Hilltop Gn NP44 .....89 E6
Hilltop Sh Ctr NP44 .14 C8
Hillview NP20 ....143 A4
Hillview Cres NP19 144 B3
Hillview Terr 🗓
 SA13 ....125 C8
Hilton Pl CF14 ......176 F3
Hinchsliff Ave CF64 214 E8
Hinter Path NP44 ...89 B1
Hinton St CF24 .....195 E5
Hirst Cres CF5 ......176 D1
Hirwain Pl CF43 .....80 C4
Hirwain St CF24 ....195 A5
Hirwain Terr CF47 ...10 E3
Hirwaun Ind Est
 CF44 ....224 C1
Hirwaun Prim Sch
 CF44 ....27 D7
Hirwaun Rd
 Aberdare CF44 ......28 F3
 Penywaun CF44 ....28 B5
Hlside Dr CF71 .....188 F1
Hobart Cl NP20 .....142 E4
Hodges Cres CF64 ..58 B2
Hodges Row CF10 ..195 B3
Hodges Sq CF10 ...195 B3
Hodges Terr NP44 ...89 C5
Hodgson's Rd SA9 ...2 A4
Hoel Cwmmamman
 SA18 ....220 D8
Hoel Gelliadra CF32 130 A3
Hoel Llwch'wr SA13 219 B6
Hoel y Mwyn Ct NP23 14 F6
Hoel-y-Graig SA12 ..99 F7
Hoel-y-Tyla SA13 ...74 D4
Hogarth Cl
 Cwmbran NP44 .....117 A8
 Newport NP19 ......143 F7
Hogarth Pl SA12 ...124 D8
Hogarth Rd NP19 ...144 A8
Holbein Rd NP19 ...144 A8
Holbrook Cl CF42 ...78 D7
Holden Rd CF11 ....194 D2
Holdings La CF71 ...175 B5
Holford St
 Aberdare CF44 ......53 C8
 Cefn Coed CF48 .....10 A4
Holford Terr 🗓 CF44 28 C3
Holgate Cl CF15 ....176 D4
Holland Cl NP10 ....142 A7
Holland St
 Ebbw Vale NP23 ....14 D7
 Port Talbot SA13 ...125 C8
Holland Way CF63 ..215 A7
Hollett Rd SA5 ......68 C4
Hollies The
 CF23 ....178 F7
Hollies The
 Blackwood NP12 ....59 D1
 Bridgend CF31 ......169 D4
 Heolgerrig CF48 .....10 B1
 Pontyclun CF72 ....173 A6
 Quakers Yard CF46 ..55 C3
Hollington Dr CF23 .161 A1
Hollins The SA11 ...72 A5
Holly Cl NP23 ....7 C5
Holly Ct CF62 ....214 C3
Holly Ct NP44 ......10 F8
Holly Gr CF14 ....160 A4
Holly Lodge Gdns
 NP44 ....90 B6
Holly Lodge Gn NP44 90 B6
Holly Lodge Rd NP44 90 B6
Holly Rd Cardiff CF5 193 D8

Holly Rd continued
 Llanharry CF72 .....172 C5
 Neath SA11 ....72 A5
 Risca NP11 ....115 B2
Holly Row CF5 .....181 E8
Holly St
 Gilfach Goch CF39 ..132 B5
 Pontardawe SA8 ....23 E5
 Rhydyfelin CF37 ...136 B5
Holly Terr
 Cardiff CF14 ....177 A2
 Newbridge NP11 .....86 F6
 Troedyrhiw CF48 ....31 B2
 Holly Ter CF47 ......10 D4
Holly Wlk CF36 .....183 C8
Hollybush NP44 .....89 D1
Hollybush Ave NP20 117 A2
Hollybush Cl
 Church Village CF38 136 A1
 Newport NP20 ......117 A2
Hollybush Gr CF23 ..90 D6
Hollybush Hts CF23 .178 D7
Hollybush Prim Sch
 NP4 ....89 C1
Hollybush Rd CF23 ..133 C8
Hollybush Terr CF23 178 D6
Hollybush View
 NP44 ....116 D8
Hollybush Villas
 CF38 ....135 F1
Hollybush Way NP44 116 D8
Hollybush Wlk NP10 117 A2
Hollycroft Cl CF5 ...193 E6
Hollyhock Dr CF31 ..169 D6
Hollylodge Cl NP44 ..90 B6
Hollyrood Cl CF62 ..214 C8
Holm View L Ctr
 CF62 ....214 D3
Holmdale 🗓 NP44 ..89 B3
Holmes St CF63 ....215 B6
Holmesdale Ct CF11 194 F2
Holmesdale St CF11 194 F2
Holmeside CF14 ....160 A3
Holms Ct CF64 .....216 A5
Holmsdale Pl CF64 .207 B3
Holmview Ct CF3 ...179 C5
Holmwood Cl CF23 .178 C4
Holst Cl NP19 ......145 A6
Holton Prim Sch
 CF63 ....215 A5
Holton Rd CF63 ....215 A5
Holy Family RC Jun & Inf
 Sch CF5 ....193 B8
Holyhead Cl CF83 ..137 C4
Holyoake Terr
 Abersychan NP4 ....37 F2
 Pontypool NP4 ......62 A8
Holyrood Terr CF40 106 E8
Holywell Rd CF38 ...136 A2
Home Farm Cl NP18 117 F2
Home Farm Cres
 NP18 ....117 F2
Home Farm Gn NP18 117 F2
Home Farm Way SA4 44 C2
Home Leigh NP11 ..86 F6
Homeland Pl NP12 ..85 F6
Homelands Rd CF14 177 C5
Homelong Ho CF14 177 F8
Homerton St CF45 ...92 B8
Homeside Ho 🗓
 CF64 ....207 B4
Homevalley Ho 🗓
 NP20 ....142 F4
Homfray St CF34 ...102 A6
Hondou Pl SA6 .....45 D1
Honeyfield Rd NP23 ..7 A4
Honeysuckle Cl
 Cardiff CF5 ....193 C3
 Ebbw Vale NP23 .....7 C5
 Merthyr Tydfil CF47 ..10 C8
Honeysuckle Way
 CF31 ....169 D5
Hong Kong Terr
 CF32 ....151 A4
Honiton Rd CF3 ....179 C7
Hoo St
 Briton Ferry SA11 ...71 C2
 Swansea SA1 ....96 B7
Hood Rd Barry CF62 214 E3
 Newport NP19 ......144 F7
Hookland Rd CF36 .183 C8
Hope Ave CF35 .....150 C4
Hope Ho CF10 ......194 E8
Hope St NP13 ....15 E5
Hopefield NP20 ....143 B7
Hopefield Ct NP20 .143 B7
Hopkin St
 Aberavon SA12 .....98 F1
 Pontardawe SA8 ...23 E5
 Treherbert CF42 ....78 A8
Hopkins Cl CF48 ....30 E4
Hopkins St SA15 ....68 C4
Hopkins Terr SA13 ..74 F6
Hopkinstown Rd
 CF37 ....109 A1
Hoppyard Mdw CF71 188 D2
Hopyard Cl NP11 ...59 B5
Horace Terr CF83 ...137 F8
Horeb Cl CF47 ......10 F3
Horeb Rd SA6 ......68 F8
Horeb St
 Merthyr Tydfil CF48 ..29 F8
 Treorchy CF42 ......78 D6

Horeb Terr CF44 ....28 E7
Horizon Pk SA6 ....69 A6
Hornbeam Cl
Caerleon NP18 ....117 E2
6 Cardiff CF23 ....180 A7
Cimla SA11 ....72 C0
Merthyr Tydfil CF47 ....10 C6
Hornbeam Wlk NP10 141 F3
Hornchurch Cl CF5 ..174 E1
Horner St CF82 ....85 A6
Horrocks Cl NP10 ....42 C4
Horsefair Rd CF31 ..169 F2
Horton St 8 SA1 ....95 C7
Horton Way CF64 ..125 E6
Horwood Cl CF24 ..195 E7
Hosea Row SA1 ....68 D4
Hosking Ind Est
CF10 ....195 B2
Hoskins St NP20 ..143 C6
Hospital Rd
Gorseinon SA4 ....66 F8
Nantyglo NP23 ....15 D8
Penllergaer SA4 ....43 E1
Penpedairheol CF82 ..84 D8
Pontypool NP4 ....62 B8
Pontypridd CF37 ..109 E1
Port Talbot SA12 ..124 E8
Hotham Cl CF23 ....161 A1
Houlson St CF48 ....11 B5
Houlston Cl CF24 ..195 F7
Housman Cl CF23 ..179 C8
Hove Ave NP19 ....144 A6
Howard Cl NP19 ....144 E6
Howard Ct
Barry CF62 ....214 C4
2 Cardiff CF10 ..195 C4
Howard Dr CF33 ....138 A5
Howard Gdns CF24 195 C6
Howard Pl 1 CF24 ..195 C6
Howard St
Cardiff CF24 ....195 D5
Tonypandy CF40 ..106 A6
Treorchy CF42 ....78 D6
Howard Terr 195 C6
Howardian Cl 4
CF23 ....178 E1
Howards Way
Ebbw Vale NP23 ....14 E3
Gorseinon SA4 ....43 C3
Howe Circ NP19 ....144 F7
Howel Rd SA11 ....71 C4
Howell Cl CF48 ....10 C1
Howell Rd CF5 ....193 C5
Howell St
Nant-y-Moel CF32 ..104 E7
Pontypridd CF37 ..109 C5
Howell's Cres CF5 ..194 B8
Howell's Row CF44 ..53 C5
Howells Row SA4 CF48 ..32 C8
Howells Rd NP23 ....7 B5
Hr Hen Dy CF5 ....177 A1
Hubert Ct CF31 ....168 F7
Hubert Rd NP19 ....143 E7
Hubert Rise
Rogerstone NP10 ..142 B4
Rogerstone NP10 ..142 B5
Hughes Ave NP19 ....7 C1
Hughes St
4 Mountain Ash CF45 ..54 E1
Tonypandy CF40 ..106 F4
Hughs Cl CF5 ....176 E3
Hugon Dr 2 CF23 ..178 E1
Humber Cl NP20 ..116 C1
Humber Rd NP20 ..116 C1
Humphrey St SA1 ....95 B7
Humphreys Terr
CF34 ....102 A8
Hunt Cl CF14 ....159 F1
Hunt Pl 1 CF63 ..215 B6
Hunter Cl NP10 ....142 A6
Hunter St Barry CF63 215 C6
Briton Ferry SA11 ..71 C1
Cardiff CF10 ....195 B1
Hunters Ridge
Cardiff CF23 ....169 C5
Cardiff CF23 ....178 B4
Tonna SA11 ....49 B1
Huntingdon Cl NP44 ..89 A3
Huntingdon Cl SA3 ..123 D8
Huntingdon Cl CF72 161 A1
Huntingdon Way SA2 ..94 B8
Huntington Cl SA3 ..123 C5
Huntsmans Cove
SA3 ....122 E7
Huntstead Cl CF14 159 C3
Hurford Cres CF37 ..109 B1
Hurford Pl CF23 ..178 C8
Hurford St CF37 ..135 A8
Hurman St CF10 ..195 B2
Huron Cres CF23 ..178 B4
Hurst Gr CF44 ....30 A2
Hutchwns Cl CF36 182 D7
Hutchwns Terr CF36 182 F7
Huxley Gn NP20 ..117 A2
Hyacinth Dr CF31 ..169 D6
Hyde St NP13 ....60 C6
Hydrangea Cl
Cardiff CF23 ....178 D7
Rogerstone NP10 ..142 B3
Hyland Pl CF44 ....27 E8
Hylton Terr CF46 ..56 A7
Hyman Pl NP4 ....37 F5
Hyssop Cl CF23 ..178 D8
Hywel Cres CF48 ..215 A6
Hywel Dda Jun & Inf Schs
CF5 ....193 B4
Hywel Ho CF47 ....30 D8

I

Ian's Wlk SA6 ....46 B4
Idencroft Cl CF23 ..161 A1
Idris Davies Rd NP22 ..12 F2
Idris Pl CF31 ....168 F7
Idris Terr SA6 ....68 E6
Idwal Pl SA5 ....68 B5
Idwal St SA11 ....72 A8
Iestyn Dr CF35 ....152 D1
Iestyn St
Aberdare CF44 ....28 E4
Cardiff CF11 ....194 D7
Iestynian Ave CF11 ..194 D7
Ifor Hael Rd NP10 ..141 F6
Ifor Jones Ct CF23 ..178 C5
Ifton St CF45 ....54 D2
Ifor Terr CF35 ....130 E3
Ilan Ave SA12 ....98 A1
Ilan Rd CF83 ....34 C8
Ilan St NP19 ....144 A1
Ilan Rd CF83 ....137 A7
Ilchester Rd CF23 ..179 C6
Ilex Cl CF14 ....177 F8
Ilfracombe Cres CF3 179 C5
Illtyd Ave CF62 ....210 A5
Illtyd Rd CF5 ....193 B6
Illtyd St Neath SA11 ..72 A8
Pontypridd CF37 ..135 B7
Ilminster Cl CF63 ..215 B6
Ilminster St CF63 ..215 B6
Ilston CF23 ....40 F4
Ilston Way SA3 ....123 A7
Ilton Rd CF23 ....178 D1
Imperial Bldgs
Cardiff CF5 ....194 A8
Glan y Nant NP11 ..85 A8
Imperial Ct CF45 ....82 C2
Imperial Ctr SA7 ....69 B7
Imperial Pk NP10 ..143 D6
Inchmarnock St
CF24 ....195 D5
Incline Rd
Aberdare CF44 ....29 F1
Abersychan NP4 ..37 F4
Incline Row SA13 ..125 D6
Incline Side CF48 ..31 B8
Incline Top CF44 ....29 F1
Industrial Terr 3
CF48 ....31 C1
Inglefield Ave CF14 177 F2
Ingles 16 NP44 ....89 B1
Inkerman Row
Blaina NP13 ....15 D5
Port Talbot SA13 ..125 D6
Inkerman St
Llanelli SA15 ....40 D5
Swansea SA1 ....95 D6
Inkerman Terr NP22 ..13 D5
Insole Cl CF5 ....193 F8
Insole Gdns CF5 ..194 A8
Insole Gr E CF5 ..193 F8
Insole Gr W CF5 ..193 F8
Insole Pl CF5 ....194 A7
Inst of Higher Ed
CF24 ....195 C6
Institute Pl CF40 ..106 E7
Institute Rd CF40 ..106 E7
Institute St CF43 ....52 A1
Institution Terr NP23 ..14 D6
Instow Pl CF3 ....179 D6
Inter-Valley Rd
SA10,SA11 ....223 D4
Intermediate Rd NP23 ..8 C5
Inverleith Terr CF40 106 E7
Inverness Pl CF24 ..196 A3
Investiture Pl CF39 133 D6
Iolo Pl CF53 ....215 B7
Iorwerth St SA5 ....68 C2
Ipswich Rd CF23 ..178 F1
Ireland Cl CF3 ....180 A5
Irene St CF45 ....81 C8
Ireton Cl CF23 ....161 A1
Irfon St CF4 ....79 F6
Iris Cl SA12 ....98 C3
Iron Bridge Rd CF5 176 C8
Iron Row NP22 ....12 D6
Iron St Cardiff CF24 195 D6
Tredegar NP22 ....13 E6
Ironworks Rd CF44 ..27 D8
Irvine Ct SA3 ....123 B4
Irving Ho 1 SA12 ..98 B3
Irving Pl CF62 ....214 E5
Is y Coed CF14 ....79 C8
Is-Fryn NP22 ....12 E6
Is-y-Bryniau SA9 ..221 B8
Is-y-Coed CF5 ....205 A6
Isaac's Pl SA12 ..124 F8
Isaf Rd NP11 ....115 B1
Isca Cl NP4 ....89 F4
Isca Ct NP18 ....118 B3
Isca Mews NP18 ..118 B2
Isca Rd NP18 ....118 C1
Iscoed SA15 ....40 B6
Isfryn Ind Est CF35 ..130 F2
Island Farm Cl CF31 168 E1
Island Farm Rd CF31 168 E1
Island Mews SA13 ..99 B1
Island Pl SA15 ....40 D5
Island Rd CF62 ....214 D4
Islawen Mdws CF35 152 E1
Islington Rd CF34 ..31 D6
Islwyn SA14 ....41 E5
Islwyn Cl
Ebbw Vale NP23 ..14 C8
Pengam NP12 ....85 B7
Ynysddu NP11 ..112 F6
Islwyn Dr CF83 ..115 B1
Islwyn Rd
Mountain Ash CF45 ..54 D3

Islwyn Rd continued
Cwmfelinfach NP11 ..113 F3
Swansea SA1 ....95 B8
Islwyn St
Abercarn NP11 ....87 A3
Cwmfelinfach NP11 113 B4
Islwyn Terr
Pontlanfraith NP12 ..86 A4
Porth CF39 ....107 D4
Islwyn Way CF63 ..215 A8
Islwyn Workshops
NP11 ....141 A8
Isyrhos SA1 ....222 B6
Itchen Cl NP20 ..116 D3
Itchen Rd NP20 ..116 D3
Iton St NP23 ....35 A7
Ivey Pl SA1 ....95 D8
Ivor John Wlk NP18 118 A4
Ivor Pk CF72 ....173 A6
Ivor St Abercarn NP11 114 C7
Barry CF62 ....214 F2
Blaenavon NP4 ....17 C6
Dowlais CF48 ....11 B4
Fleur De Lis NP12 ....85 B6
Maesteg CF34 ....102 A2
Newport NP20 ....143 C4
Pontycymer CF32 ..103 F3
Trehafod CF37 ....108 D2
Ystrad CF41 ....79 D3
Ivor Terr CF48 ....11 A5
Ivorites Row SA11 ..223 D1
Ivy Ave SA11 ....72 A8
Ivy Bush Ct SA1 ....95 E7
Ivy Cl Ebbw Vale NP23 ..7 A4
Ivy Cottage Ct NP12 ..86 A8
Ivy Dene Cl NP4 ....38 B1
Ivy Row NP24 ....58 A8
Ivy St Cardiff CF5 ..194 B6
Penarth CF64 ....207 A4
Ivy Terr CF27 ....109 A2
Ivydale CF14 ....160 A3

J

Jack-y-Ddu Rd SA11 71 B2
Jacks Pill Ind Est
NP20 ....143 D3
Jackson Cl CF62 ..213 A2
Jackson Ct 3 NP19 142 E8
Jackson Pl 2 NP19 143 E6
Jackson Rd CF5 ..193 B5
Jade Cl CF14 ....160 A4
James Cl
Fleur De Lis NP12 ....85 A6
Sarn CF32 ....150 F4
James Ct
Cardiff CF23 ....178 B5
Swansea SA1 ....69 D6
James Griffiths Rd
SA18 ....219 D7
James Pl CF37 ....135 E7
James St
Aberdagored CF81 ....58 B4
Aberdare CF44 ....53 C6
Abertillery NP13 ....36 B5
Barry CF63 ....215 D6
Bedwas CF83 ....139 A7
Blaenavon NP4 ....17 C6
Cardiff CF10 ....195 B8
Cwmdare CF44 ....28 C3
Ebbw Vale NP23 ..14 C8
3 Llanbradach CF83 ..111 F1
Llanelli SA15 ....40 E6
Maerdy CF43 ....142 A1
2 Merthyr Tydfil CF47 30 B8
8 Mountain Ash CF45 54 E1
New Tredegar NP24 ..33 E3
New Tredegar NP24 ..24 D6
Newport NP20 ....143 D2
Pontardawe SA8 ....23 D5
Pontarddulais SA4 ..19 D3
Pontypool NP4 ....62 D7
Pontypridd CF37 ..135 E7
Port Talbot SA13 ..125 B8
Tonypandy CF40 ..107 A4
Tredegar NP22 ....13 F5
Treorchy CF42 ....78 B6
Ystradgynlais SA9 ...2 F8
Ystradgynlais SA9 222 A6
James Terr
Cheltenham NP7 ....9 C6
Hengoed CF82 ....85 A3
Porth CF39 ....107 E5
James' Rd CF32 ..103 E6
James's Row NP23 ....7 C4
Jamesville NP11 ..114 B8
Jancell Ho CF33 ..148 D3
Jane Austen CF37 182 C1
Jane Ct NP10 ....163 F5
Janet St Cardiff CF24 195 E5
Pontypridd CF37 ..135 F5
Japonica Cl NP20 ..117 B3
Japonica Dr CF48 ..11 C4
Jasmin Cl SA12 ....98 C3
Jasmine Cl
Merthyr Tydfil CF47 10 C5
Swansea SA1 ....94 B7
Jasmine Dr CF3 ..180 A1
Jasper Cl CF5 ....176 E2
Jaycroft Cl CF23 ..161 B1
Jeans Cl NP20 ..117 A3
Jeddo Cl NP20 ..143 C2
Jeddo St NP20 ..143 C2
Jeffcott Pl CF44 ..207 A6
Jeffrey St
Mountain Ash CF45 ..54 D3

Jeffrey St continued
Newport NP19 ....143 E5
Jeffreys Ct SA5 ....68 B5
Jellicoe Cl NP19 ..143 F3
Jellicoe Ct 6 CF10 ..195 C4
Jellicoe Gdns CF23 178 A5
Jenkin St
Abercwmboi CF44 ....53 F4
4 Aberdare CF44 ....29 A1
2 Barry CF63 ....215 B7
Bridgend CF31 ....168 F3
Maesycwmmer CF82 ..85 B2
Jenkins Pl 18 CF47 ..30 E8
Jenkins Rd SA11 ..71 F5
Jenkins St SA11 ....71 A7
Jenkins Row
Deri CF81 ....57 B8
Rhymney NP22 ....12 F3
Jenkins Terr
Abercynon CF45 ....82 F3
Newport NP19 ....143 F3
Pontypridd CF37 ..109 A1
Porth CF39 ....107 F3
Jenkins Terr
Abergwynfi SA13 ..76 C5
Cwmfelin CF34 ..128 C8
Port Talbot SA13 ..125 D7
Jenner Rd CF62 ..214 D5
Jenner St CF63 ..215 C6
Jericho Rd SA1 ....95 E8
Jerry's La CF83 ..138 D7
Jersey Rd
Blaengwynfi SA13 ..76 C6
Swansea SA1 ....69 B4
Jersey Row SA12 ....99 E5
Jersey St
Port Talbot SA13 ..99 C1
Swansea SA1 ....68 D1
Jersey Terr
Briton Ferry SA11 ..71 B1
Pontypridd CF37 ..109 A1
Jerusalem La NP4 ..63 B4
Jerusalem La NP4 ..63 B4
Jesmond Dene CF15 158 B4
Jessop Cl NP10 ..142 B6
Jessop Rd NP10 ..142 B6
Jestyn Cl Cardiff CF5 ..194 E4
Dinas Powys CF64 ..206 B4
Jestyn St CF39 ..107 E4
Jevan Cl CF5 ....176 D3
Jewel St CF63 ..215 B5
Jewell La NP20 ..143 B8
Jim Driscoll Way
CF11 ....195 A1
Jim Harvard Ct 5
SA6 ....69 A8
Job's La CF48 ....10 A4
Jockey St SA1 ....95 D8
John Baker CI NP44 ..11 C6
John Batchelor Way
CF64 ....207 A6
John Bull Cl NP19 ..144 E6
John Croft CF62 ..212 F6
John Field Wlk
NP19 ....144 E4
John Frost Sq 2
NP20 ....143 C4
John Ireland Cl
NP19 ....144 D5
John Morgan Cl CF5 176 B3
John Penry Cres SA5 ..68 B6
John St Aberavon SA12 99 A1
Abercarn NP11 114 C8
Abercwmboi CF44 ....53 F4
7 Aberdare CF44 ....29 A1
Bargoed CF81 ....57 F3
Barry CF63 ....215 C6
Cardiff CF10 ....195 B4
Cefn Cribwr CF32 ..149 C2
Ebbw Vale NP23 ....7 C1
Hirwaun CF44 ....27 E8
Llanelli SA15 ....40 D5
Markham NP12 ....58 E7
Merthyr Tydfil CF47 ..10 D1
Mountain Ash CF45 ..54 F2
Mumbles SA3 ....123 A4
Neath CF32 ....104 F5
Newport NP20 ....143 D3
Penarth CF64 ....207 B5
Pentre CF41 ....78 F5
Pontlottyn CF81 ....56 C6
Pontypridd CF37 ....37 B7
Porth CF39 ....107 F6
Porthcawl CF36 ..182 F6
Resolven SA11 ....226 D5
3 Swansea SA1 ....95 D8
Tonyrefail CF39 ..107 F6
Treherbert CF42 ....51 A1
Ynysddu NP11 ..112 F5
John's Dr CF35 ..170 D7
John's Hill SA1 ....211 D5
John's La CF14 ....177 A2
John's Villas CF32 ..151 A5
Johnson Pl CF64 ..207 D7
Johnston Cl NP10 ..142 A7
Johnston Rd CF14 ..159 D1
Joiners Rd SA4 ....65 D1
Jolly Rd SA18 ....220 C8
Jonathans Terr CF37 137 E8
Jones Pl 3 CF37 ..109 E2
Jones Pl NP19 ....143 E4
3 Mountain Ash CF45 54 E1

Jones St continued
New Tredegar NP24 ..33 F3
Newport NP20 ....143 B4
Pontardawe SA8 ....23 E5
Pontypridd CF37 ..109 F6
Tonypandy CF40 ..106 C6
Treherbert CF42 ....78 B8
Jones Terr
Merthyr Tydfil CF47 ..10 F1
Swansea SA1 ....95 C8
Jones' Terr SA18 ..219 F8
Jonquil Cl CF23 ..180 A7
Joseph Davies' Cl 6
SA1 ....68 C2
Joseph Parry Cl
CF47 ....206 E6
Joseph Parry Ct 8
CF47 ....30 D8
Joseph Parry's Cottage
Mus CF48 ....10 C2
Joseph Row CF33 ..148 D3
Joseph St SA13 ....99 B2
Joslin Rd CF31 ....169 A7
Joslin Terr CF31 ..169 A7
Jowett Ave CF47 ....30 F8
Joyce Cl NP20 ..142 E2
Joyce Ho 2 SA12 ....98 F1
Jubilee Cres
Bridgend CF31 ..169 A3
Nantgarw SA13 ....70 F8
Sarn CF32 ....150 E4
Jubilee Ct CF43 ....80 B2
Jubilee Gdns
Barry CF63 ....215 D8
Porthcawl CF36 ..166 A2
Jubilee Ind Est CF24 195 D5
Jubilee La
Gorseinon SA4 ....66 A8
Penarth CF64 ....207 B4
Jubilee Pl NP4 ....37 F5
Jubilee Rd
Aberdare CF44 ....53 C6
Abertillery NP13 ....36 C3
Bridgend CF31 ..169 A3
New Tredegar NP24 ..34 A2
Jubilee St
Cardiff CF11 ....194 E4
Llanharan CF72 ....153 F2
Jubilee Terr NP44 ..62 A8
Jubilee Way CF33 ..148 A2
Jude Rd NP44 ....89 B1
Julian Terr SA12 ....98 F1
Julia's Cl CF82 ....84 C7
Julian's Way CF33 ..166 A7
Julius Cl NP18 ....117 F3
Junction Ind Est
CF10 ....195 D2
Junction Lock Rd
CF10 ....195 D2
Junction Rd NP19 ..143 D6
Junction Terr CF15 ..176 C5
Juniper Cl
Porthcawl CF36 ..183 E7
Swansea SA2 ....94 B8
Juniper Cres SA4 ..116 A7
Justin Cl CF23 ....178 C4

K

Kames Pl CF24 ..195 C5
Kamsley Ho 6 CF47 30 D8
Kane Cl CF14 ....177 F2
Kathleen St CF62 ..214 C4
Katie St CF32 ....103 E7
Kays & Kears Ind Est
NP4 ....17 A7
Kean Ho 3 SA12 ....98 B3
Kear Cl NP20 ....143 C4
Kear's Row SA11 ....17 F1
Keats Cl
Bridgend CF31 ..168 D6
Cwmbran NP44 ....89 D2
Newport NP20 ....142 E2
Keats Gr SA2 ....93 F7
Keats Way CF62 ..214 E8
Keble Ct CF83 ....139 D7
Keen Rd Cardiff CF24 195 D6
Keenan Cl CF24 ..195 D5
Keeni's Pl CF23 ..150 F4
Keene Ave NP10 ..142 C3
Keene St NP19 ....143 F4
Keepers Cl SA4 ....44 C2
Keepers La CF62 ..212 F6
Keir Hardie Cl NP23 ..7 D6
Keir Hardie Cres NP19
NP19 ....144 D7
Keir Hardie Dr
Newport NP10 ....163 E7
Penarth CF64 ....217 A8
Keir Hardie Rd CF83 ..178 A3
Keir Hardie Terr
NP11 ....60 A3
Keith St CF43 ....80 B4
Keller Ho 1 SA12 ....98 F1
Kelly Rd NP19 ....144 A7
Kelston Cl CF14 ..176 F5
Kelston Pl CF14 ..176 F5
Kelston Rd CF14 ..176 F5
Kelvedon St NP19 143 E4
Kelvin Cl NP20 ..117 A2
Kelvin Rd
Cardiff CF24 ....178 B1
Clydach SA6 ....22 E1
Kember Cl CF3 ..180 A6
Kemble Ho SA12 ....98 A2
Kemble St SA2 ....94 F5
Kemeys Fawr Cl NP4 ..62 D8
Kemeys Fawr Inf Sch
NP4 ....62 D1
Kemeys Rd CF62 ..213 A2
Kemp Ho 2 SA12 ....98 B3
Kemps Covert CF61 208 F5
Kemys Pl CF14 ....177 D5
Kemys Way SA1 ....69 E2
Kemys Way SA6 ....69 B7
Kemys Wlk NP44 ....89 D1
Kendal Cl CF44 ....29 D1
Kendle Dr SA2 ....94 C8
Kendon Cl CF44 ....27 D8
Kendon Rd NP11 ....59 F2
Kendrick Rd CF62 ..214 F5
Kenfig Ind Est SA13 147 B4
Kenfig Pl
Llanyravon NP44 ....90 A3
Swansea SA1 ....69 A2
Kenfig Rd CF14 ..177 D3
Kenilworth Ct
Baglan SA12 ....98 E5
Cardiff CF5 ....193 F7
Kenilworth Ho 6
CF23 ....194 F5
Kenilworth Pl
Cwmbran NP44 ....89 C1
Mumbles SA3 ....123 A8
Kenilworth Rd
Barry CF63 ....215 B6
Newport NP19 ....144 A5
Kenley Cl CF5 ....176 E1
Kenmare Mews
CF23 ....161 A2
Kenmuir Rd CF24 ..195 F7
Kennard Cres NP4 ..17 B6
Kennard Ct NP4 ....17 B6
Kennard Pl NP4 ....17 B7
Kennard St CF44 ....78 F2
Kennard Terr SA11 ..59 F1
Kennedy Cl CF38 ..156 A7
Kennedy Dr CF35 ..170 C8
Kennedy Rise CF62 ..214 C5
Kennel Row SA11 ....71 B1
Kennerleigh Rd CF3 179 A4
Kenneth Treasure Ct 2
CF3 ....179 D7
Kennington Cl
Cardiff CF11 ....159 E2
Killay SA2 ....93 D6
Kenry St
Evanstown CF39 ..132 B8
Tonypandy CF40 ..106 E5
Treorchy CF42 ....78 B8
Kensington Ave CF5 194 A6
Kensington Dr
Bridgend CF31 ..168 C6
Porth CF39 ....108 A2
Kensington Gdns 6
NP19 ....143 F6
Kensington Gr NP19 143 F5
Kensington Pl NP19 143 F5
Kenson Cl CF62 ..212 E1
Kenson Hill CF62 ..212 E6
Kent Cl NP10 ....142 A7
Kent Cres SA11 ..118 A3
Kent Gn CF62 ..214 E6
Kent Rd CF11 ....194 F2
Kenway Ave SA11 ..71 F6
Kenwood Rd CF5 ..193 B5
Kenyon Rd CF24 ..196 A7
Keppoch St CF24 ..195 C8
Keralake Terr 3
CF40 ....106 F3
Kern Cl SA12 ....98 B3
Kerrigan Cl CF5 ..176 D1
Kerrycroy St 10
CF24 ....195 D5
Kestell Dr CF11 ....207 A8
Kestrel Cl
Bridgend CF31 ..169 D3
Cardiff CF23 ....178 D7
Neath SA10 ....48 E2
Kestrel View CF3 ....84 F3
Kestrel Way
Newport NP10 ....163 E7
Penarth CF64 ....217 A8
Keswick Ave CF23 ..178 A3
Keteringham Cl
CF64 ....216 A5
Kewstoke Ave CF3 ..179 B5
Kewstoke Pl CF3 ..179 B5
Keyes Ave CF23 ....178 A5
Keyes Cl 3 CF14 ..195 C4
Keynsham Ave NP20 143 C3
Keynsham Rd CF44 ..177 C5
Keys The CF61 ..209 F6
Keyston Rd CF5 ..176 A1
Khartoum Terr SA10 222 F5
Kidwelly Cl
Blackwood NP12 ....58 E2
Newport NP44 ....90 A2
Kidwelly Cl CF83 ..137 D4
Kidwelly Gr CF48 ..225 F1
Kidwelly Rd NP44 ....90 B2
Kier Hardie CF NP19
NP19 ....144 D7
Kilcatten St 3 CF24 ..195 D5
Kildare St SA5 ....68 C3
Kilfield Rd SA3 ..122 B5
Kilgetty Cl CF5 ..194 C4
Killan Rd SA2 ....93 B8
Kiln St CF44 ....53 C8
Kilvey Rd SA1 ....95 E8
Kilvey Terr SA1 ....95 E8
Kimberley Cl SA2 ....94 D7
Kimberley Cl CF31 ..169 B4
Kimberley Pl NP4 ....31 C2
Kimberley Rd
Cardiff CF23 ....178 D1
Swansea SA2 ....94 D7
Kimberley Terr
Cardiff CF14 ....177 F8

Kimberley Terr continued
Tredegar NP22 . . . . .13 F6
Kimberley Way CF39 107 F2
Kincoed Rd NP12 . . . . . .59 B1
Kincraig St CF24 . . . . .195 B8
King Charles Rd NP11 86 D5
King Edward Ave
CF83 . . . . .138 B2
King Edward Rd
Brynmawr NP23 . . . . .2 C5
Gwaun-Cae-Gurwen
SA18 . . . . .220 F6
King Edward St
Blaengarw CF32 . . . . . .103 E5
 Merthyr Tydfil CF47 .10 D2
King Edward Terr
NP22 . . . . .12 E5
King Edward VII Ave
CF10 . . . . .195 A7
King Edward's Rd
SA1 . . . . .95 A6
King George Ave
SA15 . . . . .95 D7
King George St SA2 .94 B3
King George V Dr E
Cardiff CF14 . . . . .177 F4
CF14 . . . . .177 F4
King George V Dr N
CF14 . . . . .177 F5
King George V Dr W
CF14 . . . . .177 E4
King La NP20 . . .143 C4
King St Abercynon CF45 82 F3
Aberdare CF44 . . . . .53 C8
Abertillery NP13 . . . . . .36 B5
Abertridwr CF83 . . . . . .137 A7
Blaenavon NP4 . . . . . . .17 C7
Brynmawr NP23 . . . . . . .8 B4
Cwm NP23 . . . . .35 B6
Cwmdare CF44 . . . . . . .28 C3
Cwmfelinfach NP11 . . .113 A4
Ebbw Vale NP23 . . . . . . .7 F4
Ferndale CF43 . . . . .80 A5
Mountain Ash CF45 . . . .81 E8
Nantyglo NP23 . . . . .4 E1
Neath SA11 . . . . .71 E7
Newport NP20 . . . . . . .143 C4
Pant CF48 . . . . .121 A6
Penarth CF64 . . . . .207 B5
Pontllottyn CF81 . . . . . .12 F1
Pontypool NP4 . . . . . . .62 B7
Pontypridd CF37 . . . . . .135 E6
Port Talbot SA13 . . . . . .99 C1
 Swansea SA1 . . . . . . .95 D7
Taffs Well CF15 . . . . . .158 A3
Ton Pentre CF41 . . . . . .79 B2
Tredegar NP22 . . . . .6 A5
King Wood Cl CF23 .178 F2
King's Arms CF71 . . .176 C5
King's Head Rd SA5 . .67 F3
King's Hill
Hengoed CF82 . . . . .85 A3
Porthcawl CF36 . . . . . .183 A7
King's Par NP20 . . . .143 D2
King's Rd
Cardiff CF11 . . . . .194 D6
Radyr CF15 . . . . .176 C5
**King's Road (Heol y
Brenin)** SA1 . . . . .95 E6
Kingarth St CF24 . .195 C5
Kingcraft St CF45 . . . .54 D2
Kingdon-Owen Rd
SA11 . . . . .71 F5
Kingfisher Cl CF3 . . .179 F7
Kingfisher Ct SA15 . . .41 A5
Kingfisher Pl NP10 . .163 E7
Kingfisher Sq CF62 .210 D6
Kingleys The CF34 .102 A8
Kingrosia Pk SA6 . . . .47 A8
Kings Acre NP20 . . . . .12 E5
Kings Ave NP22 . . . . .12 E5
Kings Cl CF83 . . . . . .137 A7
Kings Coll CF24 . . . . .195 C7
Kings Ct CF64 . . . . . .206 A2
Kings La SA1 . . . . .95 D7
Kings Monkton Sch
CF24 . . . . .195 B8
Kings Rd Cardiff CF11 194 D7
Mumbles SA3 . . . . .123 A4
Kings Ride CF64 . . . .205 F3
Kings Terr CF14 . . . . .101 F6
Kingsacre CF38 . . . . .106 C6
Kingsbridge Bsns Pk
SA4 . . . . .66 C8
Kingsbury Ct CF44 . . .28 E6
Kingsbury Pl
Aberdare CF44 . . . . .52 F4
Cwmaman CF44 . . . . . . .53 A4
Llwydcoed CF44 . . . . . .28 E6
Kingsdale Ct NP20 .143 A3
Kingsfield NP23 . . . . . .7 E1
Kingshill Ct NP20 143 C4
Kingsland Cres CF63 215 A4
Kingsland Rd
Cardiff CF14 . . . . .176 F4
Cardiff CF5 . . . . .194 B6
Kingsland Terr CF37 .135 C2
Kingsland Wlk NP44 .89 B2
Kingslea NP44 . . . .209 B1
Kingsley Cl CF64 . . . .216 B5
Kingsley Pl CF83 . . . .110 F2
Kingsley Terr
Aberfan CF48 . . . . .55 C4
Merthyr Tydfil CF47 . . . .10 F1
Kingsmill Terr
NP20 . . . . .143 B4

Kingston Rd
Cardiff CF11 . . . . .194 D5
Newport NP19 . . . . . . .143 E5
Swansea SA2 . . . . .94 D7
Kingsvale NP20 . .143 C4
Kingsway
Bridgend CF31 . . . . . . .169 C2
Newport NP20 . . . . . . .143 C4
Swansea SA1 . . . . .67 C4
**Kingsway (Ffordd y
Brenin)The** SA1 . . . .95 C7
Kingsway Bldgs
CF31 . . . . .169 D2
Kingsway Ctr
NP20 . . . . .143 C4
Kingsway Ffordd y Brenin
CF10 . . . . .195 A6
**Kingswood
(Coed-y-Brenin)**
CF37 . . . . .135 A8
Kingswood Cl
Ewenny CF35 . . . . .185 E7
Hengoed CF82 . . . . .85 A3
Kinley St SA1 . . . . . . .95 F7
Kinnock Cl NP44 . . . . .90 A6
Kinsale Cl CF23 . . . .161 A2
Kipling Cl Cardiff CF23 179 B7
Penarth CF64 . . . . .206 F5
Kipling Gdns CF35 . .168 C5
Kipling Hill NP20 . . .142 G2
Kirby Daniel Ct
NP20 . . . . .143 C3
Kirby La NP20 . . . . . .143 C3
Kirkby Cl CF10 . .195 C3
Kirkhouse St CF37 . .135 B8
Kirkwall Cl CF24 . . . .195 F7
Kirton Cl CF5 . . . . . . .176 E1
Kitchener Com Jun & Inf
Sch CF11 . . . . .194 D5
Kitchener Rd CF11 .194 D5
Kitchener St NP4 . . . . .6 B1
Kittiwake Cl CF36 . . .182 D8
Kittle Gn SA3 . . . . . . .121 E7
Kittle Hill La SA3 . . . .121 E7
Kitty Hawk Dr NP19 .144 B3
Knap Car Terr CF42 .216 A2
Knelston Pl SA5 . . . . .67 F7
Knelston Prim Sch
SA3 . . . . .231 A8
Knight St NP20 .143 C3
Knight St
Aberavon SA12 . . . . . . .99 A1
 Mountain Ash CF45 .54 D3
Knighton Ct
Caerleon NP18 . . . . . . .118 B2
 Cardiff CF24 . . . . . .195 D6
Knights Rd SA13 . . . .125 E3
Knights Row CF45 . . . .82 F3
Knightswell Rd CF5 .193 A2
Knightswell Rd CF5 .193 A3
Knole Cl CF23 . . . . . .161 A1
Knoll Ave SA2 . . . . . . .94 E6
Knoll Terr CF40 . . . . .106 D7
Knowbury Ave CF64 .217 B8
Knox Rd CF24 . . . . . .195 B6
Knox St SA13 . . . . . . .125 A3
Knoyle Dr SA5 . . . . . . .68 C7
Knoyle St SA5 . . . . . . .68 C7
Kyfts La SA3 . . . . .228 E3
Kyle Ave CF14 . . . . . .177 C5
Kyle Cres CF14 . . . . .177 C5
Kymin Rd CF64 . . . . .207 B4
Kymin Terr CF64 . . . .207 B4
Kyveilog St CF11 . . . .194 D7

Laburnam Ave NP22 . . . .6 D1
Laburnam La CF48 . . .10 B6
Laburnam Terr CF48 . .31 B2
Laburnam Way CF64 206 E3
Laburnham Bush La
NP19 . . . . .144 C2
Laburnham Cl NP10 .141 E7
Laburnham Pl SA2 . . .94 B6
Laburnum Ave
Baglan SA12 . . . . .98 E7
Newport NP19 . . . . . . .144 B4
Laburnum Cl
Barry CF62 . . . . .214 F7
Ebbw Vale NP23 . . . . . . .7 C5
Merthyr Tydfil CF47 . . . .10 D4
Laburnum Ct CF37 . .136 B5
Laburnum Gr NP22 . . .85 E3
Laburnum Pl SA2 . . . .94 B6
Laburnum Terr
Abercarn NP11 . . . . .87 C4
Rhydyfelin CF37 . . . . . .136 B5
Laburnum Way CF64 206 E3
Ladies Row NP22 . . . . .6 F1
Lady Abardare Flats
SA4 . . . . .54 D4
Lady Housty Ave
SA3 . . . . .122 C5
Lady Jane St
SA12 . . . . .124 F8
Lady Margaret Ct
SA3 . . . . .178 E1
Lady Margaret Villas
SA2 . . . . .94 F3
Lady Margaret's Terr
CF24 . . . . .195 D5
Lady Mary Rd CF23 .178 B3
Lady Tyler Terr NP22 .12 E5
Ladybench NP44 . . . . .89 B1

Ladyhill Gn NP19 . . . .144 C4
Ladyhill Rd NP19 . . . .144 D5
Ladysmith Rd
Caerphilly NP12 . . . . . . .85 E6
Cardiff CF23 . . . . .178 D1
Ladysmith Terr
Tredegar NP22 . . . . .13 F6
Troedyrhiw CF48 . . . . . .31 C2
Ladywell NP44 . . . . . . .89 E5
Laing St CF33 . . . . . . .148 C1
Lake Ct SA12 . . . . . . .124 F7
Lake Hill Dr CF71 . . . .188 F1
Lake Rd Brynmawr NP23 .8 C4
Newport NP10 . . . . . . .144 C1
Port Talbot SA12 . . . . . .124 E7
Lake Rd E CF23 . . . . .178 A4
Lake Rd N CF23 . . . . .178 A5
Lake Rd W CF23 . . . . .178 A4
Lake St CF43 . . . . .79 F6
Lake View Cl
Cardiff CF23 . . . . .178 B4
Llanelli SA15 . . . . .40 C7
Lake View CF23 . . . . .178 B4
Lakefield Cl SA15 . .40 D4
Lakefield Pl SA15 . . . .40 C4
Lakefield Rd SA15 . . . .40 D4
Lakeside Barry CF62 .214 C1
Cwmdare CF44 . . . . . . .28 C2
Lakeside Cl NP22 . . . . .6 B1
Lakeside Cty Jun & Inf
Sch CF23 . . . . .178 A4
Lakeside Dr CF23 . . .178 B5
Lakeside Gdns CF48 . .10 B4
Lakeside Tech Pk
SA7 . . . . .69 B6
Lakeview Cl CF36 . . .183 A8
Lakeview Terr SA11 . . .71 E7
Lakin Dr CF62 . . . . . . .214 C8
Lakeston Cl
Barry CF63 . . . . .215 A8
 Cardiff CF5 . . . . . . .193 C4
Porthcawl CF36 . . . . . .165 E2
Laleston Ct CF32 . . . .167 C5
Lamb & Flag Cotts
SA9 . . . . .222 B7
Lamb Cl NP20 . . . . . .142 E1
Lamb La Ponthir NP18 .114 C7
Swansea SA2 . . . . .93 B7
Lamb's Sq NP23 . . . . . .7 C4
Lambert Cl NP20 . . . .143 B7
Lambert St NP20 . . . .143 B8
Lambert Terr CF44 . . .28 F2
Lamberton Way
CF24 . . . . .195 D5
Lambourne Cres
Bettws NP20 . . . . .116 D2
 Cardiff CF14 . . . . . .177 E7
Lambourne Dr SA3 . .122 F6
Lambourne Way
NP20 . . . . .116 D2
Lambourne Wlk
NP20 . . . . .116 D2
Lambs Well Cl SA3 . .123 B4
Lamby Ind Pk CF3 . . .179 C5
Lamby Way CF3,CF24 179 B1
Lamby Way Workshops
CF3 . . . . .179 C2
Lan Ave SA6 . . . .48 C2
Lan Cl CF37 . . . . .109 B2
Lan Coed SA1 . . . . . . .69 D5
Lan Deri SA1 . . . . .69 C5
Lan Manor SA6 . . . . . .48 C2
Lan St SA6 . . . . .48 F1
Lan-y-Parc CF46 . . . . .83 E4
Lancaster Cl SA1 . . . .223 C1
Lancaster Ct SA5 . . . .67 D5
Lancaster Dr CF38 . . .156 D7
Lancaster Rd NP4 . . . .63 A2
Lancaster St
Abertillery NP13 . . . . . .36 B3
Blaina NP13 . . . . .15 C3
Merthyr Tydfil CF47 . . . .10 D2
Landeg St SA6 . . . . . . .68 E5
Landings The CF64 .206 F5
Landor Ave SA2 . . . . . .93 F7
Landor Dr SA4 . . . . . . .41 A3
Landore Ave
SA13 . . . . .125 C4
Landraw Rd CF37 . . .109 A1
Landsdowne Ct SA5 . .67 D3
Landseer Cl NP19 . . .144 A7
Landwade Cl CF5 . . . .193 C7
Landwr Parc SA6 . . . . .60 A4
Lane The CF5 . . . . .192 D2
Lanelay Cl CF72 . . . . .155 A2
Lanelay Cres CF37 . .109 B1
Lanelay Ind Est CF72 155 A1
Lanelay Pk CF72 . . . . .155 B2
Lanelay Rd CF72 . . . .155 B2
Lanelay Terr CF37 . . .135 B8
Lanes The CF41 . . . . . .80 A6
Langcliff Pk SA3 . . . .123 C3
Langdale Cl CF23 . . . .178 C2
Langdon Road SA1 . . .96 A6
**Langdon Road (Heol
Langdon)** SA1 . . . . . . .95 F7
Langer Way SA1 . . . . . .22 E1
Langham Way CF11 .194 E3
Langland Bay Rd
SA3 . . . . .122 F3
Langland Cl
Hirwaun CF44 . . . . .27 D7
Mumbles SA3 . . . . .123 A4
Langland Court Rd
SA3 . . . . .122 F4
Langland Mews SA15 .40 E3

Langland Rd
Cardiff CF3 . . . . .179 C3
Llanelli SA15 . . . . .40 E3
Mumbles SA3 . . . . .123 A4
Langland Terr SA2 . . . .94 E5
Langland Villas SA3 .123 A4
Langlands Rd CF63 .215 D7
Langport Ave CF3 . . .179 D6
Langstone Bsns Vill
NP18 . . . . .145 A8
Langstone Cotts
NP18 . . . . .145 A8
Langstone Court Rd
NP18 . . . . .145 C8
Langstone Ct NP44 . . .89 C1
Langstone Jun & Inf Sch
NP18 . . . . .119 E2
Langstone La NP18 .145 B6
Lankydrock Cl
CF3 . . . . .179 F6
Lanpark Rd CF37 . . . .109 C2
Lansbury Ave
Cefn Hengoed CF82 . . .84 F4
Margam SA13 . . . . .125 E5
Lansbury Cl
Caerphilly CF83 . . . . . .137 F5
Maesteg CF34 . . . . .101 C3
Lansbury Cres CF34 .101 F1
Lansbury Park Jun & Inf
Sch CF83 . . . . .138 D4
Lansbury Rd
Brynmawr NP23 . . . . . . .8 A3
Merthyr Tydfil CF48 . . . .10 A3
Lansbury Terr NP23 . . .7 F4
Lansdale Dr CF38 . . .136 A1
Lansdown SA1 . . . . . .122 F4
Lansdowne NP4 . . . . . .62 E1
Lansdowne Ave
CF14 . . . . .177 C6
Lansdowne Ave E
CF11 . . . . .194 C5
Lansdowne Ave W
CF11 . . . . .194 B5
Lansdowne Com Jun & Inf
Sch CF5 . . . . .194 B6
Lansdowne Hospl
CF11 . . . . .194 A4
Lansdowne Rd
Caerleon NP18 . . . . . . .118 B2
Cardiff CF5 . . . . .194 B5
Ebbw Vale NP23 . . . . . . .7 D5
Newport NP20 . . . . . . .142 E4
Lanstone Rise NP18 .119 F2
Lanwern Rd CF37 . . . .135 B8
Lanwood Rd CF37 . . .109 C2
Lapwing Cl
Penarth CF64 . . . . .217 A7
Porthcawl CF36 . . . . . .182 D8
Lapwing Rd SA15 . . . .41 A5
Larch Cl Cimla SA11 . .72 C5
Merthyr Tydfil CF47 . . . .10 D5
Pontypool NP4 . . . . .63 A4
Porthcawl CF36 . . . . . .183 E7
Larch Ct Cardiff CF15 158 D1
 Newport NP20 . . .117 A3
Larch Dr CF72 . . . . . .155 F3
Larch Gr
Caerphilly CF83 . . . . . .138 C5
Cardiff CF14 . . . . .160 B3
Llanmartin NP18 . . . . .145 B6
Newport NP20 . . . . . . .117 B3
Larch Ho CF14 . . . . . .176 G4
Larches The CF71 . . .189 C8
Larchwood CF5 . . . . .205 A6
Lark Pk SA5 . . . . .67 E7
Lark Rise CF31 . . . . . .169 D5
Larkfield Ave CF48 . . .29 F6
Larkfield Cl NP18 . . . .118 A4
Larkhill SA12 . . . . .98 F7
Larkspur Cl SA10 . . . .48 E2
Larkspur Dr SA3 . . . .122 F7
Larkwood Ave CF64 .207 C4
Lascelles Dr CF23 . . .161 B1
Lasgarn La NP4 . . . . . .38 A3
Lasgarn Pl NP4 . . . . . .38 A3
Lasgarn View NP4 . . . .37 F7
Latimer Ct SA5 . . . . . . .67 E5
Latt The SA15 . . . . . . .71 E8
Lauderdale Rd SA18 .220 E7
Laugharne Ave CF3 .179 C3
Laugharne Ct
Barry CF62 . . . . .214 F7
Swansea SA2 . . . . .94 A6
Laugharne Rd CF3 . . .179 C3
Launcelot Cres CF14 159 E2
Laundry Rd CF37 . . . .109 B1
Laura St Barry CF63 . .215 A6
Pontypridd CF37 . . . . .135 D6
Laural Wlk NP44 . . . . .89 B6
Laureate Cl CF3 . . . . .179 B7
Laurel Ave
Baglan SA12 . . . . .98 E6
Rhydyfelin CF37 . . . . . .136 A4
Laurel Cl
Cwmdare CF44 . . . . . . .28 D3
Sarn CF32 . . . . .150 F4
Laurel Cres NP20 . . .117 B2
Laurel Ct Barry CF62 .214 E7
Bedwas CF83 . . . . .138 E7
Cardiff CF5 . . . . .193 D6
Laurel Dr
Ammanford SA18 . . . . .219 D7
Bassaleg NP10 . . . . . . .142 A3
Bryn NP12 . . . . .59 E7
Penperlleni NP4 . . . . . . .39 E7
Waunarlwydd SA5 . . . . .65 D4
Laurel Gn NP44 . . . . . .89 A4
Laurel Rd NP10 . . . . .142 A3

Laureldene CF72 . . . .172 B5
Laurels Bsns Pk The
CF3 . . . . .179 D2
Laurels The NP13 . . . .15 E5
Lauriston Cl CF5 . . . .193 C2
Lauriston Pk CF5 . . . .193 C2
Lavender Ct
Bridgend CF31 . . . . . . .169 D5
Swansea SA5 . . . . .68 A8
Lavender Gr CF5 . . . .193 C8
Lavender Rd CF47 . . . .10 B6
Lavender Way NP10 .141 D7
Lavernock Rd CF64 . .216 E5
Lavery Cl NP19 . . . . . .144 A7
Lavie St CF32 . . . . . . .149 D4
Lawn Terr
Newbridge NP11 . . . . . .60 A2
Pontypridd CF37 . . . . .135 E7
Rhymney NP22 . . . . . . .12 E4
Lawns Ind Est The
NP22 . . . . .78 F4
Lawrence Ave
Abertillery NP13 . . . . . .35 F7
Markham NP12 . . . . . . .58 D7
Penywaun CF44 . . . . . .28 A6
Lawrence Cl CF31 . . .168 E6
Lawrence Hill NP19 .144 B5
Lawrence Hill Ave
NP19 . . . . .144 B5
Lawrence St CF83 . . .138 E3
Lawrence Terr
SA15 . . . . .40 E5
Lawrenny Ave CF11 .194 C4
Laybourne Cl NP44 . . .89 C5
Laytonia Ave CF14 .177 E4
Le Pouliguen Way
CF61 . . . . .210 A6
Le Sor Hill CF5 . . . . . .191 E6
Le-Breos SA3 . . . . .93 F1
Le-Breos Ave SA2 . . . .94 E6
Lea Cl NP20 . . . . .116 D2
Lea Ct NP12 . . . . .86 A3
Leach Rd NP20 . . . . . .116 D3
Lead St CF24 . . . . .195 D6
Leadon Cl NP44 . . . . . .89 A4
Leamington Rd CF14 177 B6
Leas The NP44 . . . . . . .89 C5
Leckwith Ave CF11 .194 B3
Leckwith Cl CF11 . . .194 D4
Leckwith Ct
Bridgend CF31 . . . . . . .168 C4
Cardiff CF5 . . . . .193 D4
Leckwith Pl CF11 . . .194 C3
Leckwith Rd
Cardiff CF11,CF64 . . . .194 C2
Leckwith CF11 . . . . . . .194 B1
Ledbrooke Cl NP44 . . .89 C1
Ledbury Dr NP20 . . . .143 C6
Lee Cl Cardiff CF23 . .178 D4
Dinas Powys CF64 . . . .206 B4
Lee Ct CF14 . . . . .159 C1
Lee Ho CF23 . . . . .178 D4
Lee Rd CF63 . . . . .215 A6
Lee St
Pontypridd CF37 . . . . .109 B1
Swansea SA1 . . . . .95 F7
Lee Way NP19 . . . . . .144 C1
Leeway Ct NP19 . . . . .144 C1
Leeway SA3 . . . . .121 F7
Legion's Way CF82 . . . .84 F7
Leicester Dr NP44 . . . .89 A3
Leicester Rd NP19 . . .143 E6
Leicester Sq CF82 . . . .84 F7
Leigh Cl CF61 . . . . . . .210 C6
Leigh Terr CF44 . . . . . .83 A5
Leighton Cl NP44 . . . .89 C2
Leighton Rees Cl
CF37 . . . . .81 F2
Leiros Parc Dr SA10 . .48 E2
Lennard St NP19 . . . .143 E4
Lennox Gn CF63 . . . . .215 D6
Leoline Cl CF71 . . . . .188 D2
Leon Ave CF15 . . . . . .158 A3
Leonard St
Fleur De Lis NP12 . . . . .85 B6
Neath SA11 . . . . .71 F8
Leslie Green Ct
NP10 . . . . .163 E8
Leslie St SA1 . . . . .98 F1
Lesser La NP23 . . . . . . .1 E5
Lilleshall St NP19 . . . .143 E4
Lilliput La SA3 . . . . . .123 B8
Lily St CF24 . . . . .195 C7
Limburne Dr NP19 . . .143 F4
Lime Cl
Newport NP20 . . . . . . .143 C2
Radyr CF15 . . . . .176 C4
Lime Cres NP19 . . . . .144 B4
Lime Ct NP11 . . . . .87 B8
Lime Gr Bryn NP12 . . . .85 E3
Cardiff CF5 . . . . .176 B1
Cimla SA11 . . . . .72 A5
Killay SA2 . . . . .93 D7
Llanmartin NP18 . . . . .145 F7
Merthyr Tydfil CF47 . . . .10 E6
St Athan CF62 . . . . . . .211 B7
Lime Kiln La SA3 . . . .122 C6
Lime St Ferndale CF43 .79 F6
Gorseinon SA4 . . . . . . .43 C2
Rhydyfelin CF37 . . . . . .136 G5
Lime Tree Gr SA6 . .69 A8
Lime Tree Way CF38 .103 A4
Limebourne Ct CF14 177 B3
Limekiln Rd
Abersychan NP4 . . . . . .38 A3
Mumbles SA3 . . . . .123 A5
Limes Ct CF71 . . . . . .188 F2
Limes The CF71 . . . . .188 F2
Limeslade Cl
Cardiff CF5 . . . . .193 F7
Hirwaun CF44 . . . . .27 D7
Limeslade Ct SA3 . . .123 C3

Limeside Dr SA3 ...123 C3
Limestone Rd NP23 ...8 C2
Limestone Rd E NP23 ...8 C3
Linewood Cl CF3 ...179 E7
Lincoln Cl NP19 ...143 F6
Lincoln Ct
Caerleon NP18 ...118 A3
Cardiff CF23 ...178 D5
Lincoln St Cardiff CF5 194 B6
Porth CF39 ...107 E2
Lincoln Terr 2 CF47 ...30 E8
Lindbergh Cl NP19 ...144 A3
Linden Ave
Cardiff CF23 ...178 C1
Mumbles SA3 ...123 A8
Linden Cl SA10 ...48 C4
Linden Cres CF44 ...28 D2
Linden Ct
Cwmbran NP44 ...89 B1
Newport NP72 ...172 B5
Newbridge NP11 ...87 C8
Linden Gr
Caerphilly CF83 ...138 C5
Cardiff CF23 ...179 B4
Linden Lea Dr NP12 ...85 D6
Linden Rd NP19 ...144 A5
Linden Way
Porthcawl CF36 ...183 E8
Trefechan CF48 ...10 B7
Lindens The CF64 ...207 B4
Lindsay Cl CF35 ...170 C8
Lindsay Ct CF31 ...169 A3
Lindsay Gdns NP22 ...6 E1
Lindway Ct 4 CF5 ...194 B7
Lingfield Ave
Port Talbot SA12 ...98 D2
Port Talbot SA12 ...98 E1
Lingholm Cl 3 CF3 ...179 F6
Link Rd NP4 ...63 A4
Link The SA2 ...94 B6
Links Cl SA3 ...122 E3
Links The NP4 ...38 C1
Linkside SA3 ...122 E4
Linkside Dr SA3 ...121 A6
Linley Cl NP19 ...145 A6
Linnet Cl CF23 ...178 D7
Linnet Way CF31 ...169 D5
Linton Ct NP4 ...38 A3
Linton St NP20 ...143 D2
Lion Ct 1 NP4 ...17 C6
Lion St Blaenavon NP4 ...17 C6
Swansea SA1 ...68 C2
Lion Way SA7 ...69 B7
Lionel Rd CF5 ...194 B6
Lionel Terr CF37 ...135 F5
Lisbon Ct CF82 ...84 E1
Lisburn Rd CF82 ...84 E1
Lisburn Rise CF44 ...27 D8
Liscombe St NP19 ...144 A4
Liscum Way CF62 ...214 C7
Lisnagarvey Ct CF14 ...176 F8
Lister Ave 3 SA12 ...98 F1
Lister Gn NP20 ...117 A2
Lisvane Ho CF14 ...160 B2
Lisvane Rd CF14 ...160 B2
Lisvane St CF24 ...177 F1
Liswerry Cl 2 NP44 ...90 B2
Liswerry Dr NP44 ...90 B2
Liswerry Inf Sch
NP19 ...144 B3
Liswerry Jun Sch
NP19 ...144 B3
Liswerry Park Dr
NP19 ...144 C4
Liswerry Rd NP19 ...144 C4
Litchard Bglws CF31 168 F7
Litchard Cross CF31 168 F7
Litchard Hill CF31 ...168 F8
Litchard Ind Est
CF31 ...169 A7
Litchard Jun Sch
CF31 ...168 F8
Litchard Pk CF31 ...168 F8
Litchard Rise CF31 ...168 F8
Litchard Terr CF31 ...168 F7
Litchfield Ct CF11 ...194 F4
Little Ave CF5 ...191 F5
Little Brynhill La
CF62 ...214 D8
Little Dock St CF64 ...206 F5
Little Frederick St 2
CF10 ...195 B5
Little Gam St 3 SA1 ...95 C6
Little La NP23 ...4 F7
Little London SA9 ...222 B7
Little Mill CF14 ...177 A3
Little Moors Hill
CF63 ...215 C6
Little Oaks View
NP10 ...142 A6
Little Orch CF64 ...206 C3
Little Wind St 8
CF44 ...29 C1
Littlecroft Ave CF5 ...193 F6
Littledene NP44 ...89 B3
Littleton St CF11 ...41 A3
Littlewoods CF45 ...82 D2
Livale Cl NP20 ...116 E2
Livale Ct NP20 ...116 E2
Livale Rd NP20 ...116 E2
Livale Wlk NP20 ...116 E2
Liverpool St 8 NP19 143 E6
Livingstone Pl NP19 143 E5
Livingstone Way
CF62 ...211 D2
Livorno Ho CF10 ...195 C3
Llamsamlet Ind Est
SA6 ...68 F5

Llan Rd
Llangynwyd CF34 ...128 B6
Marcross CF61 ...198 E2
Llan-Fach Rd NP11 ...87 B3
Llan-Yr-Avon Sq
CF35 ...187 F7
Llan-Yr-Avon Way
NP44 ...90 A2
Llan-yr-Eos CF46 ...83 E4
Llanarth Cl CF83 ...140 B6
Llanarth Rd
Newbridge NP11 ...86 F8
Pontllanfraith NP12 ...86 A4
Llanarth Sq NP11 ...115 A1
Llanarth St
Cwmfelinfach NP11 ...113 E3
Machen CF83 ...40 B7
8 Newport NP20 ...143 C4
Llanbad CF72 ...153 D3
Llanbedr Rd CF5 ...193 E7
Llanberis Cl CF38 ...135 E2
Llanbleddian St 2
CF24 ...195 B7
Llanbradach St
Cardiff CF11 ...194 F3
8 Pontypridd CF37 ...109 B1
Llanbradach Sta
...111 H1
Llanbryn Gdns CF72 153 E3
Llancaeach Jun & Inf Schs
CF46 ...83 E3
Llancaiach Ct CF46 ...83 E5
Llancaiach Rd 4
Llancaiach View CF46 83 E5
Llancaiach-fawr CF46 83 E6
Llancarfan Prim Sch
CF62 ...202 E1
Llancayo Pk CF81 ...57 F5
Llancayo St CF81 ...57 F5
Llandaf Sta CF14 ...176 F4
Llandafen Rd SA14 ...41 B5
Llandaff Campus (UWIC)
CF5 ...177 B1
Llandaff Chase CF5 176 F1
Llandaff Cl CF64 ...207 A2
Llandaff CW Prim Sch
CF5 ...194 A8
Llandaff Rd
Cardiff CF5 ...194 C6
Ebbw Vale NP23 ...7 E3
Llandaff St NP20 ...143 A3
Llandaff Way CF39 ...133 E8
Llanddewi St CF24 ...53 C7
Llanddewi St CF24 ...53 C7
Llandegfedd Way
NP4 ...63 A3
Llandegfedd Cl
Cardiff CF14 ...159 F3
Rogerstone NP10 ...142 B7
Llandegveth Cl NP44 ...90 B6
Llandeilo Rd
Cross Hands SA14 ...218 B8
Glanaman SA18 ...220 C8
Llandennis Ave CF23 178 B6
Llandennis Gn CF23 178 B6
Llandennis Rd CF23 178 A6
Llandenny Wlk NP44 ...89 E3
Llanderfel St NP44 ...89 E5
Llandetty Rd CF5 ...193 E7
Llandilo Cf CF64 ...206 C3
Llandinam Cres
CF14 ...177 B1
Llandinam Rd CF62 214 C5
Llandogo Rd CF3 ...179 F7
Llandough Hill CF64 206 D7
Llandough Hospl
CF64 ...206 C6
Llandough Prim Sch
CF64 ...206 D7
Llandough Trad Est
CF64 ...206 D8
Llandovery Cl 12
CF5 ...193 C4
Llandovery Villas
NP13 ...15 E2
Llandow Rd CF5 ...193 D5
Llandow Trad Est
CF71 ...199 D4
Llandowlais St NP44 89 E1
Llandraw Ct CF37 ...109 A1
Llandraw Woods
CF37 ...135 A8
Llandudno Rd CF3 ...179 C4
Llandybie Rd SA18 ...219 B8
Llandyfrig Cl 9
CF4 ...206 C3
Llanedeyrn Dr CF23 178 E6
Llanedeyrn Dr CF23 178 E4
Llanedeyrn High Sch
CF23 ...178 E4
Llanedeyrn Jun & Inf Sch
CF23 ...178 E3
Llanedeyrn Rd CF23 178 E3
Llanedi Rd
Llanedi SA4 ...218 D1
Pontarddulais SA4 ...19 A7
Llandy Cty Prim Sch
SA4 ...218 D2
Llanelli Campus of the
Carmarthenshire Coll of
Tech SA15 ...40 E5

Llanelli Ent Workshops
SA15 ...40 F3
Llanelli Sta SA15 ...40 D3
Llanelli Workshops
SA14 ...41 A3
Llanerch Cotts SA15 ...40 E7
Llanerch Cres SA4 ...43 B3
Llanerch Goed CF38 135 D1
Llanerch La NP11 ...59 F4
Llanerch Path NP44 ...89 B2
Llanerch Rd
Abertillery NP11 ...59 F5
Dunvant SA2 ...93 D8
Swansea SA1 ...69 B2
Llanerch Terr SA15 ...41 A3
Llanerch Vineyard
CF72 ...173 E4
Llanewrwg Way CF3 179 E7
Llanfabon Cl CF37 ...109 F4
Llanfabon Dr CF83 ...138 F7
Llanfabon Inf Sch
CF46 ...83 E3
Llanfabon Rd CF46 ...83 D2
Llanfaes SA9 ...2 F8
Llanfair Gdns SA3 ...123 A6
Llanfair Hill CF41 ...79 A2
Llanfair Prim Sch
CF71 ...189 D1
Llanfair Rd
Cardiff CF11 ...194 C7
Pontypridd CF37 ...135 B8
Tonypandy CF40 ...107 A4
Llanfedw Cl CF83 ...138 C5
Llanfoist Cres 4 NP4 17 D7
Llanfoist Prim Sch
NP4 ...17 D6
Llanfoist St CF11 ...194 F1
Llanfrechfa Grange Hospl
SA7 ...90 C2
Llanfrechfa Way
NP44 ...90 A2
Llangattock Ct NP44 90 B5
Llangattock Rd CF5 193 E7
Llangattwg Cl NP23 ...7 E4
Llangefni Comp Sch
SA10 ...49 B3
Llangeinor Terr CF32 ...167 E6
Llangeinor Terr
CF32 ...130 E5
Llangennech Cty Prim Sch
& Inf Schs SA14 ...18 D1
Llangennech Sta
SA14 ...42 C7
Llangewydd Grange
CF32 ...167 E7
Llangewydd Rd
CF31 ...168 C5
Llangewydd Rd
Bridgend CF31 ...168 C5
Laleston CF32 ...167 E6
Llangiwg Prim Sch
NP44 ...117 A6
Llangorse Cotts NP13 36 B8
Llangorse Dr NP10 ...142 A5
Llangorse Path NP44 90 A2
Llangorse Rd
Aberdare CF44 ...29 E1
Cardiff CF23 ...178 C7
Llanyravon NP44 ...90 A2
Swansea SA5 ...68 B5
Llangrannog Pl CF14 159 F1
Llangrannog Rd CF14 159 F1
Llangwm Sch SA15 ...67 F6
Llangwm Pl CF3 ...179 C4
Llangwm Way CF38 ...182 F7
Llangybi Cl CF5 ...192 F3
Llangyfelach Prim Sch
SA5 ...45 B2
Llangyfelach Rd SA5 68 C1
Llangynidr Rd
Cardiff CF5 ...193 E7
Ebbw Vale NP23 ...7 D6
Llanharan Prim Sch
CF72 ...154 A3
Llanharan Terr
CF32 ...172 A5
Llanharry Rd
Llanharry CF72 ...172 A8
Llanharry CF72 ...172 C6
Llanhilleth Ind Est
NP13 ...60 C5
Llanidloes Rd CF14 ...177 B2
Llanilltud Faerdref Prim
Sch CF38 ...135 F1
Llanilltud Fawr Prim Sch
CF61 ...210 A5
Llanina Gr CF3 ...179 E5
Llanishen Ct CF14 ...177 F8
Llanishen Fach Inf & Jun
Sch CF14 ...159 C1
Llanishen High Sch
CF14 ...159 F1
Llanishen St CF14 ...177 F2
Llanishen Sta CF14 160 A1
Llanllienwen Cl
Swansea SA6 ...45 F4
Ynysforgan SA6 ...46 A4
Llanllienwen Rd
Swansea SA6 ...45 F3
Ynysforgan SA6 ...46 A3
Llanmaes Rd CF61 ...210 A7
Llanmaes St CF11 ...194 F2
Llanmartin Jun & Inf Sch
NP18 ...145 A6
Llanmead Gdns
CF62 ...212 F2

Llanmihangel Rd
CF71 ...200 D7
Llanmihangel Rise
CF71 ...200 D8
Llanmorlais Cty Prim Sch
SA4 ...64 B1
Llanmorlais Rd CF14 177 C1
Llannant Rd SA4 ...42 F5
Llanofer Rd SA13 ...75 D3
Llanon Rd CF14 ...89 F6
Llanover Ave NP12 ...85 E4
Llanover Cl
Blaenavon NP4 ...17 E6
Newport NP20 ...117 A1
Llanover Rd
Blaenavon NP4 ...17 E6
Cardiff CF5 ...192 F3
Cwmavon NP4 ...17 F1
Pontypridd CF37 ...109 D2
Llanover St
Abercarn NP11 ...87 A3
2 Barry CF63 ...215 B6
Ynysybwl CF37 ...81 F1
Llanpumsaint Way
NP19 ...144 C1
Llanquian Castle
CF71 ...189 D1
Llanquian Cl CF71 ...188 F1
Llanquian Rd CF71 ...189 C3
Llanrhidian Cl CF14 ...43 D6
Llanrhidian Prim Sch
SA3 ...229 D2
Llanrhyd 8 CF48 ...31 B1
Llanrumney Ave CF3 179 B5
Llanrumney High Sch
CF3 ...179 A6
Llansamlet Ind Est
SA7 ...69 B7
Llansamlet Sta SA7 ...69 B8
Llansannor Dr CF10 ...63 A6
Llansawel Cl CF14 ...43 D6
Llansawel Cres SA11 71 B3
Llanstephan Rd CF3 179 F7
Llantarnam Cl NP44 89 F2
Llantarnam Hall
Rougemont Sch
NP20 ...116 F6
Llantarnam Ind Pk
NP44 ...116 F7
Llantarnam Park Way
NP44 ...117 A6
Llantarnam Rd
Cardiff CF14 ...177 D2
Cwmbran NP44 ...89 F1
Llantarnam Sch
NP44 ...117 A7
Llanthewy Cl NP44 ...90 B6
Llanthewy Rd NP20 143 A4
Llantrisant Gardens Cl
CF72 ...155 C6
Llantrisant Ho 8
CF72 ...155 D3
Llantrisant Rd
Beddau CF38 ...155 F7
Cardiff CF5 ...176 D3
Llantrisant CF72 ...155 F3
Pentyrch CF5,CF15 ...175 C4
Pontyclun CF72 ...173 B8
Tonyrefail CF39 ...133 D6
Llantrisant Rise CF5 176 F2
Llantrisant St CF24 ...194 F8
Llantrithyd Rd CF71 ...201 D7
Llantwit Gardens Cl
CF62 ...211 D5
Llantwit Major Rd
Cowbridge CF71 ...188 C1
Llandow CF71 ...199 E4
Llantwit Rd
Neath SA11 ...72 A8
Pontypridd CF37 ...135 C5
St Athan CF62 ...211 C5
Wick CF71 ...198 D5
Llanvair St
Barry CF63 ...215 A5
Cardiff CF24 ...195 B7
Llanvair Rd NP19 ...143 D6
Llanwern St
Cardiff CF5 ...193 C5
Newport NP19 ...144 A3
Llanwern St NP19 ...143 F6
Llanwonno Cl CF37 109 A2
Llanwonno Rd
Cwmaman CF44 ...53 A3
Mountain Ash CF45 ...54 D1
Pontypridd CF37 ...109 A2
Porth CF39 ...107 F5
Tylorstown CF43 ...80 C2
Llanwood Cl
Caerphilly CF83 ...138 D5
Swansea SA5 ...67 D4
Llanwyn Glas CF48 ...168 C4
Llanwynno Rd CF37 ...177 C8
Llanybther Rd CF5 ...192 F3
Llanyrafon Farm Mus
NP44 ...90 A2
Llanyrafon Prim Sch
NP44 ...90 A2
Llanyrnewydd SA4 ...64 F3
Lle Carsi SA13 ...227 C1
Lle Hyfryd CF44 ...28 D3
Llest Terr CF38 ...156 C6
Lletty Dafydd SA11 ...226 C4
Lletty Harri SA13 ...99 C2
Lletty'r Bugail CF14 ...128 C7
Llewelin St SA9 ...147 E7
Llewellyn Ave
Cardiff CF5 ...193 B6
Neath SA10 ...48 D1
Llewellyn Cl SA13 ...125 D7
Llewellyn Ct CF41 ...79 A4

Llewellyn Dr
Caerphilly CF83 ...138 A4
Pen-y-fai CF31 ...150 D1
Llewellyn Rd CF41 ...79 A4
Llewellyn Rd SA4 ...44 A2
Llewellyn St
Aberavon SA12 ...99 A1
Aberdare CF44 ...28 E4
Barry CF63 ...215 A6
Blaencwm CF42 ...50 C2
Nantymoel SA11 ...223 D1
Hendreforgan CF39 ...132 C5
Llanelli SA15 ...40 D4
Merthyr Tydfil CF47 ...30 D2
Neath SA11 ...71 E6
Pentre CF41,CF40 ...78 F5
Tonypandy CF40 ...106 E4
Treorchy CF41 ...79 A4
Tylorstown CF43 ...80 B1
Llewellyn Terr
CF70 ...106 E7
Llewellyn's Rd SA13 125 B7
Llewelyn Ave SA13 ...99 D2
Llewelyn Circ SA13 ...95 B8
Llewelyn Circ CF5 ...173 E3
Llewelyn Ct SA14 ...28 D4
Llewelyn Park Dr SA13 68 E7
Llewelyn St
Bargoed CF81 ...58 A1
Dowlais CF48 ...11 A5
Nant-y-Moel CF32 ...104 E7
Pontypridd CF37 ...109 A2
Swansea SA2 ...94 C6
Llewitna Terr SA1 ...67 B6
Lliedi Cres SA15 ...40 E6
Llewelyn High Sch
NP19 ...144 C1
Lliw Cotts SA4 ...43 D6
Lliw Valley Cl SA4 ...66 C6
Lloyd Ave Barry CF62 214 D6
Cardiff CF5 ...193 F7
Newbridge NP11 ...60 B3
Lloyd George Ave (Rhodfa
Lloyd George) CF10 195 B3
Lloyd Pl CF3 ...180 A6
Lloyd Rd SA5 ...68 C5
Lloyd St
11 Ammanford SA18 219 B7
Llanelli SA15 ...40 C5
Maesteg CF34 ...75 D2
Newport NP10 ...144 A3
Pontardawe SA8 ...23 B2
Ton Pentre CF41 ...79 B3
Lloyd's Terr CF47 ...10 F3
Lluest SA9 ...222 A5
Llundcglyn Cl CF48 ...10 C1
Llwycelyn Cl CF48 ...30 C8
Llwyd Coed CF14 ...158 F1
Llwyd y Berth CF83 ...137 E2
Llwydarth Cotts
CF34 ...102 B1
Llwydarth Rd CF34 ...102 C1
Llwydcoed Prim Sch
CF44 ...28 E6
Llwyfen CF47 ...10 D2
Llwyfen SA18 ...220 D6
Llwyn Afanc SA6 ...45 F5
Llwyn Arosfa SA2 ...94 C7
Llwyn Bedw
Mountain Ash CF45 ...54 B6
Pencoed CF35 ...170 C8
Swansea SA7 ...54 D4
Llwyn Berry CF48 ...10 C1
Llwyn Brwydrau SA7 ...70 A6
Llwyn Bryn Melyn
CF15 ...176 A6
Llwyn Celyn
Capel Hendre SA18 ...218 D6
Cardiff CF14 ...89 D1
Ebbw Vale NP23 ...14 B8
Swansea SA5 ...67 D4
Llwyn Cl SA15 ...40 F5
Llwyn Coed NP12 ...85 D6
Llwyn Deri Cl NP10 ...141 E2
Llwyn Derw
Pontardawe SA8 ...23 E4
Swansea SA5 ...67 D4
Llwyn Du CF15 ...176 A6
Llwyn Eithin
Caerphilly CF83 ...138 D5
Swansea SA7 ...54 D4
Llwyn Glas CF48 ...168 C4
Llwyn Grug CF14 ...177 C8
Llwyn Gwern CF35 ...170 C8
Llwyn Gwyn CF72 ...172 B5
Llwyn Helig SA13 ...148 E1
Llwyn Helyg
Swansea SA5 ...67 D5
Tredegar NP22 ...6 C2
Llwyn Mallt CF15 ...176 D8
Llwyn Mawr Cl SA2 ...94 B8
Llwyn Mawr Rd SA2 ...94 B8
Llwyn On
North Cornelly CF33 ...166 A8
Risca NP11 ...115 A2

Llwyn Rd SA18 ...220 D5
Llwyn Rhedyn SA2 ...94 B8
Llwyn Rhosyn CF14 ...177 C8
Llwyn y Bioden SA6 ...45 F5
Llwyn y Gog
Cwmrhydyceirw SA6 ...46 A5
Swansea SA6 ...45 F5
Llwyn y Golomen SA6 46 A5
Llwyn y Graig SA4 ...43 F1
Llwyn y Groes CF31 ...168 B4
Llwyn y Pia Rd CF14 ...160 B3
Llwyn Ynys SA14 ...41 C4
Llwyn Yr Eos SA14 ...41 B6
Llwyn Yr Hebog SA6 ...46 A5
Llwyn Yr Iar SA6 ...46 A5
Llwyn-Bach Terr
NP12 ...34 C2
Llwyn-Crwn Rd SA7 ...69 D7
Llwyn-fan SA14 ...18 B2
Llwyn-Nant SA18 ...220 D4
Llwyn-On Cl CF33 ...137 F4
Llwyn-on Cres NP12 ...59 B1
Llwyn-On La NP12 ...59 B1
Llwyn-On Rd
Abertillery NP13 ...36 C3
Blackwood NP12 ...59 B1
Llwyn-On St CF33 ...137 F4
Llwyn-y-Bryn
Ammanford SA18 ...219 B8
Neath SA10 ...70 C6
Llwyn-y-Gelynen
CF48 ...30 C8
Llwyn-y-Grant Pl
CF23 ...178 D2
Llwyn-y-Grant Rd
CF23 ...178 D2
Llwyn-y-Grant Terr
CF23 ...178 D2
Llwyn-y-Mor SA3 ...122 E4
Llwyn-Yr-Eos
Abercanaid CF48 ...30 F4
Swansea SA6 ...45 E2
Llwynbrain Terr
CF72 ...154 A3
Llwyncarw Cl SA4 ...45 F5
Llwyncelyn
Bettws CF32 ...129 C3
Llanelli SA15 ...40 E4
Llwyncelyn Ave SA4 ...19 D4
Llwyncelyn Cl CF39 ...108 A3
Llwyncelyn Ind Est
CF39 ...108 A3
Llwyncelyn Parc
CF39 ...108 A3
Llwyncelyn Rd SA14 ...41 A5
Llwyncrwn Rd CF38 ...155 F6
Llwyncyn Cty Prim Sch
CF38 ...155 F6
Llwyncyfarthwch
SA15 ...41 A5
Llwynderi CF44 ...28 B6
Llwynderi Newport NP20 ...143 A4
Llwynderw
Gorseinon SA4 ...43 B1
Porthcawl CF36 ...182 F7
Three Crosses SA4 ...65 E1
Llwynderw Ave CF33 151 C5
Llwynderw Dr SA3 ...94 B1
Llwynderw Dr SA3 ...123 B8
Llwynderw Inf Sch
CF34 ...102 C3
Llwynderw Rd CF37 ...177 D3
Llwynderw Unit Hospl
SA6 ...45 E2
Llwynfedw Gdns
CF14 ...177 D5
Llwynfedw Rd CF14 ...177 D5
Llwynderw Rd CF72 ...173 B7
Llwynhendy Jun Sch
SA14 ...41 D5
Llwynhendy Rd SA14 ...41 D4
Llwynmadoc St CF37 109 B1
Llwynon Cl Clydach SA6 ...22 E1
Llwynon Clydach SA6 ...22 E1
Crynant SA10 ...226 A7
Risca NP11 ...115 A2
Llwynpennau Cotts
CF72 ...174 C6
Llwynrhidian Terr 3
SA14 ...40 F4
Llwynpia Hospl CF40 79 F1
Llwynpia Rd CF40 ...106 E7
Llwynpia Sta CF40 ...106 E8
Llwynpia Terr CF40 106 E8
Llygad-Yr-Haul
Glynneath SA11 ...223 B1
Neath SA10 ...48 D2
Llyn Berwyn Cl NP10 142 B6
Llyn Cau CF23 ...178 E7
Llyn Celyn Cl NP10 ...142 B7
Llyn Cl CF23 ...178 E6
Llyn Cwm CF5 ...79 F6
Llyn Cwm Llwydrew
NP13 ...36 C2

Llyn Tircoed SA4 .....44 C6
Llynfa Rd SA4 ....65 A4
Llynfi Hospl CF34 ...101 F1
Llynfi La
　Bridgend CF31 ......168 F4
　Maesteg CF34 ......102 A3
Llynfi Rd CF34 ......102 A3
Llynfi St
　1 Bridgend CF31 ...168 F4
　Tondu CF32 ....150 C5
Llynfi View CF34 ....102 B8
Llys Aaron SA4 ....19 C4
Llys Alys SA15 ....40 E5
Llys Andrew SA10 .....70 F6
Llys Aneirin SA4 .....44 C6
Llys Baldwin SA4 .....66 B6
Llys Bartlett SA11 ...71 E7
Llys Bathania SA11 ..205 D4
Llys Bethel SA14 .....41 C5
Llys Briallen CF31 ..169 D6
Llys Bryn Felin CF39 133 C5
Llys Brynteg SA4 .....43 B3
Llys Cambria CF83 ..137 F8
Llys Caradog
　Creigiau CF15 ......174 D7
　Llanelli SA14 ....41 D5
Llys Castell SA13 ...148 A6
Llys Catwg
　Glynneath SA11 ....227 C8
　Talbot Green CF72 ..155 D2
Llys Celyn CF38 .....136 A1
Llys Cennech SA14 ...41 C3
Llys Cilsaig SA14 ....41 B8
Llys Coed
　Bridgend CF31 ......168 F2
　Pontypridd CF37 ...109 D6
Llys Coed Derw
　CF38 ....156 D8
Llys Coleg **4** CF14 .177 B3
Llys Corrwg CF37 ....36 C3
Llys Cynffig CF33 ...148 B2
Llys Cynon CF44 .....227 F7
Llys Deri CF72 ......172 B5
Llys Derwen
　Llantrisant CF72 ...155 D2
　Pontypridd CF37 ...109 D6
Llys Dewi CF61 .....209 F7
Llys Dewi Dinefwr
　CF15 ....174 E7
Llys Dewi Sant
　Gorseinon SA4 .....43 C2
　3 Swansea SA1 .....95 D6
Llys Dulais SA10 ....226 A7
Llys Dur SA4 ....46 A2
Llys Dwfnant SA11 ..226 C4
Llys Dwrgi SA7 .....209 F8
Llys Dyfodwg
　Creigiau CF15 ......174 D7
　Talbot Green CF72 ..155 C2
Llys Dyfrig CF15 ....174 D7
Llys Ebwy NP23 ......14 D7
Llys Eglwys CF33 ...168 C3
Llys Eithin SA14 ....218 C8
Llys Elba SA4 ....66 B6
Llys Faen CF31 ......168 F5
Llys Felin SA10 ......49 C4
Llys Felin Newydd
　SA7 ....95 A8
Llys Fran SA11 ....40 E7
Llys Fredrick Jones
　SA9 ....2 C7
Llys Garth CF38 ....135 D1
Llys Ger y Llan SA4 ..19 D3
Llys Glan y Mor **2**
　SA15 ....180 C7
Llys Glanrafon SA8 ..23 E4
Llys Glanrhondda
　CF41 ....77 F5
Llys Glowr CF37 .....82 A1
Llys Groeswen SA13 ..156 D8
Llys Gwalia SA11 ....43 D2
Llys Gwenci SA7 .....70 D8
Llys Gwent CF63 ....215 C8
Llys Gwernen
　Cwmrhydyceirw SA6 ..46 A2
　Swansea SA6 ......45 F2
Llys Gwyn
　Bridgend CF31 ......168 F6
　Maesteg CF34 ......102 A2
Llys Gwynfaen SA4 ...42 A8
Llys Gwynfryn SA10 ..48 C5
Llys Gwynno CF15 ..174 B4
Llys Gwyrdd NP44 ...116 A7
Llys Hafn CF15 ......158 A3
Llys Hebog SA7 ......79 A3
Llys Hebron CF41 ....79 A3
Llys Iris SA10 ....98 C8
Llys Jernegan **2** SA1 .95 E6
Llys John Davies **5**
　SA1 ....95 D8
Llys Llywelyn CF38 ..156 D8
Llys Mabon NP22 ....12 D5
Llys Maelwg CF72 ...155 C2
Llys Maendy CF41 ...79 A3
Llys Nant Fer SA18 ..220 D7
Llys Nant Glas CF45 ..82 A7
Llys Nant Pandy
　CF83 ....138 A4
Llys Nazereth CF41 ..78 F5
Llys Nedd SA10 ......48 D2
Llys Onnen NP23 ....14 B8
Llys Pen Chwan SA14 ..41 F5
Llys Pendderi SA14 ..41 F5
Llys Penpant SA4 ....45 C2

Llys Pentre SA5 ......68 D4
Llys Pum Cyfair
　CF14 ....177 C2
Llys Sant Teilo SA5 ..41 D8
Llys Siloh CF41 ......78 F5
Llys Soar CF42 ......50 E2
Llys Steffan CF61 ...209 F7
Llys Tal-y-Bont Rd
　CF14 ....177 E1
Llys Teg CF31 ......168 B3
Llys Teilo
　Creigiau CF15 ......174 E6
　Llantwit Major CF61 ..209 F7
　Talbot Green CF72 ..155 C1
Llys Trenbdaant CF37 109 A7
Llys Tripp CF15 .....158 A3
Llys Tudful CF15 ....174 E7
Llys Ty Gwyn **6**
　CF7 ....109 E2
Llys Tylcha Fawr
　CF39 ....155 A3
Llys Tynewydd CF35 .169 C7
Llys Warner SA15 ....40 E7
Llys Wenallt SA11 ...49 E2
Llys Wern SA10 ......48 C2
Llys y Brenin SA4 ...66 B8
Llys y Coed
　Barry CF62 ....214 C4
　Ystrad Mynach CF82 .111 E7
Llys y Drindod SA15 .40 D3
Llys y Felin SA14 ....41 B8
Llys y Fran CF38 ....156 E8
Llys y Gof SA15 .....40 C4
Llys y Morwr SA15 ..40 D4
Llys Yr Arddd
　Morriston SA6 .....46 A2
　Swansea SA6 ......45 F2
Llys Yr Efail
　Blaina NP13 ....15 D5
　Tonyrefail CF39 ....133 C5
Llys Yr Onnen SA14 ..41 A8
Llys Yr Orsaf **7** SA15 40 C4
Llys Yr Ysgol SA18 ..23 B8
Llys-Coed SA7 ......47 B1
Llys-faen (Lisvane &
　Thornhill Sta) CF14 159 F1
Llys-Gwyn Terr SA4 ..19 C5
Llys-Le-Breos SA3 ...93 F1
Llys-Teg SA2 ....93 D8
Llys-Uchaf SA7 ......70 B8
Llys-y-Coed SA4 .....82 D1
Llys-y-Bryn SA7 .....70 B8
Llys-y-Celyn CF83 ..138 C5
Llys-y-Coed SA10 ....71 D8
Llys-y-Felin SA14 ....41 A8
Llys-y-Fedwen CF83 138 C4
Llys-y-Felin SA5 .....68 C3
Llys-y-Fran CF31 ...168 B6
Llys-y-Nant SA11 ....47 A1
Llys-yr-Eglwys **10**
　CF64 ....207 B5

Lon Brynneuadd
　SA18 ....220 D7
Lon Brynteg SA10 ....48 C1
Lon Cadog SA2 ......94 E7
Lon Cae Banc SA2 ...94 C7
Lon Camlad SA6 .....94 E7
Lon Caron SA2 ......94 E7
Lon Carreg Bica SA7 70 B8
Lon Cae Cwm SA2 ...94 E7
Lon Cedwyn SA2 ....94 E7
Lon Cefn Mably
　CF62 ....212 F1
Lon Ceiriog SA14 ....41 D5
Lon Claerwen SA6 ...68 B8
Lon Coed Bran SA2 ..94 E8
Lon Coed Parc SA2 ..94 E8
Lon Cothi SA2 ......67 C1
Lon Cwmgwyn SA2 ..94 D8
Lon Cwrt Ynyston
　CF11 ....194 C2
Lon Cynfor SA2 ......94 D7
Lon Cynlais SA2 .....94 D7
Lon Dan-y-Coed SA2 94 E8
Lon Derw SA2 ....94 D8
Lon Draenen SA2 ....94 C7
Lon Draenog SA6 ....45 C5
Lon Einon SA4 ....43 F2
Lon Eithrym SA6 .....46 D8
Lon Elai CF72 ......173 B8
Lon Enfys SA7 ....69 D6
Lon Fach
　Caerphilly CF83 ....137 E5
　Cardiff CF14 ......177 B7
Lon Fawr CF14 ......137 F2
Lon Fferm Felin
　CF62 ....194 A2
Lon Gaer SA4 ....43 F2
Lon Ganol CF14 ....177 B7
Lon Gelliddeg NP11 ..59 C4
Lon Ger-y-Coed
　Ammanford SA18 ...219 D7
　Swansea SA2 ......94 E8
Lon Glynfelin SA11 ..41 A7
Lon Gwendraeth SA6 68 B8
Lon Gwesyn SA7 ....47 A1
Lon Gwynfryn SA2 ..94 D7
Lon Hafren
　Caerphilly CF83 ....137 F1
　Swansea SA6 ......68 B8
Lon Heddwch
　Craig-Cefn-Parc SA6 ..22 B2
　Swansea SA7 ......69 E6
Lon Helyg NP44 .....94 E8
Lon Helygen CF37 ..109 D6
Lon Heulog
　Brynmenyn CF32 ..150 D6
　Hawthorn CF37 ....136 A4
Lon Hir SA8 ....23 F4
Lon Illtyd SA2 ......94 E7
Lon Iorwg SA2 ......94 C7
Lon Irfon SA2 ....67 E1
Lon Isa CF14 ....177 B7
Lon Isaf CF83 ......137 F2
Lon Ithon SA2 ....68 E8
Lon Killan SA2 ......93 C8
Lon Lilys SA14 ......28 D6
Lon Llwyd SA18 ....220 B8
Lon Llys Havard
　SA18 ....219 C6
Lon Madoc CF14 ...177 C4
Lon Mafon SA2 .....94 D8
Lon Masarn SA2 ....94 C8
Lon Mefus SA2 ......94 E8
Lon Menai SA1 ......47 A1
Lon Nant NP44 ......89 F5
Lon Nedd SA6 ......68 B8
Lon Owen SA7 ......47 A1
Lon Olchfa SA2 .....94 A6
Lon Owain CF5 .....193 B3
Lon Pen-y-Coed SA2 67 E1
Lon Penfro SA6 .....46 A4
Lon Penllyn CF14 ...177 A6
Lon Pennant NP22 ..58 E1
Lon Pinwydden
　CF71 ....209 F8
Lon Robin Goch
　SA2 ....94 E8
Lon Sawdde SA6 ....68 A8
Lon Tanyrallt SA8 ...23 E3
Lon Teify SA2 ....67 E1
Lon Tir-y-Dail SA18 219 B7
Lon Towy SA2 ....67 E1
Lon Ty'n-y-Cae
　CF14 ....177 C6
Lon Tyr Haul SA7 ...69 E6
Lon Ucha CF14 .....177 B7
Lon Uchaf CF83 ....137 F2
Lon y Bedydd **12**
　SA18 ....219 B7
Lon y Dderwen SA15 40 E8
Lon y Fran CF83 ....137 E3
Lon y Goch CF15 ...175 C6
Lon y Maes SA14 ....41 A6
Lon y Nant CF14 ...177 C7
Lon y Tresglen CF83 137 A3
Lon yr Odyn CF83 ..138 C4
Lon Yr Ysgol SA2 ...94 D7
Lon-Od-Nant CF61 ..210 A5
Lon-Werdd CF5 .....193 A5
Lon-y-Barri CF83 ...137 D3
Lon-y-Bryn SA11 ...223 D1
Lon-y-Bugail CF31 ..168 B6
Lon-y-Byrnnau CF44 28 C3
Lon-y-Cariadon
　CF33 ....148 A7
Lon-y-Castell CF15 ..193 C3
Lon-y-Celyn
　Cardiff CF14 ......176 F6
　Nelson CF46 ....83 D4

Lon-y-Coed
　Bridgend CF31 .....168 B6
　Pontardawe SA8 ...23 A5
Lon-y-Dail CF14 ....177 B7
Lon-y-Delerwen
　Cardiff CF14 ......177 B7
　Nelson CF46 ....83 D4
Lon-y-Deri
　Caerphilly CF83 ....137 F2
Lon-y-Felin
　Garnswllt SA18 ...219 B5
　Mountain Ash CF45 ..11 D5
Lon-y-Ffin CF5 .....193 A5
Lon-y-Garwa CF83 ..137 E3
Lon-y-Gors CF83 ....137 E2
Lon-y-Groes CF14 ..177 D3
Lon-y-Gruglas SA18 219 A6
Lon-y-Llwyn CF46 ...83 D4
Lon-y-Llyn CF83 ....137 F2
Lon-y-Mynydd CF17 ..137 F2
Lon-y-Odraenen
　CF83 ....137 F2
Lon-y-Parc
　Cardiff CF14 ......177 B5
　Glynneath SA11 ...223 C1
　Maesteg CF34 ......75 A2
Lon-y-Rhedyn CF83 137 F2
Lon-y-Rhyd CF14 ...177 B7
Lon-y-Twyn CF83 ...138 B2
Lon-y-Waun CF83 ..137 E2
Lon-y-Wern
　Caerphilly CF83 ....137 F2
　Pontardawe SA8 ...23 A5
Lon-y-Winci CF14 ..177 B8
Lon-yr-Afon CF83 ..112 A8
Lon-yr-Awel CF72 ..173 C8
Lon-yr-Efail CF5 ...193 B3
Lon-yr-Eglwys CF32 185 C2
Lon-Yr-Ysgol
　Llanelli SA14 ......41 A7
　Pontardawe SA8 ...24 B3
Lon-Ysgubor CF14 ..158 B1
Loncae Porth CF14 ..159 C1
Londeg SA8 ....23 D6
London CF83 ....13 E6
London Rd SA11 .....71 E7
London Row SA12 ...94 D9
London St
　Mountain Ash CF45 ..54 D3
　Newport NP19 ....143 E6
London Terr SA12 ..108 D8
Lone Rd SA6 ....22 D1
Long Acre
　Bishopston SA3 ...122 B6
　Cwmbran NP44 ....89 B1
　North Cornelly CF33 165 E7
Long Acre Ct
　Bishopston SA3 ...122 B6
　Porthcawl CF36 ...165 D2
Long Acre Dr CF36 ..165 D1
Long Cairn SA3 .....120 D8
Long Hollow **1** NP44 ..89 E4
Long House Barn Est
　NP4 ....39 E7
Long House Cl CF14 160 A2
Long Meadow Ct
　NP19 ....144 C3
Long Meadow Dr
　CF62 ....215 A7
Long Oaks Ave SA2 ..94 E6
Long Oaks Ct SA2 ...94 E7
Long Oaks Mews SA2 94 E7
Long Ridge SA1 .....68 C1
Long Row
　Ferndale CF43 ......79 F8
　Llanelli SA15 ......40 E6
　New Tredegar NP24 ..33 F2
　Pontypridd CF37 ...136 B8
Long Shepherds Dr
　SA3 ....222 A6
Long St SA9 ....222 D4
Long View Rd
　Swansea SA6 ....45 D1
　Swansea SA6 ......68 D8
Long Vue Rd SA12 ...98 C2
Longacre Ct
　Barry CF63 ....215 D8
Longbridge NP18 ..117 F6
Longcross St CF24 ..195 C5
Longditch Rd NP19 144 E1
Longfellow Dr CF31 168 D6
Longfellow Gdns
　CF83 ....139 D7
Longfield CF44 .....27 D7
Longford Cres SA1 ..96 A7
Longford La SA10 ..48 A1
Longford Rd
　Neath SA10 ....48 B2
　Neath Abbey SA10 ..71 B8
Longhouse Gr NP44 115 F8
Longlands CF123 ...148 A7
Longleat Cl CF14 ...160 B2
Longmeadow Dr
　CF64 ....206 B2
Longmede Pk CF44 224 B1
Longreach Cl CF5 ..154 D4
Longships Rd CF10 195 F1
Longspears Ave
　CF14 ....177 E3
Longtown Gr NP10 163 E5
Longueil Cl CF10 ..195 C3
Longwood Dr CF14 176 C7
Lonlas Ave SA10 ....70 D2
Lonlas Bsns Pk SA10 70 D2
Lonlas Village Workshops
　SA10 ....70 D2

Lonsdale Rd CF23 ..178 E3
Lord Pontypridd Ho **5**
　CF5 ....194 B7
Lord St Aberdare CF44 53 C8
　8 Newport NP19 143 D6
　Penarth CF64 .....207 B1
Lorraine Cl SA12 ....98 D1
Lothian Cres CF3 ..178 D3
Loudoun Sq CF10 ..195 B3
Lougher Cl CF5 ......193 E7
Lougher Gdns CF36 182 E6
Lougher Pl
　North Cornelly CF33 165 E7
　St Athan CF62 .....211 C4
Loughor Comn SA4 ..43 B2
Loughor Rd SA4 .....66 B8
Loughor Row CF46 165 F1
Louisa Pl CF10 .....195 B2
Louise Cl SA12 .....226 C4
Louise Ct **1** CF14 176 F3
Louvain Terr NP23 ..14 E8
Lovage Cl CF23 ....178 E8
Love La Cardiff CF10 195 B5
　Llanblethian CF71 ..188 E1
Loveluck Ct CF61 ..209 F6
Low Row CF45 ......54 C5
Lowdon Terr CF62 ..214 E5
Lower Acre CF5 ....193 B3
Lower Adare St
　CF32 ....103 E4
Lower Alma Pl CF41 79 A4
Lower Alma Terr
　CF37 ....135 D8
Lower Bailey St
　1 Brynmawr NP23 ..8 C4
　Wattstown CF39 ...107 E8
Lower Bridge St Nm **6** 62 C6
Lower Brynhyfryd Terr
　CF83 ....110 F2
Lower Castle St NP13 36 B4
Lower Cathedral Rd
　CF11 ....194 F5
Lower Church St
　CF32 ....103 F3
Lower Coburn St
　SA18 ....220 D6
Lower Coronation St
　NP22 ....13 E6
Lower Court Terr
　NP13 ....36 B4
Lower Cross Rd SA15 40 F5
Lower Cross St
　Hirwaun CF44 ......27 D8
　New Tredegar NP24 ..33 D3
Lower Dell The **1**
　SA11 ....40 C7
Lower Dock St NP20 143 D4
Lower Dunraven St
　CF40 ....106 F5
Lower Edward St **13**
　CF37 ....10 D2
Lower Farm CF24 ..178 E8
Lower Forest Level
　CF45 ....54 E2
Lower Glantorvaen Terr
　NP4 ....17 B6
Lower Glyn-gwyn St
　CF83 ....139 A6
Lower Guthrie St
　CF63 ....225 A8
Lower Gwastad Terr
　CF63 ....36 B8
Lower Harper's Rd
　NP4 ....37 F5
Lower Hill St **1** NP4 17 C6
Lower Holmes St
　CF63 ....215 C6
Lower James St NP12 58 F4
Lower Lancaster St
　CF44 ....224 C1
Lower Leigh Rd NP4 38 B1
Lower Llansantffraid Rd
　CF32 ....150 D4
Lower Morel St
　CF63 ....225 A8
Lower Sq NP23 ......13 E6
Lower St NP23 ......13 E6
Lower Station Rd **4**
　SA18 ....220 B8
Lower Station St **2**
　CF44 ....53 D7
Lower Stoney Rd NP4 37 F5
Lower Ten Hos NP13 15 E6
Lower Taff View
　CF37 ....109 E2
Lower Row
　Dowlais CF48 ......11 B5
　Rhymney NP22 ......12 F3
Lower Royal La NP4 36 A6
Lower Royal Lane Terr
　NP13 ....36 A6
Lower Salisbury St
　CF63 ....13 C4
Lower Sq NP23 ......13 E6

Lower Ty-Gwyn Rd
　Abersychan NP4 ....37 E6
　Abersychan NP4 ....37 E2
Lower Union St CF48 11 E4
Lower Vaynor Rd
　CF48 ....10 C5
Lower Waun St NP4 17 C4
Lower Wern Rd SA9 ..2 B6
Lower West End **1**
　SA13 ....125 C6
Lower Woodland St **1**
　NP4 ....17 D4
Lower Wyndham Terr
　NP11 ....115 B3
Lowerdale Dr CF72 ..155 E2
Lowfield Dr CF14 ...159 F2
Lowland CF38 ......136 A3
Lowlands Cres NP44 89 E6
Lowlands Ct NP44 ..89 E6
Lowlands Rd NP44 ..89 E6
Lowndes Cl NP10 ...162 F8
Lowther Rd CF24 ...195 B7
Lucania Bldgs **1**
　SA13 ....125 C4
Lucas Cl CF63 ......215 C6
Lucas Rd SA7 ....47 A5
Lucas St Cardiff CF24 178 A3
Lucerne Dr CF14 ...159 D3
Lucknow St CF11 ..194 E3
Lucy Rd SA10 ....70 D7
Ludlow Cl
　Cardiff CF11 ......195 A2
　Llanyravon NP44 ...90 B1
Ludlow La CF44 ....207 B4
Ludlow St
　Caerphilly CF83 ...138 A2
　Cardiff CF11 ......194 F2
Lulworth Rd NP18 ..118 C1
Lundy Cl Cardiff CF14 177 E8
　Porthcawl CF36 ...165 E1
Lundy Dr
　Mumbles SA3 .....122 F7
　Newport NP19 ....143 F7
Lunnon Cl SA3 .....200 C8
Lupin Cl
　Merthyr Tydfil CF47 ..10 B5
　Merthyr Tydfil CF47 ..10 C5
　Port Talbot SA12 ...98 C3
Luther La CF47 .....10 F1
Luther St CF47 .....10 F4
Luton Ho **5** CF24 ..195 C6
Luton St CF42 ......78 D6
Luton Terr **4** SA15 40 C7
Lydbrook Cl **3** SA1 68 C2
Lydford Ave SA1 ....95 E8
Lydford Cl CF14 ....177 B6
Lydstep Cres CF14 ..177 B2
Lydstep Flats CF14 ..177 B2
Lydstep Rd CF62 ...214 F2
Lydwood Cl CF83 ..140 A2
Lyle St CF45 ....54 C3
Lyn Pac Trad Est
　NP44 ....89 E5
Lynch Blosse CF15 178 E6
Lyncroft NP44 ....89 B3
Lyncroft Cl CF23 ...179 D8
Lynden SA9 ....1 D1
Lyndhurst Ave NP20 143 A2
Lyndhurst St
　Cardiff CF11 ......194 D5
　Mountain Ash CF45 ..54 D4
Lyndon Way NP10 ..142 B4
Lyne Rd
　Newport NP20 ....143 C2
　Risca NP11 ....115 A1
Lynmouth Cres CF3 179 A3
Lynmouth Dr CF64 216 A4
Lynn Davies Ave
　CF32 ....130 E5
Lynn St SA5 ....68 A2
Lynsdale Rd SA5 ....68 C4
Lynton Cl Cardiff CF3 179 B4
　Sully CF64 ....216 B5
Lynton Cl SA3 ......122 C6
Lynton Pl CF3 ......179 B4
Lynton Terr CF3 ...179 A4
Lynwood Ct
　10 Cardiff CF24 ...195 C7
　Radyr CF15 ....176 B5
Lyon Cl CF11 ....194 D1
Lyon's Pl SA11 .....226 E5
Lyric Ct SA8 ....23 E4
Lyric Way CF14 ....159 E2
Lysander Ct CF24 ..196 A7
Lystep Ho NP44 .....89 D2
Lytham Gr **1** CF3 ..180 A8

M

Maberly Cl CF14 ...178 A7
Mabon Cl SA4 ......42 C3
Macaulay Ave CF3 179 B7
Macaulay Gdns
　NP20 ....142 E1
Macdonald Ave
　CF35 ....170 D7
Macdonald Cl CF5 ..193 A4
Macdonald Pl CF5 ..193 A4
Macdonald Rd CF5 ..193 A4
Mace La CF42 ....78 B8
Macgregor Row
　CF34 ....102 A4
Machen Cl
　Cardiff CF3 ....180 A7
　Risca NP11 ....115 B1
Machen Pl CF11 ...194 E5

Machen Prim Sch CF83 ... 139 F7
Machen St
Cardiff CF11 ... 194 E3
3 Penarth CF64 ... 206 F4
Risca NP11 ... 114 F2
Machine Mdw 3 NP4 38 A1
Machynys Rd
Llanelli SA15 ... 229 E8
Llanelli SA15 ... 40 E1
Mackintosh Pl CF24 . 178 B1
Mackintosh Rd CF37 109 D1
Mackintosh St CF48 .. 55 C5
Mackintosh Terr CF46 ... 83 D6
Mackworth Ct 6 SA1 95 D7
Mackworth Dr SA11 .. 72 C5
Mackworth Rd CF36 183 A7
Mackworth St CF31 . 168 F5
Mackworth Terr SA1 .. 95 E7
Maddox St CF40 ... 106 D6
Madeline St
Pentre CF41 ... 78 F5
Tylorstown CF40 ... 80 B1
Madoc Cl
Bridgend CF31 ... 169 A5
Dinas Powys CF64 .. 206 C3
Madoc Pl SA1 ... 95 C6
Madoc Rd CF24 ... 195 F6
Madoc St
Pontypridd CF37 ... 135 C8
Swansea SA1 ... 95 C6
Madog Cl CF43 ... 80 B4
Maelfa CF23 ... 178 E4
Maelgwyn Terr CF44 .. 28 F2
Maelog Cl CF72 ... 173 B8
Maelog Pl CF14 ... 177 E1
Maelog Rd CF14 ... 177 C4
Maen Dy CF48 ... 10 A2
Maen Ganol
Trelewis CF46 ... 56 D1
Trelewis CF46 ... 83 D8
Maen Gilfach
Trelewis CF46 ... 56 D1
Trelewis CF46 ... 83 D8
Maen Moel NP23 ... 14 D6
Maendy Pl NP44 ... 89 C6
Maendy Prim Sch NP44 ... 89 E4
Maendy Rd CF71 ... 189 B4
Maendy Sq NP44 ... 89 C5
Maendy Way NP44 ... 89 C5
Maendy Wood Rise NP44 ... 89 C5
Maengwyn SA8 ... 221 B1
Maerdy Cl NP20 ... 142 F1
Maerdy Ct CF43 ... 52 A1
Maerdy Heol CF83 .. 138 D4
Maerdy Inf Sch CF43 . 52 A1
Maerdy Jun Sch CF43 79 B8
Maerdy La CF14 ... 160 C2
Maerdy Rd
Aberdare CF44 ... 52 E7
Ammanford SA18 ... 219 B5
Maerdy CF43 ... 52 B1
Maerdy Rd Flats CF43 52 B1
Maerdy Road Ind Est CF43 ... 79 D8
Maerdy View NP22 ... 13 A1
Maerdypark CF35 ... 170 D6
Maes Bedw CF39 ... 107 E2
Maes Briallu
Caerphilly CF83 ... 138 D4
Swansea SA7 ... 69 F7
Maes Bryn CF31 ... 168 B6
Maes Brynna CF44 ... 28 C4
Maes Cadwgan CF15 174 E7
Maes Collen
Cwmrhydyceirw SA6 .. 46 A3
Swansea SA6 ... 45 F3
Maes Dafydd SA4 ... 66 B8
Maes Ganol CF37 ... 136 C4
Maes Gareth Edwards SA18 ... 220 D7
Maes Glas
Barry CF62 ... 214 C5
Caerphilly CF83 ... 138 C2
Cardiff CF14 ... 177 B4
Cefn Cribwr CF32 ... 149 B2
Ebbw Vale NP23 ... 7 B4
Gorseinon SA4 ... 43 B1
Pontypridd CF37 ... 109 D6
Tondu CF32 ... 150 E5
Tredegar NP22 ... 13 E8
Maes Golau SA15 ... 40 F8
Maes Gwair CF31 ... 168 B6
Maes Gwyn CF83 ... 138 B2
Maes Hir CF83 ... 137 F5
Maes Hyfryd CF44 ... 53 F7
Maes Illtuds CF61 .. 210 A7
Maes Lan CF33 ... 148 D2
Maes Llewelyn SA18 219 F8
Maes Lliedi SA15 ... 40 F8
Maes Lloi CF71 ... 189 B3
Maes Llwynonn SA10 . 48 E1
Maes Maddock SA4 .. 43 B1
Maes Melyn St 2 SA13 ... 125 D5
Maes Pwll SA11 ... 226 B3
Maes Rhedyn SA12 ... 98 D6
Maes Rhosyn SA8 ... 24 B3
Maes Road (Heol Maes) SA14 ... 42 C8
Maes Sant Teilo SA5 .. 45 B2
Maes St SA1 ... 95 F7
Maes Talcen CF31 .. 169 B5
Maes Teg SA4 ... 19 D5
Maes Trane CF38 ... 156 A6
Maes Triasnt CF72 .. 155 C2
Maes Ty Gwyn SA14 .. 18 C1
Maes Ty-canol SA12 .. 98 E6
Maes Uchaf CF37 ... 136 C4
Maes Watford CF83 . 158 F8
Maes y Briallu CF15 . 176 A7
Maes y Celyn SA4 ... 65 D1
Maes y Coed NP12 ... 85 D6
Maes y Cornel SA8 ... 24 A3
Maes y Crofft CF15 .. 176 A7
Maes y Deri SA18 .. 220 E8
Maes y Draenog CF15 ... 158 D2
Maes y Drudwen CF83 ... 137 E2
Maes y Fedwen
Bridgend CF31 ... 168 C2
Swansea SA6 ... 45 F3
Maes y Felin SA5 ... 67 D5
Maes y Fron 1 SA18 220 B8
Maes y Gad CF5 ... 192 F7
Maes y Gollen SA2 ... 94 B6
Maes y Gors SA15 ... 40 D4
Maes y Gruffydd Rd SA2 ... 94 C8
Maes y Grug
Bridgend CF31 ... 168 C3
Church Village CF38 . 135 E1
Maes y Gwernen Cl SA6 ... 45 E4
Maes y Gwernen Dr SA6 ... 45 E4
Maes y Hedydd CF23 160 F2
Maes y Meillion SA7 .. 69 F7
Maes y Mynnydd SA10 ... 48 A1
Maes y Odyn CF15 .. 176 A7
Maes y Pandy CF83 . 138 C7
Maes y Parc
Cardiff CF14 ... 177 B6
Swansea SA5 ... 67 D5
Maes y Rhedyn CF43 . 79 B8
Maes y Siglen CF83 . 137 E3
Maes y Wennol CF23 160 F2
Maes Yr Annedd CF5 ... 194 B7
Maes yr Awel
Radyr CF15 ... 176 B6
Rhydyfelin CF37 ... 136 C4
Swansea SA7 ... 69 F7
Maes Yr Haf
Cardiff CF14 ... 176 F8
Llwydcoed CF44 ... 28 F6
Maes Yr Hafod SA10 .. 48 E1
Maes Yr Haul Cotts CF72 ... 155 E2
Maes yr Odyn CF15 . 176 A7
Maes yr Orchis CF15 176 A7
Maes-Ar-Ddafen Rd SA14 ... 41 C4
Maes-Cefn-Mabley CF72 ... 155 D4
Maes-Deri SA1 ... 69 D5
Maes-Gwyn SA12 ... 73 B5
Maes-Gwyn St SA12 124 E8
Maes-Lan SA7 ... 69 F6
Maes-Mawr Rd
Crynant SA10 ... 226 A7
Crynant SA10 ... 25 F6
Maes-rhydwen Flats 1 CF44 ... 28 E4
Maes-y-Bedw CF46 .. 55 F8
Maes-y-berllan SA18 ... 219 C6
Maes-y-Bettws SA12 ... 100 A8
Maes-y-Bryn
Colwinston CF71 ... 187 A4
Radyr CF15 ... 176 B7
Swansea SA6 ... 45 F2
Tonyrefail CF39 ... 133 C6
Maes-y-Bryn Rd CF14,CF23 ... 161 B4
Maes-y-Byrn Prim Sch CF38 ... 156 D7
Maes-y-Celyn NP4 ... 62 D4
Maes-y-Cnyw Terr NP13 ... 60 C6
Maes-y-Coed
Barry CF62 ... 214 B2
Cwmdare CF44 ... 28 C3
Gorseinon SA4 ... 66 B8
Llanelli SA15 ... 40 B6
Swansea SA6 ... 45 F2
Tredomen CF82 ... 84 D1
Trelewis CF46 ... 83 D6
Maes-y-Coed Cty Prim Sch CF37 ... 135 B8
Maes-y-Coed Rd CF14 ... 177 E6
Maes-y-Crochan CF3 ... 180 B7
Maes-y-Cwm St CF63 ... 215 A5
Maes-y-Cwrt Terr 5 SA13 ... 125 C7
Maes-y-Dail SA18 ... 219 A7
Maes-y-darren SA9 ... 2 C6
Maes-y-Dderwen
Creigiau CF15 ... 174 E6
Maesteg CF34 ... 102 A6
Penpedairheol CF82 .. 84 D7
Swansea SA6 ... 45 B2
Swansea SA7 ... 70 A6
Maes-y-Deri
Cardiff CF14 ... 177 B7
Cilfrew SA10 ... 49 C6
Pontypridd CF37 ... 109 A2
Maes-y-Deri Cl CF35 ... 170 C8
Maes-y-Dre SA11 ... 227 C8
Maes-y-Felin
Bridgend CF31 ... 168 E7
Caerphilly CF83 ... 138 B3
Cardiff CF14 ... 177 B6
Llandow CF71 ... 199 A7
Rhydyfelin CF37 ... 136 B4
Maes-y-Ffynnon
Bonvilston CF5 ... 191 B1
Dowlais CF48 ... 11 B4
Maes-y-Ffynnon Cl SA11 ... 71 E6
Maes-y-Ffynnon La CF44 ... 53 A8
Maes-y-Ffynon SA11 ... 223 C1
Maes-y-Fioled CF15 176 A7
Maes-y-Garn Rd NP12 ... 59 B1
Maes-y-Garreg
Ebbw Vale NP23 ... 7 A4
Merthyr Tydfil CF48 .. 225 F2
Maes-y-Glyn SA18 .. 220 D8
Maes-y-Gollen CF15 174 E7
Maes-y-Graig St CF81 ... 58 A2
Maes-y-Gwrnen Rd SA6 ... 45 F4
Maes-y-Meillion SA10 ... 48 C2
Maes-y-Nant CF15 .. 174 D7
Maes-y-Parc SA12 ... 99 E5
Maes-y-Pergwm SA11 ... 223 C1
Maes-y-Rhedyn
Creigiau CF15 ... 174 E6
Neath SA10 ... 48 C2
Talbot Green CF72 .. 155 B2
Maes-y-Sarn CF15 .. 157 B1
Maes-y-Tyra SA11 .. 226 E5
Maes-y-Wennol CF72 ... 173 D8
Maes-y-Wern CF35 . 170 D8
Maes-Yr Haf SA4 ... 64 E4
Maes-yr-Afon
Caerphilly CF83 ... 138 D5
Pontyclun CF72 ... 173 A6
Maes-Yr-Awel CF34 .. 75 A2
Maes-Yr-Efail
Dunvant SA2 ... 93 D8
Gorseinon SA4 ... 43 B1
Maes-Yr-Eglwys SA11 ... 223 C1
Maes-yr-eirlys CF31 168 C2
Maes-Yr-Eithin SA7 .. 47 B1
Maes-yr-Haf
Ammanford SA18 ... 219 A7
Merthyr Tydfil CF47 .. 10 F1
Rhymney NP22 ... 12 F2
Rhymney NP22 ... 13 A3
Swansea SA7 ... 69 F6
Maes-Yr-Haf Rd
Neath SA11 ... 71 E8
North Cornelly CF33 . 166 A7
Maes-yr-Hafod CF15 ... 174 E7
Maes-yr-Haul CF32 . 150 E6
Maes-yr-Helyg CF44 . 28 E6
Maes-yr-Onen CF46 . 83 D4
Maes-yr-Onnen
Creigiau CF15 ... 174 E6
Cwmrhydyceirw SA6 .. 46 A3
Maes-yr-Ysgol
Barry CF62 ... 214 E5
Pyle CF33 ... 148 D1
Maescanner Rd SA14 . 41 B7
Maescynog SA9 ... 1 F1
Maescynon CF44 ... 27 E8
Maesderi SA4 ... 18 F4
Maesderwen Cres NP4 ... 62 D5
Maesderwen Rd NP4 . 62 E5
Maesglas
Bettws CF32 ... 129 E2
Bridgend CF31 ... 168 C5
Cwmavon SA12 ... 99 D5
Penygroes SA14 ... 218 D7
Pyle CF33 ... 148 C2
Maesglas Ave NP20 . 142 F1
Maesglas Cl NP20 .. 164 A8
Maesglas Cres NP20 163 F8
Maesglas Gr NP20 .. 163 F8
Maesglas Ind Est NP20 ... 143 B1
Maesglas Jun & Inf Sch NP20 ... 164 A8
Maesglas Rd
Newport NP20 ... 142 F1
Swansea SA5 ... 68 B3
Maesglas St NP20 .. 164 A8
Maesgrenig SA18 ... 219 F8
Maesgwyn
Cwmbran NP44 ... 89 D6
Cwmdare CF44 ... 28 C4
Maesgwyn Dr SA4 ... 19 C4
Maesgwyn Hospl CF32 ... 151 A6
Maesgwyn Rd SA4 ... 19 C4
Maesgwyn Specl Sch CF44 ... 28 D4
Maesgwynne CF48 ... 10 B3
Maeshafod NP13 ... 15 E3
Maeshir SA11 ... 223 C1
Maeslan SA8 ... 23 D5
Maesllwyn SA18 ... 219 B8
Maesmelyn 4 CF44 .. 28 C3
Maestaf St CF48 ... 31 A4
Maesteg Bsns Ctr CF34 ... 101 E4
Maesteg Comp (Lower) Sch CF34 ... 102 C3
Maesteg Comp (upper) Sch CF34 ... 128 D5
Maesteg Cres CF38 . 136 A1
Maesteg Gdns CF38 . 136 A1
Maesteg Gr CF38 .. 136 A1
Maesteg Rd
Bryn SA13 ... 100 F5
Cwmfelin CF34 ... 128 C7
Cymmer SA13 ... 75 C4
Cymmer SA13 ... 75 C5
Tondu CF32 ... 150 C5
Maesteg Row CF34 .. 102 B2
Maesteg St SA1 ... 95 E8
Maesteg Terr CF36 . 183 A7
Maestir SA15 ... 40 F7
Maestref SA15 ... 40 F8
Maeswerdd SA15 ... 40 F8
Maesybedol SA18 ... 220 B8
Maesycoed SA18 ... 219 D7
Maesycoed Rd
Godrergraig SA8 ... 221 B1
Pontypridd CF37 ... 135 B8
Maesycwm SA9 ... 1 F1
Maesycwmmer Prim Sch CF82 ... 85 B2
Maesydderwen
Llangennech SA14 ... 18 D1
Ystradgynlais SA9 ... 2 E7
Maesydderwen Comp Sch SA9 ... 2 E7
Maesyfelin Cres CF72 ... 173 A7
Maesyffynon Gr CF44 . 53 B8
Maesyffynon Terr CF40 ... 107 A5
Maesyfron Terr SA9 . 222 C7
Maesyglyn SA18 ... 219 F8
Maesygors SA14 ... 218 C8
Maesyrhaf
Cross Hands SA14 .. 218 B7
Llanelli SA15 ... 40 F7
Maesyrhaf Pl SA4 ... 43 A1
Maesyrhendre SA18 . 220 B8
Maesywerin SA18 .. 220 D7
Maesywern Rd
Glanaman SA18 ... 219 F8
Glanaman SA18 ... 219 F8
Mafeking Rd CF23 . 178 D1
Mafeking Terr NP22 .. 13 F6
Mafon Rd CF46 ... 83 D3
Magazine St CF34 .. 102 A8
Magellan Cl CF62 .. 215 A8
Magna Porta Gdns NP44 ... 117 B6
Magnolia Cl
Cardiff CF23 ... 178 D7
Merthyr Tydfil CF47 .. 10 D5
Newport NP20 ... 117 B3
Porth CF39 ... 108 A3
Magnolia Dr NP12 ... 85 E5
Magnolia Way CF38 . 156 C6
Magor Rd NP18 ... 145 F8
Magor St NP19 ... 143 F3
Magpie Rd CF62 ... 210 D6
Maiden St CF34 ... 128 C8
Maillard's Haven CF64 ... 207 B1
Main Access Rd CF62 ... 211 F1
Main Ave
Bridgend CF31 ... 169 B7
Cardiff CF23 ... 178 E1
Hirwaun CF44 ... 224 C1
Peterston-Super-Ely CF5 ... 191 E5
Upper Boat CF37 ... 136 D1
Main Rd
Aberdulais SA10 ... 49 C4
Bryn-côch SA10 ... 48 C4
Cheltenham NP7 ... 9 C6
Church Village CF38 . 136 A2
Cilfrew SA10 ... 49 C5
Crynant SA10 ... 226 A8
Dyffryn Cellwen SA10 . 223 A4
Llantrisant CF72 ... 155 F3
Maesycwmmer CF82 .. 85 A2
Mountain Ash CF45 .. 82 B6
Neath SA10 ... 48 E1
Ogmore-By-Sea CF32 . 184 C3
Pontrhydyfen SA12 .. 73 A1
Taffs Well CF15 ... 157 F4
Tonna SA10 ... 49 A3
Main St Barry CF63 .. 215 B7
Newbridge NP11 ... 60 A1
Newbridge NP11 ... 86 F6
Maindee Jun & Inf Sch NP19 ... 143 D5
Maindee Par NP19 .. 143 E6
Maindee Rd NP11 .. 113 A5
Maindee Terr NP44 .. 89 D5
Maindy Cres CF41 ... 78 F4
Maindy Croft CF41 .. 78 F4
Maindy Ct CF38 ... 135 E1
Maindy Gr CF41 ... 78 F3
Maindy Rd
Cardiff CF24 ... 194 F8
Penycoedcae CF37 .. 135 B6
Ton Pentre CF41 ... 78 F3
Ton Pentre CF41 ... 79 A3
Mainwaring Terr SA1 . 68 D2
Maitland Pl CF11 ... 194 E4
Maitland St CF14 .. 177 E2
Major Cl NP44 ... 88 F2
Major Rd CF5 ... 194 D5
Major St SA5 ... 68 C2
Malcolm Sargent Cl NP19 ... 144 D4
Maldwyn St CF11 ... 194 D7
Malefant St CF24 .. 178 A1
Maliphant St SA1 ... 68 E1
Mall The NP44 ... 89 E3
Mallard Cl 8 CF3 .. 179 E7
Mallard Way
Newport NP10 ... 163 F6
Penarth CF64 ... 217 A7
Porthcawl CF36 ... 182 D7
Mallards Reach CF3 162 D1
Mallory Cl CF62 ... 211 D7
Malmesbury Cl 7 NP20 ... 143 C6
Malmsmead Rd CF3 . 179 C7
Malpas Church in Wales Jun & Inf Schs NP20 ... 117 B2
Malpas Cl 1 CF3 .. 179 F7
Malpas La NP20 ... 143 B8
Malpas Park Jun & Inf Sch NP20 ... 117 A3
Malpas Rd NP20 ... 117 A3
Malpas St NP44 ... 89 E2
Malpas Court Jun & Inf Sch NP20 ... 116 F3
Malt Hall SA3 ... 229 D3
Malthouse Ave CF23 161 A2
Malthouse La NP4 ... 62 B7
Malthouse Rd
Caerleon NP18 ... 118 A5
Ponthir NP18, NP44 . 117 D6
Maltings The CF23 .. 160 F1
Malus Ave CF38 ... 156 C5
Malvern Cl
Newport NP19 ... 144 A8
Risca NP11 ... 115 D1
Malvern Dr CF14 ... 177 D7
Malvern Rd NP19 .. 143 D5
Malvern Terr
Risca NP11 ... 115 A1
Swansea SA2 ... 94 F5
Man-Moel Rd
Ebbw Vale NP22, NP23 . 14 C5
Hollybush NP12,NP23 .. 34 F6
Manchester Ho NP13 . 59 F8
Manchester Pl CF44 .. 27 D7
Manchester St NP19 143 D6
Mandeg CF46 ... 83 D6
Mandela Ave CF31 .. 169 D5
Mandeville Pl 6 CF11 ... 194 E5
Mandeville Rd NP12 .. 85 C7
Mandeville St 7 CF11 ... 194 E5
Mandinam Pk SA2 ... 94 A7
Manest St NP22 ... 12 E4
Mangoed CF44 ... 28 A6
Manitoba Cl CF23 .. 178 C5
Manley Cl CF39 ... 133 C5
Manley Rd NP20 ... 143 A4
Manmoel Ct NP12 ... 59 C1
Manmoel Rd NP11 ... 59 C2
Mannesmann Cl SA7 . 69 C7
Manod Rd CF14 ... 177 A2
Manor Chase 2 CF38 ... 156 A5
Manor Cl CF14 ... 177 B5
Manor Ct
5 Cardiff CF14 ... 177 A6
Church Village CF38 . 135 E1
Ewenny CF35 ... 185 E7
Swansea SA5 ... 68 C3
Manor Ct Flats NP11 115 B2
Manor Dr
Bridgend CF35 ... 169 F4
Glynneath SA11 ... 223 B1
Manor Gr CF36 ... 183 D8
Manor Hill CF72 ... 173 D7
Manor Pk
Llantwit Major CF61 . 210 A5
Newbridge NP11 ... 87 A8
Newport NP10 ... 163 F6
Manor Rd
Abersychan NP4 ... 37 F4
Pontllanfraith NP12 .. 85 F3
Risca NP11 ... 115 B1
Swansea SA5 ... 68 C3
Manor Rise CF14 ... 177 C4
Manor Sq CF61 ... 210 A4
Manor St Cardiff CF14 177 F2
Port Talbot SA13 .. 125 C8
Manor View CF61 .. 210 A4
Manor Way
Abersychan NP4 ... 37 F4
Briton Ferry SA11 ... 71 D3
Risca NP11 ... 115 C1
Manorbier Cl
Blackwood NP12 ... 58 D1
Church Village CF38 . 135 F2
2 Dinas Powys CF64 . 206 C3
Manorbier Cres CF3 179 C4
Manorbier Ct CF62 . 214 F8
Manorbier Dr NP44 .. 90 A3
Mansel Ct SA4 ... 66 B5
Mansel Dr SA3 ... 122 C6
Mansel Rd SA1 ... 69 B4
Mansel St
Briton Ferry SA11 ... 71 C2
Gowerton SA4 ... 66 B5
Llanelli SA15 ... 40 E4
Newport NP19 ... 144 A5
Port Talbot SA13 ... 125 B8
Port Talbot SA13 ... 99 B1
Swansea SA1 ... 95 C7
Manselfield Rd SA3 . 122 C6
Mansell Ave CF5 ... 192 F4
Manselton Prim Sch SA5 ... 68 C3
Manselton Rd SA5 ... 68 B3
Mansfield St 11 CF11 ... 194 E5
Mansfield Terr CF47 .. 11 A1
Manston Cl 5 CF5 .. 176 E2
Maple Ave
Baglan SA12 ... 98 E7
Risca NP11 ... 115 B2
Tredegar NP22 ... 6 D1
Maple Cl Barry CF62 . 215 A7
Bryn NP12 ... 85 D3
Cimla SA11 ... 72 C6
Gorseinon SA4 ... 43 A3
Llanharry CF72 ... 172 B5
Llanmartin NP18 ... 145 E6
Merthyr Tydfil CF47 .. 10 D4
Maple Cres
Pontypool NP4 ... 62 D1
Swansea SA2 ... 94 E7
Trefechan CF48 ... 10 B6
Maple Ct CF39 ... 133 D5
Maple Dr
Aberdare CF44 ... 28 D2
Bridgend CF31 ... 169 E4
Waunarlwydd SA5 ... 66 D4
Maple Gdns NP11 .. 141 C8
Maple Gr SA2 ... 94 E6
Maple Rd Cardiff CF5 . 176 B1
Penarth CF64 ... 206 E3
Pontypool NP4 ... 62 D2
Maple Rd S NP4 ... 62 D1
Maple St CF37 ... 136 A5
Maple Terr
Abercarn NP11 ... 87 B3
Abercwmboi CF44 ... 53 F4
Maesteg CF34 ... 102 A2
Maple Tree Cl CF15 . 176 A6
Maple Way NP23 ... 7 C5
Maple Wlk CF36 ... 183 E8
Maplewood Ave 3 CF14 ... 176 F3
Maplewood Cl SA10 .. 48 C4
Maplewood Flats 2 CF14 ... 176 F3
Marayat Wlk NP20 .. 142 E1
Marblehall Rd SA15 .. 40 E5
March Hywel
Cilfrew SA10 ... 49 C5
Pontardawe SA8 ... 24 C3
Marchwood Cl CF3 . 179 C5
Marconi Ave CF64 .. 206 F6
Marconi Cl NP20 .. 116 F2
Marcross Rd CF5 .. 193 A4
Mardy CF72 ... 155 A5
Mardy Cl
Caerphilly CF83 ... 138 C3
Merthyr Tydfil CF47 .. 30 F7
Mardy Cres CF83 .. 138 C3
Mardy Ct CF11 ... 194 F4
Mardy Hospl CF47 ... 30 F7
Mardy Rd CF3 ... 179 C2
Mardy St Cardiff CF11 194 F4
Merthyr Tydfil CF47 .. 11 A1
Mardy Terr CF47 ... 30 E7
Margam Ave SA6 ... 69 A8
Margam Cl CF62 ... 211 C7
Margam Ctry Pk SA13 ... 126 E1
Margam Ho CF31 ... 168 D4
Margam Pl SA15 ... 40 E4
Margam Rd
Cardiff CF14 ... 177 D2
Margam SA13 ... 125 E4
Port Talbot SA13 .. 126 A2
Margam Row CF33 .. 148 D3
Margam St
Cymmer SA13 ... 75 B5
Maesteg CF34 ... 102 B8
Margaret Ave
Barry CF62 ... 204 F1
Newport NP19 ... 143 D7
Margaret St
Abercwmboi CF44 ... 53 F4
Abercynon CF45 ... 82 E2
Aberdare CF44 ... 28 E3
Aberdare CF44 ... 53 D6
Bargoed CF81 ... 58 A1
Bryn-côch SA10 ... 48 C4
Merthyr Tydfil CF47 .. 10 C2
Pentre CF41 ... 78 F5
Pontypridd CF37 ... 108 F2
Port Talbot SA13 ... 99 C1
Trehafod CF37 ... 108 D2
Treherbert CF42 ... 50 E2
Tylorstown CF43, CF39 ... 107 C8
Margaret Terr
Blaengwynfi SA13 ... 76 C5
Swansea SA1 ... 96 A7
Margaret's Cl SA11 .. 71 B1
Marged St SA15 ... 40 D3
Marguerites Way CF5 ... 193 A5
Maria Ct CF10 ... 195 B3
Maria St CF10 ... 195 B3
Marian St
Blaengarw CF32 ... 103 E7
Tonypandy CF40 ... 106 A7
Marianwen St NP12 .. 85 C8
Marigold Cl
Merthyr Tydfil CF47 .. 10 C5
Rogerstone NP10 .. 141 D6
Marigold Ct CF31 .. 169 D5
Marigold Pl SA10 .. 222 D4
Marina Ct 6 NP19 .. 143 E8
Marine Bldgs CF64 .. 207 B5
Marine Cl SA12 ... 98 C1
Marine Dr Barry CF62 214 B2
Ogmore-By-Sea CF32 . 184 C3
Port Talbot SA12 ... 98 C1
Marine Ho SA10 ... 97 C8
Marine Ind Est NP23 .. 35 B6

Marine Par CF64 .207 B2
Marine St Cwm NP23 .35 B6
Llanelli SA15 .40 C3
Marine Terr CF36 .182 F6
Marine Wlk
Ogmore-By-Sea CF32 .184 C3
4 Swansea SA1 .95 D5
Mariner St 8 SA1 .95 D8
Mariner Way NP19 .164 E8
Mariner's Hts CF64 .207 B5
Mariners The SA15 .40 C3
Mariners Way CF62 .212 F1
Marion Ct CF14 .160 A1
Marion Jones Ct
NP12 .85 F1
Marion Pl NP20 .143 C2
Marion St
Cardiff CF24 .195 E6
Newport NP20 .143 C2
Marionville Gdns
CF5 .193 E8
Maritime Ind Est
CF37 .135 B7
Maritime Rd
Cardiff CF10 .195 C2
Port Talbot SA13 .125 B7
Maritime St CF37 .135 B8
Maritime Terr CF37 .135 B8
Marjorie St CF40 .107 B4
Mark St CF11 .194 F5
Market Arc 1 NP20 .143 C5
Market Mews 4 SA6 .68 F8
Market Pl
Abercarn NP11 .87 B2
Cardiff CF5 .194 D6
Market Rd
Cardiff CF5 .194 C6
Nantyglo NP23 .8 C2
Market Sq
Brynmawr NP23 .8 C4
Ebbw Vale NP23 .14 D8
5 Merthyr Tydfil CF47 .10 D1
Pontypool NP4 .62 C6
Market St
7 Aberdare CF44 .29 A2
Abertillery NP13 .36 B5
Barry CF62 .214 D3
Blaenavon NP4 .17 C6
Bridgend CF31 .168 F4
Caerphilly CF83 .138 B2
Cardiff CF15 .158 C1
Dowlais CF48 .11 B4
Ebbw Vale NP23 .14 D8
Llanelli SA15 .40 D5
2 Newport NP20 .143 C5
Pontypool NP4 .62 C6
Pontypridd CF37 .109 C1
5 Swansea SA6 .68 F8
8 Swansea SA6 .69 A8
Tredegar NP22 .13 E6
Markham Cres NP12 .59 B2
Markham Prim Sch
NP12 .58 D7
Markham Terr NP12 .58 D8
Marl Ct Cardiff CF11 .194 F1
Cwmbran NP44 .89 B5
Marland Ho
1 Cardiff CF10 .195 A4
14 Cardiff CF10 .195 A5
Marlas Cl CF33 .148 B1
Marlas Rd CF33 .148 A1
Marlborough Cl
Barry CF63 .215 C7
Llantwit Fardre CF38 .156 D6
Marlborough Com Inf Sch
CF23 .195 D8
Marlborough Com Jun
Sch CF23 .195 D8
Marlborough Ho 2
CF10 .195 A5
Marlborough Rd
Abertillery NP13 .36 C3
Cardiff CF23 .195 D8
Cwmbran NP44 .89 A3
Gorseinon SA4 .66 B8
Newport NP19 .143 D5
Swansea SA2 .94 F6
Marlborough Terr
CF10 .194 E8
Marloes Cl CF62 .214 F7
Marloes Ct SA5 .67 F6
Marloes Rd CF5 .193 B5
Marloss Path 1 NP44 89 B3
Marlow Cl NP10 .142 B6
Marlowe Gdns NP20 142 E1
Marlowe Ho 4 SA12 .98 B3
Marlpit La CF36 .166 A1
Marne St NP11 .114 B8
Marquis Cl CF62 .215 A2
Marsden St 5 SA1 .68 C2
Marsh St
9 Aberavon SA12 .124 F8
Aberavon SA12 .98 F1
Llanelli SA15 .40 D4
Marshall Cl 2 CF5 .176 E2
Marshall Cres CF47 .10 F5
Marshfield Ave CF33 148 B1
Marshfield Ct
Pontllanfraith NP12 .85 F2
Tonyrefail CF39 .133 D5
Marshfield Jun & Inf Sch
CF3 .162 C2
Marshfield Rd
Abertillery NP11 .59 F5
Maerdy CF43 .79 C8
Marshfield CF3 .162 D1
Neath SA11 .71 D6
Marshfield St NP19 .144 A3
Marston Ct NP20 .143 B7
Martell St SA5 .67 E3
Martin Cl CF48 .10 A1
Martin Cres CF39 .133 C5
Martin Rd
Cardiff CF24 .196 A4
Llanelli SA15 .40 E4
Martin St Clydach SA6 .46 D7
Swansea SA6 .68 F8
Martin Terr NP4 .17 A6
Martin's Field NP11 .86 E6
Martin's La CF45 .82 E2
Martin's Terr CF45 .82 E2
Martindale Cl NP22 .6 D1
Martindale Rd NP4 .62 E2
Martins Cl CF45 .82 E2
Martins Row CF81 .32 C8
Martyn's Ave SA10 .222 C3
Marwyn Gdns CF81 .57 F2
Mary Ann St CF10 .195 B5
Mary Immaculate High
Sch (Lower) CF5 .193 B2
Mary Immaculate High
Sch (Upper) CF5 .193 B2
Mary St
Abercwmboi CF44 .53 F4
6 Aberdare CF44 .29 A1
Bedlinog CF46 .56 A7
Bedwas CF83 .139 A6
13 Blaenavon NP4 .17 C6
Blaengwynfi SA13 .76 C6
Cardiff CF14 .176 F2
Crynant SA10 .226 A7
Dowlais CF48 .11 A4
Merthyr Tydfil CF47 .30 E8
Mountain Ash CF45 .54 E2
Neath SA11 .71 D7
Pontypridd CF37 .109 F5
Porth CF39 .107 F4
Porthcawl CF36 .182 F6
Seven Sisters SA10 .222 D4
Treharris CF46 .83 B6
Treherbert CF42 .51 A1
Mary Twill La SA3 .122 E4
Maryland Rd NP11 .115 A1
Maryport Rd CF23 .178 B2
Marysfield Cl CF3 .162 E1
Masefield Mews
CF31 .168 D6
Masefield Rd CF64 .206 F4
Masefield Vale NP20 .142 F2
Masefield Way
Rhydyfelin CF37 .136 B6
Swansea SA2 .94 E6
Mason St CF44 .53 C7
Masonic St
11 Merthyr Tydfil CF47 .10 D1
13 Merthyr Tydfil CF47 .30 D8
Matexa St CF41 .78 F3
Mathew Wlk CF5 .176 E2
Mathews Terr CF37 .135 A4
Mathias Cl 1 CF23 .178 E1
Matthew Rd CF62 .212 E2
Matthew St SA1 .95 D8
Matthew Terr
Dinas Powys CF64 .206 C4
Pontypool NP4 .61 F8
Matthews' St SA13 .227 C2
Matthewson Cl CF14 177 C2
Matthysens Way CF3 179 F5
Mattie Collins Way The
CF42 .78 D5
Mattysens Way CF3 .180 A5
Maugham Cl NP20 .142 F1
Maughan La 6 CF64 207 B5
Maughan Terr 5
CF64 .207 B5
Maun Rhydd CF82 .84 D6
Maureen Ave CF5 .193 E6
Mavis Gr CF14 .177 D6
Mawsons Mead CF5 .192 A1
Maximin Rd SA13 .125 E3
Maxton Ct CF83 .138 C3
Maxwell Rd CF3 .179 C4
Maxwell St CF43 .79 F6
Maxworthy Rd 1 NP4 17 C7
May St Cardiff CF24 .178 A1
Newport NP19 .143 E5
May's Ct SA11 .71 E7
Mayals Ave SA2 .94 A1
Mayals Gn SA3 .93 F1
Mayals Prim Sch
SA3 .123 A8
Mayals Rd SA2 .94 A1
Mayberry Rd SA12 .98 D7
Maybury Ho 9 NP44 .89 B3
Mayfair CF5 .193 A2
Mayfair Dr CF14 .159 E3
Mayfield Ave
Cardiff CF5 .194 A6
Laleston CF32 .167 F4
Porthcawl CF36 .183 D7
Mayfield Pl CF72 .155 E2
Mayfield Rd CF37 .109 B2
Mayfield St 2 SA13 .125 C7
Mayfield Terr
Ebbw Vale NP23 .7 D4
Swansea SA5 .68 B3
Mayflower Ave CF14 159 D1
Mayflower Cl SA2 .94 B6
Mayflower Way
CF62 .213 A2
Mayhill Cl CF14 .159 F3
Mayhill Gdns SA1 .68 B1
Mayhill Inf Sch SA1 .95 C8
Mayhill Jun Sch SA1 .95 C8
Mayhill Rd SA1 .68 B1
Maynard Ct CF5 .194 A8
Maynes 4 NP44 .89 B1
Maytree Ave SA3 .122 F7
Maytree Cl
Loughor SA4 .42 F2
Swansea SA6 .68 D8
Maywood CF72 .153 D3
McCale Ave CF5 .193 E7
McDonnel Rd CF81 .57 F4
McLaren Cotts
Abertysswg NP22 .33 C8
Abertysswg NP22 .33 D8
McQuade Pl CF62 .214 E2
McRitchie Pl SA5 .67 F3
Mead La NP44 .89 E4
Mead The SA2 .93 D8
Meadow Ave CF33 .148 C1
Meadow Bank NP4 .39 E6
Meadow Cl
Bridgend CF35 .169 F4
Cardiff CF23 .178 D8
Hirwaun CF44 .27 F7
Llanharan CF72 .153 F3
Mountain Ash CF45 .54 B3
Pengam NP12 .85 B6
Pontypool NP4 .89 E8
Risca NP11 .114 D3
Meadow Cres
Caerphilly CF83 .138 B2
Church Village CF38 .136 A1
Risca NP11 .141 C8
Tredegar NP22 .6 D2
Meadow Croft CF62 .213 B2
Meadow Croft Cl SA5 .66 E4
Meadow Ct
Llanelli SA14 .41 D4
St Brides Major CF32 .185 D3
Meadow Dr SA4 .42 F2
Meadow La
Croesyceiliog NP44 .90 B5
Gilfach Goch CF39 .132 B6
Hirwaun CF44 .27 C8
Penarth CF64 .206 F1
Porthcawl CF36 .183 B8
Meadow Rd
Neath SA11 .71 D5
Pontllanfraith NP12 .86 A4
Meadow Rise
Brynna CF72 .153 E4
Sarn CF32 .150 F4
Swansea SA2 .94 C4
Meadow St
Aberkenfig CF32 .150 C4
Abertillery NP13 .60 B6
Bridgend CF31 .168 F5
Cardiff CF11 .194 C7
Cwmavon SA12 .99 F6
Gilfach Goch CF39 .132 B6
Maesteg CF34 .102 A3
North Cornelly CF33 .165 F8
Ogmore Vale CF32 .104 E1
Pontycymer CF32 .103 E3
Pontypridd CF37 .135 E5
Swansea SA1 .67 F2
Meadow Sweet Dr
CF3 .180 B6
Meadow Terr NP24 .33 F4
Meadow The CF71 .189 C8
Meadow Vale CF63 .215 C8
Meadow View
Barry CF63 .215 D8
Bedwas CF83 .138 C7
Blackmill CF35 .130 E2
Dunvant SA2 .93 C8
Peterstone Wentlooge
CF3 .180 F5
Swansea SA7 .70 A6
Meadow View Ct
CF64 .216 A5
Meadow Way
Caerphilly CF83 .137 D1
Penperlleni NP4 .39 E7
Meadow Wlk
Blackwood NP11 .59 D1
Bridgend CF31 .169 A5
Ton Pentre CF41 .79 B3
Meadowbank Cl CF44 29 D1
Meadowbank Ct
CF5 .176 D2
Meadowbank Res Sch
CF14 .177 B2
Meadowbrook Ave
NP44 .89 D6
Meadowcroft SA3 .121 A5
Meadowgate Cl
CF14 .176 F7
Meadowlane Prim Sch
CF3 .179 F5
Meadowlark Cl 6
CF3 .179 E7
Meadows Rd
Cross Hands SA14 .218 B7
Cross Hands SA14 .218 C6
Newport NP19 .144 D1
Meadows The
Cimla SA11 .72 C6
Corntown CF35 .186 B7
Marshfield CF3 .162 D1
Penlline CF71 .188 A5
Porthcawl CF36 .183 C7
Risca NP11 .114 D4
Meadowside CF64 .206 D3
Meads Cl NP19 .144 C2
Meadvale Rd CF3 .179 D6
Mechanic's Sq NP22 .6 E1
Medart Pl NP11 .114 D4
Medart St NP11 .114 D4
Medlock Cl NP20 .116 E2
Medlock Cres NP20 .116 E3
Medlock Wlk NP20 .116 E2
Medway Cl NP20 .116 D3
Medway Ct NP20 .116 D3
Medway Rd NP20 .116 C2
Megan Ct SA4 .43 C3
Megan St SA5 .68 A2
Meggitt Rd CF62 .214 E8
Meini Tirion CF31 .168 B6
Meirion Cl CF63 .215 B8
Meirion Pl CF24 .196 A6
Meirion St CF44 .28 F4
Meirwen Dr CF5 .193 A2
Melbourne Ct
Caerphilly NP12 .85 C6
Cardiff CF14 .177 B6
Cwmbran NP44 .89 D2
Melbourne Rd
Abertillery NP13 .36 B5
Cardiff CF14 .177 F8
Melbourne Terr
CF72 .153 D3
Melbourne Way
NP20 .142 D3
Melcorn Dr SA3 .122 E5
Melfort Gdns NP20 .142 F3
Melfort Rd NP20 .142 F3
Meliden La CF64 .206 F3
Meliden Rd CF64 .206 E3
Melin Court Waterfall
SA11 .226 D4
Melin Gwlan CF83 .137 F4
Melin Inf Sch SA11 .71 D5
Melin Jun Sch SA11 .71 D5
Melin St NP11 .113 B4
Melingriffith Dr
CF14 .176 E5
Mellon St NP20 .143 C4
Mellte Ave SA11 .223 F2
Mellte Villas CF44 .28 E6
Melrose Ave CF23 .178 D1
Melrose Cl
Cardiff CF3 .179 F8
Swansea SA6 .69 B7
Melrose Ct
Cardiff CF11 .194 C7
6 Cardiff CF23 .178 C2
Melrose Gdns CF23 .178 D1
Melrose St CF63 .215 B6
Melton Dr CF31 .168 E2
Melville Ave CF3 .179 F8
Melville Cl CF62 .204 E1
Melville Terr CF83 .138 B4
Melyn Bach Ave NP4 .39 E3
Melyn Cl SA11 .71 C5
Melyn St SA13 .227 C2
Menai Ave SA13 .75 C3
Menai Cl CF38 .135 E2
Menai Way CF3 .179 D6
Mendalgief Rd NP20 143 C2
Mendip Cl
Newport NP19 .144 D6
Risca NP11 .115 D1
Swansea SA5 .67 D3
Mendip Rd CF3 .179 A5
Mendip View CF63 .215 C6
Menelaus Sq CF48 .11 B4
Meon Cl NP20 .116 F2
Merchant St
15 Aberdare CF44 .29 A1
Pontlottyn CF81 .12 F1
Pontlottyn CF81 .32 F8
Merchant's Hill NP4 .62 B8
Merchant's Hill Cl
NP4 .62 A8
Merches Gdns CF11 .194 F4
Merches Pl CF11 .194 F4
Mercia Rd CF24 .195 F6
Mercies The CF36 .183 B7
Mere Path NP44 .89 B3
Meredith Cl NP20 .142 F2
Meredith Rd CF24 .195 F6
Meredith Terr NP11 .86 F6
Merevale CF64 .205 F3
Merfield Cl CF32 .150 E4
Merfield Ho CF32 .150 E4
Merganser Cl CF36 .182 E8
Merganser Ct CF63 .214 F5
Meridian Ct 1 CF14 .177 E2
Meridian The CF64 .207 A5
Merion St CF40 .107 A3
Merioneth Ho 5
CF64 .206 F2
Merioneth Pl CF62 .214 F7
Merlin Cl Cardiff CF14 159 E2
Penarth CF64 .217 A8
8 Pontypridd CF37 .109 B1
Porthcawl CF36 .182 E8
Merlin Cres
Bridgend CF31 .168 C6
Newport NP19 .143 F7
Swansea SA1 .94 F8
Merlin Pl CF63 .215 A7
Merret Ct CF24 .196 A7
Merrick Cotts CF5 .191 F1
Merriots Pl NP19 .143 E5
Mersey Cl NP12 .85 D3
Merthyr Dyfan Rd
CF62 .204 F1
Merthyr Rd
Abercanaid CF48 .30 F5
Aberdare CF44 .29 A8
Cardiff CF14 .177 B4
Cardiff CF14 .177 D3
Cardiff CF15 .158 C1
Hirwaun CF44 .27 D7
Llwydcoed CF44 .28 E7
Merthyr Tydfil CF44 .225 D1
Merthyr Tydfil CF47 .10 F4
Pontwalby SA11 .223 E1
Pontypridd CF37 .109 D2
Tredegar NP22 .5 F1
Tredegar NP22 .6 B1
Troedyrhiw CF48 .31 C2
Merthyr St
Barry CF63 .214 F5
Cardiff CF24 .194 F8
Pontyclun CF72 .173 B8
Merthyr Tydfil Coll 10
CF48 .10 D1
Merthyr Tydfil Ind Pk
CF48 .31 A3
Merthyr Tydfil Sta
CF47 .10 E1
Merthyr Vale Sta
CF48 .55 D3
Merthyrmawr Rd
Bridgend CF31 .168 E2
Bridgend CF32 .185 B8
Merthyr Mawr CF32 .168 D1
Mervinian Cl 13
CF10 .195 C4
Mervyn Rd
Cardiff CF14 .177 B4
Cardiff CF24 .195 F6
Mervyn St
Aberfan CF48 .55 C5
Pontypridd CF37 .135 F5
Mervyn Terr
Cwmavon SA12 .99 C5
Pontypool NP4 .62 B7
Mervyn Way CF35 .170 B8
Mescoed Rd NP10 .142 B8
Metal St CF24 .195 D6
Metcalfe St CF34 .102 B8
Meteor St CF24 .195 C6
Methodist La CF61 .209 F6
Methuen Rd NP19 .143 E5
Metro Mon Ind Est
NP44 .89 F7
Metz Cotts SA9 .222 A6
Mews The
Abercarn NP11 .114 C7
7 Barry CF63 .214 F5
Newport NP20 .143 A5
Mewslade Ave SA5 .67 E6
Meyler St CF39 .133 B2
Meyrick Rd CF5 .193 A4
Meyrick Villas CF47 .10 D3
Meyricks NP44 .116 B8
Meyricks Row CF40 .107 A1
Michael Way NP4 .62 B7
Michael's Field SA3 .123 C3
Michael's Rd CF42 .50 B2
Michaelston Cl CF63 215 B8
Michaelston Ct CF5 .192 F4
Michaelston Rd CF5 .192 F5
Michaelstone Ct SA12 99 D4
Michelston Ct 3
CF5 .193 C4
Michna St SA12 .98 F1
Mid Glamorgan Centre for
Art, Design &
Technology CF37 .135 F8
Middle Coedcae Rd
NP4 .17 D6
Middle Rd SA5 .67 F4
Middle Row
Ferndale CF43 .79 F8
Mountain Ash CF45 .54 C5
Rhymney NP22 .12 C7
Middle St
Pontypridd CF37 .109 D2
4 Tonypandy CF40 .106 F4
Middle Terr CF43 .80 C2
Middlecroft La SA3 .121 F7
Middlegate Ct CF71 .188 F2
Middlegate Wlk
CF71 .188 F2
Middleton St
Blaengwynfi SA13 .76 C6
Briton Ferry SA11 .71 C2
Swansea SA1 .95 F7
Midfield NP4 .39 E6
Midland Ct SA1 .95 E7
Midland Pl SA7 .69 D7
Midland Rd SA7 .69 D7
Midland Terr SA9 .2 D8
Midway NP4 .39 B2
Miers St SA1 .95 E7
Mikado St CF40 .106 F4
Milborough Ct SA9 .2 B7
Milborough Rd SA9 .2 B7
Milbourne Cl CF47 .30 F7
Milbourne St
Mountain Ash CF45 .82 B6
Tonypandy CF40 .107 A4
Milbourne Terr CF47 .30 F7
Milburn Cl CF62 .212 F1
Mildred Cl CF38 .156 A7
Mildred St CF38 .156 A7
Mile End Cl SA5 .67 F3
Mile End Row SA11 .71 D5
Miles Ct CF15 .158 A3
Miles La SA3 .122 C6
Miles Rd SA5 .68 C4
Miles St Llanelli SA15 .40 C7
Maerdy CF43 .52 A1
Merthyr Tydfil CF47 .10 C2
Milford Cl CF38 .135 F2
Milford Ho NP44 .89 D2
Milford Way SA5 .67 F6
Milfraen Ave NP23 .8 D1
Military Mus CF10 .195 A6
Mill Brook SA12 .98 E5
Mill Cl Caerphilly CF83 137 F4
Cardiff CF14 .160 A1
Dinas Powys CF64 .206 A3
Mill Heath NP20 .116 E3
Mill La Bridgend CF31 168 E5
Cardiff CF10 .195 A5
Cardiff CF3 .179 C8
Cardiff CF3 .179 D8
Cardiff CF5 .194 B8
Mill La *continued*
Castleton CF3 .162 C4
Llanelli SA15 .40 D6
Llanrhidian SA3 .229 D3
Llanyravon NP44 .90 B2
Mumbles SA3 .94 B2
Ystrad Mynach CF82 .111 E6
Mill Lay La CF61 .209 F4
Mill Par NP20 .143 D1
Mill Pk CF71 .188 E1
Mill Pl Cardiff CF14 .160 B3
Cardiff CF5 .193 E6
Mill Race CF72 .173 D6
Mill Race Cafn y Felin
SA10 .71 B8
Mill Rd
Caerphilly CF83 .138 A3
Cardiff CF14 .160 A2
Cardiff CF15 .158 C1
Cardiff CF5 .193 E6
Deri CF81 .57 B8
Dinas Powys CF64 .206 A3
Mountain Ash CF45 .54 C4
Neath SA10 .48 D2
Pontllanfraith NP12 .86 A3
Pontypool NP4 .62 B8
Pyle CF33 .148 A1
Ynysybwl CF37 .81 E3
Mill St Aberdare CF44 .28 E4
Aberdare CF44 .28 F4
Blaina NP13 .15 E4
Caerleon NP18 .118 C2
Cwmfelin CF34 .128 C8
Cwmfelinfach NP11 .113 A4
Gorseinon SA4 .43 C2
Gowerton SA4 .66 B5
Llanelli SA15 .40 D4
Newport NP20 .143 B5
Pen-clawdd SA4 .64 F4
Pontypridd CF37 .109 B1
Risca NP11 .115 B1
Tonyrefail CF39 .133 B4
Treharris CF46 .83 C6
Ystrad CF41 .79 D2
Mill Terr
Ammanford SA18 .219 A5
Cwm NP23 .35 A7
Glynneath SA11 .223 C1
Risca NP11 .115 B1
Mill View CF34 .102 D1
Mill's Ho 2 SA12 .98 B2
Milland Rd SA11 .71 D7
Milland Road Ind Est
SA11 .71 D6
Millands Cl SA3 .122 D5
Millbank Jun & Inf Sch
CF5 .193 F6
Millbrook Cl CF64 .206 B4
Millbrook Ct NP4 .39 E3
Millbrook Hts CF64 .206 B4
Millbrook Jun & Inf Schs
NP20 .116 F2
Millbrook Pk CF14 .160 A3
Millbrook Pl NP4 .39 E2
Millbrook Rd
Dinas Powys CF64 .206 B4
Pontllanfraith NP12 .86 A4
Millbrook St SA6 .68 D5
Millcroft Ct CF71 .201 A4
Millennium Coastal Pk
SA14, SA15 .41 B1
Millennium Stad
CF10 .194 F5
Miller Cl NP18 .119 F1
Miller's Ct SA5 .67 F6
Millers Ave CF32 .150 F5
Millers Ride NP44 .90 A3
Millfield
Bridgend CF31 .168 E5
Cardiff CF14 .160 A3
Pontyclun CF72 .173 A7
Quakers Yard CF46 .83 C6
Millfield Cl
Cardiff CF3 .179 E6
Swansea SA2 .94 B5
Millfield Dr CF71 .188 F2
Millgate CF14 .160 A1
Millheath Dr CF14 .160 A2
Millicent St CF10 .195 B5
Millrace Cl CF14 .160 A2
Millwood CF14 .160 A3
Millwood Ct 3 SA1 .68 C2
Millwood Rise CF62 .214 C4
Millwood St SA5 .68 C3
Milman St NP20 .143 C1
Milner St NP19 .143 F3
Milton Cl
Aberbargoed CF81 .58 B4
Beddau CF38 .156 A5
Cwmbran NP44 .89 D2
Ebbw Vale NP23 .14 B8
Llantwit Major CF61 .210 B5
Milton Ct NP19 .144 F6
Milton Dr CF31 .168 C5
Milton Hill NP18 .145 B5
Milton Inf Sch NP19 .144 F6
Milton Jun Sch
NP19 .144 F6
Milton Pl Cardiff CF5 .193 E8
Machen CF83 .139 C7
8 Merthyr Tydfil CF47 .30 E8
Milton Rd Barry CF62 214 E8
Newport NP19 .144 A5
Penarth CF64 .206 F4
Milton St
Cardiff CF24 .195 C7
Cwmaman CF44 .53 A4
Milton Terr
New Tredegar NP24 .33 F1
Swansea SA1 .95 C8

Milverton Rd CF3 ....179 C7
Milward Rd CF63 ....215 B6
Min y Coed Cimla SA11 72 B6
  Lewistown CF32 ....130 E5
Min y Mor SA15 ....40 C5
Min yr Afon CF35 ....140 A7
Min-y-Coed
  Bridgend CF31 ....169 C5
  Glynneath SA11 ....223 C1
  Pyle SA13 ....73 B5
  Pyle SA13 ....148 A6
  Radyr CF15 ....176 B7
Min-y-Don SA13 ....125 E3
Min-y-Mor CF62 ....214 B2
Min-y-Nant
  Cardiff CF14 ....177 B7
  Pencoed CF35 ....170 D8
Min-y-Rhos SA9 ....222 A6
Min-yr-Allt SA10 ....48 E2
Min-yr-awel CF31 ....168 D8
Minafon CF14 ....195 C2
Minavon ☒ CF14 ....177 B5
Mincing La SA15 ....40 C5
Minehead Ave CF64 216 A5
Minehead Rd CF3 ....179 C6
Miners Row CF44 ....28 E6
Minerva St CF31 ....168 F5
Minffrwd Cl CF35 ....152 E1
Minffrwd Rd
  Pencoed CF35 ....152 E1
  Pencoed CF35 ....152 F2
Mining School Hill
  NP11 ....60 A1
Minister St CF24 ....195 A8
Minny St CF24 ....195 A8
Minori Ho CF10 ....195 C2
Minories ☒ NP44 ....89 B1
Minsmere Cl CF3 ....180 B7
Minster Cl
  Barry CF63 ....215 B8
  Swansea SA6 ....69 B7
Minster Ct SA6 ....69 B7
Minster Rd CF23 ....195 E8
Minyrafon SA9 ....2 B5
Minyrafon Rd SA10 ....2 B5
Mirador Cres SA2 ....95 A6
Miskin Cres CF72 ....173 D7
Miskin Gn NP44 ....90 A3
Miskin Ho NP44 ....90 A3
Miskin Prim Sch
  CF45 ....54 D1
Miskin Rd
  Mountain Ash CF45 ....54 E2
  Mountain Ash CF45 ....54 E2
  Tonypandy CF40 ....106 F5
Miskin St Barry CF62 214 D3
  Cardiff CF24 ....195 A7
  Treherbert CF42 ....18 E2
Miskin Terr CF45 ....54 E2
Mission Rd CF34 ....102 C1
Misty Falls Cl SA4 ....65 C1
Mitchell Cl
  Cardiff CF3 ....180 A5
  Llanyravon NP44 ....90 B1
Mitchell Cres CF47 ....11 F5
Mitchell Ct ☒ CF40 106 E6
Mitchell Terr
  ☒ Pontypool NP4 ....38 A1
  Pontypridd CF37 ....135 D8
Miterdale Cl CF23 ....178 F1
Mithras Way NP18 ....118 A4
Mitre Ct CF5 ....177 A1
Mitre Pl CF5 ....177 A1
Mitre St NP13 ....36 B5
Mixen Cl SA3 ....122 F5
Model Cotts CF47 ....10 F7
Moel Fryn CF33 ....137 D6
Moel Gilau CF32,
  CF34 ....129 D5
Moir Ct CF33 ....137 F5
Moira Pl CF24 ....195 C6
Moira St CF24 ....195 C6
Moira Terr
  Cardiff CF24 ....195 C6
  Ogmore Vale CF32 ....104 E2
Mole Cl NP20 ....116 C2
Molescombe ☒ NP44 .89 B1
Mona Cl
  Cwmbran NP44 ....89 E5
  Swansea SA6 ....69 A6
Mona Rd Cardiff CF24 .195 F7
  Maerdy CF43 ....52 A2
Monastery Rd SA10 .71 B7
  Monastery Bsns Ctr
  SA10 ....71 A7
Monet Cres NP19 ....144 A7
Monger St ☒ SA1 ....68 B1
Monica St CF34 ....102 B2
Monk Ct CF14 ....29 A1
Monk's Cl CF33 ....148 B2
Monks Cl SA10 ....71 C8
Monksland Rd SA13 .94 A4
Monkstone Cl CF64 .206 E1
Monkstone Rise CF3 179 C5
Monkton Ct CF5 ....193 C7
Monmouth Cl
  Church Village CF38 ..139 F2
  Pontypool NP4 ....63 A2
Monmouth Dr CF37 ..15 B2
Monmouth Ho
  Merthyr Tydfil CF48 ..225 F1
  Newport NP20 ....144 A8
Monmouth Pl SA6 ....46 A5
Monmouth St
  Cardiff CF11 ....194 F4
  Mountain Ash CF45 ..81 F7

Monmouth View
  CF83 ....112 A1
Monmouth Way
  Barry CF62 ....214 F6
  Bowerton CF61 ....210 B7
Monmouth Wlk
  Cwmbran NP44 ....89 E3
  Markham NP12 ....58 D7
Monnow Ct NP44 ....89 A4
Monnow Ind Sch
  NP20 ....116 D2
Monnow Jun Sch
  NP20 ....116 D2
Monnow Way NP20 .116 E2
Monnow Wlk NP20 116 E2
Montague St SA11 ..36 B6
Montana Plc CF44 ....27 E7
Montana Pl SA1 ....162 A6
Montclaire Ave NP12 .85 E6
Monterey St SA5 ....68 C3
Montgomery Rd
  Barry CF62 ....214 E4
  Newport NP20 ....117 A4
Montgomery St
  CF24 ....178 C1
Montherner Rd
  CF24 ....178 A1
Monton Terr SA1 ....96 A7
Montpellier Terr SA1 .95 B7
Montreal Cl NP20 ..142 D3
Montresor Ct NP44 ..117 B7
Monumental Terr
  CF48 ....119 A4
Moor King Cl CF3 ..180 B6
Moor La
  Llangennith SA3 ....228 C2
  Porthcawl CF36 ....165 F3
Moor Rd Baglan SA12 .98 D3
  Bridgend CF31 ....169 F2
Moor View
  Bishton NP18 ....145 F3
  Ebbw Vale NP23 ....14 C8
  Ebbw Vale NP23 ....7 F1
Moorby Ct ☒ CF10 ..195 C4
Moordale Rd CF11 ..195 A2
Moore Cl CF5 ....193 C5
Moore Cres NP19 ..145 A6
Moore Rd CF5 ....193 B5
Moore's Row CF81 ..32 D7
Moorings The
  Newport NP19 ....143 F8
  Newport NP19 ....144 A8
  Penarth CF64 ....207 A5
Moorland Ave
  Mumbles SA3 ....122 E6
  Newport NP19 ....144 C3
Moorland Cl NP44 ..22 D7
Moorland Ct CF44 ..27 F7
  Moorland Gdns Jun & Inf
  Sch CF24 ....195 E5
Moorland Cres CF38 156 A7
Moorland Hts CF35 .135 E8
Moorland Pk NP19 .144 C2
Moorland Rd
  Bargoed CF81 ....57 E4
  Cardiff CF24 ....195 E6
  Cardiff CF24 ....195 F5
  Ebbw Vale NP23 ....14 C2
  Neath SA11 ....71 F5
  Port Talbot SA12 ....98 E1
  ☒ Port Talbot SA12 ..124 D8
Moorlands Rd CF31 .168 E7
Moorings The NP4 ..143 E6
Moors La CF24 ....195 D5
Moorside Rd SA3 ..122 F7
Moorside Villas
  SA10 ....222 F6
Moorview Cl SA5 ....67 E4
Moorview Rd SA6 ....67 A4
Mor-Awel SA14 ....41 C5
Morawel SA1 ....69 D5
Morden La NP19 ....143 E7
Morden Rd NP19 ..143 E6
Morel Ct CF11 ....206 F8
Morel St CF63 ....215 A5
Morfa Ave SA13 ..125 E5
Morfa CP Jun Sch
  SA15 ....40 F3
Morfa Cres SA13 ..179 E5
Morfa Glas SA11 ..223 C1
Morfa Inf Sch SA15 ..40 E2
Morfa La
  Llantwit Major CF61 .199 D1
  Reynoldston CF61 ..205 A6
Morfa Rd
  Margam SA13 ....125 E3
  Swansea SA1 ....68 C1
  Swansea SA1 ....95 D8
Morfa St CF31 ....168 F5
  Morfa Stadium (Regional
  Sports Ctr) SA1 ....68 E4
Morfydd St
  Margam SA13 ....125 E3
  ☒ Swansea SA6 ....69 B8
  Morgan Arm ☒ CF10 195 A5
Morgan Cl CF62 ....79 F1
Morgan Jones Flats
  CF83 ....138 A3
Morgan Jones Sq ☒
  CF48 ....31 C1
Morgan Rise ☒ CF42 .30 E7
Morgan St
  Abercraf SA9 ....222 D7
  Aberdare CF44 ....28 C2
  Abertillery NP13 ....36 B6
  Barry CF63 ....215 B5
  Blaenavon NP4 ....17 C6
  Caerphilly CF83 ....138 A4
  Cardiff CF24 ....195 B5
  Dowlais CF48 ....11 A4

Morgan St continued
  Llanbradach CF83 ....111 F2
  ☒ Merthyr Tydfil CF47 .10 D2
  ☒ Mountain Ash CF45 .54 E1
  New Tredegar NP24 ..33 E3
  Newport NP11 ....143 D6
  Pontardawe SA8 ....23 C2
  Pontypridd CF37 ....109 C2
  Porth CF39 ....107 F3
  Swansea SA1 ....68 D2
  Tredegar NP22 ....13 E6
Morgan Terr
  Porth CF39 ....107 F2
  Tredegar NP22 ....13 D5
  Treorchy CF42 ....19 B4
Morgan Way NP10 ..163 F6
Morgan's Rd SA11 ..71 C5
Morgan's Terr
  Briton Ferry SA11 ....71 C3
  Mountain Ash CF45 ..73 A2
Morgannwg Ho
  SA12 ....124 D8
Morgannwg St CF37 108 D2
Morgraig Ave NP10 .163 E5
Moriah Hill NP11 ....115 A2
Moriah St
  Llwydcoed CF44 ....28 E6
  Pyle CF33 ....148 D2
Moriah Rd SA5 ....68 C6
Moriah St SA5 ....68 C6
Morien Cres CF37 ..135 F6
Morlais Bldgs ☒ CF47 10 E1
Morlais Ct CF48 ....225 F2
Morlais Ct
  Caerphilly CF83 ....137 D4
  ☒ Merthyr Tydfil CF47 .30 D8
Morlais Rd
  Llangennech SA14 ..42 B7
  Margam SA13 ....125 E4
  Swansea SA5 ....68 B5
Morlais St
  Barry CF63 ....215 C6
  Cardiff CF23 ....178 B1
  Dowlais CF48 ....11 A4
  Penrheadulch CF48 ..31 A4
Morley Cl NP19 ....144 E5
Morley Rd NP13 ....36 A6
Morningside Wlk
  CF62 ....204 F1
Mornington Ct CF3 ..179 A3
Morrell St ☒ CF48 ..30 E8
Morris Ave
  Cardiff CF14 ....159 D1
  Mountain Ash CF45 ..81 F7
Morris Finer Cl CF5 .193 E5
Morris La Swansea SA1 95 E7
  Swansea SA1 ....95 F8
Morris Rise ☒ NP4 ..17 D7
Morris St
  Cwmaman CF44 ....53 A4
  Maesteg CF34 ....102 A3
  Newport NP19 ....143 E4
  ☒ Swansea SA6 ....69 A8
  ☒ Treherbert CF42 ....51 A1
Morris Terr
  Ferndale CF43 ....79 E7
  ☒ Merthyr Tydfil CF47 .10 D2
  Pontlottyn CF81 ....12 F1
  Swansea SA1 ....45 E1
  Tredegar NP22 ....13 E7
Morris Way CF5 ....193 E5
Morrison Cres SA2 ..98 D1
Morrison Ct SA12 ..98 D1
Morrison Ho ☒ SA12 .98 D1
Morrison Rd SA12 ..98 D1
Morrison St ☒ SA12 .98 D1
Morriston Comp Sch
  SA6 ....45 F4
  Morriston Hosp SA6 ..45 E5
  Morriston North Ind Est
  Swansea SA6 ....69 C8
  Swansea SA6 ....46 B1
Morriston Pl SA18 ..220 E6
  Morriston Prim Sch
  SA6 ....69 A8
  Morriston South Ind Est
  SA6 ....69 A7
Morrisville NP11 ....113 D3
Morse Row CF32 ..150 F4
Mortimer Rd CF11 ..194 D7
Morton Ct CF14 ....178 A4
Morton Terr CF40 ..106 A7
Morton Way NP20 ..116 B1
Morton's Farm NP23 ..8 A4
Moseley Terr NP44 ..89 E7
Moses Row SA11 ..226 D5
Moss Rd
  Aberdare CF44 ....29 B4
  Cwmbran NP44 ....89 B3
Moss St CF72 ....153 D3
Mostyn Mews CF37 153 D3
Mostyn Rd CF5 ....193 A4
Mostyn St CF14 ....194 A5
Mostyn Thomas Cl
  NP13 ....15 D5
Mound Rd CF37 ..135 B8
Mount Cres
  Penllergaer SA4 ....43 F2
  Swansea SA6 ....45 D2
Mount Earl CF31 ..168 E4
Mount Earl Cl CF31 .168 E2
Mount Hall St CF44 ..53 C7
Mount Libanus St
  CF42 ....51 A1
Mount Pleasant
  Aberkenfig CF32 ..150 C3
  Aberkenfig CF32 ....37 F4
  Bargoed CF81 ....57 F8
  Barry CF63 ....215 B6
  Bedling CF46 ....56 A7
  Blaengarw CF32 ..103 E7

Mount Pleasant continued
  Blaina NP13 ....15 D5
  Bridgend CF31 ....168 B5
  Cwmfelinfach NP11 ..113 A6
  Gowerton SA4 ....68 A6
  Heolgerrig CF48 ....10 A1
  Llanelli Hill NP7 ....9 C5
  Maesycwmmer CF82 ..85 B2
  Newport NP20 ....117 A3
  Pen-y-fai CF31 ....150 C1
  Pengndalfawd CF82 ..84 E8
  Pontcymer CF32 ....103 E3
  Swansea SA1 ....95 C7
  Tonna SA11 ....49 C2
  Trehafod CF37 ....108 C2
  Merthyr Vale CF48 ..55 D2
Mount Pleasant Ave
  CF3 ....179 C6
Mount Pleasant Bldgs ☒
  CF44 ....53 A1
Mount Pleasant Cl
  NP44 ....89 D5
Mount Pleasant Cotts
  Abertillery NP13 ....36 B5
  ☒ Llangeinor CF32 ..130 B5
  ☒ Mountain Ash CF45 .54 E1
Mount Pleasant Ct
  Abertillery NP13 ....60 A7
  Neath SA10 ....70 E7
  Pontypool NP4 ....62 C6
Mount Pleasant Dr ☒
  SA1 ....95 C7
Mount Pleasant Est
  NP13 ....60 B7
  Mount Pleasant Jun & Inf
  Sch NP10 ....142 A6
Mount Pleasant La
  CF3 ....179 C6
Mount Pleasant Pl ☒
  SA1 ....95 C7
Mount Pleasant Prim Sch
  CF48 ....55 D2
Mount Pleasant Rd
  Cwmbran NP44 ....89 D5
  Ebbw Vale NP23 ....7 C1
  Porth CF39 ....107 E4
  Porthcawl CF36 ....166 C4
  Risca NP11 ....115 A2
Mount Pleasant Row
  NP13 ....36 B7
Mount Pleasant Sq
  NP23 ....2 F4
Mount Pleasant St
  Aberbargoed CF81 ....58 A5
  Aberdare CF44 ....28 F3
  ☒ Barry CF63 ....215 B6
Mount Pleasant Terr
  Abercarn NP11 ....114 C5
  Mountain Ash CF45 ..54 E1
Mount Rd
  Dinas Powys CF64 ..206 A3
  Pontypool NP4 ....38 D1
  Rhigos CF44 ....224 A1
  Risca NP11 ....115 A2
Mount St
  Aberdare CF44 ....53 C7
  Ebbw Vale NP23 ....14 D6
  Gowerton SA4 ....66 B5
  ☒ Merthyr Tydfil CF47 10 D2
  Pontllotfyn CF81 ....12 F1
  Swansea SA6 ....45 E1
  Tredegar NP22 ....13 E7
Mount Stephens
  CF14 ....160 A4
Mount Stuart Sq
  CF10 ....195 B2
Mount Terr ☒ CF47 ..10 D2
Mount The
  Cardiff CF14 ....194 C7
  Dinas Powys CF64 ..206 A3
  Gowerton SA4 ....66 B5
Mount View
  Merthyr Tydfil CF47 ..11 A1
  Merthyr Tydfil CF47 ..10 F1
Mount View Terr ☒
  SA12 ....99 A1
  Mountain Ash Comp Sch
  CF45 ....54 C4
  Mountain Ash General
  Hospl CF45 ....54 D4
Mountain Ash Rd
  CF45 ....82 D2
  Mountain Ash Sta
  CF45 ....54 D4
Mountain La CF45 ..62 D3
Mountain Rd
  Aberavon SA12 ....99 A2
  Bedwas CF83 ....138 D8
  Caerphilly CF83 ....159 B8
  Craig-Cefn-Parc SA6 ..22 C1
  Cwmaman CF44 ....53 A4
  Cwmbran NP44 ....89 B7
  Pentyrch CF15 ....157 C1
  Pontypool NP4 ....62 B1
  Risca NP11 ....115 C2
  Rogerstone NP10 ..142 A8
  Tonypandy CF40 ....107 A2
  Mountain Row CF43 ..79 F8
Mountain Stream
  SA10 ....48 C1
Mountain View
  Briton Ferry SA11 ....71 B3
  Edwardsfiganot CF83 138 A6
  Machen CF83 ....139 F7
  North Cornelly CF33 .166 A7
  Pontypool NP4 ....61 F8
  ☒ Pontypridd CF37 ..135 F6

Mountain View continued
  Tonypandy CF40 ....106 F8
  Tonyrefail CF39 ....132 E5
  Treherbert CF42 ....50 E2
Mountain View Ho
  NP4 ....62 D8
Mountain Way CF46 ..83 F2
Mountbatten NP22 ..12 F3
Mountbatten Cl
  Cardiff CF23 ....178 A5
  Newport NP19 ....144 F7
Mountbatten Ct SA5 ..67 E5
Mountbatten Rd
  CF3 ....179 C6
Mountford Cl NP10 ..142 A7
Mountjoy Ave CF64 ..206 F4
Mountjoy Cl ☒ CF64 206 F4
Mountjoy Cres ☒
  CF64 ....206 F3
Mountjoy La ☒ CF64 206 F3
Mountjoy Pl
  ☒ Newport NP20 ....143 C3
  Penarth CF64 ....206 F4
Mountjoy Rd
  NP20 ....143 C3
Mountjoy St ☒
  NP20 ....143 C3
Mountside
  Mountstuart Com Jun &
  Inf Sch CF10 ....195 B1
Moxon Rd NP20 ....117 A1
Moxon St CF63 ....215 C6
Moy Rd Aberfan CF48 ..55 B5
  Cardiff CF24 ....195 B8
  Taffs Well CF15 ..158 A4
Moyle Gr NP18 ....117 F6
Mozart Dr SA12 ....98 B3
Mozart Mews ☒ SA12 98 B3
Mr Speakers Way (Ffordd
  Mr Llefarydd) CF40 107 A4
Muirfield Dr SA2 ....93 F1
Muirton Rd CF24 ..195 F6
Mulberry Ave SA3 ..122 F8
Mulberry Cl
  Llantwit Fardre CF38 .156 C5
  Rogerstone NP10 ..141 E7
Mulberry Ct CF62 ..214 C3
Mulcaster Ave NP19 144 C2
Mulgrave Way SA2 ..94 A1
Mullins Ave CF3 ....179 D5
  Multi Trad Ctr CF15 .157 F8
Mumbles Bay Ct SA4 ..66 E2
Mumbles Pier SA3 ..123 E3
Mumbles Rd
  Mumbles SA3 ....123 A7
  Mumbles SA3 ....129 A6
  Swansea SA2 ....94 D3
Mundy Pl CF24 ....195 A8
Munnings Dr NP19 ..144 A7
Munro Pl CF62 ....214 E6
Mur Gwyn CF14 ....177 C8
Murch Cres CF64 ..206 C3
Murch Rd CF64 ....206 C3
Muriel Terr
  Bedlinog CF48 ....56 B7
  Dowlais CF48 ....11 C5
Murlande Way CF62 213 C2
Murray St SA15 ....40 D5
Murray Wlk ☒ CF11 194 D5
Murrayfield Cl SA5 ..68 B6
Murrayfield Rd CF14 177 D5
Murrells Cl CF38 ..156 D6
Murrys Wlk CF32 ..167 F5
Murton La SA3 ....122 D5
Museum Ave CF10 ..195 A7
Museum Pl CF10 ..195 A7
Musselwhite Ct NP22 ..16 B4
  Mwyndy Cross Industries
  CF72 ....173 F8
Mwyndy Terr CF72 ..173 E8
Mydam La SA4 ....43 A2
Myddynfych SA18 ..219 B8
Mydrim Pl NP22 ....25 C6
Mylo-Griffiths Cl
  CF5 ....176 E3
Mynach Clos CF82 ..84 F7
Mynachdy Rd
  Cardiff CF14 ....177 D2
  Ynysybwl CF37 ....81 D3
  Mynachlog Nedd Jun Sch
  SA10 ....71 A7
Mynydd Cynffig Jun Sch
  CF33 ....148 D2
  Mynydd Cynffig Jun Sch
  CF33 ....148 C2
Mynydd Garnllwyd Rd
  SA6 ....68 D8
Mynydd Gelli Wastad Rd
  Clydach SA6 ....46 B6
  Swansea SA6 ....68 B8
Mynydd Islwyn Cl
  NP12 ....85 D4
Mynydd Maen Rd
  NP44 ....89 C6
Mynydd View
  Pontypool NP4 ....62 B4
  Pontypool NP4 ....62 B4
Mynydd y Seren
  CF39 ....133 A3
Mynydd-Newydd Rd
  SA5 ....68 A7
Mynydd-Yr-Eos
  CF40 ....107 A4
  Mynyddbach Comp Sch
  SA5 ....68 C7
Myra Hess Cl NP19 ..144 F6

N

Naddocks Pl CF31 ..168 F3
Nailsea Ct CF64 ....216 C5
Nant Arw SA18 ....218 D6
Nant Cadle SA5 ....67 E6
Nant Canna CF35 ..170 A1
Nant Celyn Cl NP44 ..89 C6
Nant Celyn Cl NP44 ..89 C6
Nant Coch Dr NP20 142 E4
  Nant Coch House
  Rougemont Sch
  NP20 ....142 E4
Nant Ddu CF83 ....138 A2
Nant Dyfed CF72 ..155 F5
Nant Eirin CF39 ....133 A4
Nant Fforwwg CF31 168 B6
Nant Glas SA4 ....44 C5
Nant Gwineu Rd
  SA18 ....220 C8
Nant Gwyn
  Porth CF39 ....107 D1
  Trelewis CF46 ....83 D6
Nant Hir SA11 ....223 B1
Nant Isaf CF5 ....205 A7
Nant Lais CF31 ....168 D5
Nant Melyn NP23 ....7 B4
Nant Melyn Terr
  CF39 ....133 D2
Nant Morlais CF48 ..11 B6
Nant Row ☒ CF44 ..29 A1
Nant Talwg Way
  CF62 ....214 B5
Nant The CF81 ....32 D7
  Nant Twyn Yr Harris
  Drive 111 E7
Nant Walla CF14 ..177 C8
Nant y Coed CF27 ..108 F2
Nant y Dowlais CF5 ..192 E4
Nant y Felin
  Efail Isaf CF38 ....156 E5
  Nant y Garth CF15 ..157 F3
  Nant y Hwyad CF83 137 E3
  Nant y parc Prim Sch
  CF83 ....110 E3
Nant y Pepra CF5 ..192 F4
Nant y Plac CF5 ....192 E4
Nant y Rhos CF5 ..192 E4
Nant y Wedal CF14 ..178 A2
Nant y Wennol CF31 168 E2
Nant yr Arthur CF5 ..192 F4
  Nant-cae'r-refail
  SA9 ....222 E8
Nant-Fawr Cl CF23 ..178 B6
Nant-Fawr Cres
  CF23 ....178 B6
Nant-Fawr Rd CF23 ..178 B6
Nant-gau NP12 ....59 B2
Nant-y-Ci Rd SA18 .218 F7
Nant-y-coed
  Thomastown CF39 ..133 A3
  ☒ Trodyrhiw CF48 ....31 B1
Nant-y-croft NP13 ....16 C6
Nant-y-Cwm NP13 ..60 C6
Nant-y-Dall Ave
  CF37 ....136 A4
Nant-y-Dderwen
  CF38 ....156 F5
Nant-y-Drope CF5 ..192 F4
Nant-y-Fedw CF41 ..82 C5
Nant-y-Fedw Rd
  SA13 ....219 ...
Nant-y-Ffyddon
  CF82 ....84 D7
Nant-y-Ffynnon
  CF31 ....169 B5
Nant-y-Gleisiad
  SA11 ....223 B8
  Nant-y-glo Round Twrs
  NP23 ....8 B1
Nant-y-Gro
  Llanelli SA14 ....41 C6
  Llangennech SA14 ..18 B1
Nant-y-Gwyddon Rd
  CF40, CF41 ....79 D2
Nant-y-Milwr Cl
  NP44 ....115 F7
Nant-y-moel Row
  CF32 ....104 E7
Nant-y-Mynydd
  Pontypridd CF37 ....109 D7
  Seven Sisters SA10 ..222 E4
Nant-y-Rhos NP12 ..85 F3

Nant-yr-Adar
- Bridgend CF31 ...... 168 B6
- Llantwit Major CF61 . 210 A5

Nant-yr-Ely CF5 ...... 192 E4
Nantcarn Rd NP11 .. 114 C8
Nantddu Terr CF44 .. 82 C6
Nantgarw China Works
CF15 .... 158 A7
Nantgarw Inf Sch
CF15 .... 157 F8
Nantgarw Rd CF83 .. 137 E2
Nantgwyddon CF17 .. 79 C2
Nantgwyn CF44 ...... 28 C4
Nantgwyn St CF40 .. 106 F4
Nanthir Rd CF32 ..... 103 E6

Nantlais
- Ammanford SA18 .... 219 B8
- Corntown CF35 ...... 186 B7

Nantong Way SA1 .... 68 F4
Nantwen SA14 .... 41 F4
Nantyboda SA14 ..... 100 E4
Nantybryn SA14 ..... 41 A7
Nantydd Terr SA14 .. 41 C5
Nantyffin N SA7 ..... 69 D7

Nantyffin Rd
- Pontarddulais SA4 ... 19 D3
- Swansea SA7 .... 69 C2

Nantyffin S SA7 ..... 69 C6
Nantyffyllon Prim Sch
CF34 .... 101 F6
Nantyffyllon Terr
CF34 .... 101 F6
Nantygalo Comp Sch
NP23 .... 8 B2
Nantyglyn Rd SA18 .. 219 F8
Nantygwenith Ct
CF48 .... 10 C1
Nantygwenith St
CF48 .... 10 C2
Nantymoel Prim Sch
CF32 .... 104 E5
Nantyrychain Terr
CF32 .... 103 F2
Napier CI CF31 ...... 169 A4

Napier St
- Machen CF83 .... 140 A7
- Mountain Ash CF45 .. 126 E4

Narberth Cres NP44 . 90 B3
Narberth Ct CF83 .... 137 C4
Narberth Rd CF5 .... 193 D5
Narberth Ct CF22 ... 214 F7
Naseby CI CF23 ..... 160 F1
Nash CI NP10 .... 142 B6
Nash Dr NP19 .... 144 B2
Nash Gr NP19 .... 144 B3
Nash Rd NP19 ...... 144 B2
Nash St CF45 .... 82 C2
Nash View CF71 ..... 187 F4
Nasturtium Way
CF23 .... 160 D1
Nat Assembly for Wales
The CF10 .... 195 C2
Nat Cricket Ctr (Canolfan
Criced Genedlaethol)
CF11 .... 194 E7
Nat Mus of Wales
CF10 .... 195 A7
Nathan Ho NP22 ..... 12 E4
Nathan St SA13 ..... 40 C3
National Bldgs
NP20 .... 143 C4
Navigation CI CF44 . 83 C7
Navigation Rd NP11 . 114 F3

Navigation St
- Bedwas CF83 .... 139 A7
- Mountain Ash CF45 .. 54 D3

Navigation Terr CF34. 75 E6
Navigation Villas 2
CF45 .... 54 E1
Navigation W CF45 .. 54 E3
Neale St CF62 .... 214 E6
Neath Abbey SA10 ... 71 B7
Neath Abbey Bsns Pk
SA10 .... 71 B8
Neath Abbey Inf Sch
SA10 .... 71 B8
Neath Abbey Rd SA10 71 C8
Neath Coll SA10 ..... 48 D1
Neath Ct NP44 ...... 89 A4
Neath General Hospl
SA11 .... 71 E2
Neath General Sta
SA11 .... 71 E7
Neath Mus & Art Gallery
SA11 .... 71 E8

Neath Rd
- Briton Ferry SA11 .... 71 C1
- Bryn-côch SA10 ..... 48 C7
- Crynant SA10 .... 226 A7
- Maesteg CF34 .... 101 E4
- Morriston SA6 ...... 46 A2
- Pontrhydyfen SA12, SA13 .... 100 C2
- Resolven SA11 ...... 226 C5
- Resolven SA11 ...... 226 D5
- Swansea SA1,SA6 ... 68 E8
- Swansea SA6 .... 69 A8
- Tonna SA11 .... 49 B1
- Ystradgynlais SA9 ... 2 F6
- Ystradgynlais SA9 ... 222 A4

Neath St CF24 ...... 195 E5
Neath Villas NP4 .... 37 E3
Nebo Ct CF41 .... 79 C3
Neerings NP44 ...... 89 A1
Neilson CI CF24 ..... 195 D5
Nelson CI CF10 ...... 195 C4
Nelson Dr NP19 ..... 144 E6

Nelson Rd CF62 ..... 215 A8

Nelson St
- Aberdare CF44 ...... 53 B5
- Ebbw Vale NP23 ..... 3 D4
- Swansea SA1 .... 95 C6

Nelson Terr
- Llanelli SA15 .... 40 C4
- New Tredegar NP24 .. 33 F1

Neol St CF44 .... 53 B4
Nesta Rd CF5 .... 194 B6
Neston Rd NP19 ..... 144 D6
Nethercourt NP44 ... 89 B3
Nettlefold Rd CF24 .. 195 D4
Neuadd Rd SA18 .... 220 C8
Neuadd St NP13 .... 36 A6
Neuadda CI NP10 ... 141 F2
Neuaddwen St CF81 . 58 B5
Nevern Wlk 3 NP44 . 90 B2
Nevill St SA15 ...... 40 C4
Nevill Terr 2 NP4 ... 17 D7
Neville Pk NP10 ..... 163 E1
Neville PI 15 CF11 .. 194 E5

Neville Rd
- Bridgend CF31 ...... 168 C2
- Porthcawl CF36 ..... 183 A7

Neville St
- Aberystwen NP4 ..... 37 E6
- Cardiff CF11 .... 194 E5

Neville Terr CF44 .... 28 F2
Nevills CI SA4 ...... 66 C6
Nevin Cres CF3 ..... 179 C4
New Barn CF62 ..... 201 B1
New Bldgs The
NP10 .... 163 C6
New Bryn Terr CF39 .107 D8
New Bryngwyn Rd
NP11 .... 86 E6
New Bryngwyn St
NP12 .... 85 B6
New Castle St 8
CF47 .... 10 E1
New Ceidrim Rd
SA18 .... 220 B8
New Century St
CF40 .... 106 F4
New Chapel Ct NP44 . 89 D1
New Chapel St CF24 . 78 D6
New Church St CF48 . 10 A5
New College Prim Sch
CF10 .... 195 B5
New Cross Bldgs 11
SA6 .... 46 A1
New Cut Rd SA1 .... 95 D8
New Cwm Terr NP23 . 35 E7
New Dock Rd SA15 .. 40 D3
New Dock St SA15 ... 40 D2
New Forest View
CF71 .... 189 A1
New George St CF10 .195 C2
New Gladstone St
NP13 .... 15 E5
New Henry St SA11 .. 71 D6
New High St NP13 ... 36 C2
New Hos Pant CF48 .. 11 B6
New House Ct SA6 .. 61 C4
New Inn Ind Sch NP4 .63 A4
New Inn PI SA11 .... 226 D5
New James St 8 NP4 .17 D6
New King St CF11 ... 79 B2
New Mill Cnr CF72 .. 173 D6
New Mill Rd SA2 .... 94 A6
New Orchard St NP20 .89 C4
New Park Ct SA1 .... 95 D8
New Park Holiday Pk
SA3 .... 231 A4
New Park Terr CF37 . 125 E3
New Pastures NP20 . 143 A2
New Quarr Rd SA5 .. 68 C5
New Quay Rd NP19 .164 E8

New Rd
- Aberystwen NP4 ..... 37 D5
- Aberystwen NP4 ..... 37 E6
- Ammanford SA18 .... 219 B6
- Argoed NP12 .... 58 F4
- Caerleon NP18 ..... 118 C1
- Cardiff CF3 .... 179 B2
- Cilfrew SA10 .... 49 C5
- Crofty SA4 .... 64 B3
- Cwmfelinfach NP11 . 113 B4
- Deri CF81 .... 57 C8
- Dowlais CF48 ...... 11 A4
- Grovesend SA4 .... 43 C6
- Gwaun-Cae-Gurwen SA18 .... 220 E7
- Hengoed CF82, NP12 . 85 A3
- Llanelli SA14 ...... 41 B6
- Llanelli SA15 ...... 40 C6
- Llansamlet SA7 .... 46 F1
- Mountain Ash CF45 .. 54 D3
- Mountain Ash CF45 .. 82 A7
- Mountain Ash CF45 .. 82 C6
- Nantglo NP23 ...... 8 C2
- Neath SA10 .... 70 C1
- Neath Abbey SA10 .. 70 F7
- Machen CF83 .... 139 C6
- Pencoed CF72 ...... 153 C1
- Pontardawe SA8 .... 23 B2
- Pontardawe SA8 .... 24 A7
- Pontardawe SA8 .... 24 B4
- Pontarddulais SA4 .. 19 B4
- Pontypool NP4 ..... 62 F3
- Porthcawl CF36 .... 183 B7

New Rd continued
- Pyle CF33 .... 148 D3
- Skewen SA10 .... 71 A7
- Swansea SA2 .... 67 D1
- Swansea SA5 .... 68 C6
- Tondu CF32 .... 150 B5
- Ynysmeudwy SA8 ... 23 F6
- Ynysybwl CF37 ..... 109 A7

New Row
- Cwmbran NP44 ..... 88 E1
- Machen CF83 .... 139 F6

New Rupera St
NP20 .... 143 C3
New School Rd SA18 .220 B8

New St
- Aberavon SA12 ..... 99 A1
- New Aberavon SA12 . 99 A1
- Aberystwen NP4 .... 37 E6
- Aberdare CF44 ..... 53 C6
- Aberkenfig CF32 .... 150 C4
- Bridgend CF31 ..... 169 B2
- Caerphilly CF83 .... 187 F4
- Cwmbran NP44 ..... 89 E5
- Ferndale CF43 ...... 80 A5
- Glynneath SA11 .... 223 D1
- Llanelli SA15 ...... 40 E2
- Neath SA11 .... 71 E8
- Newport NP20 ...... 143 D2
- Pontcymmer CF32 .. 103 F2
- Swansea SA1 ...... 95 D8
- Tonna SA11 .... 49 D3
- Treherbert CF42 .... 50 E3
- Ystalyfera SA9 ..... 2 A4

New Terr NP4 ...... 62 A8
New Tynybedw St
CF42 .... 78 E6

New Villas
- Cwmaman CF44 .... 53 A3
- Mumbles SA3 ...... 123 B4

New Well La SA3 .... 122 F5
New William St 16
NP4 .... 17 C6
New Zealand Rd
CF14 .... 177 E2
New Zealand St SA15 .40 C6
Newall St NP13 ..... 36 B5
Newborough Ave
CF11 .... 177 E8
Newbridge Comp Sch
NP11 .... 87 A6
Newbridge Ct 7
CF37 .... 109 D2
Newbridge Gdns
CF33 .... 168 E3

Newbridge Rd
- Llantrisant CF72 .... 155 E4
- Pontllanfraith NP12 .. 86 A4
- Port Talbot SA12 .... 124 E8

Newbridge Sec Sch
NP11 .... 87 A6
Newbury Hill CF11 .. 168 E4
Newcastle Hill CF31 . 168 E4
Newchurch Ct NP44 . 89 C3
Newchurch Rd NP23 . 7 D2
Newell Rd SA10 ..... 70 E8
Newent Rd CF3 ..... 179 F6
Newfoundland Rd
CF14 .... 177 E2
Newfoundland Way
NP12 .... 85 D6

Newgale CI
- Barry CF62 .... 214 F8
- Swansea SA5 .... 67 F7

Newgale Ho NP44 ... 89 F3
Newgale PI CF5 ..... 193 D4
Newgale Row NP44 . 89 F3
Newlands SA12 ..... 98 E5
Newlands Ave CF31 . 169 B7
Newlands CI CF33 .. 148 C2

Newlands Ct
- Cardiff CF14 .... 160 A1
- Penarth CF64 ...... 198 A3

Newlands Rd CF5 ... 179 F3
Newlands PI CF62 .. 214 F5
Newlyn Rd NP11 .... 87 B7
Newman CI NP19 ... 144 F5
Newman Rd NP4 .... 38 B1
Newmarket Wlk 8
CF47 .... 10 D1
Newmill Gdns CF72 . 173 D8
Newminster Rd
CF23 .... 195 C8
Newnham Cres 3 .... 94 E7
Newnham PI NP44 .. 89 C3
Newpark District
Shopping Ctr CF72 . 155 C2
Newport (Casnewydd) Sta
NP20 .... 143 B5
Newport Arc 3
NP20 .... 143 B5
Newport Castle
NP20 .... 143 C4
Newport Ctr(L Ctr)
NP20 .... 143 C4
Newport Mkt CF10 .. 143 C5
Newport Mus & Art Gal
NP20 .... 143 C4
Newport Nash Campus
NP19 .... 144 C2

Newport Rd
- Abercarn NP11 ..... 114 B8
- Bedwas CF83 .... 138 E6
- Cardiff CF3 .... 179 C4
- Cardiff CF24 .... 195 D5
- Croesyceiliog NP44 . 90 B6
- Cwmbran NP44 ..... 117 A6
- Hollybush NP22,NP12 .34 C4
- Machen CF83 .... 139 C6
- Pontllanfraith NP12 .. 85 F3
- Pontypool NP4 ..... 63 A2
- Risca NP11 .... 148 D2

Newport Retail Pk
NP19 .... 144 D2
Newport Road La
CF24 .... 195 C6

Newton Ave SA12 ... 98 F1
Newton CI CF82 ..... 84 E7
Newton Nottage Rd
CF36 .... 183 B8

Newton Prim Sch
- Mountain Ash CF45 .. 54 E2
- Mumbles SA3 ...... 122 E5
- Porthcawl CF36 ..... 183 A7

Newton Rd
- Cardiff CF11 .... 194 D4
- Clydach SA6 .... 22 D1
- Mumbles SA3 ...... 123 A5
- Rumney CF3 .... 179 F2

Newton St
- Abercanaid CF48 ... 30 F3
- Barry CF63 .... 215 B6
- Swansea SA1 ...... 95 D8

Newton Terr 9 CF47 . 30 E8
Newton Way NP20 .. 116 F2
Newton Wynd NP44 . 89 B1
Newtown CI SA14 ... 19 A7
Newtown Ct 2 CF24 . 195 C5
Newtown Ind Est
CF10 .... 195 C5
Newydd Ct CF15 .... 158 D8
Newydd The CF33 ... 148 D2
Neyland CI CF38 .... 135 F2
Neyland Ct CF62 .... 214 F8
Neyland Dr SA5 .... 67 F7
Neyland Path NP44 . 89 B2
Neyland Pl CF5 ..... 193 D4
Niagara St CF37 .... 133 B6
Nibloe Terr 2 CF47 . 10 F4
Nicander PI SA1 .... 95 B8
Nicander Rd SA1 .... 95 B8
Nicholas Ct SA2 .... 94 B6
Nicholas St NP44 ... 78 F3

Nicholl CI
- Boverton CF61 ..... 210 B6
- Mumbles SA3 ...... 123 C3

Nicholl St SA1 ...... 95 B6
Nicholls Ave CF36 .. 183 A7
Nicholls Rd CF32 ... 150 C8
Nicholson Webb CI
CF5 .... 176 D3
Nidd CI NP20 .... 116 C1
Nidd Wlk NP20 ..... 116 C1
Nidum CI SA10 ..... 71 C8

Nightingale CI
- Llanelli SA15 ...... 41 A5
- Newport NP10 ..... 163 E7

Nightingale Ho
- 3 Aberavon SA12 ... 98 F1
- Cwmbran NP44 ..... 89 D5

Nightingale Pk SA11 . 72 E1
Nightingale Pl CF48 . 30 F6
Nightingale PI CF24 . 206 C3
Nightingale St CF48 . 30 F4
Nightingale Terr NP4 . 6 C1
Nightingale's Bush
CF37 .... 135 E8
Nile Rd CF40 .... 107 B5
Nile St CF37 .... 135 D8
Nine Mile Point CI
NP11 .... 113 B4
Nine Mile Point Ind Est
NP11 .... 113 C3
Nine Mile Point Rd
NP11 .... 113 C3
Ninian Park (Cardiff City
AFC) CF11 .... 194 D4
Ninian Park Jun & Inf Sch
CF11 .... 194 E3
Ninian Park Prim Sch
CF11 .... 194 E3
Ninian Park Rd CF11 . 194 E5
Ninian Park Sta
CF11 .... 194 D4
Ninian Rd CF23 .... 178 B1

Ninian St
- Treherbert CF42 .... 51 A1
- Treorchy CF42 ..... 78 D7

Ninth Ave
- Hirwaun CF44 ..... 224 D1
- Merthyr Tydfil CF47 . 10 E5
- Swansea SA6 ...... 45 D2

Nith St 18 CF44 .... 29 A1
Nixon Terr SA6 ..... 46 A1
Nixonville CF48 .... 55 C4
Noble Sq SA12 ..... 98 F1
Nobel Square Ind Est
NP23 .... 9 B4
Noel Terr CF48 ..... 55 E1
Nolton Ct SA5 ...... 67 F6
Nolton PI NP44 ..... 89 C1
Nolton St CF31 ..... 169 B3
Nora St CF24 .... 195 D6
Norbury Ave CF5 ... 193 E7
Norbury Ct CF5 .... 193 E7
Norbury Rd CF5 .... 193 E7
Norbury Ho 6 NP44 . 89 C2
Nordale Rd CF61 ... 178 A4
Nordale Rise CF63 .. 215 C6
Norfolk CI NP44 .... 11 A3
Norfolk Ct 6 CF15 .. 176 B6
Norfolk Ho NP19 ... 143 F6
Norfolk Rd NP19 ... 143 F6
Norfolk St CF5 ..... 195 A1
Norman Rd CF14 ... 177 B4

Norman St
- Aberavon SA12 .... 99 A1
- Abertillery NP13 ... 36 B6

Norman St continued
- Caerleon NP18 ...... 118 B2
- Port Talbot CF34 .... 195 B8

Norman Terr
- Merthyr Tydfil CF47 . 10 D2
- Pentrebach CF48 .... 31 B4

Normands Ho NP44 . 116 C8
Normandy Rd SA1 .. 68 E3
Norris CI CF64 ...... 206 D5
Norsemen CI CF42 .. 212 E2

North Ave
- Aberdare CF44 ..... 28 F2
- Maesycwmmer CF82 . 85 B2
- Pyle CF33 .... 148 C2
- Pontypool NP4 ..... 6 C1

North Blackvein Ind Est
NP11 .... 114 A4
North Church St
CF10 .... 195 B4
North Clive St CF11 . 194 F3
North Ct CF31 ...... 169 E3
North Dock Bsns
Workshops SA15 ... 40 B4
North Edward St
CF10 .... 195 B6
North Hill Rd SA1 ... 95 C8
North Hills La CF3 .. 120 C6
North Lake Dr NP10 .163 C6
North Luton CF23 .. 195 C5
North Mead CF32 ... 150 B3
North Morgan St 1
CF11 .... 194 E5

North Park Rd
- Abercarn NP11 ..... 114 C6
- Aberychan NP4 .... 37 F3
- Bargoed CF81 ...... 59 F6
- Barry CF64 .... 215 E6
- Bridgend CF31 ..... 169 C3
- Cardiff CF10 .... 194 F7

North Rd
- Aberbeeg NP13 .... 11 C1
- Cardiff CF14 .... 160 A1

North St
- Abercynon CF45 .... 82 E3
- Blaenavon NP4 .... 17 B7
- Cardiff CF11 .... 194 F3
- Dowlais CF48 ...... 11 A4
- Ebbw Vale NP23 .... 3 C4
- Maesteg CF34 ..... 75 B2
- Newport NP20 ..... 143 B4
- Penydarren CF47 ... 10 F4
- Pontypridd CF37 ... 109 D2
- Port Talbot SA12 ... 125 D7

North Terr
- Llanelli SA14 ...... 41 B7
- Maerdy CF43 ...... 52 A2
- Coytrahen CF32 ... 150 C8
- Fleur De Lis NP12 ... 85 B6
- Llanbradach CF83 .. 111 F1
- Mountain Ash CF45 . 81 F8
- Ogmore Vale CF32 . 104 C1

North View CF15 ... 158 B4
North Wlk Barry CF62 214 E6
- Cwmbran NP44 ..... 89 D3
Northam Ave CF3 ... 179 A5
Northampton La NP20 95 C7
Northcliffe Dr CF64 . 207 B5
Northcote La CF24 .. 195 B7
Northcote St CF24 .. 195 B7
Northcote Terr CF63 . 215 C6

Northern Ave
- Cardiff CF14 .... 176 B8
- Cardiff CF14 .... 177 A5

Northern Avenue Ash Gr
CF14 .... 177 A6
Northern Avenue Manor
Way CF14 .... 177 C5
Northfield CI NP18 .. 118 A4
Northfield Rd NP18 . 118 A4
Northlands CF3 ..... 179 C7
Northlands Pk SA3 .. 122 A7
Northumberland Rd 2
NP19 .... 143 F6
Northumberland St
CF5 .... 194 C3

Northway
- Bishopston SA3 .... 122 B7
- Pontypool NP4 ..... 39 B2

Northway CI SA3 ... 122 A7
Northways CF36 .... 183 A7

Norton Ave
- Cardiff CF14 .... 177 D4
- Mumbles SA3 ...... 123 A6

Norton Dr SA3 ..... 123 A6
Norton Rd CF64 .... 198 E3

Norton Terr
- Glyncorrwg SA13 ... 227 D2
- Mumbles SA3 ...... 123 A6
- Pengroes SA14 .... 218 D8

Norwich Rd CF23 .. 178 E1
Norwich St CF24 ... 195 D6
Norwood CF14 ..... 159 F2
Norwood Cres CF63 . 215 C7
Norwood Ct CF14 .. 195 D7

Nottage Mead CF36 .165 E2
Nottage Mews SA3 .122 E4
Nottage Prim Sch
CF36 .... 182 F7

Nottage Rd
- Cardiff CF5 .... 193 C4
- Mumbles SA3 ...... 122 E4

Nottingham St CF5 .. 194 B6
Notts Gdns SA2 ..... 94 F7
Novello Ho SA12 .... 98 A2
Nuns Cres CF37 .... 80 A3
Nurseries The NP18 .145 D8
Nursery Cres NP22 .. 13 A2
Nursery Gdns CF31 . 168 F8
Nursery Rise CF83 .. 133 A2
Nursery Terr NP22 .. 13 E8
Nurses Cnr SA4 .... 64 F4
Nurston CI CF62 .... 212 E2
Nut Wlk CF61 ...... 210 A4
Nydfa Rd NP12 ..... 85 A3
Nythbran Terr CF39 .108 B3
Nythfa SA4 .... 44 C5

O

O'Donnell Rd CF63 .. 215 A7
Oak CI CF72 .... 155 C2

Oak Ct
- Caerphilly NP12 .... 85 F6
- Cardiff CF15 ...... 158 D2
- 1 Cardiff CF24 .... 206 E2
- Penarth CF64 ..... 206 E2
- 1 Pontypool NP44 . 38 A1

Oak Dr SA5 .... 66 D4

Oak Gr
- Cimla SA11 .... 72 B5
- St Athan CF62 ..... 211 B7

Oak Hill Pk SA10 ... 70 E8
Oak Ho CF14 ...... 176 E7
Oak La CF83 .... 140 B6
Oak PI CF81 .... 57 E2

Oak Rd
- Llanharry CF72 .... 172 B5
- Merthyr Tydfil CF47 . 10 D3
- Rogerstone NP10 .. 141 F6

Oak Ridge
- Blackmill CF35 .... 130 E2
- Swansea SA2 ...... 94 A6

Oak St
- Abercarn NP11 ..... 87 B4
- Aberdare CF44 .... 29 A1
- Aberkenfig CF32 ... 150 C4
- Abertillery NP13 ... 36 A5
- Blackwood NP12 ... 85 E7
- Cwm NP23 .... 35 A7
- Cwmbran NP44 .... 89 E2
- Ferndale CF43 ..... 79 F7
- Gorseinon SA4 .... 66 D8
- Hendreforgan CF39 . 132 C5
- Newport NP19 ..... 143 E8
- Rhydyfelin CF37 ... 136 B5
- Ton Pentre CF41 ... 79 A2
- Tonypandy CF40 ... 106 B7
- Treherbert CF42 ... 78 A8
- Treorchy CF42 ..... 78 E6

Oak Terr
- Abercarn NP11 ..... 114 C5
- Abercwmboi CF44 .. 53 E4
- Coytrahen CF32 .... 150 C8
- Fleur De Lis NP12 ... 85 B6
- Llanbradach CF83 .. 111 F1
- Mountain Ash CF45 . 81 F8
- Ogmore Vale CF32 . 104 C1

Oak Tree Ave SA2 .. 94 C6

Oak Tree CI
- Pontypool NP4 ..... 63 A5
- Radyr CF15 .... 176 A6

Oak Tree Ct
- Bridgend CF31 ..... 169 D5
- Newbridge NP11 ... 60 C1
- Newport NP19 ..... 144 B5

Oak Tree Dr
- Cefn Hengoed CF82 . 84 E5
- Porthcawl CF36 .... 183 E7
- Rogerstone NP10 .. 141 D7

Oak View
- Blaenavon NP4 .... 17 E6
- Cilfrew SA10 ...... 49 C6

Oak Way CF32 ..... 150 F4
Oak Wood Ave CF23 173 E8
Oakdale CI NP18 ... 117 F2
Oakdale Comp Sch
NP12 .... 86 A8
Oakdale Hospl SA11 . 59 A1
Oakdale Inf Sch NP12 59 B2
Oakdale Path 5
NP44 .... 89 C2
Oakdale PI NP44 ... 62 A8
Oakdale Rd CF40 ... 107 A1

Oakdale Terr
- Blackwood NP12 ... 86 A8
- Tonypandy CF40 ... 107 A2

Oakdene CI SA3 .... 93 D7

Oakdene CI
- Baglan SA12 .... 98 C5
- Cardiff CF23 .... 178 C4

Oakengates CF35 ... 183 D8

Oakfield
- Caerleon NP18 ..... 117 F3
- Pontllanfraith NP12 . 86 A4
- Radyr CF15 .... 176 A6

Oakfield Gdns
- Machen CF83 ...... 140 B6
- Newport NP20 ..... 143 A4

Oakfield Jun & Inf Sch
CF15 .... 179 E7
Oakfield PI CF37 ... 116 F8

Oakfield Rd
- Barry CF62 .... 214 D7
- Cwmbran NP44 .... 89 D1

Oakfield continued
Glanaman SA18 .... 220 B8
Newport NP20 .... 143 A4
Pontardawe SA8 .... 23 E5
Tredegar NP22 .... 13 F5
Oakfield St
Aberfan CF48 .... 55 C6
Cardiff CF24 .... 195 D7
Llanbradach CF83 .... 112 A3
Pontarddulais SA4 .... 19 C4
Ystrad Mynach CF82 ...... 84 F1
Oakfield Terr
Ammanford SA18 .... 219 C7
Ebbw Vale NP23 .... 14 E6
Nant-y-Moel CF32 .... 104 F5
Pontypridd CF37 .... 106 F8
Oakfields CF3 .... 162 D1
Oakford CF23 .... 160 E1
Oakford Pl SA5 .... 67 D6
Oakland CF3 .... 47 A5
Oakland Ct CF37 .... 109 F4
Oakland Dr SA10 .... 48 C3
Oakland Gdns CF31 .... 57 E3
Oakland Rd SA3 .... 123 A4
Oakland St
Bedlinog CF46 .... 56 B6
Mountain Ash CF45 .... 54 E1
Oakland Terr
Cwmbran NP44 .... 116 E8
Ferndale CF43 .... 80 A5
Newbridge NP11 .... 60 A1
Pontypridd CF37 .... 109 F4
Rhymney NP22 .... 12 E5
Treharris CF46 .... 83 B7

Oaklands
Bargoed CF81 .... 57 F2
Merthyr Vale CF48 .... 55 D3
Miskin CF72 .... 173 D8
Mumbles SA3 .... 122 F6
Ponthir NP18 .... 117 E6
Port Talbot SA13 .... 99 C2
Oaklands Ave CF33 .... 168 C4
Oaklands Bsns Pk
CF43 .... 80 A4

Oaklands Cl
Bridgend CF31 .... 168 D4
Cardiff CF37 .... 179 E7
Oaklands Ct SA2 .... 94 A1
Oaklands Dr
Bridgend CF31 .... 168 D4
Ton Pentre CF41 .... 79 B3
Oaklands Park Dr
NP10 .... 141 E3
Oaklands Prim Sch
CF44 .... 53 D6
Oaklands Rd
Bridgend CF31 .... 168 C4
Newport NP19 .... 143 F5
Pontllanfraith SA4 .... 44 A6
Pontypool NP4 .... 62 D1
Pontypool NP4 .... 89 D8
Oaklands Rise CF31 .. 168 C4
Oaklands Terr SA1 ...... 95 B7
Oaklands View SA4 .... 89 A3
Oakleafe Dr CF23 ...... 178 E8
Oakleigh Ct NP44 ...... 115 F8
Oakleigh House Sch
SA2 .... 94 A2
Oakleigh Rd CF11 ...... 194 F2
Oakley Pl CF11 .... 194 F2
Oakley St NP19 .... 143 F3
Oakley Terr CF37 ...... 107 A1
Oakmead Cl CF23 ...... 160 F1
Oakmeadow Ct
CF3 .... 179 E7
Oakmeadow Dr CF3 .. 179 F6
Oakridge CF14 .... 159 F2
Oakridge W CF14 ...... 159 F2
Oaks Ct NP20 .... 143 A2
Oaks Cl NP4 .... 37 F3
Oaks End Cl CF82 ...... 84 E7
Oaks Rd NP4 .... 37 F2
Oaks The
Blackwood NP12 .... 59 C1
Cardiff CF14 .... 160 B2
Croesyceiliog NP44 .... 90 B5
Llanmartin NP18 .... 145 E7
Llantwit Fardre CF38 ... 156 D8
Machen CF83 .... 100 B6
Quakers Yard CF46 .... 83 C5
Oaksford NP4 .... 89 A2
Oaktree Ct
Cwmbran NP44 .... 89 E1
Llangennech SA14 .... 42 B7
Oakway CF5 .... 193 C8
Oakwood CF34 .... 102 C1
Thomastown CF39 .... 133 B3
Oakwood Ho SA12 .... 100 A8
Oakwood Pl SA13 ..... 100 C1
Oakwood Rd
Neath SA11 .... 71 F8
Port Talbot SA13 .... 125 B8
Swansea SA2 .... 94 F6
Oakwood St
Pontypridd CF37 .... 135 C5
Port Talbot SA13 .... 99 B1
Oban St CF63 .... 215 B6
Ocean Cres 6 SA6 .... 95 D5

Ocean House Rd
CF62 .... 211 E1
Ocean St CF42 .... 78 B4
Ocean View (Golwg y
Mor) SA10 .... 97 C8
Ocean View Cl SA2 ...... 94 B3
Ocean Way
Cardiff CF24 .... 195 E4
Port Talbot SA13 .... 98 C1
Ochr-y-Waun Rd
SA9 .... 221 B7
Octavius Cl NP10 .... 163 E5
Oddfellows St SA11 .... 223 D1
Oddfellows' St
2 Bridgend CF31 .... 168 F4
Ystradgynlais SA9 .... 1 F2
Odessa St CF48 .... 11 A5
Odet Cl CF14 .... 176 E7
Odette Ho 4 SA2 .... 98 F1
Odyn's Fee CF62 .... 212 E2
Office St CF39 .... 107 F3
Offway NP44 .... 116 C8
Ogilvie Terr Deri CF81 .. 33 A2
Fochriw CF81 .... 32 D5
Ogmore Castle CF32 . 185 A6
Ogmore Comp Sch
CF32 .... 151 A6
Ogmore Cres
Bettws NP20 .... 116 C1
Bridgend CF31 .... 169 A3
Ogmore Ct
Bridgend CF31 .... 168 D2
Caerphilly CF83 .... 137 D4
Ogmore Vale CF32 .... 104 E2
Ogmore Dr CF36 .... 165 E2
Ogmore Pl
Barry CF63 .... 215 A8
1 Llanyravon NP44 .... 90 B2
Ogmore Rd
Cardiff CF5 .... 193 C4
Ewenny CF32, CF35 ..... 185 D7
Swansea SA1 .... 69 A2
Ogmore Terr
Bridgend CF31 .... 168 F4
Bryncethin CF32 .... 151 A5
Ogmore Vale CF32 .... 104 F6
Ogwen Dr CF23 .... 178 C5
Ogwen Ho NP44 .... 89 C2
Ogwr Ent Ctr CF32 ... 150 C5
Ogwy St CF32 .... 104 F5
Okehampton Ave
CF3 .... 179 C8
Olchfa Cl SA2 .... 94 A6
Olchfa Sch SA2 .... 94 A6
Old Abergavenny Rd
NP4 .... 62 A7
Old Bakery Ct CF15 ... 157 C1
Old Bakery The NP13 .. 36 A6
Old Barn 3 NP11 .... 143 F8
Old Barn Way NP13 .... 36 A6
Old Barry Rd CF64 ..... 206 E6
Old Blaen-Afon Rd
7 Brynmawr NP23 ...... 28 E4
Brynmawr NP23 .... 35 F6
Old Blaina Rd NP13 .... 35 F6
Old Brewery La NP22 . 12 D4
Old Bridge CF31 .... 168 E4
Old Brithweunydd Rd
CF40 .... 107 A5
Old Castle Rd
Llanelli SA15 .... 40 B4
Llanelli SA15 .... 40 D8
Old Chapel Rd CF48 .. 10 A4
Old Chepstow Rd
NP18 .... 145 D8
Old Church La CF82,
NP12 .... 85 B3
Old Church Rd CF14 . 177 B5
Old Church St CF48 .... 10 A4
Old Clipper Rd CF10 . 193 F3
Old Duke Rd NP11 .... 6 E2
Old Estate Yd NP4 ...... 62 E5
Old Farm Ct SA7 .... 69 F6
Old Farm La CF15 ..... 174 E7
Old Farm Mews
CF14 .... 206 A3
Old Forge The CF15 .. 191 B1
Old Furnace SA10 .... 48 C5
Old Furnace Rd SA11 . 71 F6
Old Garden St 7
CF15 .... 176 B6
Old Green Intc NP20 . 143 C5
Old Hill Cardiff CF3 ... 179 D6
Newport NP18 .... 144 D7
Old Hill Cres NP18 ... 144 D7
Old James St 6 NP4 .. 37 C6
Old Kittle Rd SA3 ...... 121 F7
Old La NP4 .... 37 F4
Old Langstone Court Rd
NP18 .... 145 B8
Old Library Flats
CF15 .... 102 A5
Old Llanharan Rd
CF72 .... 153 C1
Old Lodge SA15 .... 40 D8
Old Hill Cardiff CF14 . 160 A6
Old Market Pl SA13 ... 205 A6
Old Market St SA13 .. 205 A6
Old Market Pl SA13 ... 99 D5
Old Market St SA11 .. 161 A6
Old Mill La CF47 .... 10 D1
Old Nantgarw Rd
CF15 .... 137 B1
Old Newport Rd CF3 . 179 F8
Old Pant Rd
Newbridge NP11 .... 60 C1
Newbridge NP11 .... 87 B7

Old Parish Rd
Blackmill CF35 .... 130 F2
Bryngwyn CF32 .... 85 A3
Ynysybwl CF37 .... 109 A7
Old Parish Road Ind Est
CF37 .... 109 A7
Old Park Rd SA13 ..... 107 D7
Old Park Terr CF37 ... 135 D7
Old Pen-Rhys Rd
CF41 .... 79 E2
Old Pol Sta CF33 .... 148 D2
Old Police Sta The
CF73 .... 79 B4
Old Port Rd CF5 .... 205 A6
Old Queen St NP19 ... 17 C6
Old Rd Aberystun NP4 . 37 F3
Ammanford SA18 .... 219 B8
Baglan SA12 .... 98 C7
Llanelli SA15 .... 40 B6
Neath SA11 .... 70 F7
Neath SA11 .... 71 D4
Pontardawe SA8 .... 24 A7
Skewen SA10 .... 71 A7
Old Rectory 4 CF5 ... 194 C6
Old Road City Prim Sch
SA15 .... 40 D6
Old Row NP44 .... 88 E1
Old School Cl CF48 ..... 10 C2
Old School Ct
Aberdarun NP11 .... 114 C5
Cardiff CF15 .... 158 C1
Old School Grange
CF82 .... 84 F2
Old School Pl NP44 .... 61 F8
Old School Rd CF36 . 182 F6
Old St CF40 .... 106 D6
Old Stables CF32 ...... 184 F6
Old Station Rd CF36 . 182 F7
Old Station Yd 2
CF36 .... 83 B6
Old Stone Row SA13 . 227 C2
Old Tavern CF32 .... 130 B4
Old Vicarage Cl
Cardiff CF14 .... 177 F8
1 Glan y Nant NP12 ...... 85 A7
Old Village La CF38 ... 165 F1
Old Village Rd CF62 . 214 C3
Old Wern Rd SA9 ...... 139 D3
Old William St 12
NP4 .... 17 C6
Old Winch Fawr Rd
CF48 .... 225 F1
Old Ynysbwl Rd CF37 . 81 E2
Oldbridge Ct NP44 .... 89 A5
Oldbury Bsns Ctr
NP44 .... 89 E2
Oldbury Rd NP44 .... 89 E2
Oldcastle Cty Jun & Inf
Schs CF31 .... 168 F3
Oldmill Rd CF63 .... 215 C7
Oldway SA13 .... 122 A6
Oldwell Ct CF23 .... 178 C2
Oliphant Circ NP20 .. 145 E2
Olive Branch Cres
SA11 .... 71 B3
Olive Rd SA3 .... 122 F8
Olive St Aberavon SA12 . 99 A1
Llanelli SA15 .... 40 F3
Olive Terr CF37 .... 107 D1
Oliver Jones Cres
CF63 .... 13 D7
Oliver Rd NP19 .... 144 A3
Oliver St CF37 .... 109 A1
Oliver Terr CF37 .... 135 E6
Ollivant Cl CF5 .... 176 D3
Olway Cl NP44 .... 90 A1
Ombersley La NP20 .. 142 F4
Ombersley Rd NP20 . 142 F4
Onllwyn Rd
Coelbren SA10 .... 222 F6
Dyffryn Cellwen SA10 . 222 E5
Onslow Terr CF32 ..... 104 D6
Ontario Way CF23 .... 178 C5
Open Hearth SA4 .... 62 E2
Orange Gr CF5 .... 176 C1
Orbit St CF24 .... 195 C6
Orchard Castle CF14 . 159 E2
Orchard Cl
Aberfan CF48 .... 55 C6
Bassaleg NP10 .... 141 F3
Boverton CF61 .... 210 D5
Marshfield CF3 .... 180 D8
Penhoed CF35 .... 152 E1
Pontypool NP4 .... 38 B1
Portyenon SA3 .... 231 A4
Porth CF39 .... 108 A3
Sigingstone CF71 .... 200 A4
Wenvoe CF5 .... 205 A7
Orchard Cres CF36 ... 206 B3

Orchard Lodge CF61 . 210 C5
Orchard Mews NP19 . 143 D7
Orchard Park CF13 .. CF73 . 179 E7
Orchard Pk CF3 .... 179 E7
Orchard Pl
Cardiff CF11 .... 194 D6
Cwmbran NP44 .... 89 D2
Newport NP18 .... 144 A6
Orchard Rise CF64 ...... 206 E4
Orchard St
Neath SA11 .... 71 E7
New Tredegar NP24 .... 8 A4
Newport NP19 .... 143 D7
Pontardawe SA8 .... 23 E5
Swansea SA1 .... 95 D7
Orchard Terr SA4 ..... 229 F4
Orchard The
Aberthin CF71 .... 189 B3
Cardiff CF5 .... 193 A5
Mumbles SA3 .... 122 F5
Ponthir NP18 .... 117 F6
Orchard Way CF62 ... 211 D3
Orchid Cl Cardiff CF3 . 180 B6
Port Talbot SA12 .... 98 C2
Tir-y-Berth CF82 .... 84 F6
Orchid Ct NP44 .... 89 A1
Ordell St CF24 .... 195 D5
Oregano Cl 13 CF3 ... 180 A4
Oriel Rd NP19 .... 143 E5
Oriel Rheilffordd Railway
Gallery CF10 .... 195 C2
Orion St 6 CF24 .... 195 C4
Orion Suite The
NP20 .... 143 D3
Ormes Rd SA10 .... 70 E8
Ormond St SA11 .... 71 C3
Ormonde Cl CF23 ..... 178 E3
Ormsby Terr SA1 .... 96 A7
Orpheus Rd SA6 .... 46 D6
Osborne Cl
Bridgend CF31 .... 150 F1
Newport NP19 .... 143 E5
Osborne Ct CF32 ...... 150 E6
Osborne Rd
Aberbillery NP13 .... 59 F5
Brynmawr NP23 .... 8 A4
Pontypool NP4 .... 62 A8
Pontypool NP4 .... 62 B7
Osborne Sq SA12 .... 99 A1
Osborne St CF11 ...... 194 E3
Osborne St SA1 .... 71 E7
Osborne Terr
Nant-y-Moel CF32 .... 104 F6
Swansea SA2 .... 94 D6
Osprey Cl Cardiff CF3 179 F8
Swansea SA2 .... 72 B5
Osterley St
Briton Ferry SA11 .... 71 C2
Swansea SA1 .... 95 F7
Oswald Rd NP20 ...... 143 C2
Oswestry Cl CF3 .... 179 C3
Other St CF37 .... 81 F2
Othery Pl CF37 .... 179 C8
Otter Cl NP20 .... 143 A3
Our Lady of the Angels Rc
Prim Sch NP44 .... 89 E2
Our Lady's RC Prim Sch
CF45 .... 54 E2
Outfall La NP10 .... 181 E7
Oval The CF47 .... 10 E1
Overdale WIN NP11 .... 59 D1
Overdene NP11 .... 85 F3
Overland Cl SA3 .... 123 A4
Overland Rd SA3 ...... 123 A4
Overton Cl CF36 .... 182 A5
Overton St CF48 .... 11 A5
Ovington Terr CF5 ... 194 B7
Owain Cl Cardiff CF23 . 178 C4
Penarth CF64 .... 206 E3
Owain Ct CF62 .... 211 D4
Owen Cl NP18 .... 118 A4
Owen St CF37 .... 136 A4
Owen's La SA9 .... 221 C2
Owen's Pl SA12 .... 98 C1
Owendale Terr NP4 .... 37 F2
Owls Lodge La SA3 ..... 93 F1
Oxford Ave 10 CF10 . 195 A5
Oxford Cl NP18 .... 117 F4
Oxford Ct CF64 .... 104 E2
Oxford La CF24 .... 195 C6
Oxford PI NP20 .... 60 C6
Oxford St
Aberdare CF44 .... 28 F2
Abertillery NP13 .... 36 B6
Barry CF62 .... 216 F3
Cardiff CF24 .... 195 C7
Gelligaer CF82 .... 84 D7
Maerdy CF43 .... 54 B1
Mountain Ash CF45 .... 54 D3
Nantgarw CF15 .... 174 B1
Oxford Street SA1 .... 95 C6
Oxford Terr NP4 .... 37 F2
Oxford Terr SA9 .... 116 F6
Oxwich Cl CF62 .... 216 B4
Oxwich Cl Cardiff CF5 193 F7
Cefn Hengoed CF82 .... 85 F7
Oxwich Leisure Pk
SA3 .... 231 D5

Oxwich Rd NP19 .... 144 A1
Oyster Bend CF64 .... 216 B4
Oystermouth Castle
SA3 .... 123 A5
Oystermouth Ct SA3 123 A6
Oystermouth Prim Sch
SA3 .... 123 A5
Oystermouth Rd SA1 95 C5
Ozanam Ct SA5 .... 67 D6

P

Pace Cl CF5 .... 176 D2
Pace Rd NP44 .... 89 B1
Packers Rd CF39 ...... 107 E4
Padarn Cl CF23 .... 178 B5
Padarn Pl 8 NP44 .... 89 E5
Paddock Cl NP11 ...... 215 B7
Paddock Rise NP44 ..... 90 B1
Paddock St SA15 .... 40 D4
Paddock The
Cardiff CF14 .... 160 A3
Cardiff CF23 .... 178 C2
Cowbridge CF71 .... 189 A1
Mumbles SA3 .... 123 A8
Paddocks Cres CF72 172 F6
Paddocks The
Aberdare CF44 .... 53 C8
Blackwood NP12 .... 58 E1
Caerleon NP18 .... 117 F3
Church Village CF38 .... 135 D1
Groesfaen CF72 .... 174 C6
Llanyravon NP44 .... 90 B1
Penarth CF64 .... 217 A8
Tonna SA11 .... 49 B2
Tonyrefail CF39 .... 133 D6
Padley's Cl CF34 .... 102 D2
Page La SA1 .... 95 B6
Page St SA1 .... 95 B7
Paget La CF11 .... 194 F3
Paget Pl CF64 .... 207 B5
Paget Rd CF64 .... 214 E2
Paget St SA1 .... 207 B5
Paget St Cardiff CF11 . 194 F2
Ynysybwl CF37 .... 81 F1
Paget Terr CF64 .... 207 B5
Painter's Row CF47 ... 78 B8
Palace Ave
Cardiff CF5 .... 194 B8
Llanelli SA15 .... 40 E5
Palace Ct CF23 .... 178 C6
Palace Rd CF5 .... 194 B8
Palace Row NP13 ..... 146 B1
Palalwyf Ave CF72 ... 173 B7
Pale Rd SA10 .... 70 F6
Palleg Rd SA9 .... 1 C2
Palm Cl NP44 .... 63 B5
Palm Rd CF47 .... 10 D5
Palm Sq NP19 .... 144 A4
Palmer Ho CF14 .... 159 E4
Palmer Pl SA13 .... 207 D7
Palmer St CF63 .... 215 D7
Palmers Dr CF5 .... 194 A4
Palmers Vale Bsns Ctr
CF63 .... 215 D7
Palmerston Prim Sch
CF63 .... 215 D7
Palmerston Rd CF63 . 215 D7
Palmerston Workshops
CF63 .... 215 D7
Palmerstown Ho
CF63 .... 215 D8
Palmyra Ct SA3 .... 123 A6
Palmyra Pl 11 NP20 . 143 C4
Pamela St CF45 .... 54 E2
Pandy NP44 .... 89 C3
Pandy Bglws CF32 ... 129 F2
Pandy Cl CF37 .... 10 B3
Pandy Cres CF33 ...... 148 A1
Pandy Ind La CF82 ... 150 D4
Pandy La CF72 .... 140 A7
Pandy Pk CF32 .... 150 D6
Pandy Rd
Aberkenfig CF32 .... 150 C4
Bedwas CF83 .... 138 C7
Blackwood NP11 .... 59 D2
Pandy Rd Nant-y-Moel CF32 . 104 F6
Newport NP44 .... 89 C3
Pandy View
Abercarn NP11 .... 114 C5
Neath SA11 .... 72 A4
Trelewis CF46 .... 83 D6
Pandy-Mawr Rd
CF83 .... 138 C5
Pangbourne Cl CF36 165 E1
Pant Bach CF33 .... 148 A2
Pant Celydd SA13 .... 125 E4
Pant Cl Pant CF48 .... 10 E3
St Brides Major CF32 . 185 D3
Pant Cotts CF48 .... 11 A7
Pant Farm Cl NP11 ... 87 A6
Pant Glas
Abertillery NP13 .... 36 B6
Cardiff CF23 .... 179 A7
Llandraddch CF83 .... 112 A3
Penhoed CF35 .... 170 D8
Pant Glas Ind Est
CF37 .... 138 F5
Pant Gwyn
Bridgend CF31 .... 168 B3
Swansea SA2 .... 94 E4
Pant Gwyn Cl NP44 .. 115 F8
Pant Hirgoed CF35 ... 152 C1
Pant Hirwaun CF32 .. 151 F4
Pant Howel Ddu SA11 71 D3
Pant Howelldu SA11 . 71 D3
Pant La NP20 .... 143 B8
Pant Lasau Rd SA5,
SA6 .... 45 C4
Pant Llygodfa CF83 .. 137 D1

Pant Mawr CF31 .... 168 B3
Pant Morfa CF36 ...... 183 B8
Pant Pl CF15 .... 157 F5
Pant Poeth CF32 ...... 168 B3
Pant Rd
Newbridge NP11 .... 87 A6
Newport NP20 .... 143 B8
Pant CF48 .... 11 B6
Pant St
Pant Bargoed CF81 .... 58 B5
Pontycymer CF32 .... 103 F2
Swansea SA1 .... 96 B7
Pant Sta CF48 .... 11 B5
Pant Tawel La CF15 .. 175 F6
Pant View
Nantyglo NP23 .... 15 E7
Newbridge NP11 .... 87 A7
Pant y Brwyn SA9 .... 221 C7
Pant y Celyn SA14 .... 41 C5
Pant y Dderwen
CF72 .... 155 B1
Pant y Dwr SA4 .... 65 D1
Pant y Fedwen
Bridgend CF31 .... 168 C2
Gwaun-Cae-Gurwen
SA18 .... 220 D6
Pant Yr Hebog CF31 168 C2
Pant Yr Helys SA5 ...... 67 B6
Pant-Bach Rd CF14 . 177 C5
Pant-Du Rd CF37 ..... 106 A8
Pant-glas SA14 .... 37 D3
Pant-Teg SA5 .... 40 F8
Pant-y-Blawd Rd
SA6 .... 46 B1
Pant-y-Celyn Pl
Morriston SA7 .... 46 C8
Swansea SA6 .... 69 A8
Swansea SA7 .... 69 D8
Pant-y-Celyn Rd
CF62 .... 211 D4
Pant-y-Celyn St SA1 94 F8
Pant-y-Cerdin CF4 ..... 53 E8
Pant-y-Coed CF62 ... 212 B8
Pant-y-Deri Cl 8
CF5 .... 193 C4
Pant-y-Dwr SA4 .... 6 C2
Pant-y-Fedwen CF44 . 53 C5
Pant-y-Felin Rd SA4 . 19 C6
Pant-y-Fforest NP23 .. 14 F6
Pant-y-Ffynnon
CF35 .... 152 F1
Pant-y-Glan NP23 .... 7 F4
Pant-y-Gog CF32 .... 103 F2
Pant-y-Mynydd NP23 . 7 F4
Pant-y-Pistyll SA8 ...... 23 C5
Pant-y-Pwdyn Rd
SA18 .... 36 C4
Pant-y-Resk Rd NP11 86 F4
Pant-y-Rheol Cl
NP44 .... 115 F7
Pant-y-Sais SA10 .... 70 C1
Pant-y-Seren CF39 ... 133 B2
Pant-Yr-Arian La
SA12 .... 98 F5
Pant-Yr-Eos
Cwmbran NP44 .... 89 C4
Cwmbran NP44 .... 89 D4
Pant-yr-Odyn
Swansea SA2 .... 67 C1
Swansea SA2 .... 94 C8
Pantanas CF46 .... 83 B6
Pantaquotis Cotts
CF72 .... 173 C5
Pantbach Cotts CF14 175 C8
Pantbach Pl CF14 ..... 177 D4
Pantddu Rd NP13 .... 59 F8
Panteg Ebbw Vale NP23 . 7 D2
Pentyrch CF15 .... 175 C5
Panteg Cl CF15 .... 192 F3
Panteg Ind Est NP4 .. 62 E3
Panteg Mews 3
NP44 .... 194 B7
Panteg Terr NP11 .... 86 F6
Panteg Way NP4 .... 62 F4
Pantglas
Gorseinon SA4 .... 43 B1
Pentyrch CF15 .... 175 C8
Pantglas Fawr CF48 ... 55 C6
Pantglas Rd CF33 .... 148 D3
Pantglas View CF38 . 138 F6
Pantgwynlais CF15 .. 158 D1
Pantiago Rd SA4 .... 19 C4
Pantle Rone SA13 ..... 227 C2
Pantmawr Ct CF14 ... 176 F8
Pantmawr Rd CF14 .. 176 F7
Pant Farm Cl NP11 ... 87 A6
Pantside Prim Sch
NP11 .... 87 B7
Pantsgallog Terr
SA18 .... 219 B6
Pantybiodau Rd
SA18 .... 218 F8
Pantycefn Rd NP12 .... 58 D7
Pantycelyn Dr 3
CF35 .... 137 F5
Pantycelyn Rd CF64 206 D6
Pantycelyn Rd CF44 . 53 C5
Pantyffynnon Rd
SA18 .... 219 B6
Pantyffynnon Sta
SA18 .... 219 B5
Pantyffynon Terr SA9 2 F8
Pantyffynon Rd SA9 . 2 F8
Pantyfid Rd CF81 .... 58 B6

Pantygasseg Rd NP4 .61 D5
Pantygraigwen Rd CF37 109 A2
Pantygwydr Rd SA2 94 F6
Pantyrheol SA11 71 C4
Pantysgallog CF48 11 A7
Pantysgallog Prim Sch CF48 11 A6
Paper Mill Rd CF5, CF11 194 A6
Parade CF37 109 D2
Parade The
Barry CF62 214 C2
Cardiff CF14 176 F4
Cardiff CF24 195 C6
Cwmbran NP44 89 E3
[7] Dinas Powys CF64 206 C3
Ferndale CF43 79 E7
Llantwit Fardre CF38 156 E8
Merthyr Tydfil CF47 10 E1
Neath SA11 71 E8
Porth CF39 107 F3
Ton Pentre CF41 78 F3
Paradise Cotts SA14 41 D4
Paradise View SA1 95 A8
Parc Afon CF40 107 C4
Parc Andrew SA10 70 F6
Parc Ave
Caerphilly CF83 138 C5
Cwmbran NP44 89 D6
Swansea SA6 68 F6
Swansea SA6 68 F7
Parc Berwig SA14 41 F2
Parc Bryn Bryn NP12 85 D3
Neath SA10 70 E5
Parc Bryn Derwen CF72 153 F1
Parc Brynmawr SA15 40 E8
Parc Bwtrimawr SA18 219 C6
Parc Bychan NP23 7 E1
Parc Castell-y-Mynach
Creigiau CF15 174 E7
Creigiau CF15 174 E8
Parc Cefn Onn Ctry Pk CF14 159 F5
Parc Clwyd [2] CF63 215 C8
Parc Cotts
Bridgend CF35 151 B2
Senghenydd CF83 110 F2
Parc Cres CF31 169 F1
Parc Cwm Darran CF81 32 F3
Parc Ddiwydiannol Betws SA18 219 C7
Parc Derwen CF82 84 F5
Parc Gitto SA14 41 D4
Parc Glanffrwd [2] SA18 220 B8
Parc Glas
Cwmdare CF44 28 D3
Neath SA10 70 F6
Parc Hafod CF14 176 F6
Parc Hendy Cres SA4 64 F3
Parc Howard Ave SA15 40 D7
Parc Howard Mus SA15 40 D7
Parc Mawr Cl SA4 44 B2
Parc Menter SA14 218 C7
Parc Morlais SA14 18 C1
Parc Nant Celyn CF38 157 A6
Parc Nantgarw CF15 157 F8
Parc Newydd
Briton Ferry SA11 71 B3
Talbot Green CF72 155 C2
Parc Onen SA10 70 E6
Parc Penrhiw SA18 219 C5
Parc Plas NP12 85 D6
Parc Pontypandy CF83 138 C5
Parc Prim Sch CF42 78 C5
Parc Rd SA6 68 F6
Parc Richard SA14 41 E4
Parc St Catwg CF15 175 C8
Parc St Joseff SA12 98 E2
Parc Terr
Senghenydd CF83 110 E2
Swansea SA6 68 F7
Parc The CF31 168 F1
Parc Trostre SA14 41 A4
Parc Ty Glas CF14 177 E7
Parc Ty Glas Ind Est CF14 177 E7
Parc Wenallt CF46 83 B7
Parc Wern SA10 70 F6
Parc Wern Rd SA2 94 E7
Parc Wood CF61 208 F5
Parc-Henry La SA18 219 B8
Parc-Tyn-y-Waun CF34 128 D6
Parc-y-Bont CF32 150 F6
Parc-y-Brain Rd NP10 142 B8
Parc-y-Bryn
Creigiau CF15 174 D8
Goytre SA13 125 E8
Llantwit Fardre CF38 156 D8
Parc-y-Coed CF15 174 E7
Parc-y-Delyn SA6 45 B1
Parc-y-Deri SA10 70 E6
Parc-y-Felin CF15 174 D7
Parc-y-Felin St CF83 138 B4
Parc-y-Fro CF15 174 E8
Parc-y-Nant CF15 158 A7
Parc-y-Rhos CF35 170 D8
Parc-Yr-Helig Rd
Birchgrove SA7 47 B1
Swansea SA7 70 B8
Parcau Ave CF31 168 C4
Parcau Rd CF31 168 C4
Parclewis Cty Prim Sch CF37 135 E7
Parcyrhun SA18 219 B6
Parcyrhun Cty Prim Sch SA18 219 B6
Pardoe Cres CF62 214 E6
Pardoe-Thomas Cl [17] NP20 143 C3
Parfitt Cl CF43 80 B4
Parfitt Pl NP12 85 D7
Parfitt St NP19 144 B3
Parfitt Terr
Cwmbran NP44 89 D5
[2] Merthyr Tydfil CF47 30 F8
Parish Rd
Beddau CF38 156 A7
Blaengwrach SA11 227 C8
Park Ave Barry CF62 214 D3
Bedwas CF83 138 E6
Capel Hendre SA18 218 D6
Cardiff CF14 176 F6
Cardiff CF5 193 A2
Glynneath SA11 223 C1
Mumbles SA3 123 B4
Neath SA10 70 C7
Newport NP20 142 E1
Ogmore Vale CF32 130 E8
Porthcawl CF36 182 E7
Rogerstone NP10 141 F6
Park Cl
Cwmbran NP44 115 F8
Gorseinon SA4 43 B2
Newport NP20 142 E1
Pontarddulais SA4 19 C3
Pontypridd CF37 135 D6
Swansea SA1 69 B3
Swansea SA6 45 E1
Treherbert CF42 50 F1
Park Court Rd CF31 168 D4
Park Cres
Bargoed CF81 57 F3
Barry CF62 214 C4
Brynmawr NP23 8 B4
Cardiff CF14 176 F6
Clydach NP7 9 D7
Llanelli SA15 40 C5
[9] Merthyr Tydfil CF47 10 E1
Neath SA10 70 C7
Pontyclun CF72 173 A7
Pontypool NP4 62 D7
Porth CF39 107 E3
Treharris CF46 83 B7
Treorchy CF42 78 D5
Park Ct Barry CF62 214 C3
Bridgend CF31 168 D4
Park Dr Bargoed CF81 57 F3
Neath SA10 70 C7
Newport NP20 142 F1
Swansea SA2 94 F7
Park End NP18 145 C8
Park End Ct CF23 178 A6
Park End La CF23 178 A6
Park Eynon [6] SA15 40 D5
Park Field SA11 49 D3
Park Gdns
Blaenavon NP4 17 C6
Newport NP20 142 E1
Pontypool NP4 62 C7
Park Gr Aberdare CF44 28 F3
Cardiff CF10 195 B7
Park Hill
Mountain Ash CF45 54 D3
[11] Mountain Ash CF45 54 E1
Tredegar NP22 13 D5
Park Ho [3] SA13 125 C7
Park House Flats NP4 62 C7
Park La Aberdare CF44 28 E4
Blaengwynfi SA13 76 C5
Blaengwynfi SA13 76 C6
Brynamman SA18 220 D8
Caerphilly CF83 138 A2
Cardiff CF14 176 F6
Cardiff CF24 195 B6
Groesfaen CF72 174 B7
Llangennech SA14 42 C8
Taffs Well CF15 157 F4
Tredomen CF82 84 D1
Treharris CF46 83 A6
Park Lane Specl Sch CF44 28 E3
Park Mill Rd SA18 219 A7
Park Pl
Abercarn NP11 114 C5
Abertillery NP13 36 B5
Bargoed CF81 58 A2
Ebbw Vale NP23 14 F2
Maerdy CF43 52 A2
Newbridge NP11 86 F7
Pontypridd CF37 109 F6
Risca NP11 115 A1
Sarn CF32 150 F4
Swansea SA2 94 E5
Tonypandy CF40 106 E6
Tredegar NP22 13 F5
Treherbert CF42 50 F2
Troedyrhiw CF48 55 C8
Park Pl (Plas y Parc) CF10 195 A7
Park Prospect CF37 109 B2
Park Rd
Abercynon CF45 82 E3
Aberdare CF44 53 C7
Aberkenfig CF32 150 C3
Bargoed CF81 57 F4
Park Rd *continued*
Barry CF62 214 C3
Cardiff CF14 176 F6
Clydach SA6 46 E8
Dinas Powys CF64 206 A4
Ebbw Vale NP23 14 D4
Ebbw Vale NP23 14 E3
Ferndale CF43 80 A5
Gorseinon SA4 43 B2
Gowerton SA4 66 C4
Hengoed CF82 85 A2
Maerdy CF43 52 A2
Maesycwmmer CF82 85 A1
Newbridge NP11 86 F7
Pen-clawdd SA4 64 E4
Penarth CF64 207 B3
Pontypool NP4 62 C7
Radyr CF15 176 B6
Risca NP11 115 A1
Southgate SA3 121 A5
Tonypandy CF40 107 A4
Treorchy CF42 78 B4
Ynystawe SA6 46 C4
Park Road Ind Est NP11 115 A1
Park Row
Cwmavon SA12 99 E6
Tredegar NP22 13 E6
Park Row Gdns CF47 10 D3
Park Side La CF37 109 C1
Park Slip Nature Pk CF32 149 F5
Park Sq NP20 143 C4
Park St
Abercarn NP11 114 B5
Abercarn NP11 114 C8
Abercynon CF45 82 D1
Blaenavon NP4 17 C6
Bridgend CF31 168 D4
Brynamman SA18 220 D8
Cardiff CF10 195 A5
Glyncorrwg SA13 227 C1
Llanelli SA15 40 D5
Maesteg CF34 102 B2
[13] Mountain Ash CF45 54 E1
Mountain Ash CF45 81 E8
Mumbles SA3 123 B5
Nant-y-Moel CF32 104 F5
Neath SA11 71 F8
Pontycymer CF32 103 F4
Pontypool NP4 62 E2
Pontypridd CF37 135 E7
Port Talbot SA13 125 C7
Porth CF39 107 D4
Pyle CF33 148 C2
Skewen SA10 71 A7
Swansea SA1 95 C7
Tonna SA11 49 D3
Tonypandy CF40 106 B6
Tylorstown CF43 80 B4
Park Terr
Caerphilly NP12 85 F6
Llanharan CF72 153 F3
Merthyr Tydfil CF47 10 D2
Pontarddulais SA4 19 D2
[6] Pontypool NP4 38 A1
Swansea SA1 68 C1
Tondu CF32 150 B5
Trelewis CF46 83 D6
Treorchy CF42 78 B5
Park Terrace Prim Sch NP4 62 C6
Park The
Blaenavon NP4 17 C7
Swansea SA2 94 A7
Treharris CF46 83 B7
Park View
Abercarn NP11 114 B5
Abercynon CF45 82 E4
Bargoed CF81 57 E3
Bassaleg NP10 142 B3
Bridgend CF31 168 B5
Bridgend CF35 169 F4
Brynmawr NP23 8 B4
Cwmaman CF44 53 A3
Cwmbran NP44 89 E6
Ebbw Vale NP23 7 D4
[2] Llanbradach CF83 111 F1
Llanharan CF72 154 A2
Llantrisant CF72 155 D3
Loughor SA4 65 D8
Maesteg CF34 102 C1
Nantyglo NP13 15 E7
[1] Pontypool NP4 38 A1
Port Talbot SA13 125 C7
Ton Pentre CF41 79 A3
Tondu CF32 150 A5
Tredegar NP22 13 D6
Tylorstown CF43 80 C3
Wattstown CF39 107 E8
Park View Bglws NP12 85 F7
Park View Cl SA11 71 C1
Park View Ct
[2] Cardiff CF11 194 F5
[11] Cardiff CF14 177 A6
Park View Gdns NP10 142 B3
Park View St NP23 14 F2
Park View Terr
Abercwmboi CF44 53 E5
Aberdare CF44 29 B3
Swansea SA2 94 D6
Park Way SA2 94 B6
Park Wood Cl NP18 117 E3
Park y Brain La NP4 39 D7
Parkdale View CF72 155 E2
Parke's La NP4 62 A6
Parker Pl CF5 193 B4
Parker Rd CF5 193 B4
Parkfield Pl
Cardiff CF14 177 E1
Newport NP20 143 A5
Parkfield Rd CF44 29 D1
Parkfields CF31 168 D8
Parkfields Rd CF31 168 D4
Parkhill Cres NP23 7 E3
Parkhill Rd SA5 68 C5
Parkhill Terr SA5 68 C5
Parkland Cres CF39 133 C5
Parkland Rd CF39 133 C5
Parkland Sch SA2 94 B6
Parkland Wlk CF62 214 C4
Parklands
Blackwood NP12 85 E8
Cardiff CF24 195 C5
Corntown CF35 186 B7
Penperlleni NP4 39 F7
Parklands Cl
Cwmbran NP44 89 E6
Rogerstone NP10 142 C3
Parklands Ct
Ammanford SA18 219 A6
Swansea SA2 94 B6
Parklands Rd SA18 219 A7
Parklands View SA2 94 B5
Parklawn Cl NP44 89 E6
Parkside NP44 89 D2
Parkside Ct
[2] Cardiff CF5 194 C6
[18] Pontypool NP4 38 A1
Parkside Gdns CF23 178 B2
Parkstone Ave CF3 179 E8
Parkview Ct CF64 206 E5
Parkview Terr SA15 40 C6
Parkville NP22 13 E5
Parkwall Rd CF14, CF23 161 A3
Parkway
Blackwood NP11 59 D5
Cardiff CF3 179 D2
Parkway Sta SA13 125 B8
Parkwood SA4 66 C4
Parkwood Dr NP10 141 E2
Parr Ave SA11 71 F8
Parracombe Cl CF3 179 C7
Parracombe Cres CF3 179 C7
Parret Cl NP20 116 F2
Parret Rd NP20 116 F2
Parret Wlk NP20 116 F2
Parrish Pl CF83 110 F2
Parrot Row NP3 15 D7
Parry Cl SA10 71 B8
Parry Dr NP19 144 C5
Parry Jones Cl NP13 15 D5
Parry Rd
Port Talbot SA12 98 B3
Swansea SA6 45 E1
Parry St
[5] Cardiff CF5 194 C6
Ton Pentre CF41 78 F3
Ton Pentre CF41 79 A3
Treorchy CF43 80 B2
Parry Terr NP11 59 F1
Parrys Dr CF45 82 C5
Parson's Row NP13 15 D5
Parsons La SA11 49 C2
Part St NP13 15 E3
Partridge Ave CF40 106 F8
Partridge La CF24 195 D7
Partridge Rd
Abertillery NP13 60 A6
Cardiff CF24 195 C7
St Athan CF62 210 E6
Tonypandy CF40 79 F1
Partridge Row NP23 7 C4
Partridge St CF41 79 A3
Partridge Way NP10 163 F7
Pascal Cl CF3 180 B8
Pascall Ct [1] CF24 195 C7
Pascoes Ave CF31 168 E5
Pastoral Way SA2 94 B8
Pastures The
Barry CF62 214 E7
Llanyravon NP44 90 B3
Patagonia Wlk [5] SA1 95 D5
Patch The CF72 172 B6
Pathway Cres CF3 179 A4
Patmore Cl CF15 157 F4
Patreane Way CF5 192 F3
Patterdale Cl CF23 178 B2
Patti Cl NP19 144 F6
Patti Ho [8] SA12 98 F1
Pavaland Cl [5] CF3 179 F6
Pavia Ct CF37 109 C1
Paviland Pl SA5 67 F5
Pavilion Ct CF36 182 F6
Pavilion Est NP4 62 A8
Pavillion Bldgs CF40 106 C6
Pavin Ct CF5 177 A1
Paxton Cl CF82 84 E7
Paxton Dr SA1 95 C5
Paxton St SA1 95 C6
Paxton Wlk NP10 142 A7
Payne St SA11 71 D6
Peacehaven NP22 14 A3
Peacehaven Ct NP22 14 A3
Peach Pl [2] CF5 193 D8
Pear Tree Cl NP18 117 E2
Pearce Cl CF3 180 A5
Pearce Ct CF63 215 A8
Pearce's Ct CF48 10 A5
Pearl Pl CF24 195 D6
Pearl St Cardiff CF24 195 D6
Cardiff CF24 195 E7
Clydach SA6 46 F8
Pearson Cres CF37 109 D5
Pearson St CF24 195 C7
Pease La CF47 30 E7
Peckham Cl CF5 176 D3
Pedair Erw Rd CF14 177 D5
Pedrog Terr SA1 68 B1
Pegler St SA5 68 C3
Pelican St SA9 1 F2
Pell St SA1 95 C7
Pellau Rd SA13 125 E5
Pellett St CF10 195 B5
Pemberton Pk SA14 41 C6
Pemberton Rd SA14 41 C5
Pemberton St SA15 40 D4
Pembrey Gdns NP12 86 A4
Pembrey Rd SA15 40 C6
Pembridge Dr CF64 206 F5
Pembroke Cl
Blackwood NP12 58 D1
Church Village CF38 135 F2
[4] Dinas Powys CF64 206 C3
Merthyr Tydfil CF48 225 F1
Ystrad CF41 79 D3
Pembroke Cres CF72 155 A5
Pembroke Ct
Caerphilly CF83 137 D4
[6] Cardiff CF14 177 A6
Pembroke Gr NP19 144 A2
Pembroke Ho SA12 124 D8
Pembroke Pl
Barry CF63 214 F6
Boverton CF61 210 B6
Llanyravon NP44 90 B3
Merthyr Tydfil CF47 10 F3
[4] Swansea SA1 95 E6
Pembroke Rd CF5 194 C6
Pembroke St
Aberdare CF44 29 A2
Swansea SA5 68 B3
Tredegar NP22 6 C1
Troedyrhiw CF48 31 C2
Pembroke Terr
[10] Aberavon SA12 124 F8
Nant-y-Moel CF32 104 F6
Penarth CF64 207 B5
Varteg NP4 17 E1
Pembrook Mews CF5 194 B6
Pembrook St CF39 133 B2
Pen Bryn Hendy CF72 173 C7
Pen Coed Isaf Rd SA14 42 B4
Pen Darren CF39 107 C1
Pen Dinas CF40 107 B4
Pen Gurnos CF47 10 C5
Pen Gwern CF35 152 D1
Pen Hendy CF72 173 C7
Pen Heol-Shenkyn NP12 58 D5
Pen Isa Coed SA1 95 F7
Pen Llew Ct CF44 28 D3
Pen Locks CF46 83 A5
Pen Onnen CF31 169 C5
Pen Parcau CF32 129 D3
Pen Pentre SA10 226 A7
Pen Tyntyla CF43 80 A2
Pen y Cwm SA2 67 D2
Pen y Dre CF39 133 D8
Pen y Groes CF72 174 B7
Pen y Groes Gr NP10 141 E2
Pen y Maes SA6 45 C2
Pen y Morfa SA4 65 A4
Pen y Mynydd CF32 129 D3
Pen y Parc NP23 14 B8
Pen Yr Alltwen SA8 24 A3
Pen-Cae-Crwn Rd SA4 43 A3
Pen-Cefn-Arda Rd SA4 43 B4
Pen-clawdd Prim Sch SA4 64 E4
Pen-Deri Cl NP12 59 C1
Pen-Hill Rd CF11 194 C7
Pen-Hydd St SA12 73 A1
Pen-Llwyn Ave NP12 85 F4
Pen-Llwyn-March Rd SA5 68 A3
Pen-Mynydd NP4 17 D7
Pen-Pych Cl CF42 50 D3
Pen-Rhiw Ave NP12 59 B1
Pen-Rhiw Bengi La NP12 59 B2
Pen-Rhiw Est NP13 60 A8
Pen-Rhiw Terr
Abercarn NP11 87 C3
Blackwood NP12 59 A2
Pen-Rhiw-Garreg Rd NP13 36 C5
Pen-Twyn La NP20 116 E3
Pen-Twyn Rd CF41, CF42 78 E4
Pen-y-Banc
Bridgend CF31 169 A4
Cwmavon SA12 100 A7
Porth CF39 107 D1
Seven Sisters SA10 222 C3
Pen-y-Banc Rd SA18 219 A6
Pen-y-Bigyn SA15 40 E4
Pen-y-bont
Crynant SA10 222 A1
Penpedairheol CF82 84 D8
Tredegar NP22 6 C2
Pen-y-Bont Rd NP13 36 B7
Pen-y-Bryn
Barry CF62 214 B2
Bridgend CF31 168 C5
Caerphilly CF83 137 E6
Cwmllynfell SA9 221 B7
Pen-y-Bryn *continued*
Cymmer SA13 75 C3
Maesteg CF34 102 B8
Neath SA10 70 E6
Neath SA11 71 F5
Pontypridd CF37 109 D5
Seven Sisters SA10 222 D3
Tonna SA11 49 D3
Ystradgynlais SA9 222 A5
Pen-y-Bryn Cl
Bettws NP20 116 E2
Penllergaer SA4 44 B2
Pen-y-Bryn Ct NP11 59 D2
Pen-y-Bryn Pl CF14 177 E2
Pen-y-Bryn Rd
Cardiff CF14 177 E2
Cardiff CF23 178 C7
Pen-y-bryn Terr
Bryn NP12 85 D3
Ebbw Vale NP23 14 D6
Pen-y-Bryn View CF32 150 F4
Pen-y-Bryn Way [2] CF14 177 E2
Pen-y-byrn Jun & Inf Sch CF3 179 D7
Pen-y-Cae
Caerphilly CF83 138 D5
Ystrad Mynach CF82 111 E8
Pen-y-Cae Cl NP11 59 D1
Pen-y-Cae La SA4 42 E2
Pen-y-cae Prim Sch SA9 222 F8
Pen-y-Cae Rd SA13 125 C8
Pen-y-caeau Ct NP11 60 C1
Pen-y-Cefn CF14 159 D2
Pen-y-Craig CF82 84 E7
Pen-y-Crug NP23 7 B5
Pen-y-Cwarel Rd NP12 112 F8
Pen-y-cwm
Pentyrch CF15 157 C1
Rhymney NP22 13 A1
Pen-y-cwm Specl Sch NP23 7 F4
Pen-y-Darren Cl CF37 109 C2
Pen-y-Dre
Caerphilly CF83 137 E7
Cardiff CF14 177 B6
Ebbw Vale NP23 7 C3
Gowerton SA4 66 B4
Merthyr Tydfil CF47 10 C5
Neath SA11 71 F8
Rhymney NP22 12 E6
Pen-y-dre High Comp Sch CF47 10 D6
Pen-y-Fai La SA15 40 B8
Pen-y-Fan SA7 69 F6
Pen-y-Fan Cl NP11 59 F6
Pen-y-fan Ind Est NP11 59 D4
Pen-y-fan Pond Ctry Pk NP11,NP13 59 D6
Pen-y-Fan Way NP12 59 C1
Pen-y-Ffordd CF33 166 A7
Pen-y-Fon St SA15 40 E3
Pen-y-Fro
Cwmdare CF44 28 C3
Dunvant SA2 66 B1
Pencoed CF35 152 C1
Pen-y-Fro Cl SA2 66 B1
Pen-y-fro Prim Sch SA2 93 B8
Pen-y-gaer Cotts SA14 41 A8
Pen-y-garn
Pontsticill CF48 3 F2
Swansea SA1 69 A3
Pen-y-Graig Rd
Pontardawe SA8 23 F3
Swansea SA1 95 B8
Ystradowen SA9 221 C7
Pen-y-Graig Terr
Abertillery NP13 60 A7
Pontypool NP4 62 D5
Pen-y-Groes
Blackwood NP11 59 C2
Caerphilly CF83 137 E6
Pen-y-Groes Ave CF14 177 D7
Pen-y-Groes Rd CF14 177 D7
Pen-y-Heol SA10 70 D4
Pen-y-Lan
Ebbw Vale NP23 7 D3
Pen-clawdd SA4 64 F3
Pen-y-lan Ct CF23 178 C3
Pen-y-Lan Pl CF23 178 C1
Pen-y-Lan Rd
Aberthin CF71 189 B3
[6] Cardiff CF23 178 C1
Cardiff CF24 195 C8
Pen-y-Lan Terr
Cardiff CF23 178 D2
Newbridge NP11 86 F7
Pen-y-Llan La NP4 63 B8
Pen-y-Mead NP12 85 D4
Pen-y-Mor Rd SA5 68 C5
Pen-y-Morfa SA15 40 E3
Pen-y-Mynydd
Cymmer SA13 75 D3
Pontypridd CF37 109 D6
Pen-y-Parc CF38 156 A7
Pen-y-Peel Rd CF5 194 C6
Pen-y-pych Prim Sch CF42 50 D3
Pen-y-Rhiw
Pen-Rhiw-fawr SA9 221 B5
Ystrad CF41 79 D3

Pen-y-Turnpike Rd
CF64 ....206 B6
Pen-y-Wain Cl NP44 178 B1
Pen-y-Wain Pl CF24 178 B1
Pen-y-Wain Rd
CF24 ....178 B1
Pen-y-Waun
Dinas Powys CF64 ....206 B3
Pentyrch CF15 ....157 C1
Pen-y-Waun Cl NP44 89 D2
Pen-y-Waun Rd
Abertillery NP11 ....59 F5
Cwmbran NP44 ....89 D2
Pen-y-Werlod Rd
NP12 ....58 D8
Pen-y-werlod Terr
NP12 ....58 D8
Pen-y-Wern SA13 ....75 E3
Pen-y-Wern Rd SA6 ..46 E8
Pen-y-Wern Terr
SA1 ....68 D4
Pen-Yr-Alley Ave
SA10 ....70 E6
Pen-Yr-Allt
Caerphilly CF83 ......158 F8
Ystalyfera SA9 ....2 B8
Pen-Yr-Eglwys
CF38 ....135 D1
Pen-Yr-Grug SA7 ....2 A8
Pen-Yr-Heol
Neath SA10 ....70 E5
North Cornelly CF33 ..166 A7
Pen-y-fai CF31 ....150 C1
Penywaun CF44 ....28 B6
Pen-Yr-Heol Dr SA2 .94 B7
Pen-Yr-Heol Rd
Abertillery NP11 ....60 F5
Pontypool NP4 ....61 A4
Pen-Yr-Yrfa SA6 ....45 D1
Pen-Yr-Ysgol CF34 102 A2
Penallt Dunvant SA2 ..93 E8
Llanelli Hill NP7 ....9 D5
Penallt SA15 ....40 F6
Penallt Terr SA15 ....40 F6
Penallta Ind Est CF82 84 E5
Penallta Rd CF82 ......84 E3
Penallta Villas CF82 ..84 E3
Penally Rd CF5 ......193 E4
Penarth Ct NP44 ......90 B1
Penarth Head La
CF64 ....207 A5
Penarth Portway
CF64 ....207 B5
Penarth Rd
Cardiff CF10 ....195 A3
Cardiff CF11 ....195 A4
Cardiff CF11 ....194 D1
Cardiff CF11 ....194 E2
Cardiff CF11 ....194 E2
Llandough CF11 ......206 E7
Penarth Sta CF64 ....207 A3
Penbedw NP44 ....90 B4
Penbryn CF32 ....103 E3
Penbryn Rd SA10 ....70 F7
Penbryn Terr SA2 ....44 C8
Pencader Rd CF5 ....193 E6
Pencae Terr SA15 ....40 F5
Pencaerfenni La SA4 64 B3
Pencaerfenni Pk SA4 64 B3
Pencai Terr CF42 ......78 D5
Pencarn Ave NP10 ..163 C6
Pencarn La
Newport NP10 ....163 D6
Newport NP10 ....163 E5
Pencarn Way NP10 163 D6
Pencerrig St
Llanbradach CF83 ..111 F1
Pontypridd CF37 ....109 B1
Pencisely Cres CF5 194 A7
Pencisely Rd CF5 ....194 B7
Pencisely Rise CF5 194 B7
Pencisely Ave CF5 ..194 A7
Penclawdd CF83 ....138 D5
Penclawdd Rd SA4 ..65 C5
Pencoed Dunvant SA2 .93 E8
Tredegar NP22 ....13 D6
Pencoed Ave
Blackwood NP12 ......85 C8
Pontypridd CF37 ....109 E1
Pencoed Com Sch
CF35 ....170 E7
Pencoed Jun Sch
CF35 ....152 E1
Pencoed Pl NP44 ....89 F6
Pencoed Sta CF35 ..170 D8
Pencoedtre Rd
Barry CF63 ....205 A1
Barry CF63 ....215 B8
Pencwmdu SA18 ....221 A1
Pendarren SA8 ......221 B1
Pendarren St
Aberdare CF44 ....28 F1
Penpedairheol CF82 94 B8
Pendarvis St SA12 ..98 E1
Pendarvis Terr [6]
SA12 ....124 F8
Pendderi Rd
Bynea SA14 ....42 A4
Llanelli SA14 ....41 F5
Penderry Rd SA5 ....68 B4
Penderyn Ave SA15 125 E5
Penderyn Cty Prim Sch
CF44 ....27 B6
Penderyn Rd CF44 ..53 B8
Penderyn Rd SA13 ..75 D3
Pendinas Ave NP11 ..59 D2
Pendine Cl CF62 ....214 F8
Pendine Rd CF5 ....193 E6

Pendine Wlk NP44 ....89 B2
Pendoylan Cl CF63 .215 B8
Pendoylan Ct
[11] Cardiff CF5 ......193 C4
Cardiff CF5 ....193 E6
Pendoylan CW Prim Sch
CF71 ....190 F6
Pendoylan Wlk NP44 89 C1
Pendragon Cl CF14 159 D2
Pendraw Pl CF23 ....178 B6
Pendre Cres CF72 ..153 F3
Pendrill St SA1 ......71 D6
Pendwyallt Rd CF14 176 E7
Pendrys Ct CF11 ....194 F4
Penedre CF43 ....80 C4
Penfedw SA6 ....177 A1
Penfelyn Heol SA6 ..45 F5
Penfford CF15 ......175 C8
Penford SA15 ....68 C4
Penfilia Terr [3] SA5 68 A4
Penford CF5 [5] CF24 195 B7
Pengam Prim Sch
NP12 ....85 B7
Pengam Rd
Blackwood NP12 ......58 B2
Cardiff CF24 ....195 F8
Pengam NP12 ....85 B8
Penpedairheol CF82,
NP12 ....84 F8
Ystrad Mynach CF82 ..84 F2
Pengelli Prim Sch
SA4 ....43 C6
Penguelan Prim Sch
CF45 ....54 E1
Pengham Stp La SA4 85 A8
Pengorof St SA9 ......1 E1
Pengry Rd SA4 ....45 B2
Pengry SA6 ....42 F1
Pengwern Rd
Cardiff CF5 ....193 E6
Swansea SA6 ....68 C8
Penhedd Ely Rd CF7 109 F2
Penheolfferthyr SA1 ..41 A1
Penhevad St CF11 ..194 F2
Penhill Cl CF5 ....194 C7
Penhiwfer Prim Sch
CF45 ....133 A8
Penhydd Rd SA12 ..103 A8
Penhydd Rd SA13 ....75 D3
Penhydd-waelod Cotts
CF45 ....54 E1
Peniel Green Rd SA7 .70 A8
Peniel Rd SA5 ....68 D5
Penkin Cl NP19 ....144 D4
Penkin Hill NP19 ....144 D4
Penlan SA14 ....42 A6
Penlan Comp Sch (Boys)
SA5 ....68 A6
Penlan Cres SA2 ....94 B7
Penlan Fach SA5 ......68 C4
Penlan Gr SA5 ....68 B5
Penlan Rd
Llandough CF64 ......206 D6
Loughor SA4 ....42 F1
Neath SA10 ....70 D8
Swansea SA6 ....68 C6
Penlan Rise CF64 ..206 D6
Penlan St CF48 ....31 B4
Penlan Terr SA5 ......68 C4
Penlan View CF48 ....30 C8
Penlan NP22 ....14 B8
Penllergaer Bsns Pk
SA5 ....44 D3
Penllergaer Forest Walks
SA4 ....44 A2
Penllergaer Prim Sch
SA4 ....44 A2
Penlline Cl CF14 ....177 A5
Penlline Rd CF14 ....177 A5
Penlline St [2] CF24 195 B7
Penllwyn Ind Est
NP12 ....85 E4
Penllwynarth
Machen CF83 ....139 D7
Penllwyn Pk NP11 ..85 F4
Penllwyn Terr [1]
NP12 ....85 F4
Penllwyn Wlk CF83 139 C7
Penllwyngwent Farm Dr
SA14 ....41 F6
Penllwyngwyn Rd
SA14 ....42 A6
Penllwynhrodyn Rd
SA14 ....41 E4
Penllyn SA12 ....99 E5
Penllyn Rd
Cardiff CF14 ....177 D7
Risca NP11 ....115 D1
Pentonville NP20 ..143 B5
Pentre CF72 ....155 A5
Pentre Afan SA12 ....98 C3
Pentre Banadl SA2 ..93 E7
Pentre Cl NP44 ......116 B8
Pentre Ct SA1 ....79 A4
Pentre Fedwen SA11 72 B5
Pentre Gdns CF11 ..194 F3
Pentre Howell CF45 170 E8
Pentre La
Llantarnam NP44 ....116 E5
Penperlleni NP4 ......39 C4
Pentre Mawr Rd SA1 68 D7
Pentre Pl
Cardiff CF11 ....194 F3
Pyle CF33 ....148 C2
Pentre Prim Sch CF41 78 F5

Penmaesglas Terr [2]
CF40 ....106 F4
Pemmain St CF39 ....102 F4
Penmark Gn CF5 ....193 A4
Penmark Rd CF5 ....193 A4
Penmark Row CF44 ..27 C8
Penmynydd SA4 ......43 B1
Penmynydd Rd SA5 68 B5
Penn St CF46 ....83 E7
Pennant Cres CF23 178 C6
Pennant Cl NP21 ......86 E6
Pennant La NP11 ......86 F6
Pennant St NP11 ......86 F6
Pennant Dr SA3 ......121 A6
Pennant Pl CF14 ....177 D3
Pennard Prim Sch
SA3 ....121 E7
Pennard Rd
Bishopston SA3 ......121 E7
Southgate SA3 ......121 B5
Pennard St SA5 ......68 C3
Pennine Cl
Cardiff CF14 ....177 E7
Risca NP11 ....115 D1
Pennsylvania CF23 178 D5
Penny Cres NP20 ..116 F3
Pennyfields [2] NP44 89 B3
Pennyroyal Cl CF3 ..180 A8
Pennyquap Rd CF40 106 F4
Penplas Rd
Swansea SA5 ....67 E7
Swansea SA5 ....67 E7
Penpound La SA18 ..219 F8
Penprys Rd SA14 ....41 E7
Penprysg Rd CF35 ..152 E1
Penrhiw La CF83 ....141 A8
Penrhiw Rd
Pontypridd CF37 ....135 B7
Risca NP11 ....115 A2
Ton Pentre CF41 ......79 A2
Penrhiw SA13 ....100 E5
Penrhiw-ceibr Jun Sch
CF45 ....81 B8
Penrhiw-ceibr Rd
CF45 ....81 B8
Penrhiw-Fer Rd
CF45 ....133 B7
Penrhiwceiber Rd
CF45 ....54 E1
Penrhiwceiber Sta
CF45 ....82 A8
Penrhiwgarreg NP13 36 C4
Penrhiwgoch SA12 ..98 C8
Penrhiwgwynt Rd
CF39 ....107 F3
Penrhiwiau SA8 ......23 E3
Penrhiwtyn St SA11 ..71 C4
Penrhos General's Acad
Radyr CF15 ....176 A7
Penrhos Cres CF3 ..179 C4
Penrhos Cty Prim Sch
SA9 ....222 A6
Penrhos Pl SA5 ......67 F6
Penrhyn Ave SA5 ....68 B4
Penrhyn Cl CF5 ......179 E5
Penrhyn Cl SA5 ....46 A3
Penrhyn St SA13 ....125 D6
Penrhyn Terr NP24 ..33 E3
Penrhys Ave CF43 ....80 B2
Penrhys Inf & Jun Schs
CF43 ....80 A2
Penrhys Rd
Treorchy CF43 ....80 B2
Ystrad CF41 ....79 F2
Penrhys Uchaf CF43 80 B2
Penrice Gn [9] NP44 90 B2
Penrice St SA6 ....45 F5
Penrys St CF48 ....10 D1
Penryce St [5] SA1 ..95 D6
Pensalem Rd SA5 ....68 B5
Pensarn Rd CF3 ....179 E5
Pensarn Way
Cwmbran NP44 ......115 F8
Cwmbran NP44 ......116 A8
Penscynor SA10 ......49 B3
Penshannel
Neath SA10 ....70 F8
Neath Abbey SA10 ..47 F1
Pensidan View NP11 141 F2
Pent Lee CF23 ......178 E7
Pentewan Cl SA4 ....46 A4
Pentip Church in Wales
Prim Sch SA15 ......40 C6
Pentland Cl
Cardiff CF14 ....177 D7
Risca NP11 ....115 D1
Pentonville NP20 ..143 B5
Pentre CF72 ....155 A5
Pentre Afan SA12 ....98 C3
Pentre Banadl SA2 ..93 E7
Pentre Cl NP44 ......116 B8
Pentre Ct SA1 ....79 A4
Pentre Fedwen SA11 72 B5
Pentre Gdns CF11 ..194 F3
Pentre Howell CF45 170 E8
Pentre La
Llantarnam NP44 ....116 E5
Penperlleni NP4 ......39 C4
Pentre Mawr Rd SA1 68 D7
Pentre Pl
Cardiff CF11 ....194 F3
Pyle CF33 ....148 C2
Pentre Prim Sch CF41 78 F5

Pentre Rd
Maerdy CF43 ....52 A1
Pentre CF41 ....78 F5
Pontarddulais SA4 ....14 C2
Treorchy CF41 ....79 A5
Pentre St
Cardiff CF11 ....194 F3
Glynneath SA11 ......223 C1
Glynneath SA11 ......227 C8
Pentre Tai Rd NP10 141 E5
Pentre Terr SA13 ..125 D5
Pentre-Chwyth Rd
SA1 ....68 F2
Pentre-Dwr Rd SA7 .69 E5
Pentre-Poeth Cl
NP10 ....141 E2
Pentre-Poeth Rd
NP10 ....141 E2
Pentre-Treharne Hill
SA1 ....68 D4
Pentre-Treharne Rd
SA1 ....68 D4
Pentrebach Ind Est
CF48 ....31 A5
Pentrebane Rd
Merthyr Tydfil CF48 ..30 F6
Pontypridd CF37 ....135 E8
Pentrebach Sch CF48 31 A4
Pentrebane Rd SA10 30 F4
Pentrebane Prim Sch
CF5 ....193 C8
Pentrebane St
Caerphilly CF83 ......138 A2
Cardiff CF11 ....194 F2
Pentrebeili Pl CF32 130 E5
Pentrebeili Terr
CF32 ....130 E5
Pentrechwyth Prim Sch
SA1 ....69 A3
Pentregethin Rd SA5 67 E5
Pentreguinea Rd SA1 95 E8
Pentrehafod Comp Sch
SA1 ....68 D3
Pentrepiod Rd NP4 ..37 F1
Pentrepoeth Jun & Inf Sch
SA6 ....46 A1
Pentrepoeth Prim Sch
NP10 ....141 F3
Pentrepoeth Rd
Llanelli SA14 ....40 D8
Swansea SA6 ....45 F2
Pentrepoeth School Rd
Morriston SA6 ....46 A1
Swansea SA6 ....46 A1
Pentwyn
Bryn-y-Cwm SA10 ....48 B4
Pontypridd CF37 ....137 E6
Ebbw Vale NP23 ......14 C7
Heolgerrig CF48 ......10 A1
Neath SA11 ....71 E5
Radyr CF15 ....176 A6
Three Crosses SA4 ..65 E1
Pentwyn Ave
Blackwood NP12 ......85 E8
Mountain Ash CF45 ..82 A6
Pentwyn Baglan Rd
SA12 ....98 E5
Pentwyn Cl
Blackwood NP12 ......85 E8
Cardiff CF14 ....177 A7
Pentwyn Ct
Aberkenfig NP4 ....83 A4
Baglan SA12 ....98 E5
Cardiff CF23 ....178 F7
Pentwyn Hts NP4 ..37 F3
Pentwyn Isaf CF23 ..178 F7
Pentwyn La
Blaina NP13 ....15 E4
Caerphilly CF83 ......137 F6
Pentwyn Link Rd
CF3,CF23 ....161 B2
Pentwyn Rd
Aberystwyth NP4 ......37 F2
Abertillery NP11 ......59 F6
Blackwood NP12 ......85 E7
Cardiff CF23 ....178 E8
Cynonville SA13 ......74 B3
Pencoed CF35 ......152 E1
Quakers Yard CF46 ..83 C4
Resolven SA11 ......226 E5
Ystalyfera SA9 ....2 B7
Pentwyn Terr
Aberystwyth NP4 ......37 F3
Abertillery NP11 ......59 F6
Marshfield CF3 ....60 B8
Pentwyn Villas CF37 137 D8
Pentwyngwyn Rd
CF83 ....139 B4
Pentwynmawr Jun & Sch
NP12 ....86 D5
Pentyla Maestg CF34 101 F4
Pentyla Rd SA2 ......94 E8
Pentyla-Baglan Rd
SA12 ....99 A2
Pentyrch Prim Sch
CF15 ....175 B8
Pentyrch St CF24 ..177 F1
Penuel La CF37 ......43 A1
Penuel Rd CF15 ....175 B8
Penuel St [1] CF47 ..17 D8

Penyard Rd
Hirwaun CF44 ....27 D8
Merthyr Tydfil CF47 ..10 E2
Neath Abbey SA10 ..71 B8
Penybanc La SA4 ....A3 A4
Penybont Prim Sch
CF31 ....168 F5
Penybont Rd CF35 ..152 F1
Penybryn Llanelli SA14 41 E6
Penybryn Ave NP12 ..85 C8
Penybryn Rd
Brynmenyn CF32 ....150 E6
Gorseinon SA4 ....43 B2
Mountain Ash CF45 ..81 F7
Penybryn Senior Specl
Sch SA8 ....68 D7
Penybryn St
Aberdare CF44 ....28 F2
Henderfogran CF39 ..132 C5
Penybryn Terr
Brynmenyn CF32 ....150 E6
Mountain Ash CF45 ..81 F8
Penybryn CF82 ....84 D5
Penybryn Villas [3]
CF47 ....10 F4
Penycoedcae Rd
CF37,CF38 ....134 F2
Penydarren Dr CF14 176 E5
Penydarren Gdns
CF5 ....193 C8
Penydarren Pk CF47 ..10 E2
Penydarren Rd CF47 ..10 E2
Penydre Rd SA6 ......22 F1
Penyfai CW Prim Sch
CF31 ....150 C1
Penyfai Rd CF32 ....150 C2
Penyfan View CF47 ..10 D5
Penyffordd CF83 ....137 F4
Penygaer Prim Sch
SA14 ....40 F7
Penygaer Rd SA14,
SA15 ....40 F6
Penygarn Ind Est
NP4 ....62 D8
Penygarn Jun Sch
NP4 ....62 D8
Penygarn Rd
Cardiff CF5 ....193 D6
Pontypool NP4 ....62 D8
Tycroes SA18 ....218 F5
Penygarn Terr CF34 102 B2
Penygarreg Rd CF39 133 C2
Penygraig Prim Sch
CF72 ....155 D2
Penygraig Rd CF72 ..159 B1
Penygraig Ind Est
CF40 ....106 F4
Penygraig Inf Sch
CF40 ....106 F4
Penygraig Jun Sch
CF40 ....106 F4
Penygraig Rd
Llanelli SA14 ....41 E4
Tonypandy CF40 ....106 F3
Penygraig Terr CF37 81 F1
Penygroes Cty Prim Sch
SA14 ....218 D8
Penygroes Rd
Ammanford SA18 ..218 F8
Gorslas SA14 ....218 C8
Penylan
Bassaleg NP10 ......142 A3
Pontypool NP4 ....63 B4
Porthcawl CF36 ......182 E7
Penylan Ct
[7] Cardiff CF24 ....178 C1
Cwmbran NP44 ......116 B8
Penylan Oval CF23 ..178 C3
Penylan Rd
Aberystwyth NP4 ......37 E7
Argoed NP12 ....58 F6
Newport NP19 ......144 A5
Pontypridd CF37 ....135 B8
St Brides Major CF32 .185 D2
Penylan Way NP44 116 B8
Penylan Way NP44 116 B8
Penyrallt La SA18 ....220 C7
Penyrallt Ave CF31 ..168 F8
Penyrenglyn Inf Sch
CF42 ....78 B8
Penyrenglyn Jun Sch
CF42 ....78 B8
Penyrheol Com Sch
SA4 ....43 B3
Penyrheol Dr SA15 ..40 E8
Penyrheol Prim Sch
SA4 ....43 B3
Penyrheol Rd
Gorseinon SA4 ....43 B3
Pontypool NP4 ....62 C3
Penyrheol Terr CF71 78 F8
Penyrnimple View
CF64 ....206 D4
Penywain La NP44 ..62 B6
Penywain Rd NP44 ..62 A7
Penywain St NP44 ..62 B7
Penywain Terr NP44 62 B7
Penywarc Rd SA15 ..40 F5
Penywaun CF38 ....156 F5
Penywaun Inf Sch
CF44 ....28 B6
Penywern Llanelli SA15 40 A7
Ystalyfera SA9 ....2 A7

Penywern Rd
Neath SA10 ....48 E2
Ystalyfera SA9 ....2 A6
Penywerlod CF82 ....34 C7
Peppermint Dr CF23 160 D1
Pepys Cres CF3 ....179 B6
Pepys Gr NP20 ......142 E2
Percival Cl CF14 ....159 D2
Perclose CF64 ......206 B3
Percoed La NP10 ..153 C4
Percy Rd SA13 ....74 B3
Percy Smith Rd
CF61 ....210 C6
Percy St CF10 ......195 A4
Pergoed La NP4 ......63 F7
Pergwm St CF40 ..107 B5
Peris Rd SA5 ....68 A5
Perrington Villas
CF32 ....151 E4
Perrots Cl CF3 ......193 E8
Perrott Pl CF46 ......83 B6
Perrott St SA13 ......81 B4
Perry Cl SA11 ....71 C1
Perry St NP44 ....89 F4
Persondy La CF5 ..176 F6
Persondy Terr NP11 87 C3
Perth Ct NP12 ......85 C6
Perthcelyn Com Primary
Sch CF45 ....81 F7
Perthlwyd CF44 ......28 A6
Perthy Cl NP44 ......116 B8
Perthyleision CF44 ..55 C3
Peter Cash Ho SA1 ..95 E3
Peter Lea Prim Sch
CF5 ....176 D1
Peter St SA1 ....68 C1
Peter St SA1 ....68 C1
Peterston Castle
CF5 ....191 E5
Peterston-Super-Ely Sch
CF5 ....191 E6
Petherton Pl [1] CF3 179 C6
Pethybridge Rd CF5 193 C4
Petrel Cl CF64 ......207 A7
Pettingale Rd NP44 ..90 B5
Petunia Wlk NP10 ..141 D7
Pheasant Rd SA8 ....23 B2
Phelps Ho [3] SA12 ..98 B3
Philadelphia Cl
SA6 ....69 A8
Philadelphia La SA1 68 D2
Philadelphia Rd
CF72 ....155 D2
Philip Dr NP44 ....89 A7
Philip Ave CF31 ....168 C5
Philip Cl CF14 ......177 D6
Philip St
Cardiff CF11 ....194 D5
Newport NP19 ......144 B4
Philip's Gn NP10 ..142 B4
Philip's Wlk NP22 ..12 E5
Philippa Freeth Ct
CF63 ....215 A4
Phillip Row CF44 ....53 F8
Phillip St
Aberdare CF44 ....29 A3
Mountain Ash CF45 ..54 D3
Newport NP19 ......143 E5
Pontypridd CF37 ....135 B7
Risca NP11 ....114 F2
Phillips Terr
Senghenydd CF37 ..110 F3
Trehafod CF37 ......108 C3
Phillipstown Prim Sch
NP24 ....33 E4
Philog Ct CF14 ....177 C4
Philog The CF14 ..177 C4
Philsay Ho NP44 ..116 C8
Phoenix Ave SA13 ..125 D5
Phoenix Bsns Pk SA7 69 B7
Phoenix Ctr SA7 ......69 C7
Phoenix Ho [3] CF24 195 D6
Phoenix Way
Garngoch Ind Est SA4 .43 F1
Swansea SA7 ....69 B6
Phyllis Ave CF31 ..168 F3
Phyllis St Barry CF62 214 F3
Swansea SA4 ....68 A2
Troedyrhiw CF48 ......31 C2
Piccadilly CF71 ....200 D8
Piccadilly Sq CF83 138 B3
Picket Mead Rd SA3 122 C5
Pickerston Cl CF44 ..211 A7
Pickwick Cl CF14 ..159 F2
Picton Arc [1] SA1 ..95 C6
Picton La
Bridgend CF31 ......168 E2
Porthcawl CF36 ....182 F6
Picton Cl CF31 ....169 A2
Picton Cl CF61 ....210 A7
Picton Gdns CF31 169 A2
Picton La SA1 ......95 C6
Picton Pl
Cardiff CF11 ....194 D5
Maestg CF34 ....102 A6
Picton Rd
Aberystwyth NP4 ......37 E4
Neath SA10 ....70 F7
Rhoose CF62 ....213 A2

Picton Rd continued
Tredegar NP22 ....6 E1
Picton St
Maesteg CF34 ....102 A6
Pontlottyn CF81 ....12 F1
Pontypool NP4 ....62 E3
Pyle CF33 ....148 D3
Picton Terr
Llanharan CF72 ....154 A3
Swansea SA1 ....95 C8
Picton Wlk
🔟 Cardiff CF11 ....194 D5
Cwmbran NP44 ....89 B2
Picwic Gn NP44 ....89 B2
Pier Cl SA12 ....98 C1
Pier St SA1 ....95 E6
Pier Way SA12 ....98 C1
Piercefield Pl CF24 ....195 D6
Pierhead St
Cardiff CF10 ....195 C2
Cardiff CF10 ....195 D2
Pil Prim Sch CF33 ....148 B2
Pil-y-Cynffig CF33 ....166 A8
Pilgrims Cl SA10 ....71 C8
Pill St CF64 ....206 F5
Pill Terr SA11 ....71 B2
Pillgwenlly Jun & Inf Sch
NP20 ....144 B2
Pillmawr Circ NP20 ....117 B2
Pillmawr Rd
Caerleon NP18 ....118 A3
Newport NP18, NP20 ....117 D2
Pilton Pl CF14 ....195 D6
Pilton Vale NP20 ....117 B3
Pine Cl
Merthyr Tydfil CF47 ....10 D5
Porthcawl CF36 ....183 D7
Risca NP11 ....115 A2
Pine Cres SA6 ....45 E2
Pine Ct Cardiff CF15 ....158 D1
Llantrisant CF72 ....155 A3
Llantwit Fardre CF38 ....156 C5
Pine Gdns NP4 ....62 A6
Pine Gr Cimla SA11 ....72 B5
Newport NP10 ....163 F8
Ystrad Mynach CF82 ....84 E1
Pine St CF43 ....79 F7
Pine Tree Cl CF15 ....176 A7
Pine Tree Ho SA12 ....98 E6
Pine Tree Rd NP4 ....63 B4
Pine Tree Way CF46 ....63 C3
Pine Valley SA12 ....99 C5
Pine Walk Dr CF39 ....108 A2
Pine Wood Cres
CF23 ....178 E3
Pineacre Cl SA2 ....94 C6
Pinecrest Dr CF14 ....159 F3
Pinecroft Ave CF44 ....29 D1
Pinehurst Rd CF5 ....193 C8
Pines The
Abertillery NP13 ....36 C6
Cardiff CF14 ....177 A5
Clifrew SA10 ....49 B4
Hirwaun CF44 ....27 F7
Machen CF83 ....139 D5
Pinetree Ct SA2 ....94 C6
Pineway SA5 ....68 C6
Pinewood Ave CF37 ....136 C5
Pinewood Cl
Llandough CF64 ....206 E6
Newport NP20 ....117 B2
Pinewood Ct
Bryn NP12 ....85 E5
Llanelli SA14 ....41 D6
Pinewood Dr CF44 ....157 A2
Pinewood Hill CF72 ....155 A2
Pinewood Rd
Ammanford SA18 ....219 D7
Swansea SA2 ....94 E6
Pinewood Sq CF42 ....23 D7
Pinewood Terr SA12 ....98 D6
Pinewood View
CF37 ....109 C6
Pinkney St SA1 ....95 E7
Pinnell Pl 🔟 NP20 ....143 C3
Pintail Cl CF36 ....195 D5
Piper Cl Cardiff CF5 ....176 D2
Newport NP19 ....144 C8
Pisgah Cl NP4 ....37 E5
Pisgah Rd NP4 ....37 E5
Pisgah St CF33 ....148 C2
Pit junction Sta SA7 ....69 C6
Pit Pl 🔟 CF44 ....53 E8
Pit St CF34 ....102 B1
Pitman La CF11 ....194 E6
Pitman St CF11 ....194 E6
Pitmedden Cl 🔟 CF3 ....179 F7
Pittsburgh Ct SA5 ....67 F7
Plane Gr CF47 ....10 D5
Plane St CF37 ....101 A6
Plane Tree Cl NP18 ....117 F2
Planet St CF24 ....195 C6
Plantagenet St CF11 ....194 F5
Plantasia SA1 ....95 D7
Plantation Cl CF47 ....10 A3
Plantation Dr NP44 ....90 B4
Plantation Gdns CF45 ....82 E3
Plantation Rd CF45 ....82 E3
Plantation Row NP23 ....14 D6
Plantation Sq 🔟 CF48 ....31 B1
Plantation Terr
Fochriw CF81 ....32 C7
Rhymney NP22 ....12 F2
Plas Bryn Gomer
NP44 ....90 A6
Plas Cadwgan SA4 ....44 C2

Plas Cae Llwyd 🔟
CF83 ....111 F1
Plas Cleddau CF62 ....214 C5
Plas Craig NP44 ....89 F4
Plas Croeso SA4 ....43 B1
Plas Cwm Parc CF83 ....110 C2
Plas Dafydd CF44 ....28 E3
Plas Derwen
Croesyceiliog NP44 ....90 A4
Troedyrhiw CF48 ....31 B2
Plas Ebbw NP44 ....89 F4
Plas Essyllt CF64 ....206 B3
Plas Glen Rosa CF64 ....207 A5
Plas Grug CF63 ....137 F1
Plas Gwernfadog Dr
SA6 ....46 A5
Plas Heddwch CF33 ....166 A8
Plas Horab CF42 ....50 F2
Plas Islwyn NP44 ....89 E4
Plas Kenfig CF33 ....165 F7
Plas Melin CF14 ....176 F4
Plas Melyn SA5 ....67 F6
Plas Morlais CF33 ....166 A8
Plas Nant CF83 ....137 A7
Plas Newydd
Cardiff CF14 ....177 A4
Dunvant SA2 ....93 B8
Ebbw Vale NP23 ....14 D6
Grovesend SA4 ....43 C6
Plas Pamir CF64 ....207 B6
Plas Phillips CF83 ....137 A7
Plas Rd
Fleur De Lis NP12 ....85 B6
Grovesend SA4 ....43 C6
Pontardawe SA8 ....24 C6
Plas St Andresse
CF64 ....207 B6
Plas St Pol De Leon 🔟
CF64 ....207 B5
Plas Taliesin CF64 ....207 B6
Plas Terr NP12 ....85 B6
Plas Thomas CF83 ....137 F3
Plas Treoda CF14 ....177 B4
Plas Trosnant 🔟
NP44 ....89 E5
Plas Twyn NP44 ....116 F8
Plas Ty-Coch NP44 ....116 F8
Plas Tymawr CF31 ....168 B3
Plas View NP12 ....85 E6
Plas y Biswail CF3 ....179 F6
Plas y Coed Ave SA6 ....68 F8
Plas y Coed Rd SA6 ....68 F8
Plas y Delyn CF14 ....160 A3
Plas y Felin Inf & Jun
Schs CF83 ....138 A4
Plas y Wan NP12 ....14 B8
Plas Yr Eglwys 🔟
CF37 ....109 D2
Plas-Cadwgan Rd
SA6 ....46 C5
Plas-Gwyn Rd SA14 ....218 D8
Plas-Mawr Rd CF5 ....193 D8
Plas-y-Coed
Cardiff CF23 ....178 B3
Glynneath SA11 ....223 C1
Plas-y-Fedwen
CF37 ....109 D6
Plas-y-Fforest
Fforest SA4 ....18 F6
Penllergaer SA4 ....44 C2
Plas-y-Llan CF14 ....177 A5
Plasbach 🔟 CF5 ....193 D8
Plascoed SA9 ....1 F2
Plasdraw Ave CF44 ....29 B2
Plasdraw Pl CF44 ....29 B2
Plasdraw Rd CF44 ....29 B2
Plasgwyn SA4 ....19 D4
Plasgwyn Terr NP12 ....85 B6
Plasmarl CF44 ....29 B2
Plasmarl Prim Sch
SA6 ....68 E5
Plasmarl Terr SA6 ....68 E5
Plasnewydd Pl 🔟
CF24 ....195 C8
Plasnewydd Prim Sch
CF24 ....102 A3
Plasnewydd Rd
Cardiff CF24 ....195 B8
Cardiff CF24 ....195 C7
Plasnewydd Sq CF24 ....195 C8
Plasnewydd St CF34 ....102 A3
Plassey Ho 🔟 CF64 ....207 A5
Plassey Sq CF64 ....207 A5
Plassey St CF64 ....207 A4
Plasturton Ave CF11 ....194 D7
Plasturton Gdns
CF11 ....194 E6
Plasturton Pl CF11 ....194 E6
Plasturtwyn CF83 ....112 A3
Plasycoed Rd NP4 ....61 E7
Players Ave SA6 ....46 D8
Playford Cres NP19 ....144 F5
Plaza Ct 🔟 NP12 ....85 F4
Pleasant Cl SA4 ....42 F3
Pleasant Ct NP44 ....38 A3
Pleasant Hill
Clifrew SA10 ....49 C5
Ferndale CF43 ....80 A6
Pleasant Hts CF39 ....107 E5
Pleasant Pl CF83 ....137 E5
Pleasant Rd
Gorseinon SA4 ....43 E2
🔟 Tonypandy CF40 ....106 F3
Pleasant Row
🔟 Llanelli SA15 ....40 E5
Pleasant Sl SA6 ....68 C3
Pleasant St
Pentre CF41 ....78 F4
🔟 Swansea SA1 ....95 D7

Pleasant St continued
Swansea SA6 ....45 F1
Pleasant Terr
Tonypandy CF40 ....106 F2
Ystrad CF41 ....79 D3
Pleasant View
Aberfan CF48 ....55 C3
Aberkenfig CF32 ....150 C3
Aberkenfig CF32 ....150 C3
Aberystwn NP4 ....37 E4
Barry CF62 ....214 D8
Beddau CF38 ....156 A6
Bedlinog CF46 ....56 B8
Blackwood NP11 ....59 D2
Blackwood NP12 ....85 E8
Brynmawr NP23 ....8 B5
Brynmenyn CF32 ....150 F6
Cefn Cribwr CF32 ....149 B2
Cross Keys SA11 ....75 C5
Ebbw Vale NP23 ....14 D8
Fochriw CF81 ....32 D7
Llanelli SA15 ....40 E8
Maesteg CF34 ....75 B1
Maesycwmmer CF82 ....85 A1
New Tredegar NP24 ....33 E2
Pontypool NP4 ....61 F8
Pontypridd CF37 ....109 D2
Tonypandy CF40 ....133 A8
Trehafod CF37 ....108 C2
Treharris CF46 ....83 A6
Treorchy CF41 ....79 A4
Treorchy CF43 ....80 B2
🔟 Troedyrhiw CF48 ....31 C1
Pleasant View Terr
Swansea SA1 ....95 C8
🔟 Swansea SA6 ....68 C4
Pleasantview St CF47 ....10 C2
Plough Cnr NP12 ....86 A4
Plough Rd
Penperlleni NP4 ....39 F5
Swansea SA1 ....68 D3
Plover Cl
Newport NP19 ....144 E1
Swansea SA5 ....68 C7
Plover Way CF64 ....217 A8
Plumley Cl CF43 ....165 F8
Plunch La SA3 ....123 C3
Plunch Rd SA3 ....123 B3
Plym Wlk NP20 ....116 E2
Plymouth Dr CF15 ....176 C5
Plymouth Rd
Barry CF62 ....214 F2
Penarth CF64 ....207 B2
Pontypridd CF37 ....109 A1
Plymouth St
Merthyr Tydfil CF47 ....30 E7
Swansea SA1 ....95 C8
Plymouth Wood Cl
CF5 ....193 D6
Plymouth Wood Cres
CF5 ....193 D6
Plymouth Wood Rd
CF5 ....193 D6
Plynlimon Ave NP11 ....59 E2
Plynlimon Cl NP11 ....59 E2
Pobbles Cl SA3 ....121 A4
Pochin Cres NP22 ....14 A4
Pochin Ho NP22 ....34 C6
Pocketts Wharf 🔟
SA1 ....95 E6
Poets Cl CF37 ....136 A6
Police Row NP22 ....6 D2
Pollard Cl NP18 ....117 E2
Polo Ground Ind Est
NP4 ....62 F4
Pomeroy St CF10 ....195 B1
Pommergelli Rd
CF14 ....176 F4
Pond Mawr CF34 ....102 D1
Pond Pl CF44 ....53 F8
Pond Rd NP23 ....8 B3
Pond Row
Abercanaid CF48 ....30 E5
Abercwmboi NP11 ....114 C7
Pont Aur SA9 ....2 A7
Pont Faen Rd NP19 ....144 C3
Pont George Rd
CF33 ....148 B3
Pont Newydd CF35 ....170 D6
Pont St SA13 ....125 C8
Pont Yr Ochain
CF44 ....224 C1
Pont-Sion-Norton Prim
Sch CF37 ....109 B3
Pont-y-chun Prim Sch
CF72 ....173 A7
Pont-y-Cob Rd SA4 ....65 F6
Pont-y-Felin Ave NP4 ....62 F2
Pont-y-Felin La NP4 ....63 A2
Pont-y-Felin Rd NP4 ....62 F2
Pont-y-Garreg Jun & Inf
Sch NP23 ....7 B2
Pont-y-Glasdwr 🔟
SA1 ....68 D1
Pont-y-Goof NP23 ....7 F1
Pont-y-Shoot SA6 ....68 D5
Pontalun Cl CF63 ....215 A8
Pontamman Rd
SA18 ....219 D2
Pontardawe Ind Est
SA8 ....23 F5
Pontardawe Rd
Clydach SA6 ....47 A8
Pontardawe SA8 ....220 D3
Pontarddulais Cty Prim
Sch SA4 ....19 D3

Pontardulais Comp Sch
SA4 ....19 D5
Pontardulais Ind Est
SA4 ....19 C6
Pontardulais Junc
SA4 ....19 D5
Pontardulais Rd
Cross Hands SA14 ....218 B6
Gorseinon SA4 ....43 C4
Llangennech SA14 ....18 E2
Swansea SA5 ....67 C6
Tycroes SA18 ....218 E5
Pontardulais Workshops
SA4 ....19 D5
Pontcanna Ct CF5 ....194 C7
Pontcanna Pl CF11 ....194 C7
Pontcanna St CF11 ....194 D7
Pontcynon Terr CF45 ....82 C8
Ponthaen CF23 ....178 D8
Pontgam Terr NP11 ....112 F8
Ponthir NP18 ....118 B4
Ponthir Sch NP18 ....117 E7
Pontllanfraith Comp Sch
NP12 ....85 F4
Pontllanfraith Prim Sch
NP12 ....86 A5
Pontlliw Prim Sch
SA4 ....44 A4
Pontlottyn Inf Sch
CF81 ....32 F8
Pontlottyn Jun Sch
CF81 ....32 F8
Pontlottyn Rd CF81 ....32 D8
Pontlottyn Sta CF81 ....12 F1
Pontmorlais CF47 ....10 D1
Pontmorlais W CF47 ....10 D2
Pontneathvaughan Rd
SA11 ....223 E2
Pontnewydd Prim Sch
NP44 ....89 B4
Pontnewydd Wlk
NP44 ....89 E4
Pontnewynydd Ind Est
NP4 ....62 A8
Pontnewynydd Prim Sch
NP4 ....62 A8
Pontnewynydd Small Bsns
Ctr NP4 ....61 F8
Pontpren
Penderyn CF44 ....224 D2
Penderyn CF44 ....224 E2
Pontrhondda Ave
CF40 ....79 E1
Pontrhondda Rd CF40 ....79 F1
Pontrhydyfen Ind Est
SA12 ....73 D1
Pontrhydyrun Ho
NP44 ....90 A7
Pontrhydyrun Rd
NP44 ....89 F7
Pontrilas Cl CF5 ....192 F3
Pontsarn Cl CF48 ....10 D7
Pontsarn Flats CF48 ....10 D7
Pontshonnorton Rd
CF37 ....109 C3
Ponticsicil Sta CF48 ....4 A5
Pontycaeaf Rd CF48 ....10 A4
Pontyclun Prim Sch
(Ysgol Gynradd
Pontyclun) CF72 ....173 B7
Pontyclun Sta CF72 ....173 B7
Pontyfelin Ind Est
NP4 ....63 A3
Pontygof NP23 ....8 D5
Pontygof Jun & Inf Sch
NP23 ....8 D5
Pontygwaith Prim Sch
CF40 ....80 B1
Pontygwindy Ind Est
NP4 ....62 B3
Pontypool North Ind Est
NP4 ....62 A8
Pontypool Street Mus
NP4 ....38 A2
Pontypridd & District
Hospl CF37 ....109 E1
Pontypridd Coll
Rhydyfelin CF37 ....136 A5
Tonypandy CF41 ....79 E1
Pontypridd Historical &
Cultural Ctr (Mus)
CF37 ....109 C1
Pontypridd Rd
Barry CF62 ....214 C5
Porth CF39 ....107 F3
Pontypridd St CF63 ....215 B6
Pontypridd Sta CF37 ....109 B1
Pool La NP19 ....143 E7

Poplar Ave
Pontypool NP4 ....63 B5
Porthcawl CF36 ....183 A7
Poplar Cl Cardiff CF5 ....176 C1
Swansea SA2 ....94 B8
Poplar Cres CF34 ....183 B8
Poplar Ct Barry CF63 ....215 A7
Barry CF63 ....215 A7
Poplar Ho CF14 ....176 E6
Poplar Mews
Porthcawl CF36 ....183 A7
🔟 Troedyrhiw CF48 ....31 C1
Poplar Pl CF48 ....10 B7
Poplar Rd
Caerphilly CF83 ....138 C2
Cardiff CF5 ....176 C1
Cardiff CF5 ....193 D8
Croesyceiliog NP44 ....90 A4
Newport NP19 ....144 B5
Porthcawl CF36 ....183 A7
Rhydyfelin CF37 ....136 A5
Tredegar NP22 ....13 F5
Poplar St CF48 ....31 C1
Poplar Terr
Pentrebach CF48 ....31 A4
Pontypool NP4 ....62 A8
Poplar Way CF47 ....10 D5
Poplars SA12 ....98 E1
Poplars Ave SA11 ....72 A6
Poplars Ct NP18 ....117 F3
Poplars The
Llanharry CF72 ....172 C5
🔟 Mountain Ash CF45 ....54 D3
Mountain Ash CF45 ....54 E3
Rhiwina NP11 ....114 D3
Poppy Cl SA12 ....98 C3
Poppy Court (Llys Pabi)
SA11 ....71 E6
Poppy Pl NP10 ....141 D7
Poppyfield Cl CF3 ....179 E6
Porcher Ave CF37 ....109 D5
Porlock Dr CF64 ....216 B5
Porlock Rd CF3 ....179 C1
Porset Cl CF83 ....138 C3
Porset Dr CF83 ....138 C2
Porset Row CF83 ....138 D5
Port Madoc Rd CF3 ....179 E5
Port Mews CF62 ....204 F1
Port Rd Barry CF62 ....214 E8
Barry CF62 ....214 D7
Port Talbot General Hospl
SA12 ....124 E8
Port Talbot Ind Est
SA13 ....125 A8
Port Talbot Pl SA5 ....67 E5
Port Talbot Workshops
SA12 ....124 E8
Port Talbot Wrkshps 🔟
SA12 ....198 E8
Port Tennant Rd SA1 ....96 A7
Port Terr CF34 ....102 B1
Portal Ho 🔟 CF47 ....30 D8
Porters Rd NP23 ....8 C2
Portfield Cres CF14 ....177 F7
Porth Cty Com Sch
CF39 ....107 D4
Porth Ind Est CF39 ....107 F4
Porth Jun Sch CF39 ....107 F3
Porth Mawr Rd NP44 ....89 E4
Porth Pl 🔟 CF39 ....107 F3
Porth Sta CF39 ....107 F3
Porth-y-Castell
CF62 ....214 B2
Porth-y-Green Cl
CF71 ....188 E1
Porthamal Gdns
CF14 ....177 C6
Porthamal Rd CF14 ....177 C6
Porthcawl Comp Sch
CF36 ....182 E7
Porthcawl Prim Sch
CF36 ....183 B8
Porthcawl Rd
Cardiff CF5 ....193 C4
South Cornelly CF33 ....165 F6
Porthkerry Ctry Pk
CF62 ....214 A3
Porthkerry Pl CF14 ....177 D2
Porthkerry Rd
Barry CF62 ....214 D4
Rhoose CF62 ....213 D2
Portia Terr SA1 ....95 C8
Portland Cl CF64 ....207 B2
Portland Pl
Aberdare CF44 ....29 A1
Cwmbran NP44 ....88 F1
Swansea SA5 ....68 A5
Tonyrefail CF39 ....133 D6

Portmead Prim Sch
SA5 ....67 F5
Portreeve Cl CF72 ....155 D2
Portselwett St NP19 ....143 F3
Portway
Bishopston SA3 ....121 F7
Bishopston SA3 ....122 A7
Portway The CF36 ....182 F6
Post Office La 🔟
CF47 ....10 D1
Post Office Row 🔟
CF40 ....106 E6
Postern 🔟 NP44 ....89 E1
Potter St NP20 ....143 D2
Potters Field CF44 ....28 E4
Potters Gn CF32 ....150 E4
Pottery Pl SA15 ....40 D5
Pottery Rd
Cefn Hengoed CF82 ....84 E5
Newport NP20 ....143 D2
Pottery St 🔟 SA15 ....40 D5
Pottery Terr NP20 ....143 C2
Pound Field
Llantwit Major CF61 ....209 F6
Llantwit Major CF61 ....210 A6
Pound Hill NP10 ....162 E5
Pound La CF5 ....204 F6
Pound Rd NP23 ....8 C5
Powderham Dr CF11 ....194 E4
Powell Duffryn Way
CF62 ....214 E3
Powell St
Abertillery NP13 ....36 B5
Bedlinog CF46 ....56 A7
Swansea SA1 ....95 D8
Tir-y-Berth CF82 ....85 A6
Powell's Pl NP10 ....143 D4
Powell's Terr NP24 ....33 E4
Power St NP20 ....143 B7
Powis Cl NP12 ....58 D1
Powis View CF43 ....215 C2
Powys Ave SA1 ....95 A8
Powys Cl CF64 ....206 C4
Powys Dr CF64 ....206 B4
Powys Gdns
Dinas Powys CF64 ....206 C4
Swansea SA1 ....95 A8
Powys Ho 🔟 CF23 ....178 C2
Powys Pl
Dinas Powys CF64 ....206 C2
Pontypridd CF37 ....135 F6
Powys Rd
🔟 Cwmbran NP44 ....206 F2
Upper Boat CF37 ....136 D1
Precinct The
Bridgend CF31 ....168 F2
Church Village CF38 ....136 A1
Llantwit Major CF61 ....210 A6
Porthcawl CF36 ....165 E1
Precipitation Rd
CF62 ....211 E1
Prendergast Pl CF37 ....193 D3
Prendergast St SA15 ....40 E4
Prescelli Cl NP11 ....115 C2
Prescelli Rd SA5 ....68 A3
Prescelly Rd SA13 ....75 D3
Prescilla Terr CF46 ....83 C8
Prescoch La NP4 ....62 C4
Presswylfa Ho SA15 ....40 D3
Prestatyn Rd CF3 ....179 D5
Presteign Ave CF38 ....135 F2
Presteigne Wlk NP44 ....89 C1
Preston Ave NP20 ....142 B3
Preston St NP13 ....36 B6
Preston St NP13 ....36 B6
Preswylfa Ct CF31 ....168 E2
Preswylfa Row 🔟
SA15 ....40 D3
Preswylfa St CF5 ....194 B7
Pretoria Rd
Abertillery NP13 ....36 C3
Tonyrefail CF39 ....133 D5
Pretoria St CF32 ....103 E6
Pretoria Terr NP22 ....13 F6
Prettyman Dr SA10 ....70 D3
Price Ave CF63 ....215 B7
Price Cl
🔟 Aberdare CF44 ....29 A1
Cefn Coed CF48 ....10 A4
Pentre CF41 ....78 F5
Rhymney NP22 ....12 E5
Price's Row SA14 ....28 F2
Prichard St CF39 ....133 C5
Priest Rd CF24 ....195 D7
Priestley Cl NP10 ....142 F1
Primitive Pl NP22 ....7 A2
Primrose Bank SA10 ....48 B5
Primrose Cl
Bridgend CF31 ....169 C6
Cardiff CF3 ....179 B2
Cowbridge CF71 ....189 A1
Nelson CF46 ....83 E4
Pant CF48 ....11 A6
Primrose Ct
Cwmbran NP44 ....88 F1
Swansea SA6 ....68 A5
Tonyrefail CF39 ....133 D6
Primrose Hill
Aberdare CF44 ....28 E4
Cowbridge CF71 ....189 B1
Llantwit Major CF47 ....30 F8
Swansea SA1 ....95 B7
Primrose La
Pontardawe SA8 ....23 D5
Pontardawe SA8 ....24 B2
Primrose Rd SA11 ....71 D4

Primrose St
Swansea SA1 ... 95 B7
Tonypandy CF40 ... 106 E5
Primrose Terr
Aberdare CF44 ... 53 C8
Porth CF39 ... 107 F3
Porth CF39 ... 108 A3
Primrose Way NP10 . 141 D7
Prince Andrew Rd
NP11 ... 59 F5
Prince Charles Ct
CF64 ... 207 A5
Prince Charles Hospl
CF47 ... 10 C5
Prince Edward Cres
NP23 ... 14 D4
Prince Edward Ho 3
CF64 ... 207 A5
Prince Leopold St 1
CF24 ... 195 D5
Prince Llewellyn Ho 2
CF64 ... 207 A5
Prince Of Wales Dr
SA11 ... 71 E8
Prince of Wales Ind Est
NP11 ... 87 A2
Prince Of Wales Rd 1
SA1 ... 95 D8
Prince Philip Ave NP23 7 D5
Prince Philip Hospl The
SA14 ... 41 B7
Prince Rd CF33 ... 148 D3
Prince Rhodry Ho 1
CF64 ... 207 A5
Prince St
Blaenavon NP4 ... 17 C6
Margam SA13 ... 125 D5
Nantyglo NP23 ... 8 C1
Newport NP19 ... 143 D6
Pontypool NP4 ... 62 B7
Prince's St
2 Treherbert CF42 ... 51 A1
Treorchy CF42 ... 78 E6
Prince's Wlk NP4 ... 63 B4
Princes Ave
Caerphilly CF83 ... 138 B1
Cardiff CF24 ... 195 D7
Princes Ct
4 Cardiff CF24 ... 195 B6
Ebbw Vale NP23 ... 7 E1
Princes Rise CF83 ... 138 B1
Princes St
Barry CF62 ... 214 D4
Cardiff CF24 ... 195 D8
Princes Way CF31 ... 169 B3
Princess Cres NP13 ... 59 E6
Princess Ct
Llanelli SA15 ... 40 C5
Tredegar NP22 ... 13 E8
Princess Dr SA10 ... 48 C2
Princess Louise Rd
CF40 ... 106 F8
Princess Margaret Way
The SA12 ... 98 B1
Princess of Wales Ct
SA1 ... 69 C5
Princess of Wales Hospl
CF31 ... 169 A6
Princess St
Abertillery NP13 ... 36 B4
Ferndale CF43 ... 79 F8
Gorseinon SA4 ... 43 B2
Llanelli SA15 ... 40 C5
Maesteg CF34 ... 102 B2
Pontypridd CF37 ... 135 E7
Ton Pentre CF41 ... 79 C3
Princess Way
Bridgend CF31 ... 169 A4
Swansea SA1 ... 95 D6
Prior St SA13 ... 99 B1
Priority Bsns Pk
CF10 ... 195 A3
Priority Ent Pk CF63 215 E7
Priority Workshops
CF63 ... 215 E7
Priors Cres SA2 ... 93 B8
Priors Way SA2 ... 93 B8
Priorsgate NP12 ... 59 C2
Priory Ave CF31 ... 168 F1
Priory Cl
Bridgend CF31 ... 168 F1
Caerleon NP18 ... 117 E3
Pontypridd CF37 ... 109 B3
Priory Ct
Abercarn NP11 ... 114 B8
Neath SA10 ... 48 C2
Priory Dr NP18 ... 145 B8
Priory Gdns
Barry CF63 ... 215 B8
Bridgend CF31 ... 168 F2
Priory Oak CF31 ... 169 A4
Priory Rd CF31 ... 168 F2
Priory St NP11 ... 115 A1
Priory Terr CF34 ... 101 F3
Priory Way NP18 ... 145 B8
Pritchard Cl 1 CF5 . 176 E2
Pritchard St CF46 ... 83 B8
Pritchard Terr NP24 ... 33 E4
Pritchards Terr NP12 . 85 B4
Probert Pl NP19 ... 143 E5
Proctor Cl CF62 ... 214 C5
Promenade
Barry CF62 ... 214 C1
Barry CF62 ... 214 E1
Swansea SA1 ... 95 C7
Promenade D'orvault The
NP22 ... 13 E6
Promenade Terr
SA3 ... 123 B4
Promenade The
Abersychan NP4 ... 37 E3
Mumbles SA3 ... 123 B8
Pen-clawdd SA4 ... 64 C4
Swansea SA2 ... 94 E4
Promenade View
SA12 ... 98 C1
Prospect Dr CF5 ... 193 F8
Prospect Pl
Abertysswg NP22 ... 33 B8
Cwmaman CF44 ... 53 A4
Cwmbran NP44 ... 89 E2
Cwmllynfell SA9 ... 221 B7
Llanelli SA15 ... 40 D6
Ogmore Vale CF32 ... 104 E1
Pont Rhyd-y-cyff CF34 128 D6
Pontycymer CF32 ... 103 E3
Pontypool NP4 ... 37 F1
Pontypool NP4 ... 63 A4
Swansea SA2 ... 94 C7
Tredegar NP22 ... 13 F6
Treorchy CF42 ... 78 E6
Tylorstown CF43 ... 80 C4
Ystalyfera SA9 ... 2 B6
Prospect St NP20 ... 143 B7
Prosser La 3 NP20 ... 142 F4
Prosser St
8 Mountain Ash CF45 . 54 E1
1 Treharris CF46 ... 83 B6
Prosser's Terr SA13 ... 75 A6
Protheroe Ave CF31 . 168 C8
Protheroe St
Ferndale CF43 ... 80 A5
Maesteg CF34 ... 75 B2
Provident Cotts CF82 . 85 B2
Pryce St Llanelli SA15 . 40 C6
Mountain Ash CF45 ... 54 D3
Treorchy CF41 ... 79 A3
Pryderi Foopath SA1 . 95 B8
Prydwen Rd SA5 ... 67 B6
Pugsley Gdns CF32 ... 150 F4
Pugsley St NP20 ... 143 C6
Pum Erw Rd CF14 ... 177 D5
Pump House Rd
CF62 ... 211 E1
Pump St 7 NP20 ... 143 B5
Punch House Flats
NP22 ... 13 E6
Purbeck St CF5 ... 194 C6
Purcell Ave SA12 ... 98 A3
Purcell Rd
Cardiff CF3 ... 179 D7
Penarth CF64 ... 206 F1
Purcell Sq NP19 ... 144 C5
Purdey Cl CF62 ... 214 C7
Purple Cl SA12 ... 98 B3
Pwll Mawr Ave CF3 . 179 C3
Pwll Melyn CF35 ... 152 C1
Pwll St SA1 ... 68 D4
Pwll y Min Cres CF5 . 191 E5
Pwll-Evan-Ddu
CF35 ... 169 C8
Pwll-y-Domen Rd
SA5 ... 68 B3
Pwll-y-Glaw SA12 ... 100 A7
Pwll-y-Waun CF36 ... 183 B8
Pwll-yr-Hwyaid SA5 . 67 E6
Pwllcarn Terr CF32 ... 103 E8
Pwlldu La SA3 ... 121 F4
Pwllfa Rd CF44 ... 53 A4
Pwllglas Rd NP12 ... 85 C7
Pwllgwaun Rd CF37 . 109 B1
Pwllheli Ct CF3 ... 179 C4
Pwllhelyg CF15 ... 176 D8
Pwllmelin La CF5 ... 193 F8
Pwllmelin Rd CF5 ... 176 E1
Pwllygath St CF33 ... 148 D2
Pye Cnr NP10 ... 142 C3
Pyke St CF63 ... 215 A5
Pyle Cross CF33 ... 148 B1
Pyle Ct SA3 ... 122 A5
Pyle Inn Way CF33 ... 148 B2
Pyle Rd
Bishopston SA3 ... 122 A5
Cardiff CF5 ... 193 C4
Porthcawl CF36 ... 166 A2
Pyle CF33 ... 148 B2
Pyle Sta CF33 ... 148 A1
Pyntws Terr 2 SA15 ... 40 F4
Pyra Ct CF62 ... 214 C3
Pytchley Cl CF72 ... 155 E2

Q

Quadrangle The
Pyle CF33 ... 148 A1
Sarn CF32 ... 150 E4
Quadrant Ctr SA1 ... 95 C6
Quadrant The SA2 ... 94 E6
Quail Ct CF24 ... 195 C7
Quakers View CF46 ... 82 F6
Quakers Yard Sta
CF46 ... 82 F6
Quantock Cl NP11 ... 115 C1
Quantock Dr NP19 ... 144 C6
Quar Rd SA11 ... 71 E6
Quarella CF31 ... 168 E6
Quarella Cres CF31 . 168 E6
Quarella Rd CF31 ... 168 E6
Quarella St CF63 ... 215 B6
Quarr Dr SA6 ... 46 D7
Quarr Rd Clydach SA6 . 46 D7
Pontardawe SA8 ... 23 E5
Quarry Cl CF5 ... 193 C8
Quarry Cotts 11 CF45 . 54 D3
Quarry Cres CF5 ... 193 C7
Quarry Dale CF3 ... 179 B2
Quarry Hill Cl CF37 . 109 A1
Quarry Pl SA18 ... 220 D7
Quarry Rd
10 Mountain Ash CF45 . 54 D3
Pontypridd CF37 ... 109 A1
Swansea SA5 ... 68 D5
Tonna SA11 ... 49 C2
Quarry Row
Blaina NP13 ... 15 F6
Merthyr Tydfil CF47 ... 10 D2
Quarry St
Nantgarw CF15 ... 157 F8
11 Swansea SA1 ... 95 D8
Tylorstown CF43 ... 80 B4
Quay Par SA1 ... 95 E7
Quay Rd SA11 ... 71 E8
Quay Row CF48 ... 30 E5
Quay St
Ammanford SA18 ... 219 C7
Cardiff CF10 ... 195 A5
Quay W SA1 ... 95 D7
Quebec Cl NP20 ... 142 D3
Queen Anne Sq
CF10 ... 194 F7
Queen Charlotte Dr
CF15 ... 174 F6
Queen Mary's Wlk
SA15 ... 40 E4
Queen Sq 6 NP23 ... 8 B4
Queen St
Aberdare CF44 ... 53 C7
Abertillery NP13 ... 36 B4
Barry CF62 ... 214 D4
Blaenavon NP4 ... 17 D6
Blaengarw CF32 ... 103 E7
Blaina NP13 ... 15 E5
Bridgend CF31 ... 168 F4
Brynmawr NP23 ... 8 C5
Brynmenyn CF32 ... 150 E6
Cardiff CF15 ... 158 C1
Cwmdare CF44 ... 28 C3
Ebbw Vale NP23 ... 14 E2
Glyncorrwg SA13 ... 227 C2
Maesteg CF34 ... 102 A3
Nantyglo NP23 ... 15 D8
Neath SA11 ... 71 E7
Newport NP20 ... 143 C3
Pant CF48 ... 11 B6
Pentre CF41 ... 78 F5
Pontlottyn CF81 ... 12 E1
Pontrhydyfen SA12 ... 73 A1
Pontypool NP4 ... 62 B7
Pontypool NP4 ... 62 E3
Pontypridd CF37 ... 135 E6
Ton Pentre CF41 ... 78 F3
Treorchy CF41 ... 79 A3
Queen St (Heol y
Frenhines) CF10 ... 195 A6
Queen Street Back Rd
SA11 ... 71 E7
Queen Street Prim Sch
NP13 ... 36 C4
Queen Victoria Meml
Almshouses 11
NP20 ... 143 B4
Queen Victoria Rd
SA15 ... 40 C4
Queen Victoria St
NP22 ... 13 D6
Queen Wood Cl
CF23 ... 178 C3
Queen's Ave
Gorseinon SA4 ... 43 B1
Porthcawl CF36 ... 183 B7
Sarn CF32 ... 150 E4
Queen's Chambers 1
NP20 ... 143 B5
Queen's Cl NP20 ... 143 B6
Queen's Cres NP22 ... 12 E5
Queen's Croft NP20 . 143 B6
Queen's Hill NP20 ... 143 B6
Queen's Hill Cres
NP20 ... 143 B6
Queen's Rd
Merthyr Tydfil CF47 ... 10 E1
Mumbles SA3 ... 123 A5
Neath SA10 ... 70 F7
New Tredegar NP24 ... 34 A2
Penarth CF64 ... 207 B5
Queen's Sq NP23 ... 14 D8
Queen's Way NP18,
NP26 ... 145 D1
Queens Arc 8 CF10 . 195 A5
Queens Ct CF31 ... 169 C3
Queens Ct The SA12 124 D7
Queens Dr
Cardiff CF5 ... 193 A2
Llantwit Fardre CF38 . 156 D6
Queens Rd
Bridgend CF31 ... 169 C2
Bridgend CF31 ... 169 C3
Cymmer SA13 ... 75 D3
Newbridge NP11 ... 87 A7
Swansea SA2 ... 94 D6
Queens Rd S CF10 ... 207 D8
Queens Villas NP23 ... 7 D2
Queens W CF10 ... 195 A6
Queens Way CF63 ... 215 A3
Queensbury Rd CF23 178 E3
Queensway
Ebbw Vale NP23 ... 7 D5
Nantgarw CF15 ... 158 A7
Newport NP20 ... 143 B5
Newport NP20 ... 143 C5
Swansea SA5 ... 67 D4
Queensway Mdws
NP19 ... 144 D2
Queensway Meadows Ind
Est NP19 ... 144 C1
Queenwood CF23 ... 178 E3
Quentin St CF14 ... 177 E2
Quilter Cl NP19 ... 144 D4

R

Raby St SA15 ... 40 C6
Rachebites Hall CF48 . 55 D4
Rachel Cl CF5 ... 176 D3
Rachel Sq NP10 ... 163 E6
Rachel St 3 CF44 ... 29 A1
Radcliff Wlk CF71 ... 189 C8
Radford Terr NP23 ... 7 D4
Radnor Com Jun & Inf Sch
CF5 ... 194 C6
Radnor Dr
Church Village CF38 ... 135 F2
Morriston SA6 ... 46 B4
Radnor Gn CF62 ... 214 F7
Radnor Ho
6 Penarth CF64 ... 206 F2
Port Talbot SA12 ... 124 D8
8 Swansea SA1 ... 95 E6
Radnor Rd
Boverton CF61 ... 210 C6
Cardiff CF5 ... 194 C6
Newport NP19 ... 143 F6
Radnor Way
Cwmbran NP44 ... 89 E3
Porth CF39 ... 133 D8
Radyr Ave SA3 ... 93 F2
Radyr Comp Sch
CF15 ... 176 D4
Radyr Court Cl CF5 ... 176 F2
Radyr Court Rd
Cardiff CF5 ... 176 E3
Cardiff CF5 ... 176 F2
Radyr Court Rise
CF5 ... 176 F2
Radyr Court Sh Prec
CF5 ... 176 E3
Radyr Farm Rd CF15 176 C4
Radyr Pl CF14 ... 177 C2
Radyr Rd CF14 ... 176 F3
Radyr Sta CF15 ... 176 C5
Raglan Cl
Abersychan NP4 ... 37 E4
Blackwood NP12 ... 58 D1
Cardiff CF3 ... 180 A7
Dinas Powys CF64 ... 206 C3
Raglan Ct
Caerphilly CF83 ... 137 D4
Croesyceiliog NP44 ... 89 F6
Newport NP20 ... 143 C2
Raglan Gr CF48 ... 225 F1
Raglan Ho 4 CF10 ... 194 F5
Raglan Mews NP10 . 163 E5
Raglan Rd
Hengoed CF82 ... 85 A3
Swansea SA2 ... 94 C7
Raglan St NP11 ... 114 E3
Raglan Terr NP23 ... 7 D3
Raglande Ct CF61 ... 210 A5
Railmill La SA12 ... 99 F5
Railway Cotts SA6 ... 45 F3
Railway Cres
8 Cardiff CF24 ... 195 D6
Cymmer SA13 ... 75 B5
Railway Heritage Mus
CF62 ... 214 F2
Railway Hos
East Aberthaw CF62 ... 212 C1
Tredegar NP22 ... 34 B8
Railway Pl SA15 ... 40 C4
Railway Row CF32 ... 129 C2
Railway St
Aberdare CF44 ... 28 F3
Abertillery NP13 ... 60 B6
Cardiff CF14 ... 177 E1
Cardiff CF24 ... 195 E6
Newport NP20 ... 143 B5
Risca NP11 ... 114 F2
Trelewis CF46 ... 83 C7
Railway Terr
Abercarn NP11 ... 87 A3
Abertillery NP13 ... 59 F8
Bargoed CF81 ... 58 A2
Blaenavon NP4 ... 17 B6
Blaengarw CF32 ... 103 D7
Blaina NP13 ... 15 D5
Briton Ferry SA11 ... 71 C1
Bryncethin CF32 ... 151 E6
Caerphilly CF83 ... 138 B2
Cardiff CF11 ... 194 D5
Cardiff CF15 ... 158 C1
Cwm NP23 ... 35 B7
Cwmllynfell SA9 ... 221 B7
Cymmer SA13 ... 75 B5
Dinas Powys CF64 ... 206 C4
Fochriw CF81 ... 32 C8
Gorseinon SA4 ... 43 C1
Hirwaun CF44 ... 224 E1
Hollybush NP12 ... 34 D3
Llanelli SA15 ... 40 C4
Maesteg CF34 ... 75 B1
Merthyr Tydfil CF47 ... 30 E7
Mountain Ash CF45 ... 82 A8
New Tredegar NP24 ... 33 D3
Ogmore Vale CF32 ... 104 E1
Penarth CF64 ... 207 A4
Pontrhydyfen SA12 ... 73 D5
Pontycymer CF32 ... 103 E4
Pontypool NP4 ... 62 E1
Porth CF39 ... 107 E6
Resolven SA11 ... 226 D5
South Cornelly CF33 ... 166 A5
Swansea SA5 ... 67 E3
Ton Pentre CF41 ... 79 B3
Tonypandy CF40 ... 106 C6
Tonypandy CF40 ... 106 F4
Tredegar NP22 ... 6 A6
Treharris CF46 ... 83 C7
Treorchy CF42 ... 78 B4
Ystradgynlais SA9 ... 222 A4
Railway View
Ebbw Vale NP23 ... 14 D6
Ebbw Vale NP23 ... 7 D4
Fleur De Lis NP12 ... 85 B4
Tonypandy CF40 ... 107 A2
Tonypandy CF40 ... 79 F1
Tredegar NP22 ... 13 E8
Rainbow Bsns Ctr
SA7 ... 69 B6
Raisdale Gdns CF64 . 207 B2
Raisdale Rd CF64 ... 207 A2
Raldan Cl CF63 ... 215 B8
Raleigh Cl SA2 ... 94 C6
Raleigh Wlk 2 CF10 195 B4
Ralph St Llanelli SA15 . 40 D5
Pontypridd CF37 ... 109 D2
Ralph Terr SA15 ... 40 C4
Ramah St CF42 ... 78 C7
Rambler Cl CF14 ... 159 F3
Ramping Rd NP11 ... 114 C8
Ramsay Rd SA6 ... 22 E1
Ramsden Rd SA6 ... 46 C7
Ramsden St NP22 ... 12 F3
Ramsey Cl CF36 ... 165 D1
Ramsey Dr SA6 ... 45 D1
Ramsey Pl SA5 ... 67 E7
Ramsey Rd CF62 ... 214 F8
Ramsey Wlk
Cwmbran NP44 ... 89 C5
Newport NP19 ... 143 F7
Ramson Cl CF82 ... 84 E6
Ramsons Way CF5 ... 193 A5
Rankine Cl NP20 ... 116 F2
Ranks The NP11 ... 87 B2
Rannoch Dr CF23 ... 178 C5
Rannoch Ho 1 NP44 . 89 C2
Raphael Ave CF31 ... 169 D6
Raphael Cl NP19 ... 144 A7
Raphael Ho 3 SA12 ... 98 D1
Rassau Ind Est NP23 ... 7 A6
Rassau Jun & Inf Sch
NP23 ... 7 B4
Rassau Rd NP23 ... 7 B4
Rathbone Terr CF34 ... 75 A2
Raven Cl CF31 ... 169 B3
Raven Way CF64 ... 217 A7
Ravenhill Rd SA5 ... 67 F4
Ravenhill St CF41 ... 79 B2
Ravens Court Cl
CF23 ... 178 E2
Ravens Ct SA11 ... 72 B5
Ravens Wlk SA3 ... 122 F6
Ravensbrook CF15 ... 176 B8
Ravenscourt
1 Cardiff CF24 ... 195 B7
Cwmbran NP44 ... 89 B3
Ravensfield SA4 ... 66 D3
Ravenshoe Rd CF63 . 215 D7
Ravenswood Cl SA10 . 48 E2
Ravenswood Ct
NP11 ... 114 E3
Rawden Mews CF11 . 194 E5
Rawden Pl CF11 ... 194 E5
Rawlinson Terr NP22 . 13 F5
Raymond Terr CF37 . 135 F6
Readers La CF62 ... 213 A2
Readers Way
Rhoose CF62 ... 212 F2
Rhoose CF62 ... 213 A2
Recorder St 7 SA1 ... 95 C6
Rectory Cl
Caerphilly CF83 ... 138 A1
Dowlais CF48 ... 11 B5
Loughor SA4 ... 42 F1
Sarn CF32 ... 150 E3
Wenvoe CF5 ... 205 A6
Rectory Ct CF61 ... 210 B8
Rectory Dr CF62 ... 211 D5
Rectory Gdns CF83 ... 140 A7
Rectory Rd
8 Barry CF63 ... 215 B6
Bedwas CF83 ... 138 E7
Caerphilly CF83 ... 138 A2
Cardiff CF5 ... 194 C6
Gelligaer CF82 ... 84 C7
Neath SA11 ... 71 E7
Newbridge NP11 ... 60 C2
Penarth CF64 ... 207 B4
St Athan CF62 ... 211 D5
Rectory Road La
CF64 ... 207 B4
Red Brink Ct CF5 ... 193 C6
Red House Cl CF5 ... 193 D6
Red House Cres CF5 193 D6
Red House Pl CF5 ... 193 D6
Red House Rd CF5 ... 193 C6
Red Lion Cotts CF5 . 191 B1
Redberth Cl CF62 ... 214 F7
Redbrink Cres CF62 . 215 A2
Redbrook Ave CF83 . 139 A6
Redbrook Ct CF83 ... 138 A1
Redbrook Ho NP44 ... 89 F3
Redbrook Rd NP20 ... 142 E4
Redbrook Way NP44 ... 89 F3
Redcliffe Ave CF5 ... 194 A6
Rede Rd NP44 ... 89 B1
Redfield St CF41 ... 79 D2
Redgate Terr CF72 ... 174 C7
Redhill Cl CF44 ... 27 C8
Redland St NP20 ... 143 B7
Redlands Ave CF64 ... 206 E4
Redlands Cl CF35 ... 170 D7
Redlands Rd CF64 ... 206 E4
Redlands The NP19 . 144 C4
Redlaver St CF11 ... 194 F3
Redrose Hill CF41 ... 79 B3
Redshank Cl CF36 ... 182 D8
Redvers St NP19 ... 143 F4
Redway Rd CF5 ... 190 F1
Redwell Ct 8 CF23 . 178 C2
Redwick Ct NP44 ... 89 F2
Redwick Ho NP44 ... 89 F2
Redwood Cl
Boverton CF61 ... 210 C5
Bryn-côch SA10 ... 48 C5
Caerleon NP18 ... 117 E2
2 Cardiff CF3 ... 179 E7
Redwood Ct
Cardiff CF14 ... 177 F8
Swansea SA5 ... 68 A5
Redwood Dr
Cwmdare CF44 ... 28 D3
Llantwit Fardre CF38 . 156 C6
Redwood Meml Hospl
NP22 ... 12 E4
Redwood Pl NP23 ... 14 D6
Redwood Rd SA3 ... 122 F7
Reece's Terr NP11 ... 114 D8
Reene Ct NP19 ... 144 A3
Rees Cl NP20 ... 117 A3
Rees Ct CF61 ... 210 B6
Rees Pl Neath SA11 ... 71 E7
Pentre CF41 ... 78 F5
Rees Rd NP44 ... 89 E3
Rees Row CF32 ... 150 F4
Rees St Aberavon SA12 . 98 F1
Dowlais CF48 ... 11 B5
Ebbw Vale NP23 ... 14 D8
Merthyr Tydfil CF47 ... 30 E8
Ton Pentre CF41 ... 79 B2
Tonypandy CF40 ... 107 B1
Treorchy CF42 ... 78 E6
Rees Terr
Llanbradach CF83 ... 111 F1
Pontypridd CF37 ... 135 E6
Reevesland Ind Est
NP19 ... 144 A1
Reform St CF81 ... 32 F8
Regalia Terr SA15 ... 40 E5
Regency Cl CF61 ... 210 A7
Regency Ho 6 SA1 ... 95 C7
Regent Ave CF5 ... 193 A2
Regent St
Aberdare CF44 ... 53 C7
Abertillery NP13 ... 60 C6
Barry CF62 ... 214 F5
Dowlais CF48 ... 11 A5
Ferndale CF43 ... 79 F6
Treorchy CF42 ... 78 E6
Regent St E SA11 ... 71 C1
Regent St W SA11 ... 71 B1
Regina Terr CF5 ... 194 B7
Reginald St
Port Talbot SA13 ... 99 C1
Swansea SA1 ... 96 A7
Reginald Terr NP10 ... 142 B4
Reigate Cl CF14 ... 159 E3
Reigit La SA3 ... 122 C6
Relf Rd CF3 ... 179 C4
Rembrandt Ho 2
SA12 ... 98 E1
Rembrandt Pl 1
SA12 ... 98 E1
Rembrandt Way
NP19 ... 143 F7
Rennie St CF11 ... 194 E5
Renoir Ho 10 SA12 ... 98 D1
Renoir Rd NP19 ... 144 A7
Reservoir Cl NP10 ... 142 B4
Reservoir Rd NP23 ... 7 C5
Rest Bay Cl CF36 ... 182 D8
Restway Ct CF5 ... 176 E3
Restway Gdns CF31 . 168 E5
Restways CF36 ... 182 E7
Restways Cl CF5 ... 176 D2
Retford Ct CF14 ... 177 C4
Retreat The
Bridgend CF31 ... 168 E2
Cardiff CF23 ... 178 D2
Porthcawl CF36 ... 165 E2
Sarn CF32 ... 150 E4
Reynallt Pl CF36 ... 182 F7
Reynolds Cl
Newport NP19 ... 143 F7
North Cornelly CF33 ... 165 E8
Rhanallt St 3 SA13 . 125 D5
Rhandir SA14 ... 41 E4
Rhandir Terr SA14 ... 18 B1
Rheidol Ave SA6 ... 68 C8
Rheidol Cl
Aberdare CF44 ... 29 E1
Cardiff CF14 ... 178 A8
Treherbert CF42 ... 78 B8
Rheidol Ct SA6 ... 68 C8
Rheidol Dr CF62 ... 214 C5
Rheola Ave SA11 ... 226 D5
Rheola Ind Est CF39 . 107 E4
Rheola St CF45 ... 82 A7
Rheolau Terr CF37 ... 108 C2
Rhes Gwaith Tyn
SA15 ... 40 F2
Rhestr Fawr SA9 ... 1 F2
Rhianfa Gdns SA1 ... 95 A7
Rhianfa La SA1 ... 95 A7
Rhiannon Cl CF14 ... 159 D2
Rhigos Gdns CF24 ... 177 F1
Rhigos Prim Sch
CF44 ... 26 C8
Rhigos Rd
Blaenrhondda CF42 ... 50 E5
Hirwaun CF44 ... 224 B1
Hirwaun CF44 ... 27 A8
Hirwaun CF44 ... 27 C8
Rhiw Cae Mawr
CF31 ... 169 B5
Rhiw Ceris CF44 ... 53 E8

Roy – St M 271

oyal Glamorgan Hospl
CF72 155 B6
oyal Gwent General
Hospl NP20 143 B3
oyal Hamadryad Hospl
CF10 195 B1
oyal La NP13 36 A6
oyal London Pk The
CF31 169 E2
oyal Mint CF72 155 B6
oyal Oak CF83 140 B6
oyal Oak Cl CF83 140 B6
oyal Oak Dr NP18 144 E7
oyal Oak Gn NP44 90 B4
oyal Oak Hill NP18 144 E7
oyal Oak Ho NP11 60 C4
oyal Oak Rd SA2 94 B3
oyal Stuart La CF10 195 B2
oyal Terr CF40 107 A5
oyce Cl CF82 84 E7
oyce Wlk NP10 142 A6
oyde Cl CF5 192 E4
oyston Cres NP19 144 B4
ubens Cl NP19 143 F7
uby St CF24 195 D6
udry Cl CF83 138 E5
udry Rd
Caerphilly CF83 138 D5
Cardiff CF14 160 D5
udry St Cardiff CF11 194 E3
Newport NP19 143 C6
Penarth CF64 206 F4
ufus Lewis Ave SA4 43 A3
ugby Ave SA11 71 E7
ugby Rd
Newport NP19 143 D5
Resolven SA11 226 D5
uggles Terr SA6 45 D1
umney High Sch
CF3 179 C5
umney Jun Sch
CF3 179 B3
umney Pottery CF3 179 A2
umney Prim Sch
CF3 179 B3
umney Wlk NP44 90 B3
uncorn Cl
Barry CF63 215 D7
Cardiff CF3 179 D8
unnymede SA2 94 E7
unway Rd CF24 196 A7
uperra Cl
Bassaleg NP10 142 B3
Cardiff CF3 179 D8
uperra La NP20 143 C3
uperra St
Llantrisant CF72 155 D4
New Tredegar NP24 33 E3
Newport NP20 143 D3
Rupert Brooke Dr
NP20 142 F2
Rural Way SA2 94 B8
Rush Dr NP11 59 D5
Rushbrook Cl CF14 176 E4
Rushfield Gdns CF31 169 A6
Rushmere Rd NP12 85 E3
Rushwind Cl SA3 122 E6
Rushwind Mews SA3 122 E6
Ruskin Ave
Port Talbot SA12 124 E8
Rogerstone NP10 142 A7
Ruskin Cl Cardiff CF3 179 B7
Cwmbran NP44 89 A2
Ruskin Rise NP20 142 E2
Ruskin St SA11 71 B3
Russel Cl NP4 63 B4
Russell Cl NP10 141 F3
Russell Dr NP20 117 A2
Russell Drive Gdns
NP20 117 A2
Russell St
Cardiff CF24 195 B7
4 Cwmbran NP44 89 E5
Dowlais CF48 11 A4
Llanelli SA15 40 D3
New Tredegar NP24 34 A1
Swansea SA1 95 B6
Russell Terr 14 CF47 30 E8
Russet Cl
Langstone NP18 145 C8
Port Talbot SA12 98 B3
Rustic Cl SA2 94 B8
Ruth Rd NP4 62 F5
Ruth St CF81 57 F3
Ruthen Terr CF62 214 D5
Rutherford Hill
NP20 117 A2
Ruthin Ct CF35 169 F4
Ruthin Gdns CF24 195 A7
Ruthin Way CF38 136 A2
Rutland Cl CF62 214 C8
Rutland Pl 10 NP20 143 C3
Rutland St CF11 194 E4
Ryans Cl SA10 71 C8
Ryder St CF11 194 E6
Ryw Blodyn SA7 69 D6

S

Sable Ave SA12 98 B2
Sable Cl Cardiff CF14 160 A4
Port Talbot SA12 98 B2
Sachville Ave CF14 177 E3
Saddler St SA1 68 D4
Saffron Ct NP44 88 F1
Saffron Dr CF3 180 A8
St Aarons Dr CF72 153 F4
St Agatha Rd CF14 177 E4
St Agnes Rd CF14 177 D4
St Aidan Cres CF14 177 D4
St Aidan's Rise CF63 215 C6
St Aiden Dr SA2 93 D6
St Alban Ave CF14 177 D4
St Alban's RC High Sch
NP4 62 C6
St Alban's RC Prim Sch
NP4 62 B7
St Alban's Rd
Swansea SA2 94 F5
Treherbert CF42 50 D3
St Alban's Terr
6 Port Talbot SA13 125 C6
Treherbert CF42 50 E3
St Albans RC Prim Sch
CF24 195 F7
St Aloysius RC Prim Sch
CF47 10 D4
St Ambrose Cl 3
CF64 206 A2
St Ambrose Rd CF14 177 E4
St Andrew's Cl CF37 135 B6
St Andrew's Cres 2
CF10 195 B6
St Andrew's Inf Sch
NP19 143 F3
St Andrew's Jun Sch
NP19 143 F3
St Andrew's La 3
CF10 195 B6
St Andrew's Pl CF10 195 B6
St Andrew's Rd
Barry CF62 214 E6
Bridgend CF31 168 E7
Dinas Powys CF5 205 D3
St Andrews Cl
Cwmbran NP44 89 F7
Llantwit Fardre CF38 156 D6
Mumbles SA3 93 E1
St Andrews Ct 5
CF40 106 E6
St Andrews Dr NP12 85 E5
St Andrews Major CW
Prim Sch CF64 205 F3
St Angela Rd CF14 177 E3
St Ann St CF81 57 F2
St Anne's Ave CF64 206 F2
St Anne's Cl
Cwmbran NP44 89 E5
Mumbles SA3 123 A3
Newbridge NP11 86 D5
Rogerstone NP10 142 B4
St Anne's Cres
Bargoed CF81 58 A2
Newport NP19 143 E7
Porthcawl CF36 183 C7
St Anne's CW Inf Sch
CF24 195 C7
St Anne's Dr SA11 49 C2
St Anne's Gdns CF82 85 B2
St Anne's Terr SA11 49 C2
St Annes Ct CF72 172 F5
St Annes Dr CF38 156 D6
St Annes Gdns CF83 137 A7
St Annes Rd NP12 85 E5
St Anthony Rd CF14 177 E4
St Anthony's Cl NP4 62 D2
St Arvan's Terr NP13 15 E5
St Arvans Cres CF3 179 F7
St Arvans Rd NP44 89 F3
St Asaph Cl CF14 177 E6
St Asaph Dr SA12 98 C2
St Asaph's Way CF83 138 A1
St Asaphs Ct SA12 98 C2
St Athan Prim Sch
CF62 211 D4
St Athan Rd CF71 200 F4
St Athan's Ct CF83 137 F2
St Augustine Rd
Cardiff CF14 177 E4
Pontypool NP4 62 D2
St Augustine's Cres 11
CF64 207 B5
St Augustine's Path 9
CF64 207 B5
St Augustine's Pl 12
CF64 207 B5
St Augustine's Rd
CF64 207 B5
St Baruch Cl 4
CF64 206 A2
St Baruchs Ct CF62 214 F2
St Basil's Cres NP10 142 A3
St Basil's Stores
NP10 142 A3
St Benedict Cl NP4 62 D2
St Benedict Cres
CF14 177 E4
St Benedict Ct NP10 142 A2
St Bernadettes RC Jun &
Inf Sch CF23 178 F8
St Bleddian Cl CF71 188 D2
St Brannocks Cl
CF62 214 C5
St Briavels Mews
NP10 163 E5
St Bride's Cl CF36 165 F1
St Bride's Rd
Aberkenfig CF32 150 C4
Ewenny CF35 185 E7
St Fagans CF5 175 D1
St Bride's Way CF63 215 A8
St Brides Cl
Llanyravon NP44 90 A2
Pontarddulais SA4 19 D4
St Brides Cres NP20 163 F8
St Brides Ct 5 CF5 193 C4
St Brides Gdns
Newport NP20 142 E1
Newport NP20 163 F8
St Brides Major Church in
Wales Prim Sch
CF32 185 C2
St Brides Pl CF5 192 B8
St Brides Rd CF71 198 C5
St Brigid Rd CF14 177 E6
St Brioc Rd CF14 177 E6
St Cadoc Rd CF14 177 E5
St Cadoc's Ave CF64 206 A2
St Cadoc's Cl NP18 118 A3
St Cadoc's Hosp
NP18 118 A2
St Cadoc's Hospl
NP18 117 F2
St Cadoc's Rd NP4 38 D1
St Cadoc's Rise
CF63 215 D8
St Catherine's Cl
CF83 138 D6
St Catherine's Ct
Abercarn NP11 114 B4
Barry CF62 214 F8
St Catherine's Rd
SA12 98 E5
St Catherines Cl SA11 71 D5
St Cattwg's Ave CF82 84 C6
St Catwg Wlk SA2 94 A2
St Cenydd Cl
Bryn NP12 85 E5
Caerphilly CF83 137 E4
St Cenydd Rd
Caerphilly CF83 137 E3
Cardiff CF14 177 F6
Swansea SA5 67 F6
St Cenydd Sch CF83 137 D4
St Christopher Dr
SA2 93 D6
St Christopher's Dr
CF83 137 F2
St Christopher's Rd
Bridgend CF31 168 E8
Porthcawl CF36 183 C7
St Christophers Ct
CF35 169 B8
St Clair Ct CF10 195 C2
St Clare's Convent Sch
CF36 183 D8
St Clare's Jun Sch
CF36 183 D8
St Clares NP22 12 F2
St Clears Cl CF83 138 A2
St Clears Pl SA5 68 B7
St Curig's Cl CF62 213 A1
St Cuthbert's RC Sch
CF10 195 B2
St Cynons Ct CF40 106 F8
St Cynwyd's Ave
CF34 102 A1
St Cyres Cl CF64 206 E4
St Cyres Rd CF64 206 E4
St Cyres Sch
Dinas Powys CF64 206 C2
Penarth CF64 206 E4
St David Ave CF64 206 B4
St David Dr SA2 93 D6
St David Lewis RC Jun &
Inf Sch NP20 116 F2
St David St
Pontycymer CF32 103 E4
Ton Pentre CF41 79 A3
St David"s Est SA6 69 B8
St David's Ave
Blackwood NP12 85 F7
Llantwit Major CF61 210 A5
St David's Cl
Bridgend CF31 168 E7
Ebbw Vale NP23 14 C8
Hendy SA4 19 B4
Llanelli SA15 40 C3
Loughor SA4 42 F1
Merthyr Tydfil CF48 225 F1
Penpedairheol CF82 84 E7
Pontypool NP4 62 C7
Ton Pentre CF41 78 F3
Upper Boat CF15 157 E8
St David's Cres CF64 206 D3
St David's Ct CF3 162 E1
St David's Ctr CF10 195 A5
St David's CW Prim Sch
CF71 187 A4
St David's Dr CF83 139 C6
St David's Metropolitan
Cathedral Church
CF10 195 B5
St David's Mkt 2
CF10 195 B5
St David's Pl
Llantrisant CF72 155 E4
Maesteg CF34 102 A1
2 Swansea SA1 95 D6
St David's RC Jun & Inf
Sch NP20 142 E1
St David's Rd
Bridgend CF31 168 D6
Cardiff CF14 177 B4
Cwmbran NP44 89 F3
Maesycwmmer CF82 85 B2
Pengam NP12 85 B7
Port Talbot SA12 124 E8
Swansea SA6 69 B8
Ystalyfera SA9 2 C6
St David's Sq SA1 95 D6
St David's St SA11 71 E7
St David's Way
Caerphilly CF83 137 F1
Cardiff CF10 195 A5
Porthcawl CF36 183 B8
St David's Well
CF36 166 A2
St Davids Cl
Bridgend CF31 169 C6
Bryn NP12 85 E5
Penllergaer SA4 44 B2
Porth CF39 133 D8
Rhymney NP22 12 E4
St Davids Cres
Cardiff CF5 193 D5
Newport NP20 142 F1
St Athan CF62 211 D5
St Davids Ho 15
CF10 195 A5
St Davids Ind Est
NP12 85 B8
St Davids Pk SA13 147 C6
St Davids RC Prim Sch
Cwmbran NP44 89 F5
Mumbles SA3 123 A6
St Davids RC Sixth Form
Coll CF23 178 C2
St Davids Rd
Gwaun-Cae-Gurwen
SA18 220 E7
Miskin CF72 173 D6
St Deinols Cl NP12 85 B6
St Denis Rd CF14 177 F5
St Dials Ct NP44 89 E2
St Dials Rd NP44 89 D3
St Dogmael's Ave
CF14 177 F7
St Domlnlcs Retreat
NP4 62 B6
St Donat's Ave SA2 94 B7
St Donat's Ct
Caerphilly CF83 137 F2
Llantwit Major CF61 210 A5
St Donats Cl
Dinas Powys CF64 206 C3
Merthyr Tydfil CF48 225 F1
St Donats Ct 7 CF5 193 C4
St Donats Pl 7 NP44 90 B2
St Donats Rd CF11 194 D4
St Dyfrig Cl 1 CF64 206 B2
St Dyfrig Rd CF64 206 E2
St Dyfrig's Ct 4 CF3 179 C6
St Edeyrn's Rd CF23 178 C6
St Edeyrns Cl CF23 178 D6
St Edward St NP20 143 B4
St Edwen Gdns CF14 177 E5
St Elmo Ave SA1 95 E8
St Fagan's Ho CF83 138 A2
St Fagan's St CF11 194 F2
St Fagans Ave CF62 214 E6
St Fagans Cl CF5 193 E7
St Fagans Ct CF5 192 F4
St Fagans CW Jun & Inf
Sch CF5 192 F4
St Fagans Dr CF5 193 A7
St Fagans Gr CF48 225 F2
St Fagans Rd CF5 193 D7
St Fagans Rise CF5 193 C8
St Fagans St CF83 138 A2
St Francis Ct
Cardiff CF14 177 A5
Cardiff CF24 195 F5
St Francis Inf Sch
CF5 193 B5
St Francis Jun Sch
CF5 193 B5
St Francis RC Prim Sch
NP4 37 F4
St Francis Rd
Bridgend CF31 168 E7
Cardiff CF14 177 A5
St Gabriel & St Raphael
RC Prim Sch CF40 106 F5
St Gabriel's RC Jun & Inf
Sch NP19 144 E6
St Garmon Rd CF64 206 E2
St George SA15 41 A4
St George's Ave
CF31 168 E8
St George's Cres
NP19 143 F7
St George's Ct NP22 13 E7
St George's Terr
SA3 229 C1
St Georges Rd CF14 177 D3
St Germans Mews 4
CF24 195 D6
St Gildas Rd CF14 177 F5
St Govan's Cl CF62 214 F8
St Govans Pl SA5 66 D3
St Gowan Ave CF14 177 E5
St Gwladys Ave CF81 57 F5
St Gwladys Ct CF81 57 F4
St Gwynnos Cl CF64 206 B3
St Helen's Ave SA1 95 A5
St Helen's Cres SA1 95 A5
St Helen's Ct CF83 137 F2
St Helen's Rc Prim Sch
CF83 138 D4
St Helen's Rd
Cardiff CF14 177 D4
Swansea SA1 95 B6
St Helens Jun RC Sch
CF62 214 F6
St Helens Prim Sch
SA1 95 B6
St Helens RC Inf Sch
CF63 215 A5
St Helens Rugby & Cricket
Gd SA2 94 F5
St Helier Dr SA12 98 B3
St Hilary Ct CF5 193 D4
St Hilary Dr SA2 93 D7
St Hilda's Rd NP4 62 E2
St Ilan Comp Sch
CF83 138 A4
St Ilan's Way CF83 138 A1
St Illtyd Cl 2 CF64 206 B2
St Illtyd Rd CF38 135 E1
St Illtyd's Cl SA12 98 E5
St Illtyd's Cres SA1 96 A7
St Illtyd's Dr SA12 98 E5
St Illtyd's Jun & Inf Sch
CF61 209 F6
St Illtyd's RC Prim Sch
CF48 11 A4
St Illtyd's RC Prim Sch
SA1 69 A3
St Illtyd's Rd CF31 168 D5
St Illtyds Cl CF31 169 C6
St Illyyd's RC High Sch
CF3 179 D5
St Ina Rd CF14 177 E6
St Isan Rd CF14 177 E5
St James Cl
Caerphilly CF83 138 E5
Maesycwmmer CF82 85 B1
St James Cres CF62 214 B5
St James Ct 3 SA1 95 A6
St James Gdns SA1 95 A7
St James Pk
Bridgend CF31 169 D4
Tredegar NP22 14 A5
St James Way NP22 13 F7
St James' Cl CF48 31 A5
St James' Cres CF33 148 B2
St James' Field NP4 62 C6
St James' Rise CF31 169 A3
St James's Cres SA1 95 A6
St Joseph's Prim Sch
CF14 177 E2
St John Baptist CW Comp
Sch CF44 28 E2
St John Lloyd RC Comp
Sch SA14 41 B6
St John Lloyd RC Jun &
Inf Sch CF3 179 E5
St John St
2 Aberdare CF44 28 F4
Cardiff CF10 195 A5
Ogmore Vale CF32 130 E8
St John's Cl
Cefn Coed CF48 10 A5
Cowbridge CF71 188 F1
Maesteg CF34 102 D2
St John's Coll CF3 179 E8
St John's Cres
Cardiff CF14 177 A6
Cardiff CF5 194 D5
St John's Cres NP4 62 A7
St John's Cres NP10 141 F6
St John's Ct
2 Cardiff CF11 194 D5
Rogerstone NP10 141 F6
St John's Dr
Pencoed CF35 170 D7
Porthcawl CF36 183 C7
St John's Gdns 21
CF47 30 E8
St John's Gr CF47 10 F3
St John's La CF46 83 D3
St John's Pl
2 Cardiff CF14 177 A6
Rhoose CF62 212 E2
St John's Prep Sch
CF36 183 D8
St John's Priory
CF31 168 F3
St John's Rd
Bridgend CF31 168 D5
Clydach SA6 46 E7
Swansea SA5 68 B3
Tonyrefail CF39 133 C5
St John's St CF39 107 F2
St John's Terr SA10 71 A7
St John's View CF62 211 C5
St Johns Cl NP4 62 A7
St Johns Ct SA6 46 B1
St Johns Dr Bryn NP12 85 E5
Ton Pentre CF41 78 F4
St Johns Rd NP19 143 F5
St Joseph Pl NP44 117 B6
St Joseph's Ct 6
SA15 40 E5
St Joseph's Prim Sch
SA11 71 F6
St Joseph's Private Hospl
NP20 117 B4
St Joseph's RC Comp Sch
SA12 98 F2
St Joseph's RC Comp Sch
NP10 163 E7
St Joseph's RC Inf Sch
Aberavon SA12 99 A1
Swansea SA1 68 D1
St Joseph's RC Ju & Inf
Sch NP19 143 E6
St Joseph's RC Jun & Inf
Sch NP22 13 D7
St Joseph's RC Jun Sch
Aberavon SA12 98 F2
Swansea SA1 68 D1
St Joseph's Rc Prim Sch
Clydach SA6 47 A7
Penarth CF64 206 D3
St Joseph's School Ho 5
CF64 207 A5
St Joseph's Terr CF44 53 A3
St Josephs Pk SA12 98 E2
St Judes Cl SA5 68 C7
St Julian Cl CF63 215 C7
St Julian St NP20 143 B4
St Julian's Ave NP19 143 E7
St Julian's Comp Sch
NP19 143 E8
St Julian's Ct CF83 137 F1
St Julian's Inf Sch
NP19 144 A7
St Julian's Jun Sch
NP19 144 A7
St Julian's Rd NP19 143 F7
St Julians Ct NP19 143 E7
St Julians Hts CF82 85 A4
St Julians Lo 5
NP19 143 E8
St Julius Cres CF72 153 F3
St Katherines Ct SA1 69 D6
St Kitts Pl SA12 98 C2
St Lawrence Ct SA5 68 B7
St Leger Cres SA1 95 F7
St Leonard's Rd
CF31 168 D4
St Leonards SA3 122 F3
St Luke's Ave
Hawthorn CF37 136 A4
Penarth CF64 206 E2
St Luke's Cl
Llanharan CF72 153 F4
Pant CF48 11 A6
St Luke's Rd
Pontypool NP4 38 A1
Porth CF39 108 A3
Tredegar NP22 6 D2
St Lukes Ct SA1 69 D6
St Lythan Cl 2 CF64 206 A2
St Lythan Ct 9 CF5 193 C4
St Lythan's Rd CF62 214 C5
St Lythans Burial
Chamber CF5 204 C5
St Maddock's Cl
CF31 169 C6
St Madoc Cl NP12 85 E5
St Maelog Cl NP12 85 E5
St Malo Rd CF14 177 E6
St Margaret's Ave
Blackwood NP12 85 C7
Neath SA10 97 C8
St Margaret's Cl 10
CF14 177 A6
St Margaret's Cres 3
CF23 195 D8
St Margaret's Dr SA15 40 B7
St Margaret's Pk
CF5 193 E6
St Margaret's Pl 9
CF14 177 A6
St Margaret's RC Sch
CF44 28 F1
St Margaret's Rd
Caerphilly CF83 137 F2
Cardiff CF14 177 A6
St Margarets Cl
CF83 138 F6
St Marie St CF31 168 F3
St Mark's Ave CF14 177 E3
St Mark's Cl CF72 153 F4
St Mark's Cres NP20 143 B5
St Mark's Gdns CF14 177 E3
St Mark's Rd CF64 206 F2
St Mark's Villas
CF37 109 A1
St Martin's Cl CF64 206 F2
St Martin's Comp Sch
CF83 138 B1
St Martin's Cres
CF83 138 A1
St Martin's Rd CF83 138 A1
St Martins Cres
Cardiff CF14 177 F7
Tredegar NP22 6 C1
St Martins Ct NP20 142 F3
St Martins Row CF24 195 B8
St Mary Pl 6 SA12 99 A1
St Mary St
Aberavon SA12 99 A1
Bargoed CF81 58 A2
Newport NP20 143 B4
Pontypool NP4 62 D3
Risca NP11 114 F3
1 Swansea SA1 95 D6
Trelewis CF46 83 C7
St Mary St (Heol Eglwys
Fair) CF10 195 A5
St Mary the Virgin Jun &
Inf Sch CF10 195 B4
St Mary's (Brynmawr)
Church in Wales Jun &
Inf Sch NP23 8 C5
St Mary's Ave CF63 215 A5
St Mary's Cl
Blaengwrach SA11 227 C8
Briton Ferry SA11 71 B1
Merthyr Tydfil CF47 10 D3
Pontypool NP4 62 D3
St Mary's Cl CF42 51 A2
St Mary's Cres CF34 102 D1
St Mary's Ct
7 Newport NP20 143 B4
Porthcawl CF36 183 C8
St Mary's Day Hospl
CF64 206 C6
St Mary's Prim RC Sch
CF31 168 E5
St Mary's RC Prim Sch
CF47 30 D8
St Mary's RC Sch
CF11 194 D6
St Mary's Rd
Bryn NP12 85 E4
Cardiff CF14 177 A6
Croesyceiliog NP44 90 A5
Pontardawe SA8 24 B8
St Mary's Sq SA1 95 D6

St Mary's St CF83 138 D6
St Mary's View CF35 170 A4
St Mary's Well Bay Rd CF64 216 E4
St Marys & St Patricks RC Sch CF34 102 B3
St Marys Cl CF5 193 D3
St Marys Ct CF14 177 A5
St Marys RC Sch SA14 41 B6
St Matthew's Rd NP4 62 D5
St Matthews Ct 6 SA1 95 D8
St Mellons Ct CF83 137 F2
St Mellons Rd
Cardiff CF14 160 E2
Marshfield CF3 180 D8
St Melons Bsns Pk CF3 180 B8
St Michael Gr NP44 117 B7
St Michael St NP20 143 D2
St Michael's Ave
Pontarddulais SA4 19 B4
Pontypridd CF37 135 D7
St Michael's Cl
Cardiff CF15 158 C1
St Athan CF62 211 D5
St Michael's RC Prim Sch CF37 135 E6
St Michael's Rd
Cardiff CF5 194 A7
Cardiff CF5 194 B8
Maesteg CF34 102 A3
Porthcawl CF36 183 C8
St Michael's Sch SA14 41 E6
St Michael's Way CF31 169 C6
St Michaels Cl CF38 155 F6
St Michaels Coll CF5 194 A8
St Michaels Ct
Cardiff CF24 177 F1
Cardiff CF5 194 B8
St Michaels Gdns CF62 214 E8
St Michaels Mews NP20 143 D2
St Michaels RC Jun & Inf Sch NP20 143 C2
St Monica's Sch (Jun & Inf) CF24 194 F8
St Nicholas Cl
1 Dinas Powys CF64 206 A2
Waunarlwydd SA5 66 E3
St Nicholas Ct
Barry CF62 214 C3
Caerphilly CF83 137 F2
4 Cardiff CF5 193 C4
Swansea SA2 93 F6
St Nicholas Rd CF31 168 E8
St Nicholas Sch CF5 191 F1
St Nicholas Sq 12 SA1 95 E6
St Nicholas' Rd CF62 214 C3
St Nicolas Ct CF23 178 E8
St Non's Cl CF31 169 C6
St Oswald's Rd CF63 215 C7
St Oswalds Cl NP4 62 E1
St Osyth Ct CF62 214 C2
St Owains Cres CF71 189 C8
St Patrick's Dr CF31 168 E7
St Patrick's RC Jun & Inf Sch
Cardiff CF11 194 F3
Newport NP19 144 A4
St Paul's Ave
Barry CF62 214 E4
Penarth CF64 206 F2
St Paul's Ct CF5 177 A1
St Paul's CW Jun & Inf Sch CF11 194 F2
St Paul's Rd SA12 124 E8
St Paul's Terr SA4 66 D8
St Peter's Ave SA5 67 D3
St Peter's Cl NP11 87 B7
St Peter's Ct CF41 78 F5
St Peter's Prim Sch NP4 17 C6
St Peter's RC Prim Sch CF24 195 C7
St Peter's Rd
Mumbles SA3 122 E5
Penarth CF64 206 E2
St Peter's St CF24 195 B7
St Peter's Terr SA2 67 E2
St Peters Cl
Abercwmboi CF44 53 E4
Llanharan CF72 153 F4
St Peters Dr NP12 85 E5
St Peters Terr 1 SA15 40 C4
St Philip Evens' RC Prim Sch CF23 178 E5
St Philips NP19 143 F4
St Pierre Cl 2 CF3 180 A8
St Quentins Cl CF71 188 E1
St Quentins Hill CF71 188 D1
St Rhidan Cl NP12 85 E5
St Rhidian Dr SA2 93 D7
St Rhidian Rd SA5 67 F6
St Richard Gwyn RC High Sch CF63 215 D8
St Roberts RC Prim Sch CF32 150 C3
St Sannan Rd NP12 85 D4
St Siors Meade CF62 212 F2
St Stephen's Ave CF41 78 F5
St Stephen's Rd NP20 143 D2
St Stephens Dr CF35 152 C1
St Tanwg Rd CF14 177 E5
St Teilo Ave CF62 214 E6
St Teilo Cl 3 CF64 206 B2
St Teilo St SA4 19 C4
St TeilO's Cl
Bryn NP12 85 E5
Ebbw Vale NP23 14 C8
St Teilo's Ct SA3 121 F6
St Teilo's CW High Sch CF23 178 D3
St TeilO's Rd CF31 168 D5
St Teilo's Way CF83 137 F1
St Telio's Ct 2 CF23 195 D8
St Theodore's Way CF32 150 F5
St Therese's Prim Sch SA12 98 C1
St Thomas Cl CF31 169 C6
St Thomas Ct NP4 37 E5
St Thomas Prim Sch SA1 95 E8
St Thomas' Ct CF63 215 C6
St Tudor's View NP12 85 E6
St Tydfil's Ave CF47 10 E1
St Tydfil's Ct 10 CF47 30 D8
St Tydfils Hospl CF47 10 E1
St Vincent Cres 3 SA1 95 D5
St Vincent Rd NP19 143 C5
St Winifred's Rd CF31 168 D6
St Winifreds Cl 5 CF64 206 A2
St Woolos Ct 10 NP20 143 B4
St Woolos Gn 2 NP44 89 E4
St Woolos Hospl (General) NP20 143 B3
St Woolos Jun & Inf Sch NP20 143 B4
St Woolos Pl NP20 143 B4
St Woolos Rd NP20 143 B4
St Woolos' Cath NP20 143 B4
Salem Cotts NP22 13 E8
Salem La CF38 135 F1
Salem Rd
Cwmavon SA12 99 F6
Llanelli SA15 40 F8
Swansea SA6 68 D5
Salem Row CF15 157 F5
Salem Terr CF40 106 F8
Salisbury Ave CF64 206 F3
Salisbury Cl
Merthyr Tydfil CF48 225 F1
2 Newport NP20 143 C6
3 Penarth CF64 206 F2
Scurlage SA3 231 A6
Salisbury Ct
Cwmbran NP44 89 C3
Penarth CF64 206 F3
Salisbury Rd
Abercynon CF45 82 D2
Barry CF62 214 C4
Cardiff CF24 195 B7
Maesteg CF34 101 F3
Salisbury St NP11 114 C4
Salisbury Terr
New Tredegar NP24 34 A1
Varteg NP4 17 E1
Salmon Cl CF23 178 E1
Salmons Wood CF71 188 B8
Salop Ho 8 CF64 207 A5
Salop Pl CF64 207 B5
Salop St
Caerphilly CF83 138 B2
Penarth CF64 207 A4
Salthouse Cl SA4 64 A3
Saltmead Ct CF11 194 E4
Saltoun St SA13 125 E3
Salubrious Pl SA1 95 D6
Salvia Cl CF3 180 A7
Salway Ave NP12 58 B2
Sambucus Ave CF71 199 C4
Samlet Rd SA7 69 C8
Samlet Sh Ctr SA7 69 C8
Samson St CF61 209 F7
Samson's Ave NP4 37 E7
Samuel Cres SA5 68 A3
Samuels Rd SA9 221 B7
Sanatorium Rd CF11 194 B5
Sanctuary Ct CF5 193 A2
Sanctuary The CF5 193 A2
Sand La SA11 98 C8
Sand St 12 CF47 10 D2
Sandbrook Rd CF3 180 B6
Sanderling Cl CF36 182 D8
Sanderling Dr CF3 179 F8
Sandfields Comp Sch SA12 98 C3
Sandfields Prim Sch SA12 98 F1
Sandfields Rd
Aberavon SA12 98 F1
Aberkenfig CF32 150 D4
Sandon St CF24 195 B5
Sandown Ct CF5 193 E5
Sandown Ho 7 SA12 98 D1
Sandown Rd SA12 124 E8
Sandpiper Cl CF3 179 F8
Sandpiper Ct SA12 98 C1
Sandpiper Rd
Llanelli SA15 40 B6
Porthcawl CF36 165 D1
Sandpiper Way NP10 163 E6
Sandringham Cl
Barry CF62 214 C8
Gorseinon SA4 66 B8
Sandringham Rd CF23 178 C1
Sandwick Ct CF23 178 C7
Sandy Cl SA12 98 C1
Sandy La
Newport NP10 163 F8
Porthcawl CF36 183 A7
Southgate SA3 121 A6
Sandy Rd SA15 40 A6
Sandy Ridge SA12 98 C1
Sandybank Rd CF41 79 C3
Sandybrook Cl NP44 89 C1
Sandymeers CF36 183 A7
Sannan St CF81 58 B5
Sanquahar St CF24 195 D5
Sansom St NP11 114 F3
Sapele Dr CF24 195 D5
Sapphire St CF24 195 D7
Sarah St CF48 55 D5
Sardis Cl SA5 66 E3
Sardis Rd
Pontypridd CF37 135 B8
Pontypridd CF37 135 C8
Sarlou Cl SA3 123 C3
Sarn Helen SA11 223 E6
Sarn Hill CF32 150 E3
Sarn Pl 7 NP11 114 F3
Sarn Sta CF32 150 D3
Sarn Villas CF32 150 E3
Sarnfan Baglan Rd SA12 98 E4
Saron Cl SA4 42 F3
Saron Cotts 4 SA13 99 C1
Saron Cty Prim Sch SA18 218 E6
Saron Pl NP23 14 D6
Saron Rd
Ammanford SA18 218 F8
Bynea SA14 41 F4
Capel Hendre SA18 218 E6
Penperlleni NP4 39 C8
Saron St CF37 135 E7
Saunders Rd CF10 195 A4
Saunders Way SA2 94 B5
Saundersfoot Cl CF5 193 D3
Saville Rd CF32 104 E3
Savine NP44 89 C1
Sawel Ct SA4 19 A4
Sawel Terr SA4 19 A4
Sawtells Terr NP4 61 F8
Saxon St CF47 10 D2
Saxons Hos NP4 37 F4
Scales Hos CF44 28 E6
Scarborough Rd
1 Newport NP19 143 E8
5 Pontypridd CF37 109 E2
Scard St 5 NP20 143 B4
Scarlet Ave SA12 98 A2
Sch of Nursing & Midwifery Studies NP18 118 A2
School Ave NP23 8 D1
School Cl NP4 62 B6
School Cres NP4 62 E1
School Ct
Cwmbran NP44 89 E2
Neath SA11 71 D5
School La
Abersychan NP4 37 F4
Ebbw Vale NP23 7 B4
Newport NP20 143 C4
Penperlleni NP4 39 E6
Pontardawe SA8 23 E5
Pontypool NP4 62 B7
Rhydyfelin CF37 136 B4
Taffs Well CF15 157 F4
School Rd
Abercraf SA9 222 C7
Crynant SA10 226 A8
Cymmer SA13 75 C5
Dyffryn Cellwen SA10 223 A4
Ebbw Vale NP23 7 B4
Glais SA7 47 A5
Llanelli SA15 40 F2
Maesteg CF34 102 A2
Miskin CF72 173 D7
Miskin CF72 173 E7
Neath SA10 70 C1
Neath SA11 71 D5
Ogmore Vale CF32 104 E1
Pyle CF33 148 D3
Tonna SA11 49 C2
Troedyrhiw CF48 31 C1
Ystalyfera SA9 2 B6
Ystradgynlais SA9 2 D8
School St
Aberbargoed CF81 58 A5
Abercwmboi CF44 53 E5
Blaencwm CF42 50 B2
Blaengwrach SA11 227 B8
Brynamman SA18 220 D8
Caerphilly CF83 137 F8
Cardiff CF10 195 B4
Deri CF81 57 B8
Ferndale CF43 79 F8
Fleur De Lis NP12 85 B5
Llantrisant CF72 155 D3
Maerdy CF43 52 A1
New Tredegar NP24 33 D3
New Tredegar NP24 33 F2
New Tredegar NP24 34 A1
Pontlottyn CF81 12 F1
Pontrhydyfen SA12 73 A1
Pontyclun CF72 173 B8
Porth CF39 107 F2
School St *continued*
Porth CF39 107 F4
Senghenydd CF83 110 F3
Ton Pentre CF41 79 A3
Tonypandy CF40 107 A2
Tonyrefail CF39 133 C5
Tylorstown CF40 80 B1
School Terr
Blaengarw CF32 103 E5
Cwm NP23 35 A8
Cwmavon SA12 99 E5
Llanharan CF72 153 F3
North Cornelly CF33 165 F7
Pontycymer CF32 103 F3
Pontypool NP4 61 F8
Rogerstone NP10 141 F5
Tonypandy CF40 106 E7
Wattstown CF39 107 D8
School View
Nantyglo NP23 8 B2
Pontypool NP4 62 D5
Schooner Way
Cardiff CF10 195 C3
Cardiff CF10 195 C4
Scotch St SA13 76 C5
Scotney Way CF23 161 A1
Scott Cl
Bridgend CF31 168 D6
Newport NP20 142 E1
St Athan CF62 211 D7
Scott Ct CF23 178 B3
Scott Rd CF10 195 A5
Scott St CF42 50 E2
Scott Wlk NP10 142 A6
Scutari Row SA13 125 C6
Scwd-yr-Afon SA10 49 C4
Scwrfa Rd NP22 6 E1
Sea Breeze SA12 98 C1
Sea View SA4 64 E4
Sea View Terr
Aberavon SA12 99 A2
Barry CF63 215 C7
Swansea SA1 68 D1
Seabank Ct CF36 182 E6
Seabrook Pl SA12 124 E8
Seaforth Cl SA12 98 B3
Seager Dr CF11 206 F8
Seagull Cl CF36 165 E1
Seal Pit Rd CF62 211 E1
Sealands Dr SA3 123 C3
Sealawns CF62 214 C1
Seaside Cres 4 SA15 40 C4
Seaton St CF37 109 B1
Seaton's Pl CF37 109 B1
Seaview
Cefn Cribwr CF32 148 F2
Swansea SA1 69 C2
Seaview Ct 6 CF64 207 B4
Seaview Dr CF32 184 C3
Seaview Ind Est CF24 195 E5
Seaview Pl CF61 209 F6
Seawall Rd CF24 196 A6
Seaward Ave SA12 98 C1
Seaward Cl SA12 98 C1
Seawatch Ctr CF61 210 E1
Seaway Par SA12 98 C4
Seaway Parade Ind Est SA12 98 C5
Sebastopol St SA1 95 F7
Second Ave
Caerphilly CF83 137 F3
Cardiff CF23 178 E1
Merthyr Tydfil CF47 10 E5
Swansea SA6 68 C8
Sedd Goch CF31 169 B4
Sedgemoor Ct NP20 143 A6
Sedgemoor Rd CF3 179 C7
Sefton Ct 6 CF15 176 B6
Selby Cl NP44 90 B2
Selina Rd CF45 82 C5
Selwyn Morris Ct CF24 195 E5
Senghennydd Pl 3 CF24 195 B7
Senghenydd St CF42 78 D6
Senlan Ind Est CF23 179 A1
Senni Cl CF62 214 C6
Senny Pl SA6 46 A5
Sepia Cl SA12 98 B2
Serecold Ave SA10 70 D6
Serpentine Rd NP20 143 B5
Seven Sisters Mus & Saw Mill SA10 222 C3
Seven Stiles Ave NP19 144 D2
Sevenoaks Rd CF5 193 B5
Sevenoaks St CF11 194 F2
Seventeenth Ave CF44 224 B1
Seventh Ave
Merthyr Tydfil CF47 10 E5
Swansea SA6 45 D1
Severn Ave
Barry CF62 214 C6
Barry CF62 214 D5
Severn Cl NP11 115 B1
Severn Cres SA12 98 D1
Severn Ct CF11 194 D6
Severn Gr CF11 194 D7
Severn Rd Bryn NP12 85 D4
Cardiff CF11 194 D6
Porthcawl CF36 182 E7
Swansea SA6 68 D8
Upper Boat CF37 136 C2
Severn Road Inf Sch CF11 194 D6
Severn Road Jun Sch CF11 194 D6
Severn Terr 12 NP20 143 B4
Severn View
Abersychan NP4 37 F6
Cwmbran NP44 89 A6
Severn View Terr NP4 37 F3
Seward St CF47 10 F3
Seymour Ave CF72 154 A4
Seymour St
Aberdare CF44 29 A2
Cardiff CF24 195 E6
Mountain Ash CF45 54 D3
Seys Cl CF71 188 D2
Seys Ct CF61 210 B7
Sgubor Goch CF72 172 D5
Shackleton Cl CF62 211 D7
Shady Rd CF41 79 B2
Shaftesbury Cl CF14 159 E3
Shaftesbury St
Newport NP20 143 B7
Newport NP20 143 C6
Shaftesbury Wlk 5 NP20 143 C6
Shakespeare Ave
Bridgend CF31 168 C5
Penarth CF64 206 E4
Shakespeare Cres
Ebbw Vale NP23 14 C8
Newport NP20 142 E2
Shakespeare Ct 3 CF24 195 C7
Shakespeare Dr CF61 210 B5
Shakespeare Rd
Barry CF62 214 F8
Cwmbran NP44 89 C2
Shakespeare Rise CF37 136 A6
Shakespeare St 2 CF24 195 C7
Shamrock Rd CF5 193 C8
Shannon Cl NP12 85 D4
Shannon Rd NP20 116 F2
Shap Row NP22 6 A6
Sharpe Cl 3 CF23 178 E1
Sharpsburgh Pl SA1 68 D3
Shaw Cl Cardiff CF3 179 B7
Ebbw Vale NP23 14 A8
Shaw Gr NP20 142 E2
Shaw St SA4 66 B5
Shawley Ct 7 NP44 89 C2
Shea Gdns 24 NP20 143 C3
Sheaf La NP19 143 D6
Shearman Pl CF11 207 A8
Shears Rd CF5 193 F7
Shearwater Cl
Mumbles SA3 122 F6
Penarth CF64 217 A7
Porthcawl CF36 182 D8
Sheen Ct 2 CF82 84 F2
Sheerwater Cl 3 CF3 179 E7
Shelburn Cl CF11 194 E4
Shelley Cl
Aberbargoed CF81 58 B4
Blackwood NP11 59 D1
Shelley Cres
Barry CF62 214 E8
Penarth CF64 206 F4
Shelley Ct CF83 139 C7
Shelley Dr CF31 168 C6
Shelley Gn NP44 89 C2
Shelley Rd NP19 143 F5
Shelley Wlk
5 Cardiff CF24 195 C7
Rhydyfelin CF37 136 A6
Shelone Rd SA11 71 B2
Shelone Terr SA11 71 C3
Shepherd Dr NP18 119 E1
Shepherd's Rd SA6 68 E6
Shepherd's Terr SA4 43 A3
Shepherds Cl NP22 6 E1
Sheppard St CF37 109 B1
Sherborne Ave CF23 178 C7
Sherborne Wlk SA2 94 A1
Sherbourne Cl CF62 214 B8
Sherbourne Ct NP4 62 E1
Sherbourne Rd NP4 62 E1
Sheridan Cl
Cardiff CF3 179 B7
Newport NP20 142 E2
Sherringham Dr SA3 122 F5
Sherwood Ct CF5 176 D1
Sherwood St CF40 79 F1
Shetland Cl NP19 143 F7
Shetland Wlk NP19 143 F7
Shields Cl CF23 161 B1
Shiloh La CF47 10 E1
Shingrig Rd CF46 83 E4
Ship La CF10 195 C2
Shirdale Cl CF82 85 B2
Shire Ct CF46 83 C6
Shires The CF3 162 D1
Shirley Cl CF63 215 D7
Shirley Dr CF48 10 A1
Shirley Rd CF23 178 A2
Shoemakers' Row CF34 102 B3
Shop Hos CF44 28 F5
Shop Rd NP4 17 F1
Shop Row Blaina NP13 15 D5
Tredegar NP22 13 E6
Shopper's Wlk 1 SA1 95 C6
Shopping Ctr 1 CF44 28 A6
Short St
Briton Ferry SA11 71 C3
Clydach SA6 22 D1
Swansea SA1 95 C8
Showle Acre CF62 212 F2
Shrewsbury Ave CF39 133 D8
Shrewsbury Cl 8 NP20 143 C6
Sibrwd y Dail CF31 168 D8
Sickert Cl NP19 144 A6
Siding Terr SA10 70 D7
Sidney Ames Ct 9 CF24 195 D6
Sidney St NP20 143 B4
Siemens Way SA7 69 A5
Sierra Pines CF45 54 A3
Siloam Hill CF83 139 F7
Siloan Ct CF41 79 A2
Siloh Cres SA1 68 D4
Siloh Rd SA1 68 D4
Silurian Way CF33 148 D2
Silver Ave SA12 98 B2
Silver Birch Cl
Caerleon NP18 117 E2
Cardiff CF14 177 C3
Silver Cl
Mumbles SA3 122 F7
Port Talbot SA12 98 B3
Silver Ct 6 SA12 98 B3
Silver Fir Sq NP10 142 B3
Silver Jubilee Cotts CF5 193 D5
Silver St
Abercarn NP11 114 C6
Cardiff CF24 195 D6
Silverhill Cl CF37 109 F4
Silverstone Cl 5 CF3 179 D8
Silverton Dr CF72 155 E2
Simon St CF40 107 B2
Simpson Cl NP20 117 A3
Simpson's Way CF33 148 B2
Sims Sq NP19 144 D5
Sinclair Dr CF23 178 E1
Sindercombe Cl CF23 160 F1
Singleton Hospl SA2 94 D4
Singleton Rd CF24 195 E5
Singleton St SA1 95 C6
Sinnatts The SA10 71 C8
Sion Pl CF44 53 E8
Sion St CF37 109 C2
Sion Terr CF44 53 E8
Sir Alfred Owen Way CF83 138 A6
Sir Charles Cres NP10 163 F5
Sir Charles Sq NP10 163 F6
Sir David's Ct CF5 194 B7
Sir Ivor Pl CF64 206 C2
Sir Ivor's Rd NP12 85 F4
Sir Stafford Cl CF83 138 C5
Sirhowy Ct
Cwmbran NP44 89 B4
Tredegar NP22 6 F1
Sirhowy Hill Ind Est NP22 13 F7
Sirhowy Inf Sch NP22 6 F1
Sirhowy Valley Ctry Pk NP11 113 F2
Sirhowy View NP12 86 A3
Sitwell Way SA12 124 E7
Six Bells Est CF48 10 B1
Six Bells Rd NP13 36 B2
Sixteenth Ave CF44 224 B1
Sixth Ave
Merthyr Tydfil CF47 10 E5
Swansea SA6 45 D1
Skaithmuir Rd CF24 195 F7
Skelmuir Rd CF24 195 F7
Skenfrith Cl NP12 58 E1
Sker Ct CF36 165 E1
Sker House (rems of) CF36 165 A4
Sker Wlk CF36 165 E1
Sketty Ave SA2 94 D7
Sketty Ct SA2 94 D6
Sketty La SA2 94 D4
Sketty Park Cl SA2 94 C6
Sketty Park Dr SA2 94 B6
Sketty Park Rd SA2 94 C6
Sketty Prim Sch SA2 94 C7
Sketty Rd SA2 94 E6
Skewen Sta SA10 70 E7
Skibereen Cl CF23 161 A1
Skinner La 4 NP20 143 C5
Skinner St
Newport NP20 143 C5
Swansea SA1 68 C1
Skokholm Cl CF36 165 E1
Skomer Cl CF36 165 E1
Skomer Ct 2 CF11 194 F3
Skomer Pl SA5 67 D7
Skomer Rd CF62 215 A8
Slade Cl
Cowbridge CF71 188 F2
Sully CF64 216 B5
Slade Gdns SA3 122 F6
Slade Rd Barry CF62 214 F7
Mumbles SA3 122 F5
Slade St NP19 143 F3
Slade Wood Ho CF62 214 F8
Slate St SA6 68 F8
Slipway The CF64 207 A5
Slocombe Trust Cotts 1 CF5 194 B7
Slon La CF32 184 D2
Sloper Rd
Cardiff CF11 194 D3
Cardiff CF11 194 D4
Sluvad Rd NP4 63 C3
Smallbrook Cl NP44 89 F3
Smallwood Rd SA12 98 E5
Smeaton Cl CF62 212 E1
Smeaton St CF11 194 E5

nith Rd NP13 . . . . .36 A6
nith Row
St Nicholas CF5 . . . . .191 F1
onypandy CF40 . . . . .133 B8
nith St
Maesteg CF34 . . . . .102 B3
Ton Pentre CF41 . . . . .79 B2
nith's Rd CF24 . . . . .101 F3
nithfield Rd SA8 . . . . . . .23 E5
nithies Ave CF64 . . . . . . .216 B4
nith's Rd SA7 . . . . .47 A2
nith St CF38 . . . . .11 D5
niths Terr NP12 . . . . .36 A6
myrna Cotts SA13 . . . . . .125 D6
myrna St SA6 . . . . .68 E5
natchwood La NP44 . . . . .37 F1
natchwood Rd NP4 . . . . .37 E2
natchwood Terr NP4 . . . .37 E2
neyd St CF11 . . . . .194 D7
nipe St CF24 . . . . .195 C7
nipe St SA7 . . . . .2 E6
nowden Cl CF83 . . . . .138 C3
niths Terr NP12 . . . . . . .115 B3
nowden Rd CF5 . . . . .193 B5
nowden Cl NP11 . . . . . . .115 B2
nowden La NP44 . . . . . . .90 A5
nowden Dr SA5 . . . . .67 D6
oane Cl NP10 . . . . .142 A7
oar Cl
Croesyceiliog NP44 . . . . . .90 B6
Loughor SA4 . . . . .42 F1
oar Rd SA14 . . . . .41 A4
oar Terr SA6 . . . . .46 A1
oberton Ave CF14 . . . . . .177 F2
ofrydd Prim Sch
NP11 . . . . .60 B2
ofrydd Rd NP11 . . . . .60 B2
oho St
Newport NP19 . . . . .143 E5
Newport NP19 . . . . .143 F5
olent Cl NP12 . . . . .85 D4
olent Rd CF63 . . . . .215 C8
olva Ave CF14 . . . . .179 B8
olva Cl CF62 . . . . .214 F7
olva Rd SA6 . . . . .68 C8
omerset Cl CF48 . . . . . . .10 A5
omerset Ct CF23 . . . . . . .179 C7
omerset Rd **4** SA12 . . .98 C2
omerset Ind Est
NP44 . . . . .89 F5
omerset La
Cefn Coed CF48 . . . . .10 A5
Port Talbot SA13 . . . . . . .125 D6
omerset Pl
Cwmavon SA12 . . . . .99 F5
7 Merthyr Tydfil CF47 . .10 E1
Swansea SA1 . . . . .55 E6
omerset Rd
Barry CF62 . . . . .214 F6
Cwmbran NP44 . . . . .89 F4
Mumbles SA3 . . . . .123 A4
Newport NP19 . . . . .143 E7
omerset St **3** CF63 . . .214 F6
omerset St
Abertillery NP13 . . . . .36 B4
1 Brynmawr NP23 . . . . .8 C4
Cardiff CF11 . . . . .194 E4
Port Talbot SA13 . . . . . . .125 D6
omerset View
Ogmore-By-Sea CF32 . . . .184 D2
Sully CF64 . . . . .216 B4
omerton Cres NP19 . . . . .144 B5
omerton Ct **9**
NP19 . . . . .144 B3
omerton Jun & Inf Sch
NP19 . . . . .144 B5
omerton La NP19 . . . . . .144 A4
omerton Pk NP19 . . . . . .144 A5
omerton Pl NP19 . . . . . .144 B5
omerton Rd NP19 . . . . . .144 A3
omerville Ct SA2 . . . . . . .94 E7
ophia Cl CF11 . . . . .194 E6
ophia Wlk CF11 . . . . . . .194 E6
orel Ave 90 E8
orrel Dr
Newport NP20 . . . . .143 A6
Penpedairheol CF82 . . . . .84 E6
South Ave
Aberdare CF44 . . . . .28 F2
Cymmer SA13 . . . . .75 D3
Pontypool NP4 . . . . .62 D1
South Bank NP23 . . . . .7 F4
South Bargoed Ind Est
CF81 . . . . .57 F3
South Blackvein Ind Est
NP11 . . . . .114 B4
South Cl
Bishopston SA3 . . . . .122 A6
Cwmbran NP44 . . . . .90 B1
Pencoed CF35 . . . . .170 D8
Porthcawl CF36 . . . . .182 F7
South Clive St CF11 . . . . .194 F1
South Cornelly Ind Est
CF33 . . . . .166 A5
South Cross Way **3**
SA12 . . . . .98 C2
South Ct NP4 . . . . .62 A8
South Dr CF72 . . . . .155 E3
South Griffith Terr
NP13 . . . . .15 E2
South Lake Dr NP23 . . . .163 D5
South Loudoun Pl
CF10 . . . . .195 B3
South Luton Pl CF24 . . . .195 C5
South Market St
NP20 . . . . .143 D3
South Morgan Pl
CF11 . . . . .194 E5

South Pandy Rd
CF83 . . . . .138 A5
South Par
Maesteg CF34 . . . . .102 B3
3 Port Talbot SA13 . . .99 F1
South Park Rd
Cardiff CF24 . . . . .195 E5
Cardiff CF24 . . . . .195 F5
South Pl
Bridgend CF31 . . . . .168 F3
Porthcawl CF36 . . . . .182 F7
South Pontypool Ind Est
NP4 . . . . .62 F4
South Prospect Sal . .95 D7
South Rd
Bridgend CF31 . . . . .169 C2
Cwmbran NP44 . . . . .116 F8
Gileston CF62 . . . . .211 E1
Penybryn CF82 . . . . .85 E4
Porthcawl CF36 . . . . .182 F7
Sully CF64 . . . . .216 B5
South Rise CF14 . . . . .185 A8
South St
Abercynon CF45 . . . . .82 D2
Bargoed CF81 . . . . .57 F4
Bridgend CF31 . . . . .168 F3
Dowlais CF48 . . . . .11 B4
Ebbw Vale NP23 . . . . .7 F4
Newport NP20 . . . . .143 B7
Pontypool NP4 . . . . .62 E1
Pontypridd CF37 . . . . . . .109 D1
Port Talbot SA13 . . . . . . .125 C7
Porth CF39 . . . . .107 F3
South Terr
Cefn Coed CF48 . . . . .10 A4
Southerndown CF32 . . . .185 A1
South View
Bryncae CF72 . . . . .153 E2
Gorseinon SA4 . . . . .43 D2
Merthyr Vale CF48 . . . . . .55 D2
Pencoed CF35 . . . . .170 D8
Pontypool NP4 . . . . .62 B7
Pyle CF33 . . . . .148 D1
Croesyceiliog NP44 . . . . . .90 A6
Gowerton SA4 . . . . .65 D7
Taffs Well CF15 . . . . .158 B4
Troedyrhiw CF48 . . . . .31 C2
South View Dr CF5 . . . . .179 C5
South View Rd NP12 . . . .85 E8
South View Terr NP44 . . .33 E4
South Wlk
Barry CF62 . . . . .214 E6
Cwmbran NP44 . . . . .89 E5
Southall Ave SA10 . . . . . .70 E6
Southall St CF72 . . . . . . .153 D3
Southbourne Cl
CF62 . . . . .214 F2
Southcourt Rd CF23 . . . .178 D1
Southcross Rd SA12 . . . .98 C2
Southdown Rd SA12 . . . .98 C3
Southdown View
SA12 . . . . .98 C3
Southend
Mumbles SA3 . . . . .123 C4
Tredegar NP22 . . . . .14 A4
Southend Terr CF83 . . . .32 F8
Southern St CF83 . . . . . .138 B2
Southern Way CF23 . . . .178 F2
Southerndown Ave
SA3 . . . . .93 H1
Southerndown Rd
CF32 . . . . .185 C2
Southesk Pl CF62 . . . . . .214 C2
Southey St
Barry CF62 . . . . .214 F5
1 Cardiff CF24 . . . . . .195 C7
Southgate Ave CF72 . . . .155 E3
Southgate Rd SA3 . . . . . .121 A4
Southgate St SA11 . . . . . .71 E6
Southlands NP11 . . . . . . .15 E5
Southlands Dr SA3 . . . . .122 F6
Southminster Rd
CF23 . . . . .195 B8
Southra CF64 . . . . .206 A2
Southview Terr **15**
NP4 . . . . .17 C6
Southville Rd
6 Newport NP20 . . . .143 B6
Port Talbot SA12 . . . . . . .98 C2
Southward La SA3 . . . . . .122 F4
Southway
Bridgend CF31 . . . . .39 B1
Sovereign Arc **4**
NP20 . . . . .143 C4
Spartan Cl NP18 . . . . . . .145 C8
Speedwell Dr CF62 . . . . .212 F7
Speke St NP19 . . . . .143 E5
Spelter Site CF34 . . . . . .102 A7
Spencer Dr CF64 . . . . . . .206 D7
Spencer La CF37 . . . . . . .136 A4
Spencer Pl CF37 . . . . . . .136 A4
Spencer Rd NP20 . . . . . .143 A4
Spencer St
1 Barry CF62 . . . . . . .214 F5
Cardiff CF24 . . . . .178 A1
Cwmaman CF44 . . . . .53 A4
Ebbw Vale NP23 . . . . .7 F4
Swansea SA5 . . . . .68 C4
Spencer Terr CF5 . . . . . .177 A1
Spencer's Row CF5 . . . . .177 A1
Spien Rd SA14 . . . . .218 D7
Spillers & Bakers **12**
CF10 . . . . .195 C4
Spinney Cl CF5 . . . . .193 C6
Spinney The
Bridgend CF31 . . . . .169 D4
Bryn NP12 . . . . .85 D3
Cardiff CF14 . . . . .168 B2
Newport NP20 . . . . .117 B2
Swansea SA2 . . . . .94 A6
Spionkop Rd SA6 . . . . . . .46 C6
Spires Wlk CF63 . . . . . . .215 B8
Spitzkop CF61 . . . . .209 F6

Splott Ind Est CF24 . . . .195 E5
Splott Rd CF24 . . . . .195 E6
Spoonbill Cl CF36 . . . . . .165 E1
Spowart Ave SA11 . . . . . .40 C6
Spring Bank NP13 . . . . . .36 A6
Spring Gardens Pl
CF24 . . . . .195 E7
Spring Gardens Terr
CF24 . . . . .195 E7
Spring Gdns
Gorseinon SA4 . . . . .43 D1
Newport NP20 . . . . .143 C2
Spring Gdns N SA10 . . . .70 F7
Spring Gdns S SA10 . . . .70 F7
Spring Gr
Cardiff CF14 . . . . .159 F2
Cwmbran NP44 . . . . .89 A3
Spring La
Croesyceiliog NP44 . . . . . .90 A5
Newport NP20 . . . . .143 E7
Spring Meadow Bsns Pk
CF3 . . . . .179 C2
Spring Meadow Rd
CF3 . . . . .179 D2
Spring Meadow Trad Est
CF3 . . . . .179 C2
Spring St Barry CF63 . . .215 D6
Dowlais CF48 . . . . .11 A5
Newport NP20 . . . . .143 B7
Spring Terr SA1 . . . . .95 B6
Springbourne CF14 . . . . .66 D3
Springfield
Horton SA3 . . . . .231 B4
Maesycwmmer CF82 . . . .85 A1
Porth CF39 . . . . .107 F3
Springfield Ave
Porthcawl CF36 . . . . .182 D7
Upper Killay SA2 . . . . .93 B5
Springfield Cl
Aberdare CF44 . . . . .117 B4
Bassaleg NP10 . . . . .141 D3
Bridgend CF31 . . . . .168 F4
Croesyceiliog NP44 . . . . . .90 A6
Gowerton SA4 . . . . .65 D8
Wenvoe CF5 . . . . .205 A6
Springfield Ct
Church Village CF38 . . . .135 E1
Pontllanfraith NP12 . . . . .86 A3
Springfield Dr
Abercynon CF45 . . . . .82 F7
Newport NP20 . . . . .144 D6
Springfield Gdns
Bridgend CF31 . . . . .169 A6
Hirwaun CF44 . . . . .24 D8
Morganstown CF15 . . . . .158 B6
Springfield La
Bassaleg NP10 . . . . .141 D3
Bridgend CF31 . . . . .169 C4
Springfield Pl CF11 . . . . .194 D6
Springfield Terr
Aberavon SA12 . . . . .99 A2
Abertillery NP13 . . . . .60 B6
Hollybush NP12 . . . . .34 C2
Neath SA11 . . . . .71 E6
Nelson CF46 . . . . .83 F3
Pontllanfraith NP11 . . . . .86 C5
Pontypool NP4 . . . . .62 A8
Pontypool NP4 . . . . .63 A3
2 Pontypridd CF37 . .135 F6
Springfields
Blackwood NP11 . . . . .59 D1
Castleton CF3 . . . . .169 D2
Springfields Rd SA10 . . .40 F2
Springhurst Cl CF14 . . . .176 F7
Springvale NP44 . . . . .89 C4
Springvale Ind Est
NP44 . . . . .89 C4
Springvale Way NP44 . . .89 D4
Springwood CF23 . . . . . .175 D5
Springwood Jun & Inf Sch
CF23 . . . . .175 D5
Spruce Cl CF71 . . . . .201 C6
Spruce Tree Gr CF47 . . . .10 D4
Spruce Way SA4 . . . . .44 C2
Spytty Rd NP19 . . . . .144 C2
Square CF21 . . . . .209 F6
Square The
Abertridwr CF83 . . . . . . .136 F7
Beddau CF38 . . . . .155 F7
Bridgend CF31 . . . . .168 E5
Bryncethin CF32 . . . . . . .151 A5
Crynant SA10 . . . . .226 A7
Cwmbran NP44 . . . . .89 A6
Dinas Powys CF64 . . . . . .206 A3
Glan y Nant NP12 . . . . . . .85 A8
Laleston CF32 . . . . .167 E5
Llanharan CF72 . . . . .154 A3
Neath SA11 . . . . .71 E6
New Tredegar NP24 . . . . .33 D3
Pencoed CF35 . . . . .170 D8
2 Porth CF39 . . . . . . .107 F3
Porthcawl CF36 . . . . .182 F6
Squire Cl **11** SA1 . . . .95 D6
Squire Dr CF32 . . . . .150 F5
Squire St CF11 . . . . .187 E1
Squires Cl NP10 . . . . . . .142 B6
Squires Ct CF38 . . . . . . .156 A5

Squires Gate
Rogerstone NP10 . . . . . . .142 A6
Rogerstone NP10 . . . . . . .142 A6
Squirrel Walk (Rhodfa'r
Wiwer) SA4 . . . . .19 A5
Stable La NP22 . . . . .13 B4
Stable Row NP4 . . . . .17 C7
Stables Ct CF48 . . . . .1 A4
Stacey Com Jun & Inf Sch
CF24 . . . . .195 D7
Stacey Ct **6** CF24 . . . .195 D8
Stacey Rd
Cardiff CF24 . . . . .195 D7
Dinas Powys CF64 . . . . . .206 A3
Stack Sq **6** NP4 . . . . . .17 C7
Stadium Cl CF11 . . . . . . .194 F1
Stadwen Rd SA4 . . . . .69 E7
Stafford Comm SA4 . . . .64 E6
Stafford Rd
Cardiff CF11 . . . . .194 F4
Newport NP19 . . . . .143 E7
Pontypool NP4 . . . . .62 E4
Stafford St SA15 . . . . . . .40 D3
Stag La CF61 . . . . .209 F6
Stag St CF44 . . . . .24 A7
Staines St CF5 . . . . .179 D8
Stair St **8** SA12 . . . . . .98 E1
Stallcourt Ave
Cardiff CF23 . . . . .178 E1
Llanblethian CF71 . . . . . .188 F4
Stallcourt Rd SA13 . . . . .125 E4
Standard CF NP20 . . . . . .143 A6
Standard Signs Est
NP19 . . . . .143 D7
Standard St CF83 . . . . . .139 A6
Standard Terr CF39 . . . . .107 F7
Standard View CF39 . . . .107 F7
Standard Villas CF83 . . .139 A6
Standert Terr SA10 . . . . .222 D3
Stanfield Cl CF48 . . . . . . .30 E4
Stanfield St CF83 . . . . . . .86 B5
Stanford Rd NP19 . . . . . .144 D5
Stangate Ho **1** CF64 . .207 B4
Stanier Cl **7** CF37 . . . .107 F3
Stanley Cl
2 Newport NP20 . . . .143 B5
Treorchy CF42 . . . . .78 B5
Stanley Pl
7 Cwmbran NP44 . . . .89 E5
Neath SA10 . . . . .64 A4
Swansea SA1 . . . . .95 C7
Stanley Rd
Aberyschan NP4 . . . . .60 D4
4 Llanelli SA15 . . . . . .40 D3
Neath SA10 . . . . .70 F6
Newport NP20 . . . . .143 B5
Ton Pentre CF41 . . . . .79 B2
Stanley Sq CF43 . . . . .80 C2
Stanley St
Blackwood NP12 . . . . .59 B3
Mumbles SA3 . . . . .123 A5
Senghenydd CF83 . . . . . .110 F2
Stanley Terr SA15 . . . . . .95 C7
Stanton Way CF44 . . . . . .217 B8
Stanway Pl CF5 . . . . .193 B6
Stanway Rd CF5 . . . . .193 C5
Stanwell Comp Sch
CF64 . . . . .206 F3
Stanwell Cres CF64 . . . . .207 B5
Stanwell Rd
Penarth CF64 . . . . .207 A3
Stapleton Pl **2** SA6 . . .68 F8
Star La Pentyrch CF15 . .125 D5
Pontypool NP4 . . . . .62 B8
Pontyclun CF72 . . . . .173 B7
Tondu CF32 . . . . .150 C5
Star Rd NP4 . . . . .39 F6
Star St Cardiff CF24 . . . .195 D6
Cwmbran NP44 . . . . .89 E2
Tredegar NP22 . . . . .6 B2
Star Trad Est NP18 . . . . .118 A5
Star Villas NP18 . . . . . . .118 A5
Starbuck St CF83 . . . . . .139 B3
Starling St CF62 . . . . . . .210 D6
Station App
Bridgend CF31 . . . . .168 F4
Ebbw Vale NP23 . . . . .7 D1
Penarth CF64 . . . . .207 A3
Pontyclun CF72 . . . . .173 B7
Tredegar NP22 . . . . .6 B2
Station Bldgs **3** NP21 .85 F4
Station Farm SA4 . . . . . . .89 F5
Station Ho
Bridgend CF31 . . . . .168 F4
Maesteg CF34 . . . . .102 A3
Station Ho CF81 . . . . . . .174 E7
Station Rd NP11 . . . . .114 F2
Station Rd
Abercraf SA9 . . . . .222 D7
Abercynon CF45 . . . . .82 E2
Abergwynfi SA13 . . . . . . .76 C5
Abertysswg NP22 . . . . . . .33 C8
Abertysswg NP22 . . . . . . .14 F3
Bargoed CF81 . . . . .58 A5
Blaina NP13 . . . . .15 D5
Briton Ferry SA11 . . . . . . .71 C3
Bynea SA14 . . . . .42 A3
Caerleon NP18 . . . . .118 A1

Station Rd continued
Cardiff CF14 . . . . .176 F3
Cardiff CF14 . . . . .177 F8
Cefn Coed CF48 . . . . .10 A4
Clydach NP7 . . . . .7 F8
Coelbren SA10 . . . . .223 A6
Creigiau CF15 . . . . .174 E7
Crynant SA10 . . . . .226 A7
Cwmbran NP44 . . . . .89 B3
Cymmer SA13 . . . . .75 C5
Dinas Powys CF64 . . . . . .206 A3
Dowlais CF48 . . . . .11 B5
Ebbw Vale NP23 . . . . .11 A8
Ferndale CF43 . . . . .80 A2
Glais SA7 . . . . .47 A6
Glan y Nant NP12 . . . . . . .85 A8
Glanaman SA18 . . . . .220 A8
Gowerton SA4 . . . . .66 C5
Grovesend SA4 . . . . .43 D6
Hirwaun CF44 . . . . .27 D8
Llanbradach CF83 . . . . . .111 F1
Llanelli SA15 . . . . .40 D5
Llangennech SA14 . . . . . .42 D8
Llanmorlais SA4 . . . . .64 C2
Llantwit Fardre CF38 . . .156 F7
Llantwit Major CF61 . . . .209 F6
Llanwern NP18 . . . . .145 B4
Loughor SA4 . . . . .65 C8
Maerdy CF43 . . . . .52 A1
Nant-y-Moel CF32 . . . . . .104 E7
Neath SA10 . . . . .70 E7
New Tredegar NP11 . . . . .60 A1
Newbridge NP11 . . . . .60 B5
Pen-clawdd SA4 . . . . .64 C6
Penarth CF64 . . . . .207 A3
Pont Rhyd-y-cyff CF34 . .128 E6
Pontardulais SA4 . . . . . . .43 B6
Ponthir NP18 . . . . .117 F6
Pontrhydyfen SA12 . . . . .73 B1
Port Talbot SA13 . . . . . . .125 B8
Port Talbot SA13 . . . . . . .125 B8
Port CF39 . . . . .107 F6
Pyle CF33 . . . . .148 D3
Radyr CF15 . . . . .176 C5
Rhoose CF62 . . . . .213 A1
Risca NP11 . . . . .114 F1
Seven Sisters SA10 . . . . .222 D3
Swansea SA1 . . . . .68 D4
Swansea SA5 . . . . .67 E3
Swansea SA5 . . . . .67 E7
Tonna SA10 . . . . .49 C3
Tonyrefail CF39 . . . . .133 B5
Tredegar NP22 . . . . .6 B2
Treorchy CF42 . . . . .78 D5
Tylorstown CF43 . . . . .80 C1
Ystrad Mynach CF82 . . . .84 E2
Ystradgynlais SA9 . . . . . . .2 F8
Station Rd E CF5 . . . . . . .205 B7
Station Rd W CF5 . . . . . .205 A6
Station Row
New Tredegar NP24 . . . . .33 E2
Pontyrhil CF32 . . . . .129 F7
Station Sq CF48 . . . . .55 D4
Station St
8 Aberdare CF44 . . . . .29 A2
Aberyschan NP4 . . . . .38 A4
Barry CF63 . . . . .203 E4
Blaengarw CF32 . . . . . . .103 A6
Machen CF83 . . . . .140 A7
Maesteg CF34 . . . . .102 A2
Newbridge NP11 . . . . .86 C5
Pontllanfraith NP11 . . . . .86 C5
1 Porth CF39 . . . . . . .107 F3
Tonypandy CF40 . . . . . . .106 F4
Tonypandy CF40 . . . . . . .106 F4
Treherbert CF42 . . . . .50 F1
Station Yd CF83 . . . . .138 C7
StCadoc's RC Sch
CF5 . . . . .191 D5
Peterston-Super-Ely
CF5 . . . . .191 D5
Pontyclun CF72 . . . . .172 C6
Llantwit Fardre CF38 . . .156 D7
Maerdy CF43 . . . . .52 A1
Merthyr Vale CF48 . . . . . .55 D3
Mountain Ash CF45 . . . . . .81 F8
Nelson CF46 . . . . .83 F3
Pen-clawdd SA4 . . . . .64 F4
Penarth CF64 . . . . .207 A3
Stebonheath Cty Prim Sch
SA15 . . . . .40 F5
Stebonheath Terr
SA15 . . . . .40 F5
Steel Works Rd NP23 . . . .14 E6
Steep St **7** CF37 . . . . .207 A5
Steepfield NP44 . . . . .90 A6
Steepholm Cl CF64 . . . . .207 A2
Steer Cres NP19 . . . . . . .144 A7
Stella Cl CF14 . . . . .159 F3

Stelvio Park Ave
NP20 . . . . .142 F3
Stelvio Park Cres
NP20 . . . . .142 F3
Stelvio Park Ct NP20 . . .142 F3
Stelvio Park Dr
NP20 . . . . .142 F3
Stembridge Ave SA5 . . . .67 E5
Stenhousemuir Pl
CF24 . . . . .195 F7
Stephen's Terr CF5 . . . . .82 F3
Stephenson Ct **3**
CF24 . . . . .195 C6
Stephenson Rd SA2 . . . .93 F6
Stephenson St
Cardiff CF11 . . . . .194 E5
Newport NP19 . . . . .143 E1
Stepney La SA2 . . . . .67 D1
Stepney Pl SA15 . . . . . . .40 D5
Stepney Prec **4** SA15 .40 D5
Stepney Rd
Glanaman SA18 . . . . .220 C8
Swansea SA2 . . . . .67 D2
Waunarlwydd SA5 . . . . . .66 E3
Stepney St
1 Llanelli SA15 . . . . . .40 D5
Swansea SA5 . . . . .68 B2
Stepping Stones The
NP4 . . . . .39 E7
Sterndale Bennett Rd
NP19 . . . . .144 F5
Sterry Rd SA4 . . . . .66 B5
Stevelee NP44 . . . . .89 C1
Stevenson Cl
Rogerstone NP10 . . . . . . .142 A6
Rogerstone NP10 . . . . . . .142 B6
Stevenson Ct NP10 . . . . .142 A6
Stevenson Street Ind Est
NP19 . . . . .164 F8
Stewart Rd CF24 . . . . . . .213 A1
Stewart St Cwm NP23 . . .35 A6
Llanelli SA15 . . . . .40 C6
Steynton Path NP44 . . . .89 C2
Stiels NP44 . . . . .116 B8
Stirling Rd
Barry CF62 . . . . .214 C7
Cardiff CF5 . . . . .193 A4
Stockland St
Caerphilly CF83 . . . . .138 A2
Cardiff CF11 . . . . .194 F3
Stockton Cl **9** NP19 . .143 E8
Stockton Rd NP19 . . . . . .143 D8
Stockton Way CF62 . . . . .212 A8
Stockton-vale NP22 . . . . .13 E8
Stokes Cotts NP18 . . . . .117 F6
Stokes Ct NP18 . . . . .117 F6
Stokes La SA15 . . . . .15 D6
Stone's Hos NP13 . . . . . .15 C6
Stonebridge Rd NP23 . . . .7 A4
Stonechat Cl
2 Cardiff CF23 . . . . . .180 A6
Porthcawl CF36 . . . . .165 D1
Stonewood View
NP11 . . . . .87 B8
Stones Mus SA13 . . . . . .126 C6
Stonewell St **7**
CF23 . . . . .178 C2
Stony La CF35 . . . . .186 A6
Stony Rd NP4 . . . . .37 F5
Stormy La
Nant-y-Moel CF32 . . . . . .104 F3
North Cornelly CF33 . . . .165 E7
Storrar Pl CF24 . . . . .196 A8
Storrar Rd CF24 . . . . .196 A8
Stour St NP44 . . . . .89 A4
Stow Hill
Newport NP20 . . . . .143 B4
Newport NP20 . . . . .143 B4
Pontypridd CF37 . . . . . . .135 D7
Stow Park Ave NP20 . . . .143 A3
Stow Park Circ
NP20 . . . . .143 A3
Stow Park Cres
NP20 . . . . .143 A3
3 Cwmbran NP44 . . . .89 E5
Stow Park Rd NP20 . . . . .143 A3
Stow Park Gdns
NP20 . . . . .143 A3
Stowe Path **4** NP44 . .90 B2
Stradey Ct SA1 . . . . .40 C7
Stradey Park Ave
SA15 . . . . .40 C6
Stradey Rd SA15 . . . . . . .40 C6
Stradling Cl
Barry CF62 . . . . .214 B6
Cowbridge CF71 . . . . . . .188 D2
Sarn CF32 . . . . .150 F4
Sully CF64 . . . . .216 B5
Stradling Pl CF61 . . . . . .210 A5
Strand CF71 . . . . .157 F5
Strand Ferndale CF43 . . .79 F6
Swansea SA1 . . . . .95 D7
Strand Row SA1 . . . . .95 D7
Strand St CF45 . . . . .54 F2
Strand The
Blaengarw CF32 . . . . . . .103 E7
Cwmbran NP44 . . . . .89 E4
Llantwit Major CF61 . . . .209 F6
Stratford Ct CF36 . . . . . .182 E8
Stratford Gn **5**
CF63 . . . . .215 C8
Stratford Ho NP20 . . . . .142 E3
Strathnairn St CF24 . . . .195 B8
Strathview NP11 . . . . .86 C5
Strathy Rd CF3 . . . . .180 A4
Stratton Way SA10 . . . . . .71 C8
Strauss Rd SA12 . . . . .98 A2
Strawberry Pl SA6 . . . . . .45 F1

Stream St CF45 ....54 D2
Street No 17 SA12 ....98 B4
Street No 19 SA12 ....98 B5
Street No 21 SA12 ....98 B5
Stryd Arthur SA18 ....219 B8
Stryd Fawr SA18 ....219 C7
Stryd Harold 8
SA18 ....219 B7
Stryd Hywel Harris
CF82 ....111 E7
Stryd Margad SA18 ....219 C7
Stryd y Parc SA18 ....219 C6
Stryd-y-Coleg SA18 219 B7
Stryd-y-Gwynt SA18 219 B7
Stryd-yr-Eglwys 8
SA18 ....219 B7
Stuart Cl Cardiff CF11 194 D1
Port Talbot SA12 ....98 B3
Stuart Pl CF10 ....195 C1
Stuart St
Aberdare CF44 ....29 A1
Cardiff CF10 ....195 B1
Merthyr Tydfil CF47 ....10 D2
Pontllotyn CF81 ....12 C1
Pontyclun CF72 ....73 B2
Treherbert CF42 ....50 F2
Treorchy CF42 ....78 D7
Stuart Terr CF72 ....155 B2
Sturmi Way CF33 ....148 C1
Sturminster Rd CF23 195 E8
Stuttgarter Strasse
CF10 ....195 B6
Subway Rd CF63 ....215 A4
Sudbury Wlk 1
NP20 ....143 C6
Sudcroft St CF11 ....194 C4
Suffolk Cl CF36 ....182 F8
Suffolk Cl CF36 ....182 F7
Suffolk Ho 1 SA12 ....98 C1
Suffolk Pl
Ogmore Vale CF32 ....100 E1
Port Talbot CF42 ....182 F7
Suffolk St CF33 ....168 C3
Sullivan Circ NP19 ....144 D4
Sullivan Cl
Cardiff CF3 ....179 D7
Penarth CF64 ....206 D1
Sully Cty Prim Sch
CF64 ....216 A4
Sully Moors Rd
Barry CF64 ....215 F5
Barry CF64 ....215 F6
Sully Pl CF64 ....207 D3
Sully Rd CF64 ....206 D1
Sully Terr CF64 ....207 A2
CF64 ....207 A2
Sully View CF63 ....215 B7
Summer Pl SA7 ....69 F7
Summer's Hos NP13 ..36 B7
Summerau Ct CF5 ....194 C7
Summercliffe Chalet Pk
SA3 ....122 D4
Summerdale Cl CF38 ..51 F5
Summerfield Ave
CF14 ....177 F2
Summerfield Cl
CF40 ....107 A5
Summerfield Dr
Llantrisant CF72 ....155 E2
Porthcawl CF36 ....165 E1
Summerfield Hall La
CF82 ....85 B3
Summerfield La
CF83 ....139 C6
Summerfield Pl
Cardiff CF14 ....177 E2
Neath SA11 ....71 E7
Summerfield Rd NP23 ..7 B5
Summerfield Terr
Fleur De Lis NP12 ....85 B5
8 Merthyr Tydfil CF47 ....10 F1
Summerhill CF47 ....10 F1
Summerhill Ave
NP19 ....143 E6
Summerhill Cl CF3 ..180 A7
Summerhill St CF47 ....10 F1
Summerhill Ho 9
NP19 ....143 E6
Summerhill Pl CF47 ....10 F1
Summerland Cl
CF64 ....206 D6
Summerland Cres
CF5 ....193 B8
Summerland La SA3 122 E5
Summerland Pk SA2 ..93 E5
Summerwood Cl
CF5 ....193 B8
Summer Cl CF5 ....176 E2
Sun St CF24 ....195 D6
Sundew Cl
Cardiff CF5 ....176 D2
Penarth CF64 ....206 E5
Sunlea Cres NP44 ....62 F6
Sunningdale CF23 ....178 B4
Sunningdale Ave SA3 ..93 F1
Sunningdale Cl CF23 178 B4
Sunningdale Ct
NP19 ....144 D6
Sunningdale Rd SA12 98 E5
Sunninghill Terr SA15 40 E6
Sunny Bank
Glyncorrwg SA13 ....227 C2
Llantrisant CF72 ....155 D3
Ogmore Vale CF32 ....106 E2
Porth CF39 ....107 E5

Sunny Bank continued
Tonypandy CF40 ....106 D7
Tonypandy CF40 ....107 A3
Treharris CF46 ....83 A5
Sunny Bank Terr
CF83 ....139 F7
Sunny Cres SA13 ....75 D3
Sunny Crest NP11 ....87 A7
Sunny Hill
Llanelli SA15 ....40 D6
Maerdy CF43 ....52 A1
Rhymney NP22 ....13 A2
Sunny Rd Llanelli SA15 40 D6
Port Talbot SA12 ....124 D8
Sunny Side CF37 ....109 B2
Sunny View CF81 ....32 F8
Sunny View Terr
NP12 ....58 F4
Sunny-Mount SA12 ....98 D5
sunnybank
Bassaleg NP10 ....141 E2
Cwmbran NP44 ....115 F8
Dinas Powys CF64 ....206 C4
Merthyr Tydfil CF47 ....10 D2
Neath SA10 ....48 C1
New Tredegar NP24 ....33 E3
Pyle CF33 ....148 B2
Sunnybank Cl
Cardiff CF14 ....177 D3
Mumbles SA3 ....122 F8
Sunnybank Ct
Bridgend CF31 ....169 C5
Pontypool NP4 ....62 D3
Sunnybank Pl SA12 ..124 D8
Sunnybank Rd
Blackwood NP12 ....68 E5
Pontypool NP4 ....62 D3
Port Talbot SA12 ....124 D8
Sunnybank St CF44 ....53 B8
Sunnybank Terr
Abertillery NP13 ....92 D5
Treorchy CF42 ....78 C5
Sunnybank Way NP4 ..62 D2
Sunnybrook Ct CF5 ..176 D1
Sunnycroft CF64 ....206 B3
Sunnycroft La CF64 ..206 B2
Sunnycroft Rd SA12 198 D5
Sunnycroft Rise 4
CF64 ....206 B2
Sunnyland Cres SA10 70 FB
Sunnyside
Llanelli Hill NP7 ....9 C4
Ogmore Vale CF32 ....106 E1
Sunnyside Rd CF31 ..168 E4
Sunnyside Terr SA13 75 C6
Sunnyview NP22 ....13 D7
Surgery Rd NP13 ....15 E6
Surgery Road Bglws
NP13 ....15 E6
Surrey Pl NP19 ....143 E7
Surrey St CF5 ....194 B6
Susannah Pl CF46 ....83 A6
Sussex Cl NP19 ....144 A2
Sussex St CF11 ....194 F4
Sutherland Cres
NP19 ....144 A7
Sutherland Mans 8
CF14 ....176 F6
Sutton Gr CF23 ....160 D1
Sutton La CF32 ....184 C4
Sutton Rd
Llandow CF71 ....199 C5
Newport NP19 ....143 D8
Ogmore-By-Sea CF32 ..184 D3
Sutton Rise CF32 ....184 A4
Sutton Spring Rd
CF71 ....199 C4
Swallow Tree Cl SA10 48 E2
Swallow Way NP10 ..163 E8
Swallowhurst Cl CF5 194 A7
Swan Cres NP23 ....7 E4
Swan La SA4 ....93 E6
Swan Rd SA12 ....98 C7
Swan Sq NP4 ....37 F3
Swan St Baglan SA12 ..98 F7
Llantrisant CF72 ....155 D3
Merthyr Tydfil CF47 ....30 D8
Swansea SA1 ....95 D8
Swan Terr 7 CF40 ..106 F4
Swan Wlk SA15 ....40 B5
Swanage Cl CF3 ....180 A7
Swanbridge Farm
CF64 ....216 D3
Swanbridge Rd
CF64 ....216 C5
Swanfield SA2 ....2 C7
Swanfield Pl 8 SA15 48 D6
Swansea Castle SA1 ..95 D7
Swansea Cl SA2 ....94 D7
Swansea Coll of Art
SA1 ....95 D5
Swansea Inst of Higher Ed
(Townhill Campus)
SA1 ....94 F8
Swansea Inst of Higher
Educ (Mount Pleasant
Campus) SA1 ....95 C4
Swansea Maritime &
Industrial Mus SA1 95 D6
Swansea Mus SA1 ....95 D6
Swansea Rd
Gorseinon SA4 ....66 E7
Hirwaun CF44 ....27 E8
Llanelli SA15 ....40 E6
Penllergaer SA4 ....44 B2
Pontardawe SA8 ....23 C2
Pontlliw SA4 ....44 A4

Swansea Rd continued
Swansea SA5 ....45 B2
Waunarlwydd SA5 ....66 E4
Swansea St CF24 ....195 E5
Swansea Vale Rly
SA7 ....69 C8
Swansea West Ind Pk
SA5 ....67 C4
Sward Cl NP10 ....142 A7
Sway Rd SA6 ....46 A1
Sweet Briar La SA3 ..123 A8
Sweetwater Pk CF48 ..10 B7
Sweetwells Cotts
CF32 ....129 F7
Sweldon Cl CF5 ....193 B3
Swift Bsns Ctr The
CF24 ....195 D5
Swift Cl CF3 ....158 D2
Swilym Terr CF47 ....30 E7
Swinburne Cl NP19 ..144 A5
Swinton St CF24 ....196 A3
Swn y Mor CF32 ....185 A1
Swn Yr Adar CF31 ..168 D8
Swn Yr Aderyn CF33 148 D2
Swn Yr Afon CF42 ....78 E5
Swn yr Eos SA9 ....2 E7
Swn-y-gwent Day Hosp
SA18 ....219 B7
Swn-y-Mor
Barry CF62 ....214 A3
Port Talbot SA12 ....98 D1
Swn-y-Nant
Abergwynfi SA13 ....76 B6
Church Village CF38 ..135 E1
Crynant SA10 ....226 A8
Cwm-twrch Isaf SA9 ..1 B2
Pencoed CF35 ....152 C1
Swn-yr-Afon CF48 ....10 B4
Swn-yr-Afon
Aberdulais SA10 ....49 C4
Gilfach Goch CF39 ..132 B7
Pyle CF33 ....148 E3
Ton Pentre CF41 ....79 B3
Swn-yr-Nant CF82 ....84 D7
Sybil St SA6 ....46 E7
Sycamore Ave
Neath SA11 ....72 A6
Newport NP19 ....144 B4
Porthcawl CF36 ....183 D8
Pyle CF33 ....148 C2
St Athan CF62 ....211 B7
Tredegar NP22 ....6 D1
Sycamore Cl
Aberdare CF44 ....28 D3
Bridgend CF31 ....168 F8
Dinas Powys CF64 ..206 B2
Llandough CF64 ....206 E6
Swansea SA2 ....94 A7
Sycamore Ct
Baglan SA12 ....98 D7
Barry CF62 ....215 A7
Risca NP11 ....115 B1
Trefechan CF48 ....30 D6
Sycamore Cross
CF5 ....191 D1
Sycamore Dr
Baglan SA12 ....98 D7
Bargoed CF81 ....57 E2
Caerphilly NP11 ....85 F6
Cwmbran NP44 ....115 F8
Sycamore Dr CF48 ..107 A5
Sycamore Ho CF14 ..176 F2
Sycamore Pl
1 Cardiff CF5 ....193 D8
Cwmbran NP44 ....89 B6
Sycamore Rd
Llanharry CF72 ....172 C5
Merthyr Tydfil CF47 ....10 E4
Mumbles SA3 ....123 A8
Pontypool NP4 ....62 D3
Sycamore Rd S NP4 ..62 D1
Sycamore St
Rhydyfelin CF37 ....136 A5
Taffs Well CF15 ....158 A4
Sycamore Terr NP11 ..87 B7
Sycamore Tree Cl
CF15 ....176 A6
Sychbant Ave CF34 ..102 A1
Sydney Ct NP12 ....85 C6
Sydney St SA5 ....168 C1
Sylvan Cl Cardiff CF5 ..176 C1
Newport NP20 ....117 B3
Sylvan Way SA2 ....94 A7
Sylvia Terr SA5 ....68 C4
Symmons St SA1 ....95 D8
Syndicate Terr NP11 113 A4
Syon Park Cl CF3 ..180 A7
Siphon St CF39 ....107 C1
Syr David's Ave CF5 194 B7
Syr-Dafydd Ave NP12 ..59 B2
System St CF24 ....195 D6

T

Taf Olwg CF46 ....83 D3
Tafarnaubach Ind Est
NP22 ....6 B2
Taff Bargoed Ctr
CF46 ....56 C4
Taff Bsns Ctr CF37 ..136 C3
Taff Cl NP23 ....7 E5
Taff Cotts
Llantrisant CF72 ....155 E2
Tongwynlais CF40 ....106 E8
Taff Ct NP4 ....37 A5
Taff Emb Cardiff CF11 194 F1
Cardiff CF11 ....195 A2
Taff Fawr Ho CF48 ..10 A3
Taff Fechan Ho CF48 ..10 A3
Taff Glen View CF47 ..30 F8
Taff Gorge Countryside
Ctr CF15 ....158 D2
Taff St
8 Cardiff CF10 ....195 B5
Cardiff CF15 ....158 C1
Ferndale CF43 ....79 F7
Merthyr Vale CF48 ....55 D3
Pontypridd CF37 ....109 C1
Treherbert CF42 ....50 F2
Taff Terr
Abercynon CF45 ....82 D1
Cardiff CF11 ....195 A2
Radyr CF15 ....176 C5
Treorchy CF42 ....78 B6
Taff Vale CF46 ....82 F6
Taff Vale Ct CF47 ....10 D8
Taff Vale Flats CF37 ..135 C8
Taff Vale Prec 1
CF37 ....109 C1
Taff Workshops 8
CF10 ....195 B1
Taffs Fall Rd CF37 ..136 D2
Taffs Mead Emb
CF11 ....194 F1
Taffs Mead Rd CF37 136 C2
Taffs Well Sta CF15 158 A3
Tafwys Wlk CF83 ....138 A3
Tai Ann CF37 ....109 F5
Tai Arfryn CF31 ....168 C3
Tai Cwm CF39 ....107 F3
Tai Duffryn CF15 ....158 A7
Tai Gwalia SA4 ....221 C5
Tai Llanbedr CF5 ....191 E6
Tai Mawr Rd CF48 ....10 A3
Tai Mewn NP23 ....14 E3
Tai Newydd
Rhydyfelin CF37 ....136 B4
Ynysybwl CF37 ....81 F2
Tai Penyard CF47 ..124 D8
Tai Siriol CF46 ....83 D3
Tai Ysgol Fach CF48 ..29 F8
Tai'r Felin SA10 ....49 C4
Tai'r Heol CF37 ....109 F6
Tai Twynau CF48 ....11 B7
Tai'r Ynys Fawr SA12 ..73 C1
Tai'r-Heol CF82 ....84 D8
Tai-Canol CF48 ....10 B1
Tai-Yr-Efail CF48 ....11 A7
Taicanol SA12 ....99 E6
Tailwyd Rd
Neath SA10 ....48 B1
Neath Abbey SA10 ....71 B8
Tair Erw Rd CF14 ..177 D5
Tair Gwaen 6 CF47 ..10 F2
Tair Waun Pr CF34 ..101 E4
Tairfelin CF31 ....168 E7
Tairywaith Prim Sch
SA18 ....220 E6
Tal y Coed SA4 ....18 F3
Tal-y-Wern SA13 ....125 D5
Talana Terr CF24 ....75 A1
Talbot Cl CF72 ....155 C3
Talbot Gn SA4 ....146 D3
Talbot Green Spec Sch
CF72 ....155 C2
Talbot La NP20 ....143 C4
Talbot Rd
Llantrisant CF72 ....155 D3
Neath SA10 ....70 F6
Neath SA11 ....71 F5
Penllergaer SA4 ....43 F2
Port Talbot SA13 ....125 C7
Pyle CF33 ....148 D3
Talbot Green CF72 ..155 C2
Talbot Sq
Merthyr Tydfil CF47 ....10 F3
Talbot Green CF72 ..155 B2
Talbot St Cardiff CF11 194 B4
Gowerton SA4 ....66 B5
Llanelli SA15 ....40 D4
Maesteg CF34 ....102 A3
Ystradgynlais SA9 ....1 F4
St Mary Church CF71 ..201 A4
Talcennau Rd SA13 125 C7
Taldwyn Terr CF47 ....31 C2
Talfaen Cl NP4 ....18 C3
Talfan Rd SA1 ....69 B3
Talgarth Cl NP44 ....89 E2
Talgarth St CF24 ..102 C2
Taliesin NP44 ....89 E4
Taliesin Cl
Pencoed CF35 ....152 B1
Rogerstone NP10 ....142 B6
Taliesin Dr NP10 ....142 B6
Taliesin Pl SA4 ....42 E1
Taliesin St SA4 ....44 B5
Talley Rd SA5 ....68 B5
Tallis Ct NP44 ....88 F3
Tallis St CF24 ....195 C5
Talwrn St CF81 ....57 D8
Talybont Cl CF62 ....211 D7
Talybont Rd CF5 ....193 D5

Talyclun SA14 ....18 E2
Talycopa Prim Sch
SA7 ....69 F7
Talyfan CF72 ....154 A3
Talyfan CF72 ....188 F1
Talygarn Ct CF72 ....172 F5
Talygarn Dr CF72 ....172 F6
Talygarn St CF14 ....172 E5
Talywain SA14 ....42 B7
Tamar Cl
Bettws NP20 ....116 E2
Bryn NP12 ....85 B5
Tan House Dr NP18 ..118 C2
Tan y Bryn CF43 ....79 B8
Tan y Marian CF42 ..79 B8
Tan y Marian Rd SA1 95 B8
Tan-y-Bryn
Beddau CF38 ....156 A7
Brynna CF72 ....153 D4
Pencoed CF35 ....152 F1
Porth CF39 ....107 D2
Rhymney NP22 ....13 A2
Senghenydd CF83 ..110 F1
Senghenydd CF83 ..111 A1
Tan-y-Bryn Terr SA4 ..64 F4
Tan-y-Coed SA4 ....37 F1
Tan-y-Farteg SA9 ....2 C7
Tan-y-Fron
Barry CF62 ....214 B3
Treorchy CF42 ....78 D5
Tan-y-Gelli SA18 ....220 B8
Tan-y-graig SA9 ....222 B7
Tan-y-Groes Pl
SA13 ....125 D8
Tan-y-Groes St
SA13 ....125 D8
Tan-y-Lan Terr SA6 ..68 F8
Tan-y-Llan Terr NP22 12 E4
Tan-y-Lon SA6 ....22 D1
Tan-y-Pych CF42 ....50 D4
Tan-y-Rhiw SA10 ..222 D1
Tan-Yr-Allt CF72 ....155 E2
Tanglewood Cl CF14 160 A2
Tangmere Dr CF5 ..176 D2
Tank Farm Rd SA10 ..70 C3
Tank Farm Way
CF64 ....215 E6
Tanlan Sq NP24 ....33 F2
Tansy Cl Cardiff CF14 159 D3
Penpedairheol CF82 ..84 E6
Tanyard Pl CF44 ....53 B8
Tanybryn
Mountain Ash CF45 ....81 F8
Risca NP11 ....141 C8
Tanybryn Pl CF47 ....10 F4
Tanybryn Terr CF43 ..107 C8
Tanycoed Rd SA6 ....22 E1
Tanycoed St CF45 ....81 F8
Tanycoed Terr CF44 ..53 F4
Tanyfan SA18 ....218 E6
Tanygarth SA9 ....222 C7
Tanygraig Rd SA14 ..41 C8
Tanyrallt
Abercraf SA9 ....222 C7
Clydach SA6 ....22 D1
Tanyrallt Ave CF31 ..168 F7
Tanyrhiw Rd SA11 ..226 A6
Tanywaun SA9 ....222 B6
Tanywern La SA9 ....2 B7
Tanyrallt Ave CF31 ..168 F7
Tapley Cl CF5 ....193 C3
Taplow Terr SA1 ....68 F6
Tarragon Way CF23 ..160 E1
Tarran Workshops
CF31 ....168 A4
Tarren Terr SA12 ....100 A7
Tarrws Cl CF5 ....205 A7
Tarwick Dr CF3 ....179 E6
Tatem Dr CF5 ....193 C7
Tathan Cres CF62 ..211 D5
Taunton Ave CF3 ....179 C5
Taunton Cres CF3 ..179 C5
Tavistock Cl SA2 ....94 E7
Tavistock Rd SA2 ....94 E7
Tavistock St CF24 ..195 B7
Tawe Bsns Village
SA6 ....69 A7
Tawe Pk SA6 ....69 A7
Tawe Pl SA6 ....46 E7
Tawe Rd SA6 ....69 A7
Tawe Terr SA8 ....23 E4
Tawe View Cres SA6 ..45 F1
Tawel Fan SA14 ....41 A6
Tawelfan Nelson CF46 83 A4
Ystradgynlais SA9 ....1 F4
Tawelfryn CF48 ....225 F3
Taylor Rd CF31 ....168 C2
Taylor St NP11 ....114 F3
Taylor's Row SA1 ....71 D6
Taymuir Green Ind Pk
CF24 ....195 F8
Taymuir Rd CF24 ..195 F7
Teal Cl CF36 ....182 E8
Teal St CF24 ....195 C7
Tealham Dr CF3 ....180 B7
Teamans Row CF15 ..176 B8
Teasel Ave CF64 ....206 E5
Techniquest CF10 ..195 B1
Technology Dr CF3 ..168 E1
Ted Davies Cl CF3 ..165 F8
Tedder Cl CF14 ....177 F7
Tees Cl NP20 ....116 F2
Teg Fan SA10 ....40 E6
Tegfan
Caerphilly CF83 ....137 E3
Cardiff CF11 ....194 D6

Tegfan continued
Ferndale CF43 ....79 E1
Pontlliw SA4 ....44 E6
Pontyclun CF72 ....173 A4
Swansea SA4 ....69 F7
Tegfan Cl CF14 ....159 E3
Tegfan Ct NP44 ....115 F7
Tegid Rd SA1 ....68 A5
Teglan Pk SA18 ....218 E6
Teifi Dr CF62 ....214 C6
Teifi Pl CF5 ....193 E7
Teify Cres CF32 ....104 E4
Teilo Cres SA1 ....95 E7
Teilo Pl SA1 ....194 C1
Teilos Dr CF31 ....194 D6
Teilos Dr CF31 ....194 D6
Telekebir Rd CF37 ..109 A8
Telford Cl
Penpedairheol CF82 ..84 E6
Rogerstone NP10 ....142 B7
Telford St
Cardiff CF11 ....194 E2
Newport NP19 ....143 E6
Telor-y-Coed CF83 ..112 A4
Telyn Aur SA6 ....45 E2
Temperance Ct CF15 157 B8
Temperance Hill
NP11 ....114 F7
Temperance La SA9 ..1 F
Temperance Pl CF37 109 C2
Templar Parc CF24 ..195 C2
Temple St
Llanelli SA15 ....40 E
Maesteg CF34 ....102 B
Newport NP20 ....143 D
Swansea SA1 ....95 D
Templeton Ave CF14 159 E
Templeton Cl CF14 ..159 E
Templeton Way SA5 ..67 F
Ten Acre Wood
SA13 ....126 B
Tenby Cl
Dinas Powys CF64 ..206 C
Llanyrafon NP44 ....90 A
Tenby Ct CF83 ....137 D
Tenison Rd NP44 ....115 A
Tennison Ave NP18 145 A
Tennyson Cl CF37 ..136 A
Tennyson Cl CF37 ..136 A
Tennyson Dr CF31 ..168 D
Tennyson Rd
Barry CF62 ....214 E
Newport NP19 ....144 A
Penarth CF64 ....206 E
Tennyson Terr NP24 ..33 F
Tennyson Way
Llantwit Major CF61 ..210 B
Swansea SA2 ....93 F
Tensing Cl CF14 ....159 E
Tensing Terr 11
CF63 ....215 B
Tenth Ave
Merthyr Tydfil CF47 ....10 F
Swansea SA6 ....45 D
Teras Brynteg 11
SA18 ....219 B
Terfyn Ynysawdre
CF32 ....150 E
Tern Cl CF3 ....179 E
Tern Ct NP44 ....89 A
Tern Rd CF36 ....182 D
Terra Nova Way
CF64 ....206 F
Terrace Rd SA1 ....95 B
Terrace Road Prim Sch
SA1 ....95 B
Terrace The
Creigiau CF15 ....174 E
Rhymney NP22 ....12 E
Tetbury Cl NP20 ....143 C
Tewdric Ct NP44 ....90 B
Tewdrig Cl CF61 ....209 F
Tewends 12 NP44 ....89 B
Tewkesbury Pl CF24 178 A
Tewkesbury St CF24 178 A
Tewkesbury Wlk
NP20 ....143 C
Teynes NP44 ....89 B
Thackeray Cres CF3 179 B
Thames Cl
Bettws NP20 ....116 E
Bryn NP12 ....85 D
Thaw Cl CF62 ....212 E
Theobald Rd CF5 ..194 C
Theodora St CF24 ..195 E
Theodore Rd SA13 ..125 C
Thesiger Ct CF24 ..195 A
Thesiger St CF24 ..195 A
Third Ave
Caerphilly CF83 ....137 E
8 Merthyr Tydfil CF47 ....10 E
Swansea SA6 ....45 D
Thirlamere Terr 1
CF44 ....53 E
Thirlmere Pl 5
NP19 ....143 F
Thirteenth Ave CF24 212 E
Thistle Cl CF62 ....214 D
Thistle Ct NP44 ....88 F
Thistle Terr 1 CF40 106 E
Thistle Way
Cardiff CF5 ....194 A
Risca NP11 ....115 B
Thistleboon Dr SA3 123 C
Thistleboon Gdns
SA3 ....123 B
Thistleboon Rd SA3 123 B
Thomas Cres CF36 ..194 B
Thomas Davies Ct 5
CF3 ....179 B
Thomas Ellis Way
NP22 ....13 F

Thomas Evans Ho
SA1 . . . . .67 F1
Thomas Fields NP22 . .12 F3
Thomas Jones Sq 6
CF48 . . . . .31 C1
Thomas Row SA1 . . . . .95 D8
Thompson St
Aberavon SA12 . . . . .98 F1
Aberdargoed CF81 . . . . . .58 B5
Aberfan CF44 . . . . .29 A3
Aberfan CF48 . . . . .55 C4
Abertridwr CF83 . . . . . .137 A7
Bargoed CF81 . . . . .58 A2
Briton Ferry SA11 . . . . . .71 C1
Cardiff CF11 . . . . .194 F3
Hendreforgan CF39 . .132 C5
Llanbradach CF83 . . . . .111 F1
Llanelli SA15 . . . . .46 E6
Maerdy CF43 . . . . .52 A1
Maesycwmmer CF82 . .85 B2
Mountain Ash CF45 . . . .54 E1
Nelson CF46 . . . . .83 E3
New Tredegar NP24 . . . .33 E3
Pontardawe SA8 . . . . . . .23 E5
Pontypridd CF37 . . . . . .109 B1
Pontypridd CF37 . . . . . .109 C1
Swansea SA1 . . . . .95 E7
Tonypandy CF40 . . . . . .106 D6
Tonypandy CF40 . . . . . .106 C6
Treharris CF46 . . . . .83 B6
Treorchy CF41 . . . . .79 A5
Thomas St
Dowlais CF48 . . . . .11 A5
Resolven SA11 . . . . .226 D5
Swansea SA6 . . . . .68 E6
Thomas' Pl CF39 . . . .107 F2
Thomas's Pl CF39 . . .107 E7
Thomasville CF83 . . .137 E5
Thompson Ave
Cardiff CF5 . . . . .194 A7
Newport NP19 . . . . .144 B3
Thompson Cl
1 Cardiff CF5 . . . . .194 C6
Gorseinon SA4 . . . . .66 D8
Thompson Pl CF5 . . .194 A7
Thompson St
Barry CF63 . . . . .214 F4
Cardiff CF11 . . . . .102 A1
Ynysybwl CF37 . . . . . . .109 A8
Thompson Villas
CF37 . . . . .109 A8
Thorburn Cl SA11 . . . .71 F8
Thorley Cl CF23 . . . .178 B4
Thorncombe Rd NP22 .85 F6
Thorne Ave NP11 . . . . .86 F7
Thorney Rd SA12 . . . . .98 D7
Thornfield Mews
CF31 . . . . .150 C1
Thornhill
Brynmawr NP23 . . . . .8 C5
Cwmbran NP44 . . . . .89 B6
Thornhill Ct CF14 . . . .177 D8
Thornhill Gdns NP10 141 E7
Thornhill Prim Sch
CF14 . . . . .159 E3
Thornhill Rd
Capel Hendre SA14 . . . .218 C6
Cardiff CF14 . . . . .159 C3
Cwmbran NP44 . . . . .89 B5
Thornhill St 3 CF5 . .194 C6
Thornhill Way NP10 .141 E6
Thornleigh Rd NP11 . .59 F5
Thornton Cres CF72 .103 F2
Thornwood
Cwmbran NP44 . . . . .89 C6
Thornwood CF14 . . . . . .83 B6
Thornwood CF14 . . . . . . .83 B6
Three Arches Ave
CF14 . . . . .178 A6
Three Cliffs Dr SA3 .121 A6
Three Elms Cl CF82 . .84 F4
Three Oaks Cl CF83 .138 C7
Three Salmon St
CF47 . . . . .30 D8
Three Ships Ct SA3 .123 C3
Thrush Cl 1 CF3 . . . .180 A6
Thurston Rd CF37 . . .109 D2
Thurston St
Abercynon CF45 . . . . . . .82 E3
6 Cardiff CF5 . . . . .194 D5
Tidbeunaw Ct SA5 . . .68 C7
Tichbourne St SA3 . .123 B4
Tide Fields Rd CF24 .196 A5
Tidenham Ct CF5 . . . .193 D4
Tidenham Rd CF5 . . .193 D4
Till Gr NP18 . . . . .117 F3
Tillery Rd NP13 . . . . . .36 B1
Tillery St NP13 . . . . . . .36 B6
Tillsland NP44 . . . . . .116 C8
Timber Yd CF14 . . . . .195 D4
Timbers Sq CF24 . . . .195 D8
Timbre Pl 5 SA12 . . .186 A7
Timothy Pl CF44 . . . . .53 D8
Timothy Rees Cl
CF5 . . . . .176 D3
Tin St CF24 . . . . .195 D6
Tingle La CF35 . . . . . .186 A7
Tinkinswood Burial
Chamber CF5 . . . . .204 A7

Tintagel Cl CF14 . . . .159 D2
Tintern Cl
Cwmbran NP44 . . . . .89 F2
St Athan CF62 . . . . .211 C7
Tintern St CF5 . . . . . .194 C6
Tippett Cl NP19 . . . . .144 E5
Tir Bach Rd NP12 . . . .85 F1
Tir Capel SA14 . . . . . . .41 A6
Tir Einon SA14 . . . . . . .41 C4
Tir John North Rd
SA1 . . . . .96 C8
Tir Meibion La CF72 159 E3
Tir Morfa Prim Sch
SA12 . . . . .98 B1
Tir Morfa Rd SA12 . . .98 B1
Tir Newydd
Llanelli SA14 . . . . .41 A4
North Cornelly CF33 . .166 A8
Tir y Waun SA9 . . . . .222 A5
Tir-Aton Ct CF22 . . . .173 B7
Tir-Berllan NP12 . . . . .59 B2
Tir-Philkins NP12 . . . .86 B6
Tir-y-berth Prim Sch
CF82 . . . . .85 A6
Tir-y-Berth St CF82 . .85 A6
Tir-y-Cwm La NP11 .114 F1
Tir-y-Cwm Rd NP11 .114 F1
Tirbach Rd SA9 . . . . . . .2 C7
Tirforgan SA14 . . . . . . .41 A7
Tirfounder Rd CF44 . .53 E7
Tirgof SA14 . . . . .42 B8
Tirmynydd Rd SA2,
SA4 . . . . .92 D8
Tirpenry St SA6 . . . . . .46 A1
Tirpentwys Terr NP4 .61 F8
Tirphil Prim Sch
NP24 . . . . .33 D3
Tirpys SA18 . . . . .219 A5
Tirwaun SA14 . . . . . . .218 B7
Tirycoed Rd SA18 . . .220 A8
Tirynys SA15 . . . . .40 F8
Titan Rd CF24 . . . . . . .195 E7
Tiverton Dr CF3 . . . . .179 A4
Toft Pl SA15 . . . . .40 E6
Toftingald Ave CF44 177 D5
Toghill Dr CF15 . . . . . .158 B3
Tollgate Cl
Caerphilly CF83 . . . . . . .138 D5
Cardiff CF11 . . . . .194 D1
Tollgate Rd SA13 . . . .125 E3
Tolpath NP44 . . . . .89 A1
Tom Pentre Ind Est
CF41 . . . . .79 A3
Ton Rd Cwmbran NP44 .89 B2
Ton Rhosyn CF31 . . . .169 B5
Ton Row CF41 . . . . .79 A3
Ton Teg CF35 . . . . .170 D4
Ton The CF3 . . . . .179 D7
Ton View CF33 . . . . . .148 D2
Ton y Felin CF37 . . . . .136 A6
Ton-Bach St NP4 . . . . .17 D6
Ton-coch Terr CF44 . .54 B6
Ton-Mawr Ave NP4 . . .17 D6
Ton-Mawr Rd
Blaenavon NP4 . . . . .17 D6
Pontrhydyfen SA12 . . . .73 B5
Ton-Mawr St 17 NP4 .17 D6
Ton-y-Felin Rd
CF83 . . . . .138 B3
Ton-y-Groes CF35 . . .170 E7
Ton-y-Pistyll Rd
NP11 . . . . .86 D5
Ton-Yr-Ywen Ave
CF14 . . . . .177 E5
Tonclwyda SA11 . . . .226 B3
Tondu Prim Sch
CF32 . . . . .150 C4
Tondu Rd CF31 . . . . . .168 D6
Tondu Sta CF32 . . . . .150 D5
Tone Cl NP20 . . . . .116 D2
Tone Rd NP20 . . . . . . .116 D2
Tone Sq NP20 . . . . . . .116 D2
Tongwynlais Prim Sch
Cardiff CF15 . . . . .158 C1
Tongwynlais CF15 . . . .176 C8
Tonna Hospl SA11 . . .49 E3
Tonna Rd CF34 . . . . . .102 A7
Tonna Uchaf SA11 . . .49 D3
Tonnau Prim Sch
SA11 . . . . .49 C2
Tonteg Cl CF38 . . . . . .136 A2
Tonteg Hospl CF38 . .135 F2
Tonteg Rd CF38 . . . . .136 B3
Tontine St SA1 . . . . . . .95 D8
Tonypandy Comp Sch
CF40 . . . . .106 C4
Tonypandy Ent Ctr
CF40 . . . . .106 C5
Tonypandy Prim Sch
CF40 . . . . .106 E5
Tonypandy Sta CF40 .106 C5

Tonyrefail Comp Sch
CF39 . . . . .133 A4
Tonyrefail Prim Sch
CF39 . . . . .133 C5
Tonyrefail Rd CF37 .134 E5
Tonysguboriau Cty Prim
Sch CF72 . . . . .155 B2
Top Rd NP44 . . . . .37 F6
Topaz St CF24 . . . . . . .195 D6
Tor Ho SA3 . . . . .123 A3
Tor View
Bedwas CF83 . . . . .138 C7
Penmaen SA3 . . . . .120 B5
Torbay Terr CF42 . . . .213 A1
Tordoff Way CF62 . . .214 E6
Torfaen Terr 2 NP4 . .38 A1
Torlais St NP11 . . . . . . .86 F6
Toronto Ave SA13 . . .125 E4
Torrens Dr CF23 . . . . .178 B4
Torrington Rd
Cardiff CF3 . . . . .179 C7
Swansea SA5 . . . . .68 A3
Tothill St NP23 . . . . . . .7 C1
Tower Cl CF31 . . . . . . .169 A3
Tower Ct Swansea SA1 .67 F1
Swansea SA6 . . . . .69 B8
Tower Gdns SA1 . . . . . .67 F1
Tower Hill CF44 . . . . .207 B3
Tower Hill Ave CF44 .207 B3
Tower Rd
Gileston CF62 . . . . .211 E1
Hirwaun CF44 . . . . .27 C7
Tower St CF37 . . . . . . .135 D7
Tower Way CF44 . . . . .215 E6
Towers The
Cwmbran NP44 . . . . .89 F3
Hirwaun CF44 . . . . .27 D7
Town Hall Sq CF41 . .188 F2
Town Mill Rd CF41 . .188 E1
Town Reach NP20 . . .143 C5
Townsend Comm Sch
SA1 . . . . .95 A8
Townhill Gdns SA1 . . .94 F8
Townhill Rd SA1,SA2 .95 A8
Towy Rd CF41 . . . . . . .178 A7
Towyn Rd CF3 . . . . . . .179 C6
Towyn Way CF38 . . . .136 A2
Trade La CF10 . . . . . . .195 A3
Trade St CF10 . . . . . . .195 A4
Traeth Ffordd
Llanelli SA15 . . . . .40 B4
Llanelli SA15 . . . . .40 C4
Traethmelyn SA12 . . .98 A3
Trafalgar Cl 3 CF24 178 C1
Trafalgar Pl SA2 . . . . .94 F5
Trafalgar Rd CF23 . . .195 D8
Trafalgar St NP11 . . .115 A1
Trafalgar Terr CF41 . .79 D2
Traharne Ct SA1 . . . . .71 C8
Traharne Dr CF5 . . . . .192 F4
Trallwm Rd SA14 . . . .41 C3
Trallwm Rd SA7 . . . . . .69 E6
Trallwn Pl SA7 . . . . . . .69 E6
Trallwn Prim Sch SA7 .69 E7
Trallwn Rd SA7 . . . . . .69 E6
Tram Ct CF37 . . . . .109 D2
Tram La NP04 . . . . .117 D7
Tram Rd
Caerleon NP18 . . . . . . .118 C2
Cwmbran NP44 . . . . .89 B6
Pontlanfraith NP12 . . . .85 F4
Tram Road Side
Quakers Yard CF46 . . . .83 A4
Treharris CF46 . . . . .83 A6
Tramore Way CF23 . .161 A1
Tramroad La CF47 . . . .10 E3
Tramroad Side N
CF48 . . . . .10 E1
Tramroad Side N
CF47 . . . . .10 E1
Tramroad Side S
CF48 . . . . .30 E8
Tramroad Terr 4
CF47 . . . . .10 E1
Tramroadside
Ebbw Vale NP23 . . . . .7 A4
Newbridge NP11 . . . . . . .86 F6
Tramway CF44 . . . . . . .27 C7
Tramway Cl NP44 . . . .89 A1
Tramway Rd SA14 . . .24 B5
Tranch Rd NP4 . . . . . . .62 A6
Trannon Ct NP44 . . . . .89 A4
Tranquil Pl NP44 . . . . .89 A4
Trap Well CF83 . . . . . .138 D5
Traston Ave NP19 . . .144 B1
Traston Cl NP19 . . . . .144 B1
Traston La NP19 . . . . .144 B1
Traston Rd
Newport NP19 . . . . .144 B1
Newport NP19 . . . . .164 F8
Traverner Trad Est
NP18 . . . . .118 B3
Travis Way CF36 . . . .165 E2
Trawler Rd SA1 . . . . . . .95 D5
Traws Fynydd CF41 .169 B4
Trawsfford SA9 . . . . . . .2 E8
Trawsmawr La NP20,
SA3 . . . . .116 C4
Tre Gwilym CF44 . . . . .53 E8
Tre Newydd NP23 . . . . .7 E1
Tre Telynog CF44 . . . .53 E8

Tre Uchaf Prim Sch
SA4 . . . . .42 F1
Tre-banog Terr
CF44 . . . . .224 D2
Tre-Beferad CF61 . . . .210 C5
Tre-Edwards NP22 . . .12 E5
Tre-Herbert Rd NP44 .90 D6
Tre-Lyn La NP12 . . . . .85 A6
Tre-Pit Rd CF71 . . . . . .198 B5
Tre-York St NP22 . . . . .12 E4
Trealaw Prim Sch
CF44 . . . . .106 F5
Trealaw Rd
Tonypandy CF40 . . . . . .106 F5
Tonypandy CF40 . . . . . .106 F6
Treasure St CF42 . . . . .78 D7
Trebannws Prim Sch
SA8 . . . . .46 E8
Trebanog Cl CF3 . . . .179 E6
Trebanog Cres CF3 . .179 E5
Trebanog Row CF39 .133 D8
Treberth Est NP19 . . .144 E6
Treborth Rd CF3 . . . . .179 E5
Trecastle Ave CF14 . .159 F1
Trecenydd Ind Est
CF83 . . . . .137 F1
Trecinon Rd CF3 . . . .179 F5
Tredegar Ave
Ebbw Vale NP23 . . . . . . .14 C7
Llanharan CF72 . . . . . . .153 F3
Cardiff CF72 . . . . .153 F4
Tredegar Comp Sch
NP22 . . . . .13 C5
Tredegar Ct
Abercarn NP11 . . . . .114 B3
Cardiff CF11 . . . . .176 F5
Newport NP20 . . . . .143 C2
Tredegar Gap CF3 . . .14 D8
Tredegar House Dry
NP10 . . . . .163 E6
Tredegar House Dr
NP10 . . . . .163 D7
Tredegar Park View
NP10 . . . . .142 C4
Tredegar Rd
Ebbw Vale NP23 . . . . . . .14 C7
Gorseinon SA4 . . . . .43 C1
New Tredegar SA4 . . . . .33 E3
Tredegar St
Abercarn NP11 . . . . .114 B4
Bassaleg NP10 . . . . .141 E4
Cardiff CF10 . . . . .195 B5
Risca NP11 . . . . .114 F2
Tredegar Terr
Abergorwedd CF41 . . . . .58 A4
Risca NP11 . . . . .114 B4
Tredomen Gdns
Tredomen CF82 . . . . .84 D2
Tredomen Ind Pk
CF82 . . . . .84 D2
Tredomen Terr
Tredomen CF82 . . . . .84 D1
Tredomen CF82 . . . . .84 D2
Tree Tops Ave CF14 . .85 E8
Treetops Cl CF5 . . . . .176 B1
Tref-y-Rhyg Prim Sch
CF39 . . . . .133 A3
Trefasser Cres CF3 . .179 E6
Trefelin Cl SA14 . . . . . .28 E4
Trefelin Cres SA13 . . .99 C2
Trefelin St CF43 . . . . . .34 D3
Trefenter Rd SA13 . . .99 C2
Trefforest Cty Prim Sch
CF37 . . . . .135 E7
Trefforest Sta CF37 . .135 E6
Trefil Cl NP22 . . . . .6 A4
Treforest St CF37 . . . .135 E6
Treforest Estate Halt
CF38 . . . . .136 D1
Treforest Ind Est
Upper Boat CF15 . . . . . .157 E8
Upper Boat CF15 . . . . . .136 C2
Treforgan Rd
Cynant SA10 . . . . .222 A1
Cynant SA10 . . . . .226 A8
Treforis SA18 . . . . .219 C6
Tregare St NP19 . . . . .143 D6
Tregarn Cl NP18 . . . . .119 E2
Tregarn Ct NP18 . . . . .119 E2
Tregarn Rd NP18 . . . .119 F2
Tregare Cl SA6 . . . . . . .45 F4
Tregaron Ho SA13 . . .125 E3
Tregaron Rd CF5 . . . .193 B5
Tregarth Cl CF15 . . . .174 D8
Tregarth Ct CF15 . . . .174 D8
Tregelles Ct
Cwmrhydyceirw SA6 . .46 A4
Swansea SA6 . . . . .45 F3
Tregelles Ct SA18 . . . .48 B1
Tregenna Ct
Caerphilly CF83 . . . . . . .138 C3
Llanhari Major CF61 . . .210 B7

Trehafod Sta CF37 . . .108 C3
Treharne Dr CF31 . . . .150 D1
Treharne Flats CF37 .136 B5
Treharne Rd
Barry CF63 . . . . .215 A7
Maesteg CF34 . . . . .75 B1
Swansea SA6 . . . . .45 F1
Treharne Row CF44 . . .82 F6
Treharne Row
Maesteg CF34 . . . . .102 A4
Pontyrhyl CF32 . . . . . . .129 E8
Treharne St
Merthyr Vale CF48 . . . . .55 D5
Pentre CF41 . . . . .78 F4
Tonypandy CF40 . . . . . .106 F5
Treharris Terr CF46 . . .82 F6
Treharris St CF24 . . . .195 C7
Treherbert Hospl
CF42 . . . . .50 F2
Treherbert Inf Sch
CF42 . . . . .78 A8
Treherbert Inf Sch
CF42 . . . . .50 F2
Treherbert St CF24 .194 F8
Treherbert Sta CF42 . . .50 F2
Trehopcyn Prim Sch
CF37 . . . . .109 A2
Trelai Ct CF5 . . . . .193 C3
Trelai Jun & Inf Sch
CF5 . . . . .193 C5
Trelales Prim Sch
CF32 . . . . .167 E4
Trelawney Ave 5
CF3 . . . . .179 B3
Trelawney Cres 2
CF3 . . . . .179 B3
Trelech Cl NP44 . . . . . .89 F2
Trelewis Prim Sch
CF46 . . . . .83 D7
Trelys Cl NP12 . . . . .85 A5
Trem Powys CF63 . . . .215 C8
Trem Twynbarlwm
NP44 . . . . .89 D1
Trem y Bryn CF31 . . . .168 C2
Trem y Castell CF83 .137 D1
Trem y Coed CF63 . . .205 B1
Trem y Mor SA4 . . . . . .64 B2
Trem-y-Dyffryn
SA11 . . . . .226 C4
Trem-y-Cwm 3
CF38 . . . . .156 A6
Trem-y-Don CF62 . . .214 B2
Trem-y-duffryn
CF38 . . . . .156 A6
Trem-y-Garth CF72 .172 D5
Trem-y-Glyn CF39 . . .107 D1
Trem-y-Mor NP19 . . .169 B4
Trem-y-Mynydd
Blaenavon NP4 . . . . .17 D6
Hirwaun CF44 . . . . .27 F7
Tremadoc St CF43 . . .179 E5
Tremains Ct CF31 . . . .169 B4
Tremains Inf Sch
CF31 . . . . .169 C5
Tremains Jun Sch
CF31 . . . . .169 C5
Tremains Rd CF31 . . .168 F4
Tremarth Cl CF31 . . . .168 E6
Tremorfa Ind Est
CF24 . . . . .195 F4
Tremorfa Prim Sch
CF24 . . . . .196 A4
Trenant
Ebbw Vale NP23 . . . . . . .14 C8
Hirwaun CF44 . . . . .27 F7
Trenchard Dr CF14 . .177 F6
Trenewydd Rd CF31 . .71 F6
Trenewydd Rise SA11 .71 F6
Trenos Pl CF72 . . . . . .153 D2
Trenos St CF72 . . . . . .153 D2
Trent Rd NP20 . . . . . . .116 D3
Treochy Sta CF42 . . . . .78 D5
Treoda Ct 3 CF14 . . . .177 B5
Treoes Rd CF35 . . . . . .169 F3
Treorchy Comp Sch
CF42 . . . . .78 D6
Treorchy Ind Est CF42 .78 E5
Treorchy Prim Sch
CF42 . . . . .78 D6
Treorky Sq 4 CF24 . . .195 B8
Treowen Ave NP12 . . .85 E4
Treowen Rd NP11 . . . .59 F1
Trerobart Prim Sch
CF44 . . . . .27 C7
Treseder Way CF5 . . .193 B5
Tresillian Rd CF3 . . . .179 E6
Tresillian St CF61 . . . .209 F5
Tresillian Terr 4
CF10 . . . . .195 A4
Tresillian Way
CF10 . . . . .195 A4
Cardiff CF10 . . . . .195 A4
Tresillian Pl CF45 . . . .82 D2
Tretower Ct NP44 . . . . .90 B3
Trevallen Ave SA11 . . .72 A5
Trevannian Jun Sch
CF15 . . . . .138 C3
Llanhari Major CF61 . . .210 B7
Trevethick Ho 6
CF24 . . . . .30 D8
Trevethick St
Cardiff CF11 . . . . .194 E5
Merthyr Tydfil CF47 . . . .10 E2
Trevethin Com Sch
CF37 . . . . .62 C7
Trevine Path NP4 . . . .62 D7
Trevithick Ct NP20 . .116 F3
Trevithick Gdns CF37 .30 E8
Trevor Cl CF48 . . . . . . .11 B7

Trevor St
Aberdare CF44 . . . . .29 A1
Treorchy CF42 . . . . .78 D7
Trewartha Cl 7
CF11 . . . . .177 B5
Trewaun CF44 . . . . .27 E7
Trewen Rd
Birchgrove SA7 . . . . .47 A1
Swansea SA7 . . . . .70 A8
Trews Field Ind Site
CF31 . . . . .168 E6
Trewyddfa Comm
SA6 . . . . .68 F6
Trewyddfa Gdns SA6 .68 F6
Trewyddfa Rd SA6 . . . .68 E6
Trewyddfa Terr SA6 . .68 E6
Triangle CF62 . . . . .21 F2
Triangle Bsns Pk
CF37 . . . . .30 F5
Triangle The
Bridgend CF31 . . . . .169 B4
Mountain Ash CF45 . . . .54 D4
Tribute Ave NP11 . . . .114 C8
Trident Ct CF24 . . . . . .195 C4
Tridwr Rd CF83 . . . . . .136 F7
Trigfan Dawn SA12 . . .79 D6
Trinant Inf Sch NP11 . .59 F5
Trinant Jun Sch NP11 .59 F6
Trinant Terr NP11 . . . .59 F6
Trinity Cl
Mumbles SA3 . . . . .123 A5
Swansea SA1 . . . . .19 C3
Ystrad Mynach CF82 . . .84 E1
Trinity Ct
Newport NP20 . . . . .143 D2
Port Talbot SA12 . . . . . . .98 D2
Risca NP11 . . . . .114 F2
Swansea SA1 . . . . .95 C7
Trinity Fields Specl Sch
CF82 . . . . .84 E1
Trinity Hill NP11 . . . . .114 C6
Trinity La
Caerleon NP18 . . . . . . .117 F3
Pen-clawdd SA4 . . . . . . .64 C4
Trinity Pl
Newport NP20 . . . . .143 D2
Pontardulais SA4 . . . . . . .19 C3
5 Swansea SA1 . . . . . .95 C7
Trinity Rd
Cwmbran NP44 . . . . .89 D5
Llanelli SA15 . . . . .40 E3
Trinity St Barry CF62 .214 D4
Cardiff CF10 . . . . .195 A5
Swansea SA1 . . . . .43 C1
Trinity Terr SA15 . . . .40 D3
Trinity View NP18 . . .117 E3
Trip Terr CF41 . . . . .79 A5
Triscombe Dr CF5 . . .176 E1
Tristram Cl CF14 . . . .159 D2
Troed o Rhiw CF44 . .159 A1
Troed-y-Bryn
Blaina NP13 . . . . .15 E6
Caerphilly CF83 . . . . . . .137 E5
Troed-y-Garth CF15 .157 B1
Troed-y-Rhiw
Abercarn NP11 . . . . .87 A3
Abercraf SA9 . . . . .222 B7
Swansea SA7 . . . . .69 F6
Troed-y-Rhiw Rd
Cwmfelinfach NP11 . . .113 C4
Mountain Ash CF45 . . . .54 E3
Troed-y-rhiw Sta
CF48 . . . . .31 C1
Troedpennar Terr
CF44 . . . . .82 E3
Troedrhiw-gwair
CF44 . . . . .14 B2
Troedrhiw-trwyn
CF37 . . . . .108 F2
Troedyrhiw Jun Sch
CF48 . . . . .31 C1
Troedyrhiw Rd CF39 .107 E4
Troedyrhiw Terr CF44 .78 E6
Tros- Maen SA14 . . . . .40 F8
Troserch Rd SA14 . . . . .38 B2
Trosnant Cres CF82 . .84 D5
Trosnant Gr NP20 . . . .62 C6
Trosnant Villa NP4 . . .62 C6
Trostre Ind Pk SA14 . . .41 A3
Trostre Rd
Llanelli SA14, SA15 . . . .40 F3
Llanelli SA15 . . . . .40 F4
Trostrey NP44 . . . . . . .116 C8
Trostrey Cl SA15 . . . . .63 B4
Trostrey St NP19 . . . . .143 D6
Trotman Dickinson Pl
CF14 . . . . .177 E1
Trowbridge Gn CF3 . .179 E6
Trowbridge Inf Sch
CF3 . . . . .179 E5
Trowbridge Jun Sch
CF3 . . . . .179 E5
Troweyrhiw Inf Sch
CF48 . . . . .31 C1
Troy Rd NP13 . . . . .60 B7
Troy St SA6 . . . . .69 B4
Tucker St SA1 . . . . .71 C3
Tuckers Villas NP4 . . .85 E7
Tudno Pl SA5 . . . . .68 A5
Tudor Ave CF44 . . . . . .27 D8
Tudor Cl Cardiff CF5 .193 D7
Ebbw Vale NP23 . . . . . . .7 B5
Merthyr Vale CF48 . . . . .55 D3
Penarth CF64 . . . . .207 A1

Tudor Cres
- **7** Brynmawr NP23 . . . . .8 B4
- Rogerstone NP10 . . . . . .142 C4
- Rogerstone NP10 . . . . . .142 G4

Tudor Ct
- Aberbargoed CF81 . . . . .58 B4
- Bishopston SA3 . . . . . . .122 A6
- Cardiff CF14 . . . . .177 D5
- Llanedi SA4 . . . . .218 D1

Tudor Dr CF32 . . . . . .129 E1
Tudor Est CF34 . . . . . . .75 A1
Tudor Gdns
- Machen CF83 . . . . .139 F6
- Neath SA10 . . . . .48 C1

Tudor La CF11 . . . . . . .194 F4
Tudor Mews CF72 . . . .173 D7
Tudor Pl CF61 . . . . . . .210 A5
Tudor Rd
- Cwmbran NP44 . . . . . . .89 E3
- Newport NP19 . . . . . . .143 E8
- Swansea SA5 . . . . .68 C5
- Ton Pentre CF41 . . . . . . .79 A2

Tudor St Cardiff CF11 .194 F4
- Ferndale CF43 . . . . .79 F6
- Hawthorn CF37 . . . . . .136 A4
- **1** Port Talbot SA13 . . .99 B1
- Ystradgynlais SA9 . . . . . .2 E7

Tudor Terr
- Aberdare CF44 . . . . .28 F3
- Merthyr Tydfil CF47 . . . .10 D2

Tudor Way
- Bishopston SA3 . . . . . .122 B7
- Llantwit Fardre CF38 . . .156 C6
- Tudor Woods NP44 . . . .90 B2
- **Tudors The** CF23 . . . . .178 D1
- **Tulloch St** CF24 . . . . . .195 C4
- **Tummel Cl** CF23 . . . . .178 C5
- **Tumulus Way** CF71 . . .199 D4
- **Tunnel Rd** SA15 . . . . .40 E5
- **Tunnel Row** NP11 . . . . .86 E6
- **Tunnel Terr** NP20 . . . .143 B4
- **Turberville Cres**
  - CF31 . . . . .150 F5
- **Turberville Pl** CF11 . . .194 D6

Turberville Rd
- Cwmbran NP44 . . . . . . .89 E4
- Porth CF39 . . . . .107 E5
- **Turberville St**
  - Maesteg CF34 . . . . . . .102 C2
  - Tonypandy CF40 . . . . . .79 E7

Turberville Terr **5**
- CF40 . . . . .106 F4
- **Turbine Annexe Rd**
  - CF62 . . . . .211 E1
- **Turkey St** CF61 . . . . . .209 F7
- **Turner House Gallery**
  - CF64 . . . . .207 B3
- **Turner Rd** CF5 . . . . . .194 B6
- **Turner St** NP19 . . . . . .143 D6
- **Turners End** NP44 . . . .21 D5
- **Turnham Gn** CF23 . . . .178 E2
- **Turnpike Cl**
  - Dinas Powys CF64 . . . . .206 B4
  - Pontypool NP4 . . . . .62 F6
- **Turnpike Rd** NP44 . . . .90 B2
- **Turnstiles The** NP20 . .143 C7
- **Turnstone Ct** SA12 . . . .98 C1
- **Turnstone Rd** CF36 . . .165 E1
- **Tuscan Cl** CF64 . . . . . .206 D7
- **Twchwyn Garth**
  - CF35 . . . . .187 E8
- **Tweedsmuir Rd**
  - CF24 . . . . .195 F6
- **Tweedy La** NP19 . . . . .143 F5
- **Twelfth Ave** CF47 . . . . .10 F5
- **Twinings The** **5** NP44 .89 B3
- **Twissell's Rd** NP44 . . . .22 B4
- **Twll-Yn-y-Wal Rd** **4**
  - SA13 . . . . .125 E4
- **Twm Barlwm Cl**
  - NP11 . . . . .115 C2
- **Twm Barlwm View**
  - NP44 . . . . .90 B2
- **Twmbarlwm Rise**
  - NP44 . . . . .62 B6
- **Twmpath Gdns** NP4 . . .62 B6
- **Two Locks Rd** NP44 . . .89 D1
- **Two Stones Cres**
  - CF23 . . . . .148 D2
- **Twmpath Rd** NP4 . . . . .62 B6
- **Twyn** NP12 . . . . .85 A5
- **Twyn Bedw** CF39 . . . . .107 F2
- **Twyn Bedw Rd** SA6 . . . .46 D7
- **Twyn Carn Terr**
  - NP11 . . . . .1 C5
- **Twyn Carno** NP22 . . . . .12 C5
- **Twyn Cty Prim Sch**
  - SA18 . . . . .220 B8
- **Twyn Gdns** NP12 . . . . .85 C7
- **Twyn Gwyn Rd**
  - Cwmfelinfach NP11 . . . .113 A5
  - Tonypandy CF40 . . . . . .107 B2
- **Twyn Inf Sch** CF83 . . .108 B2
- **Twyn Jun Sch** CF83 . . .138 B2
- **Twyn Oaks** NP18 . . . . .118 D3
- **Twyn Pl** NP11 . . . . .87 C3
- **Twyn Rd**
  - Abercarn NP11 . . . . . . .87 B3
  - Ystrad Mynach CF82 . . .111 E7
- **Twyn Star** NP22 . . . . . .62 G6
- **Twyn Teg** SA10 . . . . . . .48 D1
- **Twyn The** CF83 . . . . . .138 B2
- **Twyn-gwyn Terr**
  - NP11 . . . . .86 E6
- **Twyn-y-Fedwen**
  - CF14 . . . . .177 D3
- **Twyn-y-Gored** SA12 . .100 A7

Twyn-Yr-Eos CF42 . . . .51 A1
Twyn-Yr-Ynys SA12 . .100 A7
Twyn-Yr-Ysgol SA9 . . .2 B7
Twyncarmel CF48 . . . .225 F1
Twyncarn Rd NP11 . . .114 B6
Twyncyn CF44 . . . . . . .205 F3
Twyncynghorchy NP23 .8 A4
Twyncynghorfdy Pl
- NP23 . . . . .8 A4
Twyncynghorfdy Rd
- Brynmawr NP23 . . . . .8 A4
- Ebbw Vale NP23 . . . . . . .7 F4
Twynderwyn Flats
- NP23 . . . . .8 A4
Twyni Teg SA2 . . . . . . .93 E8
Twyniago SA4 . . . . . . .198 D6
Twynrefail Pl SA18 . . .220 D6
Twynyffald Rd NP12 . . .85 D8
Twynygarreg CF46 . . . .83 B7
Twynyrodyn Inf Sch
- CF47 . . . . .10 F1
Twynyrodyn Jun Sch
- CF47 . . . . .30 E8
Twynyrodyn Rd **1D**
- CF47 . . . . .30 E8
Ty Alban CF40 . . . . . . .106 E7
Ty Box Cl NP44 . . . . . . .89 D5
Ty Box Rd NP44 . . . . . .89 D5
Ty Bruce Rd CF44 . . . . .27 E8
Ty Brunel SA11 . . . . . . .71 C2
Ty Bryn
- Aberbargoed CF81 . . . . .58 A5
Ty Bryn Rd NP13 . . . . . .36 A6
Ty Bryncoch CF15 . . . .158 A4
Ty Canol CF36 . . . . . . .165 F1
Ty Canol La CF83 . . . . .139 F7
Ty Canol Way NP44 . . . .90 A3
Ty Capel Zion CF43 . . . .80 B2
Ty Cerrig
- **6** Barry CF63 . . . . . . .215 B7
- Cardiff CF23 . . . . .178 E8
Ty Coch NP22 . . . . .12 E8
Ty Coch Distribution Ctr
- NP44 . . . . .116 E8
Ty Coch Way NP44 . . .116 E8
Ty Cornel CF81 . . . . . . .58 A5
Ty Crwyn CF38 . . . . . .156 E8
Ty Cydwel **1D** SA15 . . .40 D4
Ty Dawel CF39 . . . . . . .133 C5
Ty Ddewi CF41 . . . . . . .79 A2
Ty Dewi Sant SA4 . . . . .67 E3
Ty Draw
- Church Village CF38 . . .135 E1
Ty Draw La
- Penperlleni NP4 . . . . . . .39 E3
- South Cornelly CF33 . . .165 F6
Ty Ebenezer CF43 . . . . .80 C3
Ty Einon Day Hospl
- SA4 . . . . .42 A3
Ty Elizabeth **6** SA15 . .40 D4
Ty Ffynnon CF62 . . . . .214 F8
Ty Florence Asher
- SA4 . . . . .22 E1
Ty Fry CF44 . . . . .28 F1
Ty Fry Cl NP4 . . . . .17 C7
Ty Fry Rd
- Aberbargoed CF81 . . . . .58 B4
- Cefn Cribwr CF32 . . . . .149 A2
- **Ty Glas Sta** CF14 . . . .177 E6
Ty Gelli Genol Newydd
- SA11 . . . . .71 F7
Ty Gwenfo CF63 . . . . . .215 C6
Ty Gwyn SA4 . . . . .66 C5
Ty Gwyn Cl CF35 . . . . .152 B5
Ty Gwyn Dr CF31 . . . . .169 D4
Ty Gwyn Rd
- Cwmbran NP44 . . . . . . .89 B3
- Penperlleni NP4 . . . . . . .39 E3
- **Ty Gwyn Sch** CF23 . . .178 C3
- **Ty Gwyn Way** NP44 . . .89 B3
- **Ty Hedd-wyn** **1** SA12 .99 D5
- **Ty Howard** **7** SA15 . . .40 D4
- **Ty Isaf** CF72 . . . . .178 A7
- **Ty Llunfan** CF39 . . . . .132 C7
- **Ty Llwyd Parc** CF46 . . .83 C5
- **Ty Mawr Parc** CF37 . . .108 F2
- **Ty Mawr Uchaf** CF37 . .108 F2
- **Ty Merchant** CF35 . . . .152 F1
- **Ty Meriel** **6** SA15 . . . .40 D4
- **Ty Mynydd**
  - Blaenavon NP4 . . . . . . .17 D6
  - Cwmbran NP44 . . . . . . .89 C5
Ty Nant
- Bridgend CF31 . . . . . . .168 C5
- Caerphilly CF83 . . . . . .137 E4
- **Ty Nant Ct** CF15 . . . . .158 B1
Ty Newydd
- Cardiff CF14 . . . . .177 A4
- Machen CF83 . . . . .139 D5
- Seven Sisters SA10 . . . .222 D4
- **Ty Newydd Terr**
  - SA14 . . . . .218 B8
- **Ty Parc Cl** CF5 . . . . . .176 D3
- **Ty Penry Thomas**
  - NP23 . . . . .14 D7
- **Ty Ponthun** CF43 . . . . .140 A6
- **Ty Pucca Cl** CF83 . . . . .140 A6
- **Ty Pwca Pl** NP44 . . . . . .89 C6
- **Ty Pwca Rd** NP44 . . . . .89 C6
- **Ty Rhiw** CF15 . . . . .158 A4
- **Ty Seion** **5** SA4 . . . . . .54 D3
- **Ty Sign Inf Sch**
  - NP11 . . . . .115 A2
- **Ty Sign Jun Sch**
  - NP11 . . . . .115 A2
- **Ty Sivertsen** SA1 . . . . .95 B6
- **Ty Stafford** **9** SA15 . . .40 D4
- **Ty Trappa** NP44 . . . . . .89 C6

Ty Trappa Pl **1** NP44 . .89 C6
Ty Tudor NP44 . . . . . . .89 E3
Ty Twyn NP44 . . . . .89 E3
Ty Twyn Tag SA10 . . . . .48 D1
Ty Ysgol Ynyshir
- CF39 . . . . .107 E6
Ty'n y Wern NP44 . . . .133 C2
Ty'n Y Haul CF32 . . . . .150 G6
Ty-n-y-Bonau Rd SA4 . .42 A3
Ty-n-y-Cae Gr CF14 . . .177 C6
Ty-n-y-coed NP44 . . . . .89 E3
Ty-n-y-Coed La
- CF24 . . . . .178 B1
Ty-n-y-Coed Terr
- CF32 . . . . .150 G4
Ty-n-y-Graig Rd
- CF83 . . . . .111 F1
Ty-n-y-Pant Rd SA8 . . . .23 C5
Ty-n-y-Pant Rd CF14 . .177 A5
Ty-n-y-Pwll Rd CF14 . .177 A5
Ty-n-yr-Heol Rd SA10 . .48 C3
Tyr Felin SA5 . . . . .67 F6
Tyr Fran SA7 . . . . .47 A2
Tyr Graig Cty Prim Sch
- NP13 . . . . .60 A7
Tyr Holl St **7** CF24 . . .195 C5
Tyr Maes SA5 . . . . .67 F6
Tyr Person CF38 . . . . . .125 C1
Tyr Pobydd SA11 . . . . . .71 E6
Tyr Ysgol **6** CF24 . . . .195 C5
Tyr'r Ysgol CF71 . . . . .189 C5
Tyr-Groes Dr SA13 . . . .99 A1
Tyr-owen SA12 . . . . . . .99 C4
Tyr-Owen Row SA12 . . .99 D5
Tyr-Owen Terr **6**
- SA12 . . . . .99 D5
Tyrfelin St CF45 . . . . . .81 E8
Tyffran Ave SA11 . . . . . .40 E7
Ty-brachty Terr NP11 . .59 D2
Ty-Bwmpyn Rd NP11 . .61 D7
Ty-canol Ct NP44 . . . . .89 E1
Ty-Canol La CF83 . . . . .139 A8
Ty-Canol Row NP44 . . .89 E1
Ty-capel CF15 . . . . . . .158 A3
Ty-Cefn Rd CF5 . . . . . .193 D6
Ty-Coch Cl NP10 . . . . .141 F2
Ty-Coch La
- Cwmbran NP44 . . . . . . .116 E8
- Cwmbran NP44 . . . . . . .116 E8
Ty-coch Maisonettes
- SA2 . . . . .94 D7
Ty-Coch Rd
- Cardiff CF5 . . . . .193 C5
- Swansea SA2 . . . . .94 D7
Ty-Coch Terr NP44 . . .116 E8
Ty-Coed NP44 . . . . .16 B1
Ty-Dan-y-Wal NP13 . . .36 B7
Ty-Dan-y-Wal Rd
- Abertillery NP13 . . . . . .36 A3
- Abertillery NP13 . . . . . .36 B8
Ty-Draw
- Llandow CF71 . . . . .199 A4
- Penperlleni NP4 . . . . . . .39 E3
Ty-Draw Cres SA1 . . . . .69 B2
Ty-Draw Hill SA13 . . . . .99 F1
Ty-Draw Pl
- Cardiff CF23 . . . . .178 C1
- Port Talbot SA13 . . . . . .125 B8
- Swansea SA1 . . . . .69 B2
Ty-Draw Rd
- Aberdare CF44 . . . . .29 C2
- Cardiff CF23 . . . . .160 E1
- Cardiff CF23 . . . . .178 B2
- Swansea SA1 . . . . .69 C2
- **Ty-Draw St** SA13 . . . .125 B8
- **Ty-Fry Ave** CF3 . . . . . .179 B3
- **Ty-Fry Cl**
  - Brynmenyn CF32 . . . . .168 C7
  - Cardiff CF3 . . . . .179 C4
- **Ty-Fry Gdns** CF3 . . . . .179 C4
- **Ty-Fry Rd** Cardiff CF3 . .179 B4
  - Margam SA13 . . . . .125 E4
- **Ty-Glas Ave** CF14 . . . .177 F8
Ty-Glas Rd
- Cardiff CF14 . . . . .177 D7
- Cardiff CF14 . . . . .177 E8
- **Ty-Gwyn** NP44 . . . . . . .89 A2
- **Ty-Gwyn Ave** CF23 . . .178 C3
- **Ty-Gwyn Cres** CF23 . . .178 C3
- **Ty-Gwyn Rd**
  - Aberystwyth NP4 . . . . . .37 E7
  - Cardiff CF14 . . . . .177 C7
  - Cardiff CF23 . . . . .178 C2
- **Ty-Haulwen** NP23 . . . . .8 C2
- **Ty-Isaf** CF83 . . . . .137 D5
- **Ty-Isaf Complex**
  - NP11 . . . . .141 B8
- **Ty-Isaf Cres** NP11 . . . .141 A8
- **Ty-Isaf Inf Sch** NP11 . .115 B1
- **Ty-Isaf Park Ave**
  - NP11 . . . . .141 C8
- **Ty-Isaf Park Circ**
  - NP11 . . . . .141 C8
- **Ty-Isaf Park Cres**
  - NP11 . . . . .141 C8
- **Ty-Isaf Park Rd**
  - NP11 . . . . .141 B8
- **Ty-Isaf Park Villas**
  - NP11 . . . . .141 B8
- **Ty-Isaf Rd** CF83 . . . . . .44 D5
- **Ty-Isha Terr** NP12 . . . .85 D8
- **Ty-Llwyd Wlk** CF81 . . .58 B5
- **Ty-Llwydd Pl** NP11 . . . .86 F6
- **Ty-Mawr** SA8 . . . . .23 E4
- **Ty-Mawr Ave** CF3 . . . .179 A2
- **Ty-Mawr Ave** CF23 . . .178 F3
- **Ty-Mawr Rd**
  - Cardiff CF14 . . . . .176 E4
  - Cardiff CF3 . . . . .179 A2

Ty-myrtwydd SA4 . . . . .65 E8
Ty-Nant CF82 . . . . .84 D8
Ty-Nant Rd CF15 . . . . .176 B7
Ty-Nant St CF11 . . . . . .194 E3
Ty-Newydd Ct NP44 . . .89 E5
Ty-Newydd Rd
- Barry CF62 . . . . .214 F6
- Cwmbran NP44 . . . . . . .89 E5
- **Ty-Pica Dr** CF5 . . . . . .203 G6
- **Ty-Rosser-Gwyn** NP4 . .37 E7
- **Ty-to-Maen** CF22 . . . . .178 C8
- **Ty-To-Maen Cl** CF3 . . .179 E8
- **Ty-Verlon Ind Est**
  - CF63 . . . . .215 E7
- **Ty-Wern Ave** CF14 . . . .177 C6
- **Ty-Wern Rd** CF14 . . . . .177 C6
- **Tybryn Terr** CF35 . . . . .170 B8
- **Tycribwr Hill** CF32 . . . .150 G6
Tycroes Cty Prim Sch
- SA18 . . . . .218 F5
Tycroes Rd
- Ammanford SA18 . . . . .219 A5
- Tycroes SA18 . . . . .218 E6
Tyddyn Gwaun CF32 . .167 E4
Tydeg Anerys NP12 . . . .85 E7
Tyderwen CF34 . . . . . .102 A7
Tydfil Ho CF47 . . . . .10 D1
Tydfil Pl CF23 . . . . .178 B2
Tydfil Rd CF83 . . . . . . .138 D6
Tydfil St CF63 . . . . . . .215 B6
Tydfil Terr CF48 . . . . . . .31 C2
Tydfil Villas CF48 . . . . . .11 A7
Tydfil's Terr 2 CF47 . . .10 D1
Tydies NP44 . . . . .116 B8
Tydraw Cres CF33 . . . .166 B8
Tydraw Terr CF42 . . . . .50 D3
Tydu View NP10 . . . . . .142 B4
Tydvil Cl CF46 . . . . .83 C6
Tyfica Cres CF37 . . . . .109 C1
Tyfica Rd CF37 . . . . . . .109 C1
Tygwyn Ave CF37 . . . . .10 D7
Tygwyn Cl CF37 . . . . . .10 D7
Tygwyn Dr CF37 . . . . . .10 D7
Tygwyn Rd CF41 . . . . . .79 D3
Tyisaf Rd CF41 . . . . .79 B3
Tyisha Rd SA15 . . . . . . .40 A4
Tyla Glas CF83 . . . . . . .158 F8
Tyla Gwyn CF15 . . . . . .157 F7
Tyla La CF3 . . . . .161 B4
Tyla Rd SA11 . . . . .71 C3
Tyla Rhosyr CF71 . . . . .188 D2
Tyla Teg CF14 . . . . .176 E8
Tyla-Gwyn CF83 . . . . . .158 F8
Tylacelyn Rd CF40 . . . .106 F4
Tylacoch CF72 . . . . . . .172 B5
Tylacoch Pl CF40 . . . . .106 B1
Tylcha Fach CF39 . . . . .133 D2
Tylcha Fach Cl CF39 . . .133 D2
Tylcha Fach Terr
- CF39 . . . . .133 D2
Tylcha Ganol CF39 . . . .133 C2
Tylcha Isaf CF39 . . . . . .133 C2
Tylcha Isaf Terr CF39 . .133 B3
Tylcha Wen Terr
- CF39 . . . . .133 B3
Tyle Garw CF72 . . . . . .172 F8
Tyle Glas
- Glanaman SA18 . . . . . .220 C7
- North Cornelly CF33 . . .166 A8
Tyle House Cl CF61 . . .210 B8
Tyle Mali CF71 . . . . . . .187 E1
Tyle Teg SA6 . . . . .46 C7
Tyle'r Hendy CF72 . . . .173 C7
Tyle-Fforest CF42 . . . . .51 A1
Tylegarw Terr CF72 . . .172 F8
Tyler St CF24 . . . . .195 C6
Tyleri Gdns NP13 . . . . . .36 B6
Tyllwyd
- Bryn-côch SA10 . . . . . . .48 B6
- Pontardawe SA8 . . . . . . .23 E2
Tyllwyd Rd NP20 . . . . .142 F4
Tyllwyd St CF47 . . . . . . .10 F3
Tylors Ct CF48 . . . . .30 B8
Tylorstown Prim Sch
- CF43 . . . . .80 C3
Tymaen Cres SA12 . . . .99 F6
Tymaen Terr **3** SA12 . .99 F6
Tymawr Cl
- Cardiff CF3 . . . . .179 A2
- Ystradowen CF71 . . . . .189 C8
Tymawr Rd CF37 . . . . .108 F2
Tymawr St SA1 . . . . . . .96 B7
Tymawr Terr CF37 . . . .108 F2
Tymeinwr Ave CF42 . . .103 E5
Tymeinwr Cl CF42 . . . .103 E5
Tymynydd Cl CF5 . . . . .176 A7
Tyn y Waun Rd CF83 . .139 C3
Tyn y Wern Inf Annexe
- CF83 . . . . .138 F6
Tyn-y-Banwen Rd
- CF32 . . . . .129 E1
Tyn-y-Bettws Cl
- CF32 . . . . .149 D1
Tyn-y-Cae SA9 . . . . . . .100 B8
Tyn-y-Cae Rd SA7 . . . . .69 D7
Tyn-y-Caeau La
- CF36 . . . . .166 C1
Tyn-y-Coed CF80 . . . . .10 F8
Tyn-y-Coed Ffordd
- SA6 . . . . .47 A8
Tyn-y-Coed La CF15 . . .157 B1
Tyn-y-Cwm Rd
- NP11 . . . . .141 C8
Tyn-y-twr SA12 . . . . . . .98 F6
Tyn-y-Waun Rd CF83 . .139 C3
Tyn-y-Waun Rd SA7 . . .69 F6
Tyn-y-Wern Ct CF83 . . .139 A6

Univ Coll Cardiff
- CF5 . . . . .177 A1
Univ Coll Cardiff Llys
- Tal-y-Bont** CF14 . . . . .177 A2
Univ Coll Humanities Bldg
- CF10 . . . . .194 F8
Univ Coll Law Bldg
- CF10 . . . . .195 A7
Univ Coll of Swansea
- SA2 . . . . .94 D4
Univ Coll of Swansea (Dept of Bot & Microbiology) SA2 . . .94 A8
Univ Coll of Wales
- NP18 . . . . .118 A3
Univ Coll Redwood Bldg
- CF10 . . . . .194 F7
Univ Coll Sch of Home Economics CF10 . . . . .195 A7
Univ Hall CF23 . . . . . . .178 C3
Univ of Glamorgan
- CF37 . . . . .135 C8
Univ of Wales CF10 .195 A7
Univ of Wales Coll
- Newport NP19 . . . . . . .143 D6
- Newport NP20 . . . . . . .142 F5
Univ of Wales Inst Cardiff
- Cardiff CF23 . . . . .178 D4
- Cardiff CF23 . . . . .178 E1
- Cardiff CF24 . . . . .195 C6
Univ of Wales Inst of Science & Tech
- Cardiff CF10 . . . . .194 F7
Univ of Wales, Coll of
- Cardiff CF24 . . . . .195 B6
Universal St CF11 . . . . .194 F4
University Hospl of Wales
- CF14 . . . . .177 F3
University Pl CF24 . . . .195 E6
Uphill Cl CF44 . . . . .216 B6
Uphill Rd CF3 . . . . .179 B5
Upland Dr NP4 . . . . . . .38 B1
Upland Rd Neath SA11 .71 F6
**Pontllanfraith NP12 . . . .86 B4
Uplands Gowerton SA4 .66 B5
Gwaun-Cae-Gurwen
- SA18 . . . . .220 D5
**Newbridge NP11 . . . . . .86 F7
**Ton Pentre CF41 . . . . . .79 B3
Uplands Cres
- Llandough CF64 . . . . . .206 C6
- Swansea SA2 . . . . .94 F6
Uplands Ct
- **8** Newport NP19 . . . .143 F6
- Rogerstone NP10 . . . . .141 D6
Uplands Dr CF34 . . . . .101 E5
Uplands Rd
- Cardiff CF3 . . . . .179 A2
- Pontardawe SA8 . . . . . .23 D4
Uplands Terr
- Cwmbran NP44 . . . . . . .89 C3
- Swansea SA2 . . . . .94 F6
- Swansea SA8 . . . . .68 F8
Uplands The
- Newbridge NP11 . . . . . .86 F7
- Port Talbot SA12 . . . . . .73 A1
- Radyr CF15 . . . . .176 C6
- Rogerstone NP10 . . . . .141 F6
Upper Adare St
- CF32 . . . . .103 D8
Upper Alma Pl CF41 . . .78 F5
Upper Alma Terr
- CF35 . . . . .135 D8
Upper Arail St SA13 . . .36 B3
Upper Banks Sta SA1 . .69 A4
Upper Boat Ind Pk
- CF37 . . . . .136 C4
Upper Bridge St NP4 . .62 C6
Upper Brynhyfryd Terr
- CF83 . . . . .110 F3
Upper Canning St
- CF41 . . . . .79 F3
Upper Capel St CF81 . . .57 F4
Upper Church Pk
- SA3 . . . . .123 B4
Upper Church St
- Bargoed CF81 . . . . .57 F4
- **3** Pontypridd CF37 . . .109 C1
Upper Clifton St 8
- CF24 . . . . .195 D2
Upper Coedcae Rd
- NP4 . . . . .17 D7
Upper Colbren Rd
- SA18 . . . . .220 D6
Upper Colliers' Row
- Heolgerrig CF48 . . . . . . .10 B1
- Merthyr Tydfil CF48 . . . .30 C8
Upper Cosmeston Farm
- CF64 . . . . .217 A7
Upper Court Terr
- NP13 . . . . .60 B6
Upper Cross Rd SA14 . .35 A1
Upper Cross St SA25 . .33 D3
Upper Cwmbran Rd
- NP44 . . . . .89 C6
Upper Cwmbran Rd
- NP44 . . . . .89 B8
Upper Dock St NP20 .143 C5
Upper Edward St 7
- CF41 . . . . .10 D2
Upper Elizabeth St
- CF48 . . . . .11 A4
Upper Fforest Way
- Swansea SA6 . . . . .46 E4
- Swansea SA6 . . . . .69 B8
Upper Forest Level
- CF45 . . . . .54 E2

U

Ullswater Ave CF23 . . .178 A3
Ullswater Cres SA6 . . . .68 E7
Ullswater Ct NP44 . . . . .89 C3
Under Cardiff Rd
- CF81 . . . . .58 A3
Underhill Dr CF38 . . . .136 A1
Underhill La SA3 . . . . . .231 B4
Underhill Mans 3
- CF14 . . . . .176 F6
Underhill Villas CF44 . .53 B8
Underwood CF83 . . . . .138 B1
Underwood Ave CF82 .85 A1
Underwood Rd
- Blackwood NP12 . . . . . .86 A8
- Tonna SA10 . . . . .49 A3
Underwood Terr
- Abertridwr CF83 . . . . . .137 B7
- Cardiff CF24 . . . . .195 C5
Union Bldgs SA15 . . . . .40 D7
Union Pl
- Merthyr Tydfil CF47 . . . .10 F1
- Tylorstown CF43 . . . . . .80 B4
Union St
- Aberdare CF44 . . . . .28 F4
- Aberychan NP4 . . . . . . .37 F3
- Ammanford SA18 . . . . .219 C2
- Ferndale CF43 . . . . .79 F6
- Merthyr Tydfil CF47 . . . .10 E1
- **8** Mountain Ash CF45 .54 D3
- Pontllotyn CF81 . . . . . . .12 F1
- Pontypridd CF37 . . . . . .135 C8
- Swansea SA1 . . . . .95 C6
- Ton Pentre CF41 . . . . . .79 B3
- Tredegar NP22 . . . . .11 D6
United World Coll of the Atlantic CF61 . . . . . .208 F5
Unity St CF44 . . . . .28 F1
Univ Coll (Dept of Music)
- CF10 . . . . .194 F7

Upper Francis St
CF83 ....136 F7
Upper Garn Terr NP44 .16 F8
Upper Gendros Cres
SA5 ....68 A3
Upper Gertrude St
CF45 ....82 E2
Upper Glyn Gwyn St
Bedwas CF83 ....139 A7
Bedwas CF83 ....139 A7
Bedwas CF83 ....139 A7
Upper Griffin St NP13 .36 C3
Upper Gwastad Terr
NP13 ....36 C8
Upper Gwyddon Rd
NP11 ....87 B2
Upper Gynor Pl
CF39 ....107 E5
Upper Heathfield Rd
SA8 ....23 E6
Upper High St
Bargoed CF81 ....58 A4
Bedlinog CF46 ....56 A7
Merthyr Tydfil CF48 .225 F3
Rhymney NP22 ....12 E6
Upper Hill St NP4 ...17 D6
Upper Inkerman St ▋
SA15 ....40 D5
Upper James St NP12 .58 F4
Upper Kincraig St
CF24 ....195 C8
Upper King's Head Rd
SA5 ....67 A4
Upper Mdw CF5 ......193 B3
Upper Mill SA15 ....40 E6
Upper Mill Rd SA4 ...19 D4
Upper Mount Pleasant ▋
CF48 ....31 C1
Upper North Rd CF81 .57 F5
Upper Park St ▌
SA15 ....40 D5
Upper Park Terr 62 C6
Upper Power St
NP20 ....143 B7
Upper Rd NP24 ....34 A1
Upper Regent St ▐▌
CF44 ....29 A1
Upper Rhymney Prim &
Inf Schs NP22 ....12 E5
Upper Robinson St ▐▐
SA15 ....40 E5
Upper Row CF44 ......11 B5
Upper Royal La NP13 .36 A1
Upper Salisbury St
NP22 ....13 E6
Upper St NP24 ....101 F3
Upper St Alban's Rd
CF42 ....50 D3
Upper Stanley Terr
NP44 ....33 F2
Upper Station Rd ▐
SA18 ....220 B8
Upper Strand SA1 .....68 D1
Upper Taft Cl SA1 ....50 F1
Upper Tennyson Rd
NP19 ....144 A5
Upper Terr CF43 ......80 C2
Upper Thomas St ▋
CF47 ....10 E1
Upper Trelyn Rd
NP12 ....85 D4
Upper Tribute Ave
NP11 ....114 C8
Upper Trosnant St
NP4 ....62 C6
Upper Ty' n-y-parc Terr
CF14 ....177 B6
Upper Union St CF48 .11 B8
Upper Vaughan St ▐
CF37 ....109 B1
Upper Viaduct Terr
NP11 ....60 A2
Upper Wain St NP4 ...17 C7
Upper West End ▋
SA13 ....125 C6
Upper William St ▐
SA15 ....40 E5
Upper Wood St CF81 .57 F3
Upper Woodland St
NP4 ....17 D7
Uppercliff Cl CF3 ....207 C5
Uppercliff Dr CF64 ..207 C5
Uppingham Ct CF5 ..193 E6
Upton La CF47 ....142 F4
Upton Pl CF38 ....156 A6
Upton Rd NP20 ......142 F4
Upton St
Blaengwynfi SA13 .....76 C6
Porth CF39 ....107 E4
Upton Terr
Swansea SA1 ....96 A7
Tonypandy CF40 ....106 D8
Urban St CF47 ....10 F4
Usk Cl Cwmbran NP44 .89 B4
Caerphilly CF83 .....177 A6
Usk Pl
Cwmrhydyceirw SA6 .46 A5
Blaenavon NP23 ......7 C5
Usk Rd Bargoed CF81 .57 F1
Caerleon NP18 ......118 C3
Cardiff CF14 ....178 A8
Pontypool NP4 ....39 D3
Pontypool NP4 ....62 F6
Usk St NP19 ....143 D6
Usk Vale Cl NP18 ...118 B3
Usk Vale Ct NP4 ......62 F6
Usk Vale Dr NP18 ...118 B3
Usk Vale Mews
NP18 ....118 B3
Usk View NP19 ......144 A6

Usk Way Barry CF62 .214 C6
Newport NP20 ....143 D1
Uskley Ct CF3 ....179 E6
Uxilla Terr CF31 .....169 A3

V

Vachell Ct CF61 .....210 B6
Vachell Rd CF5 ......193 D5
Vaendre Cl CF3 ......162 A1
Vaindre Cl ▐ CF3 ...180 A8
Vaindre Dr ▐ CF3 ...180 A8
Vaindre La
Cardiff CF3 ....179 F8
Cardiff CF3 ....180 A8
Valarian Cl CF3 .....180 B6
Vale Ct
Cowbridge CF71 .....189 A1
Dinas Powys CF64 ..206 B3
Vale Ent Ctr CF64 ...215 F5
Vale Gdns CF37 .....109 B2
Vale Of Neath Bsns Pk
SA10 ....48 E1
Vale Of Wern Terr
SA1 ....96 B7
Vale Rd CF24 ....195 C7
Vale Reach CF35 ....152 E2
Vale St SA62 ....214 C3
Vale Terr NP22 ....13 F5
Vale Veiw NP19 .....144 A7
Vale View
Bargoed CF81 ....57 F2
Barry CF62 ....214 D8
Bridgend CF31 ......169 C6
Ebbw Vale NP23 ......7 A4
Vale View Cl CF44 ..206 D6
Vale View Cres CF44 .206 D6
Vale View Rd CF45 ..81 E8
Vale View Terr CF45 .81 E8
Valegate Ret Pk CF5 .192 F2
Valentine Rd NP4 .....38 A3
Valeview Terr CF47 .104 F7
Valley Inheritance Mus
The NP4 ....62 C7
Valley Rd NP23 ....7 D1
Valley View
Abertillery NP13 ......59 F6
Bryn NP12 ....85 E3
Cardiff CF14 ....179 E4
Cefn Hengoed CF82 ..84 F5
Neath SA11 ....62 A2
Vicarage Terr
Abercynon NP4 ....38 A5
Maesteg CF34 ....101 F3
Treorchy CF42 ....95 E7
Vickery Ho ▐▐ SA12 .98 F1
Victor Cl CF64 ....207 A3
Victor St CF5 ....194 C2
Victoria Ave
Cardiff CF5 ....194 B6
Mumbles SA3 ....123 A5
Newport NP19 ....143 F6
Penarth CF64 ....207 A3
Porthcawl CF36 ......182 A6
Swansea SA1 ....95 A5
Victoria Bldgs
Abercarn NP11 ....87 A2
Cwmfelin CF32 ......150 C8
1 Troedyrhiw CF48 ..31 C1
Victoria Cl ▐▐ NP20 .143 C4
Victoria Cres NP20 .143 B4
Victoria Ct
Mumbles SA3 ....122 D4
Newport NP19 ....143 D5
Victoria Gdns SA11 ..71 E7
Victoria La NP19 ....143 F6
Victoria Mews
▋ Cardiff CF14 .....177 E2
Pontyclun CF72 .....173 B8
Victoria Park Rd E
CF5 ....215 C6
Victoria Park Rd W
CF5 ....194 B6
Victoria Pl
Aberystwyth NP4 .....37 F5
Bargoed CF81 ....58 A2
▐ Newport NP20 ...143 C4
Victoria Prim Sch
Aberystwyth NP4 .....37 F4
Penarth CF64 ....206 F4
Victoria Quay SA1 ...95 D6
Victoria Rd
Aberystwyth NP4 .....37 F5
Abertillery NP13 ......36 B1
Aberystwyth NP4 .....37 F4
Cardiff CF14 ....177 A5
Ebbw Vale NP23 ......14 D5
Fleur De Lis NP12 ....85 A4
Gowerton SA4 ....66 B7
▐ Newport NP20 ...143 C4
Pen-clawdd SA4 ......64 E3
Penarth CF64 ....207 A3
Pontypool NP4 ....62 D5
Port Talbot SA12 ....124 E8
Pyle CF33 ....148 D3
Rhymney NP22 ....12 C4
Waunarlwydd SA5 ....65 E6

Verdi Rd SA12 ....98 B2
Vere Pl CF81 ....58 A1
Vere St Bargoed CF81 .58 A1
Barry CF63 ....215 C6
Cardiff CF24 ....195 C7
Verig St SA5 ....68 C3
Verland Cl CF5 ......194 A8
Verland Ct CF5 ....194 A8
Verland Way CF5 ....170 C8
Verlands The CF71 ..188 D2
Verlon Cl CF63 ......215 E7
Vermeer Cres NP44 .111 A7
Vernon Cl
Merthyr Tydfil CF47 ..10 F2
Pontllanfraith 44 A5
Vernon Pl
Blackwood NP11 .....59 D1
Briton Ferry SA11 ...71 B1
Vernon Rd CF36 .....183 A7
Vernon St
Bridgend CF31 ......169 A5
Briton Ferry SA11 ...71 C2
Swansea SA1 ....68 D1
Verona Pl CF63 ......215 C7
Verona Cl NP10 .....142 B3
Versil Terr SA4 ....65 F8
Vervain Cl CF5 ......193 A5
Verwey Rd NP23 .....15 D8
Vetch Field (Swansea City
Fball Gd SA1 ....95 C6
Viaduct Rd
Aberystwyth NP4 .....37 E5
Bridgend CF31 ......215 B4
Viaduct Terr NP11 ....60 A2
Vibernum Rise CF38 .156 C5
Vicarage Cl
Bargoed CF81 ....57 F4
Bassaleg NP10 ......142 B2
Ystrad CF41 ....107 A4
Vicarage Ct CF38 ...135 F2
Vicarage Dr SA8 ......23 F6
Vicarage Gdns
Marshfield CF3 ......162 D1
Rogerstone NP10 ...141 F6
Vicarage Hill NP20 .143 B4
Vicarage La
Abercynon NP4 ....37 F5
Bargoed CF81 ....57 F4
Pontllanfraith CF81 ..32 F8
Swansea SA5 ....68 A2
Vicarage Rd
Ebbw Vale NP23 ....123 B4
Mumbles SA3 ....123 A8
Penarth CF64 ....207 B3
Villas The
Markham NP12 ....58 D7
Newbridge NP11 ......86 E6
Villiers Ct
Briton Ferry SA11 ...71 B1
▐ Port Talbot SA12 .99 B1
Villiers Rd
Ammanford SA18 ...219 B6
Blaengwynfi SA13 ...76 C6
Swansea SA1 ....71 A7
Villiers St
Briton Ferry SA11 ...71 C1
Port Talbot SA12 .....99 C1
Swansea SA1 ....68 D1
Vincent Ave NP23 .....8 D1
Vincent Cl CF63 .....215 C7
Vincent Ct CF5 ......193 E5
Vincent Rd CF47 .....10 D2
Vincent Rd CF5 .....193 E5
Vincent St
▋ Blaenavon NP4 ...17 C7
Swansea SA1 ....95 B6
Vine Pl ▐ NP19 ....143 E6
Vine Row SA9 ....2 A6
Vine St NP11 ....87 B3
Viola Rd SA12 ....98 C2
Violet Cl CF14 ....177 D4
Violet Row CF24 .....195 B8
Violet St CF44 ....53 B8
Violet Wlk NP10 ....141 D7
Virgil St SA1 ....194 E3
Virginia Cl CF83 ....138 B4
Virginia View CF83 .138 B4
Virtumu Jones A Jun &
Inf Sch CF44 ....4 C3
Vishwell Rd
Cardiff CF5 ....194 B7
Wenvoe CF5 ....205 A5
Vista Ct ▐ CF64 ....207 B5
Viola Rise CF5 ......176 D2
Vivian Cl SA3 ....36 C3
Vivian Ct
Aberavon SA12 .....124 F8
Swansea SA12 ....94 D7
Vivian Mans SA2 .....94 D7
Vivian Rd SA12 ....98 D2
Vivian Park
Newport NP19 ....143 E4
Swansea SA2 ....94 D7
Vivian St
Abertillery NP13 ......36 B4
Tylorstown CF43 ......80 B3
Vivian Terr SA12 .....98 F1
Voss Park Cl CF61 ..210 B6
Voss Park Dr CF61 ..210 B6
Voylart Cl SA2 ....93 C8
Voylart Rd SA2 ....93 C8
Voysey Pl CF5 ....193 C7
Vulcan Rd CF47 ......10 D2

Victoria Row SA4 .....64 E4

W

Wade Ave SA9 ....2 B6
Wades The ▐▐ NP44 ..89 B1
Waen-Fawr NP44 ......8 B2
Waengron NP13 ....15 E5
Wagner Rd SA12 ......98 B3
Wagtail Rd CF62 ....210 E6
Wain Cl CF23 ....161 B1
Wainfelin Ave NP4 ...62 B7
Wainfelin Rd NP4 ....62 B7
Wakehurst Pl CF3 ...179 F7
Walden Grange Cl
NP19 ....144 B5
Waldhof Ct SA4 ....67 E7
Walford Davies Dr
NP19 ....144 C5
Walford Pl CF11 .....194 D5
Walford St NP20 ....143 B7
Walk Farm Dr CF3 ..168 E1
Walk The
Cardiff CF44 ....29 B3
Cardiff CF24 ....179 D4
Walk La SA6 ....69 A7
Water St
Aberavon SA12 .....125 A8
Bridgend CF31 ......168 C3
Gwaun-Cae-Gurwen
SA18 ....220 D6
Llanelli SA15 ....40 D6
Margam SA13 ....147 C4
Monksash CF71 .....198 C2
Neath SA11 ....71 E8
Waterfall Cotts
SA13 ....125 D6
Waterfall Mews
CF61 ....210 A4
Waterfall Rd SA11 ..226 D4
Waterfall Terr SA11 .226 D4
Waterfalls Wlk SA11 .223 E2
Waterford Ct CF11 ..194 E4
Waterhall Rd
Cardiff CF5 ....176 D2
Cardiff CF5 ....148 C3
Waterhouse Dr CF11 .194 E3
Waterloo NP12 ....59 B2
Waterloo Cl ▐ CF23 .178 E1
Waterloo Ct NP4 .....89 E8
Waterloo Gdns CF23 .195 D8
Waterloo Pl
Aberdare CF44 ....28 F4
Aberystwyth NP4 .....37 E4
Machen CF83 ....139 D5
Swansea SA2 ....94 F5
Waterloo Rd
Abercynon NP4 ....37 F4
Cardiff CF23 ....178 D1
Newport NP20 ......143 A3
Penygroes SA14,SA18 218 D7
Waterloo St
Aberdare CF44 ....29 F1
Llanelli SA15 ....40 D4
Neath SA11 ....71 D5
Waterloo Terr Rd
CF23 ....139 D5
Waters La NP20 .....143 C5
Waterside Cl NP12 ..142 A7
Waterside Ct
Cwmbran NP44 ....89 E2
Newport NP20 ......143 C8
Waterside Wlk W
NP44 ....142 A6
Waterston Rd CF14 .177 B2
Waterton Cross
CF31 ....169 B2
Waterton Ind Est
CF31 ....169 E2
Waterton Rd
Bridgend CF31 ......169 D2
Bridgend CF31 ......169 F3
Waterworks La NP4 ..38 A5
Watery La CF71 .....189 D5
Watford Cl CF3 ......137 F1
Watford Rd
Caerphilly CF83 .....158 F8
Cardiff CF24 ....195 F8
Watford Rise CF83 ..138 A1
Watkin La ▐ NP20 ..142 F4
Watkins Terr SA9 ...222 B6
Watson Rd CF14 ....177 A2
Watson Row CF81 ....57 B8
Watson St CF63 .....215 A5
Watson Terr CF81 ....57 B8
Watton Cl CF14 .....177 D8
Watts Cl NP10 ......142 B6
Waun Ave SA13 .....227 C1
Waun Bant Rd CF32 .148 D2
Waun Borfa Rd NP22 .85 C8
Waun Cl CF83 ....38 A2
Waun Daniel SA8 .....24 B2
Waun Dew NP23 ....7 F4
Waun Erw CF83 .....138 B5
Waun Fach CF23 ....178 E2
Waun Fach Terr
CF83 ....104 F5
Waun Fawr NP23 ......7 F4
Waun Ganol St CF83 .138 B4
Waun Goch Rd CF83 .84 C5
Waun Goch District
NP23 ....7 D4
Waun Gorse Terr
Ebbw Vale NP23 ......7 D4
Nant-y-Moel CF32 ..104 F5

Waun Gron
Llantwit Major CF61 ....210 A7
Pontardawe SA8 ....25 D8
Waun Gyrlais SA9 ....222 A6
Waun Hir CF38 ....156 F5
Waun Hywel Rd NP44 ...89 C6
Waun Illtuds CF61 ....210 A7
Waun Las SA10 ....48 C1
Waun Lee Ct CF23 ....178 E8
Waun Lwyd Terr
CF32 ....104 F5
Waun Newydd CF35 .152 B5
Waun Penlan SA8 .....23 D7
Waun Rd
Cwmbran NP44 ....89 C1
Llanelli SA15 ....40 D7
Loughor SA4 ....65 F8
Morriston SA6 ....46 A2
Swansea SA6 ....45 F2
Tonypandy CF40 ......106 D6
Waun St SA13 ....176 A5
Waun The SA12 ....99 F6
Waun Wen
Cwmavon SA12 ....99 F6
Porth CF39 ....107 E4
Waun Wen Prim Sch
SA1 ....68 C2
Waun Wen Terr
CF32 ....104 F5
Waun y Felin SA4 .....65 A4
Waun-Ebbw Bglws
NP23 ....8 B2
Waun-Ebbw Rd NP23 ..8 B2
Waun-Fawr Rd
CF14 ....177 D6
Waun-Gron Cl SA5 ....68 C6
Waun-Gron Park Halt
CF5 ....193 F7
Waun-Gron Rd
Cardiff CF5 ....193 F7
Cardiff CF5 ....194 A7
Swansea SA5 ....68 C6
Ammanford SA18 .....219 D6
Waun-Wen Rd SA1 ....68 C1
Waun-Wen Terr SA1 ..68 C1
Waun-y-Groes Ave
CF14 ....177 D7
Waun-y-Groes Rd
CF14 ....177 D7
Waun-y-Pistyll SA5 ...68 C6
Waun-y-Pound Ind Est
NP23 ....7 A2
Waun-y-Pound Rd
NP23 ....7 B2
Waunarlwydd Prim Sch
SA5 ....66 D3
Waunarlwydd Rd SA2,
SA5 ....66 F2
Waunbant Ct CF44 ...225 F2
Waunceirch Prim Sch
SA10 ....48 C2
Waunddu NP44 ....61 F8
Waundeg NP22 ....6 B2
Waunfach CF32 ....129 E3
Waunfach Flats
CF83 ....138 A4
Waunfach St CF83 ....138 A4
Waunfain CF83 ....137 F6
Waunfarlais Rd
SA18 ....219 A8
Waunfawr SA18 ....219 A7
Waunfawr Gdns
NP11 ....114 C4
Waunfawr Jun Sch
NP11 ....114 C4
Waunfawr Park Rd
NP11 ....114 C4
Waunfawr Terr
NP11 ....114 C4
Waungoch Rd NP12 ...59 C1
Waungron
Bettws CF32 ....129 E3
Glynneath SA11 ......223 D1
Waungron Rd SA6 ....46 D8
Waunhafog Rd SA18 219 A8
Waunheulog NP23 ....23 B1
Waunllanyrafon SA15 .40 C5
Waunllwydion SA18 ..220 D7
Waunlapria NP7 ......9 A5
Waunllwyd 2 CF44 ...28 A6
Waunllwyn Cres
NP12 ....85 D7
Waunlon CF36 ....183 C8
Waunlwyd Jun & Inf Sch
NP23 ....14 F3
Waunrhydd Rd CF39 133 B5
Waunscil Ave CF5 ....169 A4
Wauntreoda Rd
CF14 ....177 C4
Wavell Cl CF14 ......177 F6
Wavell Dr NP20 ......117 A3
Waveney Cl NP20 ....116 C2
Waverley Cl CF64 ....206 E6
Waverley Ct CF63 ....213 A4
Waverley Dr SA3 .....123 A5
Waverley Sq CF10 ...195 B1
Waverley St SA6 .....46 D7
Waverley Pk SA6 ....46 F8
Waycock Cross CF62 214 B6
Waycock Rd CF62 ....214 C4
Wayfield Cres NP44 ..89 E5
Wayne Cotts CF44 ...53 C7
Wayne St
Aberdare CF44 ....28 F3
Porth CF39 ....107 E4

Wayne St continued
Trehafod CF37 ....108 C2
Weare Cl NP20 ....116 C2
Weatheral St 4 CF44 .29 C2
Weavers Ho 6 SA1 ...95 E6
Webb Pl SA12 ....124 E7
Webbons Way SA1 ...67 F2
Webley Cl NP18 .....118 A4
Webley Gdns NP18 ..118 A4
Webster St CF46 .....83 B7
Wedal Rd CF14 ......194 C1
Wedgewood Ct
CF83 ....138 D3
Wedmore Rd CF11 ...194 E4
Wednesbury St
NP19 ....143 F4
Weekes Cl SA1 ......179 D7
Weig Fach La SA5 ...67 D3
Weig Gdns SA5 ......68 A4
Weig La SA5 ....67 F3
Weig Rd SA5 ....67 F3
Weir View NP22 ......67 F3
Welby Rd 4 CF5 ....194 D5
Welcome La SA1 .....118 A4
Welford St CF62 .....214 D3
Well Field SA2 ....93 E8
Well La CF5 ....191 F2
Well Pl CF44 ....29 D1
Well Rd CF62 ....212 A2
Well St
Abercynon CF45 ......82 D2
Brynmawr NP23 ......8 B4
Cefn Coed CF48 .....10 B4
Laleston CF32 ....167 H4
Merthyr Tydfil CF47 ...10 D2
Porthcawl CF36 .....182 F6
Well The CF32 ......167 E4
Welland Circ NP20 ..116 C2
Welland Cres NP20 ..116 C2
Wellfield
Beddau CF38 ....156 A8
Bishopston SA3 .....121 F6
Resolven SA11 ......226 D4
Wellfield Ave
Neath SA11 ....71 F6
Porthcawl CF36 .....183 A7
Wellfield Cl SA4 .....43 A8
Wellfield Cres CF36 .183 A7
Wellfield Ct
Barry CF63 ....205 B1
Church Village CF38 .135 E1
Marshfield CF3 ......180 D8
Wellfield La NP4 .....62 D1
Wellfield Mews
CF38 ....156 A8
Wellfield Pl 2 CF24 .195 C8
Wellfield Rd
Aberavon SA12 ......99 A2
Cardiff CF24 ....178 C1
Marshfield CF3 ......180 E8
Wellfield Sq CF38 ....59 D2
Wellington Ct
CF11 ....194 E5
Wellington Dr NP44 .89 A3
Wellington Mews
CF11 ....194 E5
Wellington Pl 11
SA12 ....124 F8
Wellington Rd
Abersychan NP4 .....37 E4
Newport NP20 ....142 D3
Wellington St
Aberdare CF44 ......29 A3
Cardiff CF11 ....194 E5
Swansea SA1 ....158 C1
Wellington Terr NP24 .33 F1
Wellington Way NP22 12 F2
Wellpark Cl CF47 ....10 D6
Wellright Rd CF5 ....193 D7
Wells Cl Baglan SA12 .98 E5
Newport NP20 ......142 E1
Wells Rd SA12 ....98 E5
Wells St CF11 ....194 E5
Wellspring Terr
NP11 ....115 A1
Wellwood CF23 .....178 E8
Wellwood Dr CF44 ...206 A2
Welsh Coll of Music &
Drama (Coleg Cerdd a
Drama Cymru)
CF10 ....194 F6
Welsh Folk Mus CF5 192 F7
Welsh Hawking Ctr
CF62 ....214 A7
Welsh Ind & Maritime
Mus CF10 ....195 C1
Welsh Inst of Sport
(Athrofa Chwaraeon
Cymru) CF11 ....194 F7
Welsh Miners Mus
CF24 ....195 D4
Welsh Office CF10 ...194 F7
Welwyn Rd CF14 ....177 C5
Wembley SA11 ....71 D4
Wembley Ave SA10 ..222 F5
Wembley Rd
Cardiff CF5 ....194 C5
Ystalyfera SA9 ......2 A6
Wenallt Ct
Aberdare CF44 .....29 B3
Cardiff CF14 ....177 B8

Wenallt Rd
Caerphilly CF83 .....137 E3
Cardiff CF14, CF83 .159 A3
Tonna SA11 ....49 D2
Wengraig Rd CF40 ..106 F5
Wenham Pl SA11 ....71 F7
Wentlloog Rd
Cardiff CF3 ....179 B3
Cardiff CF3 ....179 D3
Peterstone Wentlooge
CF3 ....180 C3
Wentloog Ave
Cardiff CF3 ....179 F2
Cardiff CF3 ....179 F2
Wentloog Cl
Cardiff CF3 ....179 F2
Cwmbran NP44 ......89 E3
Wentloog Corporate Ind
Pk CF3 ....179 F4
Wentloog Cres CF3 ..179 B3
Wentsland Cres NP4 .62 A6
Wentsland Rd NP4 ...62 A6
Wentwood Cl NP44 ..89 C3
Wentwood Rd NP18 117 E2
Wentworth Cl
Bassaleg NP10 ......141 F3
Cardiff CF3 ....180 A8
Wentworth Cres SA3 .93 E1
Wentworth La CF3 ...180 A8
Wenvoe Cl CF5 ......205 A6
Wenvoe Ct 5 CF5 ...193 C4
Wenvoe Terr CF62 ..214 D4
Weobley Castle SA3 227 B3
Weobley Ct SA1 .....67 F6
Werfa Cl CF44 ......29 D4
Werfa La CF44 ......29 D3
Werfa St CF23 ......178 B1
Wern Cres Neath SA10 70 E5
Nelson CF46 ....83 F4
Wern Ddu CF32 .....160 D1
Wern Deg CF35 .....170 D8
Wern Fach Ct NP44 115 F8
Wern Fawr La CF3 ..179 E8
Wern Fawr Rd
Pencoed CF35 ....152 E5
Swansea SA1 ....96 E4
Wern Fraith SA10 ...48 C1
Wern Gethin La CF3 179 F6
Wern Goch E
Cardiff CF23 ....178 D5
Cardiff CF14 ....178 C5
Wern Goch W CF23 178 D6
Wern Hill NP4 ......62 C1
Wern Ind Est
Rogerstone NP10 ...141 F5
Rogerstone NP10 ...142 A5
Wern Isaf CF48 .....11 C5
Wern La CF48 ....30 C8
Wern Olau SA10 ....49 B6
Wern Rd
Cefn Coed CF48 .....10 A4
Glanaman SA18 .....220 B8
Llanelli SA15 ....40 E5
Llanmorlais SA4 ....64 C1
Margam SA13 ......125 E4
Neath SA10 ....70 E2
Pontypool NP4 ......62 E1
Swansea SA1 ....68 D4
Tonypandy CF40 ....106 C5
Ystalyfera SA9 ......2 A6
Wern School Cl NP4 .62 E1
Wern St CF40 ....106 B7
Wern Terr
Ammanford SA18 ...219 D6
Cymmer SA13 ....75 D4
Pontypool NP4 ......62 B6
Rogerstone NP10 ...141 F6
Swansea SA1 ....96 C7
Wern View SA11 ....73 A2
Wern-Ddu La SA18 ..219 C7
Wern-Ddu Rd SA18 ..219 D8
Wern-Ddu Row
CF83 ....138 E1
Wernddu Ct CF83 ...138 D2
Werngoch Rd CF23 ..178 C6
Wernlys Rd CF31 ....150 D1
Wernoleu Rd SA18 ..219 C7
Wernwood Rd SA9 ...2 B6
Wesley Ave CF62 ....212 F1
Wesley Bldgs NP23 ..8 C2
Wesley Cl
Abernant SA18 .....89 D2
Dowlais CF48 ....11 A4
Wesley Ct Cardiff CF3 179 C5
Dinas Powys CF64 ..206 A3
Wesley Hill CF83 ....139 F7
Wesley La CF10 .....195 B5
Wesley Pl
Merthyr Vale CF48 ..55 D4
Risca NP11 ....114 F1
Treorchy CF41 ......79 A4
Wesley Rd
Blackwood NP12 ....85 E7
Caerphilly CF83 .....137 D1
Wesley St
Abercynon CF45 .....82 D2
Carmarthen NP44 ..89 E2
Llantwit Major CF61 209 F6
Maesteg CF34 ......75 B1
Wesley Terr
Abertillery NP11 ...114 F4
Pontypool NP4 .....62 D7
Wesleyan Flats CF39 107 F4
Wesleyan Pl NP23 ..7 D4
Wesleyan Row NP23 .7 D1
Wessex Pl CF62 .....214 C2
Wessex St CF5 ......194 B6
West Acre CF61 .....210 B8

West Ave
Caerphilly CF83 .....137 E3
Cefn Cribwr CF32 ...140 B2
Maesycwmmer CF82 ..85 B2
Pontypool NP4 ......62 C6
West Bank
Abertillery NP13 .....36 B8
Llanyravon NP44 ....90 B2
West Bank Cl 1 NP44 .38 A1
West Bute St CF10 ..195 C2
West Canal Wharf 6
CF10 ....195 A4
West Cl CF10 ....195 B2
West Cliff SA3 ....121 A3
West Crossways SA8 .23 D6
West Ct 2 CF64 .....207 A4
West Dr
Porthcawl CF36 .....182 E6
St Donat's CF61 ....208 F5
West End 4 Llanelli SA15 .40 C6
Pen-clawdd SA4 ....64 B4
Port Talbot SA13 ...125 C6
West End Ave
Pontypool NP4 .....37 F2
Porthcawl CF36 ....182 F5
West Farm Cl CF3 ..184 D2
West Farm Ct CF3 ..184 D2
West Farm Rd CF37 184 C2
West Gr Cardiff CF24 195 B4
Merthyr Tydfil CF47 ..10 D3
West Grove Ct 5
CF24 ....195 B6
West Hill NP22 ......13 D7
West Hill Rd NP4 ...38 B1
West House Rd
CF31 ....168 D4
West Lee CF11 ......194 E6
West Luton Pl 4
CF24 ....195 C5
West Market St
9 Newport NP20 ...143 D3
Newport NP20 .....143 D3
West Monmouth Sch
NP4 ....62 C5
West Mount Cres
CF38 ....136 A1
West Orchard Cres
CF5 ....194 A7
West Park Dr CF36 .165 E1
West Park La 1
NP20 ....142 F4
West Park Prim Sch
CF64 ....206 D8
West Park Rd NP20 142 F4
West Point Ind Est
CF64 ....206 D8
West Rd
Bridgend CF31 ......168 D4
Cardiff CF14 ....176 F3
Penyrheol CF82 ....85 D5
Porthcawl CF36 ....165 E2
West Rhondda CF32 129 F7
West Rise CF14 ....178 A8
West Roedin NP44 ..116 C8
West St
Abercynon CF45 .....82 E3
Aberkenfig CF32 ...150 C4
Bargoed CF81 ......17 F4
Gorseinon SA4 .....43 B1
Llantwit Major CF61 209 F6
Maesteg CF34 ......102 A2
Monknash CF71 ....198 C3
Newport NP20 ......143 B4
Pontypridd CF37 ...109 D2
Port Talbot SA13 ...125 C5
Waunarlwydd SA5 ..66 D3
West View
Bettws CF32 ....129 E1
Newbridge NP11 ...86 F6
Pentre CF41 ....155 B8
West View Cres
Blackwood NP12 ...59 A1
Trelewis CF46 .....83 D6
West View Terr
Abercarn NP4 .....87 B7
Ebbw Vale NP23 ..14 E6
West View Villas
CF81 ....58 E2
West Way (Ffordd y
Gorllewin) SA1 ....95 C6
West Wlk NP20 ....143 B1
West Wlk CF62 ....214 D6
Westbourne Cl
CF14 ....176 F4
Westbourne Ct
Cardiff CF3 ....179 C2
Penarth CF64 .....207 A1
Porthcawl CF36 ...182 E7
Westbourne Gr SA2 94 C7
Westbourne Pl
Merthyr Tydfil CF47 30 E7
Mumbles SA3 .....123 B4
Porthcawl CF36 ...182 E7
4 Troedyrhiw CF48 31 B1
Westbourne Rd
Cardiff CF14 ....176 F4
Penarth CF64 .....207 A2
Penrhiwtyn SA11 ..71 C4
Swansea SA2 .....94 C7
Westbourne Sch
Penarth CF64 .....207 A3
Penarth CF64 .....207 A4
Westbourne Terr
CF72 ....153 E2
Westbury Bglws SA15 40 E3
Westbury Cl CF61 ..215 B7
Westbury St
Llanelli SA15 ....40 E3

Westbury St continued
Swansea SA1 ....95 A6
Westbury Terr CF5 ..194 B5
Westcliff SA3 ....123 C3
Westcliff Mews SA3 123 C3
Westcross Ave SA3 123 A6
Westcross La SA3 ..122 F7
Westdale Rd SA5 ...40 C2
Western Arc CF62 ..214 E1
Western Ave
Bridgend CF31 ......169 C3
Brynmawr NP23 .....8 A4
Cardiff CF14,CF5 ..196 B8
Newport NP20 ......142 C3
Port Talbot SA12 ..98 C2
Western Ave N CF14 177 C2
Western Bsns Ctr
CF5 ....193 F6
Western Cl SA3 ....123 B4
Western Cres NP22 ..13 D7
Western Ct
10 Barry CF63 .....215 B6
Bridgend CF31 ......168 D4
Western Dr
Bargoed CF81 ......57 E2
Cardiff CF14 ....177 C2
Western Est
Caerleon NP18 .....118 B4
Caerphilly CF83 ....137 E2
Western La SA3 ....123 B4
Western Rd
Clydach SA6 ....46 C6
Pontardawe SA8 ...23 D4
Western St
Swansea SA1 ....95 B6
Trehafod CF37 .....108 D2
Western Terr
Abercarn NP11 .....114 B5
Blaengwynfi SA13 ..75 D5
Cwmfelinfach NP11 .113 A4
Ebbw Vale NP23 ...7 D1
Mardy CF43 ....152 D8
Western Valley Rd
NP10 ....142 C3
Westernmoor Rd
SA11 ....71 F6
Westfa Rd SA2 .....94 F7
Westfield Ave
Bridgend CF31 ......168 D5
Cardiff CF14 ....177 C5
Newport NP20 ......117 A2
Westfield Cl NP18 ..117 F4
Westfield Cres CF36 165 F1
Westfield Cres CF72 155 E2
Westfield Dr
Newport NP20 ......117 A2
Penarth CF64 ......206 E2
Westfield (Lower Specl)
Sch NP20 ....117 A2
Westfield Rd
Caerleon NP18 .....117 F3
Cardiff CF14 ....177 C4
Newport NP20 .....143 A5
Pontypridd CF37 ...109 C5
Westfield Specl Upper
Sch NP20 ....163 F8
Westfield Way NP20 117 A2
Westgate CF71 ......188 E2
Westgate Cl CF36 ..165 F1
Westgate St NP18 ..118 B2
Westgate St (Heol y
Porth) CF10 ....195 A5
Westgi Pen Ffordd
NP12 ....85 D8
Westgrove Ct SA4 ..43 B4
Westhill Dr CF72 ....155 E2
Westhill St CF61 ....209 F6
Westland Ave SA3 ..122 E7
Westland Cl
Cardiff CF24 ....196 A2
Loughor SA4 ....42 E1
Westlands SA12 ....98 D4
Westminster Cres
CF23 ....178 C7
Westminster Dr
Cardiff CF23 ....178 C8
Sully CF64 ....216 B5
Westminster Way
CF31 ....168 C6
Westmoor Cl NP19 .144 C3
Westmoreland St
CF5 ....194 C4
Weston Ave CF64 ..216 B4
Weston Rd
Tonypandy CF40 ....107 B1
Weston Sq CF63 ...215 C6
Weston St 7 CF63 ..215 B6
Weston Terr
Porth CF39 ....107 E6
Treorchy CF42 ......78 B4
Westray Cl NP19 ...143 F7
Westside Rd CF63 ..110 E2
Westview Terr
Abertillery NP11 ...36 C2
Caerphilly CF83 ...138 D5
Westville Rd NP20 ..33 B7
Westville Wlk 8 NP20 142 F4
Westward Cl
9 Newport NP20 ...142 F4
Westward Pl
Bridgend CF31 .....168 B6
Swansea SA1 ......94 A1

Westward Rise CF62 214 B3
Westwinds SA3 ......122 E3
Westwinds Cl SA5 ...66 E3
Westwood Ct 9
CF44 ....207 A4
Westwood Dr CF46 ..83 A6
Wexford Ct CF23 ....161 A2
Wharf La NP19 ......143 E5
Wharf Rd NP19 .....143 E5
Wharfedale Rd CF23 178 F8
Wharton Cl CF62 ..212 E2
Wharton St CF10 ...195 A5
Wheate Cl The CF62 213 A2
Wheatfield Terr SA1 .68 C1
Wheatley Ave SA12 124 E8
Wheatley Rd
Blackwood NP12 ....85 D8
Merthyr Tydfil CF47 ..30 F7
Wheatley Rd
Cardiff CF5 ....193 C5
Neath SA11 ....71 D4
Wheatsheaf Dr SA6 ..46 A4
Wheatsheaf La CF47 10 D1
Wheeler Ct CF24 ...195 E6
Wheeler St NP20 ...143 C6
Whimbrels The
CF36 ....182 D8
Whinberry Way CF5 193 A5
Whinchat Cl 8 CF3 180 A7
Whistle Rd NP4 .....9 D1
Whistler Cl NP19 ...145 F7
Whitaker Rd CF24 ..196 A8
Whitby Pl NP19 ....143 D6
Whitchurch High Sch
(Lower) CF14 ....177 B5
Whitchurch High Sch
(Upper) CF14 ....177 A5
Whitchurch Pl 1
CF24 ....178 A1
Whitchurch Psychiatric
Hospl CF14 ....176 F5
Whitchurch Rd CF14 177 F2
Whitchurch Sta
CF14 ....177 A6
Whitcliffe Dr CF64 ..217 B8
Whitcombe St 3
CF44 ....29 A2
White Ash Glade
NP18 ....117 F2
White Ave NP10 ....163 E5
White Barn Rd CF14 177 D8
White City Rd SA5 ..67 D4
White Cl SA12 ......95 B8
White Gates Ct SA10 71 A7
White Gr SA3 ....122 E7
White Hall La NP44 .90 B1
White Hart Cotts
CF34 ....128 B6
White Hart Dr CF83 139 E7
White Ho CF62 .....214 C1
White Horse CF19 ..36 B7
White House Cl
CF61 ....209 F5
White House Rd NP44 90 A5
White Lion Cotts NP22 .6 C2
White Oaks Dr CF3 .179 E8
White Rose Way NP24 33 E2
White St
Caerphilly CF83 .....138 B2
Dowlais CF48 ....11 A5
Swansea SA1 ....95 B7
White Walls SA1 ....95 D6
Whitecare Cl CF14 ..159 F2
Whitebeam Cl CF47 ..10 D3
Whitebrook Way
NP44 ....89 F2
Whitefield Cl SA11 ..223 C1
Whitefield Rd CF14 177 A2
Whitefield St CF41 ..78 D3
Whiteford Rd SA5 ...67 F6
Whitehall Ave CF3 ..179 B3
Whitehall Cl CF5 ...204 F7
Whitehall Par CF5 ..179 A3
Whitehall Pl CF3 ....179 A3
Whitehall St NP44 ..118 C1
Whitehead Cl CF37 109 B2
Whitehead St CF37 109 B2
Whitesands Rd CF14 159 D1
Whiteshell Dr SA3 ..122 E4
Whitestone Ave SA3 122 A5
Whitestone Cl SA3 ..122 A5
Whitestone Cty Prim Sch
SA3 ....122 E7
Whitestone La SA3 .122 E5
Whitethorn Ct SA4 ..67 F5
Whitethorn Dr CF33 169 B4
Whitethorn Pl SA2 ..94 B6
Whiteways CF61 ....210 B7
Whitewell Dr CF61 ..210 A5
Whitewell Rd CF62 .214 E7
Whitland
Cardiff CF5 ....176 D1
Swansea SA5 ....67 F6
Whitland Cres CF5 .176 E1
Whitley Rd SA4 .....42 F1
Whitmore Park Dr
CF62 ....214 C7
Whitson Rd NP19 ...144 B7
Whitstone Rd NP19 144 B6
Whittan Cl CF62 ....212 E1
Whitting St SA11 ...223 D1
Whitting Terr CF39 ..107 E5
Whittington St
Neath SA11 ....71 E6

Whittington St continued
Tonna SA11 ....49 D3
Whittington Terr SA4 .43 D2
Whittle Ct NP20 ....117 A3
Whittle Dr NP20 ....117 A3
Whittle Rd CF11 ....194 D3
Whitworth Ct CF11 ..194 F4
Whitworth Terr NP22 .13 F5
Wick & Warcross Prim
  Sch CF71 ....198 D5
Wick Rd
Castle-upon-Alun CF35 186 B4
Ewenny CF35 ......185 F7
Llantwit Major CF61 .199 B2
Llantwit Major CF61 .209 E7
Llantwit Major CF61 .209 E7
St Brides Major CF32 .185 D1
Wicken Cl CF3 .....180 A7
Wicklow Cl CF23 ...161 A1
Widecombe Dr CF3 .179 A3
Widgeon Cl CF36 ...165 E1
Wigan Terr CF22 ...151 A5
Wigmore Cl CF14 ..159 C5
Wild Gardens Rd
  CF23 ....178 B5
Wild Mill La CF31 ..168 E7
Wildbrook SA13 ...125 D8
Wilden Ave SA13 ..125 D5
Wildfowl & Wetlands Ctr
  SA14 ....41 C2
Wilfred Brook Ho
  CF11 ....194 F2
Wilfred St CF63 ...215 B5
Wilkins Terr
Caerphilly CF83 ....137 F6
Caerphilly CF83 ....138 A6
Wilkinson Cl CF24 .195 C5
Wilks Row 1 SA1 ..95 C8
Willenhall St NP19 .143 E4
Willesden Rd CF11 .168 C6
Willet Cl SA11 .....71 F8
William Adams Ct
  CF3 ....14 D8
William Belcher Dr
  CF3 ....180 A5
William Bowen Cl
  SA4 ....66 A5
William Brown Cl
  NP44 ....1 A7
William Ct
  5 Swansea SA1 ..95 C6
  Ystrad CF41 .....79 C3
William Dennis Ave
  SA4 ....66 A8
William Forbes Bnglws
  CF81 ....58 A6
William Harris Bglws
  CF83 ....137 A7
William Lovett Gdns 1
  NP20 ....143 B4
William Morris Dr 1
  NP19 ....144 D6
William Morris Gdns
  SA1 ....96 B7
William Nicholls Dr
  CF3 ....179 E8
William Pl CF39 ...107 E3
William St
Aberbargoed CF81 ..58 B4
Abercwmboi CF44 ..52 E4
Abercynon CF45 ....82 E2
Abertridwr CF83 ...137 A7
Bargoed CF81 ......58 A2
Bedwas CF83 ......139 A6
Cardiff CF11 ....194 D7
Cwm NP23 ....35 A7
Cwmfelinfach NP11 .113 B3
Fleur De Lis NP12 ..85 B5
5 Merthyr Tydfil CF47 .10 D2
6 Merthyr Tydfil CF47 .30 E8
Mumbles SA3 ....123 A5
Newbridge NP11 ....59 F1
Pontardawe SA8 ...23 B1
Pontycymer CF32 ..109 F5
Pontypridd CF37 ...109 F5
Porth CF39 ....107 F6
Swansea SA1 ......95 C6
Tir-y-Berth CF82 ...85 A6
Treherbert CF42 ...50 F2
Ystrad CF41 ....79 C3
Ystradgynlais SA9 ..2 E7
William Thomas Meml
  Chapel NP11 ....113 B3
Williams Ave SA11 .226 D5
Williams Cl
  CF32 ....150 E6
Williams Cl 8 NP20 .143 C3
Williams Cres
Barry CF62 ....214 E5
Sarn CF32 ....150 F5
Williams Pl
Merthyr Tydfil CF47 .10 F3
Upper Boat CF37 ...136 C3
Williams St
Blackwood NP12 ....85 F7
Brynna CF72 ....153 C3
Hollybush NP12 ....34 D4
Pontarddulais SA4 ..19 C4
Tonypandy CF40 ...106 F8
Williams Terr
Treharris CF46 .....83 B7
6 Merthyr Tydfil CF47 .30 E8
Williams Way CF48 .10 C2
Williamstown Prim Sch
  NP23 ....40 C7
Willie Seager Cotts
  CF23 ....178 D1
Willins NP44 ......116 B8
Willins Rd CF3 ....95 C7

Willow Bank SA4 ....66 D3
Willow Cl
Beddau CF38 ....155 F5
Bridgend CF35 .....169 F3
Ebbw Vale NP23 ....7 C1
Newport NP19 .....142 B1
Penarth CF64 ......206 E3
Porthcawl CF36 ....183 E8
Rogerstone NP10 ..141 D7
Willow Ct
12 Cardiff CF24 ....195 C7
Newbridge NP11 ....87 C8
Tredegar NP22 .....6 C2
Willow Dr
Caerphilly NP12 ...85 F6
Llanmartin NP18 ..145 E6
8 SA NP18 ....117 F3
Willow Gr
Aberdare CF44 .....28 E2
Baglan SA12 ....98 E6
Cardiff CF3 ....180 A8
Willow Herb Cl CF3 .180 B6
Willow Parc NP11 ..59 D1
Willow Rd
Blackwood NP11 ....59 D3
Llanharry CF72 ....172 C5
Newport NP19 .....142 B1
Willow Rise CF82 ..84 D7
Willow St CF37 ....136 A5
Willow Terr CF45 ..81 F8
Willow Tree Cl CF15 .175 F6
Willow Way SA12 ..98 D6
Willow Wlk
Cimla SA11 ....72 C6
Cowbridge CF71 ...188 F2
Willowbrook Dr CF3 179 E6
Willowbrook Gdns
  5 ....93 F1
Willowbrook Jun & Inf
  Sch CF3 ....180 A6
Willowbrook Laboratory
  Units CF3 ....179 F7
Willowdale Cl CF5 .193 C8
Willowdale Rd
Cardiff CF5 ....193 B8
Cardiff CF5 ....193 C8
Willowdene Way
  CF3 ....180 A8
Willowfield Ct CF23 178 C6
Willowford CF15 ..157 E8
Willowmere CF64 .206 D7
Willows Ave CF24 .195 F6
Willows Com High Sch
  CF24 ....196 A6
Willows Cres CF63 215 A7
Willows Pl SA1 ....95 C7
Willows The
Abertillery NP13 ...36 C4
Bedwas CF83 ......138 E7
Bridgend CF31 .....169 A4
Croesyceiliog NP44 .90 A5
Laleston CF32 .....167 E4
Llanelli SA15 ......40 C7
St Athan CF62 .....211 D4
Willowtown Jun & Inf Sch
  NP23 ....11 A8
Willowturf Ct CF32 150 E4
Wills Ct CF62 ......213 A1
Wills Row NP10 ...142 B4
Wilmot St SA11 ....71 E6
Wilson Ct 2 CF47 ..30 D8
Wilson Pl Cardiff CF5 193 C4
Maerdy CF43 ......52 A1
Wilson Rd Cardiff CF5 193 B5
Newport NP19 ....144 A7
Wilson St
Cardiff CF24 ......195 E7
Newport NP20 ....143 A1
Wilton Terr 7 CF47 .30 E8
Wimble Wood Cl
  SA3 ....123 A7
Wimborne Cl
  CF64 ....216 B5
Wimborne Rise NP44 89 C5
Wimborne Rd CF14 152 E1
Wimborne St CF48 .11 A5
Wimbourne Bldgs
  CF63 ....215 C4
Wimbourne Cl CF61 209 F5
Wimbourne Gdns
  CF35 ....152 E1
Wimbourne Rd CF35 215 C6
Wimbourne Terr
  CF39 ....57 A1
Wimmerfield Ave SA2 93 E7
Wimmerfield Cl SA2 .93 E7
Wimmerfield Cres
  SA2 ....93 E7
Wimmerfield Dr SA2 .93 F7
Winch Ave CF48 ...10 A3
Winch Fawr Rd CF48 225 F1
Winch Fawr Rd
  CF48 ....10 A3
Winch Wen Ind Est
  SA6 ....69 C6
Winchester Ave
  CF23 ....178 D2
Winchester Cl
Barry CF62 ....214 D5
Newport NP20 ....143 A1
Wind Rd SA9 ......2 C3
Wind St Aberdare CF44 29 A1
6 Swansea SA1 ....95 C6

Windermere Ave
  CF23 ....178 A3
Windermere Cl CF44 29 D1
Windermere Cres SA6 68 E7
Windermere Rd SA6 .68 E7
Windermere Sq 4
  NP19 ....143 E8
Windflower Cl 1
  CF3 ....180 A7
Windhover Cl 8
  CF3 ....180 A6
Windlass Ct CF10 ..195 C3
Windmill Cl
Cardiff CF14 ......159 E2
Llantwit Major CF61 210 A7
Wick CF71 ....198 D5
Windmill Ind Area
  CF63 ....215 D4
Windmill La
Llanblethian CF71 ..188 E1
Llantwit Major CF61 210 A7
Windmill Sq 7
  NP20 ....143 C3
Windmill Terr SA1 ..95 E8
Windrush Cl NP20 ..116 E2
Windrush Pl 6 CF5 193 D8
Windsor Arc 8 CF64 207 B4
Windsor Ave
Newbridge NP11 ....86 F6
Radyr CF15 ....176 B6
Windsor Cl
Boverton CF61 .....210 B6
Cardiff CF5 ....176 B6
Windsor Clive Inf Sch
  CF5 ....193 C5
Windsor Clive Jun Sch
  CF5 ....193 C5
Windsor Cres
Cardiff CF15 ......176 C5
Windsor Ct
4 Cardiff CF24 ....195 C6
Penarth CF64 .....207 B3
Pontyclun CF72 ...173 B8
Radyr CF15 ....176 B6
6 Swansea SA1 ...95 C7
Ynysybwl CF37 ....81 F1
Windsor Dr CF72 ..173 B7
Windsor Espl CF10 195 B1
Windsor Gdns
Beddau CF38 ......156 A8
Cardiff CF5 ....193 E6
Windsor Gn CF5 ...193 E6
Windsor Gr CF15 ..176 B6
Windsor Ho 6 CF10 194 F5
Windsor La
7 Cardiff CF10 ...195 B6
Penarth CF64 .....207 A5
Windsor Mews 1
  CF24 ....195 C5
Windsor Pl
Abertridwr CF83 ...136 F7
Cardiff CF10 ......195 B6
Merthyr Vale CF48 .55 D4
Mumbles SA3 .....123 B5
Pant CF48 ....11 B6
1 Penarth CF64 ...207 A4
Pentre CF41 ......78 F4
Rogerstone NP10 ..142 B4
Senghenydd CF83 .110 F2
Treharris CF46 ....83 B6
Ynysybwl CF37 ....81 F1
Windsor Rd
Cwm NP23 ....35 B8
Penarth CF64 .....207 A5
Radyr CF15 ....176 B6
Windsor St
Cardiff CF24 ......195 C7
Merthyr Vale CF48 .55 D4
Mumbles SA3 .....123 B5
Pant CF48 ....11 B6
7 Penarth CF64 ...207 A4
Windsor Terr
Aberbeeg NP13 ....36 C4
Cardiff CF10 ......195 B6
Merthyr Tydfil CF47 10 D1
Mumbles SA3 .....123 B5
Pant CF48 ....11 B6
7 Penarth CF64 ...207 A4
Windsor Terrace La
  CF64 ....207 B4
Windsor Village SA12 98 D3
Windway CF5 .....94 A2
Windway Rd CF5 ..94 A2
Windyridge CF64 ..206 C2
Wine St
Llantwit Major CF61 209 F6
Pontypridd CF37 ..12 F1
Wingate Dr CF14 ..177 F6
Wingate St NP20 ..143 C1
Wingfield Ave CF38 155 F7
Wingfield Cl CF37 .109 E1
Wingfield Cres CF83 112 A3
Wingfield Rd CF14 177 A4
Wingfield Rise CF46 83 B5
Wingfield St SA8 ..36 A3
Wingfield Terr CF46 83 B5
Winifred Ave CF62 214 E8

Winifred Rd SA10 ..70 E7
Winifred St
Dowlais CF48 ......11 A5
Mountain Ash CF45 81 F8
Winifred Terr NP13 36 B8
Winnipeg Dr CF23 178 C5
Winni Cl NP44 ....216 C4
Winslade Ave CF39 133 C6
Winston Ave CF5 ..193 A2
Winston Rd CF62 ..214 E8
Winston St SA1 ....95 C8
Winstone Cotts NP4 54 F5
Winstone Rd NP4 ..38 B1
Wistaria Cl NP20 ..117 B3
Wiston Path NP44 .89 B2
Witham St NP19 ..143 E4
Witherdene Rd CF43 80 C2
Withy Pk SA3 .....122 A6
Withycombe Rd CF3 179 C7
Witla Court Rd CF3 179 C5
Wolfe Cl CF63 .....215 C7
Wolffe Cl CF71 ....188 D2
Wolfs Castle Ave
  CF14 ....159 E1
Wolseley St
Newport NP20 ....143 C1
Newport NP20 ....143 C1
Womanby St CF10 195 A5
Wood Cl Cardiff CF14 160 B1
Llanyravon NP44 ..90 B1
Neath SA11 ....71 D4
Wood Cres NP10 ..142 A7
Wood Path NP44 ..90 A6
Wood Rd
Abercynon CF45 ..82 E2
Pontypridd CF37 ..135 D7
Wood St
Abercarn NP11 ...114 B8
Bargoed CF81 .....58 A4
Cardiff CF10 ......195 A4
Ferndale CF43 ....79 F7
Gilfach Goch CF39 132 B5
Maerdy CF43 ......52 A2
Maesteg CF34 ....102 B2
Penarth CF64 .....207 A4
Pontycymer CF32 .103 F3
Pontypridd CF37 ..109 F5
Port Talbot SA13 .125 D6
Wood View SA11 ..72 B6
Wood View Cl SA11 71 C1
Wood View Cres
  NP11 ....115 A1
Wood View Terr NP11 115 A2
Woodbine Cotts
  SA11 ....226 C4
Woodbine Rd NP12 85 F7
Woodburn Dr SA3 123 A6
Woodcock St CF24 195 C7
Woodcote SA4 ....43 C7
Woodend Rd SA15 40 D8
Woodfield Ave
Pontlliw SA4 ......44 A5
Radyr CF15 ....176 C4
Woodfield Bldgs
  CF39 ....107 F4
Woodfield Cross
  NP22 ....13 F4
Woodfield Park Cres
  NP11 ....85 F6
Woodfield Rd
Cwm NP23 ....35 B8
Pontypool NP4 ....63 A4
Talbot Green CF72 155 A2
Tredegar NP22 ....13 F5
Woodfield St
Bryncae CF72 .....153 E2
1 Morriston SA6 ...46 A1
Pontllanfraith NP12 86 A6
1 Port Talbot SA13 125 C6
Swansea SA6 .....68 F8
Woodfield Terr
Mountain Ash CF45 81 F8
Porth CF39 ....107 F4
Tir-y-Berth CF82 ..84 F6
Trehafod CF37 ....108 C2
Woodfieldside Bsns Pk
  NP12 ....86 E6
Woodford Cl CF5 ..176 E1
Woodford Rd SA5 .67 E7
Woodham Cl CF24 214 D6
Woodham Pk CF62 214 D6
Woodham Rd CF24 215 A4
Woodland Ave
1 Margam SA13 ...125 E4
Mumbles SA3 .....122 F7
Pencoed CF35 ....170 D8
Porthcawl CF36 ...183 B8
Woodland Cotts CF46 56 A7
Woodland Cres
Abercynon CF45 ..82 F3
Cardiff CF23 ......178 C4
Creigiau CF15 ....174 E8
Cwmfelinfach NP44 90 A4

Woodland Park View 5
  NP19 ....143 F6
Woodland Pk
Glynneath SA11 ...223 D1
Penderyn CF44 ....224 D2
Ynystawe SA6 .....46 B5
Woodland Pl
Bargoed CF81 .....58 A1
Bedlinog CF46 ....56 B7
7 Cardiff CF24 ...195 C7
Cefn Hengoed CF82 84 F4
8 Merthyr Tydfil CF47 10 E1
North Cornelly CF33 166 A7
Penarth CF64 .....207 A4
Pengam NP12 .....85 B7
Woodland Rd
Beddau CF38 ......156 B6
Cardiff CF14 ......176 F4
Croesyceiliog NP44 90 A4
Crynant SA10 .....226 A7
Glyncorrwg SA13 227 C2
Llansamlet SA6 ...46 C5
Mountain Ash CF45 54 C3
Neath SA10 ......70 E8
Neath SA11 ....71 F7
Newport NP19 ....143 F6
Pontllanfraith NP12 80 B2
Ystradowen SA9 ..221 C7
Woodland Rise CF31 150 D1
Woodland Row SA12 99 D6
Woodland St
Blaenavon NP4 ...17 D7
Cwmbran NP44 ...89 D4
Mountain Ash CF45 54 C3
Pontardawe SA8 ..23 F5
Woodland Terr
Abercanaid CF48 ..87 A3
Abercanaid CF48 ..53 C6
Abertillery NP13 ..36 A1
Abertillery NP13 ..36 B8
Abertridwr CF83 ..136 F7
Bargoed NP12 ....58 F8
Merthyr Tydfil CF47 10 E1
Mountain Ash CF45 54 C3
Nantyglo NP23 ...8 C1
Neath SA10 ......48 F2
New Tredegar NP24 13 B5
Pantywaen CF32 ..130 D4
Pontyclun CF72 ..172 F8
Pontypool NP4 ....61 F8
Pontypridd CF37 ..135 B8
Senghenydd CF83 110 F3
Treorchy CF42 ....78 B4
Treorchy CF42 ....78 C7
Woodland Vale CF42 78 D7
Woodland View
Abersychan NP4 ...37 E7
Cwmfelinfach NP11 113 F3
Pontypool NP4 ....62 B8
Woodland Way
Merthyr Tydfil CF48 30 A8
Sarn CF32 ....150 E3
Woodland Wlk NP18 145 C4
Woodlands
Beddau CF38 ......156 B7
Gowerton SA4 ....66 C5
Tredegar NP22 ....6 C1
Woodlands Ave
Clydach SA6 ......46 F8
Treharris CF46 ....83 B6
Woodlands Bsns Pk
  SA9 ....2 D2
Woodlands Cl CF71 188 D2
Woodlands Cres CF46 83 B5
Woodlands Ct 4
  CF62 ....214 F5
Woodlands Dr NP20 117 A4
Woodlands Gdns CF72 104 E6
Woodlands Jun & Inf Sch
  NP44 ....89 B5
Woodlands Park Dr
  CF37 ....193 C3
Woodlands Pk
Ammanford SA18 ..219 C6
Pencoed CF35 ....170 C8
Pyle CF33 ....148 D1
Woodlands Rd
Barry CF62 ....214 F5
Loughor SA4 .....42 F1
Woodlands Rise
  CF31 ....168 C4
Woodlands Spcl High
  Sch CF5 ....193 E5
Woodlands St CF32 104 E3
Woodlands Terr
Cross Hands SA14 218 B7
Maesteg CF34 ....75 A1
Resolven SA11 ...226 C5
Swansea SA1 .....95 B7
Woodlands The
Abersychan NP4 ..37 E5
Bridgend CF31 ....169 C5
Cardiff CF14 ......160 B2
Pontypool NP4 ....62 B8
Woodlands Workshop Ctr
  CF72 ....155 A1
Woodlawn Way
  CF14 ....159 E2
Woodmans Terr SA9 2 B6
Woodpecker Sq
  CF62 ....210 E6
Woodridge Ct SA3 122 F4
Woods Gelliwion
  CF37 ....135 A8
Woodside
Newport NP10 ....163 E7
Tonna SA11 ....49 A3

Woodside Ave
Bridgend CF31 ....168 F8
Neath SA11 ....71 F7
Swansea SA2 .....93 E6
Woodside Cl
Bishopston SA3 ...122 A5
Swansea SA2 .....93 E6
Woodside Cres
Clydach SA6 ......46 C8
Swansea SA3 .....14 D6
Woodside Ct CF14 160 A1
Woodside Rd
Cwmbran NP44 ...89 C4
Pontypool NP4 ....38 B2
Woodside Terr
Abertillery NP13 ..60 B6
Newbridge NP11 ..60 B2
Woodside Way NP44 89 C4
Woodstock Cl CF62 214 D5
Woodstock Gdns
  CF35 ....152 D1
Woodstock Mews
  CF71 ....188 E2
Woodvale Ave CF23 178 D7
Woodview Cl NP44 89 B4
Woodview Ct NP4 ..62 B6
Woodview Pl SA5 ..67 E6
Woodview Terr
Bryn-côch SA10 ..48 C4
Nantgarw NP11 ...59 F2
Pontypool NP4 ....62 B6
Woodville Ct 6
  CF24 ....195 A8
Woodville Pl
Ebbw Vale NP23 ..14 C6
Ferndale CF43 ....79 F7
Woodville Rd
8 Cardiff CF24 ...178 A1
6 Cardiff CF24 ...195 A7
Mumbles SA3 .....123 A4
Newport NP20 ....142 F4
Woodville St SA4 ..19 C5
Woodville Terr NP12 58 F5
Woodward Ave
  NP11 ....114 B4
Woodward Rd NP11 114 C4
Woolacombe Ave
  CF3 ....179 C6
Woolaston Ave CF23 178 C5
Woolascott Dr SA3 122 D5
Woollacott Mews
  SA3 ....122 D5
Wooller Ho 9 SA12 98 F1
Woolmer Cl CF5 ..176 D2
Woolpitch SA4 ....89 B3
Woosnam Cl CF23 178 E1
Worcester Cl
Heolgerrig CF48 ..10 A1
Llanyravon NP44 ..90 A3
Worcester Cres
  SA6 ....144 A8
Worcester Ct
Cardiff CF11 ......194 F1
Swansea SA2 .....69 C7
Worcester Dr SA3 123 A4
Worcester Path NP44 90 A3
Worcester Pl SA1 .95 D7
Worcester Rd SA3 123 A4
Worcester St
Brynmawr NP23 ..8 C4
Cardiff CF11 ......194 F2
Wordsworth Ave
Bridgend CF31 ....168 C6
Cardiff CF24 ......195 C7
Penarth CF64 .....206 F4
Wordsworth Cl
Cwmbran NP44 ...89 D2
Ebbw Vale NP23 ..14 B8
Llantwit Major CF61 210 B6
Wordsworth Gdns
  CF37 ....136 B6
Wordsworth Rd
  NP19 ....144 A5
Wordsworth St
Cwmaman CF44 ...53 A4
1 Swansea SA1 ...95 C8
Working St CF10 ..195 A5
Works Rd SA5 .....23 E4
Worle Ave CF3 ....179 B5
Worle Pl CF3 ......179 B5
Wren Ave SA11 ...72 B5
Wren Bank SA11 ..71 B2
Wren Cl
Bridgend CF31 ....169 C4
Cardiff CF3 ....180 A6
Wren Rd CF62 ....210 E6
Wrexham Ct CF3 ..179 C5
Wrgant Pl CF43 ...52 A2
Wright Cl NP19 ...144 B3
Wroughton Pl CF5 193 E6
Wychtree St SA6 ..69 A7
Wychwood Cl SA3 123 A4
Wye Cl Barry CF62 214 C6
Swansea SA1 .....95 A7
Wye Cres NP20 ...116 C2
Wye St NP20 .....144 B4
Wyeverne Rd
Cardiff CF24 ......195 A8
1 Newport NP19 ..144 A5
Wyfan Pl CF14 ....177 D2
Wyncliffe Rd CF23 179 A8
Wynd St CF63 ....215 B6
Wyndham Arc 8
  CF10 ....195 A5
Wyndham Cl
Bridgend CF31 ....169 C6
Pontarddulais SA4 19 C3

Wyndham Cres
7 Aberdare CF44 . . . . .53 D7
Bridgend CF31 . . . . .127 B8
Cardiff CF11 . . . . .194 D6
Wyndham Park Way
CF5 .191 E5
Wyndham Pl CF11 . . . . . .194 E5
Wyndham Rd CF11 . . .194 D6
Wyndham St
Barry CF63 . . . . .215 A5
Bridgend CF31 . . . . .168 A4
Cardiff CF11 . . . . .194 E5
Cardiff CF11 . . . . .194 E5
Cardiff CF15 . . . . .158 C1
Dowlais CF48 . . . . .11 A4
Evanstown CF39 . . . . . . .132 B8
Machen CF83 . . . . .140 A7
Newport NP20 . . . . .143 C6
Ogmore Vale CF32 . . . .104 E4
8 Port Talbot SA13 . .125 C7
Porth CF39 . . . . .107 F2
Swansea SA1 . . . . .95 B6
Ton Pentre CF41 . . . . .79 A2
Tonypandy CF40 . . . . . . .106 F4
Treherbert CF42 . . . . .50 E2
Troedyrhiw CF48 . . . . . . .31 C1
Wyndham Terr
Cardiff CF14 . . . . .178 A8
Risca NP11 . . . . .115 B1
Wyngarth SA1 . . . . .69 D5
Wynnstay Cl CF11 . . . .194 E3
Wynter Ct SA5 . . . . .68 C6
Wyon Cl CF5 . . . . .176 D3
Wyvern Ave SA12 . . . . .98 C2
Wyvern Ho 1 SA12 . . .98 C2

Y

Y Berllan Cimla SA11 . .72 B6
Dunvant SA2 . . . . .93 D7
Swansea SA6 . . . . .45 C2
Ystradgynlais SA9 . . . . . . .2 D7
Y Bont Faen Prim Sch
CF71 . . . . .188 E1
Y Bwthyn SA15 . . . . .40 A4
Y Cedrwydden NP12 . .85 D5
Y Cilgant CF83 . . . . .137 E6
Y Clos
Cwmllynfell SA9 . . . . . . .221 B7
Llanelli SA15 . . . . .41 A5
Y Cyswllt SA4 . . . . .44 C5
Y Dderwen CF34 . . . . .128 D7
Y Deri CF38 . . . . .156 C6
Y Dolau SA6 . . . . .45 C2
Y Dolydd CF83 . . . . . . .137 F1
Y Felin Ffrwd CF83 . .137 F4
Y Fron SA14 . . . . .218 A8
Y Ganolfan CF48 . . . . . .11 A4
Y Garn SA4 . . . . .44 A2
Y Garth CF44 . . . . .28 C4
Y Gefnen SA7 . . . . .69 F6
Y Gilfach SA9 . . . . .2 B7
Y Gilwern SA9 . . . . .2 B6
Y Glyn
Cefneithin SA14 . . . . . . .218 A8
Dunvant SA2 . . . . .93 D7
Maesycwmmer CF82 . . .85 A1
Y Goedlan
Cwm-twrch Uchaf SA9 .221 C6
Cwmfelin CF34 . . . . .128 C8
Y Goedwig CF14 . . . . .177 A8
Y Gorlan SA2 . . . . .93 D7
Y Graig CF48 . . . . .11 A7
Y Groes Cardiff CF14 .177 B7
Sarn CF32 . . . . .150 F3
Y Gwernydd SA7 . . . . . .46 F6
Y Lan CF35 . . . . .132 E7
Y Llest CF31 . . . . .150 C1
Y Llwyn SA15 . . . . .41 A5
Y Llwyni SA6 . . . . .45 C2
Y Pant Comp Sch
CF72 . . . . .155 C1
Y Parc CF72 . . . . .174 B7

Y Rhodfa CF62,CF63 . .214 F4
Y Rhos SA15 . . . . .40 F7
Y Waun Llanelli SA14 . .41 C6
Ynysybwl CF37 . . . . .81 F2
Y Waun Fach SA6 . . . . .45 B2
Y Wern CF32 . . . . .129 E3
Y Wern Prim Sch SA9 . .2 B6
Y-fan SA14 . . . . .41 C5
Y-Gaer SA14 . . . . .41 A8
Y-Wern SA6 . . . . .45 B2
Yalton SA3 . . . . .122 F7
Yard Coal Rise NP11 . .59 C3
Yard Row NP23 . . . . .7 D3
Yarrow CF15 . . . . .193 A5
Yellow Row NP22 . . . . . .6 E2
Yeo Cl NP20 . . . . .116 E1
Yeo Rd NP20 . . . . .116 E1
Yeo St SA11 . . . . .226 D5
Yew Cl CF47 . . . . .10 C5
Yew Gr Caerphilly NP12 .85 F6
Pontllanfraith NP12 . . . .86 A6
Yew St
Aberbargoed CF81 . . . . . .58 B5
Merthyr Tydfil CF47 . . . . .30 E8
Taffs Well CF15 . . . . .158 A4
Troedyrhiw CF48 . . . . . . .31 C1
Yew Tree Cl CF71 . . . .187 B4
Yew Tree Ct
Barry CF62 . . . . .214 C3
Cardiff CF23 . . . . .178 C2
Yew Tree La NP18 . . . .118 B3
Yew Tree Terr
Aberbargoed CF81 . . . . . .90 A5
Cwmbran NP44 . . . . .89 C2
Yewberry Cl NP20 . . . .117 B2
Yewberry La NP20 . . .117 B2
Yewtree Cl
Cardiff CF5 . . . . .193 C8
Munbles SA3 . . . . .62 B8
Yewtree Gr CF62 . . . . .211 B7
Yewtree Rd NP11 . . . . .87 A7
Ymyl-yr-Afon SA10 . . .49 C4
Yniscedwyn Rd SA9 . . . .2 E8
Ynisderw Rd SA8 . . . . . .23 E4
Ynisaf Cotts SA9 . . . . .222 A6
Ynisyddarren Rd SA9 . .2 B6
Ynys Cadwyn SA11 . . .227 C8
Ynys Ct CF37 . . . . .135 C6
Ynys Ct
Glyncorrwg SA13 . . . . . .227 C1
Swansea SA6 . . . . .69 B7
Ynys Fach Ave SA11 .226 E5
Ynys Fawr Ave SA11 .226 E5
Ynys Glyd St CF82 . . .111 F7
Ynys Hir CF37 . . . . .109 D7
Ynys Hywel Visitor Ctr
NP11 . . . . .113 B3
Ynys La NP44 . . . . .90 A5
Ynys Las CF46 . . . . .83 D4
Ynys Nedd SA11 . . . . .226 E5
Ynys Newydd Rd SA2 .94 B6
Ynys Park Cotts CF41 .79 A3
Ynys St
Port Talbot SA13 . . . . .99 C1
Porth CF39 . . . . .107 F7
Ynys Terr CF37 . . . . . . .135 F5
Ynys y Coed CF5 . . . . .194 A8
Ynys-bydafau SA9 . . .222 B7
Ynys-Cedwyn Lodge
SA9 . . . . .2 F7
Ynys-Gyfeillon Rd
CF37 . . . . .109 C2
Ynys-Las SA14 . . . . .41 C5
Ynys-Lee SA13 . . . . .99 E4
Ynys-Lwyd St CF44 . . .53 C8
Ynys-Meudwy Rd SA8 .24 B8
Ynys-Penllwch Rd
SA6,SA7 . . . . .46 F7
Ynys-y-Coed NP12 . . . .86 B8
Ynys-y-Cwm Rd SA15 .40 C7
Ynys-y-gwial SA9 . . . . . .1 F5
Ynys-y-Mond Rd
Glais SA7 . . . . .47 B7
Pontardawe SA8 . . . . .23 E2

Bridgend CF31 . . . . .169 B2
Newport NP19 . . . . .143 B7
York St Aberdare CF44 .53 C6
Abertillery NP13 . . . . .36 A5
Cardiff CF5 . . . . .194 C5
Cardiff CF5 . . . . .194 C6
Mountain Ash CF45 . . . .54 D1
Porth CF39 . . . . .107 F3
Swansea SA1 . . . . .95 D6
York Terr Cwm NP23 . .35 B7
Tredegar NP22 . . . . .13 F6
Youldon Ho CF64 . . . .206 B3
Yr Allt
Llangennech SA14 . . . . . .18 B1
Llantrisant CF72 . . . . . . .155 D3
Yr Aran SA2 . . . . .93 D8
Yr Efail CF35 . . . . .170 B1
Yr Elain SA2 . . . . .93 D8
Yr Hafan CF32 . . . . .103 E1
Yr Hafod Llanelli SA15 .40 E7
Swansea SA6 . . . . .45 C2
Yr Hendre
Nantgarw CF15 . . . . .158 A8
Pyle CF33 . . . . .148 D3
Yr Ysfa CF34 . . . . .102 A2
Yr-Hen-Lawnt CF40 . .106 B3
Yryswen Terr SA10 . . .222 A1
Ysbryd-y-coed
Pen-y-Fai CF31 . . . . .168 D8
Pen-y-Fai CF31 . . . . .168 D8
Ysbyty Gymuned
Ystradgynlais SA9 . . . . . . .2 E7
Ysbyty'r Tri Chwm
NP23 . . . . .7 C3
Ysgol Bro Eirwg CF3 .179 A4
Ysgol Bryn Castell Sch
CF31 . . . . .168 D5
Ysgol Bryn Onnen y
Farteg NP4 . . . . .37 F8
Ysgol Crug Glas SA1 .95 D8
Ysgol Cwmgors
SA18 . . . . .220 D5
Ysgol Gymraed Ystrad
Mynach CF82 . . . . .84 E1
Ysgol Enw'r Delyn
CF64 . . . . .206 D3
Ysgol Gyfun Bryntirion
CF31 . . . . .158 D8
Ysgol Gyfun Cwm Rhymni
CF81 . . . . .57 F3
Ysgol Gyfun Cwm Rhymni
(Ysgol Isaf) CF81 . . . . .58 B4
Ysgol Gyfun Cymer
Rhondda CF39 . . . . .107 E2
Ysgol Gyfun Gwynllyw
NP4 . . . . .37 B1
Ysgol Gyfun Gwyr
SA4 . . . . .66 C5
Ysgol Gyfun Gymraeg
Glantaf CF14 . . . . .177 A2
Ysgol Gyfun Gymraeg
Glantaff CF5 . . . . .176 F2
Ysgol Gyfun Gymraeg
Plasmawr CF5 . . . . .176 D1
Ysgol Gyfun Llanhari
CF72 . . . . .172 A5
Ysgol Gyfun Maes Yr Yrfa
SA14 . . . . .218 A8
Ysgol Gyfun Rhydfelen
CF37 . . . . .135 F5
Ysgol Gyfun Rhydyfelin
CF37 . . . . .136 A5
Ysgol Gyfun Rhydywaun
CF44 .27 F7
Ysgol Gyfun y Strade
SA15 .40 A6
Ysgol Gyfun Ystalyfere
SA9 . . . . .2 E7
Ysgol Gymraeg Bro Ogwr
CF31 .79 F6
Ysgol Gymraeg
Bryn-y-mor SA2 . . . . .94 F5
Ysgol Gymraeg Brynmawr
Jun & Inf Schs NP23 . .8 B4
Ysgol Gymraeg
Casnewydd NP18 . . . . . .144 E4

Ysgol Gymraeg Cwm
Gwyddon NP11 . . . . .87 B2
Ysgol Gymraeg Cwmbran
Jun & Inf Sch NP44 .89 D2
Ysgol Gymraeg Cwmtwrch
SA9 . . . . .1 B1
Ysgol Gymraeg Dewi Sant
SA14 .40 F7
Ysgol Gymraeg Melin
Gruffydd & Eglwys Wen
Prim Sch CF14 . . . . .177 A4
Ysgol Gymraeg Pwll Coch
CF11 . . . . .194 C4
Ysgol Gymraeg
Ynysgedwyn SA9 . . . . .2 F8
Ysgol Gynradd Brynnau
CF72 . . . . .153 D3
Ysgol Gynradd Cymraeg
Cwm Nedd SA11 . . . . . .223 D1
Ysgol Gynradd
Gwaelod-y-garth**
CF15 . . . . .157 F4
Ysgol Gynradd Gymraeg
Caerphilly CF83 . . . . .138 B4
Tonyrefail CF39 . . . . .133 C5
Treorchy CF42 . . . . .78 B7
Ysgol Gynradd Gymraeg
Bargod CF81 . . . . .58 A1
Ysgol Gynradd Gymraeg
Bodringallt CF41 . . . . . . .79 D3
Ysgol Gynradd Gymraeg
Bronllwyn CF41 . . . . .79 A2
Ysgol Gynradd Gymraeg
Bryniago SA4 . . . . .19 D4
Ysgol Gynradd Gymraeg
Castell Nedd SA11 . .71 F7
Ysgol Gynradd Gymraeg
Castellau CF38 . . . . .155 F7
Ysgol Gynradd Gymraeg
Cwm Garw CF32 . . . . . .103 E4
Ysgol Gynradd Gymraeg
Cynwyd Sant CF34 .102 A2
Ysgol Gynradd Gymraeg
Evan James CF37 . . .109 B1
Ysgol Gynradd Gymraeg
Felindre SA5 . . . . .20 F2
Ysgol Gynradd Gymraeg
Garth Olwg CF38 . . .135 E1
Ysgol Gynradd Gymraeg
Llwyncelin CF39 . . . . .108 A3
Ysgol Gynradd Gymraeg
Lon Las SA7 . . . . .69 D8
Ysgol Gynradd Gymraeg
Pont-Sion-Norton
CF37 . . . . .109 E3
Ysgol Gynradd Gymraeg
Pontarddawe SA8 . . . . .23 E6
Ysgol Gynradd Gymraeg
Pontybrenin SA4 . . . . . . .66 B8
Ysgol Gynradd Gymraeg
Tyle'R Ynn SA11 . . . . . . .71 B4
Ysgol Gynradd Gymraeg y
Login Fach SA5 . . . . .66 F3
Ysgol Gynradd Trebannws
Prim Sch SA8 . . . . .23 C2
Ysgol Hendre Specl Sch
SA10 .48 C5
Ysgol Heol Goffa
SA15 .40 E7
Ysgol Heol-y-Celyn
CF37 . . . . .136 A5
Ysgol Ifor Bach CF83 .110 F3
Ysgol Iolo Morgannwg
CF71 . . . . .188 F1
Ysgol Llanilltud Fawr
CF61 . . . . .210 A5
Ysgol Llyn-y-forwyn
CF43 .79 F6
Ysgol Maes Dyfan
CF63 . . . . .215 A7
Ysgol Mynydd Bychan
CF14 . . . . .177 F2
Ysgol Pen-y-garth
CF64 . . . . .206 D5

Ysgol Pencae CF5 . . . .176 F2
Ysgol Pl NP44 . . . . .89 C4
Ysgol Rhiwfawr Sch
SA9 . . . . .221 B5
Ysgol Sant Curig
CF62 . . . . .214 E5
Ysgol St SA1 . . . . .96 B7
Ysgol Synradd Cymraeg
Aberdar CF44 . . . . .29 B1
Ysgol Thomas Stephens
CP Sch SA11 . . . . .223 F3
Ysgol Ty Coch CF38 .136 B1
Ysgol y Babanod
SA14 .41 A8
Ysgol y Castell CF83 .138 / 2
Ysgol y Ferch Sger
Corneli CF33 . . . . .165 F8
Ysgol y Glyn SA18 . . .220 E8
Ysgol y Lawnt NP22 . .1 . . .3
Ysgol Yr Ynys SA14 . . .41 C6
Ysgol-y-Graig Prim Sch
CF48 .10 A5
Ysgubor Fach CF83 . .139 F7
Ysgubor Fach St SA1 .68 C2
Ysguborwen NP22 . . . . .6 F1
Ysguthan Rd SA12 . . .124 F8
Yspitty Rd SA14 . . . . . . .42 B1
Ystad Celyn CF34 . . . .102 A1
Ystad Deri NP22 . . . . . . .6 E2
Ystcil-Garu CF71 . . . . .199 F8
Ysticlau Rd SA10 . . . . .222 D4
Ystrad Bldgs CF83 . . .139 A6
Ystrad Cl CF3 . . . . .180 A7
Ystrad Einon SA4 . . . . .43 B2
Ystrad Fawr CF31 . . . .168 D5
Ystrad Mynach Coll
CF82 . . . . .111 E8
Ystrad Mynach Hosp
CF82 . . . . .111 E8
Ystrad Mynach Inf Sch
CF82 .84 E1
Ystrad Mynach Jun Sch
CF82 .84 E1
Ystrad Mynach Sta
CF82 .84 E1
Ystrad Rd
Swansea SA5 . . . . .67 B4
Ton Pentre CF41 . . . . . . .79 B4
Ystrad Rhondda Sta
CF41 .79 D0
Ystrad St CF11 . . . . . . .195 A1
Ystrad Sta CF41 . . . . . . .79 A3
Ystrad Terr
Abercarn NP11 . . . . .87 C4
Ton Pentre CF41 . . . . . . .79 B3
Ystrad-Fawr Villas
SA9 . . . . .222 A5
Ystradbarwig Terr
CF38 . . . . .156 C6
Ystradgynlais Workshops
SA9 . . . . .2 E8
Ystradowen CP Sch
SA9 . . . . .221 C7
Ystwyth Pl SA6 . . . . . . .45 D1

Z

Zammit Cres SA15 . . . .41 A5
Zephaniah Way NP13 .15 D5
Zig-Zag La CF36 . . . . . .166 B2
Zinc St CF24 . . . . .195 D6
Zion Ct CF38 . . . . .156 A7
Zion Pl NP23 . . . . .14 D5
Zion Row SA15 . . . . .40 D6
Zion St NP23 . . . . .14 D6
Zion Terr CF40 . . . . .106 A6
Zoar Ave CF34 . . . . .102 A4
Zoar Pl CF34 . . . . .102 A4
Zoar Rd Neath SA11 . . .71 D8
Ystalyfera SA9 . . . . .2 E4
Zoar Terr CF46 . . . . .83 A5
Zouch St SA5 . . . . .68 C3